The Blue Guides

D1343221

Tuscany

Alta Macadam

A&C Black • London
WW Norton • New York

Fourth edition
Published by A & C Black Publishers Limited
37 Soho Square, London W1D 3QZ

A CIP catalogue record of this book
is available from the British Library.

ISBN 0–7136–5997–1

Published in the United States of America by
WW Norton and Company, Inc
500 Fifth Avenue, New York, NY 10110

Published simultaneously in Canada by
Penguin Books Canada Limited
10 Alcorn Avenue, Toronto, Ontario M4V 3B2

ISBN 0–393–32345–5 USA

The author and the publishers have done their best to ensure the accuracy of all the information in Blue Guide Tuscany; however, they can accept no responsibility for any loss, injury or inconvenience sustained by any traveller as a result of information or advice contained in the guide.

Alta Macadam has been a writer of Blue Guides since 1970. She lives in Florence with her family, the painter Francesco Colacicchi and their children, Giovanni and Lelia. Combined with work on writing the guides she has also been associated in Florence with the Bargello Museum, the Alinari photo archive, and Harvard University at the Villa I Tatti in Florence. As author of the Blue Guides to Rome, Venice, Sicily, Florence, Tuscany, and Umbria she travels extensively in Italy every year to revise new editions of the books.

The Historical Introduction © **John Law** (M.A. D.Phil. F.R. Hist.S.). Dr Law is Senior Lecturer in History at the University of Wales, Swansea. He edits the journal, *Renaissance Studies* and co-wrote, with Denys Hay, *Italy in the Age of the Renaissance* (London, 1989). He is currently working on the 'despots' of Renaissance Italy and the 'discovery' of the Italian Renaissance in 19C Britain.

Cover picture: the walled city of Siena, detail from the *Adoration of the Magi* by Bartolomeo di Fredi, in the Pinacoteca di Siena. The Art Archive. Dagli Orti.
Frontispiece: the fortifications at Magliano in Toscana.

A&C Black uses paper produced with elemental chlorine-free pulp, harvested from managed sustainable forests.

Printed and bound in Great Britain by Butler and Tanner Ltd, Frome and London.

Contents

Practical information

Background information

The guide

Maps and plans

Introduction

Tuscany (in Italian Toscana) is the most famous of the twenty regions of Italy. It has an area of 22,991 square kilometres, and a population of about 3,473,000. It lies between the Apennines and the Tyrrhenian sea, bordered on the north by Emilia and Liguria, on the east by the Marche and Umbria, and on the south by Lazio. It includes the famous towns of Florence, Siena, and Pisa, as well as numerous beautiful and interesting small towns such as Lucca, Cortona, Volterra, Massa Marittima, Pienza, Montepulciano, San Gimignano, and Montalcino.

It is well known for its splendid landscape, particularly that of the Chianti region between Florence and Siena with its charming low hills covered with olive groves, vineyards, woods, and isolated cypress trees, and dotted with beautiful old farmhouses. The region also includes the Apuan Alps, white with snow and marble, which form a dramatic background to the coastal plain of Versilia. The high Monte Amiata is almost always prominent in the southern Tuscan landscape. Other areas of particular natural beauty, and with their own special characteristics, include the Casentino with its country churches and castles (below the forest of Camaldoli), the Mugello, the hilly wooded area north of Florence with numerous villas and churches, and the remote areas around Pitigliano, near the southern border of Tuscany.

Although the sea coast of Versilia, which first became popular for its bathing resorts in the 18C, has lost much of its charm, beautiful stretches of coastline can still be found in the Maremma (notably the Monti dell'Uccellina) and on Monte Argentario. The island of Elba retains some unspoilt parts, and Capraia, another lovely island in the Tuscan archipelago, can be visited.

Tuscany derives its name from the inhabitants of ancient Etruria—the Etruscans—known in Latin as *Etrusci* or *Tusci*, who probably landed at Tarquinia (now in Lazio) in the 8C BC. In *Etruria Propria* they formed themselves into a Confederation of twelve principal cities, of which Chiusi (Clevsins) was the most important in present-day Tuscany. Other member cities included Cortona, Vetulonia, Volterra (Velathri), Arezzo (Arretium), Populonia, Roselle (Rusellae), and Fiesole (Faesulae). The other four cities were Tarquinia (Tarxuna)—the most important; Veii (Veio)—the largest; Cerveteri (Caere)—all three in present-day Lazio; and Perugia (Perusia) in present-day Umbria. There were also important Etruscan settlements in the Maremma, and around Pitigliano, and Saturnia. Numerous Etruscan remains, including tombs and walls, can still be seen in these places, and important finds from excavations are exhibited in museums all over the region.

In the Middle Ages Lucca was a powerful independent town, and Pisa, at the head of its Maritime Republic, was one of the most important cities in Europe in the 12C. Siena reached the height of its power in the 12C–13C, and is still one of the most beautiful medieval towns in Italy. Numerous small hill towns survive in Tuscany as testimony to the rise of independent communes in the Middle Ages, the most famous of which is San Gimignano.

Many beautiful country churches can be seen all over the region, as well as the splendid 12C Romanesque abbey of Sant'Antimo and the 13C Gothic ruins of San Galgano. Important Tuscan monasteries and charter houses include Monte

Oliveto Maggiore, La Verna, Camaldoli, Vallombrosa, the Certosa del Galluzzo (outside Florence) and the Certosa di Pisa (near Calci).

Siena, Lucca, and Pisa (as well as Florence) have some of the most beautiful Gothic and Romanesque buildings to be seen in Italy. The early 14C Sienese school of painting produced masters such as Duccio, Simone Martini and Pietro and Ambrogio Lorenzetti. In the 13C and early 14C the great sculptors Nicola Pisano and his son Giovanni were active in Pisa.

Florence is world famous for its Renaissance buildings, but other Renaissance monuments in Tuscany include the piazza in Pienza, Santa Maria del Calcinaio in Cortona, and Santa Maria delle Carceri in Prato. Delightful enamelled terra-cotta works by the Florentine Della Robbia family are to be found all over the region (in Florence, Pistoia, Lucca, Impruneta, La Verna, the Valdarno, and the Casentino). The great Florentine school of painting had a wide influence over local masters whose works are preserved in country churches and small towns. Luca Signorelli left some masterpieces in his native city of Cortona, and in Arezzo and Borgo San Sepolcro some of the best works of Piero della Francesca can be seen.

Apart from the fundamental importance to western civilisation of the Florentine Renaissance, Tuscany also produced some of the greatest artists and writers of all time: Giotto, Masaccio, Brunelleschi, Donatello, Leonardo da Vinci, Michelangelo; Dante, Boccaccio, Poliziano, and Petrarca.

Towns interesting for their 19C architecture include Viareggio and Livorno, and the spa of Montecatini has elaborate buildings dating from the beginning of the twentieth century.

Numerous travellers (including poets and writers) have come to Tuscany over the centuries, and Florence, Livorno, Pisa and Bagni di Lucca have particular Anglo-American associations. Florence was an important part of the Grand Tour itinerary for British travellers in the 18C, many of whom came by boat to Livorno. The consul Sir Horace Mann and his friend Horace Walpole presided over the English community in Florence in the latter part of the century. The English colony in Pisa in the early 19C included Byron and Shelley (who drowned off Viareggio in 1822). The Brownings lived in Florence from 1847 until Elizabeth's death in 1861 and Henry James also lived there towards the end of the century. Tuscany was the setting for two of E.M. Forster's novels published at the beginning of the 20C, when Aldous Huxley and D.H. Lawrence spent much of their time writing in Tuscany.

The inhabitants of some of the larger towns in Tuscany retain notable individual characteristics, and often rivalry is strong between them. Pisa has traditionally been the enemy of Florence, and Lucca proudly independent of the two. Carrara has been an active centre of the Anarchist movement since the beginning of the twentieth century.

Tuscany has more museums than any other region in Italy, and an increasing number of interesting small local museums are being opened, including those at Certaldo, Vetulonia, Montepulciano, Montalcino, Pienza, San Casciano Val di Pesa, Empoli, Tavarnelle, and Montelupo Fiorentino, to name but a few. Tuscany is known for its gardens and it is now becoming easier to visit those in private hands. In summer there are numerous music and theatre festivals in small villages throughout the region.

Acknowledgements

As for previous editions of this guide **Françoise Pouncey Chiarini** checked the text for southern Tuscany, the Maremma and the Chianti district, after making numerous trips in the interests of the guide. I am extremely grateful to her for her generous help and meticulous professional editorial work. We received help from the Soprintendenze per i Beni Artistici e Storici of Siena (particular thanks to Bruno Santi) and of Florence (particular thanks to Rosanna Caterina Proto Pisani). The local tourist offices throughout Tuscany provided assistance, and in particular those of the Mugello (special thanks to Piera Ballabio of the Comunità Montana Mugello), Monte Amiata, Pienza, Arezzo, and Prato.

How to use the Guide

The guide is divided into **chapters** which describe the main towns, with their environs, in the various provinces of Tuscany. In addition, certain areas of the region known for their distinctive landscape are given separate chapters. Itineraries on foot are provided for the main towns, with separate descriptions for the major monuments and museums. An exhaustive section at the beginning of the book lists all the **practical information** a traveller is likely to need in preparation for and during a visit to Tuscany. This information is integrated with specific details at the beginning of each chapter and at the beginning of the description of each town. Information has been given both for those who visit the area by car and those who travel by public transport.

A small selection of **hotels** has been given at the beginning of each chapter, with their official star rating, in order to give an indication of price. In making the choice for inclusion, generally speaking the smaller hotels have been favoured, those in the centre of towns, or in particularly beautiful positions in the countryside. For further information, see under 'Where to Stay' in the Practical Information section.

On the double page **town plans** of Florence, Siena and Pisa hotels have been marked with a number which corresponds to the key in the text (i.e. Map II;3;4, or Map I;3;5) given with the list of hotels at the beginning of the description of the town. Since there are two plans for Siena (called Siena I and Siena II) the first number in the key refers to the Plan (I or II), the second number to the square, and the third number to the number which marks the position of the hotel. For Pisa and Florence hotels the first number refers to the square on the plans and the second number to the number which marks the position of the hotel. On some of the single page plans hotels have been marked with a number (which corresponds to the key in the text; i.e. Map 5).

Restaurants have also been listed at the beginning of each chapter, and these have been divided into three categories which reflect price ranges in 2002:

€€€ Luxury-class restaurants where the prices are likely to be about €30 a head (and sometimes well over €50 a head). These are the most famous restaurants in Tuscany and they usually offer international cusine.

€€ First-class restaurants where the prices range from about €25 and above. These are generally comfortable, with good service, but are not cheap.

€ Simple trattorie and pizzerie where you can eat for around €13–€20 a head, or even less. Although simple, and by no means smart, the food in this category, which often includes local specialities, is usually the best value.

For further information, see under Eating out on p 24.

The **most important monuments and works of art** in Tuscany have been highlighted in bold capital letters or bold type throughout the text, and **asterisks** have been used to indicate works of art which are particularly beautiful or interesting. The 'Highlights' section on page 11 singles out the major monuments which should not be missed.

Bold type has also been used in **churches** to differentiate the various parts of the building (such as the façade, south side, east end, and important chapels). All churches are taken as being orientated, with the entrance at the west end and the altar at the east end, and the south aisle on the right and the north aisle on the left.

In Florence, Pisa, and Siena all the main monuments have been keyed (ie. Pl.2) against the double page **town plans** which are gridded with numbered squares. On the **ground plans** of museums and churches figures or letters correspond with the description in the text.

The **local tourist boards** (*Agenzia per il Turismo*, shortened to APT) are usually extremely helpful and it is only through them that you can secure up-to-date information on the spot about opening times and accommodation. They have all been listed with their telephone numbers and e-mail addresses on pages 14 and 30, and the information offices are listed at the beginning of each chapter and in each town. On the town maps they are marked with **i**, the symbol which is used on local signposts throughout Italy.

Opening times of museums and monuments have been given throughout (ie. 09.00–14.00; fest. 09.00–13.00), with the abbreviation 'fest.' showing times for Sundays and holidays. The times vary and often change without warning, and it is best to consult the local APT on arrival about up-to-date times. For further information, see p 32. Almost all churches close at midday and do not reopen again until 15.00, 16.00, or even 17.00 hours.

Although detailed town plans are provided, every traveller to Tuscany whether driving or using public transport, will also need a large scale **map** of the region: the best are those produced by the TCI (details on p 15).

Currency The Euro replaced the Italian lire as the official monatary unit in Italy on 1 January 2002. The fixed exchange rate for one Euro was Lire 1936.270. For further information, see p 15.

Abbreviations and symbols used in the guide

ACI	Automobile Club Italiano
APT	Agenzia per il Turismo (official local tourist office)
b.	born
C	century
c	circa (about)
CAI	Club Alpino Italiano
d.	died
✉	email/website
ENIT	Ente Nazionale per il Turismo

📠	fax
FAI	Fondo per l'Ambiente Italiano (founded in 1975 on the model of the British National Trust)
fest.	*festa*, or festival (ie. holiday, including Sunday)
fl.	*floruit* (flourished)
FS	Ferrovie dello Stato (Italian State Railways)
☎	phone
St	Saint
TCI	Touring Club Italiano

Highlights

Famous towns

The most famous towns of Tuscany—Florence, Siena, Pisa, Lucca, Arezzo, and San Gimignano—have many of the most important buildings, works of art, and museums in the region. The Campo of Siena and the Piazza del Duomo of Pisa are unforgettable sights.

Lesser known small towns and villages

The region also has numerous less well known small towns which are extremely interesting and pleasant places to visit (and much less crowded in spring and summer than the more famous towns). These include Cortona, Pienza, Montepulciano, Volterra, Massa Marittima, Montalcino, San Quirico d'Orcia, Pitigliano, Sansepolcro and Colle Val d'Elsa. Near Florence the towns of Prato and Pistoia, often overlooked, have much of interest.

Small **well preserved villages** in lovely countryside include (in the order they appear in the book): Uzzano, Barga, Bolgheri, Tirli, Caldana, Montepescali, Capalbio, Montefioralle, San Gusmé, Monteriggioni, Certaldo Alto, Torri, Bagno Vignoni, Castiglione d'Orcia, Cetona, Magliano in Toscana, Pereta, Sovana, Sorano, Poppi, Cennina, Anghiari, Civitella in Val di Chiana, and Lucignano.

Small museums

Besides the large museums in the famous towns, there are often excellent small museums in lesser known places such as Cortona and Volterra. Other particularly fine museums include the Museo della Collegiata di Sant'Andrea at Empoli, the museum at San Casciano in Val di Pesa, the Pinacoteca Comunale at Castiglion Fiorentino, the Museo della Cattedrale di San Zeno in Pistoia, the Museo Civico and Diocesano at Montalcino, and the Museo della Cattedrale in Pienza.

Masterpieces by famous artists

Numerous masterpieces by great artists are to be found all over the region, including the best works of Duccio, Simone Martini, Pietro and Ambrogio Lorenzetti, Fra Angelico, Filippo Lippi, Piero della Francesca, Luca Signorelli, and the sculptors Nicola and Giovanni Pisano, Donatello, and the Della Robbia family. These can easily be found by reference to the index of artists at the back of the book.

Landscape

Some of the most beautiful landscape in Tuscany can be found in the Chianti region, the Casentino, the forest of Camaldoli, the Mugello, the Garfagnana (the Parco Naturale delle Alpi Apuane and the Parco dell-Orecchiella), Monte Amiata, the Maremma (particularly in the Parco dell'Uccellina, and near Capalbio and Pitigliano, at the nature reserve of Bolgheri, the Lago di Burano, and Cala Martina and Cala Violina on the coast near Follonica). Fine countryside can also be found in parts of Monte Argentario (and the Tombolo di Feniglia), Elba, and Capraia. For details on the **gardens** and the **coast** of Tuscany, see pages 34–36.

Archaeological sites and collections

Etruscan sites and tombs in interesting towns or lovely countryside include those at Chiusi, Cortona, Vetulonia, Volterra, Arezzo, Populonia, Roselle, Fiesole, Pitigliano, Saturnia, and Artimino. **Roman** monuments are to be found at Lucca, Arezzo, Fiesole, Volterra, Cosa and Roselle. **Archaeological collections** with prehistoric, Etruscan and Roman material are kept in museums in the following towns or localities: Florence, Fiesole, Artimino, Pistoia, Pontremoli, Pisa, Siena, Volterra, Grosseto, Arezzo, Cetona, Cortona, and Chiusi.

Romanesque churches

The following are some of the most important Romanesque churches in Tuscany (apart from those in Florence, Pisa, Siena, and Lucca): Sant'Antimo, San Galgano, San Godenzo, the Duomo of Prato, the Duomo of Barga, San Piero a Grado, Abbadia Isola, the Pieve di Santa Maria a Chianni, the Collegiata of San Gimignano, the Pieve di Cellole, Mensano, the Pieve di San Lazzaro a Lucardo, the Duomo of Massa Marittima, the Collegiata of Sant'Agata at Asciano, the Collegiata of San Quirico d'Orcia, the Pieve di Romena, Gropina, the Pieve di Santa Maria in Arezzo, and San Pietro a Cedda.

Monasteries and charterhouses

Monasteries and charterhouses in Tuscany in beautiful natural settings, interesting also for their works of art, include: Monte Oliveto Maggiore, La Verna, Camaldoli, Vallombrosa, the Certosa del Galluzzo, the Certosa di Pisa, Montesenario, Sant'Anna in Camprena, Abbadia San Salvatore, Rosano, Badia a Passignano, and Lecceto.

Renaissance architecture

Masterpieces of Renaissance architecture (apart from those in Florence) include Santa Maria delle Carceri in Prato, the Tempio di San Biagio at Montepulciano, Santa Maria del Calcinaio at Cortona, and the Renaissance town of Pienza.

PRACTICAL INFORMATION

 Planning your trip

When to go

The best time to visit Tuscany is in spring or autumn. In these seasons the countryside is at its best, covered with wild flowers in the spring and bright with orange and yellow leaves in the autumn. However, spring can be unexpectedly wet until well after Easter, and Easter itself should be avoided if possible as it is the most crowded time of year throughout Italy. Autumn is often dryer and can be quite warm throughout October and even in early November. At the height of summer Tuscany can be extremely hot, and at these times it is best to go to the mountains, or to the hill towns (those above 500 metres). The coast of Versilia, and the seaside resorts in the Maremma, and the island of Elba can be extremely crowded with Italian holiday makers in July and August. As all over Italy, Tuscany is crowded with Italian school parties from March until early May. The special charm of a visit to Tuscany in winter is that even the most famous sights can be totally deserted.

Passports

These are necessary for all travellers from Britain and North America entering Italy. Visitors from Australia and New Zealand do not require visas, but those from South Africa do. A lost or stolen passport can be replaced by the relevant embassy in Rome (see p 38).

Italian Tourist Boards

The *Italian State Tourist Office* (*ENIT, Ente Nazionale Italiano per il Turismo*) provides detailed information about Italy at ✉ www.italiantourism.com and addresses of tourist offices in Italy, and abroad at www.enit.it/otp.asp. or at the following addresses:

Australia c/o Italian Chamber of Commerce and Industry, Level 26, Market St, Sydney, ☎ 0061 292 662 1666, 🖷 0061 292 621 677.

Canada 1 Place Ville Marie, Suite 1914, Montreal, Quebec, H3B 2C3, ☎ 001 514 8867667, 🖷 001 514 392 1429, ✉ initaly@ucab.net.

Netherlands Stadhoudeskade 2, 1054 ES Amsterdam, ☎ 003 120 616 8244, 🖷 003 120 618 8515.

UK 1 Princes Street, London W1R 8AY, ☎ 020 7408 1254 or 020 7355 1557, 🖷 020 7493 6695, ✉ enitlond@glabolnet.co.uk.

USA 630 Fifth Avenue, Suite 1565, New York, NY 101111, ☎ 001 212 245 5633, 🖷 001 212 586 9249, ✉ enitny@italiantourism.com.
500 North Michigan Avenue, Suite 2240, Chicago I, IL 60611, ☎ 001 312 6440996, 🖷 001 312 644 3012.

12400 Wilshire Blvd, Suite 550, Los Angeles, CA 90025, ☎ 310 820 1898, ▯ 310 820 6357, ✉ enitala@earthlink.net.

For the addresses of the official local tourist boards (*APT*) in Tuscany, see below and p 30.

Web sites on Tuscany

Region of Tuscany
www.regione.toscana.it

Local *APT* tourist offices in Tuscany
Abetone - Pistoia - Montagna Pistoiese aptpistoia@comune.pistoia.it
Amiata info@amiata.turismo.toscana.it
Arcipelago Toscano info@arcipelago.turismo.toscana.it
Arezzo info@arezzo.turismo.toscana.it
Chianciano Terme - Valdichiana info@chianciano.turismo.toscana.it
Firenze info@firenze.turismo.toscana.it
Grosseto aptgrosseto@grosseto.turismo.toscana.it
Livorno info@livorno.turismo.toscana.it
Lucca aptlucca@lucca.turismo.toscana.it
Massa Carrara apt@massacarrara.turismo.toscana.it
Montecatini Terme e Valdinievole apt@montecatini.turismo.toscana.it
Pisa info@pisa.turismo.toscana.it
Prato apt@prato.turismo.toscana.it
Siena aptsiena@siena.turismo.toscana.it
Versilia bacchi@versilia.turismo.toscana.it

Tour operators
Among the many UK tour operators offering inclusive holidays to Tuscany from the UK are the following:

Abercrombie & Kent Travel, Sloane Square House, Holbein Place, London SW1W 8NS, ☎ 020 7559 8500, ▯ 020 7730 9376, ✉ info@abercrombie kent.co.uk, www.abercrombiekent.co.uk.

Ace Study Tours, Babraham, Cambridge CB2 4AP, ☎ 01223 835055, ▯ 01223 837394.

Alternative Travel Group Ltd, 69–71 Banbury Road, Oxford OX2 6PE, ☎ 01865 315678, ▯ 01865 315697 specialises in walking holidays.

Citalia (CIT Holidays Ltd), Marco Polo House, 3–5 Lansdowne Road, Croydon, Surrey CR9 1LL, ☎ 020 8686 5533, ✉ www.citalia.co.uk.

CTS Travel (UK) Ltd, 44 Godge Street, London W1P 2AD, ☎ 020 7436 4878, ▯ 020 7580 5675, ✉ www.ctstravel.co.uk.

Magic of Italy, King's House, 12–42 Wood Street, Kingston-upon-Thames, Surrey KT1 1JF, ☎ 02700 270 500 for reservations, 0990 462 442 for brochures, ✉ www.magictravelgroup. co.uk.

Martin Randall Travel Ltd, 10 Barley Mow Passage, London W4 4PH, ☎ 020 8742 3355, ▯ 020 8742 7766, ✉ info@martinrandall.co.uk.

Prospect Music & Art Tours Ltd, 36 Manchester Street, London W1U 7LH, ☎ 020 7486 5704, ▯ 020 7486 5686, ✉ enquiries@prospecttours.com.

Travelscene, 11–15 St Ann's Road, Harrow Middlesex HA1 1LQ, ☎ 020 8863 2787, ▯ 020 8861 5083, ✉ www.travelscene.co.uk.

Maps

Although detailed town plans have been included in this book, it has not been possible, because of the format, to provide an atlas of Tuscany adequate for those travelling by car. The maps at the end of the book are only intended to be used when planning an itinerary. The Italian Touring Club publishes several sets of excellent maps: these are constantly updated and are indispensable to anyone travelling by car in Italy. They include the *Grande Carta Stradale d'Italia* on a scale of 1:200,000. This is divided into 15 sheets covering the regions of Italy: Tuscany is covered on the sheet (No. D39) entitled *Toscana*. These are also published in a handier form as an atlas (with a comprehensive index) called the *Atlante Stradale d'Italia* in three volumes (the one entitled '*Centro*' covers Tuscany). These maps can be purchased from the Italian Touring Club offices and at many booksellers; in London they are obtainable from **Stanfords**, 12–14 Long Acre, WC2E 9LP, ☎ 020 7836 1321, ✉ www.stanfords.co.uk.

Health and insurance

British citizens, as members of the EU, have the right to claim health care in Italy if they have the E111 form issued by the Department of Health and Social Security. There are also a number of private holiday health insurance policies, certainly advisable for visitors from outside the EU. Keep the receipt (*ricevuta*) and medical report (*cartella clinica*) to present to your insurer if you have to make a claim.

Currency

On 1 January 2002 the Euro (€) replaced the Italian Lire as the official monatary unit. The fixed exchange rate for one Euro was Lire 1936.270. There are bank notes of 5, 10, 20, 50, 100, 200 & 500 Euro, and coins of 1, 2, 5, 10, & 50 Eurocents as well as 1 & 2 Euro. The Lire was withdrawn from circulation at the end of February 2002.

Travellers' cheques and Eurocheques are the safest way of carrying money while travelling, and most credit cards are now generally accepted in shops, hotels, and restaurants, and at some petrol stations. Outside banks in towns there are numerous cashpoints called Bancomat (check with your own bank about any charges associated with their use), and also automatic machines which change foreign bank notes.

Disabled travellers

Italy is at last catching up with the rest of Europe in the provision of facilities for the disabled. All new public buildings (including museums) are now obliged by law to provide access for the disabled, and specially designed facilities. In the annual list of hotels in each province of Tuscany published by the *APT*, hotels which are able to provide hospitality for the disabled are indicated. Airports and railway stations in Italy provide assistance, and for rail travel the disabled are entitled to a 'carta blu' which allows a discount on the price of the fare. Trains equipped to carry wheelchairs are listed in the railway timetable published by the FS and available at newstands. Access is allowed to the centre of towns (normally closed to traffic) for cars with disabled people, where parking places are reserved for them. The *VAMI Association* (*Associated Volunteers for Italian Museums*) is a non-profit association which organises educational activities and guided tours devoting particular attention to the problems faced by the visually-impaired:

their headquarters in Florence are at the Museo Marino Marini, ☎ 055 219 432 or 055 681 8214. For all other information concerning disabled visitors, contact local *APT* offices, or *Chance* (☎ 045 806 0110) or *Si...viaggiare* (☎ 06 232 67504).

Getting there

By air
Air services from the UK Flights between London Stansted and Gatwick and Pisa airport are operated by *Alitalia* (☎ 0870 544 8259, ✉ www. alitalia.co.uk), *British Airways* (☎ 0990 444000 or 0345 222111, ✉ www. brit-airways.com), and *Ryanair* (☎ 0870 156 9569, ✉ www. ryanair.com). At present the cheapest flights are often offered by *Ryanair* on the web. *Meridiana* (☎ 020 7839 2222, ✉ www.meridana.it) flies from Gatwick to the small airport of Florence (Amerigo Vespucci at Peretola). There are also flights from Manchester, Glasgow, and Dublin to Pisa.

Other companies with flights to Italy include *British Midland* (☎ 0870 6070 555, ✉ www.iflybritishmidland.com), *Buzz* (☎ 0870 240 7070, ✉ www.buzz-away.com) and *Go* (☎ 0845 605 4321, ✉ www.go.fly.com).

Details of charter flights are available through travel agents and listings sections in many of the national newspapaers, especially the Sunday newspapers, the *London Evening Standard* and *Time Out*. *Citalia* (☎ 020 8686 0677) has fly-drive schemes.

Air services from the USA Non-stop services from New York, Boston, Chicago and Los Angeles to Rome are operated by *Alitalia* (☎ 1 800 223 5730, ✉ www.alitaliausa.com). Flights from New York to Rome are also operated by *Continental* (☎ 1 800 231 0856, ✉ www.continental.com), *Delta* (☎ 1 800 241 4141, ✉ www.delta-air.com) and *TWA* (☎ 1 800 892 4141, ✉ www. twa.com). *United Airlines* (☎ 1 800 5382 929, ✉ www.ual.com) operate between Washington DC, and Rome. *British Airways*, *Air France*, *KLM*, *Lufthansa*, and *Sabena* offer flights connecting through London, Paris, Frankfurt, Amsterdam and Brussels to Rome or Milan which are often more economical than direct flights. From Rome and Milan there are internal flights to Pisa or Florence airports.

Airports
Pisa (☎ 050 500 707) is the main international airport in Tuscany, 85km west of Florence. There is a railway station in the airport (tickets are bought in the air terminal) which has a direct train service to Florence (Santa Maria Novella station) in 1 hour (via Pisa central and Empoli): however, recently the number of trains a day has been drastically reduced (apparantly in an attempt to promote the small Florence airport, criticised for its proximity to the centre of Florence and its cramped site), and so unfortunately this excellent service is no longer as useful as it used to be. In summer there is also a direct *SITA* coach service between the airport and Florence (also in 1 hour). Otherwise you have to take a

town bus (no. 3; every 15 minutes) from the airport to Pisa central station where there are other train services to Florence. Taxis for the centre of Pisa are also available (or ☎ 050 541 600). For return flights from Pisa an air terminal (☎ 055 216 073) operates from 06.00 to 16.30 at Florence railway station (on platform no. 5, near which the airport trains depart). Luggage can be checked in here for all flights except *Ryanair*, and boarding cards obtained (not later than 15 minutes before the departure of the airport train).

Florence The small airport of Florence (Amerigo Vespucci at Peretola, ☎ 055 315 874 or 055 373 498), a few kilometres north of Florence, has some flights from Europe (including London Gatwick, and Amsterdam, Barcelona, Brussels, Frankfurt, Munich, Paris, and Vienna), as well as internal domestic flights. *ATAF/SITA* shuttle bus every 30 mins from the arrivals terminus to the *SITA* bus station next to the railway station of Santa Maria Novella in under 30 minutes. Tickets can be bought on board. Taxis are also usually available (otherwise ☎ 055 4798, 055 4390). For baggage lost and found, ☎ 055 308023.

Bologna airport, across the Apennines in Emilia-Romagna, also has direct flights from London. It is at Borgo Panicale, 7km northwest of the city. There is an excellent bus service (*Aerobus*) every 20 minutes to Bologna station in about 10 minutes which runs from the station 05.55–22.30 and from the airport 08.30–23.45. From Bologna station there are trains (on the main Rome–Milan line) in 60–75 minutes to Florence.

Rome The nearest intercontinental airport to Tuscany is Rome (Fiumicino) which has direct flights from numerous cities in the USA as well as from Europe. Non-stop trains run from the airport to Rome (Stazione Termini) every half hour in 30 minutes, and from there it takes under 2 hours to Florence by fast train (Eurostar).

By rail

From the UK *Eurostar* trains (from Waterloo, London, or Ashford, Kent) operate services to the Gare du Nord, Paris where there is an overnight sleeper to Florence. For information, contact *European Rail Ltd* (☎ 020 7387 0444; ▤ 020 7387 0888; ✉ www.raileurope.co.uk). Overnight car sleeper services run May–September once a week from Calais to Bologna (for information and booking, ☎ 0272 544 350 or 051 630 3589).

Rail websites
www.trenitalia.com (Italian State Railways)
www.freedomrail.co.uk
www.itwg.com/home.asp
www.railchoice.co.uk (arranges rail travel between London and Italy via Paris, and will also supply tickets for travel within Italy).

From the USA and Canada In North America, contact the following *Citalia* offices.
CIT **New York**: 15 West 44th Street, 10th Floor, New York, NY 10036, ✉ tour@cittours.com.
CIT **Chicago**: 9501 West Devon Avenue, Suite 1, E. Rosemont, Il. 60018, ✉ rail@cit-rail.com.
CIT **Montreal**: 1450 City Counselers St Quebec, Montreal H3A 2E6, ☎ 361 7799 for the Montreal area, local area dial 514 845 9101.

CIT **Toronto**: 130 Merton Street, ☎ 416 746 2890.
For general information call ☎ 8488 88088; ✉ www.trenitalia.com.

In Italy the main line from Milan and Bologna to Rome has stations at Prato, Florence and Arezzo (although not all trains stop at Prato and Arezzo). The coastal line from Turin and Genoa serves Massa Carrara and Versilia, Pisa, Livorno, and Grosseto.

The main station in Florence (**Stazione di Santa Maria Novella**) is very close to the centre of the city. *Information Office* open 07.00–21.00, or ☎ 8488 88088).

The slower trains also stop at **Stazione Campo di Marte**, when coming from the south, and **Stazione Rifredi** , when coming from the north. Some overnight sleeper trains only stop at Stazione Campo di Marte.

By coach

For details of the coach services available from the UK to Florence, contact *Eurolines* (☎ 01582 404 511; ✉ www.eurolines.com). In Florence, ☎ 055 357 110. Services operate from London's *Victoria Coach Station* on Mon, Wed, Fri, and Sun (usually five days a week in summer) at 09.00 and arrive at Florence, Piazza Adua the next afternoon at 15.00 (change bus in Milan). However, the fare is high when compared to the cut-price air tickets now available between Italy and Britain.

By car

The easiest approaches by road are the motorways through the Mont Blanc (closed for repairs until 2002), St Bernard, or Mont Cenis tunnels, over the Brenner pass, or along the south coast of France. The A1 motorway from Milan and Bologna to Rome runs through Tuscany from Prato to Florence, the Valdarno, Arezzo, Valdichiana, and Chiusi. The coastal motorway from the south of France and Genoa enters Tuscany at Massa Carrara and continues south through Versilia to Lucca and Pisa. The Via Aurelia (now double carriageway all the way to Civitavecchia near Rome) continues south along the coast of Tuscany via Grosseto.

British drivers taking their own cars by any of the routes across France, Belgium, Luxembourg, Switzerland, Germany, and Austria need the vehicle registration book, a valid national driving licence (accompanied by a translation, issued free of charge by the *Italian State Tourist Office*), insurance cover, and a nationality plate attached to the car. If you still have an old-style green driving licence you will also need an International Driving Licence. If you are not the owner of the vehicle, you must have the owner's written permission for its use abroad.

A Swiss motorway pass needed for that country is obtainable from the *RAC, AA,* the Swiss Tourist Board in London or at the Swiss border. The continental rule of the road is to drive on the right and overtake on the left. The provisions of the respective highway codes in the countries of transit, though similar, have important variations, especially with regard to priority, speed limits, and pedestrian crossings.

Membership of the *AA* or *RAC* entitles you to many of the facilities of affiliated societies on the Continent. Temporary membership of the *Automobile Club d'Italia* (*ACI*) can be taken out on the frontier or in Italy. They provide a break-down service (*Soccorso ACI,* ☎ 116).

AA ☎ 01256 29123
RAC membership and insurance ☎ 01345 3331133
    route information ☎ 01345 333 222
Additional route information is available from 📧 www.autostop.it/.

Motorway routes to Italy from Europe

The main routes from France, Switzerland, and Austria are summarised below.

From France, by-passing Geneva The direct motorway route from France, enters Italy through the Mont Blanc Tunnel (closed for repairs until 2002). The road from Courmayeur to Aosta has not yet been improved. At Aosta the A5 motorway begins: it follows the Val d'Aosta. Just beyond Ivrea is the junction with the A4/5 motorway: the A5 continues south to Turin, while the A4/5 diverges east. At Santhia the A4 motorway from Turin is joined for Milan via Novara, or the A26/4 can be followed south via Alessandria, reaching the coast at Voltri, just outside Genoa.

For Tuscany there is a choice between the *Autostrada del Sole* (A1) from Milan or the Florence–Pisa motorway from Genoa. Alternatively the AI can be taken to near Parma where the A15 diverges for the coast at La Spezia. The two latter routes avoid the Apennine pass between Bologna and Florence which carries very heavy traffic and can be subject to delays. This stretch of motorway can also be avoided when approaching from the north by continuing along the A14 beyond Bologna for Cesena, and from there taking the E45 superstrada through Romagna into eastern Tuscany (Sansepolcro and Arezzo).

To Turin from France The most direct approach is through the Mont Cenis Tunnel from Modane in France to Bardonecchia. A road continues via Oulx where a motorway continues via Susa to Turin. From Turin a motorway (A6) descends direct to the coast at Savona, or the motorway (A21, A26) via Asti and Alessandria leads to Genoa; either one joins directly the coastal motorway for Pisa and Florence. Alternatively, the A4 motorway leads from Turin east to Milan for the *Autostrada del Sole*.

The coastal route from the South of France This follows the A10 motorway through the foothills with frequent long tunnels to enter Italy just before Ventimiglia. The motorway continues past Alassio, Albenga, and Savona (where the motorway from Turin comes in), to Voltri (where the A26 motorway from Alessandria comes in) and Genoa (with the junction of the the A7 motorway from Milan). The coastal motorway continues beyond Rapallo and La Spezia into Tuscany past the resorts of Versilia, and at Viareggio divides. The left branch (A11) continues via Lucca to Florence (and the *Autostrada del Sole*), while the coastal branch (A12) continues to Pisa and Livorno and links up with the Aurelia superstrada which runs south along the Tuscan coast via Grosseto.

From Switzerland (Lausanne). The approach to Italy is usually through the Great St Bernard Tunnel (or by the pass in summer) which only becomes motorway at Aosta (see above).

Another motorway route from Switzerland is via the St Gotthard Tunnel (closed for repairs in 2002) and Lugano. The motorway (A9) enters Italy at Como and continues to Milan where the *Autostrada del Sole* (A1) begins for central Italy.

From Germany and Austria (Innsbruck) The direct approach to Italy is by the motorway over the Brenner Pass. The motorway (A22) continues down the Isarco valley to Bolzano and the Adige valley via Trento to Verona. Here motorways diverge west for Brescia and Milan, or east for Vicenza and Venice, or continue south via Mantua to join the A1 motorway just west of Modena for Florence and central Italy.

For tips about driving once you are in Italy, and a description of Italian roads, etc. see p 26.

Where to stay

Hotels

Hotels in Italy are classified by stars as in the rest of Europe. There are five official categories of hotel from the most expensive luxury 5-star hotels to the cheapest and simplest 1-star hotels. However, these categories are bound to disappoint many travellers: the categories are now defined by the services offered (i.e. television in each room, private telephone, 'frigo-bar', etc) and often do not reflect quality. 5-star and 4-star hotels in some localities are not always on a par with hotels with the same designation in the other places in Europe.

A small selection of hotels in Tuscany has been given at the beginning of each chapter of the guide. They have been listed with their official star rating (and keyed with numbers on the town plans) in order to give an indication of price. In making the selection for inclusion, smaller hotels have been favoured, and those in the centre of towns, or in particularly beautiful positions in the countryside. For hotel e-mail addresses, consult the APT web sites (see p 14).

Each local tourist board (*APT*) issues a free list of hotels giving category, price, and facilities. Local tourist offices help you to find accommodation on the spot; it is however advisable to book well in advance, especially at Easter and in summer. To confirm the booking a deposit is usually required (this can normally be made by using a credit card): you have the right to claim the deposit back if you cancel the booking at least 72 hours in advance.

Hotels equipped to offer hospitality to the disabled are indicated in the APT hotel lists.There are now numerous agencies and hotel representatives in Britain and America who specialise in making hotel reservations (normally for 5-star and 4-star hotels only). Accommodation may also be booked through agencies in the **UK** including *HPS Hotel Reservations*, Archgate, 823–825 High Road, Finchley, London N12 8UB, ☎ 020 8446 0126, 📠 020 8446 0196, 📧 www. hotel-reserve.com and *Hotel Connect*, Birkley House, 18–24 High Street, Edgware HA8 7RP, ☎ 020 8381 3131, 📧 enquiries@hotelconnect.co.uk, 📧 www.go-fly.com (via *Go* airline's website). The *Italian Connection* (☎ 020 7486 6890, 📠 020 7486 6891).

Up-to-date information about hotels and restaurants can be found in numerous annual specialised guides to Italy. These include *Alberghi d'Italia,* a selection of 3-star hotels published by Gambero Rosso, *Alberghi e Ristoranti d'Italia* published by the *Touring Club Italiano*, and the red guide *Italia: Hotel-Ristoranti,* published by Michelin.

Every hotel has to declare its prices annually (and these are published in the local provincial *APT* hotel lists, and cannot be exceeded). The total charge for the room (excluding breakfast) should be exhibited on the back of the door of the hotel room, and in the foyer there should be a list of all the rooms in the hotel with their prices. Prices usually change according to the season, and can be considerably less in off peak periods. Hotels in the more famous towns of Tuscany such as Florence and Siena are bound to be a lot more expensive than hotels of the same category in the less well known localities.

In all hotels the service charges are included in the rates. You should beware of extra charges added to the bill. The drinks from the 'frigo-bar' in your room are extremely expensive (it is always best to buy drinks outside the hotel). Telephone calls are also more expensive if made from your room; there is usually a pay telephone (see p 40) in the lobby which is the most economical way of telephoning (and more convenient than using the public telephones in the streets). Hotels are now obliged by law (for tax purposes) to issue an official receipt to customers: you should not leave the premises without this document.

Breakfast (which can be disappointing and costly) is by law an optional extra charge, although a lot of hotels try to include it in the price of the room. When booking a room, always specify if you want breakfast or not. If you are staying in a 2-star or 3-star hotel in a town, it is usually well worthwhile going round the corner to the nearest pasticceria or bar for breakfast. However in the more expensive hotels there are now some good buffet breakfasts provided. But even here the standard of the 'canteen' coffee can be poor: you can always ask for an 'espresso' or 'cappuccino' instead. There is a large supplement if you order breakfast in your room.

Agriturismo and self-catering

This has recently been developed throughout Italy, and provides accommodation in farmhouses (*aziende agrituristiche*) in the countryside, although many of them are no longer on working farms. There are now some 1450 farmhouses in Tuscany which provide accommodation. Terms vary greatly from bed-and-breakfast, to self-contained flats. These are highly recommended for travellers with their own transport, and for families, as an excellent (and usually cheap) way of visiting Tuscany. Some farms require a stay of a minimum number of days. Cultural or recreational activities are sometimes also provided, such as horse-back riding.

Agriturist accommodation is now usually listed in the local *APT* hotel brochures; otherwise a list of them is supplied by the local *APT* offices. More information about such holidays from the **Regione Toscana**, Via di Novoli 26, 50127 Firenze (▨ 055 438 3064, ✉ www.agriturismo.regione.toscana.it. They produce a brochure entitled *Tuscany farm holidays*, available from their office, and publish an official annual list (*Annuario Officiale Regione Toscana: Agriturismo Toscana*), also in English. Associations which provide information and publish annual guides include: **Agriturist Toscana**, Piazza San Firenze 3, Florence, ☎/▨ 055 287 838, www.agriturist.it (*Guida dell'ospitalità rurale*); **Turismo Verde Toscana**, Viale Lavagnini 4, Florence, ☎ 055 20022 or 055 462 2611; ▨ 055 234 5039, ✉ cia-toscana@interbusiness.it (*Turismo Verde*); and **Terranostra**, Via della Villa Demidoff 64; ☎ 055 324 5011; ▨ 055 324 6612; ✉ www.terranostra.it (*Country house holidays in Tuscany*), terranostra.toscana@coldiretti.it.

Accommodation in historic buildings

A new type of hotel has been introduced into Italy, called a *residenza d'epoca*. They are normally in a building, or group of houses, of historic interest, often a castle or monastery. They may have only a few rooms, and sometimes offer self-catering accommodation. They are listed separately in the *APT* hotel lists, with their prices.

Renting accommodation

This has become easier and better organised in the last few years. Villas, farm-houses, and apartments can be rented for holidays and short periods through specialised agencies. Information from *ENIT* offices abroad, and *APT* offices in Italy. Specialised agencies in the USA include: *The Parker Company Ltd*, 319 The Lynnway, Lynn, MA 01901-1810 (☎ 1 800 280 2811).

Camping

Camping is now well organised throughout Italy. In Tuscany, campsites are listed in the local *APT* hotel lists, giving details of all services provided, as well as the size of the site. In some sites caravans and campers are allowed. The sites are divided into official categories by stars, from the most expensive 4-star sites, to the simplest and cheapest 1-star sites. Their classification and rates charged must be displayed at the campsite office. Some sites have been indicated in the text, with their star ratings. It is advisable to book in advance.

Full details of the sites in Italy are published annually by the *Touring Club Italiano* (*TCI*) in *Campeggi e Villaggi Turistici in Italia*. The *Federazione Italiana del Campeggio* has an information office and booking service at Via Vittorio Emanuele 11, Calenzano, 50041 Florence (☎ 055 882 391, 🖹 055 882 5918). There are also two websites for further information: *Easycamping* is at 🖾 www.icaro.it/ and *Faita* is at 🖾 www.camping.it/italy/.

Hostels

Religious organisations sometimes run hostels or provide accommodation at extremely advantageous prices. Information from local *APT* offices.

Youth hostels

The *Italian Youth Hostels Association* (*Associazione Italiana Alberghi per la Gioventù*), Via Cavour 44, 00184 Rome (☎ 06 487 1152, 🖹 06 488 0492) publish a free guide to the 61 hostels all over the country. A membership card of the *AIG* or the *International Youth Hostel Federation* (🖾 www.hostels-aig.org) is required for access to Italian youth hostels. Details from the *Youth Hostels Association*, Trevelyan House, 8 St Stephen's Hill, St Albans, Herts AL1 2DY, and the *American Youth Hostel Inc*, National Offices, PO Box 37613, Washington DC 20013-7613. The regional office in Tuscany is at the *Ostello Villa Camerata*, Viale Augusto Righi 2, Florence (☎ 055 601 451, 🖹 055 610 300).

In Tuscany there are at present youth hostels open at: Florence (see above); Marina di Massa: *Apuano*, Viale delle Pinete 89, Partaccia; Abetone: *Renzo Bizzarri*; Lucca: *San Frediano*, Via della Cavallerizza 12; Prato: *Villa Fiorelli*, Parco di Galceti; Castelfiorentino: *Castelfiorentino*, Viale Roosevelt 26; and Tavarnelle Val di Pesa: *Ostello del Chianti*, Via Cassia.

Food and drink

Tuscan food is traditionally excellent, but now good genuine cuisine is becoming less and less easy to find.

First courses

A classic first course is *minestrone,* a thick vegetable soup. In winter this is made in a richer version, called *ribollita* or *zuppa di pane,* with white beans, black cabbage, and bread. Another vegetable soup, often found in the Maremma (and the Casentino), is *acquacotta,* made with onions, basil, celery, and greens (first lightly fried) with the addition of tomatoes, toasted bread, pecorino cheese, and eggs.

A summer salad (*panzanella*) has dry bread, tomatoes, fresh onions, cucumber, basil, and capers (sometimes with the addition of finely chopped green *radicchio*). *Pappa al pomodoro* is also made in summer, a thick tomato soup with bread, seasoned with basil, etc. *Crostini* are a typical hors-d'oeuvre: fresh chicken-liver paste and other 'homemade' paté of mushrooms, aubergine, etc. spread on bread and often served with cold cuts of ham and salami (*affettati*). *Prosciutto e melone* (raw Parma ham with melon) is particularly good as a first course in summer. *Bresaola* is cured beef often served with *rughetta* (rocket).

In the autumn (usually in October) *fettunta* or *bruschetta* is served: toasted bread with garlic and oil straight from the olive press; if it is topped with hot black cabbage it is called *cavolo con le fette.* Regional first course dishes include *tortelli di patate* (or *topini*), made with potatoes (found especially in the Casentino and Mugello), *pici* or *pinci,* handmade spaghetti (found in Siena), *tortelli maremmani,* fresh pasta filled with ricotta and spinach, *pappardelle alla lepre,* short pasta with a rich hare sauce. Black and white truffles (*tartufi*) are an expensive delicacy, often served with pasta in southern Tuscany.

Second courses

Second course meat dishes are often stewed slowly in a tomato sauce, called *in umido.* In the Maremma, wild boar (*cinghiale*) is often served, sometimes with polenta. *Scottiglia* is a traditional dish of various meats (including chicken and lamb) chopped up and cooked in oil, sage, hot pepper, and tomato, served on toast. *Rosticciana* is grilled spare ribs. The famous *bistecca alla fiorentina,* a T-bone steak cooked over charcoal, has been banned because of 'mad cow' disease.

Traditional Florentine dishes include *fagioli all'uccelletto,* haricot beans in a tomato sauce, and *trippa alla fiorentina,* tripe in a tomato sauce with parmesan cheese. Fresh mushrooms, especially *porcini,* are served all over Tuscany in the autumn. Another good seasonal dish, often served in early spring, is *tortino di carciofi,* baked artichoke pie.

Fish dishes, for which Livorno is particularly famous, include *baccalà alla Livornese,* salt cod cooked in tomatoes, black olives, and pepper, and *cacciucco alla Livornese,* a stew of fish in a hot sauce. In Versilia *seppie in zimino* are often served, cuttlefish cooked with spinach.

Sweets

Tuscany is not famous for its sweets, although two excellent puddings produced in the autumn are *castagnaccio*, a chestnut cake with pine nuts and sultanas, and *schiacciata all'uva*, a bready dough baked in the oven, filled and topped with black grapes and sugar and seasoned with fennel. *Torta della Nonna* is a custard tart with pine nuts. *Frittelle di San Giuseppe* are fritters made with rice, eggs, milk, and lemon rind; *cenci* are simpler fritters. In Livorno *torta* is sold, a delicious thin pizza-like bread cooked with chick-peas. This is also found in Volterra, where it is called *cecina*. *Biscotti di Prato* (or *cantuccini)* are hard biscuits with almonds which are dipped in *vin santo* or *morellino* (a sweet red wine).

Tuscan wines

The best known Italian wine, **Chianti**, is produced in Tuscany. The name is protected by law and only those wines from a relatively small district which lies between Florence and Siena are entitled to the name Chianti Classico (for a fuller description, see p 141). Chianti Classico Gallo Nero (distinguished by a black cock on the bottle) is usually considered the best, but Chianti Putto and Chianti Grappolo are also very good. Other Chianti wines from different parts of Tuscany are: Chianti Montalbano, Chianti Rufina, Chianti Colli Fiorentini, Chianti Colli Senesi, Chianti Colli Aretini, and Chianti Colline Pisane.

In Tuscany the red table wine is usually of better quality than the white. Excellent red wines (not cheap) are *Brunello di Montalcino* and *Vino Nobile di Montepulciano*. Good red wine is also produced at Carmignano near Florence, and around Lucca. The most famous white wine of Tuscany is the *Vernaccia di San Gimignano*, but other good white wines are produced around Pitigliano, Montecarlo, and in the Val d'Arbia. White and rosé wines are also found in the region of Bolgheri. Elba used to produce excellent wines (now hard to find), including *Aleatico*, a dessert wine. *Vin Santo* is another dessert wine (see p 141).

More and more estates which produce wine are opening their cellars to the public, and allowing wine tasting: many of these are on country roads entitled Strade del Vino. Some of the best known are mentioned in the main text. Further information about those in the Chianti region is available from *Consorzio Vino Chianti*, Lungarno Corsini 4, Florence (☎ 055 210 168), *Consorzio Chianti Classico*, Via Scopeti 155, Sant'Andrea in Percussina (☎ 055 822 8245), and *L'Associazione Nazionale Città del Vino*, Via Massetana Romana 34, Siena (☎ 0577 271 556, 🖷 0577 271 595, with an office at Suvereto, ☎ 0565 829 923). There is a wine museum at Rufina, and *enoteche* open in the fortresses of Siena and Montalcino.

Eating out

Restaurants in Italy are called *ristoranti* or *trattorie*; there is now usually no difference between the two, although a *trattoria* used to be less smart (and usually cheaper) than a *ristorante*. Italian food is usually good and not too expensive. The least pretentious restaurant almost invariably provides the best value. Nearly every locality has a simple (often family run) restaurant which caters for the local residents; the decor is usually very simple and the food excellent value. This type of restaurant does not always offer a menu and the choice is usually limited to three or four first courses, and three or four second courses, with only fruit as a sweet. The more sophisticated restaurants are more attractive and comfortable and often larger and you can sometimes eat at tables outside. They display a menu outside, and are also usually considerably more expensive. In all restaurants it is acceptable to order a first course only, or skip the first course and have only a second course. Note that fish is always the most expensive item on the menu in any restaurant.

Meal times Lunch is normally around 13.00 or 13.30, while dinner is around 20.00 or 21.00. Some restaurants still have a cover charge (*coperto*, shown separately on the menu) which is added to the bill (although this has officially been discontinued). Prices include service, unless otherwise stated on the menu. Tipping is therefore not strictly necessary, but a few Euro can be left on the table to convey appreciation. Restaurants are now obliged by law (for tax purposes) to issue an official receipt to customers; you should not leave the premises without this document (*ricevuta fiscale*).

Restaurant prices

In each chapter a small selection of restaurants open in Tuscany in 2002 has been given, which is by no means exhaustive. The restaurants have been divided into three categories (€€€, €€ and €) to reflect price ranges in 2002.

€€€: luxury-class restaurants where the prices are likely to be around €50 a head. These are the most famous restaurants in Tuscany and they usually offer international cuisine.

€€: first class restaurants where the prices are around €30. These are generally comfortable, with good service, but are not cheap.

€: simple trattorie and pizzerie where you can eat for around Lire €13–€20 a head, or less. Although simple and by no means 'smart', the food in this category, which often includes local specialities, is usually the best value.

Restaurant guides

Some of the best annual guides to eating in Italy (but only in Italian) are published by Gambero Rosso (*Ristoranti d'Italia*) and Slow Food (*Osterie d'Italia*, a guide to cheaper eating). Specialised annual guides to restaurants (mostly in the €€€ and € categories as described above) include the red Michelin guide (*Italia: hotel-ristoranti*); *I Ristoranti di Veronelli*, and *Alberghi e Ristoranti* (Touring Club Italiano). Website: www.e-ristoranti.it.

Pizzerie and self-service restaurants

Pizze (a popular and cheap food throughout Italy) and other excellent snacks are served in a *pizzeria*, *rosticceria* and *tavola calda*. Some of these have no seating accommodation and sell food to take away or eat on the spot.

For **picnics**, sandwiches (*panini*) are made up on request (with ham, salami, cheese, anchovies, tuna fish.) at *pizzicherie* and *alimentari* (grocery shops). *Fornai* (bakeries) often sell delicious individual pizzas, bread with oil and salt (*focaccia* or *schiacciata*), and puff pastry topped or filled with cheese, spinach, tomato, salted anchovies, ham, etc; they also usually sell good sweet buns, rolls, and cakes. Some of the most pleasant places to picnic in towns have been indicated in the guide below.

Bars and cafés (caffè or pasticcerie)

These are comfortable and pleasant places to have a good snack. A selection of these (in towns) is listed below. They are open all day, and most Italians eat the excellent refreshments they serve standing up. You pay the cashier first, and show the receipt to the barman in order to get served. In almost all bars, if you sit at a table you are charged considerably more (at least double) and are given waiter service (and you should not pay first). However, some simple bars have a few tables which can be used at no extra charge (it is always best to ask before sitting down). Black coffee (*caffè or espresso*) can be ordered diluted (*alto, lungo or americano*) or with a dash of milk (*macchiato*), with hot milk (*cappuccino or caffè-latte*) or with a liquor (*corretto*). In summer, cold coffee (*caffè freddo*) or cold coffee and milk (*caffè-latte freddo*) are served. A wide selection of soft drinks, wines, and spirits are also available. A *pasticceria* (usually also a caffè) always sells the best cakes since they are made on the premises. Ice-creams are always best in a *gelateria* where they are made on the spot: bars usually sell packaged ice-cream only.

Getting around

By car

Tuscany has an excellent network of roads, and it is almost always best to avoid motorways and *superstrade* and use the secondary roads which are usually well engineered and provide fine views of the countryside. Buildings of historic interest are often indicated by yellow or brown signposts. White road signs sometimes indicate entry into a municipal area which is (confusingly) often a long way from the town of the same name. In the larger towns the traffic tends to be chaotic, the roads congested, and parking difficult. Always try to park outside the centre and explore towns on foot. Hotels and restaurants are usully clearly signposted (yellow signs). Information offices are marked with a yellow 'i' symbol.

Motorways (*autostrade*). Italy probably has the finest motorways in Europe, although in the last few decades too many have been constructed to the detriment of the countryside. Tolls are charged according to the rating of the vehicle and the distance covered. There are service areas on all autostrade (open 24 hours), with cafés and restaurants. Most autostrade have SOS points every two kilometres. Contrary to French roads, motorways in Italy are indicated by green signs (and normal roads by blue signs). At the entrance to motorways, the two directions are indicated by the name of the most important town (and not by the nearest town) which can be momentarily confusing. The *Autostrada del Sole* (AI) which runs through Tuscany is less wide than some of the more recent motorways and carries very heavy traffic (including numerous lorries), especially between Bologna and Florence. Driving on this road is easier on Saturdays and Sundays when lorries are banned.

Superstrade are dual carriageway fast roads which do not charge tolls. They do not usually have service stations, SOS points, or emergency lanes. They are also usually indicated by green signs, but sometimes by blue signs (*quattro corsie*, meaning four lanes). In Tuscany the superstrada between Florence and Siena is particularly busy at 08.00, 18.00 and on Sunday late afternoon and evening, and it is a poorly engineered road, and rather narrow.

Petrol stations are open 24 hours on motorways, but otherwise their opening times are 07.00–12.00, 15.00–20.00; winter 07.30–12.30, 14.30–19.00. There are now quite a number of self-service petrol stations open 24hrs operated by bank notes or credit cards. Unleaded petrol is now available all over Italy. Petrol in Italy costs less than in England, and a lot more than in America.

Car parking Almost every town in Tuscany (as in the rest of Italy) has taken the wise step of closing its historic centre to traffic (except for residents). This makes them much more pleasant to visit on foot. Access is allowed to hotels and for the disabled. On approaching a town, the white signs for *centro* (with a bull's eye) should be followed towards the historic centre. Car-parks are also sometimes indicated by blue 'P' signs; where parking is a particular problem, the best places to park near the centre have been mentioned in the main text. Some car parks are free, while others charge an hourly tariff. In some towns mini-bus services connect car parks with the centre. With a bit of effort it is almost always possible to find a place to leave your car free of charge, away from the town centre. It is forbidden to park in front of a gate or doorway marked with a *passo carrabile* (blue and red) sign. Always lock your car when parked, and never leave anything of value inside it.

Car hire is available in the main towns and at Pisa and Florence airports. Arrangements for the hire of cars in Italy can also be made through Citalia, Alitalia or British Airways (at specially advantageous rates in conjunction with their flights).

Rules of the road Italian law requires that you carry a valid driving licence when travelling. It is obligatory to keep a red triangle in the car in case of accident or breakdown. This serves as a warning to other traffic when placed on the road at a distance of 50 metres from the stationary car. It is compulsory to wear seat-belts. Driving in Italy is generally faster (and often more aggressive) than driving in Britain or America. Road signs are now more or less standardised to the international codes, but certain habits differ radically from those in Britain or America. Unless otherwise indicated, cars entering a road from the right are given precedence (also at roundabouts). If a driver flashes his headlights, it means he is proceeding and *not* giving you precedence. In towns, Italian drivers are very lax about changing lanes without much warning. Some crossroads in small towns have unexpected 'stop' signs. Italian drivers tend to ignore pedestrian crossings. In towns, beware of motorbikes, mopeds and Vespas, the drivers of which seem to consider that they always have the right of way.

The police (see p 37) sometimes set up road blocks on country roads to check cars and their drivers: it is important to stop at once if you are waved down by a policeman at the side of a road and you must immediately show them your driving licence and the car documents.

By train

The *Italian State Railways* (*FS—Ferrovie dello Stato*; ☎ 8488 88088; ✉ www.trenitalia.com) run various categories of trains:

ES—*Eurostar*. International express trains running between the main Italian and European cities. They have a special supplement, approximately 30 per cent of the normal single fare, and no standing passengers are permitted. Booking is obligatory (and included in the price of the ticket). First and second-class carriages.

EC and IC—*Eurocity* and *Intercity*. International and national express trains, with a supplement (but cheaper than the Eurostar supplement).

Espressi. Long-distance trains (both classes) not as fast as the Intercity trains.

Diretti. Although not stopping at every station, a good deal slower than Espressi.
Interregionali. Local trains stopping at most stations.
Regionali. Local trains stopping at all stations, mostly with second-class carriages only.

Buying tickets and booking a seat Tickets (valid for two months after the day sold) must be bought before the journey, otherwise a fairly large penalty has to be paid to the ticket-collector on the train. In order to validate your ticket it has to be stamped at an automatic machine in the railway station before starting the journey (there is always a machine at the beginning of each platform and sometimes half way up it). If, for some reason, you fail to do this, try to find the ticket conductor on the train before he finds you. Once the ticket has been stamped it is valid for 6 hours for distances up to 200 km, and for 24 hours for distances over 200km.

The most convenient way of buying rail tickets (and making seat reservations) is from a travel agent (but this is only possible through those who are agents for the Italian State Railways), as there are often long queues at the station ticket offices. Some trains charge a special supplement (see above), and on some, seats must be booked in advance; when buying tickets you therefore have to specifiy which category of train you intend to take as well as the destination. Trains in Italy are usually crowded especially on holidays and in summer; and it is now always advisable to book your seat for long-distance journeys. There is a small booking fee (€3.00) and the service is available from 2 months to 3 hours before departure. There is no extra charge for booking a seat on a Eurostar train. In the main stations the better known credit cards are now generally accepted. Use the special ticket window when buying a ticket with a credit card. In main towns such as Florence and Rome you can now buy a ticket by telephone (☎ 199 166 177) 24 hrs before departure (with delivery to your address for a small extra charge).

Fares and reductions In Italy fares are still much lower than in Britain. Children under the age of 4 travel free, and between the ages of 4 and 12 travel half price. There are also some reductions for families. For travellers over the age of 60 (with senior citizen railcards; show your card when buying your ticket), the *Carta Res* (valid one year) offers a 30 per cent reduction on *international* rail fares. The Inter-rail card (valid 1 month) which can be purchased in Britain by young people up to the age of 26, is valid in Italy (and allows a reduction of 50 per cent on normal fares). If you purchase the *Carta d'Argento* (for those over 60) or the *Carta Verde* (for those between the ages of 12 and 26), both valid one year, you are entitled to a reduction on rail fares.

A *Chilometrico* ticket is valid for 3000km (and can be used by up to five people at the same time) for a maximum of 20 journeys. A *Eurodomino* ticket is valid for one month's travel in a number of European countries (for 3,5, or 10 days). There is no age limit for either of these tickets.

You can claim reimbursement (on payment of a small penalty) for unused tickets and sleepers not later than 24 hours before the departure of the train. If a Eurostar train is over 25 minutes late, you are entitled to a 50% refund. Bicycles are allowed on most trains (except Eurostar trains): a day ticket costs marginally less on slow trains. A *Carta Blu* is available for the disabled, and certain trains have special facilites for them (information from the main railway stations in Italy).

Timetables The timetable for the train services changes on about 26

September and 31 May every year. Excellent timetables are published twice a year by the *Italian State Railways* (*In Treno*; one volume for the whole of Italy) and by Pozzorario in several volumes (*Sud e Centro Italia* or *Nord e Centro Italia* cover Tuscany). These can be purchased at news-stands and railway stations.

Left luggage offices are usually open 24 hours at the main stations; at smaller stations they often close at night, and for a few hours in the middle of the day.

Porters are entitled to a fixed amount (shown on notice boards at all stations) for each piece of baggage, but trolleys are now usually available.

Restaurant cars (sometimes self-service) are attached to most international and internal long-distance trains. Also, on most fast trains, snacks, hot coffeee and drinks are sold thoughout the journey from a trolley wheeled down the train. Sometimes you can buy snacks from the train window from trolleys on the platform of large stations.

Sleeping cars, with couchettes, or first and second class cabins, are carried on certain long-distance trains, as well as 'Sleeperette' compartments with reclining seats (first-class only).

Train services in Tuscany are generally good. All the towns which can be easily reached by train are indicated in the text below. The main line from Milan to Rome has stations at Prato, Florence, Arezzo, and Chiusi, as well as numerous smaller towns (slow trains only). The main line down the coast from Genoa to Rome has stations at Massa, Viareggio, Pisa, Livorno, and Grosseto, as well as the smaller towns (slow trains only). There is a line from Florence via Empoli to Pisa, and via Empoli to Siena, and a secondary line from Florence to Prato, Pistoia and Lucca.

There has been interest in recent years in preserving some of the historic and most scenic railway lines in Tuscany, including the line from Asciano to Monte Antico, which is sometimes open for special excursions in May and October (for information ☎ 055 235 6194 or 0577 207 413). The pretty Faentina line between Florence and the Mugello has been reopened (and it also has steam train excursions on certain days of the year).

By bus

Local country buses abound between the main towns in Italy, and offer an excellent alternative to the railways. It is difficult to obtain accurate information about these local bus services outside Italy. Details have been given in the text. The main bus companies operating in Tuscany are: *SITA*, Via Santa Caterina da Siena 15, Florence (☎ 800 373 760 or 055 214 721), and Sansepolcro (☎ 0575 742 999); *Lazzi*, Piazza Stazione 4, Florence (☎ 055 351 061); *COPIT* and *CAP*, Largo Alinari 9, Florence (☎ 055 214 637); *LFI*, Via Guido Monaco 37, Arezzo (☎ 0575 39881); *TRA-IN*, Via Trento 33, Poggibonsi (☎ 0577 937 207); *CPT* in the province of Pisa (☎ 050 505 511).

Town buses Now that most towns have been partially closed to private traffic, town bus services (the details of which have been given in the text) are usually fast and efficient. You buy a ticket before boarding (at automatic machines, tobacconists, bars, newspaper kiosks, and information offices) and stamp it on board at automatic machines.

By bicycle

Bicycles can be transported on trains except Eurostars (see p 27). In Florence bike hire firms which also have mountain bikes, include *Alinari*, Via Guelfa 85, ☎ 055 280 500 and *Florence by Bike*, Via San Zanobi 120, ☎ 055 488 992.

Taxis

Taxis (white in colour) are provided with taximeters; make sure these are operational before hiring. There are no cruising taxis so they have to be hired from ranks or by telephone. You are not expected to leave a tip, but most Italians 'round off' the fare. A supplement for night service, and for luggage is charged. There is a heavy surplus charge when the destination is outside the town limits (ask roughly how much the fare is likely to be). Women travelling alone in the evening are sometimes entitled to a reduced rate.

Local tourist offices

Tuscany is divided into sectors, each with a local tourist information office, the *Agenzia per il Turismo* (*APT*) which provides invaluable help to travellers on arrival: they supply a free list of accommodation (revised annually), including hotels, agriturist accommodation, youth hostels, and camping sites; up-to-date information on museum opening times and annual events; and information about local transport. They also usually distribute, free of charge, illustrated pamphlets about each town, sometimes with a good plan.

The headquarters are normally open Monday–Saturday 08.00–14.00, but in the towns of particular interest there is sometimes a separate *APT* information office which is also often open in the afternoon.

APT offices in Tuscany (the e-mail addresses of these offices are given on p 14):
Abetone-Pistoia-Montagna Pistoiese, Via Marconi 28, San Marcello Pistoiese (☎ 0573 630 145).
Amiata, Via Adua 25, Abbadia San Salvatore (☎ 0577 775 811).
Arcipelago Toscano, Calata Italia 26, Portoferraio, Elba (☎ 0565 914 671).
Arezzo, Piazza Risorgimento 116, Arezzo (☎ 0575 23952).
Chianciano Terme-Valdichiana, Via Sabatini 7, Chianciano Terme (☎ 0578 63538).
Firenze, Via Manzoni 16, Florence (☎ 055 23320).
Grosseto, Via Monterosa 206, Grosseto (☎ 0564 454 510).
Livorno, Piazza Cavour 6, Livorno (☎ 0586 898 111).
Lucca, Piazza Guidiccioni 2, Lucca (☎ 0583 491 205).
Massa Carrara, Lungomare Vespucci 24, Marina di Massa (☎ 0585 240 046).
Montecatini Terme-Valdinievole, Viale Verdi 66, Montecatini Terme (☎ 0572 772 244).
Pisa, Via Pietro Nenni 24, Pisa (☎ 050 929 777).
Prato, Via Muzzi 51, Prato (☎ 0574 35141).
Siena, Via di Città 43, Siena (☎ 0577 42209).
Versilia, Piazza Mazzini 22, Viareggio (☎ 0584 48881).

Language

Although many people speak a little English, some basic Italian is helpful for everyday dealings. If you are able to say a few words and phrases your efforts will be much appreciated. See Food and wine section for relevant vocabulary.

good morning *buon giorno*
good afternoon/good evening *buona sera*
good night *buona notte*
goodbye *arrivederci*
hello/goodbye (informal) *ciao*
see you later *a più tardi*

yes/no *si/no*
okay *va bene*
please/thank you *per favore/grazie*

today *oggi*
tomorrow *domani*
yesterday *ieri*
now *adesso*
later *più tardi*
in the morning *di mattina*
in the afternoon/evening *di pomeriggio/di sera*
at night *di notte*

Monday *lunedì*
Tuesday *martedì*
Wednesday *mercoledì*
Thursday *giovedì*
Friday *venerdì*
Saturday *sabato*
Sunday *domenica*

spring *primavera*
summer *estate*
autumn *autunno*
winter *inverno*

January *gennaio*
February *febbraio*
March *marzo*
April *aprile*

May *maggio*
June *giugno*
July *luglio*
August *agosto*
September *settembre*
October *ottobre*
November *novembre*
December *dicembre*

what is your name? *come si chiama/come ti chiami?* (informal)
my name is ... *mi chiamo ...*

I would like *vorrei*
do you have ...? *ha ...?/avete ...?* (plural)

where is ...? *dov'è ...?*
what time is it? *che ore sono?*
at what time? *a che ora?*
when? *quando?*

how much is it? *quanto è?*
the bill *il conto*
where are the toilets? *dove sono i gabinetti?*

do you speak English? *parla inglese?*
I don't understand *non capisco*

cold/hot *freddo/caldo*
with/without *con/senza*
open/closed *aperto/chiuso*
cheap/expensive *economico/caro*

left/right/straight on *sinistra/destra/diritto*

Museums, galleries and churches

The opening times of museums and monuments are given in the main text but they sometimes vary and often change without warning; when possible it is always advisable to consult the local tourist office (*APT*) on arrival about the up-to-date times. The opening times of state-owned museums and monuments are in the process of change: many museums and archaeological sites in Tuscany are now open seven days a week (although if they have a closing day it is still usually Monday). However, there is no standard timetable and you should take great care to allow enough time for variations in the hours shown when planning a visit to a museum or monument. Some museums in the larger cities now usually stay open on the main public holidays (1 January, Easter, 1 May, 15 August, and Christmas Day). In Florence, the Uffizi, Palazzo Pitti and Galleria dell'Accademia are open in the evenings in summer (when they are usually less crowded).

Admission charges vary, but are now quite high (the Uffizi costs €6.5). There are often cumulative tickets allowing entrance to a number of museums and monuments (sometimes valid for several days) which are almost always worth purchasing.

Reductions Citizens of member countries of the EU under the age of 18 and over the age of 65 are entitled to free admission to State-owned museums and monuments in Italy (on production of an identity card proving your age). EU students between the ages of 18 and 26 are now entitled to a reduction (usually 50%) to State-owned museums, and some other museums have special tickets for students.

For one week during the year (the *Settimana per i Beni Culturali e Ambientali*), usually in early December or March, there is free entrance for everyone to all state-owned museums in Italy, and others are opened specially. Website for state-owned museums: www.beni-culturali.it (☎ 800 991 199).

In Florence, there is now a booking service (*Firenze Musei*, ☎ 055 294 883, ▤ 055 264 406) for visiting the state-owned museums, particularly useful for the Uffizi and Galleria dell'Accademia which can have extremely long queues.

Churches
Although they usually open very early in the morning (at 07.00 or 08.00), churches are normally closed for a considerable period during the middle of the day. Almost all churches close at 12.00 and do not reopen until 15.00, 16.00, or even 17.00 hours. Cathedrals and some of the larger churches (indicated in the text) may be open without a break during daylight hours. Smaller churches and oratories are often open only in the early morning, but it is sometimes possible to find the key by asking locally. Ask the sacristan to see closed chapels, crypts, and cloisters (he sometimes expects a tip). Some churches now ask that sightseers do not enter during a service. Normally visitors who are not in a tour group may do so, provided they are silent and do not approach the altar in use. You sometimes have to pay a small entrance fee to see treasuries, cloisters, and some chapels. Lights (operated by coins) have now been installed in many churches to illuminate frescoes and altarpieces, but a torch and binoculars are always useful. Sometimes you are not allowed to enter important churches or religious sanctuaries wearing shorts or with bare shoulders.

Festivals

There are a number of traditional festivals in Tuscan towns which are of the greatest interest. At these times, the towns become extremely lively, and, apart from the central race or competition, numerous celebrations take place on the side, and local markets are usually held at the same time. The most important local festivals have been described in detail in the text, but a summary is given below, in case you are able to choose a period in which to visit Tuscany when some of them are taking place. They are particularly exciting events for children. Information from local **APT** offices.

Spring Carnival celebrations at Viareggio, Cerreto Guidi, Borgo San Lorenzo, and Bibbiena. Easter: *Scoppio del Carro* (when a carriage 'explodes' with fireworks outside the Duomo) on Easter Day in Florence, Good Friday passion play at Grassina. Ascension Day: *Festa del Grillo* (a fair in the Cascine park) in Florence. Other festivals include: *Palio* (horse race)at Fucecchio; *Balestro del Girifalco* (falcon crossbow contest) at Massa Marittima; *Maggiolata* (May fair) at Castiglione d'Orcia; *Palio dei Somari* (donkey race)at Torrita di Siena.

Summer The *Palio* (horse race) at Siena, the most splendid and exciting of all annual festivals in Italy (see p 359). *Calcio in Costume* ('football' game in 16C costume)in Florence; *Palio del Cerro* (athletic contests in 16C costume) at Cerreto Guidi; *Corpus Domini* procession in Prato; *Giostra del Saracino* (a tournament) in Arezzo; *Balestro del Girifalco* (falcon crossbow contest) at Massa Marittima. Marine festivities, with procession of boats at Porto Santo Stefano, Porto Ercole, Orbetello, Isola del Giglio, and Castiglione della Pescaia. Rodeo at Alberese; *Palio* (horse race) at Piancastagnaio; *Fiera di Sant'Antonino* and *Palio Marinaro* (rowing contest) in Livorno; *Palio degli Arcieri* (archery contest) in Piombino; *Disfida fra gli arcieri di Terra e Corte* (archery contest) at Fivizzano; *Festa di San Ranieri* (regatta) and *Gioco del Ponte* (a sham fight on the Ponte di Mezzo) at Pisa; *Giostra dell'Orso* (a tournament)at Pistoia; *Bravio delle Botti* (a barrel rolling contest) at Montepulciano.

Autumn *Festa della Rificolona* (a fair when paper lanterns are carried through the streets) in Florence; *Festa dell'uva* (wine festival) and *Fiera di San Luca* (cattle fair) in Impruneta; *Sagra dei Marroni* (chestnut festival) at Marradi; display of the *Sacro Cingolo* (Holy Girdle) in Prato; *Palio della Balestra* (crossbow contest) in Sansepolcro; *Palio* (race) at Castel del Piano; *Astiludio* (flag throwing contest) at Volterra; *Sagra del Tordo* (gastronomic 'thrush' festival) at Montalcino.

Summer music and theatre festivals in Tuscany include: *Maggio Musicale* in Florence; *Estate Fiesolana* in Fiesole; *Festival di Pentecoste* at Badia a Passignano; *Festival del Teatro* at Sorano; Puccini opera festival at Torre del Lago; *Settimana musicale senese* at the Accademia Musicale Chigiana, Siena; music festival at Montepulciano; theatre festival (*Teatro Povero di Monticchiello*) at Monticchiello; chamber music festival at La Foce (*Incontri in Terra di Siena*); music and theatre festival at Radicondoli; buskers' festival (*On the Road*) at Pelago. Concerts are usually held at Sant'Antimo, Cennina, and Montalcino. Summer opera courses are held by the British Institute of Florence (see p 37) in Massa Marittima.

Sport and leisure

Swimming

Much of the **coast of Tuscany** has been intensely developed for tourism and the beaches can be overcrowded particularly in Versilia, where Viareggio is the most popular seaside resort on the west coast of Italy. Forte dei Marmi and I Ronchi nearby are elegant resorts with beaches crowded with Florentines and Milanese in July and August. Here there is limited free access to the beaches since at the *stabilimenti* or *bagni attrezzati* you are charged for the hire of cabins and deck chairs and there is usually a refreshment kiosk. There is free access only to the *spiaggie libere* which are often crowded and less easily accessible. However everyone is allowed to within five metres of the edge of the sea at all beaches.

The Parco Naturale Migliarino-San Rossore-Massaciuccoli between Viareggio and Livorno is a protected area of coastline (limited access). The mouth of the Serchio at Marina di Vecchiano is well preserved. There are beaches south of Livorno at Il Romito and Quercianella, at the resort of Castiglioncello, and between Cecina and Piombino (particularly attractive at Baratti and around Populonia. Cala Martina and Cala Violina are beautiful bays near Portiglione south of Follonica. The wooded headland of Punta Ala has some exclusive resorts, and the sand is particularly golden at Castiglione della Pescaia. The best preserved stretch of coastline in Tuscany (and one of the best in Italy) is near Grosseto at the foot of the Monti dell'Uccellina (protected as the Parco Naturale della Maremma), accessible from Marina di Alberese.

Further south, the promontory of Monte Argentario has fine stretches of coast and elegant resorts (with good free beaches on the Tombolo di Feniglia). The beach near Talamone is also attractive and south of Ansedonia there is a very extensive sandy beach. The islands which form the Tuscan archipelago are now mostly protected as a national park: Elba is the most famous, with an attractive coastline crowded with holidaymakers particularly from Florence in summer (and from Germany in September), Capraia has a rocky shore (frequented by skin-divers), and Giglio also has pleasant beaches. The *TCI* and *Legambiente* publish a guide to the best beaches in Italy, called *Guida Blu* (www.legambiente.com).

There are also municipal **swimming pools** open in summer throughout Tuscany. Numerous three and four-star hotels in Tuscany (and 'agriturist' hotels) now have swimming pools (and some also tennis courts).

Walking

Hiking and walking have become more popular throughout Italy in recent years and more information is now available locally. Details have been given in the relevant chapters. The areas of Tuscany particularly suitable for walking are the Garfagnana, the Mugello, the Casentino (Monte Falterona, and the Foreste Casentinesi), and Monte Amiata. Specialist guides to walking in Tuscany are now published with detailed maps (including *Landscapes of Tuscany*, by Elizabeth Mizon, Sunflower Books). The Tuscan Region and the *WWF* publish a guide to walking in Tuscany called *Cammina Toscana* (Arcadia). Another guide, in 2 volumes, is *A Piedi in Toscana* (ed. Iter; only available in Italian). For walking excursions, contact *CAI* (*Club Alpino Italiano*), Via dello Studio 5, Florence, ☎ 055 239 8580. Good maps on a scale of 1:100,000, 1:50,000 and 1:25,000 are produced by the *Istituto Geografico Militare*, invaluable for the detailed exploration of the country. They can be bought at Viale Filippo Strozzi 10, Florence.

Walking tours of Tuscany are organised by specialist agencies in the UK and North America, including *Alternative Travel Group Ltd*, 69–71 Banbury Road, Oxford (☎ 01865 310399).

Protected areas of particular natural beauty

In Tuscany these include two national parks: the Parco Nazionale di Monte Falterona, Campigna e Foreste Casentinesi, created in 1991 and the Parco Nazionale dell'Arcipelago Toscano, created in 1996. There are also three regional parks (the Parco Naturale delle Alpi Apuane incorporating the Parco dell'Orecchiella reserve, the Parco Naturale di Migliarino-San Rossore-Massaciuccoli, and the Parco Naturale della Maremma), and a number of small nature reserves and local protected areas. The *Tuscany Region* (*Regione Toscana*), Dipartimento delle Politiche Territoriali e Ambientali, Via di Novoli 26, Firenze; 🖾 www.regione.toscana.it) issues a free map and publishes a guide to the protected areas in Tuscany (*Parchi, Riserve e aree protette della Toscana*, 2000). The *World Wide Fund for Nature* (*WWF*) oases (for information, ☎ 055 477 876) include Bolgheri (in the Maremma marshes near the coast), Lago di Burano, Orbetello and the Orti di Bottagone, the wooded area of Bosco di Rocconi (province of Grosseto), and further north (province of Lucca), the Oasi del Bottaccio. *Legambiente Toscana* (Via G. Orsini 44, Flirence, ☎ 055 681 0330; www.legambientetoscana.it) is a society for the protection of the environment. It opened its first reserve in 1998 at Bosco di Tanali in the Padule di Bientina (province of Pisa).

A local office of the *Club Alpino Italiano* (*CAI*), the *Comunità Montana*, the *WWF*, and the *APT* all provide information.

Cycling

Cycling tours of Tuscany are becoming more and more popular. With the enormous increase in agriturism accommodation in the countryside in the last few years it has become much easier to plan a holiday by bike. Areas particularly suitable to cycling include the Mugello (the Comunità Montana have published an excellent little guide to the best routes, see p 124), the Chianti region, and the Val d'Orcia. There are now specialist agencies in the US and UK which organise cycling trips. Mountain bikes can be hired in Florence (see p 30). For maps, see p 15.

Golf

There is an 18-hole golf course at *Ugolino*, 12km southeast of Florence on the Strada Chiantigiana, beyond Grassina (☎ 055 230 1009). It has reciprocal arrangements with two other Tuscan 18-hole golf courses nearby, *Le Pavoniere* at Prato (Via della Fattoria 6, Località Tavola), designed by Arnold Palmer, ☎ 0574 620 855, and *Poggio dei Medici* at Cignano near Scarperia in the Mugello, ☎ 055 843 0436.

There are other 18-hole courses at *Punta Ala*, Via del Golf 1, 58040 Punta Ala (Grosseto), ☎ 0564 922 121); *Versilia*, Via della Sipe 40, 55045 Pietrasanta (Lucca), ☎ 0584 881 574; and *Montecatini*, Via dei Brogi, Località Pievaccia, 51015 Monsummano Terme (Pistoia), ☎ 0572 62218.

Tuscan gardens

Gardens are a special feature of Tuscany, and it is becoming possible to visit an increasing number of private gardens, usually by previous appointment. Those described (with their opening times) are included in the following list.

In and around Florence: Giardino di Boboli, Villa di Castello, Villa della Petraia, the botanical gardens (Giardino dei Semplici), and the Giardino dell'Orticoltura. In May and June the Giardino dell'Iris and the Giardino delle Rose are open. The Villa Medici in Fiesole and Villa della Gamberaia in Settignano charge an entrance fee. The private gardens of Villa I Tatti, Villa La Pietra (at present being restored), Villa Le Balze, Villa Capponi, and Villa I Collazzi can sometimes be seen by previous appointment. In the environs of Florence gardens surround the Villa di Poggio a Caiano and Villa Corsi Salviati (Sesto Fiorentino).

In the Mugello, the private garden of the Castello del Trebbio is only sometimes open by previous appointment. One of the most famous gardens in Tuscany is that of the Villa Garzoni at Collodi. In Lucca the Botanical Gardens are open regularly, and in the environs there are well-known private gardens open at the Villa Reale di Marlia, Villa Mansi, and Villa Torrigiani. A camellia festival is held in March at Pieve di Compito, when more villa gardens are open, and there is a flower show and market. In the Apuan Alps, there is an alpine garden at Pania di Corfina. The Botanical Gardens at Pisa are one of the most important in Tuscany, and between Pisa and Florence there are gardens at the Villa Medici of Cerreto Guidi, and private gardens which can sometimes be visited at Bibbiani and the Villa di Belvedere at Crespina. There is a rose garden at Cavriglia open in May. Siena has a Botanical Garden, and in the environs there are private gardens at Villa di Vicobello, Celsa, and Cetinale (open by previous appointment). The Horti Leonini at San Quirico d'Orcia are open as public gardens, and at Pienza the hanging garden of Palazzo Piccolomini is usually open (but is at present being restored). Also in the Val d'Orcia the beautiful garden of La Foce is now open to the public one day a week.

Lesser known gardens include Villa La Fratta (near Torrita di Siena), La Peschiera at Santa Fiora, the Villa Rinuccini di Torre a Cona near San Donato in Collina and Villa Chigi on the outskirts of Castelnuovo Berardenga. Penelope Hobhouse has published a guide to the *Gardens of Italy* (1998).

 Additional information

Banking services

Banks are usually open Monday–Friday 08.30–13.30, 14.30–15.30 (or 14.45–15.45). They are closed on Saturday and holidays, although a few banks now open on Saturday morning. They all close early (about 11.00) on days preceding national holidays. The commission on cashing travellers' cheques can be quite high. Outside many banks there are cashpoints and also machines which change foreign banknotes. Money can be changed at exchange offices (cambio), in travel agencies, some post offices, and main stations. At some hotels, restaurants, and shops money can be exchanged (but usually at a lower rate).

The British Institute of Florence

This is a non-profit making independent Institution, which was founded in 1917 by a group of Anglo-Florentines including Arthur Acton, Edward Hutton, G.M. Trevelyan, Lina Waterfield, and Gaetano Salvemini, and received a Royal Charter in 1923. Its scope is to promote British culture in Italy and Italian culture to English-speaking visitors and to maintain a library of English books in Florence.

The Institute runs a language school and courses in art history in Florence at Piazza Strozzi 2 (☎ 055 284 033; ✉ info@britishinstitute.it), and summer courses at Massa Marittima. Its excellent lending library (c 50,000 volumes, the largest collection of English books in Italy) is in Palazzo Lanfredini, Lungarno Guicciardini 9 (☎ 055 284 032; ✉ library@britishinstitute.it). Since 1989 it has been named after its benefactor Harold Acton, who died in Florence in 1994. It can be used for a small fee, and retains the atmosphere of a 19C general browsing library. The reading room has English newspapers and periodicals. Interesting public lectures are also held here. ✉ www.britishinstitute.it for information.

Crime and personal security

For all emergencies, ☎ 113 or 112.

It is always advisable not to carry valuables in handbags (thieves often operate on mopeds or Vespas), and always watch out for pick-pockets on public transport.

Help and advice is given to British and American travellers in Italy who are in difficulty by the British and American embassies and consulates, see below. The embassies replace lost or stolen passports.

Cash and documents can be left in hotel safes. It is a good idea to make photocopies of all important documents in case of loss. You are strongly advised to carry some means of identity with you at all times while in Italy, since you can be held at a police station if you are stopped and found to be without one.

There are three categories of policemen in Italy: *Vigili Urbani*, the municipal police (who wear blue uniform in winter and white during the summer and hats similar to London policemen); *carabinieri*, the military police who have local offices in every town and small village (and who wear black uniform with a red stripe down the side of their trousers); and the *Polizia di Stato*, State police (who wear dark blue jackets and light blue trousers).

Crime should be reported at once, theft to either the Polizia di Stato or the Carabinieri. A detailed statement has to be given in order to get an official document confirming loss or damage (*denuncia di smarrimento*), which is essential for insurance claims. Interpreters are usually provided.

To report the loss of theft of a credit card, call:

Visa, ☎ 800 862 079.

Mastercard, ☎ 800 870 866.

American Express, ☎ 06 72282.

Dress

If you are wearing shorts or miniskirts, or have bare shoulders you can be refused admission to some churches.

Electric current
The electricity supply is 220 watts. Visitors may need round, two-pin Continental plugs for some appliances.

Embassies and consulates

Consulates
United Kingdom Lungarno Corsini 2, Florence, ☎ 055 284 133.
United States of America Lungarno Vespucci 38, Florence, ☎ 055 239 8276.

Embassies in Rome
Australia Corso Trieste 25/c, ☎ 06 852 721.
Canada Via Zara 30, ☎ 06 4459 8421.
Netherlands Via M. Mercati 8, ☎ 06 321 5827.
New Zealand Via Zara 28, ☎ 06 440 4035.
Republic of Ireland Piazza Campitelli 3, ☎ 06 697 9121.
South Africa Via Tanaro 14, ☎ 06 852 541.
United Kingdom Via XX Settembre 80/A, ☎ 06 4890 3777.
United States of America Via Veneto 121, ☎ 06 46741.

Emergency services
For all emergencies, ☎ 113: the switchboard will coordinate the help you need.
For first aid and ambulance mergencies, ☎ 118
First aid services (*pronto soccorso*) are available at hospitals, railway stations, and airports.
Fire brigade, ☎ 115.
Road assistance, ☎ 116.
For all other emergencies, see under Crime above.

Internet centres
There are now numerous internet centres in the larger towns in Tuscany. One of the best known is *Internet Train.*

Markets
Street markets take place once a week in country towns, and local fairs are held in Florence (*Festa dell'Annunziata*), Vicchio (*Fiera Calda*), Piancastagnaio, Sansepolcro, Monte San Savino, Carmignano, and Filetto (Villafranca Lunigiana). Specialist fairs include the antiques fair (*Fiera Antiquariato*) at Arezzo, the first Saturday and Sunday of the month, and the cattle market at Alberese in spring. Wine fairs are held all over Chianti in autumn.

Newspapers
National papers include *Corriere della Sera* (of Milan), *La Stampa* (of Turin), and *La Repubblica*. Foreign newspapers are obtainable at most kiosks. The *International Herald Tribune*, published daily in Bologna, carries news on Italy.

Free publications which give up to date information on the larger towns (also in English) are usually produced in larger towns, and are available through the *APT* information offices, hotels, and agencies.

Opening hours

Shops (including clothes, hardware, and hairdressers) are generally open from 09.00–13.00, 16.00–19.30, including Saturday, and for most of the year are closed on Monday morning. Food shops usually open from 08.00–13.00, 17.00–19.30 or 20.00, and for most of the year are closed on Wednesday afternoon. From mid-June to mid-September all shops are closed instead on Saturday afternoon.However many shops in tourist centres now stay open all day. For banking hours, see above.

Pensioners

There is free admission to all State-owned galleries and monuments for British citizens over the age of 65 (you should carry your passport for proof of age and nationality). For concessions on international rail travel, see p 28.

Pharmacies

Pharmacies or chemists (*farmacie*) are identified by their street signs, which show a luminous green cross. They are usually open Monday–Friday 09.00–13.00, 16.00–19.30 or 20.00. Some are open 24hrs a day. A few are open on Saturdays, Sundays (and holidays), and at night: these are listed on the door of every chemist.

Photography

Rules about photography vary in museums, so it is always best to ask first for permission (the use of a flash is often prohibited).

Public holidays

The main holidays in Italy, when offices and shops are closed, are as follows:

1 January	New Year's Day
25 April	Liberation Day
Easter Monday	
1 May	Labour Day
15 August	Assumption
1 November	All Saints' Day
8 December	Immaculate Conception
25 December	Christmas Day
26 December	St Stephen

Each town keeps its patron Saint's day as a holiday.

Museums are usually closed on Easter Sunday and 15 August, although sometimes some of the State museums are kept open on these days. There is usually no public transport on 1 May and the afternoon of Christmas Day. For annual festivals, see above.

Public toilets

There is a notable shortage of public toilets in Italy. All bars (*caffès*) should have toilets available to the public (generally speaking the larger the bar, the better the facilities). Nearly all museums now have toilets. There are also toilets in railway stations and and bus stations.

Students and young visitors

EU members under 18 are allowed free entrance to State-owned museums, and EU students between the ages of 18 and 26 are now entitled to half-price tickets for State-owned museums, and sometimes reductions for the young are available in other museums. For youth hostels, see p 40.

Telephones and postal services

There are public telephones all over Italy in street kiosks, and in some bars and restaurants, although many of these have been dismantled now that so many people use mobile phones. Most pay phones are operated by telephone cards which can be bought from tobacconists displaying a blue 'T' sign, bars, some newspaper stands, and post offices, although a few old-style telephones still operate with coins. For international calls there are also now various prepaid telephone cards (available as above) which you do not insert in the public telephones, but they can be used from any telephone by dialling a toll free number.

Tipping

Most prices in hotels and restaurants include a service charge, and so tipping is far less widespread in Italy than in North America. Even taxi-drivers rarely expect anything much above the charge (which officially includes service). In restaurants prices are almost always inclusive of service, so always check whether or not the service charge has been added to the bill before leaving a tip (if in doubt, ask the waiter for explanation). In hotels, porters who show you to your room and help with your luggage, or find you a taxi, usually expect a small tip.

BACKGROUND INFORMATION

An historical introduction

By John Law

The allure of Tuscany

Tuscany has long fascinated foreign visitors. For this its cultural history provides a principal explanation. The region's contribution to the visual arts and architecture has been astounding in quantity and quality, in terms of technical mastery and innovation. The importance and influence of this contribution can also be gauged from the fact that Tuscany largely created the Renaissance as both a historical phenomenon and as an idea. A revealing figure here is the painter, architect and art historian Giorgio Vasari (1511–74). He came from Arezzo and his compendious and influential *Lives of the Artists*, first published in 1550, propagated the concept of the Renaissance, a period of rebirth.

Vasari shared in the belief that civilisation had reached a high point with the Roman Empire, only to decline with the barbarian invaders and the iconoclasm of early Christianity. Its eventual revival, or rebirth, Vasari located largely in Tuscany and attributed to a succession of gifted painters, sculptors and architects, most of whom were Tuscan. For Vasari, the process began with remarkable pioneers, Cimabue (c 1240–1302?) and Giotto (c 1267–1337). It reached further heights with artists like the painter Masaccio (1401–28), the sculptor Donatello (c 1386–1466) and the architect Filippo Brunelleschi (1377–1446). It attained its peak with Vasari's friend and hero, Michelangelo Buonarotti (1475–1564). And not only were most of the leading participants Tuscan; Vasari also assigned a key role in the recognition and support of talent to the Medici family, prominent in Florence from the 15C. Cosimo I, Duke of Florence from 1537 and Grand-Duke of Tuscany from 1569, was among Vasari's own patrons.

Vasari's work has had considerable bearing on the interpretation of European cultural history, and while the main focus of his attention was the fine arts and architecture, the concept of Renaissance was applied to other areas. For the poet and Latinist Francesco Petrarch (1304–74) and his humanist followers—of whom many of the leading lights were again Tuscan—literature, moral philosophy and the study of history also underwent a Renaissance, distancing the modern era in cultural terms from the Middle Ages. Moreover, the recovery of the values of ancient Rome and Greece was believed by those involved to be of more than academic or antiquarian interest. The Renaissance, and the study of the humanities, were thought to have a wider relevance for society as a whole.

But the cultural contribution of Tuscany goes beyond even the important and influential channels opened up by humanism and the Renaissance. Petrarch was a fine poet in the vernacular, and here again the Tuscan contribution was remarkable. The poets Dante Alighieri (1265–1321) and Petrarch, and the story-teller Giovanni Boccaccio (1313–75) not only raised Italian to a literary language of the highest level; they also had a profound effect on the literature of the rest of Europe. The prestige of Latin and Greek as the languages of scholarship somewhat eclipsed Italian in the 15C, but it continued as the expressive vehicle for a remarkable number of chroniclers, diarists and letter writers from the Tuscan political and mercantile elite. In the 16C the vernacular re-emerged as the language of another generation of influential writers of whom the Florentine historians and political thinkers Niccolò Machiavelli (1469–1527) and Francesco Guicciardini (1483–1540) are among the most famous.

Of course, it would be misleading to suggest that the entire course of Tuscan history can match the achievements of the period c 1300 to c 1550. However the legacy of the Renaissance continued to inspire later generations of craftsmen, artists, architects, men of letters, and their patrons. It also encouraged salons, libraries, art collections and learned societies. The Accademia della Crusca of Florence is a good example; it was established in 1582 to champion the purity of the Italian language. The Accademia Etrusca was founded in Cortona in 1727 to study the pre-Roman civilisation of the region. In its turn, this tradition inspired generations of foreign artists, connoisseurs and scholars to visit Tuscany; in the 18C Florence became a principal stopping point for travellers on the Grand Tour, as Tobias Smollett vividly recalls in his *Travels through France and Italy* (1766). In the 19C and 20C the history and civilisation of Tuscany have been intensely studied. Moreover, research, curiosity and taste have not been satisfied with the major cities, the principal artists or the Renaissance period alone.

There are other reasons for foreign interest in Tuscany. Although generally a satellite of Habsburg power from 1530 to 1859, the region never sank to provincial status, like the provinces of the Papal States. This was largely due to the fact that the Medici ruled from Florence, as Dukes and then Grand-dukes; in 1737 they were succeeded by the House of Lorraine which lasted—with interruptions during the Revolutionary and Napoleonic periods—down to 1859. The survival of an active court preserved a source of patronage and attracted foreign visitors, diplomats, adventurers and political exiles; Prince Charles Edward Stuart resided in Florence from 1775 to 1788. And there were other autonomous states within the boundaries of Tuscany. The city of Lucca preserved its republican constitution from the end of the Middle Ages to 1805, when it became a principality ruled by various dynasties down to 1859. Minor principalities, which also changed hands, were centred at Massa and Piombino on the Tyrrhenian coast. More famously, Napoleon was ruler of Elba from May 1814 to February 1815.

To captains of industry, however, Elba was better known for its iron ore. Deposits on the island and the mainland had been worked from pre-Roman times; the name 'Elba' was often given to foundries in 19C Britain. This introduces the point that Tuscany remained of economic importance in the modern era, if its cities had lost the commercial, financial and industrial pre-eminence they had acquired in Europe between the 12C and 14C—a phenomenon to be discussed below. Marble and alabaster were quarried in its hills. Abroad, the reputation of its olive oil preceded that of its wine. Luxury items were manufactured for export, ceramics and silk for example. From the 18C there was a growing international market for its works of art. Some of the Grand-dukes actively encouraged the Tuscan economy, for example by draining the Maremma region to improve health and agricultural production, or by developing Livorno as an international port where Jewish and Protestant communities could trade and worship unmolested. The second commercial railway in Italy was built by Robert Stevenson between Livorno and Pisa (1841–44).

For a variety of reasons, therefore, Tuscany did not have to await the invention of 'Chiantishire' or the introduction of the summer school or the art trail to become familiar to foreign visitors and residents.

Furthermore, the evidence of the rich travel literature and the many descriptions devoted to Tuscany—and, more poignantly, the evidence of the English cemetery in Florence—suggest that a simple categorisation of such foreign travellers and residents would be hard to make. The writer Frances Trollope (1780–1863) is buried in Florence. Visits to that city in 1860 and 1861 gave George Eliot material for her historical novel *Romola* set in Florence in the 15C. John Ruskin (1819–1900) studied the region's medieval art and architecture; he particularly admired the Gothic church of Santa Maria della Spina in Pisa. Other champions of the medieval past were Frederick Stibbert (1838–1906), whose Florentine home is now a museum, largely of arms and armour, and John Temple Leader (1810-1903), whose restored castle of Vincigliata near Settignano attracted distinguished visitors like Queen Victoria. One of Temple Leader's properties, the Villa I Tatti, was later acquired by the art historian, collector and dealer Bernard Berenson (1865–1959).

Tuscany, the 'paradise of exiles', attracted bohemian rebels (like Shelley and Byron in Pisa, 1821–22); others aimed for a more aristocratic lifestyle (like the Sitwells at Montegufoni, 1909–74). The historian Janet Ross (1842–1927) made herself a model of estate management at Poggio Gherardo on the outskirts of Florence. Peter Tchaikovsky's love of the city is expressed in his *Souvenirs of Florence* (1892). The power of the poet Dante attracted his admirers, like the British historian Thomas Macaulay (1800–59) and the American writer Charles Eliot Norton (1827–1908), while Tuscany's remarkable artistic legacy drew a succession of aspiring artists, like the Pre-Raphaelite George Frederick Watts (1817–1904)

If the relatively liberal policies of the Tuscan Grand-dukes encouraged merchants and engineers, they also gave hope to Protestant preachers and teachers who planted churches and schools in the principal resorts and cities of the region in the 19C. Health could also be a motive for visiting or taking up residence; the indefatigable Scottish writer Margaret Oliphant (1828–97) moved to Florence in 1859 in the hope that the climate would prove beneficial to her husband. Ancient spas like Bagni di Lucca were revitalised. Viareggio was an early resort for sea bathing. While some visitors were consumed by the dangers, frustrations, temptations and responsibilities of living abroad, others found them a source of inspiration. E.M. Foster's novels *Where Angels Fear to Tread* (1905) and *Room with a View* (1908) were set in Tuscany. In the 19C, the politics of the *Risorgimento* were a source of inspiration and excitement, encouraged when Florence became for a few years capital of Italy (1865–71); the poetess Elizabeth Barrett Browning (1806–61) was an enthusiastic supporter of Italian unification. A later generation was introduced to Tuscany by the war against Fascism and German occupation, and the heavy battles on the Gothic Line (1943–45). The period is captured in the writings of Iris Origo (*War in the Val d'Orcia*), Eric Newby (*Love and War in the Apennines*) and Stuart Hood (*Carlino*).

Wartime Tuscany was also the setting for Michael Ondaatje's *The English*

Patient (1992), filmed by Anthony Minghella in 1997. Films have been made of *Room with a View* (James Ivory, 1985) and *Where Angels Fear to Tread* (Charles Sturridge, 1991). Franco Zeffirelli made the—partly—autobiographical *Tea with Mussolini*, with its dramatic finale in San Gimignano, in 1999. Attempts to capture on film the self-indulgent, sybaritic and introspective character of the foreign community in Florence were made with *Stealing Beauty* (Bernardo Bertolucci, 1995) and *Up at the Villa* (Philip Haas, 2000, based on a Somerset Maugham short story of 1941). John Mortimer, who coined the expression 'Chiantishire' to tease the English enthusiasm for Tuscany, made that the setting for his novel *Summer's Lease* (1988), turning it into a TV serial the following year.

Etruscans and Romans

Tuscany (*Toscana*) is derived from the Roman and early medieval name *Tuscia* which in turn comes from Etruria, the land of the Etruscans (*Tusci, Etrusci*). Etruscan power and civilisation were at their height from the 8C to the 4C BC. Quite apart from being seafarers with trading connections across the Mediterranean, the Etruscans settled and influenced other peoples in the Italian peninsula well beyond the frontiers of the modern region. They settled north of the Apennines and deep into what is now Umbria. They also spread southwards, through Lazio to Rome and beyond; the Tarquin rulers of Rome for around 100 years from 616 BC were an Etruscan dynasty. Lars Porsena who beseiged Rome in 508 BC was an Etruscan chieftain from Chiusi.

But the Etruscans did not create a centralised state; their civilisation was a city-based federation whose unity lay more in language, customs and religion than in political power. Eventually this proved a weakness and exposed the Etruscans to Roman conquest in the 4C BC. But although there were battles and rebellions, and Roman colonies were established (e.g. Florence, Lucca, Pisa), the Etruscans were not displaced. Their religion was respected. Some of the southern cities (Arezzo, Cortona) had welcomed Rome as an ally and Etruscan communities were accorded rights of self-government. The region did not desert Rome for Hannibal during the darkest days of the Second Punic War (217 BC), and in 90 BC its inhabitants were granted Roman citizenship. In the 3C and 2C BC, links with the capital had been strengthened with improvements and extensions to the road system, but the surviving identity of the Etruscans resulted in Tuscany being recognised as the seventh region of Italy under the emperor Augustus. Diocletian united it with Umbria in the late 3C AD, with Florence as the capital. Whatever its frontiers, Roman regional administration was overwhelmed by the barbarian invasions, though between 535 and 553 Byzantine armies from the eastern Roman Empire had success in regaining imperial territory from the Ostrogoths. But these gains were swept aside in the late 6C by the Lombards who occupied all Tuscany and created a duchy with its capital at Lucca (568–774).

The Middle Ages ~ development and recession

The next fundamental change in the balance of power was created by the entry of the Franks to Italy under Pepin III (751–68) and Charlemagne (768–814) as papal champions, eventually conquering the Lombard duchy of Tuscany in 774. In 800, Pope Leo III (795–816) tried to secure his ally by crowning Charlemagne as emperor in Rome. Tuscany became part of this new western empire, and a Frankish march, or frontier province, was established with its capital at Lucca.

However, as in other parts of western Christendom in the age of feudalism, effective authority was wielded from the centre only fitfully and real power was exercised by lay and ecclesiastical landlords, great monastic houses and, increasingly, by the cities.

The rise of the cities to a position of prominence in late medieval and Renaissance Tuscany was a phenomenon of such importance that it demands some explanation. Of course, none of the major centres were purely medieval foundations; all proudly claimed a Roman past, but some went back to Etruscan times and even earlier (Volterra, Chiusi, Fiesole). Whatever their precise origins, towns and cities were founded for a variety of reasons: for security, on defensive sites (Volterra); on river crossings (Florence); near good anchorages (Pisa). In Tuscany, the continuity of urban life was never broken despite the instability following the fall of the Roman Empire and the Saracen raids that intensified with the break-up of Charlemagne's empire in the 9C. A fundamental reason for urban growth—and indeed survival—was the wealth of the countryside in terms of agricultural production and raw materials. The insanitary conditions of urban life, the readiness with which their inhabitants were afflicted by famine and disease, meant that such communities depended on a steady flow of immigrants from their hinterlands. But this did not depopulate the countryside, where the majority of the population continued to live until relatively modern times. The intensity, age and variety of rural settlement—from monastic houses to villas, from medium-size towns to isolated households—points to the wealth of much of the region.

But the principal cities of Tuscany developed in economic terms far beyond the role of local market towns and centres of industry. A lead in this process was taken by Pisa which turned defensive warfare against Saracen raiders into expansion overseas, settling colonies on Corsica, Sardinia and the Balearic Islands in the 10C and 11C, participating in the crusading movement in the eastern Mediterranean and becoming a commercial and naval power of international importance.

The population of Pisa rose from around 12,000 in the mid-12C to around 20,000 in the early 13C and to around 40,000 in the late 13C, small by modern standards but large in the context of medieval Europe. The other cities of Tuscany also expanded rapidly over the same period; the economic revolution in which Pisa took part caused, and was sustained by, the development of its neighbours, Florence, Lucca, Siena. The first two became industrial giants for the production of textiles (woollen cloth and silk). All three became centres of finance, and Tuscan bankers and money-changers operated on an international scale by the 12C and 13C. For example, on the security of royal customs receipts, the Riccardi bankers of Lucca lent vast sums to Edward I of England, financing, among much else, the construction of castles in Wales. Again, the remarkably rich commercial and personal archive left by Francesco Datini (1335–1410), the merchant of Prato so vividly evoked by Iris Origo, shows business acumen at work on a local and international scale.

However, the economic upswing demonstrated most dramatically by the leading Tuscan cities was not sustained. Natural disasters intervened gradually or suddenly. The port of Pisa began to silt up and the population became increasingly exposed to malaria from the 14C. The economies of all the Tuscan cities were disrupted by the Black Death of 1348–49; its arrival in Florence was graphically described by Boccaccio in his *Decameron*. Though precise statistics are lacking, it seems likely that the plague, which became endemic, was a major factor in reducing the populations of Tuscany by at least one third.

Other checks on the economy were man-made. As in the 20C so in the 13C and 14C, heavy advances to demanding foreign clients could place the lenders in the hands of their debtors, as relations between Florentine banking houses and Edward III of England demonstrate, the English king defaulting on his debts in 1345. The Tuscan cities also faced competition, first on an Italian and later on an international scale. The rivalry of Genoa, Venice and Florence seriously weakened the naval and commercial power of Pisa; the last rival subjected Pisa to its rule in 1406. Furthermore, the commercial revolution so linked to Tuscan enterprise encouraged the development of other centres of industry, commerce and finance in Europe (e.g. Barcelona, Flanders, the Rhineland). The Medici bank, the leading Florentine finance house of the 15C, counting the papacy among its clients, did not have the resources of its 14C predecessors, and political considerations and mismanagement at the centre and branch level gradually reduced the scope of its operations. Finally, the growth of the Atlantic powers and the Ottoman Empire from the late 15C further reduced the relative importance of Tuscany in the economies of Europe and the Mediterranean. It was only in the 19C that Florence—the largest city in the region—saw its population pass the 100,000 mark, the level that it had reached c 1300.

The Communes

The economic development of Tuscany earlier in the Middle Ages, its agricultural wealth and its relative accessibility by land and sea were principal reasons for the growing autonomy of its towns and cities, and their emergence in the 11C and 12C as self-governing communes. There were other factors. The authority of the emperor's representatives in the region, the marquisses of Tuscany, was only spasmodically effective and came to an end with the death of Matilda in 1115. The emperors themselves, though certainly capable of effective military and political intervention down to the 13C and even beyond, were generally distant overlords with many other preoccupations. Their struggles with the papacy, particularly intense in the late 11C, 12C and early 13C, for control of the personnel and wealth of the Church proved very debilitating.

The communes that benefited from this conflict and the collapse of central authority could be represented, particularly by historians in the 19C, in a heroic and sometimes patriotic light. They could be seen in terms of a people fighting for freedom from alien rule, and as devoted allies of the papacy and the cause of the Church. The communes could also be portrayed as breaking the repressive, reactionary, medieval power of the feudal aristocracy with weapons and policies derived from more modern economies, and social and legal attitudes.

However, historians have now become more cautious, even sceptical, when discussing the phenomenon. It was not until 1859 that Tuscany ceased to be a satellite of the Holy Roman Empire. In the medieval period some communes—Siena, Lucca, Pisa—could have pro-imperial, or Ghibelline, regimes that continued to look to the emperors for protection and privileges. The confrontation once seen between feudal aristocrats and bourgeois entrepreneurs is now regarded as overdrawn. Great landowners of ancient pedigree could also have interests in banking and commerce, like the Piccolomini of Siena. Upwardly mobile bourgeois families enthusiastically adopted an aristocratic life-style and acquired titles, coats of arms, country estates and well-connected marriages. If the communes of Tuscany did try to control with force and legislation the political and military influence of noble clans, they could not end it as the castles of the Tuscan countryside show. Moreover, they often turned to such families for support, for example when in need of leaders and resources in time of war.

Furthermore, the communes were far from being democracies. The participation of such bodies as the *popolo* and guilds in the 13C and 14C may have widened government, but it did not end the ascendancy of a *de facto* oligarchy of the wealthier and longer-established families. In 14C Florence, for example, the *Arti Maggiori*, or greater guilds of bankers, merchants, lawyers maintained a predominance over the *Arti Minori* representing the much more numerous artisans and retailers. In none of the communes was the bulk of the rural or urban population ever admitted to government. In conditions of economic hardship this could result in violence; in July 1378 the unenfranchised day labourers of Florence, the Ciompi, tried and failed to win for themselves a place in government.

But violence was not confined to resentful workers and peasants. Within communal government there was little sense of loyal opposition; a regime's enemies faced legal and fiscal penalties, fines, exile, imprisonment or death. Beyond the borders of a city state, exiles could gather in vengeful contrary commonwealths, though others could choose a more solitary path. Most famously, faction in Florence condemned Dante Alighieri to exile in 1302; the poet gradually distanced himself from other exiled Florentines and their allies, though his bitterness never left him.

Dante's career also points to other sources of instability in the political and social life of the communes of Tuscany. His family shared, and continued, his exile; a strong sense of kin, often intensified by local loyalties founded on the parish or quarter of a city, meant that patron-client relationships, a reliance on the clan, could undermine public authority. Secondly, internal faction could have a wider, even international, dimension as Guelfs (nominally pro-papal) fought Ghibellines (nominally pro-imperial) for control of the cities of Tuscany in the 13C and 14C.

Lastly, if communes were jealous of their own authority they were less prepared to recognise the liberties of others. For reasons of military and economic security, the towns and cities of Tuscany all sought to extend the area of their jurisdiction, or *contado*. The larger communes also sought to bring their rivals under their dominion. This was markedly the case with Florence whose self-centred belief in liberty encouraged rather than inhibited its expansion in Tuscany: Prato, 1350; Pistoia, 1351; Volterra, 1361; Arezzo, 1384; Pisa, 1406; Cortona, 1411; Livorno, 1421.

The achievements of the Communes

But it can be as anachronistic to belittle as to exaggerate the achievements of the communes. In a Europe largely dominated by monarchical forms of government and a hierarchic view of society, they did represent an alternative: a concept of popular sovereignty; republican constitutions; more open, answerable, forms of government; greater social mobility. Such an alternative view found expression in books of statutes and the resolutions and debates of governing councils. It shaped political thought, attitudes to history and forms of propaganda. It informed the astounding range of often vivid and detailed chronicles and diaries produced in the cities of late medieval Tuscany. Even more tangibly, it was expressed in the construction of public buildings, the *palazzi*, where councils and courts met and archives and treasuries were stored. The communes also tried to improve the quality of life: establishing markets, building bridges, paving streets and squares, regulating private building, installing fountains, passing legislation on hygiene. They tried to encourage public education, the more enlightened communes supporting universities (Pisa from the 12C, Siena from the 13C). They tried to further security: fortifying the city with walls and gates; curbing powerful families who sought to build towers and castles for themselves in town and country; regulating the carrying of weapons; placing garrisons in strategic fortresses.

The sense of community could also be expressed in religious terms with the communes supporting the Church, charitable institutions and the cults associated with saints and relics. The main focus of attention was generally the cathedral, but the commune could also support hospitals and the churches associated with religious orders and local cults. The case of Siena can be taken to illustrate these general points: from ambitious plans to enlarge and embellish the cathedral and its baptistry (14C and 15C), to support for the central hospital of Santa Maria della Scala; from the construction of the seat of government, the Palazzo Pubblico (1297–1310) to its decoration with frescoes expressing civic pride, piety and political beliefs; from the paving of the central Piazza del Campo (1327–49), to the engineering feat of installing in it a public fountain, the Fonte Gaia (1409–19).

It is in the Campo that the famous horse race, the *palio* between rival *contrade*, or districts, of the city is still run. This serves to introduce a further point. Loyalty to parish, family or guild was not necessarily incompatible with the common good of the wider community. Competition could be expressed in a civic context as the patronage of the guilds of Florence for the shrine of Or San Michele in the early 15C clearly demonstrates. The foundation (1495) of the beautiful Piccolomini library in the cathedral of Siena by Cardinal Francesco Piccolomini (later Pius III, 1503) was in part intended to celebrate the family name and the achievements of his uncle Aeneas Sylvius (Pius II, 1458–64). It was also intended to enrich the church and contribute to learning.

As a form of government, republicanism failed to survive the Renaissance other than in Lucca. The political instability of the region had earlier seen communes come under the rule (*signoria*) of a native or foreign lord (*signore*). In some instances, such lordship could be largely nominal, like that of the Angevin kings of Naples over Florence in the early 14C. However, some *signori* were sustained by real economic and military power and the support of a faction or party of the population. This was the case with the military leader Castruccio Castracane (1281–1328) who, from a base in Lucca over which he was made duke (1327), extended his rule over a number of Tuscan cities.

The rise of principalities

But the strength of republicanism in the region and the jealousy of other families prevented signorial regimes from being more than interludes, though principalities did take root at Massa and Piombino. With the Renaissance the situation changed. In the course of the 15C, and particularly after 1434, the Medici established an ascendancy in Florence. This was not based on force, nor was the family's influence formalised in terms of office or title; they remained private citizens. Medici power was based on wealth, family alliances and patronage in the broadest sense. It depended crucially on the political and diplomatic skills of the Medici themselves, and more particularly the heads of the leading household: Cosimo (1389–68), Piero (1418–69), Lorenzo the Magnificent (1449–92). When these qualities were lacking, as happened after the death of Lorenzo, republicanism quickly re-established itself. Moreover, the Medici regime had lost credibility due to its misreading and mismanagement of foreign policy following the invasion of Italy by the king of France, Charles VIII, in 1494.

However informal their hold on power in the 15C, abroad the Medici had established themselves as Italian princes, and two members of the dynasty became pope: Leo X (1513–21) and Clement VII (1523–34). Papal support helped sustain the family in its periods of exile and also contributed—along with the armies of the emperor Charles V—to its eventual return in 1530, first as lords of the city and then as dukes (1532). Not only was the Medici hold on power formalised and given some legitimacy; they also inherited the ascendancy Florence had achieved over Tuscany. Thanks again to Habsburg arms, the Medici state was enlarged by the Treaty of Cateau-Cambrésis (1559) with the addition of Siena and the commune of Montalcino, both of which had put up a heroic defence of Tuscan republicanism against superior forces. In 1569 Cosimo I was created Grand-duke of Tuscany.

But if the rule of the Medici, their transformation from private citizens to princes and the construction of fortresses and citadels in Florence and elsewhere brought about the end of republican government in most of Tuscany, the legacy of the republican past was not destroyed. The civic sense and cultural vitality generated in the Middle Ages survived in Florence and the other cities of Tuscany, informing and moderating the relatively enlightened and liberal Grand-dukes down to Tuscany's unification with the kingdom of Italy in 1860.

Further reading

Some contemporary sources

D. Alighieri, *The Divine Comedy*.

G. Boccaccio, *The Decameron*.

G. Brucker, ed., *Two Memoirs of Renaissance Florence* (New York, 1967).

G. Brucker, ed., *The Society of Renaissance Florence: a documentary study* (New York, 1971).

N. Machiavelli, *The Prince*.

N. Machiavelli, *History of Florence*.

J. Ross, *Lives of the Early Medici* (London, 1910).

R.E. Selfe and P.H. Wicksteed, eds, *Villani's Chronicle* (London, 1906).

G. Vasari, *Lives of the Artists*.

Some histories and descriptions

E. Armstrong, *Lorenzo De' Medici* (London, 1927).

J. Burckhardt, *The Civilisation of the Renaissance in Italy*

B. Duffy, *The Tuscan Republics* (London, 1892).

J.C.L. De Sismondi, *History of the Italian Republics.*

E. Gardner, *The Story of Siena* (London, 1902).

E. Gardner, *The Story of Florence* (London, 1910).

M. Oliphant, *The Makers of Florence* (London, 1891).

J. Ross, *Old Florence and Modern Tuscany* (London, 1904).

J. Ross and N. Ericksen, *Pisa* (London, 1909).

C. Roth, *The Last Florentine Republic* (London, 1925).

F. Schevill, *Siena* (New York, 1910; rpr. 1964).

J.A. Symonds, *The Renaissance in Italy* (London, 1907).

P. Villari, *The Life and Times of Girolamo Savonarola* (London, 1897).

P. Villari, *The Life and Times of Niccolo Machiavelli* (London, n.d.).

P. Villari, *History of Florence* (London, 1908).

Some more modern histories and descriptions

C. Ady, *Lorenzo dei Medici and Renaissance Italy* (London, 1955).

J. Bentley, *Italy: the Hill Towns* (London, 1990).

A. Brown, *The Renaissance* (London, 1996).

G. Brucker, *Renaissance Florence* (New York, 1969).

G. Brucker, *Florence. The Golden Age* (Berekely, 1998).

E. Borsook, *Florence* (London, 1997).

G. Gilbert, *Machiavelli and Guicciardini* (Princeton, 1965).

J.R. Hale, *Florence and the Medici* (London, 1977).

J.R. Hale, ed., *A Concise Encyclopedia of the Italian Renaissance* (London, 1981).

D. Hay, ed., *The Longman History of Italy* (London, 1981—).

H. Hearder and D.P. Waley, eds, *A Short History of Italy* (Cambridge, 1962).

H. Hearder, *Italy: a Short History* (Cambridge, 1990).

C. Hibbert, *The Rise and Fall of the House of Medici* (London 1974).

C. Hibbert, *Florence. Biography of a City* (London, 1997).

G. Holmes, *The Florentine Enlightenment* (London, 1969).

G. Holmes, *Dante* (Oxford, 1986).

J. Hook, *Siena* (London, 1979).

J. Keates, *Tuscany* (London, 1988).

M. Levey, *Florence. A Portrait* (London, 1996).

I. Origo, *The Merchant of Prato* (London, 1963).

M. Phillips, *The Memoir of Marco Parenti, A Life in Medici Florence* (London, 1990).

G. Ridolfi, *The Life of Giovanni Savonarola* (London, 1959).

G. Ridolfi, *The Life of Niccolo Machiavelli* (London, 1963).

G. Ridolfi, *The Life of Francesco Guicciardini* (London, 1967).

F. Schevill, *The Medici* (New York, 1960).

D.P. Waley, *The Italian City Republics* (London, 1978).

D.P. Waley, *Siena and the Sienese* (Cambridge, 1991).

Social history

G. Artrom Treves, *The Golden Ring. The Anglo-Florentines* (London, 1956).

K. Beevor, *A Tuscan Childhood* (London, 1995).

G. Brucker, *Giovanni and Lusanna: Love and Marriage in Renaissance Florence* (Berkeley, 1986).
C.L. Dentler, *Famous Foreigners in Florence* (Florence, 1964).
O. Hamilton, *The Divine Country* (London, 1982).
C. Hibbert, *The Grand Tour* (London, 1969).
M. MacCarthy, *The Stones of Florence and Venice Observed* (Harmondsworth, 1979).
F. Mayes, *Under the Tuscan Sun* (London, 1996).
I. Origo, *Images and Shadows* (London 1998).
J. Pemble, *The Mediterranean Passion* (Oxford, 1988).
L. Waterfield, *A Castle in Italy* (London, 1961).

Art history: the Renaissance

C. Avery, *Florentine Renaissance Sculpture* (Fakenham, 1982).
J. Beck, *Italian Renaissance Painting* (New York, 1981).
B. Berenson, *The Italian Painters of the Renaissance* (Oxford, 1930).
A. Chastel, *Italian Art* (London, 1983).
B. Cole, *Giotto and Florentine Painting* (New York, 1976).
E. Gombrich, *Story of Art* (London, 1985).
C. Gould, *An Introduction to Italian Renaissance Painting* (London, 1957).
F. Hartt. *History of Italian Renaissance Art* (New York, 1987).
M. Hollingsworth, *Patronage in Renaissance Italy* (London, 1994).
M. Hollingsworth, *Patronage in Sixteenth Century Italy* (London, 1996).
L. Murray, *The High Renaissance and Mannerism* (London, 1991).
P. Murray, *The Architecture of Renaissance Italy* (London, 1986).
P. & L. Murray, *The Art of the Renaissance* (London, 1963).
J.T. Paoletti and G.M. Radke, *Art in Renaissance Italy* (London, 1997).
E. Welch, *Art in Renaissance Italy* (Oxford, 1997).

Place names in Italian towns and cities

Many of the place names in Italian towns and cities have ancient origins; the names assigned to public buildings, market places, towers, bridges, gates and fountains frequently date back to the Middle Ages. Especially near the centre of town, they may reflect the crafts and trades practised, the dominant local families, the venerated saints and cults of centuries ago. But the practice of formally naming all streets and squares began in the 19C. Frequently local—even parochial—patriotism determined the choice as the community celebrates its own history and its own political, literary, religious and scientific figures, as well as famous foreign visitors. However, in the case of Tuscany, a remarkable number of local artists and writers have acquired a national and even international significance, figures like Dante, Petrarch, Michelangelo—the list is a long one.

But the choice of place names can reflect other concerns, and events and figures from later Italian national history are prominently represented. Thus a united republican Italy can be celebrated in terms of concepts (e.g. Via della Repubblica, della Libertà, della Vittoria), events (e.g. Via del Plebiscito, recalling the vote that preceded a region uniting with the Kingdom of Italy in the 19C), or by drawing on the gazetteer of Italian rivers, mountains, seas and cities.

Broadly speaking the national figures and events chosen tend to be representative of four phases in recent Italian history. Probably the most emotive and frequently commemorated is the *Risorgimento* (the Resurgence), the movement that led to the unification and independence of Italy in the 19C; among the battles commemorated are: Custoza, Lissa, Solferino, Magenta, Montebello, Mentana. For some historians, Italy's entry to the First World War represents the final phase in the pursuit of national unity; the battles and campaigns between Italy, and her allies, and the Central Powers are also frequently recorded in place names: the Isonzo; Monte Pasubio; Caporetto; Monte Grappa, the Piave; Vittorio Veneto. Opposition to Fascism and the ending of the Second World War are also commemorated in this way, as are the statesmen and events associated with the country's reconstruction, economic development and membership of the EC. Casualties in Italy's successful struggle against political terrorism (Aldo Moro, murdered by the Red Brigades in 1978) and the less successful war with organised crime (Alberto della Chiesa, killed by the Mafia in 1982) are also being so honoured.

Largely censored and deleted from the record are the events and personalities closely linked to Fascism, Italy's empire and the reigns of the last two members of the House of Savoy, Vittorio Emanuele III (1900–46) and Umberto II (1946). However, the keen-eyed observer might be able to identify traces of Fascist insignia and the Fascist system of dating (1922, when Mussolini was invited to lead the government, is year 1) on public buildings and monuments, and some street names still recall territories once ruled from Rome (e.g. Istria, Dalmazia, Albania, Libia).

Below are listed a selection of the more prominent figures and events from recent Italian history the traveller is likely to encounter time and again.

Prominent people

ALFIERI Vittorio (1749–1803), poet and dramatist.

BATTISTI Cesare, Italian patriot executed by the Habsburg regime in Trent, 12 July 1916.

CARDUCCI Giosuè (1835–1907), patriotic poet and literary critic.

CAVOUR Camillo (1810–61), statesman and cautious architect of Italian unification.

CRISPI Francesco (1818–1901), statesman.

FOSCOLO Ugo (1778–1827), poet and patriot.

GARIBALDI Giuseppe (1807–82), inspirational political and military leader in the *Risorgimento*.

GRAMSCI Antonio (1891–1937), political thinker, Marxist, opponent of Fascism.

MANIN Daniele (1804–57), Venetian patriot and statesman, defender of that city against Habsburg forces, 1848–49.

MARCONI Guglielmo (1874–37), electrical engineer and radio pioneer.

MARGHERITA of Savoy (1851–1926), wife of King Umberto I, noted for her piety, good works and cultural patronage.

MARTIRI DELLA RESISTENZA (or DELLA LIBERTÀ), opponents of Fascism and German occupation, 1943–45.

MATTEOTTI Giacomo (1885–1924), socialist politician, assassinated by Fascists.

MAZZINI Giuseppe (1805–82), leading republican figure of the *Risorgimento*.

OBERDAN Guglielmo (1858–82), Italian patriot, executed by the Habsburg regime in Trieste.

RICASOLI Bettino (1809–80), Florentine statesman, instrumental in securing Tuscany's adherence to the Kingdom of Italy in 1860.

SAFFI Aurelio (1819–1890), man of letters and hero of the *Risorgimento*.

UMBERTO I of Savoy, King of Italy, 1878–1900.

VERDI Giuseppe (1813–1901), prolific opera composer whose output was often associated with cause of a united Italy. His surname could be read as the initials of Vittorio Emanuele Re d'Italia.

VITTORIO EMANUELE II of Savoy, King of Sardinia-Piedmont from 1849, King of Italy 1861–78.

Historic events

XI FEBBRAIO: 11 February 1929, formal reconciliation between the papacy and the kingdom of Italy.

XXIX MARZO: 29 March 1943, armistice between Italy and the Allies.

XXVII APRILE: 27 April 1945, Benito Mussolini captured by partisans in northern Italy. The Fascist leader was quickly tried and executed on 28 April.

XI MAGGIO: 11 May 1860, Garibaldi landed with 1000 men at Marsala (Sicily) and launched the military campaign that led to the Unification of Italy.

XXIV MAGGIO: 24 May 1915, Italy enters the First World War.

II GIUGNO: 2 June 1946, referendum designed to favour a republican constitution.

XX GIUGNO: 20 June 1859, papal forces and their supporters violently suppressed a pro-Unification rising in Perugia.

XIV SETTEMBRE: 14 September 1860, the forces of the Kingdom of Italy entered Perugia.

XX SETTEMBRE: 20 September 1870, Italian forces enter Rome, overthrowing papal rule.

IV NOVEMBRE: 4 November 1918, proclamation of the armistice between Italy and Austria.

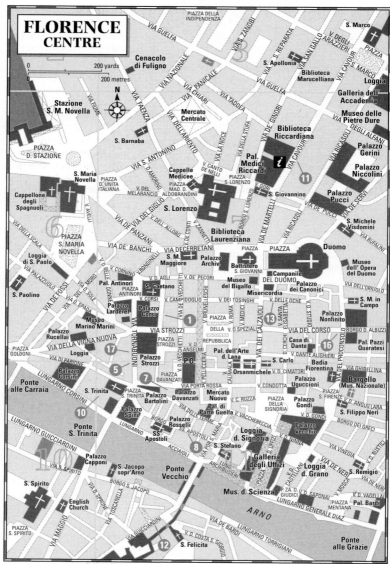

FLORENCE CENTRE

0 ____ 200 yards
0 ____ 200 metres

N

S. Marco
PIAZZA
V. DEGLI ARAZZIERI
Loggia
Galleria dell' Accademia
Museo delle Pietre Dure
Palazzo Gerini
Palazzo Niccolini
Palazzo Pucci
S. Michele Visdomini

Cenacolo di Fuligno
VIA GUELFA
VIA NAZIONALE
VIA PANICALE
VIA CHIARI
VIA TADDEA
VIA DE' GINORI
PIAZZA DELLA INDIPENDENZA
VIA S. ZANOBI
VIA S. REPARATA
S. Apollonia
S. Marco
Biblioteca Marucelliana
Biblioteca Riccardiana
VIA CAVOUR

Stazione S. M. Novella
VIA FIUME
VIA FAENZA
Mercato Centrale
S. Barnaba
VIA DELL'ARIENTO
VIA S. ANTONINO
VIA S. AMBROGIO

PIAZZA D. STAZIONE

S. Maria Novella
Cappellone degli Spagnuoli
PIAZZA S. M. UNITA' ITALIANA
VIA DELLA SCALA
VIA DE' BANCHI
VIA DE PANZANI
VIA DEL GIGLIO
VIA DE' CONTI
VIA DELL'ALLORO

Cappelle Medicee
S. Lorenzo
PIAZZA MAD. D. ALDOBRANDINI
V. DEL MELARANCIO
V. CANTO DE' NELLI
BORGO S. LORENZO
Pal. Medici Riccardi
PIAZZA S. LORENZO
S. Giovannino
VIA DE' MARTELLI
VIA DE' PUCCI
VIA DE' SERVI

i 11

Biblioteca Laurenziana

Museo dell'Opera del Duomo
Duomo
Campanile
PIAZZA DEL DUOMO
Battistero S. Giovanni
Palazzo dei Canonici
Misericordia
Palazzo del Bigallo
S. M. MAGGIORE
Palazzo Archivi
PIAZZA S. M. MAGGIORE
VIA DECRETANI
VIA DE' CERRETANI
VIA DE' PECORI

S. M. in Campo
Palazzo Nonfinito
VIA DELL'ORIUOLO
VIA BUFALINI

Pal. Antinori
PIAZZA ANTINORI
S. Gaetano
V. CORSI
V. D. AGLI
Palazzo Corsi
Palazzo Larderel
Museo Marino Marini
Palazzo Rucellai
VIA DELLA VIGNA NUOVA
17
Loggia
Palazzo Corsini
Ponte alle Carraia
LUNGARNO CORSINI

S. Paolino
S. Trinita
5 7
Palazzo Strozzi
PIAZZA STROZZI
VIA STROZZI
Palazzo dell'Arte d. Lana
Orsanmichele
S. Carlo
VIA DEL CORSO
Casa di Dante
Badia Fiorentina
16
Pal. Pazzi Quaratesi
Bargello (Mus. Nazionale)
S. Filippo Neri

PIAZZA DELLA REPUBBLICA

P.O.
Pal. dell'Arte d. Lana
VIA PORTA ROSSA
Mercato Nuovo
Palazzo Davanzati
Pal. di Parte Guelfa
Palazzo Bartolini
PIAZZA S. TRINITA
S. Trinita
Palazzo Spini
Palazzo Rosselli
SS Apostoli
Ponte S. Trinita
10
LUNGARNO GUICCIARDINI

Palazzo Capponi
S. Jacopo sopr'Arno
BORGO S. JACOPO
Ponte Vecchio
8
S. Stefano
Loggia d. Signoria
Palazzo Vecchio
Galleria degli Uffizi
Palazzo Gondi
Palazzo Uguccioni
PIAZZA DELLA SIGNORIA
VIA DE' NERI
S. Remigio
Pal. Bardi

S. Spirito
English Church
PIAZZA S. SPIRITO
VIA MAGGIO
Ponte Vecchio
Mus. d. Scienza
Loggia d. Grano
ARNO
LUNGARNO GENERALE DIAZ
Ponte alle Grazie

LUNGARNO TORRIGIANI
12
S. Felicita
VIA GUICCIARDINI
Palazzo Pitti

THE GUIDE

Florence

Florence, in Italian *Firenze*, is one of the most famous cities in Italy. As the birth-place of the Renaissance it preserves some of the greatest works of art and most beautiful buildings in the world. From the fifteenth century onwards it became a centre of learning in the arts and sciences unparalleled since classical times. It is now a small city (380,000 inhabitants), the regional capital of Tuscany, with nearly all its beautiful buildings concentrated within a relatively small area. The famous museums of the Uffizi, Palazzo Pitti, and Bargello contain the master-pieces of Florentine art. The delightful low hills which surround the city have been preserved from new buildings. The best time to visit Florence is in the winter: it can be unpleasantly crowded with tourists in the spring and unbearably hot in July and August. The river Arno, a special feature of the city, has caused disastrous floods throughout its history (last in 1966). *For a fuller description of the city, see Blue Guide Florence.*

Practical information

 Getting there and getting around
By air

The nearest large international airport is at **Pisa** (see p 246). Direct train service in 1 hour to Florence Santa Maria Novella station (which has an Air Terminal). In summer there are also *SITA* bus services (also in one hour).

The small **Florence** airport (Amerigo Vespucci), a few kilometres north of Florence, has some flights from Europe. *ATAF/SITA* bus every 30 mins from the arrivals terminus to the *SITA* bus station next to the railway station of Santa Maria Novella in under half an hour.

Bologna airport also has interna-tional flights (airport bus every 20 mins in 15 mins to Bologna station, and from there trains to Florence in 60–75mins).
By car

Most of the centre of Florence (within the *Viali*, and in the Oltrarno; see the Plan) is closed to private cars (from 08.30–19.30), except for residents and temporary access to hotels. Parking is difficult. At present the only large car parks with long-term parking (with hourly tariff) near to the centre of the city are at the Fortezza da Basso, Piazza Stazione (underground), Parterre (underground), and inside the walls near Porta Romana. Smaller car parks include Piazza Beccaria and Lungarno della Zecca Vecchia.
By train

Santa Maria Novella (**Map 6**) for nearly all services. The slower trains also stop at *Campo di Marte* station (beyond **Map 8**) when coming from the south, and *Rifredi* station (north of **Map 2**) when coming from the north. Some overnight sleeper trains only stop at *Campo di Marte*.

By bus

Although the centre of the town is very small and best visited on foot, there are four small **electric bus services** which provide an excellent view of the historic centre: line **A** & **D** both start from the railway station: line **A** traverses the city north of the Arno and line **D** the city south of the Arno. Line **B** follows the Lungarno north of the Arno and line **C** connects Piazza San Marco, Piazza Santa Croce, and Ponte Vecchio. Tickets have to be bought before boarding from newsagents, bars (*tabacchi*), or automatic machines. **Information office**, Piazza Stazione (07.00–20.00, ☎ 800 424 500; www.ataf.net).

For services to the **environs**, see p 105–123. There is a wide network of **country bus services** in Tuscany, operated by *Lazzi*, Piazza Stazione 4 (☎ 055 351 061), *SITA*, Via Santa Caterina da Siena 15 (☎ 800 373 760), *COPIT* and *CAP*, Largo Alinari 9 (☎ 055 214 637).

Information offices

APT, Via Cavour 1 (red) **Map 7**; ☎ 055 290 832; ✉ infoturismo@provincia.fi.it. and ✉ info@firenze.turismo.toscana.it), Borgo Santa Croce 29 (red) (**Map 11**), Piazza Stazione (beneath the bus shelter on the right side of the railway station), and Florence airport. **Hotel booking office** (*ITA*) at the railway station, on the motorway approaches to Florence (Chianti Est and Peretola Sud), and at Pisa airport.

Where to stay
Hotels

It is essential to book well in advance at Easter, September and October, and in the summer.

☆☆☆☆☆ *Helvetia e Bristol*, **Map 7**;*1*, Via de' Pescioni 2 (☎ 055 287 814; 055 288 353).

☆☆☆☆ *J & J*, Via di Mezzo, **Map 8**;*2*, Via di Mezzo 20 (☎ 055 234 5005,

055 240 282); *Monna Lisa*, **Map 8**;*3*, Borgo Pinti 27 (☎ 055 247 9751, 055 247 9755).

☆☆☆ *Annalena*, **Map 14**;*4*, Via Romana 34 (☎ 055 222 402, 055 222 403); *Beacci Tornabuoni*, **Map 11**;*5*, Via Tornabuoni 3 (☎ 055 212 645, 055 283 594); *Loggiato dei Serviti*, **Map 7**;*6*, Piazza Santissima Annunziata 3 (☎ 055 289 592, 055 289 595); *Porta Rossa*, **Map 11**;*7*, Via Porta Rossa 19 (☎ 055 287 551, 055 282 179); *Torre Guelfa*, **Map 11**;*8*, Borgo Santi Apostoli 8 (☎ 055 239 6338, 055 239 8577).

☆☆ *Boboli*, **Map 14**;*9*, Via Romana 63 (☎ 055 229 8645, 055 233 7169); *Bretagna*, **Map 11**;*10*, Lungarno Corsini 6 (☎ 055 289 618, 055 289 6119); *Casci*, **Map 7**;*11*, Via Cavour 13 (☎ 055 211 686, 055 239 6461); *La Scaletta*, **Map 11**;*12*, Via Guicciardini 13 (☎ 055 283 028, 055 289 562); *Villani*, **Map 7**;*13*, Via delle Oche 11 (☎ 055 239 6451, 055 215 348).

☆ *Azzi*, **Map 2**;*14*, Via Faenza 56 (☎/ 055 213 806); *Brunetta*, **Map 8**;*15*, Borgo Pinti 5 (☎/ 055 247 8134); *Marie Luisa de' Medici*, **Map 7**;*16*, Via del Corso 1 (☎/ 055 280 048); *Scoti*, **Map 7**;*17*, Via Tornabuoni 7 (☎/ 055 292 128).

Hotels **outside the centre** of Florence include: ☆☆☆☆ *Torre di Bellosguardo*, Via Roti Michelozzi 2 (☎ 055 229 8145, 055 229 008), and ☆☆☆ *Villa Montemartino*, Via Gherardo Silvani 151 (☎ 055 223 520, 055 223 495). For hotels in the environs, including Fiesole, see pp 105–123.

Youth hostel ~ Ostello per la Gioventù

Villa Camerata, Viale Righi 2 (☎ 055 601 451, 055 610 300).

Campsite

☆☆ *Italiani e Stranieri*, Viale Michelangelo.

Eating out
Restaurants

€€€€ *Enoteca Pinchiorri*, Via Ghibellina 87, one of the most famous and expensive restuarants in Italy.

€€€ *Taverna del Bronzino*, Via delle Ruote; *Oliviero*, Via delle Terme 51; *Orient Express*, Borgo Allegri 9.

€€ *Latini*, Via Palchetti 6; *Cocco Lezzone*, Via del Parioncino 26; *Il Troia*, Via Porcellana 29; *Quattro Leoni*, Via Toscanella; *La Pentola dell'Oro*, Via di Mezzo 24 (a club; membership by previous appointment; annual subscription) is run by a scholar of Renaissance cuisine who produces excellent traditional Tuscan dishes.

€ *Antico Ristoro di' Cambi*, Via Sant'Onofrio 1; *Benvenuto*, Via Mosca 16; *Diladdarno*, Via de' Serragli 108; *Borgo Antico*, Piazza Santo Spirito 6; *Da Sergio*, Piazza San Lorenzo 8; *Al Tramvai*, Piazza Tasso 14.

Simple cheap trattorie

La Casalinga, Via Michelozzi 9; *Mario*, Via Rosina 2; *Sabatino*, Via Pisana 2 (Porta San Frediano); *Salumeria/Vini*, Via Ghibellina 27 (red) (lunch only). For pizza: *Ciao Bella*, Piazza del Tiratoio 18.

Cafés

Cafés which have comfortable tables (also outside) include *Rivoire* in Piazza Signoria (famous for its chocolate, but rather grand and you pay extra for your surroundings). *Procacci*, an elegant little old fashioned café on Via Tornabuoni has good truffle sandwiches and cheeses. *Cibreo*, Via Andrea del Verrocchio 5, and *La Via del Tè*, Piazza Ghiberti 22, are both small cafés with a few tables outside near the market of Sant'Ambrogio. *Caffelatte*, Via degli Alfani 39, is a simple little café with home-made snacks, and *La Pergola*, Via degli Alfani 27, is an excellent Sicilian snack bar.

The best **cake shop** (*pasticceria*) in Florence is *Dolci e Dolcezze*, 8 Piazza Beccaria. The *Forno Sartoni*, Via dei Cerchi 34, sells exceptionally good simple traditonal Florentine cakes and buns (as well as pizzas and other snacks), at reasonable prices. The *Pasticceria Alcedo Falli* in Fiesole (Via Gramsci 29) also makes particularly good cakes and pastries. One of the the best **ice-cream shops** in Florence is *Vivoli*, Via Isola delle Stinche 7 (near Santa Croce).

Picnics

There are lovely places to **picnic** in the hills surrounding Florence, but very few places in the centre of the city. North of the Arno you can picnic in the Giardino dell'Orticoltura, the parks of Villa il Ventaglio and Villa Stibbert; and south of the Arno in the gardens below San Miniato al Monte or off Viale Machiavelli.

Admission to museums

The telephone booking service for State-owned museums (☎ 055 294 883) is highly recommended, especially for the Uffizi and the Accademia where there can be very long queues. Cumulative tickets also available.

A carnet can be purchased which allows a 50 per cent reduction to the museums owned by the Comune (including Palazzo Vecchio and the Cappella Brancacci).

British and American Consulates and churches

British Consulate, Lungarno Corsini 2 (**Map 10**).

American Consulate, Lungarno Vespucci 38 (**Map 5**).

Anglican Church, St Mark's, Via Maggio 16.

American Episcopalian, St James, Via Bernardo Rucellai 9.

Institutes

British Institute, Piazza Strozzi 2 (Italian language courses), with an excellent library and reading room at Lungarno Guicciardini 9B (see p 37);

Institut Français, Piazza Ognissanti 2; *German Institute of Art History*, Via Giuseppe Giusti 44, with the best art history library in Florence (post-graduate students); *Dutch Institute*, Viale Torricelli 5; *Harvard University Center for Italian Renaissance Studies*, Villa I Tatti, Ponte a Mensola, Settignano (with a good library, open to post-graduate students); *Centro Linguistico Italiano Dante Alighieri*, Via de'Bardi 12 (Italian language courses).

Concerts and drama

Teatro Comunale (**Map 5**), Corso Italia 16, symphony concerts and opera. The Maggio Musicale, an annual music festival (May–July) is held here. *La Pergola* (**Map 7**), Via della Pergola 12 (drama season, and chamber music concerts organised by the *Amici della Musica* in January–April and October–December). Concerts are often given by the *Orchestra Regionale Toscana* and the *Orchestra da Camera Fiorentina*.

Annual festivals

The *Scoppio del Carro*, on Easter Day, is a traditional religious festival held in and outside the Duomo. On 24 June, St John's Day (St John is the patron saint of Florence), a local holiday is celebrated with fireworks at Piazzale Michelangelo. A football game in 16C costume (*Calcio in costume*) is held in three heats during June. An Antiques Fair (the *Mostra Mercato Internazionale dell'Antiquariato*) is held biennially in the autumn.

History of Florence

The Roman colony of Florentia was founded in 59 BC by Julius Caesar. The city was built on the Arno where the crossing is narrowest, and it flourished in the 2C and 3C AD. The commune of Florence came into being in the first decades of the 12C, and there followed a long drawn-out struggle between Guelfs and Ghibellines. By the middle of the 13C Florentine merchants, whose prosperity was largely based on the woollen cloth industry, were established in a privileged position in trade and commerce, and the florin, first minted in silver c 1235, and soon after in gold, was used as the standard gold coin in Europe. In the 14C Florence was one of the five largest cities in Europe. By this time Palazzo Vecchio had been built by Arnolfo di Cambio, and the two churches of Santa Maria Novella and Santa Croce were erected. Giotto's works in the city prepared the way for a new spirit of Humanism.

The city's greatest moment of splendour came in the 15C when a new conception of art and learning symbolised the birth of the Renaissance, under the brilliant leadership of Cosimo de' Medici and, later, under his famous grandson Lorenzo il Magnifico. The Renaissance found its highest expression in the works of Brunelleschi, Donatello, and Masaccio. Numerous great artists worked together in Florence in the 15C creating remarkably beautiful paintings, buildings, and statuary. Among them were Lorenzo Ghiberti, Luca della Robbia, Beato Angelico, Filippo Lippi, and Paolo Uccello. In the later 15C Pollaiolo, Verrocchio, and Sandro Botticelli produced splendid works, and they were followed by the 'universal' artist Leonardo da Vinci. The fame of Michelangelo, who was favoured by the patronage of Lorenzo il Magnifico, spread throughout Europe and he was recognised as the greatest artist of his time.

Despite opposition from Republican exiles, enlightened Medici rule continued into the 16C when they became grand-dukes of Tuscany. Andrea del Sarto, Pontormo, Giambologna, Benvenuto Cellini, and Bronzino represent the Mannerist era of art in the city.

The Medici were succeeded in 1737 by Austrian grand-dukes. From 1861 to 1875 Florence was the capital of the Italian kingdom. All the bridges except Ponte Vecchio were blown up in the Second World War, and in 1966 a disastrous flood of the Arno caused severe damage to the city and its works of art.

Piazza del Duomo

The Baptistery of San Giovanni

The **Baptistery of San Giovanni (**Map 7**; open 12.00–18.30; fest. 08.30–13.30) is one of the oldest and most revered buildings in the city, called by Dante his *bel San Giovanni*. It was probably built in the 6C or 7C, and in any case not later than the 9C. It is a domed octagonal building of centralised plan derived from Byzantine models. In the 11C–12C the **exterior** was entirely encased in white and green marble from Prato in a classical geometrical design, which became a prototype for numerous other Tuscan Romanesque religious buildings. The cupola was concealed by an unusual white pyramidal roof (and the 11C lantern placed on top), probably in the 13C.

The bronze doors

The building is famous for its three sets of gilded bronze doors. The two doors by Lorenzo Ghiberti were erected after he won a competition in 1401, often taken as a convenient point to mark the beginning of the Florentine Renaissance.

The *south door* (1336) is by Andrea Pisano with reliefs illustrating the history of St John the Baptist. The bronze frame was added by Vittorio Ghiberti (1452–64). Over the doorway are statues of the Baptist, the Executioner, and Salome, by Vincenzo Danti (1571).

The *north door*, by Lorenzo Ghiberti (1403–24) contains scenes of the Life of Christ, the Evangelists, and the Doctors of the Church. The beautiful frame is also by Ghiberti, and his self-portrait appears in the fifth head on the left door. The sculptures above of St John the Baptist, the Levite, and the Pharisee are by Francesco Rustici (1506–11), from a design by Leonardo da Vinci.

The **east door** is the most celebrated work of Lorenzo Ghiberti, the completion of which took him most of his life (1425–52). It is said to have been called by Michelangelo the Gate of Paradise. The pictorial reliefs (see below), no longer restricted to a Gothic frame, depict each episode with great conciseness, and the workmanship of the carving is masterly. A copy of the door made from casts taken in 1948 was set up here in 1990, and the original panels are exhibited in the Museo dell'Opera del Duomo (although four of them are still being restored). The subjects are: 1. *The Creation and the Expulsion from Paradise*; 2. *Cain and Abel*; 3. *Noah's Sacrifice and Drunkenness*; 4. *Abraham and the Angels and the Sacrifice of Isaac*; 5. *Esau and Jacob*; 6. *Joseph sold and recognised by his Brethren*; 7. *Moses receiving the Tablets of Stone*; 8. *The Fall of Jericho*; 9. *Battle with the Philistines*; 10. *Solomon and the Queen of Sheba*. The frame contains beautiful statuettes of Prophets and Sibyls, and medallions with portraits of Ghiberti himself and his contemporaries. The splendid bronze door-frame is also by Ghiberti. Above, the sculptural group of the Baptism of Christ, attributed to Andrea Sansovino and Vincenzo Danti, with an Angel added by Innocenzo

Spinazzi (18C), is a cast of the original now in the Museo dell'Opera del Duomo.

The harmonious **interior** is designed in two orders, of which the lower has huge granite columns from a Roman building, with gilded Corinthian capitals, and the upper, above a cornice, a gallery with divided windows. The walls are in panels of white marble divided by bands of black, in the dichromatic style of the exterior. The oldest part of the splendid mosaic ***pavement** in *opus tessellatum* (begun 1209) is near the Gothic font. Beside the 13C high altar is an elaborate paschal candlestick delicately carved by Agostino di Jacopo (1320). The ***tomb of the antipope John XXIII** (Baldassarre Coscia, who died in Florence in 1419) by Donatello and Michelozzo is one of the earliest Renaissance tombs in the city. This beautifully carved monument in no way disturbs the architectural harmony of the building.

The ***mosaics** in the vault are remarkably well preserved. The earliest (c 1225) are in the *scarsella* above the altar; they are signed by the monk Jacopo, who is also thought to have begun the main dome, the centre of which is decorated with early Christian motifs. Above the apse is the ***Last Judgement*** with a huge (8m) figure of Christ attributed to Coppo di Marcovaldo. The four bands of the cupola illustrate the ***Story of Genesis***, the ***Story of Joseph*** (the design of some of the scenes is attributed to the Maestro della Maddalena), the ***Story of Christ***, and the ***Story of St John the Baptist*** (some of the early episodes are attributed to Cimabue). Work on the mosaics was well advanced by 1271, but probably continued into the 14C.

The Duomo

The *Duomo (**Map 7**) the cathedral dedicated to the Madonna of Florence, **Santa Maria del Fiore**, fills Piazza del Duomo; a comprehensive view of the huge building is difficult in the confined space. It produces a memorable effect of massive grandeur, especially seen from its southern flank, lightened by the colour and pattern of its beautiful marble walls (white from Carrara, green from Prato, and red from the Maremma). The famous dome, one of the masterpieces of the Renaissance, rising to the height of the surrounding hills (from which it is nearly always visible), holds sway over the whole city.

• Open 10.00–17.00; fest. 13.00–17.00. Excavations of Santa Reparata open 10.00–17.00 exc. fest. Ascent of the dome, entrance from the south door, 08.30–18.20; Sat 09.30–17.00; first Sat of month 08.30–15.00; closed fest.

View of Florence with the Duomo

History of the Duomo

The early Christian church, dedicated to the Palestinian Santa Reparata, is thought to have been founded in the 6C–7C, or possibly earlier. The Bishop's seat, formerly at San Lorenzo, was probably transferred here in the late 7C. By the 13C a new and larger cathedral was deemed necessary, and in 1294 Arnolfo di Cambio was appointed as architect. In 1355 Francesco Talenti continued work on the building, probably following Arnolfo's original design of a vaulted basilica with a domed octagon flanked by three polygonal tribunes. By 1417 the octagonal drum was substantially finished. The construction of the cupola had long been recognised as a major technical problem, and after a competition Brunelleschi was appointed to the task, and had erected the dome up to the base of the lantern by 1436 when Pope Eugenius IV consecrated the cathedral.

The majestic **cupola, the greatest of all Brunelleschi's works (1420–36), is a feat of engineering skill. It was the first dome to be projected without the need for a wooden supporting frame to sustain the vault during construction, and was the largest and highest of its time. The cupola has two concentric shells, the octagonal vaults of which are evident both on the exterior and the interior of the building; the upper section is built in bricks in consecutive rings in horizontal courses, bonded together in a herring-bone pattern. The lantern was begun a few months before the architect's death in 1446, and carried on by his friend Michelozzo. In the late 1460s Verrocchio placed the bronze ball and cross on the summit. Brunelleschi also designed the four decorative little exedrae with niches which he placed around the octagonal drum between the three domed tribunes. The balcony at the base of the cupola added by Baccio d'Agnolo was never completed, according to Vasari, because of Michelangelo's stringent criticism. The dome has been under constant surveillance since 1980 when alarm was raised about its stability (the main problem seems to be the weight of the dome which has caused fissures in the drum).

The building of the cathedral was begun on the south side where the decorative pattern of marble can be seen to full advantage. The Porta dei Canonici has fine sculptural decoration (1395–99). On the north side, the *Porta della Mandorla** (1391–1405) is by Giovanni d'Ambrogio, Piero di Giovanni Tedesco, Jacopo di Piero Guidi, and Nicolò Lamberti. In the gable is an *Assumption of the Virgin* in an almond-shaped frame by Nanni di Banco (c 1418–20) which had an important influence on early Renaissance sculpture.

The **façade**, erected to a third of its projected height by 1420, was demolished in 1587–88; the present façade in the Gothic style, was designed by Emilio De Fabris and built in 1871–87.

Interior

The Gothic interior is somewhat bare and chilly after the warmth of the colour of the exterior, whose splendour it cannot match. The huge grey stone arches of the nave reach the clerestory beneath an elaborate sculptured balcony. The massive pilasters which support the stone vault have unusual composite capitals. Three dark tribunes with a Gothic coronet of chapels surround the huge dome. The beautiful marble **pavement** was designed by Baccio d'Agnolo, Francesco da Sangallo and others.

West wall Mosaic of the *Coronation of the Virgin*, attributed to Gaddo Gaddi. Ghiberti designed the three stained glass windows. The huge clock was decorated with four heads of prophets by Paolo Uccello in 1443. The recomposed tomb of Antonio d'Orso, Bishop of Florence (d. 1321) by Tino da Camaino includes a fine statue.

South aisle In a tondo is a bust of Brunelleschi by Buggiano, his adopted son (1446). On the side altar, statue of a *Prophet* attributed to Nanni di Banco. The bust of Giotto by Benedetto da Maiano bears an inscription by Poliziano. On the second altar, statue of Isaiah by Ciuffagni.

Steps lead down to the **excavations of Santa Reparata** (opening times, see above). Through a grille to the left at the bottom of the steps the simple tomb slab of Brunelleschi, found here in 1972, can be seen. The architect of the cupola was the only Florentine granted the privilege of burial in the cathedral. The complicated remains of Santa Reparata (shown in a model), on various levels, include Roman edifices on which the early Christian church was built (a fine mosaic pavement of which survives), and remains of the pre-Romanesque and Romanesque reconstructions. Here are displayed finds from the excavations, including fresco fragments and plutei.

East end of the church (mostly reserved for private worship). Above the octagon the great **dome** soars to a height of 91m. The fresco of the *Last Judgement* by Vasari and Federico Zuccari (1572–79) was restored in 1981–94. The stained glass in the roundels of the drum was designed in 1443–45 by Paolo Uccello, Andrea del Castagno, Donatello, and Ghiberti. Against the pillars stand 16C statues of Apostles by Jacopo Sansovino, Vincenzo de'Rossi, Andrea Ferrucci, Baccio Bandinelli, Benedetto da Rovezzano, Giovanni Bandini, and Vincenzo de'Rossi.

The marble **sanctuary** by Bandinelli (1555), with bas-reliefs by himself and Bandini, encloses the high altar, also by Bandinelli, with a wood *Crucifix* by Benedetto da Maiano. Each of the three apses is divided into five chapels with stained glass windows designed by Lorenzo Ghiberti. Above the entrance to the South Sacristy is a large lunette of the *Ascension* in enamelled terracotta by Luca della Robbia.

In the central **apse** are two graceful kneeling angels, also by Luca, and a bronze reliquary ***urn** by Lorenzo Ghiberti with exquisite bas-reliefs.

Over the door into the **north sacristy** is another fine relief by Luca della Robbia of the ***Resurrection**. This was his earliest important work (1442) in enamelled terracotta. The doors were his only work in bronze. It was in this sacristy that Lorenzo il Magnifico took refuge on the day of the Pazzi conspiracy in 1478 in order to escape the death which befell his brother, Giuliano. The ***interior** has beautiful intarsia cupboards dating from 1436–45 by artists including Lo Scheggia and Antonio Manetti. The end wall was continued by Giuliano da Maiano in 1463 (possibly on a cartoon by Antonio del Pollaiolo). The carved frieze of putti is by various artists probably including Benedetto da Maiano. On the entrance wall is a fine marble lavabo by Buggiano probably based on a design by Brunelleschi.

In the pavement of the left apse is Toscanelli's huge gnomon (1475) for solar observations.

Ascending the dome The ascent is highly recommended (for opening times see p 60). The climb (463 steps) is not specially arduous, and it follows a labyrinth of corridors, steps, and spiral staircases (used by the builders of the cupola) as far as the lantern at the top of the dome. During the ascent the structure of the dome can be examined, and the views of the inside of the cathedral from the balcony around the drum (45.5m in diameter), and of the city from the small windows and from the lantern, are remarkable. On the way down, there is a room with instruments used during the construction of the dome.

North aisle The painting of Dante holding a copy of his *Divina Commedia* with an interesting view of Florence (1465) is by Domenico di Michelino. On the side altar, *King David* by Bernardo Ciuffagni. The two splendid frescoed ***equestrian memorials** to the famous *condottieri*, the Englishman Sir John Hawkwood (Giovanni Acuto) who commanded the Florentine army from 1377 until his death in 1394, and Nicolò da Tolentino (d. 1434), are by Paolo Uccello and Andrea del Castagno. The bust of the organist Antonio Squarcialupi is by Benedetto da Maiano. On the last altar, the prophet *Joshua* attributed to Donatello (traditionally thought to be a portrait of the humanist friend of Cosimo il Vecchio, Poggio Bracciolini), originally on the façade of the Duomo.

The Campanile

The *Campanile (**Map 7**; open 09.00–18.50 or 19.30), nearly 85m high, was begun by Giotto in 1334 when, as the most distinguished Florentine artist, he was appointed city architect. It was continued by Andrea Pisano (1343), and completed by Francesco Talenti in 1348–59. It is built of the same coloured marbles as the Duomo, in similar patterns, in a remarkably well-proportioned design. The original bas-reliefs and statues of Prophets and Sibyls in the niches are in the Museo dell'Opera del Duomo.

The ascent of the bell-tower via 414 steps is interesting for its succession of views of the Duomo, the Baptistery, and the rest of the city. Although lower than the cupola, the climb is steeper.

Between the Baptistery and the Campanile is the little Gothic ***Loggia del Bigallo** built in 1351–58 probably by Alberto Arnoldi, who carved the reliefs. Beneath the loggia lost and abandoned children were shown for three days before being consigned to foster-mothers.

The **Museo del Bigallo** (open only by appointment, ☎ 055 230 2885) is the smallest museum in the city, but one of the most charming. It preserves most of the works of art commissioned over the centuries by the Misericordia and the Bigallo from Florentine artists, including a portable triptych by Bernardo Daddi. Across Via dei Calzaiuoli is the **Misericordia**, a charitable institution which helps those in need, and runs an ambulance service. The lay confraternity, founded in 1244, continues its work through some 2000 volunteers who still wear distincive black capes and hoods. The Oratory contains an altarpiece by Andrea della Robbia and a statue of St Sebastian by Benedetto da Maiano. Other works of art can sometimes be seen on request.

Museo dell'Opera del Duomo

At Piazza del Duomo 9 is the *Museo dell'Opera del Duomo (**Map 7**; open 09.30–18.30; fest. 08.00–14.00), in a building which has been the seat of the Opera del Duomo (responsible for the maintenance of the cathedral) since the beginning of the 15C. It contains material from the Duomo, the Baptistery, and the Campanile, including important sculpture.

Ground floor Roman fragments, Gothic statues by Tino da Camaino, a marble bust of Brunelleschi attributed to Giovanni Bandini or Buggiano, and sculptures from the Porta della Mandorla. In the courtyard, recently covered with a glass roof, are displayed six of the ten **gilded bronze *panels** by Lorenzo Ghiberti, removed from the east door of the Baptistery (described on p 59), which are masterpieces of the early Renaissance. Each exquisitely carved panel describes in continuous narrative various episodes from Old Testament stories. Here also is the large statuary group of the Baptism of Christ begun by Andrea Sansovino which used to be above the door. A large hall displays ***sculptures** by Arnolfo di Cambio from the old façade of the Duomo (it was never completed and demolished in 1587), and **four seated Evangelists** added to the lower part of the façade by Nanni di Banco (St Luke), Donatello (*St John the Evangelist), Bernardo Ciuffagni (St Matthew), and Niccolò di Piero Lamberti (St Mark). Another room contains marble *panels from the choir of the Duomo by Baccio Bandinelli and Giovanni Bandini (1547).

On the stair landing is the famous ******Pietà*** by **Michelangelo**. A late work, it was intended for the sculptor's own tomb. According to Vasari, the head of Nicodemus is a self-portrait. Dissatisfied with his work, Michelangelo destroyed the arm and left leg of Christ, and his pupil Tiberio Calcagni restored the arm and finished the figure of Mary Magdalen.

First floor The first room is dominated by the two famous ***cantorie** made in the 1430s by **Luca della Robbia** and **Donatello** for the Duomo. The original sculptured panels by Luca are displayed beneath the reconstructed Cantoria. The children (some of them drawn from classical models), shown dancing, singing, or playing musical instruments, are exquisitely carved within a beautiful architectural framework. Donatello's Cantoria provides a striking contrast, with a frieze of running putti against a background of coloured inlay. Around the walls are the sixteen statues from the niches on the Campanile by Donatello (two *Prophets*, *Abraham and Isaac*, ******Geremiah***, ******Habbakuk***), Nanni di Bartolo, and Andrea Pisano.

On the right is a room which displays Donatello's expressive statue in wood of ******St Mary Magdalen***, thought to be a late work (formerly in the Baptistery). The magnificent ***altar of silver-gilt** also from the Baptistery, is a Gothic work by Florentine goldsmiths finished in the 15C. The statuette of the *Baptist* is by Michelozzo; the reliefs (at the sides) of the Beheading of the Saint, and of his birth are by Verrocchio and Antonio del Pollaiolo. The silver ***Cross** is the work of Betto di Francesco, Antonio del Pollaiolo, and others. Also displayed here are needlework ***panels** from a liturgical tapestry worked by the craftsmen of the *Arte di Calimala* and designed by Antonio del Pollaiolo, and a portable diptych from Constantinople made in miniature mosaics, a rare Byzantine work of the early 14C.

On the other side of the Cantoria room the original ***bas-reliefs from the Campanile** are exhibited. The lower row are charming works by Andrea Pisano (some perhaps designed by Giotto) illustrating the *Creation of Man*, and the *Arts and Industries*. The last five reliefs (on the right wall) were made in the following century by Luca della Robbia. The upper row of smaller reliefs, by pupils of

Pisano, illustrate the seven *Planets*, the *Virtues*, and the *Liberal Arts*. The *Seven Sacraments* are by Alberto Arnoldi. The lunette of the *Madonna and Child* and two statuettes of the Redeemer and St Reparata are by Andrea Pisano. In the corridor is a display which reconstructs a building site thought to be similar to that set up by Brunelleschi when working on the dome of the cathedral, with some of the apparatus which may have been used in its construction, together with the original brick moulds. The wooden model of the lantern is thought to have been made by Brunelleschi as the (winning) entry in the competititon of 1436. His death mask is also preserved here. Off the next corridor are three rooms relating to the architecture of the Duomo, including models of the cupola, and projects made in 1587 for a new façade, and drawings for the façade of 1860.

Beside the Baptistery is the **Pillar of St Zenobius**, erected in the 14C to commemorate an elm which came into leaf here when the body of the bishop saint (d. c 430) was translated from San Lorenzo to Santa Reparata in the 9C.

Via de' Calzaioli (**Map 7**), on the line of a Roman road, was the main thoroughfare of the medieval city, linking the Duomo to Palazzo Vecchio and passing the guildhall of Orsanmichele. On the right is **Piazza della Repubblica** (**Map 7**), on the site of the Roman forum, and still in the centre of the city. It was laid out at the end of the 19C after the demolition of many medieval buildings. Much criticised at the time, it remains a disappointing intrusion into the historical centre of the city. It has several large cafés with tables outside.

Orsanmichele

The tall rectangular church of *Orsanmichele (**Map 7, 11**) was built as a market by Francesco Talenti, Neri di Fioravante, and Benci di Cione in 1337. The arcades were enclosed by huge Gothic windows by Simone Talenti in 1380. The upper storey was intended to be used as a granary. The decoration of the exterior was undertaken by the Guilds (or *Arti*) who commissioned statues of their patron saints for the canopied niches. They competed with each other to command work from the best artists of the age, and the statues are an impressive testimony to the skill of Florentine sculptors over a period of some two hundred years. Since 1984 restoration of the statues and niches has been underway: the restored statues are now exhibited inside the building: those which have not been replaced in situ by copies are indicated below.

The **statues**, beginning at Via de'Calzaioli (corner of Via de'Lamberti) and going round to the right are: *St John the Baptist* (1414–16), by Lorenzo Ghiberti, the first life-size statue of the Renaissance to be cast in bronze (to be replaced by a copy); *Incredulity of St Thomas* (1466–83), by **Verrocchio**, in a tabernacle by Donatello (the *stemma* above is by Luca della Robbia); *St Luke*, by Giambologna (1601; awaiting restoration), in a tabernacle by Niccolò Lamberti; *St Peter* (1408–13) attributed to Bernardo Ciuffagni; tabernacle and *St Philip* (c 1415) by Nanni di Banco; tabernacle, relief, and statues of *four soldier saints* (the *Quattro Santi Coronati*), modelled on Roman works, by **Nanni di Banco** (c 1415; to be replaced by a copy), and *stemma* above by Luca della Robbia; *St George* by Donatello (the original statue and relief are in the Bargello); tabernacle and *St Matthew* (1419–22; awaiting restoration) by **Ghiberti**; *St Stephen* by **Ghiberti** (1428; awaiting restoration); *St Eligius* and bas-relief by Nanni di Banco; *St Mark* by **Donatello**; *St James the Greater* and bas-relief attributed to Niccolò Lamberti; Gothic tabernacle attributed to Simone Talenti, with a *Madonna and Child* attributed to **Giovanni Tedesco** (to be replaced by a copy), and *stemma* by Luca della Robbia; *St John the Evangelist* by Baccio da Montelupo (1515; awaiting restoration).

The **interior** of the dark rectangular hall now serves as a church (closed 12.00–16.00), and contains interesting frescoes (14C–16C), and fine Gothic stained glass windows. The Gothic *tabernacle by **Andrea Orcagna** (1349–59) is a masterpiece of all the decorative arts. A beautiful frame of carved angels encloses a painting on the altar of the *Madonna* by **Bernardo Daddi**. On the other altar is a statue of the *Madonna and Child with St Anne*, by Francesco da Sangallo (1522).

The **Museo di Orsanmichele** (opened daily on request at Orsanmichele at 09.00, 10.00, and 11.00 except the first and last Monday of the month) is reached by an overhead passageway from **Palazzo dell'Arte della Lana**, built in 1308 by the Guild of Wool Merchants but arbitrarily restored in 1905. At the base of the tower is the little 14C oratory of Santa Maria della Tromba, with a painting of the *Madonna* by Jacopo del Casentino. On the upper floor of Orsanmichele the **restored statues** from the exterior niches (described above) are beautifully exhibited. From the second Gothic hall on the floor above there are fine views of Florence.

Palazzo dell'Arte dei Beccai, also facing Orsanmichele, the headquarters of the Butchers' Guild until 1534, is now the seat of the Accademia delle Arti del Disegno (the Academy of the three trade guilds of painters, architects, and sculptors, predecessor of the Academy of Fine Arts) founded in 1563 by Vasari and his contemporaries.

On Via Porta Rossa is the 16C loggia of the **Mercato Nuovo (Map 11)**, the Florentine straw-market (with stalls also selling leather goods, cheap lace, and souvenirs). It is known to Florentines as *Il Porcellino* from the popular statue here of a bronze boar (a copy by Tacca from an antique statue in the Uffizi).

Via Porta Rossa continues to **Palazzo Davanzati (Map 11**; closed since 1995 for major structural repairs), the Museo della Casa Fiorentina Antica, and the best surviving example of a medieval nobleman's house in Florence (despite numerous restorations). It is particularly interesting as an illustration of Florentine life in the Middle Ages. The typical 14C façade consists of three storeys above large arches on the ground floor. The interior, of great interest for its architecture and contemporary wall paintings (rare survivals of a decorative form typical of 14C houses) has been beautifully arranged with the furnishings of a Florentine house of 15C–17C (including tapestries, lacework, ceramics, sculpture, paintings, decorative arts and domestic objects). The 16C–17C furniture is a special feature of the house. At present only the entrance hall is open where a few of the contents are temporarily displayed.

Via Pellicceria leads to **Palazzo di Parte Guelfa**, built as the official residence of the Captains of the Guelf party in the 13C. The palace was enlarged by Brunelleschi who added a hall. Nearby is **Palazzo dell'Arte della Seta**, with a beautiful *stemma* in the style of Donatello (the palace belonged to the guild of silk-workers).

Via delle Terme, and the parallel Borgo Santi Apostoli to the south, are both pretty medieval streets with numerous towers and old palaces.

Santi Apostoli (**Map 11**), one of the oldest churches in the city, has a Romanesque stone façade. The basilican interior (open 10.00–12.00, 15.00–17.00) has fine green marble columns and capitals. It contains a *sinopia* of a fresco of the Madonna by Paolo Schiavo formerly on the façade; the Tomb of Prior Oddo Altoviti by Benedetto da Rovezzano; and a *tabernacle by Andrea della Robbia.

Across Via Porta Santa Maria (rebuilt after 1944) is the church of **Santo Stefano al Ponte** (**Map 11**), another very old church, now used as a concert hall. The interior was altered by Ferdinando Tacca in 1649. The altar-steps are by Buontalenti, and it contains altarpieces by Santi di Tito and Matteo Rosselli. In the canonry, to the right of the church the **Museo Diocesano di Santo Stefano al Ponte** (open only by appointment, ☎ 055 225 843) displays works of art from churches in the diocese, including interesting 14C–15C Tuscan works.

Piazza della Signoria

*Piazza della Signoria (**Map 11**), dominated by Palazzo Vecchio, the town hall, has been the political centre of the city since the Middle Ages. Here, from the 13C onwards, the *popolo sovrano* met in *parlamento* to resolve crises of government. It is now usually crowded with tourists as well as Florentines. By 1385, when it was paved, the piazza had nearly reached its present dimensions. The 18C pavement was virtually destroyed when it was renewed in 1991.

Loggia della Signoria

The huge *Loggia della Signoria (**Map 11**), also known as *Loggia dei Lanzi* and *Loggia dell' Orcagna*, with its three beautiful lofty arches, was built in 1376–82 by Benci di Cione and Simone Talenti (probably on a design by Orcagna). It was intended to be used by government officials during public ceremonies and as an ornament to the square.

Since the end of the 18C the loggia has been used as an open-air museum of sculpture. The magnificent bronze *Perseus* was commissioned from Cellini by Cosimo I in 1545 (restored in 2000). Perseus is shown trampling Medusa and exhibiting her severed head. The original bas-relief and statuettes from the pedestal are now in the Bargello. The *Rape of a Sabine* (1583), a three-figure group, is Giambologna's last work, and one of the most successful Mannerist sculptures (it is to be removed to the Accademia after its restoration and replaced here by a copy). Also here are two lions, one a Greek work, the other a 16C copy; **Hercules and the Centaur**, by Giambologna; the **Rape of Polyxena**, by Pio Fedi; and Roman statues.

Michelangelo's famous **David** was commissioned by the city of Florence in 1501 and set up in front of Palazzo Vecchio in 1504 as a political symbol representing the victory of Republicanism over tyranny. It was removed to the Accademia in 1873 and replaced here by a copy. The colossal statue of **Hercules and Cacus**, an unhappy imitation of the David, was sculpted in 1534 by Bandinelli. Donatello's statue of **Judith and Holofernes** has been replaced by a copy (original inside Palazzo Vecchio, see below).

The **Neptune Fountain**, by Ammannati, is dominated by a colossal flaccid figure of Neptune, known to Florentines as '*il Biancone*' (the 'white giant'). The

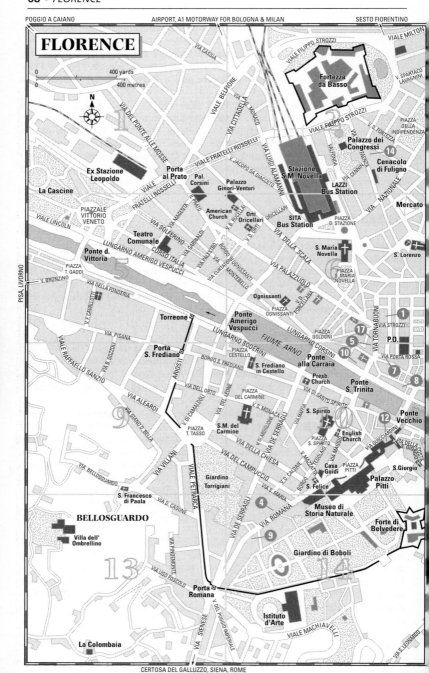

FLORENCE

0   400 yards
0   400 metres

N

VIALE MILTON
V. SPARTACO LAVAGNINI
VIALE FILIPPO STROZZI
Fortezza da Basso
VIA CASSIA
VIALE BELFIORE
VIA CITTADELLA
VIA DI MONACO
VIALE FILIPPO STROZZI
VALFONDA
PIAZZA DELLA INDIPENDENZA
V. D. FORTEZZA
Palazzo dei Congressi
Cenacolo di Fuligno
VIALE FRATELLI ROSSELLI
VIA LUIGI ALAMANNI
V. JACOPO DA DIACCETO
VIA NAZIONALE
VIA CENNINI
Ex Stazione Leopoldo
Porta al Prato
Pal. Corsini
Palazzo Ginori-Venturi
Stazione S.M. Novella
LAZZI Bus Station
La Cascine
VIALE FRATELLI ROSSELLI
VIA IL PRATO
American Church
Orti Oricellari
SITA Bus Station
PIAZZA D. STAZIONE
Mercato
PIAZZALE VITTORIO VENETO
VIALE LINCOLN
VIA SOLFERINO
VIA MAGENTA
VIA GARIBALDI
VIA PALESTRO
BORGO OGNISSANTI
VIA DELLA SCALA
S. Maria Novella
S. Lorenzo
Teatro Comunale
CORSO ITALIA
Ponte d. Vittoria
PIAZZA T. GADDI
V. BRONZINO
VIA DELLA FONDERIA
VIA F. CAVALLOTTI
VIA PISANA
LUNGARNO AMERIGO VESPUCCI
CURTATONE
MONTEBELLO
VIA PALAZZUOLO
PIAZZA S. MARIA NOVELLA
Ognissanti
PIAZZA OGNISSANTI
V. D. PORCELLANA
VIA TORNABUONI
VIA STROZZI
Torreone
Ponte Amerigo Vespucci
FIUME ARNO
LUNGARNO CORSINI
PIAZZA GOLDONI
P.O.
Porta S. Frediano
LUNGARNO SODERINI
PIAZZA CESTELLO
S. Frediano in Cestello
Ponte alla Carraia
VIA PORTA ROSSA
VIA RAFFAELLO SANZIO
ARIOSTI
BORGO S. FREDIANO
VIA DELL' ORTO
VIA DEL LEONE
Presb. Church
Ponte S. Trinita
VIA ALEARDI
VIA GIANO D. BELLA
VIA V.S. MONACA
PIAZZA DEL CARMINE
S.M. del Carmine
S. Spirito
English Church
Ponte Vecchio
VIA BELLOSGUARDO
VIA DI CAMALDOLI
VIA DELLA CHIESA
PIAZZA T. TASSO
PIAZZA S. SPIRITO
V. MAGGIO
VIA GUICCIARDINI
VIA DELLA COSTA
S. Giorgio
S. Francesco di Paola
VIA VILLANI
VIA DEL CAMPUCCIO
VIA S. MONACA
Casa Guidi
PIAZZA PITTI
Palazzo Pitti
BELLOSGUARDO
Villa dell' Ombrellino
VIALE PETRARCA
Giardino Torrigiani
VIA DE' SERRAGLI
S. Felice
VIA ROMANA
VIA D. CASONE
VIA S. MARIA
Museo di Storia Naturale
Forte di Belvedere
VIA UGO FOSCOLO
VIA PINDEMONTE
Giardino di Boboli
La Colombaia
Porta Romana
VIA SIENESE
VIA DEL POGGIO IMPERIALE
Istituto d'Arte
VIALE MACHIAVELLI
V.S. LEONARDO

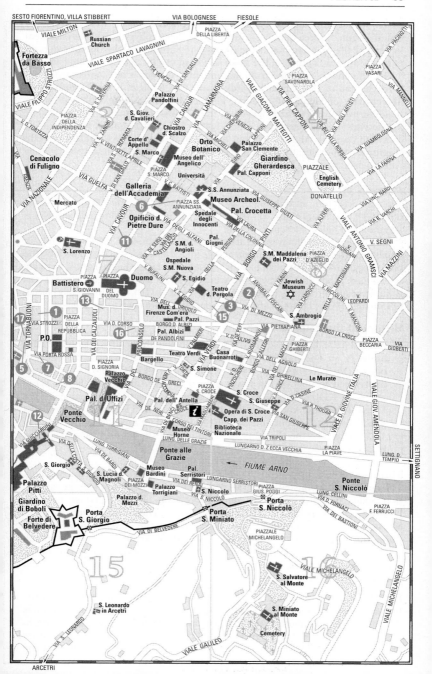

more successful elegant bronze groups on the basin were carved by Giambologna, Andrea Calamech, and others. The porphyry disk in the pavement in front of the fountain marks the spot where Savonarola, the Dominican prior of San Marco, was burnt at the stake as a heretic after his excommunication in 1498. The fine bronze equestrian monument to Cosimo is by Giambologna.

At the end of the piazza, towards Piazza San Firenze, is the **Tribunale di Mercanzia** (or Merchants' Court), founded in 1308 and established in this building in 1359. Palazzo Uguccioni (no. 7) has an unusual but handsome façade attributed to Mariotto di Zanobi Folfi (1550), with a bust of Francesco I by Giovanni Bandini. Above a bank at no. 5 was displayed the **Collezione Della Ragione**, a representative collection of 20C Italian art left to the city in 1970 by Alberto della Ragione, but this is to be moved.

Palazzo Vecchio

*Palazzo Vecchio, also known as *Palazzo della Signoria* (**Map 11**; open 09.00–19.00; Thurs & fest. 09.00–14.00), the medieval Palazzo del Popolo, is still the town hall of Florence.

On a design traditionally attributed to Arnolfo di Cambio (1298–1302), it is an imposing fortress-palace built in *pietra forte* on a trapezoidal plan and became the prototype of many other town halls in Tuscany. The façade has remained virtually unchanged: it has graceful two-light windows and a battlemented gallery. It was the tallest edifice in the city until the 15C; the tower (1310), asymmetrically placed, is 95m high. Many of the rooms on the upper floors are open to the public.

History of the Palazzo Vecchio

The palace stands on part of the site of the Roman theatre of Florence built in the 1C AD. The *priori* (priors) lived here during their two months' tenure of office in the government of the medieval city. In 1433 Cosimo il Vecchio was imprisoned in part of the tower known as the Alberghetto, before being exiled. In 1540 Cosimo I moved here from the private Medici palace in Via Larga. It became known as Palazzo Vecchio after 1549 when the Medici grand-dukes moved out and took up residence in Palazzo Pitti. From 1865 to 1871 it housed the Chamber of Deputies and the Foreign Ministry when Florence was capital of the Kingdom of Italy.

There is a second entrance in Via della Ninna on the right side of the building. The **courtyard** reconstructed by Michelozzo (1453), and the elaborate decoration added in 1565 by Vasari on the occasion of the marriage between Francesco, son of Cosimo I, and Joanna of Austria. The fountain bears a copy of Verrocchio's putto, now inside the palace. The statue of *Samson killing the Philistine* is by Pierino da Vinci. In the 14C **Sala d'Arme** exhibitions are held. Near the 15C weather vane with the Marzocco lion removed from the top of the tower, is the ticket office. The rest of the ground floor is taken up with busy local government offices.

First floor A monumental double grand staircase by Vasari ascends to the immense *Salone dei Cinquecento, built by Cronaca in 1495 for the meetings of the Consiglio Maggiore of the Republic. Leonardo da Vinci and Michelangelo were commissioned to paint huge murals of the Florentine victories at the battles of Anghiari (over Milan) and Cascina (over Pisa) on the two long walls. Only the cartoons and a fragment by Leonardo were ever completed; these were copied and studied by contemporary painters before they were lost. The room was transformed by Vasari in 1563–65 when the present decoration was carried out in honour of Cosimo I, and the Florentine victories over Siena and Pisa, by Giovanni Stradano, Jacopo Zucchi, and Giovanni Battista Naldini. **Michelangelo's** *Victory*, a strongly knit two-figure group, was intended for a niche in the tomb of Julius II in Rome. Giambologna's *Virtue overcoming Vice* was commissioned as a pendant (the original plaster model is displayed here). The statues of the *Labours of Hercules* are Vincenzo de'Rossi's best works.

From an inconspicuous door on the entrance wall the charming *Studiolo of Francesco I* can be seen. This tiny study is a masterpiece of Florentine Mannerist art created by Vasari and his school. It is entirely decorated with paintings and bronze statuettes celebrating Francesco's interest in the natural sciences and alchemy, by Il Poppi, Bronzino, Vincenzo Danti, Vasari, Santi di Tito, Giovanni Battista Naldini, Giovanni Battista Stradano, Alessandro Allori, Giovanni Bandini, Maso di San Friano, Giambologna, Vincenzo de'Rossi, Giovanni Maria Butteri, Alessandro Fei, Bartolomeo Ammannati, and Jacopo Zucchi.

The **Quartiere di Leone X** was decorated for Cosimo I by Vasari, Marco da Faenza, Giovanni Stradano, and others with paintings illustrating the political history of the Medici family. Only the Sala di Leone X is at present open.

Second floor Stairs lead up to the **Quartiere degli Elementi**, also decorated by Vasari and assistants. In a little room here is displayed the original of Verrocchio's *Putto with a dolphin*, removed from the courtyard. In some of the rooms are fine cabinets in *pietre dure*. The **Terrazza di Saturno** has a good view of Florence.

A balcony leads across the end of the Sala dei Cinquecento. The apartments of Cosimo I's wife are known as the **Quartiere di Eleonora di Toledo**. The *chapel* was entirely decorated by Bronzino. In the **Sala di Ester** is a painting of 1557 which shows the lost fragment of the *Battle of Anghiari* by Leonardo, probably the best copy that has survived. Beyond the **Cappella della Signoria** decorated by Ridolfo del Ghirlandaio is the **Sala d'Udienza** with a superb *ceiling by Giuliano da Maiano and assistants. The *doorway crowned by a statue of Justice is by Benedetto and Giuliano da Maiano. The mural paintings (1545–48) are by Salviati. The **Sala dei Gigli** (decorated with Florentine lilies) has another magnificent *ceiling, and frescoes by Domenico Ghirlandaio. Here is displayed Donatello's bronze statue of *Judith and Holofernes*, removed from Piazza della Signoria after its restoration. It is one of his last and most sophisticated works. The **Cancelleria** (chancellor's office) was Niccolò Machiavelli's office when he was government secretary. The **Sala delle Carte Geografiche** contains 57 maps illustrating the entire known world by Fra Ignazio Danti and Stefano Bonsignori (1563–81).

The **Collezione Loeser** (which includes a *portrait of Laura Battiferri*, wife of Bartolomeo Ammannati, by Bronzino and a tondo by Alonso Berruguete) is displayed on a mezzanine floor below.

Other interesting parts of the building are shown on guided tours of the 'percorsi segreti' ('secret itineraries') which it is best to book in advance, ☎ 055 276 8224. These include the Studiolo (see above) and Tesoretto (a tiny private study of Cosimo I) and the remarkable roof of the Salone dei Cinquecento. A delightful Children's Museum (**Museo dei Ragazzi**) was opened in 2000 in other rooms of the palace, to illustrate certain historical periods through a theatre workshop, or to explain architectural principles of scientific theories to teenage children run by a group of enterprising young people. There is also a section with games for infants (for information and booking, ☎ as above).

Galleria degli Uffizi

The massive *Palazzo degli Uffizi (**Map 11**) extends from Piazza della Signoria to the Arno. The unusual U-shaped building with a short façade on the river front was begun in 1560 by Vasari, and completed according to his design by Alfonso Parigi the Elder and Bernardo Buontalenti. It was commissioned by Cosimo I to serve as government offices (*uffici*, hence uffizi). Resting on unstable sandy ground, it is a feat of engineering skill. The use of iron to reinforce the building permitted extraordinary technical solutions during its construction, and allowed for the remarkably large number of apertures.

- Gallery open winter 08.30–18.50; fest. 08.30–19.00; summer 08.30–21.00; fest. 08.30–20.00; closed Monday. To book in advance, ☎ 055 294883, see p 57. **Corridoio Vasariano** and **Collezione Contini-Bonacossi**, visits by appointment only, ☎ 055 265 4321. There is a **café** with a terrace on the third floor.

The ****Galleria degli Uffizi** is the most important collection of paintings in Italy and one of the great art collections of the world. The origins of the collection go back to Cosimo I, and numerous members of the Medici dynasty continued to add works of art in the following centuries. The last of the Medici, Anna Maria Lodovica, bequeathed her inheritance on the people of Florence in 1737. All the works are well labelled and the collection is arranged chronologically by school. The following description includes only some of the most important paintings and sculptures. More rooms are to be opened on the first floor and the collection rehung, and a new exit constructed on Piazza Castellani.

A series of large rooms on the **ground floor** house ticket offices (separate one for pre-booked visits), bookshops, information centres, and cloakrooms. Beyond the staircase, in a hallway, is a detached fresco of the **Annunciation* by Botticelli. A room nearby (at present closed) incorporates the remains of the church of **San Pier Scheraggio** (founded c 1068), and a series of *frescoes of illustrious Florentines by Andrea del Castagno are displayed.

There is a lift for the picture galleries on the third floor (although it is now officially reserved for the use of the disabled and the gallery staff). The staircase, lined with antique busts and statues, leads up past the **Prints and Drawings Room**, with one of the finest collections in the world, particularly rich in Renaissance and Mannerist works (shown in *Exhibitions).

Third floor
The **vestibule** (**A**) contains good antique sculpture. The long U-shaped gallery provides a fine setting for the superb collection of antique sculptures (mostly Hellenistic works).

Room 2 contains three famous paintings of the **Maestà* by Cimabue, Duccio di

Boninsegna (both c 1285), and Giotto (painted some 25 years later).

Room 3 displays works of the 14C Sienese school including, the Lorenzetti brothers, and an *Annunciation*, one of Simone Martini's most famous works.

Room 4 Florentine school of the 14C (Giottino, Bernardo Daddi, Nardo di Cione, and Giovanni da Milano).

Rooms 5 & 6 Works by Lorenzo Monaco and Gentile da Fabriano, including two charming *Adoration of the Magi*.

Room 7 (Florentine school of the early 15C). Domenico Veneziano, *Madonna enthroned with saints*; Piero della Francesca, *portraits of Federico di Montefeltro* and *Battista Sforza*; Paolo Uccello, *Battle of San Romano*.

Room 8 contains some lovely *works by Filippo Lippi (including the *Predella of the Barbadori Altarpiece* and *Madonna and Child with two angels*). His son Filippino is represented by a lovely Adoration of the Child and two large altarpieces.

Room 9 Paintings by Piero and Antonio del Pollaiolo (*Six Virtues, and Saints Vincent, James, and Eustace*, from San Miniato), and two exquisite small panels illustrating the *Story of Holofernes* by Botticelli.

Rooms 10–14 displays the masterpieces of **Botticelli**, including the famous *Primavera* and *Birth of Venus*. The *Primavera* (c 1478) is an allegory of Spring, painted for Lorenzo di Pierfrancesco de' Medici, cousin of Lorenzo il Magnifico (who may be represented in the figure of Mercury). In a dark orange grove, the Garden of Hesperides of Classical myth, in a meadow of exquisite spring flowers, Zephyr chases Flora and transforms her into Spring, who is shown bedecked with flowers. In the centre is Venus, with Cupid above her, and beyond the beautiful group of the Three Graces united in dance, is the figure of Mercury. The *Birth of Venus* is perhaps the most famous of all Botticelli's works, also probably painted for Lorenzo di Pierfrancesco. The pagan subject is taken from a poem by Politian and illustrates Zephyr and Chloris blowing Venus ashore while Hora, her fluttering dress decorated with cornflowers and daisies, hurries to cover her nakeness. The elegant figures are painted with a remarkable lightness of touch. Other famous works by Botticelli here include: *Adoration of the Magi*, *Calumny*, *Pallas and the Centaur*, *Madonna of the Magnificat*, and a late *Annunciation*. Also here is the *Triptych* commissioned by the Portinari family in Bruges from Hugo van der Goes in 1475 and shipped back to Florence. There are also three works by Domenico Ghirlandaio in this room.

Room 15 The early Florentine works of Leonardo da Vinci (*Annunciation*, and the *Adoration of the Magi*, an unfinished composition), together with paintings by his master Verrocchio (*Baptism of Christ*) are displayed here. Also works by Perugino and Luca Signorelli.

Room 18 The beautiful octagonal *Tribuna* was designed by Buontalenti, and contains the most important *classical sculptures* owned by the Medici (the famous *Medici Venus*, a copy of the Praxitelean *Aphrodite of Cnidos*; the *Arrotino*; the *Dancing Faun*; the *Wrestlers*; and *Apollino*). Around the walls are a remarkable series of distinguished court *portraits*, many of them of the family of Cosimo I commissioned from Bronzino.

Room 19 Works by Luca Signorelli, Perugino, and Lorenzo di Credi.

Room 20 is devoted to Dürer (*Adoration of the Magi*) and the German School, including Lukas Cranach the Elder (*Adam and Eve*).

Room 21 Venetian works by Giovanni Bellini (*Sacred Allegory*), and Giorgione.

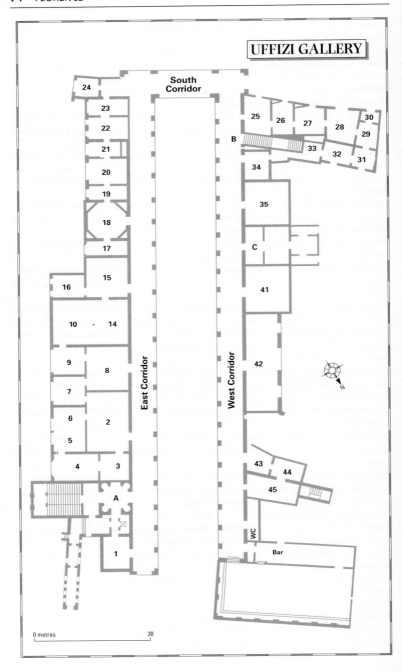

Room 22 contains German and Flemish *portraits by Hans Memling, Hans Holbein the Younger, and Joos van Cleve the Elder.

Room 23 *triptych* by Mantegna; and works by Correggio.

The short **south corridor** (good view of the Arno) displays some more fine ancient sculpture.

Room 25 contains the famous ***Tondo Doni** of the *Holy Family*, the only finished tempera painting by Michelangelo. Painted for the marriage of Agnolo Doni with Maddalena Strozzi (1504–05) when the artist was 30 years old, it breaks with traditional represenations of this familiar subject and signals a new moment in High Renaissance painting.

Room 26 has some famous works by Raphael: *Madonna del Cardellino*, *Leo X with Cardinals Giulio de'Medici and Luigi de'Rossi*, and a *self-portrait*. Fine portraits by Pontormo are displayed in **Room 27**, together with works by Bronzino, and Rosso Fiorentino.

Room 28 is devoted to Titian, including some of his masterpieces (*Flora* and *Venus of Urbino*) and some very fine portraits. Also displayed here is the *Death of Adonis* by Sebastiano del Piombo.

Rooms 29–30 are devoted to Dosso Dossi and Parmigianino and the 16C Emilian school.

Room 31 displays works by Paolo Veronese (*Annunciation*, *Holy Family with St Barbara*) and the Veneto school, including Tintoretto is also represented in **room 32**.

Room 33 has works by the **French school**, including François Clouet (equestrian portrait of Francis I). **Room 34** has more works by the Venetian school, including Lorenzo Lotto and Giovanni Battista Moroni (*Count Pietro Secco Suardi*).

Room 35 has some good works by Federico Barocci.

Room 41 contains two huge canvases illustrating *Scenes from the life of Henri IV*, very fine works by Rubens, as well as his self-portrait and that of his wife *Isabella Brandt. The portraits by Van Dyck include an *equestrian portrait of the Emperor Charles V*. There is also a well-known *portrait of Galileo* by Sustermans.

Room 42 The **Niobe Room** was designed in 1779 to house the Roman statues of Niobe and her children, copies of Greek originals of the school of Skopas (early 4C BC) and the neo-Attic Medici vase. In the corridor outside the Wounded Warrior is a Greek original of the 5C BC.

Room 43 exhibits works by Caravaggio including the *Sacrifice of Isaac*, and works by Annibale Carracci, Claude Lorraine and Guido Reni.

Room 44 has three *portraits by Rembrandt (two of them self-portraits), as well as Dutch and Flemish works (Jan Steen, Jacob Ruysdael). The 18C works in **room 45** include Venetian genre scenes and portraits by Giovanni Battista Tiepolo, Francesco Guardi, Canaletto, Alessandro and Pietro Longhi, as well as portraits by Etiene Liotard, Chardin and Goya.

On the landing by the **stairs** down to the exit is a sculptured boar (copy of a Hellenistic original).

Corridoio Vasariano

The Corridoio Vasariano (**B**) is a covered passageway built by Vasari in 1565 to connect Palazzo Vecchio, via degli Uffizi and Ponte Vecchio, with Palazzo Pitti (for admission, see p 72). It offers unique views of the city, and is hung with notable paintings including 17C works, and a celebrated ***collection of self-portraits** (begun by Cardinal Leopoldo), by Vasari, Bronzino, Salvator Rosa, Rubens, Rembrandt, Van Dyck, Velazquez, Hogarth, Reynolds, David, Delacroix, Corot, Ingres, and many others.

The **Collezione Contini-Bonacossi** is arranged in a wing of the Uffizi (entrance on Via Lambertesca; for admission, see p 72). It contains Italian paintings (many by artists not represented elsewhere in the Uffizi), Spanish works, and 15C–17C majolica and furniture, ceded to the Italian state in 1974. Among the most important works are Madonnas by Duccio di Buoninsegna, Sassetta, and Andrea del Castagno.

Ponte Vecchio

The fame of Ponte Vecchio (**Map 11**; open to pedestrians only), lined with quaint medieval-looking houses, saved it from damage in 1944. It was the only bridge over the Arno until 1218. The present bridge of three arches was reconstructed after a flood in 1345 probably by Taddeo Gaddi (also attributed to Neri di Fioravante). The excellent jewellers here continue the traditional skill of Florentine goldsmiths whose work first became famous in the 15C. Their shops have pretty fronts with wooden shutters and awnings; they overhang the river supported on brackets. Above them on the left side the round windows of the Corridoio Vasariano can be seen. From the opening in the centre there is a view of Ponte Santa Trìnita.

On the south side of Ponte Vecchio Via Guicciardini continues towards Piazza Pitti; on the left opens Piazza Santa Felicita with a granite column of 1381 marking the site of the first Christian cemetery in Florence. Here is **Santa Felìcita** (**Map 11**), probably the oldest church in Florence after San Lorenzo. The early-Christian church, dedicated to the Roman martyr, St Felicity, was last rebuilt in 1736 by Ferdinando Ruggeri in a 15C style. The fine interior is notable chiefly for the superb *works (1525–27) by Pontormo in the **Cappella Capponi** (an altarpiece of the *Deposition*, and frescoes of the *Annunciation*, and the *Evangelists*).

The Pitti Palace and the Boboli Gardens

The Pitti Palace

*Palazzo Pitti (**Map 10**) still contains the apartments used for four centuries by the grand-dukes and rulers of Florence and Tuscany, as well as the works of art acquired by them. It houses a number of important museums, including the Galleria Palatina, with one of the finest collections of paintings in Italy, the Museo degli Argenti, the Galleria d'Arte Moderna, and the Galleria del Costume. The state apartments used by the Medici and Lorraine grand-dukes, have been restored to their appearance in 1911 when occupied by the royal house of Savoy. Other suites of rooms will be opened to the public after their restoration.

• **Admission** Tickets for all the museums in the palace are sold from the right side of the courtyard, left of the main staircase leading up to the Galleria Palatina and Museo d'Arte Moderna (advance booking service, ☎ 055 294 883). A combined ticket, valid for 3 consecutive days, can also be bought (cheaper after 16.00). The rooms are not numbered: the numbers

given in the description below refer to the floor plan of Palazzo Pitti on p 78.
Galleria Palatina (ticket valid also for the **Appartamenti Reali**) 08.30–18.50; fest. 08.30–13.50; closed Mon.
Galleria d'Arte Moderna and **Galleria del Costume** (second floor) and **Museo degli Argenti** (entered from the left side of the courtyard) daily 08.30–13.50; closed the second and fourth Sun of every month and the first, third and fifth Monday of every month.

History of the Pitti Palace

The palace was built by the merchant Luca Pitti, an effective demonstration of his wealth and power to his rivals, the Medici. The majestic golden-coloured palace is built in huge rough-hewn blocks of stone of different sizes. Its design is attributed to Brunelleschi although it was begun c 1457, after his death. The palace remained incomplete on the death of Luca Pitti in 1472; by then it consisted of the central seven bays with three doorways. Bartolomeo Ammannati, and then Giulio and Alfonso Parigi the Younger completed the building, and the two side wings (the rondò) were added in the 18C and 19C.

In 1549 the palace was bought by Eleonora di Toledo, wife of Cosimo I. It became the official seat of the Medici dynasty of grand-dukes after Cosimo I moved here from Palazzo Vecchio. The various ruling families of Florence continued to occupy the palace, or part of it, until 1919 when Vittorio Emanuele III presented it to the State.

The splendid *courtyard by Ammannati serves as a garden façade to the palace. It is a masterpiece of Florentine Mannerist architecture, with bold rustication in three orders.

Galleria Palatina

The **grand staircase** by Ammannati ascends to the first floor with the entrance to the celebrated **Galleria di Palazzo Pitti** or **Galleria Palatina**, formed in the 17C by the Medici grand-dukes, and installed here in the 18C. The splendid ceilings in the reception rooms on the *piano nobile* were decorated in the 17C by Pietro da Cortona for the Medici grand-dukes. They contain the masterpieces of the collection, including numerous famous works by Raphael and Titian. The arrangement of the pictures (most of them richly framed) still preserves to some extent the character of a private royal collection of the 17C–18C, the aesthetic arrangement of the rooms being considered rather than the chronological placing of the paintings. This produces a remarkable effect of magnificence even though in some cases the pictures (all of which are well labelled) are difficult to see on the crowded walls.

From the three reception rooms (straight ahead—1, 2, and 21), there is a view of the courtyard and Boboli gardens. Beyond these are the 'minor' rooms of the gallery (rooms 22–23 and 10–19). The six reception rooms (4–9) overlooking Piazza Pitti which contain the famous masterpieces of the collection, are visited at the end.

From the **Sala del Castagnoli** (**21**), containing a magnificent 19C circular table in *pietre dure*, is the entrance to the so-called **Volterrano wing** (sometimes closed). Here the **Sala delle Allegorie** (**22**) contains works by Volterrano and Giovanni da San Giovanni. The rooms beyond (23–31) contain works by Cigoli, Carlo Dolci, Empoli, Lorenzo Lippi, Cristofano Allori, Jacopo Ligozzi, Jacopo Vignali, Giovanna

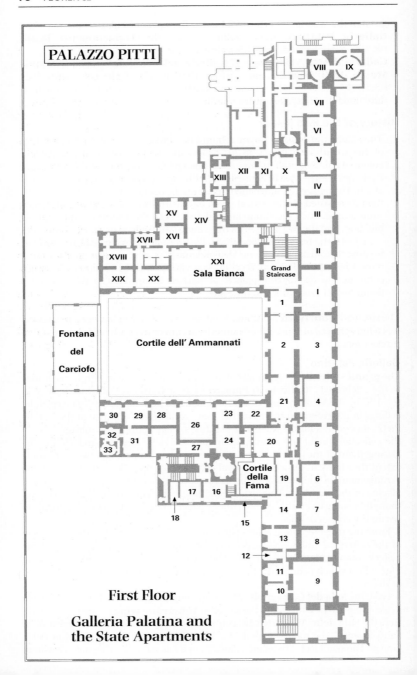

PALAZZO PITTI

VIII
IX
VII
VI
V
XIII XII XI X
IV
XV
XIV
III
XVII XVI
II
XVIII
XXI
Sala Bianca
Grand
Staircase
XIX XX
I

**Fontana
del
Carciofo**

Cortile dell' Ammannati

1
2   3
21   4

30   29   28
23   22
26
32
31
24
20
33
27

**Cortile
della
Fama**
19
5
6
17   16
14   7
18
15
13   8
12
11
9
10

First Floor

**Galleria Palatina and
the State Apartments**

Garzoni, Francesco Furini, Giovanni Bilivert, Francesco Curradi, and Salvator Rosa.

From the Sala del Castagnoli (see above) is the entrance to a series of rooms decorated in the neo-Classical style which contain the smaller works in the collection. The **Sala di Musica** (**20**) was built in 1811–21. The **Galleria del Poccetti** (19) displays portraits by Rubens, Pontormo, Peter Lely, and Niccolò Cassana.

The **Sala di Prometeo** (**14**) contains: *Dance of Apollo with the Muses* by Baldassarre Peruzzi; a *Tondo of the Madonna and Child*, one of the best works of Filippo Lippi; *Young Bacchus* by Guido Reni; *Portrait of a Man* by Botticelli; and the *Eleven Thousand Martyrs* by Pontormo. Rooms 15–18 are not always open. A **corridor** (**15**) with small Flemish paintings leads to the **Sala della Giustizia** (**16**) with a *Portrait of a man* by Titian (thought to be Vincenzo Mosti). The **Sala dei Putti** (**18**) contains still-lifes by Rachele Ruysch and a small monochrome painting of the *Three Graces* by Rubens.

The **Sala di Ulisse** (**19**) contains portraits by Moroni, *Death of Lucrezia* by Filippino Lippi, and the *Madonna dell'Impannata* by Raphael. Beyond the delightful **Empire Bathroom** (**12**) the **Sala dell'Educazione di Giove** (**21**) contains *Judith with the head of Holofernes* by Cristofano Allori, and the *Sleeping Cupid*, a late work by Caravaggio. The *Sala della Stufa* (**10**) is beautifully frescoed by Pietro da Cortona showing the *Four Ages of the World*, his first work in the palace (1637).

To the left is the entrance to the six rooms on the *piano nobile* overlooking Piazza Pitti which house the masterpieces of the collection. The **Sala dell'Iliade** (**23**) contains portraits by Sustermans, Francesco Pourbus the Younger, Ridolfo del Ghirlandaio, and Joos van Cleve; Andrea del Sarto, two large paintings of the *Assumption*; **Titian**, *Philip II of Spain*, *Diego de Mendoza*; **Raphael**, *Portrait of a woman expecting a child*.

The next five reception rooms (**24–28**) have beautiful Baroque *ceilings decorated in the 1640s by Pietro da Cortona for Ferdinando II. **Sala di Saturno** (24) contains some masterpieces by Raphael: *Madonna della Seggiola*, a beautifully composed tondo, among the artist's most mature and most popular paintings; *Maddalena Doni and her husband*; *Vision of Ezekiel*; *Madonna del Baldacchino*; *Cardinal Tommaso Inghirami*; and the *Madonna del Granduca*, an early work showing the influence of Leonardo. Also here is *Deposition* by Perugino.

The **Sala di Giove** (25) has the most beautiful ceiling of this suite of rooms. Here is another masterpiece by Raphael, his *Portrait of a lady (La Velata)*. The *Three Ages of Man* by the Venetian school is usually attributed to Giorgione. The exquisite small *Head of St Jerome* may be by Verrocchio, and the *Young St John the Baptist* is by Andrea del Sarto, and the *Deposition* by Fra Bartolomeo.

The **Sala di Marte** (**26**) has a huge allegorical painting, the *Consequences of War* by Rubens, who also painted *The Four Philosophers* (represented by Rubens himself, his brother Filippo, Justus Lipsius, and Jan van Wouwer). The splendid portrait of *Cardinal Ippolito de'Medici* is by Titian, and there is another fine portrait by Paolo Veronese. The two beautiful small works with scenes from the *Life of Joseph* are by Andrea del Sarto.

In the **Sala di Apollo** (**27**) there is a *Portrait of a gentleman*, a masterpiece by Titian, who also painted the *Mary Magdalen*.

The **Sala di Venere** (**28**) is named after the *Venus Italica*, sculpted by

Canova, and presented by Napoleon in exchange for the Medici *Venus* which he had carried off to Paris. Here are more superb works by **Titian**: the **Concert* (a famous work, also attributed to Giorgione); **Pietro Aretino*, a splendid portrait; and **Portrait of a lady*, known as *La Bella*. The two lovely landscapes (*Ulysses in the Phaecian Isle*, and **Return from the hayfields*) are by Rubens.

Appartamenti Reali
The other half of the *piano nobile* along the façade of the palace is occupied by the royal apartments (closed Jan–Apr). These lavishly decorated rooms were used as state apartments from the 17C onwards by the Medici and Lorraine grand-dukes and later by the royal house of Savoy. They were beautifully restored in 1993 to their appearance in 1880–1911. The contents, which reflect the eclectic Victorian taste of the Savoy rulers, as well as the neo-Baroque period of the 19C Lorraine grand-dukes, include splendid silk curtains, drapes, wall hangings and furnishings made in Florence and France; sumptuous gilded chandeliers, neo-Classical mirrors and frames; early 19C carpets from Tournai, huge oriental vases; furniture decorated with *pietre dure*; and portraits of the Medici by Sustermans. The Appartamenti degli Arazzi (XV–XX) were reopened in 2000, and are open in winter when the Appartamenti Reali are closed. It contains Gobelins and Florentine tapestries.

    Second floor The **Galleria d'Arte Moderna** (adm. see p 77), beautifully displayed in rooms decorated around 1825 for the Lorraine grand-dukes, is particularly representative of Tuscan art of the 19C, notably the Macchiaioli school (including Giovanni Fattori, Silvestro Lega, Telemaco Signorini). In every room there is a detailed catalogue of the works displayed which cover the period from the mid-18C up to the end of the First World War. They are arranged chronologically and by schools.

    In the Palazzina della Meridiana, the southern wing of the palace, which was begun in 1776 by Gaspare Maria Paoletti, is the beautifully arranged **Galleria del Costume** (adm. see p 77), founded in 1983 and the only museum of the history of fashion in Italy (exhibits mostly from the 18C to the early 20C).

Museo degli Argenti
The **Museo degli Argenti (for admission, see above), arranged in the summer apartments of the grand-dukes, is entered from the left side of the courtyard. Although always known as the 'silver' museum it contains a great miscellany of decorative arts. The main room contains exuberant and colourful frescoes by Giovanni da San Giovanni. In the **Sala Buia** is displayed the magnificent **collection of vases in *pietre dure* which belonged to Lorenzo il Magnifico, most of which date from the late Imperial Roman era. The reception rooms are decorated with trompe l'oeil frescoes by Angelo Michele Colonna and Agostino Mitelli.

    The rooms towards the gardens were the living quarters of the grand-dukes. Here, and on the mezzanine floor, are displayed their eclectic collection of personal keepsakes, gifts presented by other ruling families, objets d'art made specially for them, and the **jewellery collection* of the electress Anna Maria Lodovica de' Medici.

Boboli Gardens
On the hillside behind Palazzo Pitti lie the magnificent **Boboli Gardens (**Map10**, 14), laid out for Cosimo I by Tribolo and extended in the early 17C.

• Open 09.00–sunset; except first and last Mon of the month. The main entrance is in the courtyard of Palazzo Pitti (ticket office also in the courtyard); there are three other entrances (and exits) at the Annalena Gate in Via Romana, and the Porta Romana gate.

The biggest park in the centre of Florence, it is laid out on two main axes. The lower gardens, with 17C arboured walks on either side of a splendid long cypress avenue (the *Viottolone*) and the *Isolotto* with its fruit trees in pots, are the most attractive. The vegetation is predominantly evergreen with tall double hedges and ilex woods. About 170 statues decorate the walks, many of them restored Roman works and others dating from the 16C and 17C (some are removed for restoration or replaced by copies). The **amphitheatre** was designed by Ammannati in imitation of a Roman circus.

At the top of the garden in the secluded Giardino del Cavaliere (charming views) is the **Museo della Porcellana** (open 09.00–13.50, exc. 1st, 3rd 5th Mon & 2nd and 4th Sun of month) displaying 18C–19C porcelain. Near Piazza Pitti exit is the 16C ***Grotta Grande** (closed for restoration).

Galleria dell'Accademia and Museo di San Marco

The Galleria dell'Accademia

The entrance to the *Galleria dell'Accademia (**Map 3, 7**) is at Via Ricasoli 58. Open 08.30–18.50 exc. Mon; in summer it is sometimes also open in the evenings; booking service, ☎ 055 294 883, see p 57.

The gallery is visited above all for its famous works by Michelangelo, but it also contains an important collection of Florentine paintings. The collection was formed in 1784 with a group of paintings given, for study purposes, to the Academy by Pietro Leopoldo I. Since 1873 some important sculptures by Michelangelo have been housed here, including the *David*.

The galleria contains ****sculptures** by **Michelangelo**. The four *Slaves* or *Prisoners* (c 1521–23) were begun for the tomb of Julius II in Rome which was never finished. The *St Matthew* (1504–08), one of the twelve apostles commissioned from the sculptor by the Opera del Duomo, was the only one he ever began. These are all magnificent examples of Michelangelo's unfinished works, some of them barely blocked out, the famous *non-finito*, still much discussed by scholars.

The **Tribune** was specially built in 1882 to exhibit the *David by Michelangelo (1501–04) when it was removed from Piazza della Signoria. It is perhaps the most famous single work of art of western civilisation, and has become all too familiar through endless reproductions, although it is not the work by which Michelangelo is best judged. It was commissioned by the city of Florence to stand outside Palazzo Vecchio where its huge scale fits its setting. The figure of David, uncharacteristic of Michelangelo's works, stands in a classical pose suited to the shallow block of marble, 4.10m high. The hero, a young colossus, is shown in the moment before his victory over Goliath. A celebration of the nude, the statue established Michelangelo as the foremost sculptor of his time at the age of 29.

The Pinacoteca. At the end of the hall to the left of the *David* is a huge room which displays 19C works by Academicians, including plaster models by Lorenzo Bartolini. Off the hall are three rooms containing early Tuscan works of the

13C–14C, including the Orcagna brothers and followers of Giotto. The **first floor**, with a *Pietà* by Giovanni da Milano, also has Florentine paintings of the 14C and 15C, including works by Lorenzo Monaco, and an exquisite embroidered altar frontal of 1336.

Off the Galleria (see above) is the entrance to three rooms with 15C Florentine paintings including: a *frontal of a *cassone* or marriage-chest of the Adimari family showing a wedding scene in front of the Baptistery, by Lo Scheggia and two *Madonnas by Botticelli. The last room contains early 16C works including a plaster model by Giambologna of his Rape of the Sabine in the Loggia dei Lanzi, and a *Descent from the Cross* by Filippino Lippi and Perugino.

Part of the very fine **Museum of Musical Instruments** (with stringed instruments by Stradivari, Guarneri, Arnati, and Ruggeri, and a harpsichord by Cristofori) collected by the Medici, was opened here in 2001.

At Via Alfani 78 is the **Museo dell' Opificio delle Pietre Dure** (open 09.00–14.00 exc. fest.), which documents the history of the Opificio founded in 1588 by the Grand-duke Ferdinando I. The refined craft of working hard or semi-precious stones (*pietre dure*) was perfected here. Beautiful mosaics were made to decorate cabinets and table-tops, some of which are exhibited here. This is also the seat of a State restoration and conservation laboratory, and restoration school.

Nearby is the **Rotonda di Santa Maria degli Angeli** (now used by the university; no adm.), one of the first centralised buildings of the Renaissance begun by Brunelleschi in 1434 and left unfinished.

Via dei Servi is lined with a number of handsome 16C palaces, including Palazzo dei Pucci attributed to Ammannati. The church of **San Michele Visdomini** (or San Michelino) contains a *Holy Family* by Pontormo. The street tabernacle here encloses a fresco by Cosimo Rosselli. Via dei Servi leads to Piazza Santissima Annunziata (described below).

Via Ricasoli (see above) leads from the Galleria dell'Accademia to **Piazza San Marco** (Map 3), one of the liveliest squares in the city. Here, beneath the Loggia dell'Ospedale di San Matteo, is the seat of the Accademia di Belle Arti, an art school opened in 1784.

Museo di San Marco

The north side of the square is occupied by the Dominican church and convent of San Marco. The convent contains the *Museo di San Marco (**Map 3**; open 08.30–13.50; Sat & Sun 08.30–19.00; closed 1st, 3rd, and 5th Sunday and the 2nd and 4th Mon of the month), famous for its works by the **Blessed Fra' Angelico** who was a friar in the convent.

Cosimo il Vecchio founded a public library here, the first of its kind in Europe. Antonino Pierozzo (1389–1459) and Girolamo Savonarola (1452–98; see p 70) were famous priors of the convent.

The beautiful **Cloister of St Antonino** was built by Michelozzo. The lunettes with scenes from the life of St Antonino are by Bernardino Poccetti. In the corners are frescoes by Fra Angelico. The **Pilgrims' Hospice**, also by Michelozzo, contains a superb *collection of paintings by Fra Angelico, mostly dating from the 1430s and very well preserved. Many of them come from Florentine churches (all well labelled). The *Tabernacle of the Linaioli* has a marble frame designed by

Ghiberti. The **Great Refectory** and adjoining rooms display 16C and 17C works (some by Fra Bartolomeo). The **Chapter House** contains a large *Crucifixion and Saints* by Fra Angelico and assistants, and the Small Refectory a charming *Last Supper* by Domenico Ghirlandaio and his workshop.

First floor The *dormitory consists of 44 small monastic cells beneath a huge wooden roof, each with their own vault and adorned with a fresco by Fra Angelico or an assistant. The *Annunciation, at the head of the stairs, is justly one of the most famous works of the master. Among the most beautiful frescoes are those in Cells 1, 3, 6, and 9, and the *Madonna enthroned* in the corridor. **Savonarola's cell** contains two portraits by Fra Bartolomeo. The *library, a light and delicate hall, is one of the most pleasing of all Michelozzo's works; it contains illuminated choirbooks and psalters. At the end of the hall is the Sala Greca, added in 1457.

On Via La Pira can be seen the **Giardino dei Semplici** (open 09.00–12.00; entrance at 3 Via Micheli), a botanical garden laid out in 1545–46 by Tribolo for Cosimo I.

In Piazza San Marco is the **church of San Marco** (Map 3) which contains a *Madonna and saints* by Fra Bartolomeo; an 8C mosaic of the *Madonna in prayer*; and the tomb slabs of the famous humanist scholar and Platonic philosopher Pico della Mirandola (1463–94) and his friend the poet Poliziano (Angelo Ambrogini, 1454–94).

Just out of Piazza San Marco, in Via Cavour (Map 7, 3) is the **Casino Mediceo**, built by Buontalenti and now occupied by the law courts. This was the site of the Medici Garden where Cosimo il Vecchio and Lorenzo il Magnifico collected antique sculpture, and where the sculptor Bertoldo is said to have held a school of art in the mid 15C. At no. 69 is the **Chiostro dello Scalzo** (Map 3; open Mon, Thur & Sat 08.30–14.00), with fine *frescoes in monochrome by Andrea del Sarto and Franciabigio.

A short way west of Piazza San Marco is the former convent of **Sant' Apollonia** (Map 3; open 08.30–13.50 exc. 1st, 3rd & 5th Sun of month, and 2nd & 4th Mon) which contains a *Last Supper*, the masterpiece of Andrea del Castagno, and other works by him.

Piazza Santissima Annunziata

*Piazza Santissima Annunziata (**Map 7**), designed by Brunelleschi, is surrounded on three sides by porticoes. It is the most beautiful square in Florence. The equestrian statue of the Grand-duke Ferdinando I is by Giambologna, and the two fountains by Tacca.

The *Spedale degli Innocenti, opened in 1445 as a foundling hospital, the first institution of its kind in Europe, is still an institute dedicated to the education and care of children. Brunelleschi began work on the building in 1419, and the *Colonnade of nine arches is one of the first masterpieces of the Renaissance. It takes inspiration from classical antiquity as well as from local Romanesque buildings. In the spandrels are delightful *medallions, perhaps the best known work of Andrea della Robbia (1487), each with a baby in swaddling-clothes against a blue background.

The Convent may be visited to see the Museo dello Spedale degli Innocenti (open 08.30–14.00 except Wed). Among Brunelleschi's works are the Chiostro degli Uomini (with a lunette by Andrea della Robbia), and the oblong *Chiostro delle Donne*, with 24 slender Ionic columns beneath a low loggia. Stairs lead up to the pinacoteca displayed in a long gallery, with 15C Florentine paintings, including the splendid *Adoration of the Magi* by Domenico Ghirlandaio. The *Madonna and Child* is one of the most beautiful works by Luca della Robbia.

The church of Santissima Annunziata

The church of the *Santissima Annunziata (**Map 7**), was founded by the seven original Florentine members of the Servite Order in 1250 and rebuilt, along with the cloister, by Michelozzo and others in 1444–81. The series of frescoes on the walls of the **Chiostrino dei Voti** is particularly interesting since most of them were painted in the second decade of the 16C by the leading painters of the time: (right to left): Rosso Fiorentino, *Assumption*; Pontormo, *Visitation*; Franciabigio, *Marriage of the Virgin*; Andrea del Sarto, *Birth of the Virgin, Coming of the Magi*. The frescoes by Alesso Baldovinetti (*Nativity*) and Cosimo Rosselli (*Vocation and Investiture of San Filippo Benizzi*) are earlier works. The last five frescoes (damaged) are works by Andrea del Sarto.

The heavily decorated and dark interior has a highly venerated shrine of the Madonna. The huge *tabernacle* was designed by Michelozzo and executed by Pagno di Lapo Portigiani. On the south side, monument to Orlando de'Medici, by Bernardo Rossellino, and a *Pietà* by Bandinelli who is buried here. The fine organ is by Domenico di Lorenzo di Lucca (1521).

The unusual circular **tribune** was begun by Michelozzo and completed in 1477 by Leon Battista Alberti. In the cupola is a fresco by Volterrano. The high altar dates from the 17C. Near the *tomb of Bishop Angelo Marzi Medici, signed by Francesco da Sangallo (1546), is the burial place of Andrea del Sarto. In the semicircular chapels which radiate from the **sanctuary** are paintings by Alessandro and Cristofano Allori, Bronzino (*Resurrection*), and a statue of *St Roch* by the famous German sculptor (born around 1450) Veit Stoss. The east chapel is the burial place of Giambologna; it contains reliefs and a *Crucifix* by him, and statues by his pupils including Francavilla. The *Madonna* is attributed to Bernardo Daddi.

The **sacristy**, with a fine vault, was built by Portigiani from Michelozzo's design. On the **north side**, statue of the Baptist by Michelozzo; an *Assumption* by Perugino; and a *Crucifixion* by Giovanni Stradano. The *Last Judgement* by Alessandro Allori is derived from Michelangelo's fresco in the Sistine Chapel. The last two chapels contain a *Holy Trinity with St Jerome*, and *St Julian and the Saviour* (behind the Baroque altar) is by Andrea del Castagno.

The **cloisters** have memorial stones, and, over a side door into the church, is the *Madonna del Sacco*, one of the best works by Andrea del Sarto. The other lunettes contain 17C frescoes by Andrea Mascagni, Bernardino Poccetti, Matteo Rosselli, and Ventura Salimbeni. The **Cappella di San Luca** has belonged to the Accademia delle Arti del Disegno since 1565. It contains works by Vasari, Pontormo, Alessandro Allori, Luca Giordano, and Montorsoli.

Just out of the square, at Via Gino Capponi 4, is the **Cloister of the ex-Compagnia della Santissima Annunziata (or di San Pierino)**. There is a lunette by Santi Buglioni over the portal, and a delightful little cloister with frescoes (c 1585–90) by Bernardino Poccetti and others.

Archeological Museum

East of the square, at Via della Colonna 38, is the ***Museo Archeologico** (Map 7; open Mon 14.00–19.00; Tues and Thurs 08.30–19.00; Wed, Fri, Sat & Sun 08.30–14.00), with one of the most important collections of Etruscan antiquities in existence and a very fine Egyptian musum. The Etruscan, Greek and Roman sections have been undergoing rearrangement for years.

On the **first floor** is the **Egyptian Museum**, one of the most important in Italy, recently rearranged. The well-labelled exhibits, in thirteen rooms, include statues, bas-reliefs, papyri, canopic jars, Coptic fabrics, sarcophagi, funerary stele, mummy cases, and finds from Thebes, including a Hittite Chariot in wood and bone from a tomb of the 14C BC.

In the **Etruscan, Greek and Roman** sections of the museum, a long gallery contains three important bronze statues: an Etruscan ex-voto probably dating from the end of the 5C or beginning of the 4C BC representing a mythical animal known as the *Chimera* (found outside Arezzo in the 16C); *Minerva*, a Roman or Etruscan work (removed for restoration); and the *Arringatore*, a votive statue of an orator dating from the late Republican era. The Etruscan funerary sculpture includes urns, the *Mater Matuta*, a canopic vase (c 440 BC), and the tomb of the noblewoman Larthia Seianti (150 BC). The *collection of precious stones, gems, cameos and jewellery, displayed in a long covered passageway, includes classical pieces as well as works from the 15C–18C, arranged by subject matter. A modern pavilion displays Hellenistic jewellery, and a rare silver amphora, with 132 concave medallions in bas relief, thought to date from 380–390 AD and attributed to a Syrian silversmith. On the **second floor** is an outstanding collection of *Attic vases, beautifully arranged in eleven rooms, including the famous *François Vase, made in Athens c 570 BC. There is also a temporary display of Greek and Roman bronzes here: the Greek originals include a torso of an Athlete (c 470 BC), and a *horse's head (2C–1C BC). In a corridor are displayed two fine Archaic Greek kourai, and the famous bronze *Idolino (probably a Roman copy of a Greek original).

Piazza San Lorenzo

San Lorenzo

Piazza San Lorenzo (**Map 7**) around the church of the same name, is filled with a busy street market (with cheap leather-goods and clothing). The church of *San Lorenzo (**Map 7**; open 10.00–12.00, 15.30–17.30; fest. 15.30–17.30) was intimately connected with the Medici after they commissioned Brunelleschi to rebuild it in 1425–46. It is the burial place of all the principal members of the family from Cosimo il Vecchio to Cosimo III. Thought to be the earliest church in Florence, a basilica on this site was consecrated by St Ambrose of Milan in 393. The grandiose façade designed by Michelangelo was never built; the exterior remains in rough-hewn brick.

The grey cruciform interior, built with *pietra serena*, with pulvins above the Corinthian columns in *pietra forte*, is one of the earliest and most harmonious architectural works of the Renaissance. It was completed on Brunelleschi's design by Antonio Manetti (1447–60) and Pagno di Lapo Portigiani (1463).

In the south aisle, *Marriage of the Virgin* by Rosso Fiorentino, and *taberna-cle by Desiderio da Settignano. The two bronze *pulpits in the nave are the last works of Donatello, finished by his pupils Bertoldo and Bartolomeo Bellano. Beneath the dome a simple inscription, with the Medici arms, marks the grave of Cosimo il Vecchio *Pater Patriae*.

Off the north transept is the *Old Sacristy (usually open Mon, Wed, Fri & Sat 10.00–11.45; Tues & Thurs 16.00–17.45) by Brunelleschi, one of the earliest and purest monuments of the Renaissance (1420–29), with a charming vault. The decorative details are by Donatello (the *tondi in the pendentives and lunettes, the reliefs above the doors, and the doors themselves). In the centre is the sarcophagus of Giovanni di Bicci de'Medici and Piccarda Bueri, by Buggiano. Set into the wall is the magnificent porphyry and bronze sarcophagus of Giovanni and **Piero de'Medici** by Verrocchio. In a chapel in the north transept is an *Annunciation* by Filippo Lippi, and a 19C monument marking the burial place of Donatello.

Biblioteca Laurenziana

From the 15C cloister a staircase ascends to the *Biblioteca Laurenziana (**Map 7**: open 09.00–13.00 exc. fest.); a library begun by Michelangelo c 1524 to house the collection of MSS made by Cosimo il Vecchio and Lorenzo il Magnifico.

The heavily decorated **vestibule**, filled with an elaborate staircase was constructed by Vasari and Ammannati on Michelangelo's design. The peaceful reading room provides an unexpected contrast. The collection is famous above all for its Greek and Latin MSS. *Exhibitions are held every year.

The Cappelle Medicee

The entrance to the Medici Chapels (**Map 7**) is from outside San Lorenzo, in Piazza Madonna degli Aldobrandini. They are open 08.30–16.30 except the 2nd & 4th Sun, and the 1st, 3rd, and 5th Mon of the month. The drawings attributed to Michelangelo in a room beneath the Sagrestia Nuova can only be seen by appointment at the ticket office 09.30–12.00.

From the crypt a staircase leads up to the *Cappella dei Principi, the opulent, if gloomy, mausoleum of the Medici grand-dukes begun by Matteo Nigetti (1604). Its minor details were completed only in the 20th century. It is a tour de force of craftsmanship in *pietre dure*. A passage to the left leads to the so-called *Sagrestia Nuova (or New Sacristy), begun by Michelangelo and left unfinished when he departed from Florence in 1534. It is built in dark *pietra serena* and white marble in a severe and idiosyncratic style. Here are the famous **Medici tombs** of Lorenzo, Duke of Urbino, and Giuliano, Duke of Nemours with statues of the dukes, and allegorical figures of *Dawn* and *Dusk*, *Night* and *Day*, all superb works by Michelangelo. On the entrance wall is the *Madonna and Child*, also by Michelangelo, intended for the monument to Lorenzo il Magnifico and his brother Giuliano.

On the walls behind the altar, architectural graffiti have been uncovered, attributed to Michelangelo and his pupils including Tribolo. Nearby is a little room (for adm. see above) where charcoal *drawings of great interest were discovered on the walls in 1975, attributed by most scholars to Michelangelo himself.

Palazzo Medici-Riccardi

On the corner of Piazza San Lorenzo, behind a statue of Giovanni delle Bande Nere by Baccio Bandinelli, is *Palazzo Medici-Riccardi (**Map 7**), the town mansion of the Medici, built for Cosimo il Vecchio by Michelozzo after 1444. It remained their residence until 1540 when Cosimo I moved into Palazzo Vecchio. Its rusticated façade, facing Via Cavour, served as a model for other famous Florentine palaces. The courtyard, decorated with medallions ascribed to Bertoldo, the famous little chapel frescoed by Benozzo Gozzoli and the galleria frescoed by Luca Giordano can be visited (entrance is at Via Cavour 3; open 09.00–19.00 exc. Wed).

A staircase leads up to the dark little *chapel, the only unaltered part of Michelozzo's work, with a beautiful ceiling and marble inlaid floor. The walls are entirely covered with decorative *frescoes, the masterpiece of Benozzo Gozzoli of the *Procession of the Magi to Bethlehem*, which includes portraits of the Medici (shown with their emblem of the three ostrich feathers). The decorative cavalcade is shown in a charming landscape with hunting scenes. The **gallery** (lift) has a vault fresco by Luca Giordano (1683), and a *Madonna and Child* by Filippo Lippi.

The back of Palazzo Medici-Riccardi stands on Via de' Ginori, with a number of fine palaces and the **Biblioteca Riccardiana** (1718).

Near the Cappelle Medicee and the east end of the church of San Lorenzo the animated Via dell'Ariento with numerous market stalls leads past the huge **Mercato Centrale** (in a cast-iron hall built in 1874), the biggest food market in Florence, to the busy Via Nazionale. In Via Faenza, just to the left, is the so-called **Cenacolo di Fuligno** (Map 2; open 09.00–12.00) with a fresco of the *Last Supper* by Perugino. At the station end of Via Nazionale, at Largo Alinari 15 is the headquarters of **Fratelli Alinari**, a firm founded in 1852 and famous for its black and white photography. Alinari's photo archive and a museum here are open to the public.

Piazza Santa Maria Novella

Santa Maria Novella

*Santa Maria Novella (**Map 6**; open 09.30–16.30; fest. & Fri 13.00–17.00) is the most important Gothic church in Tuscany. The Dominicans were given the property in 1221 and building was begun in 1246 at the east end. The Dominican friars, Sisto and Ristoro are thought to have been the architects of the impressive nave, begun in 1279. The church was completed under the direction of Fra Jacopo Talenti in the mid 14C.

The lower part of the beautiful marble *façade, in a typical Tuscan Romanesque style, is attributed to Fra Jacopo Talenti. In 1456–70 Leon Battista Alberti was commissioned by Giovanni di Paolo Rucellai to complete the upper part of the façade. Its classical lines are in perfect harmony with the earlier work. To the right of the façade are the Gothic *avelli* or family-vaults of Florentine nobles, which extend around the old cemetery (with the present entrance to the church). The campanile, also attributed to Fra Jacopo Talenti, was grafted onto an ancient watch tower.

The spacious nave has remarkably bold stone vaulting, its arches given prominence by bands of dark grey *pietra serena*. Here hangs a *Crucifix, an early work by Giotto (restored in 2001). The stained glass in the rose window at the west end is thought to have been designed by Andrea di Bonaiuto (c 1365). Over the west door is a good fresco of the *Nativity*, thought to be an early work by Botticelli.

In the south aisle are 16C altarpieces. In the south transept are Gothic tombs including that of Joseph, Patriarch of Constantinople, who died in Florence in 1440, with a contemporary fresco of him.

Steps lead up to the **Cappella Rucellai** (light on left) which contains a marble *statuette of the *Madonna and Child* signed by Nino Pisano, and the bronze tomb slab of Francesco Leonardo Dati, by Ghiberti. The walls have traces of 14C frescoes.

The **Cappella dei Bardi** has damaged frescoes in the lunettes attributed to Cimabue, and an altarpiece by Vasari.

Cappella di Filippo Strozzi. Exuberant *frescoes by Filippino Lippi illustrate stories from the *Life of St Philip the Apostle and St John the Evangelist*. Behind the altar, *tomb of Filippo Strozzi, exquisitely carved by Benedetto da Maiano. In his *Decameron* Boccaccio uses this chapel as the meeting-place of a group of young people during the Plague year of 1348.

On the main altar is a bronze *Crucifix* by Giambologna.

In the **sanctuary** (entrance allowed every hour on the hour) are delightful *frescoes commissioned by Giovanni Tornabuoni. They are the masterpiece of Domenico Ghirlandaio; he was assisted by his brother Davide, his brother-in-law, Sebastiano Mainardi, and his pupils (including perhaps the young Michelangelo). In the scenes from the life of St John the Baptist, and of the Virgin, many of the figures are portraits of the artist's contemporaries, and the whole cycle mirrors Florentine life of the late 15C. On the end wall are the two kneeling figures of the donors, Giovanni Tornabuoni and his wife Francesca Pitti.

North transept. The Cappella Gondi with marble decoration by Giuliano da Sangallo contains the famous wood *Crucifix by Brunelleschi traditionally thought to have been carved to show Donatello how the Redeemer should be represented. The Cappella Gaddi has a cupola decorated by Alessandro Allori and a painting by Bronzino. At the end of the transept the *Cappella Strozzi is a remarkably well-preserved example of a Tuscan chapel of the mid-14C. The *frescoes of the *Last Judgement*, *Paradise*, and *Inferno* are the most famous work of Nardo di Cione (c 1357). The fine *altarpiece is by his brother, Orcagna.

The **sacristy** has a fine cross-vault by Fra Jacopo Talenti and stained glass windows dating from 1386. The lavabo is by Giovanni della Robbia.

The altarpieces in the **north aisle** are by Alessandro Allori, Vasari, and Santi di Tito. Also here is the famous *fresco of the *Trinity with the Virgin and St John the Evangelist and donors*, a remarkable work by Masaccio (restored in 2001). It is thought that his friend Brunelleschi designed the accurate linear perspective of the painted architecture.

Museo di Santa Maria Novella

To the left of the church is the entrance to the *Museo di Santa Maria Novella (open 09.00–14.00 exc. Fri). The Romanesque *Chiostro Verde has damaged *frescoes by Paolo Uccello (c 1446) painted in *terraverde* and illustrating stories from Genesis: (in the East walk) the *Creation of Adam*, and the *Animals*, and the *Creation* and the *Temptation of Eve*, and *Flood*, the *Recession of the Flood (with Noah's ark), and the *Sacrifice* and *Drunkenness of Noah*. The other frescoes in the cloisters also date from the first half of the 15C.

Off the cloister opens the ***Cappellone degli Spagnuoli**, or Spanish Chapel. It received its name in the 16C when it was assigned by Duchess Eleonora di Toledo to the Spanish members of her suite. It was originally the chapter house built by Jacopo Talenti in the mid-14C with a splendid cross-vault. It is entirely covered with colourful *frescoes by Andrea da Bonaiuto (Andrea da Firenze) dating from c 1365. They represent the *Mission, Works,* and *Triumph of the Dominican Order* (including the artist's vision of the completed Duomo), and the *Triumph of Catholic doctrine personified in St Thomas Aquinas*. In the Chiostrino dei Morti are frescoes dating from the mid 14C.

The large **refectory** has fine cross-vaulting. The fresco of the *Manna in the Desert* by Alessandro Allori surrounds a good fresco of the *Madonna and Child* attributed to a follower of Agnolo Gaddi. Here, and in the adjoining chapel, are displayed church silver, charming reliquary busts by the Sienese school, and vestments.

Piazza Santa Maria Novella, with its irregular shape, was created by the Dominicans at the end of the 13C. The two obelisks were set up in 1608 (resting on bronze tortoises by Giambologna) as turning posts in the course of the annual Palio dei Cocchi. Beneath the 15C Loggia di San Paolo is a beautiful *lunette showing the *Meeting of Saints Francis and Dominic* by Andrea della Robbia. In the house on the corner of Via della Scala Henry James wrote *Roderick Hudson* in 1872. The **Farmacia di Santa Maria Novella** at Via della Scala 16 is (open 09.00–13.00, 15.30–19.30 except Saturday afternoon and Monday morning) was decorated in neo-Gothic style in 1848. The charming old chemist's shop has 17C vases.

Ognissanti

Via della Porcellana leads out of Via della Scala to Borgo Ognissanti with the church of Ognissanti (**Map 6**), founded in 1256 by the Umiliati, a Benedictine Order skilled in manufacturing wool. The church was rebuilt in the 17C; the façade rebuilt in travertine in 1872, incorporates a terracotta attributed to Benedetto Buglioni.

On the south side are two early frescoes by Domenico Ghirlandaio: the *Madonna of the Misericordia* protects the Vespucci whose family tombstone (1471) is in the pavement. Between the third and fourth altars, on the north and south side are *St Jerome* by Domenico Ghirlandaio, and *St Augustine's vision of St Jerome*, by Botticelli, both painted c 1481. Elsewhere in the church are altarpieces by Santi di Tito and Matteo Rosselli, Botticelli (Filipepi) is buried in the south transept.

From the **cloisters** (entrance on the left of the façade, Mon, Tues & Sat 09.00–12.00), with 17C frescoes by Jacopo Ligozzi and Giovanni da San Giovanni, is the entrance to the **refectory** with a *Last Supper* (*cenacolo*) by Domenico Ghirlandaio. The **sacristy** (shown on request by the custodian) has early 14C wall paintings, and a large painted *Crucifix* attributed to Giotto (removed for restoration).

In the piazza is Palazzo Lenzi (now the French Consulate and French institute) built c 1470, with restored graffiti.

Via Tornabuoni

Ponte Santa Trìnita (described on p 97) crosses the Arno at the beginning of Via Tornabuoni (**Map 7**), the most elegant street in Florence with fashionable shops. Here is ***Palazzo Spini-Feroni** (1269), one of the best preserved and largest private medieval palaces in the city.

Santa Trìnita

Opposite is the church of *Santa Trìnita (**Map 11**), dating in its present Gothic form from the end of the 14C. The façade was added by Buontalenti in 1593.

On the west wall, the interior façade of the Romanesque building survives. **South aisle**. The fourth chapel is entirely frescoed by Lorenzo Monaco, who also painted the beautiful *altarpiece of the *Annunciation*.

The ***Sassetti Chapel** (on the right of the choir) contains delightful frescoes of the *Life of St Francis* by Domenico Ghirlandaio. They include views of Florence and portraits of the Medici and personages of the Renaissance city. The *altarpiece of the *Adoration of the Shepherds*, also by Ghirlandaio, is flanked by the donors, Francesco Sassetti and his wife Nera Corsi. Their tombs are attributed to Giuliano da Sangallo.

In the sanctuary is a triptych by Mariotto di Nardo and remains of vault frescoes by Alesso Baldovinetti. In the second chapel left of the altar is the *tomb of Benozzo Federighi by Luca della Robbia (1454–57), with a beautiful marble effigy surrounded by an exquisite frame of enamelled terracotta mosaic.

North aisle, Fifth chapel, *Mary Magdalen*, a wooden statue by Desiderio da Settignano (finished by Benedetto da Maiano). The fourth chapel has works by Neri di Bicci and the second chapel, paintings by Ridolfo del Ghirlandaio.

In Piazza Santa Trìnita, with the **Column of Justice**, a granite monolith from the Baths of Caracalla in Rome, are **Palazzo Buondelmonti**, with a façade attributed to Baccio d'Agnolo, and, perhaps, his best work, **Palazzo Bartolini Salimbeni**. Beyond several more handsome palaces rises the huge ***Palazzo Strozzi** (**Map 7**; used for exhibitions), the last and grandest of the magnificent Renaissance palaces in Florence, built for Filippo Strozzi by Benedetto da Maiano in 1489 (and finished by Cronaca).

At Via Tornabuoni **Palazzo Larderel**, attributed to Giovanni Antonio Dosio, is a model of High Renaissance architecture. Opposite is the huge church of **San Gaetano**, the most important 17C church in the city (often closed). The façade is by Pier Francesco Silvani, and the interior was built in *pietra serena* in 1604–49 by Matteo Nigetti and Gherardo Silvani. Nearly all the frescoes and altarpieces were painted in the 1630s and 1640s by Jacopo Vignali, Matteo Rosselli, Giovanni Bilivert, Lorenzo Lippi, and others.

*Palazzo Antinori (**Map 7**), attributed to Giuliano da Maiano (1461–69), is one of the most beautiful smaller Renaissance palaces in Florence. Nearby, on Via de'Cerretani is the Gothic Cistercian church of **Santa Maria Maggiore** (open 07.00–12.00, 15.30–17.30). It contains frescoes by Mariotto di Nardo, a Byzantine relief in painted wood of the **Madonna enthroned* attributed to Coppo di Marcovaldo (removed for restoration), and an effigy of Bruno Beccuti attributed to Tino da Camaino.

Via della Vigna Nuova leads out of Via Tornabuoni past the home (1614) of Sir

Robert Dudley, and the house where George Eliot stayed while gathering material for *Romola*, to ***Palazzo Rucellai** (Map 6; no admission). This was designed for Giovanni Rucellai by Leon Battista Alberti and executed by Bernardo Rossellino (c 1446–51). The design of the dignified façade with incised decoration and classical features had a lasting influence on Italian architecture.

Behind the palace, the former church of **San Pancrazio**, with a fine classical porch by Alberti, has been converted into the **Museo Marino Marini** (open 10.00–17.00; fest. 10.00–13.00; closed Tues) displaying sculptures by Marino Marini (1901–80), who bequeathed them to the city.

At Via della Spada 18 is the entrance to the remarkable **Cappella di San Sepolcro** (usually open only on Sat at 17.30 exc. July–Sept) built in 1467 also by Alberti for Giovanni Rucellai. It contains a *model in inlaid marble of the Sanctuary of the Holy Sepulchre.

Museo Nazionale del Bargello

*Palazzo del Bargello (**Map 11**), a massive battlemented medieval fortified building in *pietra forte*, was erected in 1250 as the Palazzo del Popolo. Building was continued in the 14C and it was well restored in the 19C. At first the seat of the *Capitano del Popolo*, it became the residence of the Podestà, the governing magistrate of the city, at the end of the 13C. From the 16C, as the police head-quarters, it became known as the *Bargello*. The palace now contains the **Museo Nazionale del Bargello, famous for its superb collection of Florentine Renaissance sculpture, including numerous works by Donatello and the della Robbia family. 16C Florentine sculpture is well represented by Michelangelo, Cellini, and Giambologna, among others, and an exquisite collection of small Mannerist bronzes. There is also a notable collection of decorative arts (open 08.30–13.50; closed the 1st, 3rd & 5th Sun, and the 2nd & 4th Mon of the month).

The fine **hall** (right) contains 16C sculptures by Michelangelo and his Florentine contemporaries. Works by Michelangelo include: *Bacchus drunk (an early work; c 1497); *tondo of the Madonna and Child with the infant St John made for Bartolomeo Pitti; *bust of **Brutus** (c 1539–40); and *Apollo (or David). Other sculptors well represented here include Jacopo Sansovino *(Bacchus)*, Bartolomeo Ammannati, Bandinelli (bust of Cosimo I, **Adam and Eve**), De'Rossi (*Dying Adonis*), Cellini (**Narcissus, Apollo** and **Hyacinth**, *bronzes from the pedestal of his statue of **Perseus**, bust of Cosimo I), and Giambologna (*Mercury*).

The Gothic **courtyard** displays more 16C sculptures. A room off the court-yard displays 14C sculpture (Arnolfo di Cambio and Tino da Camaino).

First floor

The **Loggia** contains more works by Giambologna. The **Salone del Consiglio Generale**, a fine vaulted hall, displays superb sculptures by Donatello and his con-temporaries. The works by Donatello include some of his most famous sculptures in bronze, marble and terracotta. In the middle of the room is the *Marzocco*, the Florentine heraldic lion, in *pietra serena*. On the end wall, in a reconstructed tabernacle, *St George from Orsanmichele (c 1416), with its remarkable very low relief below of *St George and the Dragon*. The bronze statue of *David, was one of the earliest and most beautiful free-standing male statues of the Renaissance, probably made between 1430 and 1440 for the courtyard of the Medici palace. The other *David*, in marble, is an early work. The enigmatic bronze putto, known as *Atys-Amorino*, and splendid terracotta *bust of Niccolò da Uzzano, are also by Donatello. Desiderio da Settignano is well represented with two *busts of a young woman and a boy (in the centre), a low relief of a *Madonna and Child*, and (against the far wall) another bust of a youth with a medallion at his neck. There is a very fine relief of a battle scene by Donatello's pupil Giovanni di Bertoldo displayed close to the two trial *reliefs of the *Sacrifice of Isaac* by Ghiberti and Brunelleschi made for the competition for the second bronze doors of the Baptistery (won by Ghiberti); and a *reliquary urn, also by Ghiberti. There are charming *reliefs of the *Madonna and Child* by Agostino di Duccio and Michelozzo, and numerous delightful enamelled terracotta *Madonnas by Luca della Robbia.

The other rooms on this floor contain a beautifully displayed *collection of **decorative arts** (seals, glass, enamels, ecclesiastical ornaments, jewellery, goldsmiths' work, *ivories, and majolica). The Cappella del Podestà contains restored frescoes begun by Giotto in the year of his death (1337) and continued by his assistants.

Second floor

The room at the top of the stairs contains a number of colourful enamelled terracottas by Giovanni della Robbia and cases of bronze medals and plaquettes (early 15C–18C). The small adjoining room displays beautiful *works by Andrea della Robbia, including a charming bust of a boy and tabernacles with the Madonna. Another room has sculptures by Verrocchio including his bronze *David*, and marble *bust of a *Lady holding flowers*. Also here are a number of fine Renaissance *portrait busts by Antonio del Pollaiolo, Mino da Fiesole, Benedetto da Maiano (*Pietro Mellini); Antonio Rossellino; and Francesco Laurana (*Battista Sforza).

The collection of Italian medals begun by Lorenzo il Magnifico, including works by Pisanello, is exhibited in two rooms, which also contain busts by Bernini and Algardi.

The **Salone del Camino** contains a superb display of small *Renaissance bronzes, by Antonio del Pollaiolo (*Hercules and Antaeus*), Cellini, Giambologna, Tacca, Tribolo, Bandinelli, Il Riccio, and Danese Cattaneo. The fine *chimneypiece is by Benedetto da Rovezzano. The anatomical figure made in wax by Ludovico Cigoli was cast by Giovanni Battista Foggini. Also on this floor is a magnificent collection of *arms and armour, some of it from the Medici collections.

In Piazza San Firenze is *Palazzo Gondi** by Giuliano da Sangallo (c 1489), and **San Firenze**, a large building now occupied by the law courts, by Francesco Zanobi del Rosso (1772). Next door is the church of **San Filippo Neri** with an interior of 1712.

The Badia Fiorentina

Opposite the Bargello, in Via del Proconsolo, is the Badia Fiorentina (**Map 11**), the church of a Benedictine abbey founded in 978 by Willa, the widow of Uberto, Margrave of Tuscany. The graceful, slender campanile (undergoing a lengthy restoration) is Romanesque (1307) below and Gothic (after 1330) above.

The 17C interior (at present only open Mon 15.00–16.00) contains a painting of the *Madonna appearing to St Bernard* by Filippino Lippi; a sculpted altarpiece, the tomb of Bernardo Giugni, and (north transept), *monument to Ugo, Margrave of Tuscany*, all by Mino da Fiesole.

The Chiostro degli Aranci, by Bernardo Rossellino, has an interesting fresco cycle with scenes from the Life of St Benedict by an artist known as the Maestro del Chiostro degli Aranci (c 1430).

Via Dante Alighieri leads left from Via del Proconsolo to Piazza San Martino with the splendid 13C Torre della Castagna, and the little chapel of **San Martino del Vescovo** decorated with charming frescoes by the workshop of Ghirlandaio illustrating the life of St Martin and works of charity. The area is traditionally associated with the great Florentine poet Dante Alighieri, who was probably born on the street that now bears his name. The so-called Casa di Dante is in a group of houses restored in the 13C style in 1911. In the little church of **Santa Margherita de'Cerchi** Dante is supposed to have married Gemma Donati (it contains an altarpiece by Neri di Bicci).

At Via del Proconsolo 10 is the handsome Palazzo Pazzi-Quaratesi attributed to Giuliano da Maiano. Here begins ***Borgo degli Albizi**, one of the most handsome streets in the city, lined with numerous fine palaces, including two (nos 28 and 26) by Bartolomeo Ammannati. Across the borgo is Palazzo Nonfinito, begun in 1593 by Buontalenti. It now houses the **Museo Nazionale di Antropologia ed Etnologia** (open 09.30–12.30 exc. Sun), founded in 1869 by Paolo Mantegazza, and probably the most important museum of its kind in Italy. The most interesting material comes from Africa, North Pakistan, South America, Mexico, Asia. The exhibits from the Pacific Ocean were probably acquired by Captain Cook on his last voyage.

At Via dell'Oriuolo 24 is the **Museo di Firenze com'era** (Map 7; open 09.00–14.00 exc. Thurs), a topographical historical museum of the city. The maps, paintings, and prints displayed in several rooms of the old Convento delle Oblate illustrate the life of the city since the 15C. Nearby is the hospital of **Santa Maria Nuova** founded in 1286 by Folco Portinari with a portico by Buontalenti, and the 15C church of **Sant'Egidio**.

Around Piazza Santa Croce

Piazza Santa Croce (Map 11), an attractive and spacious square, is the centre of a distinctive district of the city. Some houses in the piazza have projecting upper storeys resting on *sporti*. Palazzo dell'Antella, built by Giulio Parigi, has a worn polychrome façade painted in 1619. Palazzo Cocchi (Serristori) at the end of the square is attributed to Giuliano da Sangallo.

Santa Croce
The church of *Santa Croce (**Map 11, 12**), the Franciscan church of Florence, was rebuilt c 1294 possibly by Arnolfo di Cambio. The neo-Gothic façade dates from 1863. The huge, wide **interior** (open 09.00–17.30 or 18.30; in winter 08.00–12.30, 15.00–17.30) has an open timber roof. The Gothic church was rearranged by Vasari in 1560. For five hundred years it has been the custom to bury or erect monuments to notable citizens of Florence in this church; it is the burial place of Ghiberti, Michelangelo, Machiavelli, and Galileo.

South aisle. First pillar, *Madonna del Latte* a relief by Antonio Rossellino. The **tomb of Michelangelo** was designed by Vasari. The neo-Classical cenotaph to **Dante** (buried in Ravenna) is by Stefano Ricci. The *pulpit is by Benedetto da Maiano. There follow monuments to Vittorio Alfieri (by Antonio Canova), and to **Niccolò Machiavelli** (by Innocenzo Spinazzi, 1787). The altar-pieces in this aisle are by Vasari, Alessandro del Barbiere (*Flagellation of Christ*), and Andrea del Minga (*Agony in the Garden*). By the side door is the *Cavalcanti tabernacle** with a beautiful high relief of the *Annunciation* by Donatello. The *tomb of Leonardo Bruni** by Bernardo Rossellino (c 1446–47) is one of the most harmonious and influential sepulchral monuments of the Renaissance. Bruni was an eminent Florentine humanist, a Greek scholar, historian of Florence, and Chancellor of the Republic.

South transept. The **Castellani Chapel** contains decorative *frescoes by Agnolo Gaddi and assistants. The **Baroncelli Chapel** has *frescoes by Taddeo Gaddi (father of Agnolo), a pupil of Giotto. The restored altarpiece of the *Coronation of the Virgin* is by Giotto and his workshop. Also here is a 15C fresco of the *Madonna* by Sebastiano Mainardi, and a 16C statue of the *Madonna and Child* by Vincenzo Danti.

The *sacristy** has frescoes by Taddeo Gaddi, and, in the **Rinuccini Chapel**, *frescoes by Giovanni da Milano, one of the most gifted followers of Giotto. The **Medici Chapel** by Michelozzo contains an *altarpiece by Andrea della Robbia.

East chapels. Two small rectangular vaulted chapels right of the sanctuary are famous for their frescoes by Giotto, his most important works in Florence, probably dating from the 1320s. They had a fundamental influence on Florentine painting, as can be seen especially in other frescoes in this church by Taddeo Gaddi, Maso di Banco, and Giovanni da Milano. The *Peruzzi Chapel** contains scenes from the life of *St John the Evangelist* and of *St John the Baptist* (unfortunately damaged and in very poor condition), while the *Bardi Chapel** frescoes illustrating the story of *St Francis* were designed by Giotto, but some of them may have been executed by his pupils. The painting of *St Francis* on the altar dates from the 13C.

The **sanctuary** is frescoed with the *Legend of the Cross** by Agnolo Gaddi (c 1380), who also designed the fine stained glass lancet windows. The polyptych was designed in 1869 using panels by various hands including Niccolò Gerini, and Giovanni del Biondo, and Lorenzo Monaco. The *Crucifix* above is by the Maestro di Figline. In the last two east chapels are frescoes of the *Lives of St Lawrence and St Stephen* by Bernardo Daddi, and colourful and well-preserved frescoes of the *Life of St Sylvester* by Maso di Banco.

North transept. The **Niccolini Chapel** designed by Giovanni Antonio Dosio, has frescoes by Volterrano. The second **Bardi Chapel** contains a wooden *Crucifix* by Donatello. In the **Salviati Chapel** is the *tomb of Princess Sofia Czartoryska (d. 1837) with a Romantic effigy by Lorenzo Bartolini.

North aisle. By the side door, *monument to Carlo Marsuppini** (d. 1453) by Desiderio da Settignano. The classical sarcophagus may be the work of Verrocchio. In the pavement between the fifth and fourth altars is the handsome tomb-slab with niello decoration of Lorenzo Ghiberti, and his son Vittorio. The **monument to Galileo Galilei** (1564–1642) was set up by Giovanni Battista Foggini in 1737 when the great scientist was allowed Christian burial inside the church. In the nave is the tomb-slab of his ancestor and namesake, a well-known physician in 15C Florence. There are two altarpieces in this aisle by Santi di Tito (*Supper at Emmaus* and *Resurrection*).

Museo dell'Opera di Santa Croce

On the right of the church is the entrance to the conventual buildings and the Museo dell'Opera di Santa Croce (**Map 12**; open 10.00–18.00 or 19.00 exc. Wed).

In the first cloister (14C) is the charming ***Cappella dei Pazzi**, one of the most famous works of Brunelleschi (1442–46). The portico may have been designed by Giuliano da Maiano; the shallow cupola bears delightful enamelled terracotta decoration by Luca della Robbia, who also made the medallion with *St Andrew over the door.

The beautiful calm **interior** is one of the masterpieces of the early Renaissance. The twelve *roundels of the seated Apostles are by Luca della Robbia; the polychrome roundels of the Evangelists may have been designed by Donatello. The ***second cloister** is another beautiful work by Brunelleschi.

Off the first cloister is the entrance to the Museo dell'Opera di Santa Croce. In the fine Gothic **refectory** is displayed Cimabue's great *Crucifix* which has been restored after it was almost completely destroyed in the flood of 1966. The huge *fresco of the *Last Supper* on the end wall and below the *Tree of the Cross* is by Taddeo Gaddi. Also here are fragments of a large fresco by Orcagna of the *Triumph of Death and Inferno* detached from the nave of the church, and several other fine 14C–15C frescoes (including one with a view of the Baptistery and Duomo). In a reconstructed tabernacle is Donatello's colossal gilded bronze *St Louis of Toulouse, from Orsanmichele. The other rooms contain more frescoes (14C–17C), della Robbian terracottas, interesting large sketches detached from walls of the Cappella dei Pazzi, and sculptures by Tino da Camaino. Beneath the colonnade, just before the exit from the cloister, is a memorial to Florence Nightingale, named after the city where she was born.

To the right of Santa Croce is the huge **Biblioteca Nazionale**, an important library, the main building of which dates from 1911–35. At the other end of Piazza Santa Croce **Via dei Benci**, with its old rusticated houses, runs towards the Arno. **Palazzo Mellini Fossi** (no. 20) has a frescoed façade (beautifully restored in 1996) dating from 1575. The polygonal 13C Torre degli Alberti has a 15C loggia below. Opposite, Palazzo Bardi alle Grazie (no. 5) is an early Renaissance palace attributed to Brunelleschi; no. 1, Palazzo Malenchini was reconstructed on the site of a 14C palace of the Alberti where the great architect Leon Battista died in 1472.

Museo Horne

Palazzo Corsi, at no. 6, attributed to Cronaca, houses the Museo Horne (**Map 11**; open 09.00–13.00, exc. fest.). The interesting collection of 14C–16C paintings, sculptures, and decorative arts (notable furniture and majolica) was presented to the nation, along with his house, by the English art historian Herbert Percy Horne (1864–1916). A handlist is lent to visitors. Off the lovely **courtyard** a room exhibits a selection of the drawings collected by Horne (Renaissance and 16C and early 17C works).

On the first floor the main room has paintings by Dosso Dossi, Pietro Lorenzetti, and a tiny work depicting the *Story of St Julian* by Masaccio (very damaged). Another room displays an important painting of *St Stephen* by Giotto, and the last room a tondo of the *Holy Family* by Beccafumi. The second floor has 15C furniture, and paintings by the Master of the Horne Triptych and Neri di Bicci, and a portable diptych attributed to Simone Martini.

Off the interesting old Via dei Neri, a road (right) leads to the **church of San Remigio** (**Map 11**), founded in the 11C. The fine Gothic interior (often closed) contains a *Madonna and Child* by a follower of Cimabue known as the Master of San Remigio. Nearby is the interesting medieval Piazza Peruzzi, and Via dei Bentaccordi which takes its shape from the curve of the Roman amphitheatre (2C–3C AD) once on this site. The **church of San Simone**, founded in 1192–93, has a fine interior by Gherardo Silvani (1630), and an altarpiece of *St Peter enthroned* (1307); opposite is Palazzo da Cintoia, one of the best preserved medieval palaces in the city.

Casa Buonarroti

From the north side of Santa Croce Via delle Pinzochere leads to Via Ghibellina, where, at no. 70 is the *Casa Buonarroti (**Map 12**; open 09.30–13.30 exc. Tues); a charming museum, usually uncrowded, and extremely well maintained. Three houses on this site were purchased in 1508 by Michelangelo who left the property to his only descendant, his nephew Leonardo.

The **ground floor** is used for exhibitions. Also displayed here are: a collection of Etruscan and Roman works (including two well preserved Etruscan stelae from Fiesole) collected by Michelangelo's descendants; paintings and sculptures based on works by Micelangelo (the statue of *Venus* is attributed to Vincenzo Danti), and a *love scene, a copy of a lost work by Titian.

First floor. Two early works by Michelangelo: *Madonna of the Steps*, a marble bas-relief, carved at the age of 15 or 16, and a **battle relief**, modelled on a Roman sarcophagus. The wooden model for the façade of San Lorenzo was designed by Michelangelo (but never carried out). The *torso, a model in clay and wood for a river god, is also by Michelangelo. A selection of his **drawings** owned by the museum are shown in rotation.

The four charming rooms decorated in 1613 by Michelangelo Buonarroti the Younger in celebration of his great-uncle and his family, contain paintings by Cristofano Allori, Giovanni Biliverti, Empoli, Giovanni da San Giovanni, Matteo Rosselli, and Jacopo Vignali. Also here: portrait of Michelangelo attributed to Giuliano Bugiardini, a predella by Giovanni di Francesco, and a bust of Michelangelo the Younger by Giuliano Finelli. The room to the right of the stairs displays *bozzetti in wax, terracotta, wood and plaster attributed to Michelangelo and his circle (the *Two Wrestlers* in terracotta in the centre of the room is recognised as by the hand of Michelangelo). The last rooms are dedicated to the cult of Michelangelo in the 19C.

The church of **Sant'Ambrogio** (**Map 8**), to the north, was rebuilt in the late 13C. It contains a number of interesting frescoes including a *Madonna enthroned with Saints*, attributed to the school of Orcagna. In the chapel on the left of the high altar is an exquisite *tabernacle by Mino da Fiesole (who is buried here), and a large *fresco by Cosimo Rosselli of a procession with a miraculous chalice (preserved here) in front of the church. On the north side, *Angels and

Saints by Alesso Baldovinetti surrounding a *Nativity* by his pupil Graffione. Cronaca (d. 1508) and Verrocchio (d. 1488) are both buried here.

Nearby is the produce **market of Sant'Ambrogio** and the *Mercatino*, a flea market in Piazza dei Ciompi, with Vasari's graceful Loggia del Pesce (removed from the Mercato Vecchio). Lorenzo Ghiberti lived in Piazza dei Ciompi, and Cimabue lived in Borgo Allegri which was given this name, according to Vasari, after his painting of the *Maestà* (now in the Uffizi) left his studio in a joyous procession down the street.

To the north, beyond the huge **Synagogue** (1874–82) with a green dome (and a small museum), is the ex-convent of **Santa Maria Maddalena dei Pazzi** (**Map 8**), on Borgo Pinti (no. 56). The *cloister is by Giuliano da Sangallo. The church has a fine Baroque sanctuary (1675, by Ciro Ferri) and altarpieces by Carlo Portelli, Matteo Rosselli, Domenico Puligo, and Santi di Tito. In the **Chapter House** (usually open 09.00–12.00, 17.00–19.00; or ring at no. 58) is a beautiful and very well preserved *fresco of the *Crucifixion and Saints* by Perugino, one of his masterpieces.

Along the Arno

Ponte alla Carraia (**Map 10**), first constructed in 1218–20, was the second bridge to be built over the Arno. It was rebuilt and repaired several times, and reconstructed after it was blown up in 1944. At the north end, Lungarno Vespucci, opened in the 19C, leads away from the centre of the city towards the park of the Cascine past two modern bridges.

The **Cascine** (**Map 1, 5**) is a huge public park (not as well maintained as it might be, and not safe at night) which skirts the Arno for 3.5km. It was used as a ducal chase by the Medici grand-dukes in the 17C, and festivals were held here. It was first opened regularly to the public c 1811. In these gardens the *Ode to the West Wind* was conceived and chiefly written by Shelley in 1819. At the far end is a monument to the Maharajah of Kolhapur who died in Florence in 1870. From here the view is dominated by a suspension bridge (1978) over the Arno.

Lungarno Corsini leads past the huge **Palazzo Corsini** (**Map 1, 5**) built between 1656 and c 1737 in a grandiose Roman Baroque style. It contains the most important private art collection in Florence (adm. by appointment only at 11 Via Parione). In rooms frescoed by Alessandro Gherardini and Antonio Domenico Gabbiani it is particularly interesting for its paintings of the 17C Florentine school. It also contains a *Madonna* by Pontormo, a *Crucifix* by Giovanni Bellini, and a cartoon attributed to Raphael of his portrait of Julius II. The palace is also now used for important exhibitions.

Farther on is **Palazzo Masetti** (now the British Consulate) where the Countess of Albany, widow of Prince Charles Edward Stuart, lived from 1793 to her death.

*Ponte Santa Trìnita (**Map 10**) was first built in 1252. The present bridge is an exact replica of the bridge begun by Ammannati in 1567 and destroyed in 1944. The high flat arches (catenaries) which span the river recreate the unique curve of a chain suspended from two terminal points. They are perfectly proportioned and the bridge provides a magnificent view of the city. The statue of *Spring* on the parapet is the best work of Pietro Francavilla (1593).

Lungarno Acciaioli continues to **Ponte Vecchio** (described on p 76). The modern buildings on both banks of the river near the bridge replaced the medieval houses which were blown up in 1944 by the Germans in order to render Ponte Vecchio impassable.

Museo di Storia della Scienza

Beyond the Uffizi lies Piazza dei Giudici with the medieval Palazzo Castellani which now contains the *Museo di Storia della Scienza (**Map 11**), open 09.30–17.00 exc. Tues & Sat when it is open 09.30–13.00; closed fest. exc. the 2nd Sun of the month (10.00–13.00), a beautifully displayed and well maintained collection of scientific instruments. A large part of the collection was owned by the Medici grand-dukes. Excellent hand-lists are lent to visitors.

First floor Room I: astrolabes, quadrants, solar clocks, and mathematical instruments. Room II: German instruments, and navigational instruments, including some invented by Sir Robert Dudley. Room III: scientific instruments made for the Medici grand-dukes. Room IV: precious collection of instruments which belonged to Galileo, including his compass, the lens he used in discovering the four largest moons of Jupiter (cracked by him before he presented it to Ferdinando II), and the Giovilabio; models of his inventions. Room V: astronomy, including Galileo's two wooden telescopes. Room VI: lenses and prisms. Room VII: globes, including the armillary sphere made by Antonio Santucci in 1588. Room VIII: microscopes. Room IX: material relating to the Accademia del Cimento, an experimental academy founded by Cardinal Leopoldo in 1657 (including elaborate glass). Room X: barometers, thermometers and rain gauges. Room XI: astronomy in the 18C and 19C (large telescopes).

Second floor Room XII: mechanical clocks. Room XIII: mathematical instruments (18C–19C). Room XIV: magnetic and electrostatic machines. Room XV: pneumatic apparatus. Rooms XVI–XVII: demonstration models made in 1775 illustrating mechanical principals. Room XVIII: surgical instruments and anatomical models. Room XIX: history of pharmaceutical research. Room XX: instruments concerning fluids and gases. Room XXI: weights and measures.

Upstream is **Ponte alle Grazie (Map 11)**, first built in 1237 and replaced after 1944 by a modern bridge. Via dei Benci leads northwards away from the bridge past the Museo Horne, described on p 95.

Across the river, at the other end of the bridge is Piazza dei Mozzi, with the large Palazzo Bardini (no. 1), built by the famous antiquarian and collector Stefano Bardini in 1883. It houses his huge art collection, bequeathed to the city in 1923 as the **Museo Bardini (Map 11)**. It is closed for radical restoration and rearrangement. Bardini's eclectic collection includes medieval and Renaissance architectural fragments, classical, medieval and Renaissance sculpture (including reliefs attributed to Donatello), paintings (including *St Michael* by Antonio Pollaiolo), the decorative arts, furniture, ceramics, carpets, arms and armour, and musical instruments. Many of the rooms were built specially to contain the fine doorways, staircases, and ceilings from demolished buildings.

The **Palazzi dei Mozzi**, on Via de'Bardi, built in the 13C–14C are among the most splendid private houses of medieval Florence. The severe façades in *pietra forte* have arches on the ground floor. The building, together with a huge collection of decorative arts, was left to the State in 1965 by Ugo, son of Stefano Bardini, and there are long-term plans to open it to the public, along with the huge garden which climbs the hillside behind.

Via di San Niccolò, a narrow medieval street, leads left to the church of **San Niccolò Sopr'Arno** (**Map 11**), with several interesting 15C frescoes, including the *Madonna della Cintola* (in the sacristy), attributed to Alesso Baldovinetti, and *St Ansano*, attributed to Francesco d'Antonio. The road continues past the pretty 14C Porta San Miniato (right) to the massive Porta San Niccolò with a high medieval tower (c 1340).

The winding *Via de'Bardi* leads right from Piazza dei Mozzi past a series of fine old town houses back to Ponte Vecchio.

The Oltrarno

In the characteristic district on the south bank of the Arno known as the *Oltrarno*, the two most important churches are Santo Spirito and Santa Maria del Carmine, and around them focuses the life of this part of the city.

Santo Spirito

The church of *Santo Spirito (**Map 10**; open 10.00–12.00, 16.00–18.00 exc. Wed pm) was rebuilt by Brunelleschi in 1444. Building was continued after his death by Antonio Manetti and others. The slender campanile is by Baccio d'Agnolo (1503), and the modest façade dates from the 18C.

The *interior*, designed by Brunelleschi, was executed mostly after his death and modified in the late 15C. It is remarkable for its harmonious proportions, its solemn colour, and the perspective of the colonnades and vaulted aisles. The plan is a Latin cross with a dome over the crossing. The columns, with fine Corinthian capitals, are carried round the transepts and east end forming an unbroken arcade with 38 chapels in semi-circular niches.

The Baroque high altar by Giovan Battista Caccini disturbs the harmony of the architecture. The interior façade was designed by Salvi d'Andrea (1483–87), and the stained glass oculus is from a cartoon by Perugino.

South aisle chapels. 2nd chapel, a free copy of Michelangelo's famous *Pietà* in St Peter's by Nanni di Baccio Bigio; 4th chapel, *Christ expelling the money-changers from the temple* by Giovanni Stradano; 6th chapel, *Martyrdom of St Stephen* by Passignano.

South transept chapels. 10th chapel, *Madonna del Soccorso*, a painting of the early 15C; 12th chapel, *Madonna and Child, with the young St John, saints, and donors*, one of the finest works of Filippino Lippi; 13th chapel, *Vision of St Bernard*, a copy of a work by Perugino (now in Munich), by Felice Ficherelli; 14th chapel, *Marriage of the Virgin*, the best work of Giovanni Camillo Sagrestani (1713).

Chapels at the east end. 15th chapel, *Madonna and Saints*, a good painting in the style of Lorenzo di Credi; 16th chapel, polyptych by Maso di Banco; 17th chapel, *Epiphany* byAurelio Lomi, 18th & 19th chapels, *Martyred Saints* and *Christ and the adulteress*, both by Alessandro Allori.

North transept chapels. 24th chapel, *St Monica and Augustinian nuns in black habits*, traditionally attributed to Botticini, but possibly by Verrocchio;

25th chapel, *Madonna enthroned between Saints* by Cosimo Rosselli; 26th chapel, sculpted *altarpiece by Andrea Sansovino; 27th chapel, *Trinity with Saints*, a good painting of the late 15C, by the Mazziere brothers; 29th chapel, *Madonna enthroned with Saints* by Raffaellino dei Carli.

A door beneath the organ in the north aisle leads into a grandiose *vestibule built by Cronaca in 1491. The *sacristy, taking its inspiration from Brunelleschi, was designed by Giuliano da Sangallo. Here, since 2000, is displayed a *Crucifix attributed to Michelangelo, found in the church in 1963 and believed to be the Crucifix known to have been made by Michelangelo for the Augustinians.

To the left of the church, at no. 29, is the entrance to the **Cenacolo di Santo Spirito** (at present closed) in the refectory of the 14C convent; the only part of it of this date to survive. Above a fresco of the *Last Supper* (almost totally ruined) is a huge *Crucifixion, both of them painted c 1360–65 and attributed to Andrea Orcagna and his bottega. Also displayed here is the **Fondazione Salvatore Romano**, an interesting collection of sculpture, notable for its Romanesque works.

Piazza Santo Spirito is one of the most attractive little squares in the city, the scene of a small daily market. *Palazzo Guadagni** (no. 10) was probably built by Cronaca c 1505. Via Sant'Agostino leads to Via de' Serragli, a long straight road with handsome 17C–18C palaces. Via Santa Monica continues past a tabernacle by Lorenzo di Bicci into **Piazza del Carmine**.

Santa Maria del Carmine
Here is the rough stone façade of the church of Santa Maria del Carmine (**Map 10**), famous for its frescoes by Masaccio in the Cappella Brancacci, which escaped destruction in a fire in 1771 that ruined the rest of the first church.

The huge, broad **interior** was rebuilt in an undistinguished late Baroque style. At the end of the north transept is the sumptuous *Chapel of Sant'Andrea Corsini** by Pier Francesco Silvani, one of the best Baroque works in Florence. The ceiling is by Luca Giordano, and the marble and silver reliefs by Giovanni Battista Foggini.

The Brancacci Chapel
The **Brancacci Chapel, in the south transept, is now entered at no. 14 in the piazza through the early 17C cloisters. It is open 10.00–17.00; fest. 13.00–17.00; closed Tues. The **frescoes** illustrating the life of St Peter were commissioned by Felice Brancacci c 1424 from **Masolino** and **Masaccio**. Seriously damaged in the 18C and 19C, they were restored in 1983–89, and many of the details formerly obscured by surface mould can now be seen. The design of the whole fresco cycle may be due to Masolino, but his pupil Masaccio seems to have continued work on them alone in 1428. Later that year Masaccio himself broke off work abruptly on the frescoes and left for Rome where, by the end of the year, he had died at the early age of 27. The frescoes were at once recognised as a masterpiece and profoundly influenced Florentine art of the Renaissance. All the major artists of the 15C came here to study the frescoes which combine a perfect application of the new rules of perspective with a remarkable use of chiaroscuro. The cycle was completed only some 50 years later by Filippino Lippi (c 1480–85) who carefully integrated his style with that of Masaccio, possibly following an earlier design.

The frescoes are arranged in two registers. **Upper row** (right to left): Masolino, *Temptation of Adam and Eve*; Masolino, *St Peter, accompanied by St John, brings Tabitha to life and heals a lame man* (the figures on the extreme left may be by Masaccio); Masaccio, **St Peter baptising*; Masolino, *St Peter preaching*; Masaccio, **The Tribute money*, perhaps the painter's masterpiece; Masaccio, **Expulsion from Paradise*, one of his most moving works.

Lower row (right to left): Filippino Lippi, **Release of St Peter from prison*; Filippino Lippi, *Saints Peter and Paul before the proconsul*, and *Crucifixion of St Peter*; Masaccio, *Saints Peter and John distributing alms*; Masaccio, **St Peter, followed by St John, healing the sick with his shadow*; Masaccio, **St Peter enthroned with portraits of friars*, his last work, and *St Peter bringing to life the Emperor's nephew*, finished by Filippino; Filippino Lippi, *St Peter in prison visited by St Paul*. The altarpiece of the *Madonna del Popolo* is a Tuscan Byzantine work of the mid-13C attributed to Coppo di Marcovaldo.

Borgo San Frediano (Map 10, 9), at the north end of the piazza, gives its name to a characteristic district with numerous artisans' houses and workshops. The large church of **San Frediano in Cestello** with its main entrance on the Arno was rebuilt with a fine dome in the 17C by Antonio Maria Ferri. It contains late 17C and early 18C paintings and frescoes.

The fortified **Porta San Frediano** (Map 5, 9) is the best preserved part of the last circle of city walls built by the commune in 1284–1333. The gate, built in 1324, perhaps by Andrea Pisano, has a high tower and huge wooden doors.

Via di Santo Spirito (**Map 10**) runs parallel to the Arno in the other direction, past the 17C Palazzo Rinuccini, Palazzo Manetti with a 15C façade (the home of Sir Horace Mann in 1740–86 while he was serving as English envoy to the Tuscan court), and Palazzo Frescobaldi. On Lungarno Guicciardini (**Map 10**) is Palazzo Lanfredini by Baccio d'Agnolo with bright (restored) graffiti decoration. On the first floor is the library of the **British Institute** (see p 37). A non-profit making independent institution, it was founded in 1917, and received a royal Charter in 1923. Its scope is to promote British culture in Italy and Italian culture to English-speaking visitors. The excellent lending library (c 50,000 volumes) has the largest collection of English books in Italy. The institute also runs a well-known language school at Piazza Strozzi 2.

From the foot of Ponte Santa Trìnita the handsome **Via Maggio** (Map 10) leads away from the Arno. Its name (from *Maggiore*) is a reminder of its origin as the principal and widest street of the Oltrarno. Palazzo Ricasoli (no. 7) was built at the end of the 15C. Palazzo Machiavelli (no. 16–18) was bought in 1877–1905 by **St Mark's Anglican Church**. The church, in part of the ground floor, was designed in 1877–79 for Anglo-Catholic zealots led by the Rev. Charles Tooth, and its pre-Raphaelite decoration survives virtually intact. It can usually be visited on request (10.00–12.00) at the vicar's residence on the floor above, and services are held every Sun at 10.30 am. Palazzo di Bianca Cappello (no. 26), with good graffiti decoration attributed to Bernardino Poccetti, was built by the Grand-duke Francesco I for Bianca Cappello. Palazzo Ridolfi (no. 13) dates from the late 16C, and Palazzo Commenda di Firenze (no. 42), first built in the late 14C, was reconstructed in the 16C.

Via Maggio ends in **Piazza San Felice** (Map 10). No. 8 is the 15C **Casa Guidi** (open Apr–Nov, Mon, Wed & Fri 15.00–18.00; ring the bell), where Robert and Elizabeth Barrett Browning rented a flat on the first floor and lived after their secret marriage in 1846 until Elizabeth's death in 1861. Since 1993 it has been owned by Eton College and is leased to the Landmark Trust. It has been restored as far as possible to its simple appearance in the Brownings' day: during their stay here both poets wrote some of their most important works, including Elizabeth's *Casa Guidi Windows*, and Robert's *The Ring and the Book*.

San Felice is a Gothic church with a Renaissance façade by Michelozzo. It contains a large *Crucifix* almost certainly by Giotto, and a *Triptych* very close to the style of Botticelli.

Via Romana continues southwest to Porta Romana (**Map 13**), a well-preserved gate built in 1327 on a design by Andrea Orcagna. No. 17, Palazzo Torrigiani, was built in 1775 as a natural history museum, known as **La Specola**. Here in 1814 Sir Humphry Davy and Michael Faraday used Galileo's great burning glass to explode the diamond. It now contains a **Zoological Museum** (open 09.00–13.00 exc. Wed) with a remarkable collection of anatomical models in wax, many of them by Clemente Susini (1775–1814).

In **Piazza Pitti**, dominated by the huge Palazzo Pitti (see p 76), the pretty row of houses facing the palace includes the home of Paolo dal Pozzo Toscanelli (1397–1482), the famous scientist and geographer. While staying at no. 21 in 1868 Dostoyevsky wrote *The Idiot*.

Via Guicciardini continues to Ponte Vecchio; on the left is the ancient Borgo San Jacopo with the Torre Marsili di Borgo, a fine towerhouse, and the church of **San Jacopo sopr'Arno** with an interior decorated in 1709 and an 11C portico transported here in the 16C from a demolished church.

To San Miniato

San Miniato can be reached directly from the Santa Maria Novella station and Porta Romana by bus 12, or on foot by the steps from Porta San Niccolò (**Map 12**). However, if you have time, the following route on foot is highly recommended (and Bus 13 can be taken back from San Miniato to Porta Romana and the station of Santa Maria Novella).

Near Ponte Vecchio the narrow Costa San Giorgio (**Map 11**) winds up the hill towards Forte di Belvedere past the pretty Costa Scarpuccia (left). The church of **San Giorgio sulla Costa** has a good Baroque interior by Giovanni Battista Foggini. Beyond the house (no. 19) purchased by Galileo for his son Vincenzio, the road reaches **Porta San Giorgio** with a fresco by Bicci di Lorenzo. Built in 1260 this is the oldest gate in the city to have survived. Here is the entrance to *Forte di Belvedere** (**Map 11, 15**), a huge fortress designed by Buontalenti for Ferdinando I in 1590. It is closed for restoration until 2003.

*Via di San Leonardo** (**Map 15**), one of the most beautiful country roads on the outskirts of the city, is well worth exploring on foot. It passes the church of **San Leonardo in Arcetri** which contains an early 13C *pulpit*, and several 15C paintings, and some beautiful old villas, and joins another lovely old road which continues to the village of Arcetri (see p 112).

*Via di Belvedere (**Map 15**), a picturesque country lane, follows the straight line of the city walls (first built in 1258) from Forte di Belvedere to Porta San

Miniato. From here Via del Monte alle Croci or Via di San Salvatore al Monte return uphill.

San Miniato al Monte

Across the busy Viale Galileo, a monumental flight of steps leads up past a cemetery (1839) to *San Miniato al Monte (**Map 16**; open 08.00–12.00, 14.00 or 14.30–18.00 or 19.00).

The finest of all Tuscan Romanesque basilicas, it is one of the most beautiful churches in Italy. Its position on a green hill above the city is incomparable. Deacon Minias is thought to have been martyred c 250 during the persecutions of Emperor Decius and buried on this hillside. The church was built in 1013 by Bishop Hildebrand on the site of Decius' tomb.

The *façade, begun c 1090, is built of white and dark greenish marble in a beautiful geometrical design reminiscent of the Baptistery. The mosaic (restored) of *Christ between the Virgin and St Minias* dates from the 13C. The tympanum is crowned by an eagle, emblem of the Arte di Calimala (the cloth-importers guild) who looked after the fabric of the building.

The fine *interior built in 1018–63, with a raised choir above a large hall crypt, is practically in its original state. In the centre of the pavement are seven superb marble intarsia *panels (1207) with signs of the zodiac and animal motifs. At the end of the nave is the *Cappella del Crocifisso, an exquisite tabernacle by Michelozzo (1448). The painted panels are by Agnolo Gaddi, and the enamelled terracotta roof and ceiling by Luca della Robbia.

In the aisles are a number of 13C–15C frescoes. On the north wall is the *Chapel of the Cardinal of Portugal, begun by Antonio Manetti in 1460. The exquisitely carved *tomb of the Cardinal is by Antonio Rossellino and the ceiling, with five *medallions, by Luca della Robbia. The altarpiece of *Three Saints* by Antonio and Piero del Pollaiolo is a copy of the original in the Uffizi. The *Annunciation is by Alesso Baldovinetti. Before the choir is a beautiful marble *transenna dating from 1207, and *pulpit. The low columns in the choir have huge antique capitals. The large apse mosaic, representing *Christ between the Virgin and St Minias* (1297), was first restored in 1491 by Alesso Baldovinetti.

The **sacristy** (south side) is entirely frescoed with scenes from the *Life of St Benedict, one of the best works of Spinello Aretino (restored in 1840). The 11C Crypt has slender columns with antique capitals, and its original altar which contains the relics of St Minias. The frescoes are by Taddeo Gaddi.

The massive stone **campanile** was begun after 1523, but never finished. During the siege of Florence (1530) Michelangelo mounted two cannon here, and protected the bell-tower from hostile artillery by a screen of mattresses. The battlemented Bishop's Palace dates from 1295 (restored). There is a splendid **view** from the terrace in front of the church.

In a grove of cypresses on the side of the hill is the church of **San Salvatore al Monte**, a building of gracious simplicity by Cronaca. Steps lead down to **Piazzale Michelangelo** (**Map 16**), a celebrated viewpoint usually crowded with coaches and tourists. From the balustrade on the huge terrace is a remarkable panorama of the city. **Viale dei Colli** (bus 13), a fine roadway 6km long, was laid out by Giuseppe Poggi in 1865–70. It is one of the most panoramic drives near Florence.

The Viali

The wide avenues (or *viali*) form a ring-road busy with traffic around the centre of the city, north of the Arno. They were laid out in 1865–69 by Giuseppe Poggi after he had demolished the last circle of walls built in 1284–1333; he left some of the medieval gates as isolated monuments.

Viale Filippo Strozzi skirts the huge **Fortezza da Basso** (Map 2). This massive fortress, on a grand scale (with its exterior wall still intact), was built for Alessandro de'Medici in 1534 by Antonio da Sangallo. It became a symbol of Medici tyranny, and Alessandro was assassinated here by his cousin Lorenzino in 1537. It is now used partly as a restoration laboratory for paintings, by the Opificio delle Pietre Dure—one of the two official schools of restoration in Italy—and partly as an international exhibition centre. Public gardens have been laid out on the glacis.

From the Fortezza a bus (no. 4 from Piazza Unità Italiana near the station) runs northeast to the ***Museo Stibbert** (open Mon, Tues, and Wed 10.00–14.00; Fri, Sat & Sun 10.00–18.00; closed Thurs; tours begin every 30 minutes and last 1 hour). The museum was created by Frederick Stibbert (1838–1906) in this building which he erected in 1878–1905, and used partly also as his residence. With an Italian mother, he was born in Florence. His eclectic collection, with an extraordinary variety of objects, is crammed into 57 period rooms designed by him, producing a remarkably bizarre atmosphere. Stibbert was particularly interested in armour and costume, and the museum is famous for its armour (including a remarkable collection of Asiatic armour). The park, also created by Stibbert, is open daily (09.00–dusk except Thurs).

Across Viale Strozzi is Palazzo dei Congressi (1964), an international conference centre. At no. 14 is the Istituto Geografico Militare, the most important cartographical institute in Italy. Viale Lavagnini continues towards Piazza della Libertà. In Via Leone X (left) is the delightful **Russian Church** (Map 3) built in 1904 by Russian architects. It is owned by the Russian Orthodox community of Florence and is open for services on the third Sunday of the month. In the arcaded **Piazza della Libertà** is the medieval Porta San Gallo and a triumphal arch erected in 1739.

To the north of the square is Ponte Rosso near which is the entrance to the **Giardino dell'Orticoltura**, a horticultural garden created in 1859 (open daily) with an elaborate greenhouse (1880; by Giacomo Roster). Via Bolognese begins here and leads uphill out of the city (bus 25) past a number of villas including **Villa La Pietra** (no. 120), the former residence of the aesthete and historian Sir Harold Acton (1904–94) and left by him to New York University. The beautiful *garden created by Sir Harold's father Arthur in 1904–37 in imitation of a 16C Tuscan garden, is being restored. Arthur Acton also collected a notable group of early Tuscan paintings here, which is one of the most interesting private art collections in Florence (no admission).

The Viali continue to **Piazza Donatello**, in the centre of which is the **English Cemetery** (Map 4; open Mon 09.00–12.00; Tues–Fri 15.00–18.00) on a mound shaded by cypresses. Elizabeth Barrett Browning, Walter Savage Landor, Frances Trollope (Anthony's mother), the American preacher Theodore Parker of Lexington, Robert Davidson, the German historian of Florence and Gian Pietro Vieusseux the Swiss bibliophile are buried here.

San Salvi

From the next square, **Piazza Beccaria (Map 8, 12)**, the ex-convent of San Salvi is reached (bus 6 from Via Tornabuoni and Piazza San Marco). In the refectory (entrance at Via San Salvi 16; open 08.30–13.50 exc. Mon) is the celebrated *Cenacolo di San Salvi* by Andrea del Sarto (c 1520–25), a masterpiece of Florentine fresco, remarkable for its colouring, and one of the most famous frescoes depicting the *Last Supper* in Italy. 16C altarpieces and other works by Andrea del Sarto are displayed in the conventual buildings.

Nearby is the sports ground of Campo di Marte with the **Stadio Comunale**, a remarkable building (1932) by Pier Luigi Nervi (enlarged in 1990).

Environs of Florence

For a full description of the places in the immediate environs of Florence mentioned below, see *Blue Guide Florence.*

San Domenico and Fiesole

The small town of Fiesole is the most famous place in the immediate environs of Florence and is a particularly pleasant place to stay (especially in summer when it is cooler than Florence) since most of the hotels are in good positions with gardens. It is interesting for its Etruscan walls, Roman theatre, archaeological museum, collection of Attic vases, and the little Museo Bandini. The country lanes near the town are particularly beautiful.

Practical information

Getting there
By car from Florence

From Piazza della Libertá (**Map 3, 4**) Viale Don Minzoni leads across the railway to Piazza delle Cure. From here Viale Volta leads to (6.5km) Via San Domenico which climbs up to San Domenico. From here the main road to Fiesole continues uphill to end in the piazza of Fiesole (8km). **Car parking** in Fiesole can be difficult. There are free car parks in Piazza Mercato and Via Giovanni Duprè (below the Teatro Romano); the central car park in Piazza Mino has an hourly tariff.

By bus

No. 7 about every 20 mins (from the station and Piazza San Marco) via San Domenico.

Information office
Via Portigiani 3, Fiesole (☎ 055 598720).

Where to stay
Hotels

✩✩✩✩ *Villa San Michele*, Via Doccia 4, with restaurant and swimming pool (☎ 055 59451, 🗏 055 598734); *Villa Aurora*, Piazza Mino 39, with restaurant (☎ 055 59100; 📠 055 59587).

⁂ *Villa Bonelli*, Via Poeti 1, with restaurant (☎ 055 59513; 📠 055 598942); *Bencistà*, Via Benedetto da Maiano 4 (☎ & 📠 055 59163).

⁂ *Villa Baccano*, 4 Via Bosconi (☎ & 📠 055 59341).

Campsite

⁂ *Panoramico*, Via Peramonda 1.

Eating out
Restaurants

MAIANO €€ *La Graziella* (☎ 055 599963).
SAN DOMENICO € *Pizzeria San Domenico* (☎ 055 59182).

Lovely places to **picnic** include the park below San Francesco; near the Roman theatre; near Maiano; and off the *Strada dei Bosconi* (en route to Vincigliata).

San Domenico di Fiesole

From Viale Alessandro Volta (where the park of **Villa il Ventaglio** is open daily) in Florence, Via di San Domenico ascends the hillside offering a beautiful view of Fiesole and its villas to San Domenico di Fiesole, a little hamlet with several handsome private villas.

The 15C church of **San Domenico** has a 17C portico and campanile (by Matteo Nigetti). It contains a *Madonna with Angels and Saints* (c 1430) by Fra Angelico. The architectural background was added by Lorenzo di Credi in 1501, when the frame was redesigned (the saints are by a follower of Lorenzo Monaco). There are also altarpieces by Lorenzo di Credi (*Baptism of Christ*) and Jacopo da Empoli (*Annunciation*).

In the Convent of San Domenico, St Antoninus and Fra Angelico were both friars. In the little Chapter House (ring at no. 4) is a *Crucifixion* and *Madonna and Child* by Fra Angelico.

The narrow Via della Badia descends (left; beware of traffic) from San Domenico to the *Badia Fiesolana*, in a beautiful position. The cathedral of Fiesole until 1028, it was rebuilt in the 15C under the direction of Cosimo il Vecchio. The European University Institute was established in the conventual buildings in 1976. The rough stone front incorporates the charming *façade of the smaller Romanesque church with inlaid marble decoration. The simple cruciform *interior (open for services) is attributed to a close follower of Brunelleschi.

From San Domenico the prettiest way up to Fiesole on foot is by the beautiful old Via Vecchia Fiesolana (very narrow and steep), lined with fine villas and beautiful trees, and with splendid views of Florence (described on p 108).

Fiesole

Fiesole (295m) is a little town (15,000 inhab.) set in a magnificent position on a thickly wooded hill overlooking the valleys of the Arno and the Mugnone. It has always been a fashionable residential district with fine villas, gardens and stately cypress groves. An Etruscan city, its foundation preceded that of Florence by many centuries, and, with its own local government, it is still proudly independent of the larger city. It is crowded with Florentines and visitors in summer when its position makes it one of the coolest places in the neighbourhood of the city.

History

Excavations have proved that the hill was inhabited before the Bronze Age. The site of Faesulae, on a hilltop above a river valley, was typical of Etruscan settlements. Probably founded in the 6C or 5C BC from Arezzo, it became one of the chief cities of the Etruscan confederacy. It was the most important town in Etruria after its occupation by the Romans. After a decisive battle in 1125 Florence finally gained control of the older city.

The bus from Florence (no. 7; see above) terminates in Piazza Mino da Fiesole, the main square. The **cathedral**, founded in 1028, was over-restored in the 19C. The tall battlemented bell-tower dates from 1213. The bare stone interior has a raised choir above a hall crypt. The massive columns have fine capitals (some of them Roman). Above the west door is a statue of St Romulus in a garlanded niche by Giovanni della Robbia. In the Cappella Salutati (right of the choir) are frescoes by Cosimo Rosselli, and the *tomb of Bishop Salutati with a fine portrait bust, and an *altar-frontal, both superb works by Mino da Fiesole. Over the high altar is a large *altarpiece by Bicci di Lorenzo. In the crypt, with interesting primitive capitals, there is an early 13C painted *Madonna*.

At the upper end of the piazza is the old **Palazzo Pretorio** next to the church of **Santa Maria Primerana**, with a quaint porch. The equestrian monument (1906) in the square celebrates the meeting between Vittorio Emanuele II and Garibaldi at Teano. At the opposite side of the piazza, Via San Francesco, a very steep paved lane, climbs up the hill past the Cappella di San Jacopo with goldsmiths' work, and a terrace with a fine *view of Florence.

The ancient church of **Sant'Alessandro** (open only for exhibitions) contains cipollino marble *columns with Ionic capitals and bases from a Roman building. At the top of the hill (345m), on the site of the Etruscan and later Roman acropolis are the convent buildings of **San Francesco**. The church contains altarpieces by Neri di Bicci, Piero di Cosimo, and Raffaellino del Garbo. A small missionary **museum** contains Eastern objets d'art. The wooded hillside is a public park.

Roman theatre and museum

From Piazza Mino the street behind the apse of the cathedral leads to the entrance to the *Roman theatre and museum (open 09.30–19.00; winter 09.30–17.00; closed Tues in winter; ticket also valid for the Museo Bandini).

From the terrace there is a good comprehensive view of the excavations, which were begun in the 19C, in a plantation of olive trees. The **Roman theatre** (1C BC) held 3000 spectators (the seats on the right side are intact; the others have been restored). To the right are the **Roman baths**, reconstructed in 1892, probably built in the 1C AD and enlarged by Hadrian. A small terrace provides a fine view of a long stretch of **Etruscan walls** which enclosed the city. Northwest of the theatre is a **Roman temple** (1C BC), and, on a lower level, remains of an Etruscan Temple (3C BC).

The **museum**, built in 1912, contains a topographical collection (well labelled) from Fiesole and its territory, including a she-wolf in bronze, Bronze Age material, Etruscan stelai, urns, architectural fragments from the theatre and temples, and the Stele Fiesolana (5C BC). Also displayed here is the splendid *Costantini Collection of Greek vases.

In Via Dupré is the small **Museo Bandini**, a collection of 13C–15C Florentine paintings, including works by Bernardo Daddi, Neri di Bicci, Taddeo Gaddi,

Lorenzo Monaco, and Bicci di Lorenzo in a pretty little palace built for the collection in 1913.

The hills around Fiesole

There are many beautiful old roads in the vicinity of Fiesole.

From Piazza Mino, Via Santa Maria and Via Belvedere climb up the hill (with superb views) to the wall along the east limit of the Etruscan city. Below are the beautiful woods of Montececeri crossed by footpaths.

*Via Vecchia Fiesolana descends steeply from the Piazza Mino and passes the

Villa Medici built by Michelozzo for Cosimo il Vecchio. The beautiful garden (at its best after Easter) is one of the earliest of the Renaissance, and has a superb view of Florence. The entrance is on the main road at Via Beato Angelico 2; it is privately owned but willingly shown, usually on weekdays 09.00–15.00, and on Sat 09.00–12.00. Opposite (no. 26) is **Villa Le Balze**, owned by Georgetown University since 1979, with a beautiful garden designed by Cecil Pinsent (which can sometimes be seen on request). A pretty by-road leads to **Fontelucente** where there is a church built over a spring. In Via Dupré is **Ville Le Coste** (no. 18) where the painter Primo Conti (1900–88) lived, and which contains a collection of his works (open 09.00–13.00 except fest.)

Via Benedetto da Maiano diverges from the main Florence road below Fiesole for the hamlet of **Maiano**. The **Villa di Maiano** was restored in 1863 as the residence of John Temple Leader, who acquired many farms and villas between Fiesole and Settignano, and planted the woods in this district. Nearby are disused quarries of *pietra serena*.

Via Benedetto da Maiano continues to Ponte a Mensola (see below).

From Piazza Mino in Fiesole (see above) the main street continues uphill and, beyond Borgunto, the Strada dei Bosconi leads out of the town with increasingly beautiful views over the wide Mugnone valley to the north. It continues to L'Olmo where it joins Via Faentina which leads north for the Mugello valley (see p 124), while, soon after leaving Fiesole, a by-road diverges right for Montebeni and Settignano. It runs along a ridge round the north shoulder of Monte Ceceri through magnificent woods, planted by John Temple Leader in the 19C. Just beyond **Villa di Bosco di Fontelucente**, with an interesting garden redesigned after the Second World War by Paolo Peyron (sometimes shown on request), there is a superb view of Florence. The road climbs to a fork; the road on the right continues past

Castel di Poggio (sometimes open by appointment). It was rebuilt in the late 15C and a wing added in 1820 (and restored in the neo-Gothic style in 1922). There are splendid views. The road descends, lined with magnificent cypresses, past the **Castello di Vincigliata**, the ruins of which were rebuilt in neo-Gothic style in 1855 by John Temple Leader. Privately owned, it is sometimes shown by appointment (☎ 055 599556). The castle was used by Temple Leader as a museum. The road goes on downhill past Villa I Tatti for Settignano (see below).

On the Via Faentina which follows the Mugnone valley below Fiesole, just beyond the village of **Le Caldine** is the convent of the **Maddalena**. Probably built by Michelozzo it has several frescoes by Fra Bartolomeo who lived here.

Ponte a Mensola and Settignano

Getting there
By car from Florence

From Lungarno del Tempio (**Map 12**) the roads are signposted for Settignano, approached by via Gabriele d'Annunzio which passes through (5km) San Martino a Mensola on its way uphill to end in (7.5km) Settignano. **Car parking** in Piazza Desiderio.
By bus

No. 10 (from the station and Piazza San Marco) via **Ponte a Mensola** (service about every 20 mins, journey time about 30 mins).

Eating out
Restaurants

€€ *Osvaldo*, Ponte a Mensola.
€ *La Capponcina*, Via San Romano, Settignano 17.
There are numerous places to **picnic** near Ponte a Mensola and Settignano.

Ponte a Mensola

At the foot of the hill of Settignano in the village of Ponte a Mensola, Via Poggio Gherardo branches left from the main road past the Villa di Poggio Gherardo, traditionally thought to be the setting for the earliest episodes in Boccaccio's *Decameron*. In 1888 it was purchased by Janet and Henry Ross. (Janet wrote some excellent books on Tuscany and created a lovely garden here.)

***San Martino a Mensola** is a Benedictine church of the 9C, founded by St Andrew, thought to have been a Scotsman and archdeacon to the bishop of Fiesole, Donato, who was probably from Ireland. In the graceful 15C interior is a ***Triptych of the Madonna enthroned with two female Saints** by Taddeo Gaddi, and, on the high altar, a triptych with the donor Amerigo Zati by a follower of Orcagna (1391), known as the Master of San Martino a Mensola. In the north aisle is an ***Annunciation** by a follower of Fra Angelico, and a ***Madonna and four saints** by Neri di Bicci. A wooden *casket, which formerly contained the body of St Andrew and his reliquary bust (late 14C) are also preserved here.

Nearby is **Villa I Tatti** (entrance on Via Vincigliata), the former home of Bernard Berenson (1865–1959), the art historian and collector, and left by him to Harvard University as The Center of Italian Renaissance Studies. It contains his library (open to post-doctorate scholars), his *collection of Italian paintings, and a beautifully kept Italianate garden, laid out by Cecil Pinsent in 1911–15. The house and garden are shown to scholars with a letter of presentation, only by appointment.

The pretty by-road continues up the hill through woods past the castles of

Vincigliata and Poggio to Fiesole (see above). In Via Vincigliata at the bottom of the hill are two plaques commemorating the writers and artists who lived and worked in the neighbourhood. The **Villa Boccaccio** (Via di Corbignano) was owned by the father of Giovanni Boccaccio who probably spent his youth here.

Settignano

From Ponte a Mensola the road continues up to Settignano winding across the old road; both have fine views of the magnificent trees on the skyline of the surrounding hills. Settignano (178m), a peaceful village, is known for its school of sculptors, most famous of whom were Desiderio and the brothers Rossellino. In the church is a *Madonna and Child with two angels*, attributed to the workshop of Andrea della Robbia. In the lower Piazza Desiderio there is a superb view of Florence.

The numerous narrow lanes in and around Settignano, mostly with splendid views over unspoilt countryside are well worth exploring on foot.

In Via Capponcina is **Villa Michelangelo** (no. 65; no admission) where Michelangelo passed his youth. Via Rossellino diverges right from the narrow main road of Settignano to **Villa Gamberaia** (no. 72) which has a famous *garden (open weekdays 09.00–17.00; entrance fee; ring), remarkable for its topiary, azaleas, and ancient cypresses and pine trees.

Villamagna

Getting there
By car from Florence
From Piazza Ferrucci (**Map** 16) follow the one-way system signposted for Bagno a Ripoli and Villamagna, which is above the Arno, about 11km from Florence.
By bus
No. 33 from the station to Bagno a Ripoli (c every 20 mins in 45 mins), and from there bus no. 48 (infrequent service, about every hour) to Villamagna (in about 45 mins).

Where to stay
Hotel
☆☆☆☆☆ *Villa La Massa*, at Candeli, with restaurant and swimming pool (☎ 055 6510101, 🖷 055 6510109).

Above the Arno to the east of Florence is **Vicchio di Rimaggio** with the church of **San Lorenzo** (only open on Sunday). The portico has a good fresco of *St Lawrence with two angels* by the circle of Cosimo Rosselli over the door. Inside there are two 15C ciborium and a *Madonna and Child* attributed (from this work) to the Maestro di Vicchio di Rimaggio (c 1300).

Farther east, above woods, is **Villamagna** with the church of **Pieve di San Donnino** (if closed, ring at the priest's house at no. 1 in the lane above the church to the right). The church was in existence by the 11C, and it preserves its Romanesque appearance.

In the **south aisle** is a stucco relief of the *Madonna and Child* surrounded by a 17C painting, and a triptych by Mariotto di Nardo, and the body of the Blessed Gherardo in a 16C urn. At the east end of the south aisle, frescoes attributed to the Maestro di Signa, and near the high altar, 16C *Crucifix*.

At the east end of the **north aisle** *Madonna and Child with two Saints* by Francesco Granacci, who was born in Villamagna. On the north altar, fine 15C painting of the *Madonna and Saints* in its original frame, and above the 16C font, a 14C painting of *Saints John the Baptist and Anthony Abbot*. A road (about 2km) leads uphill ending at the church of **Incontro** which offers a splendid view (557m).

Poggio Imperiale and Pian de' Giullari

Getting there
By car from Florence
Viale del Poggio Imperiale (**Map 13, 14**) leads in a few hundred metres to the villa. Pian de'Giullari is signposted off Viale Galileo (**Map 15, 16**), approached by Via Gramontino and Via di Torre del Gallo, about 4km from the centre of Florence.
By bus
No. 11 (every 5–10 mins) from Piazza San Marco and Via Serragli for Poggio Imperiale (in about 20 mins). Also bus no. 38 (request service only, ☎ 800 019 794) from Porta Romana for Poggio Imperiale (Largo Fermi) and for Pian de' Giullari (in about 10 mins).

Eating out
Restaurant
€€ *Omero*, Via Pian de' Giullari 11.

Outside Porta Romana (**Map 13, 14**) Viale del Poggio Imperiale, a long straight cypress avenue lined with handsome villas surrounded by gardens leads up to the huge **Villa di Poggio Imperiale** (now a school; adm. readily granted by previous appointment) with a neo-Classical façade by Pasquale Poccianti and Giuseppe Cacialli (1814–23). After 1565 this was the residence of the grand-dukes of Florence. Some of its rooms are decorated by Matteo Rosselli (1623), and others by Giuseppe Maria Terreni (1773).

To the left of the villa, in Largo Fermi, is the entrance to the **Observatory of Arcetri**, founded in the 19C and with a high international reputation in the scientific field.

Via San Leonardo (see p 102) leads back towards Florence while Via Guglielmo Righini winds up past **Villa Capponi** (no. 3), with a beautiful 16C *garden (privately owned) to **Torre del Gallo**, reconstructed in medieval style by Stefano Bardini in 1904–06.

The road continues to the pretty little village of **Pian de' Giullari** where **Villa di Gioiello** (no. 42; not open to the public) was the house where the aged Galileo lived, practically as a prisoner, from 1631 onwards. After he was condemned by the Inquisition in 1633 he avoided imprisonment through the good offices of Grand-duke Ferdinando II but was constrained to live here for the rest of his life; he died in 1642.

Lovely walks can be taken from Pian de' Giullari along Via San Matteo in Arcetri, and Via Santa Margherita a Montici.

Monteoliveto and Bellosguardo

Getting there
By car from Florence

Via Bellosguardo (**Map** 9) is the approach to Bellosguardo and Via di Monte Oliveto (off Viale Raffaello Sanzio, **Map** 9) for Monte Oliveto, both about 1km from the Oltrarno.

By bus

For **Monteoliveto** bus no. 12 from the station to Viale Raffaello Sanzio and to Piazza Torquato Tasso for **Bellosguardo** (**Map** 9; a walk of about 20 mins). Bus no. 42 (infrequent service) for **Bellosguardo** (going on to Marignolle, in about 15 mins) departs from Porta Romana.

On the south bank of the Arno, near Ponte della Vittoria (**Map 5**) is the thickly wooded hill of **Monteoliveto**. It is reached via Viale Raffaello Sanzio and (right) Via di Monteoliveto (**Map** 9; a walk of about 15 mins). A military hospital occupies the convent of the church of **San Bartolomeo** (for adm. ring at no. 72A). It contains frescoes by Bernardino Poccetti and Sodoma (*Last Supper*; very damaged), and an altarpiece by Santi di Tito. The road ends in front of an entrance to the **Villa Strozzi** (open daily, 09.00–dusk), a wooded park.

Bellosguardo

The adjoining hill to the south is aptly called Bellosguardo (**Map 9**), which offers superb views of Florence. It can be reached by foot (in about 15 mins) from Monteoliveto by the pretty Via di Monteoliveto, but the most direct approach from the centre of Florence is from Piazza San Francesco di Paola (**Map** 9).

In the piazza is an ex-convent (no. 3; no adm.) bought by the sculptor Adolf Hildebrand in 1874, surrounded by a beautiful park, and the fantastic Villa Pagani built by Adolfo Coppedè in 1896. Via di Bellosguardo climbs uphill, with a view (right) of **Villa dello Strozzino** a beautiful Renaissance villa. On the right, beside a group of pine trees, is **Villa Brichieri-Colombi** (no. 20) owned in 1849–73 by Miss Isa Blagden who was often visited here by the Brownings. Henry James wrote *The Aspern Papers* while staying at the villa in 1887.

A road on the left leads to the **Torre di Bellosguardo** (now a hotel) with a delightful garden. From the quiet Piazza di Bellosguardo is the entrance to the **Villa dell'Ombrellino,** where Violet Trefusis lived until her death in 1973. It was ostentatiously restored in 1988 as a trade centre. Via San Carlo leads out of the opposite side of the piazza to **Villa di Montauto** where Nathaniel Hawthorne stayed in 1859. Via Piana continues from Piazza di Bellosguardo to Via di Santa Maria a Marignolle: on the left, at no. 2, is **Villa La Colombaia**, now a convent school, where Florence Nightingale was born (plaque).

Pretty walks can be taken from here along Via delle Campora and Via di Santa Maria a Marignolle.

The Certosa del Galluzzo

Getting there
By car from Florence

Follow the signs for the Siena superstrada and A1 motorway (Certosa exit) from Porta Romana (**Map** 13). The Certosa is just above the road beyond Galluzzo (7km).
By bus

No. 37 from the station (every 20 mins)

to a request stop below the Certosa (in about 30 mins).

Where to eat
Restaurant

€€ *Da Bibe*, Via delle Bagnese 1, Ponte all'Asse.

Outside Porta Romana, Via Senese (**Map 13**) climbs uphill, and continues through the village of Galluzzo, just beyond which, on a picturesque hill to the right of the road, is the *Certosa del Galluzzo (open 09.00–11.30, 15.00–17.30 exc. Mon. Tours are given by a monk). The monastery was founded in 1342 by Niccolò Acciaioli.

A Della Robbian tondo in the Great Cloister of the Certosa del Galluzzo

On the upper floor of the **Palazzo degli Studi**, a fine Gothic hall, is a picture gallery with five frescoed *lunettes of the Passion cycle by Pontormo, detached from the cloister and painted while he was staying in the monastery in 1522. There are also 14C and 15C Florentine paintings. In the church and chapter house are fine tombs (the one of Cardinal Agnolo II Acciaioli is probably by Francesco da Sangallo). The secluded **Great Cloister** with tondi by Andrea and Giovanni della Robbia, is surrounded by the monks' cells (one of which can be visited).

The Medici Villas of Careggi, La Petraia and Castello

Getting there
By car from Florence

The Villa di Careggi is reached by one-way roads north of the Fortezza da Basso (**Map** 2) well signposted for the Ospedale di Careggi (4km). The villas of La Petraia and Castello are off the busy main road to Sesto Fiorentino, about 7km from the centre of Florence.

By bus

No. 14C (every 10 mins) from the station or Via Martelli to the **Villa di Careggi** (the penultimate request stop before the terminus, in about 30 mins). Bus no. 28 from the station (every 5–10 mins), for the Medici villas of **La Petraia** and **Castello** (the second 'Castello' request stop for La Petraia, and the last 'Castello' request stop for

Castello; in about 35 mins).
A bus is recommended to cross the uninteresting northern suburbs of Florence, but pretty country walks may be taken in the hills behind Careggi, La Petraia, and Castello.

Where to eat
Restaurants

CERCINA €€ *Trianon*, and *I Ricchi*. **SERPIOLLE** €€ *Strettoio*, Via di Serpiolle 7 and *Dulcamare Club*, Via Dante da Castiglione 2. € *Osteria della Fettunta*, Via Reginaldo Giuliani (near Villa della Petraia).

Villa di Careggi

In the northern suburbs, beside the Careggi hospital buildings is the Medici Villa di Careggi. Set in a well-wooded park, it is now used as offices by the hospital (open 08.00–18.00; Sat 08.00–14.00; closed fest.). A 14C castellated farmhouse here was enlarged (and a loggia added) by Michelozzo for Cosimo il Vecchio in 1434. This was the literary and artistic centre of the Medicean court, and the meeting place of the famous **Platonic Academy** which saw the birth of the humanist movement of the Renaissance. Cosimo il Vecchio, Piero di Cosimo, and Lorenzo il Magnifico all died in the villa. In 1848 it was restored by Francis Sloane.

There are pretty country lanes in the hills behind Careggi, especially towards **Cercina** where there is a fine Romanesque church.

Villa della Petraia

Villa della Petraia (open 09.00–dusk except on the 2nd and 3rd Mon of the month) was once a castle of the Brunelleschi but the villa was rebuilt in 1575 for the Ferdinando I by Buontalenti. In 1864–70 it was a favourite residence of Vittorio Emanuele II, and in 1919 it was presented to the State by Vittorio Emanuele III. A pretty **garden** and moat (filled with carp) precede the villa, which still preserves a tower from the old castle. On the upper terrace is a very fine copy of a beautiful fountain by Tribolo and Pierino da Vinci. A magnificent **park**, with ancient cypresses, extends behind the villa to the east.

The courtyard of the **villa** has decorative *frescoes illustrating the history of the Medici family, by Volterrano and Cosimo Daddi. In a room here is displayed the bronze group of *Antaeus and Hercules* by Ammannati from the fountain in Villa di Castello. The rooms were furnished as state apartments in the 19C. On the first floor the private apartments, decorated in neo-Classical style, contain the original bronze statue of *Venus* by Giambologna, removed from the fountain in the garden. The gaming room is a remarkable period piece hung with 17C paintings.

In Via della Petraia is **Villa Il Bel Riposo** where Carlo Lorenzini (Collodi) lived while writing *Pinocchio*, and the **Villa Corsini** rebuilt in 1698 by Antonio Ferri, with an interesting Baroque façade. A plaque records the death here in 1649 of Sir Robert Dudley (see p 299). The villa and garden are to be opened to the public.

Villa di Castello

In front of Villa Corsini, Via di Castello leads shortly to Villa di Castello (admission to the gardens only, times as for La Petraia), now the seat of the Accademia della Crusca, founded in 1582, for the study of the Italian language. The villa was acquired by Giovanni and Lorenzo di Pierfrancesco de'Medici, Lorenzo il Magnifico's younger cousins, around 1477. Here they hung Botticelli's famous

Birth of Venus. The typical Tuscan ***garden**, described by numerous travellers in the 16C and 17C, was laid out by Tribolo for Cosimo I in 1541, and is now beautifully kept. At its best from April to June, it has one of the most important collections of citrus fruit trees in the world, with over 100 varieties, grown in some 1000 terracotta tubs (kept in the orangery in winter). The ***fountain** by Tribolo has been removed for restoration, and the bronze group by Ammannati is at present exhibited in Villa della Petraia. Above the splendid ***grotto**, full of exotic animals and encrusted with shell mosaics, on the upper terrace in ilex woods there is a pool with a colossus by Ammannati. There is also a charming little **secret garden** (admission on request) created in the late 17C where a rare creamed-coloured jasmine grows. The beds have recently been replanted with antique roses and about 400 varieties of aromatic and medicinal herbs.

Lovely country walks may be taken in the lanes on the hillside above Via Giovanni da San Giovanni.

Sesto Fiorentino

 ### Getting there
By car from Florence
From the Fortezza da Basso (**Map 2**) follow the signs north to Sesto Fiorentino (9km).
By bus
No. 28 (every 5–10 mins) from the station terminates at Sesto Fiorentino (in about 45 mins).

 ### Where to stay
Hotel
☆☆☆☆ *Villa Villoresi*, Via Ciampi 2, Colonnata, with restaurant and swimming pool (☎ 055 443212, 🖷 055 442063).

Sesto Fiorentino is a small town (41,000 inhab.) in the northern suburbs of Florence. On the main approach road is **Villa Corsi Salviati,** with an 18C garden. Next to the Ginori porcelain factory, entered at Via Pratese 31, is the **Museo delle Porcellane di Doccia** (open Tues, Thur, and Sat 09.30–13.00, 15.30–18.30 except in Aug) in a fine building by Piero Berardi (1965). It contains a large well-displayed *collection of porcelain made in the famous Doccia factory founded by Carlo Ginori in 1735. The firm, known as Richard-Ginori since 1896, continues to flourish. Across the road, in an inconspicuous one-storey warehouse, Ginori seconds can be purchased.

At the foot of the wooded slopes of **Monte Morello** (934m), traversed by paths and a panoramic road, is the **Villa Ginori** at Doccia, with a huge park and cypress avenue, created by Leopoldo Carlo Ginori in 1816.

Pratolino and Montesenario

Getting there
By car from Florence

Pratolino is about 10km north of Florence, reached by the Via Bolognese (which leaves the city north of Piazza della Libertà, **Map** 3). From Pratolino a pretty road (about 6km) climbs up to Montesenario.

By bus

No. 25 (every 25 mins) from the station and Piazza San Marco for Pratolino (in about 45 mins); there is no public transport to Montesenario.

Where to stay
Hotels

PRATOLINO ✯✯✯✯ *Villa Demidoff*, with pool (☎ 055 409772; ▤ 055 409781).
BIVIGLIANO ✯✯✯ *Giotto* (☎ 055 406608; ▤ 055 406730).
Campsite

BIVIGLIANO ✯✯ *Poggio degli Uccellini*.

Eating out
Restaurant

PRATOLINO €€ *Villa Vecchia*.

Villa Demidoff ~ Pratolino

The entrance to the huge park of Villa Demidoff is at Pratolino. Some 17–18 hectares of the splendid well-kept park belong to the Province (open March on fest. 10.00–18.00; Apr–Sept on Thur, Fri, Sat & Sun 10.00–20.00; and in Oct on fest. 10.00–19.00).

A remarkable garden with numerous fountains was created here in 1569 for Francesco I de' Medici by Buontalenti, the most famous of which was Giambologna's colossal statue (about 10 metres high) of **Appennino* (1579–80), which is still one of the most extraordinary sights in Italy (the huge figure symbolising the Apennine mountains crouches on a natural rock above a pool surrounded by trees). Other areas of the gardens have been or are being restored. The Paggeria (servants' quarters) of the Medici villa was restored as the residence of the Demidoff family when they bought the estate in 1872 and transformed the park.

6km further north is the little hill resort of **Bivigliano** where the church of San Romolo (open at weekends) contains a della Robbian terracotta, and a 15C wooden statue of *St John the Baptist*. The 16C Villa di Bivigliano, surrounded by a large park, where concerts are sometimes held, can be visited by appointment (☎ 055 406717).

Convent of Montesenario

On a hill-top (817m), 3km from Bivigliano, is the convent of Montesenario. The **views* are superb, and on a clear day you can see the whole of the Mugello valley. Seven Florentine merchants became hermits here and established the Servite Order of mendicant friars in 1233. In the piazzale are two statues of Saints (1754) by Pompilio Ticciati.

The church and convent were enlarged by Cosimo I in 1539, and then rebuilt in 1717. The **church** has an 18C interior with elaborate stuccoes and a vault fresco by Antonio Domenico Gabbiani. In the sanctuary is a *Crucifix* in polychrome stucco by Ferdinando Tacca and in the choir are paintings by Giuseppe Bezzuoli (*Assunta*, 1849), and Pietro Annigoni (*Seven founders of the*

Order, 1985). The Oratory of San Filippo contains a 15C polychrome terracotta *Deposition* group. The Chapel of the Seven Founders was added in 1933 in a neo-Gothic style by Giuseppe Cassioli. Above the Sacristy door is a 14C painting of the *Madonna and Saints*. In the refectory of the **convent** is a frescoed *Cenacolo* by Matteo Rosselli.

Rovezzano, Santa Brigida, Pontassieve

Getting there
By car from Florence
The road for Pontassieve follows the Arno east of the city from Ponte San Niccolò (**Map** 12). It passes (7km) Rovezzano, and a by road which leads up into the hills to Santa Brigida (10km).
By train
Pontassieve has a railway station (slow trains only stop here, in about 10 mins from Santa Maria Novella).

By bus
No. 14 (every 10 mins) from the station and Piazza Duomo for Sant' Andrea a Rovezzano (in about 30 mins).

Eating out
Restaurants
CONSUMA € *Dal Consumi* for good snacks.
SANTA BRIGIDA € pizzeria.
MONTELORO €€ *Da Orlando*, with tables outside (☎ 055 8309056).

To the east (on the outskirts) of Florence, on the main road which follows the Arno, is **Rovezzano**. In Piazzetta Benedetto da Rovezzano is a tabernacle with a *Crucifixion* by Franciabigio. The church of **San Michele** (rebuilt in 1840) contains a painted *Crucifix* dated 1400, and a *Madonna enthroned* by the Maestro della Maddalena. The church of **Sant'Andrea a Rovezzano** has a fine Romanesque campanile. In the neo-Classical interior with frescoes by Luigi Ademollo, is a beautiful relief of the *Madonna* (c 1450) by Luca della Robbia, and an early 13C painting of the *Madonna and Child*. Just before **Compiobbi** is the **Florence British Military Cemetery**, with 1551 graves from the Second World War. A pretty country road diverges from the main road towards Fiesole via **Gricigliano** where the 15C–16C Villa Martelli, with a fine garden, is now a monastery (the monks sell produce and Mass is held here in Gregorian chant on Sundays at 11.00), and the hamlet of **Monteloro**.

Between Compiobbi and Pontassieve is the locality of **Le Sieci**, with the **Pieve di San Giovanni Battista a Remole** with a fine tall campanile. The church is usually open 16.00–18.30; if closed ring at the priest's house in the garden beyond the portico. In the right aisle is the font composed of various coloured marbles in 1753, behind a 15C balustrade. On the wall is a statuette of *St John the Baptist* by the bottega of Giovanni della Robbia. At the end of the aisle is a 15C ciborium in pietra serena. On the east wall, *Crucifixion, with the Madonna and St John*, attributed to the school of Botticelli. In the chapel to the left is a *Madonna and Child*, attributed to the Master of Remole, who acquired his name from this work.

North of Le Sieci is the castle of **Torre a Decima**, approached by a pretty road lined on one side by cypresses. It was owned by the Pazzi family from the 13C, and was restored in 1950. The wine cellars can sometimes be visited by appointment.

Higher up, in a beautiful position, is **Doccia** where the church of Sant'Andrea (entrance through the little courtyard behind) contains a tiny della Robbian tabernacle and a *Madonna and Saints* by the school of Ghirlandaio. The *Crucifix and saints* by Ignazio Hugford is in very poor condition. Outside is a medieval well, now covered with posters. A narrow road below Doccia is signposted for Santa Brigida. It winds up and down through woods and lovely rolling hills, with a view left of the castle of Torre a Decima. Beyond Fornello is La Villa with a handsome villa, where another road comes in from Molino del Piano.

Santa Brigida has a church with a square tower and an unusual plan. It contains a *Madonna and Child with two Saints* attributed to the Maestro di San Martino alla Palma, a 16C painted *Crucifix*, and a little carved tabernacle of 1483. On the intrados of the choir arch there are unusual carvings. At the west end are two 16C polychrome busts in niches. The apse has interesting frescoes. From the terrace there is a lovely view of the unspoilt countryside.

Below Santa Brigida is the **Castello del Trebbio** (not to be confused with the Castello del Trebbio outside San Piero a Sieve described on p 129), right on the road. It was built by the Pazzi family in the 13C but has been restored. Visitors are invited into the courtyard. On the floor of the valley is the *pieve* of **Lubaco** with a Romanesque apse.

Pontassieve (16,500 inhab.), an important centre of the *Chianti Rufina* wine trade, stands to the east of Florence at the confluence of the Sieve and Arno Rivers. The old Medici bridge (1555; attributed to Bartolomeo Ammannati) across the Sieve, can be seen upstream from the main road bridge. The town was severely damaged in the Second World War.

From Pontassieve begins the road for the Casentino—the beautiful wooded upper valley of the Arno (described on p 508)—across the Consuma Pass. Off this road is **Nipozzano**, a picturesque hamlet spread out along a ridge backed by cypresses, with the 17C Villa Albizi (Frescobaldi) behind a low wall, a church, and remains of an 11C castle. There are pretty farmhouses in the vicinity and views all the way to Vallombrosa. The farm produces a well-known wine (the cellars can be visited).

Diacceto, also surrounded by vineyards, has the church of San Lorenzo (open only at weekends), rebuilt in 1872, which contains a della Robbian *Madonna and Child with Saints*. At nearby **Pelago**, a festival (called On the Road) of buskers and street players is held in July. Opposite a little Oratory preceded by a portico (and containing a small 15C wood *Crucifix*), a road leads into Piazza Ghiberti, named after the great sculptor Lorenzo, who was born here, probably in 1378. This delightful ancient **market square** preserves its old pump and a medley of houses. Via Roma leads out of the piazza past an old tower, and steps continue up past the handsome town hall and beneath two arches to the tiny Piazza Cavalcanti at the top of the village. In the church of San Clemente a small museum preserves works from churches nearby including a triptych by Niccolò di Pietro Gerini.

The main road continues to Borselli. Near Borselli, on the Pomino road, is the Romanesque church of **Tosina** which contains a beautiful triptych by Mariotto di Nardo (1389). **Consuma**, a summer and ski resort is a few metres below the Pass (1023m) connecting the Pratomagno with the main Apennine chain.

Southwest of Pontassieve (see above) is the Villa of **Altomena**. A Guidi family castle and a church have been incorporated into the villa which is surrounded by extensive vineyards and olive groves. The church contains a *Madonna and Child with Saints* attributed to the circle of Domenico Ghirlandaio.

A by-road leads across the Arno from Pontassieve to the village of **Rosano**, in a peaceful position by the river. By a pretty tabernacle a narrow road leads shortly to the well-kept Benedictine convent of Santa Maria, founded in 780, and now housing some seventy nuns (ring for admission on the right of the courtyard at the closed order).

The **church** has a Romanesque façade and a fine 11C–12C campanile. Mass is celebrated with Gregorian chant at 7am on weekdays and at 10am on holidays. The presbytery is raised above the pretty crypt which has a 12C altar. In the right aisle is a font (1423) and to the right of the high altar, *Annunciation* by Giovanni dal Ponte (1434). On the east wall is a fine painted *Crucifix* (in very poor condition) by an unknown master of the late 12C or early 13C. In the chapel at the base of the campanile, *Annunciation* by Jacopo di Cione. The nuns have a laboratory for the restoration of books. A beautiful road climbs to Villamagna (described above).

Bagno a Ripoli

Getting there
By car from Florence
Bagno a Ripoli (5km) is well signposted from Ponte San Niccolò (**Map** 12), on the south side of the Arno.

By bus
No. 33 from the station (every 20 mins) to Bagno a Ripoli in about 45 mins.

South of the Arno, approached across Ponte San Niccolò, is the large scattered Comune of Bagno a Ripoli, a pleasant residential area on low hills with fine views. On the approach, beyond the district of Sorgane, much criticised when it was built in 1962–70, is the **Pieve a Ripoli** (San Pietro), first mentioned in the 8C, with a beautiful interior.

North of the centre of Bagno a Ripoli, at Quarto, is the church of **Santa Maria**, restored in 1930 by Giuseppe Castellucci. It contains a triptych with a central panel by Bicci di Lorenzo, and side panels by the bottega of Bernardo Daddi, as well as a painting signed and dated 1391 by a certain Francesco.

Near the Arco di Camicia, is the church of **Santo Stefano a Paterno** rebuilt in 1934. It contains a painted *Crucifix* by a follower of Cimabue (late 13C). From **L'Apparita** there is a good view of Florence.

The church of **San Quirico a Ruballa** (1763) contains a *Madonna and Child with the young St John* by Domenico Puligo, a painted *Cross* of c 1330, and a small wooden 14C statue of the *Madonna and Child*. Close to the motorway (at Osteria Nuova) is the church of **San Giorgio a Ruballa**, restored by Nicolò Matas in 1863. It contains a *Madonna and Child with Saints* dated 1336, and a painted Cross, a late work by Taddeo Gaddi.

San Donato in Collina is in a beautiful position, with fine villas. To the northeast is the splendid 18C **Villa Rinuccini di Torre a Cona** with a medieval tower. It has a cypress avenue and Italianate garden surrounded by a fine park (not open to the public). **Palazzolo**, has a neo-Gothic church, and nearby is the Romanesque church of **San Lorenzo a Cappiano** (open Sunday morning only) with an 18C interior and a *Madonna and Child* attributed to the Maestro di Barberino.

Antella, Grassina and Impruneta

Getting there
By car from Florence
Antella (5km) and Grassina (10km) are near the Firenze Sud exit of the A1 motorway. The prettiest approach to Impruneta (17km) is along the Via Chiantigiana (N 222) sign-posted off Viale Europa which is approached from Piazza Ferrucci (Map 16).
By bus
No. 32 from the station (about every 10 mins) to Ponte a Ema and Antella (in about 35 mins); bus 31 from the station (about every 10 mins) to Grassina (in about 45 mins). For Impruneta, services run by *CAP* c every hour (Largo Alinari, off Piazza della Stazione) in 40 mins.

Information office
Open Apr–Dec at Impruneta: Via Mazzini 1 (☎ 055 2313729).

Where to stay
Campsite
☆☆ *Camping Internazionale*, open in summer, at Bottai near Impruneta.

Eating out
Restaurant
I Tre Pini, at Pozzolatico, near Impruneta.

Florence is left by Piazza Ferrucci at the south end of Ponte San Niccolò (**Map 12**). The road signposted to Grassina crosses a piazza in front of the **Badia a Ripoli**, a pretty 16C porticoed church flanked by its tall campanile. A Benedictine convent, founded in 790, it became a Vallombrosan monastery in the 12C. Since its suppression in 1808 it has been a parish church. The interior, enlarged in 1598, has a Latin cross plan with a crypt. It was restored to its original state in 1930 when the later painted decoration and stuccowork was destroyed.

The altarpieces include: *St John Gualberto* by Agostino Veracini (c 1744); *Crucifixion and Saints* by Nicodemo Ferrucci; *Madonna and Child* by Jacopo Vignali, (1630); *Scene from the life of Countess Matilda* by Giovanni Camillo Sagrestani (1706), and *Madonna and Child in glory* by Francesco Curradi. In the sacristy are fine inlaid cupboards and a frescoed frieze attributed to Bernardino Poccetti (1585). There is another fresco by Poccetti (a lunette showing the *Marriage at Cana*), signed and dated 1603–4 in the refectory of the convent.

Near **Ponte a Ema** at Rimezzano is the **Oratorio di Santa Caterina dell'Antella** (for admission, ☎ 055 6390356 or 055 6390222). The stone façade was originally frescoed (the lunette over the doorway representing the *Madonna and Child* is by Spinello Aretino). The nave is divided into two bays with cross-vaults containing figures of the Evangelists. On the walls is a *cycle of frescoes of the *Life of St Catherine* by Spinello Aretino (c 1390). Flanking the apse are figures of *Saints Anthony* and *Catherine* attributed to Pietro Nelli (c 1360). Another cycle of frescoes (c 1360) also devoted to St Catherine and attributed to the Maestro di Barberino decorates the apse. The original altarpiece is by Agnolo Gaddi.

Grassina is a large village which is famous for its Good Friday Passion play. The golf-course at **Ugolino** (18 holes) was created in 1933 mainly for the British colony in Florence (the first golf course was made in the grounds of one of the Demidoff properties in 1889). The Club House was built by Gherardo Bosio and the greens beautifully landscaped between olive trees, cypresses, and pines.

Impruneta

Impruneta (correctly, L'Impruneta; 275m), is a large village (13,600 inhab.) on a plateau, where the great cattle fair of St Luke is still celebrated (mid-October), although it has now become a general fair. The clay in the soil has been used for centuries to produce terracotta for which the locality is famous. The kilns here still sell beautiful pottery (flower pots, floor tiles, etc).

The Collegiata

In the large central piazza (where the fair is held) is the Collegiata (Santa Maria dell'Impruneta), with a high 13C tower, and an elegant portico by Gherardo Silvani (1634). After severe bomb damage in 1944, the **interior** was restored to its Renaissance aspect which it acquired in the mid-15C under the Pievano Antonio degli Agli. At the west end is the 16C organ and early 18C cantoria. **South side**. First altar, *Martyrdom of St Lawrence* by Cosimo Gamberucci; second altar, *Birth of the Virgin* by Passignano. In the nave chapel, where the Pievano Antonio degli Agli lies buried, there is a bronze *Crucifix* by Felice Palma. At the entrance to the presbytery are two chapels (c 1452) attributed to Michelozzo, with beautiful *decoration in enamelled terracotta by Luca and Andrea della Robbia. They had to be reconstructed and restored after bomb damage. The chapel on the right was built to protect a relic of the True Cross given to the church by Pippo Spano in 1426. It contains an enamelled terracotta ceiling and an exquisite relief of the *Crucifixion with the Virgin and St John* in a tabernacle, flanked by the figures of St John the Baptist and a bishop saint. Beneath is a charming predella of adoring angels. The chapel on the left protects a miraculous painting of the *Virgin* traditionally attributed to St Luke which was ploughed up by a team of oxen in a field near Impruneta. For centuries it was taken to Florence to help the city in times of trouble. It had to be restored in the 18C by the English painter Ignazio Hugford. The beautiful ceiling is similar to the one in the other chapel. The frieze of fruit on the exterior incorporates two reliefs of the *Madonna and Child*. The figures of Saints Luke and Paul flank a tabernacle which contains the image of the *Madonna and Child* (usually covered; exposed only on religious festivals). The silver altar frontal designed by Giovanni Battista Foggini replaces a 15C relief now exhibited in the treasury (see below).

Five large 18C paintings depicting *Miracles of the Virgin* include two fine works by Gian Domenico Ferretti. The large high altarpiece (1375) was partially recomposed after it was shattered in the Second World War. The carved and inlaid choirs stalls date from 1522.

On the **north side** of the nave are altarpieces by Matteo Rosselli (*Martyrdom of St Sebastian*) and Empoli (*Calling of St Peter*), and a 16C cantoria. In the baptistery is a late 16C font with a 14C relief of the *Baptism of Christ*. A door beneath the portico on the right leads into two cloisters; off the second (left) is the little crypt (11C), with sculptural fragments. In the sacristy is a Crucifixion group in wood and bronze, by the bottega of Pietro Tacca (restored in 2000).

The della Robbia family

The art of enamelled terracotta was invented in the 1440s by Luca della Robbia. The secret of the chemical composition he used for the enamelling (a lead glaze with the addition of oxides) was handed down through three generations of his family (who had their kiln and workshop in Via Guelfa in Florence), and then lost. Tuscany is full of these colourful luminous works, usually blue and white, used in the decoration of buildings and for altarpieces and numerous half-length Madonna reliefs which became popular for private devotion.

Luca (1399/1400–82) started life as a highly skilled and sensitive marble sculptor (his earliest work and masterpiece is the Cantoria now in the Museo dell'Opera del Duomo in Florence) and was very successful in his very long life. He is generally recognized as one of the most important early Renaissance sculptors, and was clearly influenced by classical art. His best enamelled terracotta works can be seen in Florence (in the Bargello Museum, the Duomo, and Cappella Pazzi), Pistoia (the *Visitation* in the church of San Giovanni Fuorcivitas), and here at Impruneta.

His nephew **Andrea** (1435–1525) worked with him, and then went on to produce his own very beautiful works at La Verna, the Spedale degli Innocenti in Florence, and at the Osservanza outside Siena. Some of his finest works are also in the Bargello Museum in Florence. He had five children, all of whom produced enamelled terracotta works. The most skilful one was **Giovanni** (1469–1530) who made use of more colours as can be seen in his numerous works in Tuscany (including those in Florence, in the Bargello Museum, and in the cloister of the Certosa di Galluzzo in the environs). There was a revival of interest, particularly in England, in della Robbian works in the late 18C and they were imitated with some success in the 19C.

The entrance to the **treasury** is on the left of the church door (open Fri, 10.00–13.00, Sat 15.00–18.30; Sun 10.00–13.00, 15.00–18.30; in summer: Thur and Fri 10.00–13.00, Sat and Sun 10.00–13.00, 16.00–19.30). Above the portico of the church are displayed a gilded silver *Cross attributed to Lorenzo Ghiberti (c 1420–25); two paxes attributed to Antonio di Salvi; a Cross of the 13C and 14C; fifteen silver votive vases of 1633; and 17C and 18C church silver. The marble schiacciato relief (c 1448) attributed to a follower of Donatello or the circle of Filarete shows the discovery of the miraculous painting of the *Madonna of Impruneta* (see above). In two other rooms are displayed eleven *illuminated choirbooks including one attributed to Lippo di Benivieni (c 1310–20), five attributed to the bottega of Pacino di Bonaguida (mid-14C), and three by Antonio di Girolamo da Ugolino (1537–39). The patchwork cushion and linen and silk veil were found in the tomb of Antonio degli Agli (d. 1477; see above) in 1944. Vestments are to be exhibited in another room.

The Mugello and the Val di Sieve

The Mugello is the area north of Florence which extends either side of the Sieve river. The beautiful landscape consists of wooded hills rising above the cultivated valley. Numerous churches and villas are dotted around the hills. The small towns of Borgo San Lorenzo, San Piero a Sieve, and Scarperia contain interesting buildings, and Vicchio is famous as the birthplace of Giotto. The Alto Mugello extends up to the Apennine passes and the border with Emilia-Romagna. The whole area offers numerous attractions to nature lovers and hikers and cyclists, and there are many farms which offer pleasant accommodation and good restaurants. The *Comunità Montana Mugello* is a particularly efficient tourist office which provides excellent brochures, maps and guides, and detailed information for visitors. The Val di Sieve is the area northeast of Florence around the wine-growing centres of Pontassieve and Rufina.

Practical information

Getting there
By car from Florence

There are two direct roads from Florence to the **Mugello**: the Via Faentina (N302), the most attractive road, and the Via Bolognese (N65) which offers a slightly faster approach. The Faentina can also be joined at l'Olmo from a beautiful secondary road which leads along the hills beyond Fiesole (see p 106).

The **Val di Sieve** can be reached directly from Florence east along the Arno on the busy Arezzo road (N69) as far as Pontassieve, and then by N67 which follows the Sieve north to Rufina and Dicomano.

By train

The secondary Faentina line (via Le Caldine and Vaglia) from Florence (Campo di Marte station) to San Piero a Sieve and Borgo San Lorenzo. The scenic journey takes about 45 mins. From Borgo another secondary line (from Faenza) runs via Vicchio, Dicomano and Rufina to Florence (Santa Maria Novella station) in about 1hr.

By bus

SITA and *CAP* provide a frequent service from Florence to San Piero a Sieve (in 50mins) and to Borgo San Lorenzo (in 1 hour). Other services connect Borgo San Lorenzo to San Piero a Sieve, Cafaggiolo, and Scarperia as well as Vicchio and Dicomano.

Information offices
Comunità Montana Mugello, Via Togliatti 45, Borgo San Lorenzo, ☎ 055 849 5346; ✉ turismo@cm-mugello.fi.it; www.turismo.mugello.toscana.it. *Associazione Turismo Ambiente*, Via Bandini 6, Borgo San Lorenzo, ☎ & 📠 055 845 8793.

Where to stay
Agriturismo

BORGO SAN LORENZO *Collefertile*, Via Arliano, La Sughera 37, Montegiovi, ☎ 055 849 5201; ✉ info@collefertile.com; *La Topaia*, Via San Giovanni Maggiore 57, ☎ 055 840 8741; ✉ salsedo@tin.it; *Sanvitale*, Via Campagna 20, località San Giorgio, Luco di Mugello, ☎ 055 840 1158; ✉ sanvitale@dada.it. **FIRENZUOLA** *Badia di Moscheta*, Via di Moscheta 8, ☎ 055 814 4015;

✉ www.ischetus.com/moscheta.htm. In a beautiful isolated position, with a good restaurant.

MARRADI *Piano Rosso*, Via Piano Rosso, Biforco, ☎ 055 804 5345; ▤ 055 804 2807.

PALAZZUOLO SUL SENIO *Badia di Susinana*, Via Badia di Susinana 36, ☎ 055 804 6630; ▤ 055 804 6660; *Ca' Nova*, Via Bibbiana 21, ☎ & ▤ 055 804 6569; *Fantino*, Piedimonte 29, località Fantino; ☎ 055 804 6708; ✉ www.paginegialle.it/fantino; *Le Panare*, Via Lozzole, Piedimonte, ☎ 055 804 6346; ✉ lepanare@tin.it.

Residence

BORGO SAN LORENZO *Monsignor Della Casa*, Via di Mucciano 7, ☎ 055 896 4770; ✉ www.monsignore.com.

PALAZZUOLO SUL SENIO *Antico Borgo I Cancelli*, Località I Cancelli, ☎ 055 804 6578; ▤ 055 804 6063.

Hotels

PALAZZUOLO SUL SENIO ☆☆☆ *Senio*, Borgo dell'Ore 1, ☎ 055 804 6019; ▤ 055 804 6485, with restaurant (see below).

VICCHIO ☆☆☆ *Hotel Villa Campestri*, Via di Campestri 19, ☎ 055 849 0107; ▤ 055 849 0108. In a beautiful villa near Sagginale at Campestri.

Campsites

PALAZZUOLO SUL SENIO ☆☆ *Visano*, Via Faggiola 19, ☎ 055 804 6106.

SAN PIERO A SIEVE ☆☆☆ *Mugello Verde*, Via Massorondinaio 39, at La Fortezza, ☎ 055 848 511, ✉ www.florencecamping.com.

BARBERINO DI MUGELLO ☆☆ *Il Sergente*, Via Santa Lucia 24, Monte di Fò, ☎ 055 842 3018; ✉ info@campingilsergente.it.

FIRENZUOLA ☆☆ *Lo Stale*, Bruscoli Postiglione, ☎ 055 815 297.

VICCHIO ☆☆ *Vecchio Ponte*, Via Costoli 18, ☎ 055 844 8306, and *Valdisieve*, Via Rossoio Caldeta, ☎ 055 844 256.

Eating out
Restaurants

BORGO SAN LORENZO
€€€ *Gli Artisti*, Piazza Romagnoli 1. In the historic centre; €€ *Teatro dei Medici*, località La Torre. In a Medici villa outside Borgo on the road to San Piero a Sieve. €€ *Collefertile*, località Arliano. Good snack bars for lunch include *I Bachiacca*, Viale Pecori Geraldi 52 and *Valecchi*, Via Mazzini.

VICCHIO €€ *L'Antica porta di Levante*, Piazza Vittorio Veneto 4; € *La Casa del Prosciutto*, Ponte a Vecchio.

SAGGINALE € *La Bottega di Sagginale*, Via Belvedere 23. Famous for *tortello di patate*.

MARRADI €€ *Il Camino*, Viale Baccarini 38.

PALAZZUOLO SUL SENIO €€€ *Locanda Senio*, Borgo dell'Ore 1.

VAL DI SIEVE (Pontassieve) €€ *La Casellina*, Via Colognese 28.

Cake-shops

BORGO SAN LORENZO has some excellent pasticcerie including *Aurelio*, Corso Matteotti (which produces its own chocolate) and *Cesarino*, Piazza Martiri della Libertà. *La Piazzetta* (Piazza Garibaldi) has good ice-creams.

Shopping
Market at Borgo San Lorenzo on Tuesdays.

Borgo San Lorenzo

Borgo San Lorenzo (14,800 inhab.), in the Sieve valley, is the main town of the Mugello, with a pleasant old town centre. Up until the 1950s it was a thriving market town, and since the 1960s numerous small industries have set up factories on the plain, towards Scarperia. The famous Chini ceramic factories, founded by two cousins Galileo and Chino Chini, both natives of Borgo, were active here from 1906–44, producing very fine ceramic decoration and stained glass, much of it still to be found in the town, and in the museum dedicated to their work.

History

Of ancient foundation, Borgo San Lorenzo was once a possession of the Ubaldini, and from the 10C was owned by the Bishop of Florence. In a central position, on a crossing of the Sieve, it became a dominion of Florence after 1290. It suffered a severe earthquake in 1919.

In the centre of the town **Palazzo del Podestà** has numerous well-preserved coats of arms on its façade (including della Robbian works).

Nearby is the large **Pieve di San Lorenzo**, first mentioned in 941 and rebuilt in the 12C. It was restored in 1937 after earthquake damage.

The pretty side altars were erected in 1503. North aisle: second altar, *Madonna and Saints Domenic and Francis* by Matteo Rosselli; third altar, *Saints Benedict, Sebastian, and Dominic* attributed to Bachiacca; fourth altar, *Madonna in glory with Saints* by Jacopo Vignali. Over the high altar, 14C painted *Crucifix*, and in the apse, mural painting by Galileo Chini (1906) of the *Redeemer and Saints*. At the end of the south aisle is a *Madonna*, a ruined fragment of a *Maestà*, almost certainly a very early work by Giotto thought to date from 1290–95. Fourth altar, *Madonna enthroned with Angels* attributed to Agnolo Gaddi; third altar, *St Michael* by Paolo Colli (d. 1822), and a 15C polychrome terracotta bust of St Lawrence. The second altarpiece of the *Lamentation over the Dead Christ* is by Cesare Velli (1591).

Outside the church is the tabernacle of St Francis, brightly decorated in 1926 with paintings and polychrome terracotta by the Chini workshop.

Corso Matteotti divides the old town roughly in half. Just before it passes beneath a gate with a clock tower (which still keeps the hours) a side street right leads to the foot of the unusual **campanile of San Lorenzo**, built in 1263 above the apse. It is circular beneath and irregularly hexagonal above.

Corso Matteotti continues towards a less attractive part of the town past the police station in a building of 1930 (with a ceramic eagle by the Chini workshop) and some way further on ends beside the **Santuario del Santissimo Crocifisso** on the edge of town. This centrally-planned building was built by Girolamo Ticciati in 1714–43 on the site of an oratory dedicated to a *Crucifix*, believed to work miracles and venerated since c 1400. It had to be reconstructed after the earthquake of 1919.

The fine high altarpiece of the guardian angel protecting Borgo from the earthquake of 1835 is by Giuseppe Bezzuoli. Behind it is kept the miraculous *Crucifix* attributed to the school of Giovanni Pisano, exhibited only on the first Sunday of every month. The eight paintings of the *Passion of Christ* are by Luigi Sabatelli and the right altarpiece (the *Baptism of Constantine*) is by Ignazio Hugford. The Cappella della Compagnia, off the left side of the church, has stained glass by the Chini workshop (1922).

On the left of the sanctuary is the deconsecrated Gothic church of **San Francesco** (ring for adm. at the ex-convent) with an interesting Cistercian interior and restored Giottesque frescoes. Nearby is the large **Villa Pecori-Giraldi**, with a 16C façade and a 19C tower, surrounded by a park (being restored). It is now the seat of **Museo della Manifattura Chini** (open Fri, Sat & fest. 15.00– 18.00; Tues & fest. 10.00–13.00; in summer: Wed, Fri, Sat & fest. 16.00–19.00; Tues and Sat 10.00–13.00). The villa preserves some of its fireplaces and frescoed decorations by the Chini (including *St George and the Dragon* by Galileo). It also has a delightful Art Nouveau staircase. The museum has a fine collection of majolica, ceramics, tiles, and stained glass made by the Chini manufactory in Borgo San Lorenzo from 1900 to the 1930s, many of them by Galileo, Augusto, and Tito. There is also the reconstruction of a ceramic workshop, and a collection of works donated by the painter Pietro Annigoni (died 1988).

On the other side of the town, in Piazza Dante (with a public garden), is the headquarters of the **Misericordia** (1908) with a neo-Gothic exterior and a majolica *Pietà* by Galileo Chini over the doorway. Inside the chapel are two side altars and two kneeling angels in enamelled terracotta by Galileo Chini, who also painted the apse.

The Alto Mugello

The Via Faentina leads north from Borgo San Lorenzo to the town of Marradi, near the border with Emilia-Romagna. The district is known as the Alto Mugello. An annual running race known as the *100 kilometri del passatore* is held on this road from Faenza to Florence in spring.

A few kilometres north of Borgo San Lorenzo, just off the Via Faentina, is the church of **San Giovanni Maggiore** (open Sun 09.00–12.00), surrounded by farm buildings. It has a portico and an 11C octagonal campanile. Founded in the 10C, the church was rebuilt by Francesco Minerbetti in 1520–30 and transformed in the 19C. It contains an elegant 12C ·ambone. The stained glass is by the Chini factory, and the nave was frescoed in 1843 by Pietro Alessi Chini.

Further north, near **Ronta**, a quiet little summer resort, is the **Madonna dei Tre Fiumi** in a fine position. Here an interesting privately-owned water mill, the **Antico Mulino Margheri** which is still in operation can be visited on request (☎ 055 840 3051). The **Colla di Casaglia** (913m) is the hill dividing the Sieve and Lamone valleys.

Marradi lies in a narrow stretch of the Lamone valley, at the foot of the Apennines on the border between Tuscany and Emilia-Romagna. It came under Florentine rule from 1428 onwards. Its capture by the Allies in 1944 made a breach in the German Gothic line (see p 130). The Piazza Le Scalelle is named after a mountain pass which was the scene of a victory of the citizens of Marradi in 1358 over Corrado Lando, a count from Württenberg who was forced to lead his mercenary army south via the territory of Marradi in order to avoid Florence. Since he willfully damaged the town, he was ambushed by the angry citizens; Carrado's brother died and he himself was wounded and taken prisoner.

On the outskirts of the town is the **Teatro degli Animosi**, built in 1792 by Giulio Mannaioni. Outside the town is **Badia del Borgo** (first documented in 1025), reconstructed in 1741–65. In the sacristy are 15C paintings attributed to the Master of Marradi (it can be seen by appointment, ☎ 055 804 5498).

Palazzuolo sul Senio

A winding mountain road connects Marradi with Palazzuolo sul Senio in the Senio valley to the northwest. It was ruled by the Ubaldini family until 1362 when it came under Florentine control. In the picturesque 14C Palazzo dei Capitani is the **Museo delle Genti di Montagna**, a fine local ethnographical museum (open March–Dec on fest. 15.00–18.00; in July and Aug daily exc. Mon 16.00–19.00). Next to it, above a garden, is the church of Santi Carlo e Antonio with an interesting 17C interior. The parish church of Santo Stefano contains Florentine 16C–17C paintings, decorations by Dino Chini (1945). The medieval **Pieve di Misileo** (rebuilt in 1781), near Palazzuolo, preserves a Romanesque crypt and a 15C painting of the *Madonna and Saints*.

Another road leads north from Borgo San Lorenzo via **Luco di Mugello** (where the hospital, in a former monastery, has a beautiful Renaissance court-yard), to **Grezzano**. Here in the **Casa d'Erci**, an old farmhouse, is a delightful private museum (open on fest. 15.00–19.00; summer also on Sat 15.00–19.00; or by appointment, ☎ 055 845 7197) of agricultural implements and artisans' tools, all of them still in working order, illustrating life in the Mugello up until the last War. It is organised by a group of local volunteers.

San Piero a Sieve

A valley in the Mugello

To the west of Borgo San Lorenzo is San Piero a Sieve at a crossroads connecting the Mugello plain with the Apennine passes via Scarperia and Barberino del Mugello, and where the river Sieve meets the Carza. The **Pieve di San Pietro**, at the entrance to the village on the main road from Vaglia, was founded in the 11C and altered in the 18C. The baptismal font is a fine work by the della Robbia. Above the high altar is a wood *Crucifix* attributed to Raffaello da Montelupo. Outside is a statue of *St Peter* by Girolamo Ticciati (1768). Across the main road Via della Compagnia ascends past a little 13C oratory to Palazzo Adami with terracotta decorations.

A country track continues up to the large 16C **Fortezza di San Martino**, surrounded by pine woods. It was designed for the Medici by Bernardo Buontalenti to guard Florence from the north. It is one of the most interesting examples of Renaissance military archi-tecture left in Tuscany and is to be restored and eventually opened to the public.

From Palazzo Adami, Via dei Medici descends through Piazza Gramsci past the large **Villa Schifanoia** (formerly Medici) built in terraces on the hillside with a dovecot in the tower, and (right) an ancient house with arches, past the **Municipio** with polychrome majolica decoration (1925), into the central Piazza Colonna.

Bosco ai Frati

Outside the village, just after a bridge over the Sieve, a by-road (signposted) leads left to Bosco ai Frati, a charming little convent (four friars live here) in pretty wooded country (known locally for its mushrooms). Visitors are shown around by one of the friars (closed 12.00–15.00). The convent was founded before 1000 and the Franciscans came here in 1212. In 1273 St Bonaventura was staying in the convent when Gregory X appointed him Cardinal. The story is told that the saint was washing dishes in the scullery and told the messenger to hang his cardinal's hat on a tree nearby. The convent was purchased by Cosimo il Vecchio in 1420 and he employed Michelozzo to restore it (and add the fine porch behind the church). Off the cloister a little museum contains a remarkable *Crucifix*, attributed to Donatello.

The Medici villas of Trebbio and Cafaggiolo

A few kilometres west of San Piero a Sieve are the delightful Medici fortified villas of Trebbio and Cafaggiolo. They are reached off the main road (N65) to Barberino di Mugello. The **Castello del Trebbio**, in a lovely elevated position, is surrounded by a hamlet and pretty woods (privately owned; for adm. ☎ 055 845 8793 *Turismo e Ambiente*, Mon, Wed or Fri). The castle, surrounded by cypresses, was built by Michelozzo for Cosimo il Vecchio in 1461 as a country residence. It remained the property of the Medici until 1644. A beautiful Italianate 15C **garden** with a long 17C pergola survives. The villa was the residence of Giovanni Dalle Bande Nere and Maria Salviati, and Amerigo Vespucci may have been a guest here in 1476. The kitchen and a small living room on the ground floor are also usually shown.

The **Villa di Cafaggiolo**, a huge castle behind a garden railing can be seen from the main road (privately owned; adm. as for Trebbio). It is surrounded by a park with some fine trees. This was the first country villa that Michelozzo built for Cosimo il Vecchio. It was erected in 1451 on the site of a castle. In 1500, Pierfrancesco de' Medici founded a ceramic manufactory in the buildings to the left of the villa. It was famous for its production, especially up to c 1520. Leo X stayed here in 1515, and it was the favourite country house of Ferdinando I and of the Lorraine grand-dukes. It was bought by the Borghese family in 1864.

The impressive exterior, with corbelling below the eaves and decorated with battlements, formerly had two towers and was once surrounded by a moat. The interior is less interesting, although it has some 19C decorations restored in 1887 by the Chini brothers on the ground floor.

Beyond Cafaggiolo, towards Barberino, is the huge artificial lake of **Bilancino** built between 1984 and 1998 to contain some 69 million cubic metres of water, with an area of about 5 sq km. The dam here was designed to control the waters of the Sieve (and their confluence with the Arno at Pontassieve in times of flood), and to increase Florence's supply of drinking water, but it proved extremely costly and there are now doubts about how effective it would be in preventing another disastrous Arno flood. However, for the time being the lake is very pretty, and there are plans to use it for boating and wind-surfing.

Galliano, off the road to the right, was founded in 1048 by the Ubaldini family at the foot of an Apennine pass (remains of its fortifications survive). The *pieve* has a dome frescoed by Tito Chini (1920). Inside is a *Madonna and Child* attributed to Margaritone di Arezzo and a *Madonna and Child with Saints* attributed to the school of Ghirlandaio. In the adjoining oratory is an *Annunciatory Virgin* by Davide Ghirlandaio. In the church of **Santo Stefano a Rezzano** nearby is a *Madonna and Saints* attributed to Filippino Lippi.

Barberino di Mugello is well known because of its vicinity to the Florence–Bologna motorway. A hamlet grew up here in the 11C around a castle belonging to the Cattani family. Of great strategic importance on an Apennine pass, it was sacked by many armies, including that of Sir John Hawkwood (in 1364); see p 481. It was badly damaged in the last war. Palazzo Pretorio, in Piazza Cavour, has a portico attributed to Michelozzo. The *pieve* of **San Silvestro** contains a precious organ (16C–19C), and the oratory next door has good carved woodwork.

The church of **Cavallina**, south of the town, contains a fine carved tabernacle attributed to Mino da Fiesole, and a 16C *Madonna and Child with Saints.*

Also just outside Barberino is the **Badia di Santa Maria a Vigesimo** with a fine façade and interior of 1740–47. Beneath the organ of 1744 is a Rococo cantoria. The paintings include a 15C *Virgin Annunciate* and a *Birth of the Virgin* by Ignazio Hugford.

The church of Sant'Andrea at **Camoggiano**, across the motorway, has a pretty façade (1470) with a little portico, and, inside, late 14C frescoes by the Florentine school. Next door is the Renaissance Palazzo Cattani with a good courtyard.

North of Barberino is the *pieve* of **San Gavino Adimari** rebuilt in 1267, with an 18C interior and an interesting tomb slab carved with Christian symbols. Beyond **Panna**, where mineral water is bottled, is the **Passo della Futa** (903m) one of the main Apennine passes. In the autumn of 1944 during the Second World War the strongest German defences in the 'Gothic line' (which stretched across the ridge of the Apennines between Versilia and Rimini) were established here, only finally broken by the Allies in the spring of 1945 after heavy fighting. Just beyond **Pietramala** (851m), a summer and winter holiday resort is the **Passo della Raticosa** (968m) with an old custom-house on the border with Emilia, see *Blue Guide Northern Italy.*

Scarperia

North of San Piero a Sieve is Scarperia (5700 inhab.) which was founded in 1306 by the Florentines to protect her territories from invading armies from across the Apennines. The town preserves its interesting rectangular plan laid out on either side of the main road which connected Florence to Bologna (now Via Roma) with the castle in the centre. In 1415 it became the seat of a vicariate of the Florentine Republic, with jurisdiction over the whole of the Mugello. In 1542 the village suffered from an earthquake, and after the Lorraine grand-dukes opened the new road across the Futa Pass in 1752, Scarperia lost its importance.

At the entrance to the town is the little **Oratorio della Madonna dei Terremoti** with a charming fresco of the *Madonna and Child enthroned* (c 1448) attributed to the circle of Francesco d'Antonio (or the school of Filippo Lippi). Beyond the little public garden (with a view) is the lovely walled garden of the **Torrino**, a 15C tower restored in 1930 (adm. by appointment with *Turismo e Ambiente*, ☎ 055 845 8793 Mon, Wed, or Fri.) It contains a private museum with an eclectic collection, including Etruscan vases, medieval urns and paintings on nine floors and Art Nouveau tiled decoration by the Chini workshop.

The main road runs straight up to the centre of the town with the splendid *Palazzo dei Vicari, now the seat of the **Museo dei Ferri Taglienti** (open Sat & fest. 10.00–13.00, 15.00–18.30; mid June–mid Sept daily exc. Mon 16.00–19.00; Sat & fest. 10.00–13.00), which illustrates the history of the craft of making knives which has been practised here probably since the 14C; it was a flourishing industry in Scarperia from the 15C up until the early 20C. The palace was built in 1306 perhaps on a design by Arnolfo di Cambio, and it has a very tall tower and numerous coats of arms all over its façade, some in enamelled terra-cotta by the della Robbia family and Benedetto Buglioni. The imposing atrium (restored in 1889 by Gaetano Bianchi), covered with more coats of arms and late 14C frescoes (including a *Madonna and Child*), leads into the long rectangular courtyard which stretches as far as the hillside. The staircase leads up past a huge fresco of *St Christopher* (c 1412) to the first floor. Here is a fine fresco of the *Madonna and Child with Saints* by the school of Ridolfo del Ghirlandaio (1554). The Sala del Consiglio has more frescoes (15C–19C) with coats of arms. The Sala del Sindaco, with 14C and 15C paintings, a 16C fireplace, and polychrome terracotta relief of the *Madonna and Child*, may also be visited.

In the piazza, opposite Palazzo dei Vicari, is the parish church of **Santi Jacopo e Filippo** founded in the 14C but rebuilt, with a neo-Gothic campanile.

Left side: first altar, *Crucifixion and Saints* by Matteo Rosselli; second altar, *Annunciation*, a fine painting attributed to Giovanni Balducci. In the chapel to the left of the main altar, small marble tabernacle, an early work by Domenico Rosselli and a small wooden *Crucifix* attributed to Jacopo Sansovino. In the apse, late 15C wooden *Crucifix*. In the chapel to the right of the main altar is a beautiful marble tondo of the *Madonna and Child* by Benedetto da Maiano (in its original wooden frame). The second altarpiece on the right side (*Birth of the Virgin*) is by Matteo Rosselli, and on the wall is a fragment of a 15C fresco. Also in the piazza, with a large window, is the **Oratorio della Madonna di Piazza** (door usually unlocked) with a Gothic tabernacle enclosing a fine painting of the *Madonna and Child* by Jacopo del Casentino, within a 15C marble frame.

To the right of Palazzo dei Vicari, at Via Solferino 15 is the **Bottega del coltellinaio**, an artisan's workshop used for making knives (admission as for Palazzo dei Vicari). From the public gardens (see above) a road runs down the edge of the hillside by the **Oratorio della Madonna del Vivaio** built on a design by Alessandro Galilei in 1724–41. It is a centrally-planned church surmounted by a tall drum and lantern, with an interesting neo-Classical interior (although it has been closed since 1960, funding has arrived for its restoration).

The district of Scarperia

Sant'Agata, a short way west of Scarperia, has an interesting *pieve*, thought to date from the 5C, but documented since 984. The exterior is prettily decorated and the low tower has a clock. The interior is remarkable for its unusual columns on huge square bases which rise directly to the wooden roof beams. The plan of the original church can be seen in the pavement. At the west end the baptismal font is enclosed by Romanesque marble intarsia panels (1165; formerly part of an ambone damaged in an earthquake in 1542). On the wall is a Romanesque statuette of an angel. On the triumphal arch are two tabernacles with the *Madonna and Annunciatory Angel* attributed to Cristofano Allori. Over the west door, Romanesque statue of *St Agata*. On the west wall painting of *Saints* and a reliquary assembled in the 17C (two Saints are by Jacopo di Cione, c 1377).

In the oratory next door is the **Museo d'Arte Sacra di Sant'Agata** (open fest. 10.00–12.00, 15.00–17.00; in summer also on Sat). The paintings include a Madonna enthroned signed by a certain Nicolaos (1345), *Mystical Marriage of St Catherine*, a fine painting by Bicci di Lorenzo enclosed in a 16C wooden tabernacle, an altarpiece by the school of Ridolfo del Ghirlandaio (1514), *Christ* *in pietà* by the 16C Florentine school, a tabernacle by Giovanni della Robbia, the *sinopia* and fresco from a tabernacle by Ambrogio di Baldese, and *St Catherine of Alexandria* by the Maestro di Signa (c 1460). There is also church silver and a Cross of 1379, as well as 14 engravings of the *Stations of the Cross* by Luigi Sabatelli. In two rooms off the cloister is an interesting collection of finds made in prehistoric sites in the vicinity by a local archaeological group.

Beside the 17C Palazzo Salviati, Chiasso Salviati leads out of the village into open country. Below the church is a Romanesque bridge and old water mill. Just outside the village there is a delightful little private museum, **Sant'Agata Artigiana e Contadina** (open fest. 15.00–18.00) with mechanical tableaux made by Faliero Leprino of local peasant life (1920–50).

Just to the south of Scarperia is the church of **Santa Maria a Fagna**. Founded before 1018, the façade and interior were decorated in 1770. The church (for the key ring at the house on the right) contains a handsome 12C *ambone and font and an *Assumption of the Virgin*, signed and dated 1587 by Santi di Tito.

Another country road from Scarperia (signposted Luco di Mugello) passes the isolated little church of **San Michele a Figliano** which contains a font and altar by the Chini factory (who also designed the war memorial outside). Nearby is the **Villa Frescobaldi a Corte** with a fine park (no adm.).

To the north of Scarperia is the neo-Classical **Villa il Pelagio** (left), once a residence of the Borghese family, with a garden. Beyond the **Giogo di Scarperia** (882m), an Apennine pass, is **Firenzuola**, a 14C Florentine colony, with a gateway at either end of its arcaded main street. The town was laid out on symmetrical lines within rectangular bastions, designed by Antonio da Sangallo the Elder, but it was very badly damaged in the Second World War. The German Gothic line (see p 130) was pierced here by the American fifth Army in September 1944 after heavy fighting. In the castle is the **Museo della Pietra Serena** (open mid June–mid Sept Mon, Fri, Sat 16.00–19.00; fest. 11.00–13.00; winter Sat 15.00–17.00; fest. 11.00–13.00, 14.00–17.00). It illustrates the traditional methods of quarrying *pietra serena* found in the interesting rock formations along the Santerno river valley just to the north of Firenzuola. This fine-grained dark grey sandstone is particularly easy to carve, and although generally not sufficiently resistant for the exterior of buildings, it was used to decorate many Renaissance interiors in Florence. The museum also contains numerous artefacts made locally from *pietra serena*.

The **Abbazia di Moscheta** in a beautiful position in the countryside, houses the **Museo del Paesaggio Storico dell'Appenino** (open Sat 15.00–17.00; fest. 11.00–13.00, 14.00–17.00; summer: Thurs, Fri, Sat 16.00–19.00; fest. 11.00–13.00, 16.00–19.00) which illustrates the characteristics of the mountainous landscape of the Mugello. To the north, on the Emilian border just outside Moraduccio is a British Military Cemetery.

South of Borgo San Lorenzo

South of Borgo San Lorenzo, in beautiful countryside off the two roads from Florence between Polcanto and Vaglia, is the **Badia di Buonsolazzo**, a Benedictine foundation with a worn 18C façade. At **Faltona**, on the Via Faentina, is the church of Santa Felicità, with a tall tower. Nearby is the well-kept, privately-owned 18C **Villa Guiducci a Serravalle** (with a painted coat of arms on the bright yellow façade).

On the south bank of the river Sieve, is **Santa Maria ad Olmi**, a conspicuous church with a bell tower, next to an elegant villa. The church dates from the 16C and contains a 15C tabernacle which encloses a 14C fresco, and paintings by Alessandro Allori and Carlo Portelli (if closed, ring at no. 4). Francesco I and Bianca Cappello stayed in the villa in 1585 when Alessandro Allori painted Bianca's portrait in fresco (detached in 1871 and now exhibited in the Tribuna of the Uffizi).

From Olmi a road leads south through an unspoilt valley to the little village of Poggiolo-Salaiole past the **Villa de Le Viterete** (1624), the buildings of which line the edge of the road next to a little chapel (the garden façade, difficult to see, has a loggia), and the 15C **Villa La Bartolina** with a fine ground floor loggia of four arches.

On the left of the Sagginale road is **Lutiano Nuovo**, a little group of houses with a roadside tabernacle protecting a ceramic *Madonna and Child* by the Chini (1914). A road diverges right for the church of **San Cresci** in a lovely position above the valley. It has a splendid tall campanile with windows on four stories. Founded in the 9C, it was rebuilt in 1701–04 by Giovanni Battista Foggini (and reconstructed after the earthquake in 1919).

Near Sagginale is **Barbiana** where Don Lorenzo Milani (1923–67) was parish priest. He was also a writer and educator and founded a remarkable local school here for children from poor families based on the development of liberty and socialisation. Together with his pupils he wrote *Lettera ad una professoressa* (*Letter to a teacher*), published in 1967.

Vicchio

Vicchio was the birthplace of Giotto and Fra Angelico. Benvenuto Cellini had a house here from 1559–71 (on Corso del Popolo; plaque). A picturesque bridge crosses the Sieve. Part of the medieval walls (1324) survive. In Piazza della Vittoria is the polygonal Torre dei Cerchiai beside a neo-Classical loggia. The centre of the little town is Piazza Giotto which has a bronze monument to the painter by Italo Vagnetti (1901). The **Museo di Arte Sacra e di religiosità popolare 'Beato Angelico'** (open Tues & Thur 15.00–17.00; Sat & fest. 10.00–12.00) has an interesting collection of works of art from churches in the region, including: a beautiful painting of the *Madona and Child* by the Maestro della Madonna Strauss (from San Cresci); a bust of *St John the Baptist* by Andrea della Robbia; church silver including a reliquary attributed to Massimiliano Soldani Benzi; an *Annunciation* by Francesco Furini, a mid-15C stained glass window of *St Felicity and her children* attributed to the circle of Andrea del Castagno, *St John the Baptist* attributed to Bernardo Daddi, a 15C *Madonna and Child* attributed to Pesellino, *Madonna and Child with Saints* by Neri di Bicci, a head of Christ in wax by Clemente Susini, a 15C frescoed street tabernacle, an enamelled terracotta font attributed to Benedetto Buglioni; two terracotta busts of Bartolomeo Medici Minerbetti and Tommaso Minerbetti (c 1523); vestments; an *Assumption* by Cosimo Rosselli (the lower part attributed to Piero di Cosimo), and a polyptych by the Maestro di Montefloscoli.

A few kilometres outside Vicchio, signposted off the main road to Borgo San Lorenzo, is **Vespignano** where the house in which Giotto is thought to have been born is open: in summer on Tues, Thur, Sat, and Sun, 15.00–19.00; and in winter on Sat and Sun, 15.00–19.00. It contains photographs of his major works.

Giotto di Bondone

Giotto di Bondone (1266/7–1337) introduced a new style of painting which was to have a profound influence on the course of Italian art. It had a realism, monumentality and sense of volume which had never been achieved in medieval painting or by his master Cimabue. He was immediately recognised by his contemporaries as a great painter: admired by Petrarch and Boccaccio, his friend Dante mentions him in his *Divina Commedia* (*Purgatorio*; Canto XI, 91–92):

Credette Cimabue, nella pittura,
Tener lo campo, ed ora ha Giotto il grido...

Cimabue thought he commanded the field in painting,
and now Giotto has the acclaim...

Among his famous masterpieces are the fresco cycles in the Scrovegni chapel in Padua, and in the upper church of San Francesco in Assisi, and in the Peruzzi and Bardi chapels in Santa Croce in Florence. One of his most beautiful paintings is the *Maestà* painted for the church of Ognissanti in Florence and now in the Uffizi. As capomaestro of the cathedral works in Florence he designed the campanile. He is also known to have worked for the papacy in Rome, the Anjou in Naples and the Visconti in Milan. His art was closely studied by Masaccio, Leonardo, and Michelangelo. A fragment of a painting of the Madonna attributed to him can be seen near Vicchio in the *pieve* at Borgo San Lorenzo.

On the hillside above the house is the church of San Martino which contains a *Madonna and Child* by Paolo Schiavo and a tabernacle by Mino da Fiesole. A path leads across fields to the little Cappellina della Bruna protected by cypresses, which preserves a damaged fresco attributed to Paolo Schiavo.

Dicomano

Dicomano is a flourishing small market town of ancient origins, with some arcaded streets. The town hall occupies a large neo-Classical building (1888). A road leads up above the town to the 12C Romanesque **Pieve di Santa Maria** with a squat campanile (if closed ring at the priest's house, no. 25 on the left). The small interior has low stone arcades and a wooden roof. On the south wall is a Della Robbian relief of the *Marriage of St Joachim and Ann*. At the end of the south aisle, the *Nativity* attributed to the school of Bronzino, is in a splendid Mannerist frame.

On the east wall, *Assumption* by Francesco Curradi in another fine frame. Behind the altar is a tiny della Robbian polychrome tabernacle. **North aisle**. *Madonna and Saints* attributed to Giorgio Vasari, and a beautiful 14C triptych of the *Madonna with Saints*.

On the north side of the town is the **Oratorio di Sant'Onofrio**, a splendid neo-Classical building by Giuseppe del Rosso (1796), preceded by a portico of four columns. The church of **Sant'Antonio** (rebuilt in 1938; usually locked) contains a Della Robbian relief (1504; heavily restored after damage in 1919) and a 14C *Madonna and Child with Saints*.

Important Etruscan excavations (6C BC) have taken place southeast of Dicomano at **Frascole**.

A road leads northeast from Dicomano to the Passo del Muraglione on the border with Emilia-Romagna passing **San Godenzo**. The town is noted for its *abbey church, a massive Romanesque building founded in 1028 by Jacopo il Bavaro, Bishop of Fiesole. It stands above the main street, in Piazza Dante Alighieri. In 1308 a meeting took place in the abbey of members of the Guelf party in exile from Florence, including Dante.

The plain stone interior has the presbytery raised above the crypt. On the parapet is a pretty frieze of inlaid marble. The polyptych of the *Madonna and Saints* attributed to Bernardo Daddi was repainted in 1533. The apse mosaic of the *Coronation of the Virgin* is by Giuseppe Cassioli (1929). In the left aisle is an *Annunciation* attributed to Franciabigio, and a wooden *statue of *St Sebastian* by Baccio da Montelupo (1506).

Nearby is **Castagno d'Andrea**, thought to have been the birthplace of the painter Andrea del Castagno (1417 or 1419–57). In the parish church (rebuilt after the Second World War) are frescoes of the *Crucifixion* by Pietro Annigoni (1958). Here is an entrance to the **Parco Nazionale delle Foreste Casentinesi, Monte Falterona e Campigna** (see p 512), an extensive protected wooded area of the Apennines.

The **Passo del Muraglione** (907m), an Apennine pass above the border with Emilia-Romagna, is named after the massive wall erected here in 1836 by Leopoldo II to shelter travellers from snow and icy winds. To the north, where the Troncalosso and Acquacheta rivers meet, is the charming **Acquacheta** waterfall (130m), sung by Dante (*Divina Commedia; Inferno*, XVI, 94–102).

South of Dicomano is **Londa** (where Etruscan remains have been found) on a secondary road which leads to Stia in the Casentino (see p 510). Farther south, a beautiful by-road winds up through vineyards past some lovely old farmhouses to **Castiglioni**, with a 12C church (altered in 1926) from where there is a view below of the tiny little fortified borgo of Castello di Castiglioni.

Beyond **Petrognano**, with a church rebuilt in 1925 and the 18C Villa Budini Gattai, and Rimaggio, the tower of the *pieve* of **San Bartolomeo in Pomino** is conspicuous ahead. The church was founded in the 12C–13C (if closed, ring at no. 60). It has an attractive tall basilican interior with stone arches and a raised chancel. On the left altar, *Madonna and Saints Sebastian and Anthony Abbot*, a fine work attributed to the Master of San Miniato, and on the wall a della Robbian *Madonna and Child with two Saints*. On the right wall is a detached fresco of *St James* with its *sinopia*. The stained glass and mosaic lunette of the *Madonna with two angels* outside the west door date from 1933. **Rufina** has been famous as a wine-growing centre since 1760 (*Chianti Rufina* is bottled here). Above the town (but hidden by its park) is the 16C Villa di Poggio Reale, approached by a long cypress avenue. In the wine cellars dating from the 1930s is the **Museo della Vite e del Vino** (open Sat & fest. 15.00–18.00; summer Sat & fest. 10.00–13.00, 16.00–19.00). This well arranged collection of objects from the late 19C to the present day illustrate the history of wine making in the area.

The tall 12C tower of **Montebonello** is conspicuous on the other side of the river where a road leads to **Santa Maria in Acone**. The road crosses a stream and then narrows to climb uphill. An unsurfaced road leads past a farm and ends in front of the church (key at the house next door). The lunette over the main door, the apse and the high altar were decorated by the Chini at the beginning of this century.

The Chianti

The beautiful hilly region between Florence and Siena is known as the Chianti district. Its characteristic landscape includes numerous carefully tended vineyards, orchards, and olive groves, as well as wilder wooded areas. It is perhaps at its most beautiful in autumn when the leaves of the vines and deciduous trees turn to gold and stand out amidst the silver olive trees, and dark green cypresses and pines. It is at this time that the vintage (*vendemmia*) takes place. Picturesque villages and castles often dominate the hills and offer spectacular panoramas. Some of the most typical and beautiful parts of the countryside can be explored on white unsurfaced roads. Also in this area are many old Romanesque country churches (*pieve*). Vineyards surround the typical, elegant farmhouses known as *case coloniche*. Many of them were built in the 18C during the agricultural reforms carried out by Grand-duke Pietro Leopoldo, and they are often beautifully sited with characteristic towers (formerly dovecots). Some of them have been carefully restored in the last few decades, often by foreigners. The northwestern district of the Chianti region is described on p 144.

The name 'Chianti' is probably of Etruscan origin. The boundary between the Province of Florence (north) and that of Siena (south) divides the Chianti district roughly in half. Most of the castles originated as part of the *Lega del Chianti* (Chianti League): they were fortified strongholds built by the Florentines in the 12C against the Sienese and owned by rich Florentine families and landowners.

Towns and castles were lost and won (the Florentines were heavily defeated at Montaperti in 1260) but in 1559 Siena, and her entire territory, was forced to capitulate to the grand-duke of Tuscany, Cosimo I de'Medici.

Practical information

Getting there
By car

The prettiest road from Florence is the Via Chiantigiana (N222) via Grassina near Impruneta (see p 122) to Greve in Chianti, Panzano, and Castellina in Chianti. South of Panzano another lovely road traverses beautiful countryside in the heart of the Chianti region via Radda and Gaiole.

By bus

Frequent services run by *SITA* from Florence (*SITA* bus station, Via Santa Caterina da Siena 15, off Piazza Stazione) to Greve in 1hr. Some services leave Florence by Porta Romana, and run via Galluzzo and the Cassia as far as Terme di Firenze, and others leave Florence by Piazza Beccaria, and run via Ponte a Ema, Grassina, Ugolino, and Strada in Chianti. From Greve the bus continues to Panzano (and, infrequently, to Lamole, Radda and Castellina). Another *SITA* service (once or twice a day) runs via Grassina, Greve, and Panzano to Radda and Gaiole (in 2hrs).

Information offices

APT of Florence (☎ 055 290 832) for Greve, and Panzano; and *APT* of Siena (☎ 0577 280 551) for Radda, Gaiole, Castellina in Chianti, and Castelnuovo Berardenga. There is a local tourist office in Greve (Via Luca Cini, ☎ 055 854 5243).

Where to stay
Hotels

There are a number of fine hotels in beautiful quiet positions in the country, mostly three and four star, and nearly all of them with swimming pools. There is however a scarcity of cheaper hotels and campsites.

GREVE IN CHIANTI ☆☆☆ *Del Chianti*, Piazza Matteotti 86 (☎ & ▤ 055 853 763).

PASSO DEI PECORAI ☆☆ *Da Omero*, Via Giovanni Falcone 68 (☎ & ▤ 055 850 716).

PANZANO ☆☆☆ *Villa Sangiovese*, Piazza Bucciarelli 5 (☎ 055 852 461; ▤ 055 852 463), and *Villa Le Barone*, Via San Leolino 19 (☎ 055 852 621; ▤ 055 852 277).

RADDA IN CHIANTI ☆☆☆☆ *Relais Fattoria Vignale*, Via Pianigiani 8 (☎ 0577 738 300; ▤ 0577 738 592); ☆☆☆ *Vescine (Il Relais del Chianti;* ☎ 0577 741 144; ▤ 0577 740 263).

GAIOLE IN CHIANTI ☆☆☆☆ *Castello di Spaltenna* (☎ 0577 749 483; ▤ 0577 749 269); ☆☆☆ *Residence San Sano* at Lecchi, 6km south (☎ 0577 746 130; ▤ 0577 746 156).

CASTELNUOVO BERARDENGA ☆☆☆☆ *Relais Borgo San Felice* (☎ 0577 359 260; ▤ 0577 359 089); *Villa Arceno*, località Arceno (near San Gusmè (☎ 0577 359 292; ▤ 0577 359 276); ☆☆☆ *Il Fortilizio*, on the Chiantigiana at il Colombaio (☎ 0577 552 29; ▤ 0577 561 70).

CASTELLINA IN CHIANTI ☆☆☆☆ *Villa Casalecchi* (☎ 0577 740 240; ▤ 0577 741 111) and *Tenuta di Ricavo* (☎ 0577 740 221; ▤ 0577 741 014); ☆☆☆ *Belvedere di San Leonino* (☎ 0577 740 887; ▤ 0577 740 924); *Colle Etrusco Salivolpi* (☎ 0577 740 484; ▤ 0577 740 998); *Il Colombaio*, Strada Chiantigiana 29 (☎ & ▤ 0577 740

444). *Palazzo Squarcialupi*, in an historic palazzo, Via Ferruccio 26 (☎ 0577 741 186; ▤ 0577 740 386).

Agriturismo

Numerous localities including Greve, Radda, Gaiole, and Castellina in Chianti offer *Agriturismo* accommodation (listed in the *APT* hotel lists. Information also from *Agenzia Colline Verdi*, Via della Rocca 12, Castellina in Chianti, ☎ & ▤ 0577 740 620).

Youth hostel

GREVE *Villa San Michele*, Via Casole 40, ☎ & ▤ 055 851 034.

Campsite

CASTELLINA IN CHIANTI ☆☆ *Luxor srl* (☎ 0577 743 047) open in summer, with swimming pool and restaurant.

Eating out

Restaurants also tend to be expensive in the Chianti region. Some of the cheaper ones are listed below.

MONTEFIORALLE € *Taverna del Guerrino*. Via Montefioralle 39.

STRADA IN CHIANTI €€ *Il Padellina*. Corso del Popolo 54.

LA PANCA € *Trattoria Le Cornacchie*.

PASSO DEI PECORAI € *Casprini da Omero*.

RADDA IN CHIANTI € *Le Vigne*, Podere Le Vigne.

GAIOLE € *Il Carlino d'oro*, San Regolo.

VOLPAIA *Osteria la Bottega di Volpaia* (snacks).

CASTELNUOVO BERARDENGA € *La Bottega del 30*, Via S. Caterina 2 (at Villa a Sesta) and *Nonna Luisa* at Corsignano.

CASTELLINA IN CHIANTI € *La Torre*, Piazza del Comune 15.

Wine tasting

In many of the larger estates the **wine cellars** (*cantine*) may be visited, and

wine purchased. Wine-tasting and snacks are also often provided by appointment (telephone numbers are given in the text below where this applies: booking is usually necessary at least three days in advance).
Information from local tourist offices and the *Consorzio del Chianti*,

Lungarno Corsini, Florence 4 (☎ 055 212 333), and the *Consorzio del Marchio Storico Chianti Classico*, Via Scopeti 155, Sant'Andrea in Percussina, San Casciano Val di Pesa (☎ 055 822 8245). **Annual wine festival** in the third week of September in Greve in Chianti.

Greve in Chianti

Greve in Chianti, a pretty market town (10,000 inhabitants), is one of the centres of the wine trade. It has an attractive triangular **piazza**, with porticoes along two sides, which provides a perfect setting for the annual fair. The monument commemorates Giovanni da Verrazzano (d. 1528), the explorer of the North American coast. The church of **Santa Croce**, rebuilt in the neo-Classical style, has a painting by Bicci di Lorenzo. In Piazza Matteotti is a little puppet theatre which gives regular performances for children in summer.

On a hill, just outside the town, is the little church of **San Francesco** containing a glazed terracotta *Deposition* by Santi Buglioni. The conventual buildings are to house a local museum for works of art from churches in the neighbourhood. These will include altarpieces by Francesco Granacci, Raffaellino del Garbo, and Francesco Curradi, some interesting 14C–15C sculptures, liturgical objects, and an archaeological section.

To the west is the charming little village of **Montefioralle**, the birthplace of the Vespucci family. Amerigo Vespucci (1415–1512), a Melici agent in Seville, gave his name to America having made two voyages in 1494 and 1501–02 following the route charted by his Italian contemporary Columbus. It is perched on a hill, partly surrounded by its old walls, and has remains of a medieval castle. The village has preserved its medieval character and there are fine views all around. In the church of Santo Stefano is a large icon of the *Madonna and Child* by a 13C Florentine painter, and paintings of the *Trinity with four Saints* and an *Annunciation with Saints John the Baptist and Stephen*, both 15C Florentine works.

On a nearby hill is **San Cresci**, a Romanesque church in a beautiful position. The 12C façade has the unusual feature of a narthex and brick decoration round the entrance and window arches. The interior has undergone numerous alterations over the centuries and what we see is mostly 19C. Some damaged remains of early frescoes have been uncovered under whitewash. A beautiful unsurfaced road continues, through woods, to Badia a Passignano (see p 149).

The area around Greve is particularly rich in medieval castles, mostly privately owned, each surrounded by its estate which produces its own wine.

To the north, by-roads lead off on the right to the former castle of **Uzzano** (☎ 055 853 032), now transformed into a villa with a porticoed courtyard. The drive uphill through woods and cypress trees offers some splendid views.

Nearby is the romantic-looking fortified farmhouse of **Colognole** (private) at the end of a long cypress alley. Beyond is the elegant **Villa Calcinaia**, for centuries the property of the Capponi family, with fine gardens (☎ 055 853 008).

Further north are the castles of **Verrazzano** (☎ 055 853 049) and **Vicchiomaggio** (☎ 055 853 003), both in fine positions. On the main road is the **Passo dei Pecorai** (344m), off which is the castle of **Gabbiano** (☎ 055 821 053) with four round corner towers and an impressive towered entrance. On the road to Impruneta are terracotta furnaces at **Ferrone**.

On the Via Chiantigiana, 2km beyond Chiocchio, is a pretty road running parallel to the Sezzate river. The impressive castle of **Mugnana** (private), surrounded by cypress trees, faces the little medieval village of **Sezzate** across the valley. Further along is the villa and little church of **Cintoia** with its castle, or fortified village, on the hill. Just before reaching La Panca, a by-road leads to the Vallombrosan abbey of **Montescalari** (698m), incorporated into 17C farm buildings.

Off the road to San Polo in Chianti are by-roads for **Castel Ruggero** (☎ 055 642 976), **Villa Tizzano** with the little church of Santo Stefano, and the **Fattoria di Vitiano** (☎ 055 855 037), all with fine views. The main road continues via Strada and Grassina to Florence.

Panzano

Panzano (498m), originally a medieval castle, still preserves some of its old walls and towers. Its strategic and picturesque position is best appreciated on the approach from San Casciano. There is one main street leading to the church of **Santa Maria** which was completely renovated a century ago. It has a late Gothic *Madonna and Child* attributed to Bernardo di Stefano Rosselli encased in a larger picture with saints and angels. In the nearby oratory is an *Annunciation* attributed to Michele di Ridolfo del Ghirlandaio.

Approximately 1km south of Panzano is its *pieve*, **San Leolino**, beautifully situated on a hill. This fine Romanesque church (the elegant portico was added in

---

Agriculture in the Chianti region

The agricultural landscape of Tuscany has changed since the 1950s and 1960s when the centuries old sharecropping (*mezzadria*) system of farming came to an end. Until then the peasant families of Tuscany had lived on small holdings (*poderi*) taking a proportion of the crops in return for their work for the landowner. As a result the land was intensely cultivated, often in terraces, with small vineyards, olive groves, and orchards of fruit trees and vegetables. White oxen were used to till the land. With the growth of industrialisation and the booming economy in the post-war years many tenant farmers left the rural life of the country for the towns. Although a few small *poderi* can still be seen, characterised by the variety of crops grown in a small area, with the vines often strung between olive and fruit trees, most of the cultivated land in Tuscany is now owned by large estates surrounded by extensive vineyards which have considerably altered the look of the countryside, particularly in the Chianti region. Many producers now sell their wine and other products directly from their farms (*fattorie*). The beautiful old farm houses (*case coloniche*) and their outhouses, where once the peasants lived with their familes above the stables and barns, are now being restored and bought up by wealthy Italians and foreigners or developed for agriturist accommodation.

the 16C) has a nave and two aisles terminating in three apses; a little door in the right aisle leads to the cloister. The church has several interesting works: an altarpiece of the *Madonna between Saints Peter and Paul*, and stories from their lives, attributed to Meliore di Jacopo (mid-13C), a triptych by the Maestro di Panzano (15C), a *Madonna enthroned with two angels* of the 15C Florentine school, a polyptych over the high altar by Mariotto di Nardo, and two glazed terracotta tabernacles attributed to Giovanni della Robbia. On the left wall is a reliquary bust of St Euphrosynus. This bishop saint was venerated in a nearby oratory, 1km further south off the main road, behind which is a little Romanesque chapel with a carved altar over a well, whose waters were believed to be miraculous.

All around Panzano are numerous villas and *case coloniche* in beautiful countryside. To the north is the 15C villa of **Vignamaggio**, which has a fine Italian garden (it can be visited, together with the cellars, by appointment ☎ 055 854 4840). The road continues towards the hills to the picturesque village of **Lamole**, with a pretty church in the piazza which has a 15C polyptych.

West of Panzano, off the road to Badia a Passignano, is **Rignana** (☎ 055 852 065), a little group of farm buildings and a medieval tower. Concerts are given in summer in the nearby church of Santa Maria.

Radda in Chianti

Radda in Chianti, another major wine centre, was the principal castle of the Chianti League in the 13C. Although something survives of its walls and fortifications, the medieval hill town has been extensively transformed. In the central piazza is the 15C **Palazzo del Podestà** which has numerous coats of arms on its façade; there is a fine view from the main hall. Opposite are steps leading to the heavily restored church of **San Niccolò**. Outside the town, near the sport fields, is the church of **Santa Maria al Prato**, originally Romanesque but rebuilt in the 17C with the addition of a portico. The adjoining convent of **San Francesco** is destined to become a museum for works of art from churches in the district.

The **Castello di Volpaia** (☎ 0577 738 066) stands in a splendid panoramic position (617m). Wine has been produced here since the 11C. In the tiny fortified hamlet there is a small Renaissance church called La Commenda. Modern art exhibitions are held here in September.

South of Radda is the **Villa Vistarenni** (☎ 0577 749 439). Its monumental 16C façade rises majestically above the surrounding vineyards. The villa originally belonged to the Strozzi family and has fine cellars excavated in the underlying rock, which can be visited.

The **Badia di Coltibuono** (628m), a former Vallombrosan abbey, is surrounded by beautiful oak and pine woods. The monastery has been transformed into a villa (with a restaurant and wine cellars). The main structure in grey stone dates from the 11C–12C and it has an impressive crenellated tower; the church can also be visited.

Gaiole in Chianti owes its importance as a market town to its position as a crossroads between the Chianti district and the upper Arno valley. The surrounding area is very beautiful. On a hill to the west is the medieval castle of **Vertine**. Just east of Gaiole is the village of **Barbischio**, picturesquely perched on a hill covered with rocks and wild vegetation. The impressive castle of **Meleto** (private), to the south, is one of the best preserved castles originally forming part

The wines of Tuscany

The world-famous **Chianti red wine** is produced from a careful blend of white and black grapes perfected over many centuries: it was already exported to England in the 17C. The blend is composed of black *Sangiovese* grapes, black *Canaiolo* grapes (traditionally grown in Tuscany), and white *Trebbiano* and *Malvasia* grapes. Only wine produced from grapes grown in a limited geographical area (first officially established in 1716 and the boundaries redrawn in 1932) can bear the label of the black rooster on a yellow ground in a red circle and be called *Chianti Classico gallo nero*. This area, which is strictly controlled, includes San Casciano Val di Pesa, Greve, Castellina, Radda, Gaiole, Castelnuovo Berardenga, Barberino Val d'Elsa, Tavarnelle and Poggibonsi. The other Chianti wines, some of which rival the *classico*, include *Chianti Colli Aretini*, *Chianti Colli Fiorentini*, *Chianti Colli Senesi*, *Chianti Montalbano*, and *Chianti Rufina*. The bright ruby-red Chianti is drunk younger than most French wines. It has between 11.5 and 13 degrees of alcoholic content, and normally is unsuitable for long storage.

The soil and climate of this area of Tuscany is particularly adapted for the vines, which have been planted here since Etruscan times. The grape harvest (*vendemmia*) takes place for a few weeks, usually in late September or early October when the grapes are fully ripe and the weather sunny and dry. The wine-making process usually includes a double fermentation (known as the *governo*).The very best wine is produced in small orchards where the vines are strung between olive trees and the land between them cultivated. However, nowadays most of the wine is produced in extensive vineyards, intensely cultivated on the hillsides. Sulphite free wine is now unfortunately difficult to find, although often it is possible to purchase excellent locally produced wine which is not bottled but can be bought in bulk from small farms. The larger estates now often only sell bottled wine, and organise wine tasting and tours of the cellars (see p 137).

Vin Santo is an amber dessert wine (17–18 degrees of alcoholic content) produced in Tuscany and Umbria, in particular in the Chianti region (and at Carmignano), similar in taste to an excellent sherry. It is made from selected white bunches of grapes which are laid out on cane mats to dry in the autumn sun after the *vendemmia*. After a few months, usually before Christmas, they are pressed two or three times and the grape-juice or must (*mosto*) is then stored in small casks (*caratelli*), preferably made out of chestnut or oak, and sealed with cement. It is then aged for a minimum of three years (but sometimes for as long as 20 years) in a room, usually indoors under the eaves of the roof (in a place subject to the varying temperature of the seasons) rather than in a wine cellar.

Vin Santo is thought to have acquired its name through its association with Holy Week (*La Settimana Santa*) when the wine was usually transferred to bottles, but others maintain that it was called 'Santo' because it was the wine which was normally used at Mass. Yet another theory is that the name comes from the Greek island of Xanthos where a similar wine was made.

Many small wine producers still make excellent Vin Santo for home consumption, but it is also produced on a commercial scale. It is often served with dry almond biscuits (*biscotti di Prato* or *cantuccini*) at the end of a meal.

of the Chianti League. It has two massive circular towers, one of which still has its original defences, dominating extensive vineyards. The interior was transformed into a villa in the 18C.

On the road between Radda and San Sano, in a beautiful setting, is one of the oldest Romanesque churches in the Chianti district, **San Giusto in Salcio**. Together with its impressive bell-tower, it has been extensively restored in recent times.

San Polo in Rosso (☎ 0577 746 070) is another interesting early *pieve*. It was formerly situated on the boundary separating the territories of Florence and Siena and was therefore incorporated into a fortified *castello*, probably in the 13C. The picturesque group of buildings includes an interesting bell tower and a cloister.

One of the most impressive castles in the Chianti is the **Castello di Brolio** (open daily, except Fri, 10.00–12.00, 15.00–18.00), the home of the Ricasoli family since the 12C, and well-known for its wine. Strategically placed at the south end of the Chianti hills, it was for centuries disputed between Florence and Siena. The impressive fortifications surrounding the castle date in part from the 15C–16C but were heavily restored in the 19C. The palace was rebuilt in 1862–72 by Pietro Marchetti in Sienese Gothic style for Bettino Ricasoli, the eminent statesman and philanthropist, who died here in 1880. The 14C chapel contains a polyptych by Ugolino di Nerio (14C); in the crypt are the family tombs. The dining room was modelled on the medieval hall of an English castle and contains paintings by Pietro Aldi (1876). The magnificent view to the south stretches from Monte Amiata to Siena and the hills beyond.

To the south is **San Gusmé**, one of the most picturesque villages in the area, surrounded by its original walls complete with two gateways. An excellent white wine (Val d'Arbia) is produced in this area.

Further south is **Castelnuovo Berardenga**, where little survives of the 15C castle, except for the clock-tower and a stretch of walls and a watch tower. The church of **Santi Giusto e Clemente** has a neo-Classical façade. Inside is a *Madonna and Child* by Giovanni di Paolo, signed and dated 1426 and a *Madonna* by Andrea di Niccolò, removed from the nearby Pieve di Pacina. The **Villa Chigi** has gardens which may be visited on Sundays (10.00–dusk).

At **Montaperti**, west of the river Arbia, is the hill where the Florentine Guelf army was defeated by Siena and Florentine exiles on 4 September 1260 in the battle, dramatically referred to by Dante (*La Divina Commedia*; *Inferno*, X, 85). A pyramid commemorates the battle. Nearby is the **Pieve di Sant'Ansano** (founded in the 7C). A footpath leads to an octagonal chapel over the spot where St Ansanus, first patron saint of Siena, was allegedly martyred in the 4C.

Castellina in Chianti

Castellina in Chianti (578m) is a small well kept medieval town, with a 15C castle and town gate, which dominates the Arbia, Elsa, and Pesa valleys, with spectacular views of woods, vineyards, olive groves, and scattered *case coloniche*. It has a modern suburb which meets the demands of the expanding wine trade, and smart shops which cater for its many visitors. On the northern side the 15C defence walls are relatively well preserved, and a remarkable walkway (Via delle Volte) follows the eastern line of walls. The castle (now the town hall) has a tower and battlements;

Olive oil

Some of the best Italian olive oil is produced in Tuscany, much of it in this region. The olives, which are at first green and then turn black as they ripen, are still harvested by hand so as not to damage the trees: ladders are propped up against the trees from which the olives are picked into baskets, and sheets (sometimes parachutes left over from the Second World War) spread out on the ground beneath to collect the olives as they fall. The harvest, in late autumn, usually takes many weeks or even months. The olives are then taken to an olive press, once a stone mill worked by mules, but now mechanically operated. To facilitate the pressing the olives are usually slightly heated, but purists make sure the temperature of the olives is not altered. The oil straight from the first pressing is the best and can be labelled *olio extra vergine di oliva* if its acidity is less than 1 per cent. When newly pressed it has a bright green colour and a particularly aromatic flavour. Its qualities are especially appreciated on garlic toast (*bruschetta* or *fettunta*) or as a dip for raw vegetables (*pinzimonio*).

The land is usually left to rest until February when the soil is dug and loosened around the large roots of the olive trees and then fertilised. The pruning of the trees in March is a very long and laborious process done with a hand-saw and secateurs. The branches are then sprayed with copper sulphate.

The olive oil of Tuscany is considered one of the best in Italy, with a particularly strong flavour, and this is the most northerly part of the country where olive trees thrive (in northern Italy the climate is too cold, except for a few very limited areas such as Liguria and around Lake Garda). The trees, if carefully tended, usually flourish and bear fruit for hundreds of years, although an exceptionally harsh winter in 1984 killed numerous olive trees in Tuscany (many of these have been replanted and are beginnng to bear fruit). Low hills are the ideal terrain for olives. Olive oil, which is expensive even in Italy, is recognised for its exceptional nutritional value and as one of the most healthy vegetable oils, both in its raw state and when heated for cooking or frying. It is the basis of Italian cuisine, and replaces butter in the Mediterranean diet. Local recipes provide numerous different ways of preserving or pickling the olives both when still green and when they ripen and become black, to be eaten as hors-d'oeuvre.

it houses a small Etruscan museum. In the parish church (rebuilt after the last war) is a detached fresco of the *Madonna and Child* by Lorenzo di Bicci, and the shrine of St Fausto, invoked either in times of torrential rain or drought.

Just outside the town is the impressive Etruscan tomb of **Montecalvario** (7C BC) surrounded by pine trees. The tumulus has a diameter of 50 metres and has four tombs connected by covered passages. Remains of the Etruscan town walls and a well have also been discovered.

A particularly beautiful road descends westwards to Poggibonsi (see p 420) past the little 12C Romanesque church of **San Pietro a Cedda**. It has carved architraves over the front and side doors, a square bell-tower, and an apse decorated with blind arcades. The simple interior (open only for Mass on Sat at 17.30, and Sun at 10.30) is built entirely of stone, with a timber roof. A large transversal arch resting on the elaborately carved capitals of two half columns divides the nave. The apse has a lancet window and delicately carved decoration. There are two frescoes of saints (15C) and a reproduction of a triptych now in the Museo Civico of Colle Val d'Elsa. A little beyond is a fine view of the castle of Strozzavolpe on a hill to the left (described on p 420).

The Via Chiantigiana south of Castellina runs along a ridge offering a variety of extensive views, passing the little hamlet of **Fonterutoli** and crossing the village of **Quercegrossa**. Here, in the Romanesque church is a group of painted terracotta figures attributed to Francesco di Giorgio Martini representing the *Lamentation of the dead Christ*.

Farther south, in beautiful countryside and with a lovely view of Siena, is the **Certosa di Pontignano**, a monastery founded in 1343 and enlarged in the 15C and 16C. It is now attached to Siena University and used for conferences. A fine Renaissance cloister leads to a smaller cloister surrounded by a portico and an upper loggia. A third cloister has remains of frescoes by Bernardino Poccetti. The church also has frescoes by Poccetti and other artists and some fine carved choirstalls by Domenico Atticciati all dating from the 16C. Another chapel has a *Crucifixion* by Francesco Vanni and works by Giuseppe Nicola Nasini.

San Casciano in Val di Pesa and Tavarnelle

This beautiful district, offering spectacular views of the delightful countryside, is also in the Chianti area (see p 136). The chapter focusses on places near the Via Cassia (N1), a Roman road from Rome to Florence, paved c 154 BC, which runs through splendid countryside and passes many places of interest. Both San Casciano and Tavarnelle now have interesting small diocesan museums, and San Donato in Poggio is a particularly well preserved village.

Practical information

Getting there
By car

The Via Cassia or the Via Chiantigiana (see p 136) are by far the most pleasant routes between Florence and Siena. The **superstrada** which runs roughly parallel to the Cassia and has exits at all the main places of interest, is a poorly engineered road, with no emergency lane, and is usually very busy. It has no service stations.

By bus

Frequent bus services run by *SITA*. From Florence via Porta Romana, Galluzzo, San Casciano, San Donato in Poggio, to Tavarnelle in 1hr 20mins; also via Sant'Andrea in Percussina to San Casciano and Mercatale.

Information offices

APT of Florence (☎ 055 290 832). Local tourist offices in San Casciano Val di Pesa (☎ 055 822 9558) and Tavarnelle (☎ 055 807 7832).

Where to stay
Hotels

SAN CASCIANO IN VAL DI PESA ✦✦✦ *L'Antica Posta*, Piazza Zannoni 1 (☎ 055 822 313; 📠 055 822 278).
TAVARNELLE ✦✦ *Torricelle Zucchi*, a particularly well-run hotel, Via Cellini 32 at Sambuca (☎ 055 807 1780; 📠 055 807 1102).

Agriturismo

Agrirismo accommodation is widely available (information from the local tourist offices).

Youth hostel

TAVARNELLE *Ostello del Chianti*, Via Roma 137 (☎ 055 807 7009).

Campsites

BARBERINO VAL D'ELSA ✦✦ *Semifonte*, Via Ugo Foscolo 4 (☎ & 📠 055 807 5454; open March–Nov).
MARCIALLA *Toscana Colliverdi* (☎ 0571 669 334; open March–Sept).

Eating out
Restaurants

SAN CASCIANO €€ *Cantinetta del Nonno*, Via IV Novembre 18; *Nello*, Via IV Novembre 64; *Malia sul Ponte*, Via Scopeti 130;

and *Matteuzzi*, Via Certaldese 8. For restaurants in **Cerbaia**, see p 153.
SANT'ANDREA IN PERCUSSINA €€ *Scopeti*.
MERCATALE €€ *Il Salotto del Chianti*, Via Sonnino 92.
BARGINO €€ *del Pesce*, excellent fish restaurant.
TAVARNELLE €€ *La Gramola*, Via delle Fonti 1; at La Romita, 3km north: €€ *La Fattoria*; at **MARCIALLA** 4km west: € *Il Frantoio*.
BADIA A PASSIGNANO €€ *La scuderia*; at Rignana, 3km south. €€ *La Cantinetta*.
SAN DONATO IN POGGIO €€ *Villa Francesca* and €€ *La Toppa*. An excellent cheap pizzeria at the Circolo open at weekends in winter; in summer it is operated by volunteers from the Unione Sportiva next to the playing field (daily in June and July). Between San Donato and Panzano at La Piazza, €€ *Osteria della Piazza*.
LUCARDO € *C'era una volta*.
BARBERINO VAL D'ELSA €€ *La Bustecca* (also pizzeria); € *Pizzeria l'Archibugio*.

Annual festivals

At Badia a Passignano a **chamber music festival** is held at Pentecost (early June); information from the *Amici della Musica*, Tavarnelle Val di Pesa (☎ 055 807 6426). A three-day **country fair** (*Giardino in fiore*) is held in late September at Villa Le Corti near Mercatale.

San Casciano in Val di Pesa

San Casciano in Val di Pesa is a small town (14,500 inhab.) situated on a hill which dominates the beautiful hilly landscape of the Chianti district with extensive views all around. From a signposted car park steps lead up to the town centre. Inside the walls it is a short walk to Piazza Pierozzi where an archway, beneath the clock-tower, leads to the **Collegiata**, rebuilt in 1793 on the site of a Romanesque church. Over the baptismal font is a fresco of the *Madonna and Child with Saints John the Baptist and Stephen* by an early 15C Florentine master. Above the high altar is a painted wood *Crucifix* by the workshop of

Baccio da Montelupo, and, in the choir, *Glory of St Cassiano* by Luigi Pistocchi. On the altar to the left is a detached fresco of the *Madonna and Child* (c 1500) and on the left wall of the nave, an *Annunciation* by Fra Paolino.

The church of **Santa Maria del Gesù** (known as Il Suffraggio), in Via Roma, is now the **Museo di Arte Sacra** (open Sat 16.30–19.00; fest. 10.00–12.30, 16.00–19.00). The museum contains works from San Casciano and from many of the nearby country churches. Inside, on the high altar, *Madonna and Child* by Lippo di Benivieni, and other 15C and 16C paintings including a *Coronation of the Virgin* by Neri di Bicci (1481) in the nave. In a little room to the right is a polychrome marble statue of the *Madonna and Child* inscribed Gino Micheli (1341).

In the adjoining **oratory** are two important paintings: a *Madonna and Child* by Ambrogio Lorenzetti, one of the artist's earliest works, dated 1319, and the **San Michele altarpiece**, a rare 13C Florentine work, attributed to Coppo di Marcovaldo, both from the church of Sant' Angelo at Vico l'Abate. Other interesting gold-ground panels include *Madonnas* by the Master of the Horne Triptych, Jacopo del Casentino and Cenni di Francesco, a *Crucifix* attributed to the Master of San Lucchese, a triptych by the Master of San Iacopo a Mucciana and the *Martyrdom of St Lucy* by Simone Pignoni. The marble pedestal, possibly of a baptismal font, is composed of carvings representing the *Annunciation, Nativity*, and *Annunciation to the Shepherds*, attributed to the Master of Cabestany (French or Spanish, second decade of the 12C). There are a number of showcases on the upper floor, displaying liturgical objects, church silver, and vestments.

From Piazza Pierozzi Via Morrocchesi leads to the church of the **Misericordia** (Santa Maria del Prato), a 14C Gothic church rebuilt in the late 16C (if closed, entrance through the adjacent Confraternity). The church has several fine works (well labelled): a painted *Crucifix with the mourning Virgin and St John* by Simone Martini (c 1325); *Madonna and Child, St Francis and St Peter* by Ugolino di Nerio; an enthroned *Madonna with Saints and Angels*, dated 1516, by a Florentine artist; other 17C paintings by Francesco Furini, Rutilio Manetti and Jacopo Vignali; marble **pulpit** with reliefs representing the *Annunciation* by Giovanni di Balduccio (1339).

Outside the old walls, next to a terrace with a fine view, is the church of **San Francesco** (founded 1492). The church was renovated and the portico added in the 18C. Inside, on the left, is an altarpiece of the *Madonna and Child between Saints Francis and Mary Magdalen* by Biagio d'Antonio, and, right, a Sienese *Crucifix* (c 1360).

Environs of San Casciano

On the pretty road leading west to Cerbaia are several Romanesque churches in picturesque settings. They are generally open only for services on Sunday morning, but at other times ring at the priest's house. Most of their contents have been removed for safe keeping to the museum in San Casciano (see above).

Just outside San Casciano a narrow by-road diverges steeply left (signposted Vivai Orlandi) to **Santa Maria ad Argiano**, a Romanesque church largely rebuilt in the 18C. The church of **San Martino ad Argiano** has a Romanesque façade with terracotta decorations and an 18C portico. Next to it is the Oratory of the Santissima Annunziata, which has fine 17C furniture, an *Annunciation* by Cesare Dandini and a painting of *Saints Augustine, Ambrose, and Carlo Borromeo* by

Fabrizio Boschi. A cypress avenue leads to the villa and church of **San Pietro a Montepaldi**, with a simple Romanesque façade and Baroque interior.

Near Talente is **San Giovanni in Sugana**, one of the oldest and most important Romanesque churches in the diocese of Florence. It was considerably restored and provided with a cupola in the 16C. It contains some glazed terracotta works by the della Robbia and Buglioni, and a *Crucifixion* by Pier Dandini. It preserves parts of its original structure and has an elegant 16C cloister with an upper loggia, carved doorways and a two-light Romanesque window. **Cerbaia**, on the Via Volterrana, is described on p 155.

To the north of San Casciano, in woods, is the hamlet of **Sant'Andrea in Percussina** with the *Albergaccio* where Niccolò Machiavelli lived in exile from Florence in 1513 and wrote *Il Principe*. The hostelry (☎ 055 828 471) here succeeds the one frequented by the politician and writer. The Romanesque church of Sant'Andrea has an elegant Renaissance interior with a small dome, a 17C *Presentation in the Temple* and some fragmentary frescoes (14C–15C).

Nearer Florence, at Spedaletto, a path leads to **Santa Maria a Casavecchia**, a Romanesque church beautifully situated with a view of Brunelleschi's dome in the distance. Inside is a relief of the *Assumption* in glazed terracotta by Benedetto Buglioni (c 1515). Off the Via Cassia, following the road to Greve just beyond Tavarnuzze is the **US Military Cemetery** with the graves of 4403 American soldiers who died in service north of Rome in 1944–45 (open daily 08.00–17.00). At the **Terme di Firenze** there is a public swimming pool.

On the northern outskirts of San Casciano is the Romanesque church of **Santa Cecilia a Decimo**. A church existed here in the time of Charlemagne, but the present structure, including an impressive bell-tower, dates from the 12C. The portico was added in the 16C. The interior, elegantly decorated with stuccowork (1728) has a nave and two aisles separated by arches. On the altar is a *Madonna and Child with Saints Lawrence and Cecilia* by Michele di Ridolfo del Ghirlandaio. The small fresco of the *Madonna and Child* is by Cenni di Francesco. Behind the church are picturesque old farm buildings.

A pretty road leads south from San Casciano to Certaldo. It passes the tiny village of **San Pancrazio**. In a little piazza at the top of the hill is the Romanesque *pieve* (10C) beside a fortified tower (the key may be obtained from the priest's house next door). It has a 17C portico, but the nave and aisles and two small apses correspond to the original structure. The paintings include a *Crucifixion* by Santi di Tito, 1590. In a nearby room are frescoes of the Liberal Arts and representations of Virgil, Dante and Petrarch attributed to Cosimo Gheri who also painted two altarpieces for the church.

Lucardo, a hamlet with remains of a castle, is beautifully situated on a hill overlooking the Pesa and Elsa valleys. The interior of the church of San Martino (key from the canonica) was renewed in the Baroque period and decorated with stucco-work. There are several paintings, including a *Madonna and Child with Saints Peter, John the Baptist, Martin, and Justus* attributed to Ridolfo del Ghirlandaio. A record of the castle, of which only a tower and parts of the walls now survive, dates from the 8C.

A little further south, beyond a handsome *casa colonica* with a tower, an unsurfaced road leads to the **Pieve di San Lazzaro a Lucardo**, dating from the late

11C. It is a fine example of early Romanesque architecture, surrounded by medieval buildings and an impressive tower (the upper part is restored) next to the remains of the former cloister. The church is built entirely of sandstone and has a basilican plan with a nave and two aisles divided into seven bays by pillars, and a raised chancel terminating in three apses. The crypt was discovered during restoration work. There are frescoes on the left wall and on two pilasters by Cenni di Francesco. The porch over the entrance was added in the 19C. The road continues through rolling countryside, with a view of San Gimignano, as it approaches Certaldo (see p 156).

On the road to Mercatale, east of San Casciano, is the 16C **Villa Le Corti**, attributed to Santi di Tito, belonging to the Corsini family (a country fair, 'Giardino in fiore' is held here in September). Just before reaching Mercatale an unsurfaced road diverges left to **Luiano**. Here, near a group of houses beside a villa, is the small Romanesque church of Sant'Andrea (11C) at the end of a footpath. It is one of the earliest churches in the Florentine diocese, and maintains its Romanesque structure and plan. The exterior, in white *alberese* stone, is well preserved. There is a fine view towards Impruneta.

Beyond Mercatale, at the crossroads known as Le Quattro Strade, the road to the right leads past an old fortified farmhouse to **Santo Stefano a Campoli**, dating from the 12C. It has a 17C portico, and the interior was remodelled in the 18C (key in the afternoons from the house next door). It contains a *Madonna and Child with Saints*, attributed to Franciabigio and a small 15C *Madonna and Child with the infant St John*. From Le Quattro Strade there is a beautiful road to Panzano (see p 139).

Tavarnelle

The main road runs through the long village of Tavarnelle at the south end of which is the church of **Santa Lucia a Borghetto**. This Franciscan church, first recorded in the 13C, is one of the few examples of Gothic architecture in the district. Typically sober in form, and built from simple bricks and pebbles, it contains fresco fragments and a 14C Florentine painted *Crucifix*. Something survives of the former cloister on the right. The façade was considerably restored at the beginning of the 20C.

Off the main road at the north end of Tavarnelle, beyond the turning for Morrocco, is the Romanesque church of **San Pietro in Bossolo** in a lovely position. The church, preceded by a portico, is flanked by a tall bell-tower and the canonica which houses the **Museo di Arte Sacra**. The interior of the church, restored to its original aspect, is very simple and opens onto a small cloister.

The museum contains works of art and liturgical objects from churches in the district (open Sat 16.00–19.00; fest. also 09.00–13.00). The paintings include a *Madonna and Child* attributed to Meliore (c 1280); *Madonnas* by Rossello di Jacopo Franchi and the Master of Marradi; several altarpieces by Neri di Bicci from the convent of Morrocco (see below) which were commissioned in 1473–75 by Niccolò Sernigi whose portrait was also painted by the artist. There are paintings by the Master of Tavarnelle, Lorenzo di Bicci, Jacopo da Empoli, and a number of works by later Florentine artists. The liturgical objects include two **13C processional crosses**. There is a fine collection of church plate (15C–19C), vestments, ex-votos, and reliquaries.

At **Morrocco** is the Carmelite convent of Santa Maria del Carmine, founded in

1460. Since 1982 it has housed a small community of Discalced Carmelite sisters from Australia (Sunday Mass at 09.30; ☎ 055 807 6067). The church is flanked by a loggia with remains of 15C frescoes. Inside is a glazed terracotta della Robbian lunette of the *Annunciation* and a portrait in a garlanded tondo of Niccolò di Giovanni Sernigi, founder of the convent, by Andrea della Robbia.

Badia a Passignano

Near Sambuca a pretty by-road (signposted) leads uphill to the Badia a Passignano (341m), in a delightful setting, enclosed by cypress trees and surrounded by vineyards and olive groves. The monastery was founded in 1049 by an abbot of the Vallombrosan Order created by St Giovanni Gualberto, who died here in 1073 and was canonised in 1193. Little survives of the original monastery, except perhaps the crypt of the church of San Michele. The oldest parts, including the church façade and bell-tower, date from the later 13C but are much restored. The outer walls and cloisters were added in the mid-15C when the monastery was enlarged and later embellished with numerous frescoes. The two smaller towers and battlements we see today were added in the late 19C after the abbey was sold at auction and bought by a certain Count Dzieduszycki. The

Badia a Passignano

present Vallombrosan community was reinstated here in 1986 (the monastery is open to the public Sun afternoon, or on request, ☎ 055 807 1622). A **music festival** is held in the abbey in June (see Festivals, p 145).

At the end of a cypress avenue, beyond an arched doorway, is a large court-yard, with the abbey church of San Michele Arcangelo (described below). Opposite is the entrance to the **monastery**, giving on to a terrace and an Italian garden. A fine 15C stone doorway with a carved and inlaid door gives access to the **cloister**. The upper loggia, which was enclosed and provided with windows in the 18C, has frescoes of the *Life of St Benedict* by Filippo d'Antonio Filippelli (1483). The red brick dome of the church (described below), visible from the cloister, was added in 1602. The large **refectory** has a painted *cenacolo*, a life-size fresco representing the *Last Supper*, covering the end wall, by Domenico and Davide Ghirlandaio, dated 1476. The two lunettes above of *Adam and Eve driven out of Paradise* and *Cain slaying Abel* (1474) are by Bernardo di Stefano Rosselli. There are also remains of other frescoes, a carved stone pulpit and corbels and a monumental fireplace.

A small chapel, with a fresco of the *Annunciation* by Filippelli, has stairs leading to the church of **San Michele Arcangelo**. Originally Romanesque, it was remodelled in the late 16C. The choir-stalls were carved by a Vallombrosan monk, Michele Confetto, in 1549; the two altarpieces, separating the choir from the nave, representing the *Nativity* and the *Three Archangels* are by Michele di Ridolfo del Ghirlandaio. The impressive statue of St Michael the Archangel defeating the Dragon is a rare 13C marble sculpture which originally stood on the roof above the entrance to the church. It is the only important surviving work from the Romanesque monastery.

The spacious **sacristy**, off the south transept, dates from the 15C. It contains a stone tabernacle with painted wooden shutters made for St Giovanni Gualberto's reliquary bust. This superb work, composed of a silver and silver gilt head resting on a gilded base, was made in Siena in 1324–32. It is decorated with scenes from the saint's life in coloured enamel. The fine sacristy cupboards are by Domenico Atticciati (1580) and the eight small paintings are attributed to Francesco Curradi.

In 1598–1602 Domenico Cresti, the artist known as 'Il Passignano', who was born in the village, remodelled the east end of the church creating three chapels, a transept and a dome (frescoed by Giuseppe Nicola Nasini in 1706). Passignano was responsible for all the frescoes in the central chapel dedicated to St Michael: *God the Father in Glory* in the vault, the four *Cardinal Virtues* in the spandrels, and the *Evangelists* in painted niches. He also painted the three large altarpieces representing the *Apparition of St Michael on Mount Gargano* (right), the *Apparition of the Madonna* (centre), and *St Michael defeating Lucifer* (left). The statues of *Saints Peter and Paul* are by Andrea Ferruzzi.

The chapel on the right is dedicated to St Sebastian and St Atto, a Vallombrosan abbot. All the paintings, including the frescoes in the south transept illustrating the life of Atto, are by Benedetto Veli (1600).

The left-hand chapel is dedicated to St Giovanni Gualberto and contains his tomb which lies beneath a reclining marble figure by Giovanni Caccini (1580). The design of the chapel and the *Glory of the Saint* frescoed in the vault are by Alessandro Allori (1580), who also painted, with assistants, the scenes of the saint's life in the north transept, and the large fresco of the *Transportation of the Relics*, depicting numerous portraits of members of the clergy and congregation. The altarpiece of the chapel which shows Pope Celestino III proclaiming the saint's canonisation in 1193 is by Giuseppe Nicola Nasini (1709). The two other altarpieces representing the *Ordeal by Fire of St Peter Igneus* (right) and *Giovanni Gualberto forgiving his brother's murderer and praying before the Crucifix of San Miniato* (left) are by Giovanni Butteri (1600). Steps lead down to the small 10C crypt.

The little village church of **San Biagio**, approached by a flight of steps outside the abbey walls, dates from the 14C and has some remains of frescoes inside.

San Donato in Poggio

This is a charming fortified medieval village in a beautiful setting. A main street connects the two gates with the piazzetta in the centre, containing an elegant Renaissance palace, a well and a little Gothic church. There are remains of the old walls and many of the houses still preserve their original character.

Just outside the village is the *pieve*, a beautiful Romanesque church of the late 12C, with three apses, built out of large blocks of cream-coloured *alberese* stone. The upper part of the square crenellated tower is of darker stone. Inside, simple piers divide the aisles from the nave, which is considerably higher. A little chapel on the right contains a baptismal font by Giovanni della Robbia (1513) with reliefs of the *Life of St John the Baptist*, and a small collection of paintings among which is a *Coronation of the Virgin* by Giovanni del Biondo. Over the high altar is a *Crucifix* by a follower of Giotto.

On the road between San Donato and Castellina is the sanctuary of the **Madonna di Pietracupa** (open daily 11.00), a late-Renaissance church (1595) surrounded by a portico. Inside are three altarpieces by Passignano; the one on the high altar encloses a venerated image of the *Madonna*. The road continues to Castellina in Chianti (see p 142) along a ridge, with magnificent views across the Elsa valley towards San Gimignano and the hills beyond.

Just south of Tavarnelle is the little village of **Barberino Val d'Elsa**. It preserves its medieval defence walls and a gateway at either end of the main street, which is named after the poet Francesco da Barberino (1264–1348). The 14C **Ospedale dei Pellegrini** (pilgrims' hospice), just inside the walls, is now the public library. There are several elegant palaces (restored), including the **Palazzo Pretorio** with coats of arms on the façade. The church of **San Bartolomeo** was rebuilt by Giuseppe Castellucci at the beginning of this century. A *Madonna and Child* by Bicci di Lorenzo and a bronze bust of Beato Davanzato by Pietro Tacca are preserved in the canonica.

   South of Barberino is the **Pieve di Sant'Appiano**, a 10C Romanesque church extensively rebuilt in brick in the 12C after its tower fell down, destroying much of the original building. The interior is finely proportioned with brick columns separating the nave from the aisles, and carved capitals. To the right of the entrance from the Romanesque cloister is a marble tomb slab carved with the effigy of Raffaello Gherarduccio dei Gherardini (1331). The chapel left of the choir has remains of frescoes and a *Madonna and Child with Saints* by a 16C Florentine artist. Against the wall on the left is the shrine of St Appiano, which was originally under the main altar. According to tradition, St Appiano was the first evangeliser of the Val d'Elsa. In the nave are three frescoes of saints by the school of Ghirlandaio.

   The cloister, which still preserves a fine door and three windows of the original sacristy, leads to the canonica. It has a 15C hall with fresco decoration and the arms of the Catellini family, protectors of the *pieve*, and a small collection of paintings awaiting restoration. In front of the simple façade of the church are four columns which were part of the former baptistery (pulled down in the early 19C) which had an unusual octagonal plan with a dome and crypt. Next to the cloister an **antiquarium** contains Etruscan and Roman objects from the surrounding district (open Sat and Sun, 15.00–19.00). Nearby is the picturesque medieval village of **Linari**.

   A by-road leads west through beautiful countryside from Barberino Val d'Elsa to Certaldo passing the Villa di Petrognano before reaching a crossroads where there is a circular chapel surrounded by cypresses. It is known as **La Cupola** since it reproduces in miniature Brunelleschi's cupola of Florence cathedral. It has been restored, and forms a charming landmark. It was built in 1597 by Santi di Tito to commemorate the former town of **Semifonte**. Originally enclosed in star-shaped walls, in a strategic position close to the Francigena and Volterrana roads, Semifonte was the stronghold of the powerful Conti Alberti. It became such a threat to Florence that it was razed to the ground after a siege lasting four years which ended in 1202. Nearby is the church of **Santa Maria a Bagnano**. Its precious paintings are now in the museum at Certaldo (see p 157).

Castelfiorentino and Certaldo

These two small towns, both in the province of Florence, although little visited, contain important works of art. Castelfiorentino has frescoes by Benozzo Gozzoli and 18C Florentine artists, and Certaldo, where Boccaccio spent the last years of his life, has more frescoes by Gozzoli. Interesting early 16C sculptures can be seen at San Vivaldo.

Practical information

Getting there
By car

The Via Volterrana, considered one of the most beautiful roads in Tuscany, which links Florence to Volterra, runs through Castelfiorentino, and passes Cerbaia, Montespertoli, Gambassi Terme and Il Castagno. Certaldo is 9km south of Castelfiorentino on the N429.

By train

Services from Florence to Empoli in 20mins. From Empoli (with some through trains from Florence) to Castelfiorentino (in 15 mins) and Certaldo (in 30 mins).

By bus

Buses run by *SITA* (infrequent daily service) from Florence (via Porta Romana and Galluzzo) to Cerbaia, Montespertoli, Castelfiorentino, and Certaldo (in 1hr 40 mins). A service links Florence to Volterra along the Via Volterrana once a day (in 2hrs 40 mins).

Information office
APT of Florence (☎ 055 290 832). *Pro-loco* in Certaldo, Via Boccaccio 16 (☎ 0571 664 944).

Where to stay
Hotels

CASTELFIORENTINO ☆☆ *Lami*, Piazza Gramsci 82 (☎ & 📠 0571 640 76).
CERTALDO In Certaldo Alto: ☆☆ *Il Castello*, restaurant (☎ & 📠 0571 668 250) and *Osteria del Vicario*, rooms to let (☎ 0571 668 228).
GAMBASSI TERME has ☆ hotels.
MONTAIONE ☆☆☆ *Vecchio Molino* (☎ & 📠 0571 697 966).

Youth hostels

CASTELFIORENTINO *Ostello Castelfiorentino*, Via Roosevelt 26 and *Il Grande Prato*, Via dei Renai 11 (☎ 0571 617 44).
MONTAIONE *Peter Pan*, Via Marconi 25 (☎ 0571 628251, 📠 0571 629 176).
GAMBASSI TERME *Il Castagno*, Via Volterrana 28, località Castagno (☎ & 📠 0571 678 048).

Campsite

☆☆ *Toscana Colliverdi* (☎ 0571 669 334), 10km west of Certaldo at Marcialla (open March–Sept).

Eating out

MONTESPERTOLI €€ *La Terrazza*, Viale Matteotti. At Montagnana (Via Volterrana nord 145) €€ *Il Focolare*; € *Baccaiano* at Baccaiano.

CERBAIA €€€ *Tenda Rossa*, Piazza Monumento 9, considered by many to be one of the best restaurants in Tuscany.

Castelfiorentino

Castelfiorentino (population 17,500) is an industrial town on the river Elsa, with the old walled town above on a rocky spur. Originally a castle in a strategic position for the defence of Florence (hence its name), Castelfiorentino owed its importance to its position on the pilgrim road to Rome, the Via Francigena.

Santa Verdiana and the lower town

At the entrance to the lower town is the church of Santa Verdiana rebuilt in the 18C on the site of the former Romanesque church of Sant'Antonio. The elegant façade, with a portico, is by Bernardo Fallani and Giuseppe Manetti.

The interior is entirely decorated with frescoes by a group of 18C Florentine artists to an overall architectural design by Foggini which forms a unique and charming complex of exceptional freshness and luminosity. The nave vault, the twelve hemispherical domes of the side chapels and the paintings of the apse and altars depict the legend, miracles and apotheosis of Santa Verdiana. This local saint, after making a pilgrimage to Santiago di Compostela and another to Rome, chose to live the rest of her life as an anchoress in a walled-up cell (in the church crypt). Renowned for her holiness, Verdiana died c 1242 after living 34 years in the company of two snakes which were sent, in answer to her prayers, to try her patience.

The *Glory of St Verdiana* in the nave vault is by Alessandro Gherardini (1708), with painted architecture by Lorenzo del Moro. The cupola above the transept representing the saint received into heaven, is by Matteo Bonechi (1716). The small domes were frescoed by Giovanni Camillo Sagrestani, Agostino Veracini, Ranieri del Pace, Antonio Puglieschi, and Niccolò Lapi. The altarpieces include, Jacopo da Empoli, *Assumption of the Virgin* (enlarged by Gherardini a century later with the addition of putti); Orazio Fidani, *Ecstasy of St Francis* (1644); Simone Pignoni, *Charity of St Thomas of Villanova* (1664); Giovanni Martinelli, *Three Saints*; and Giovanni Domenico Ferretti, two *Scenes from the life of St Verdiana*.

Three large paintings dating from the 1630s (*Reclusion of St Verdiana* by Giovanni Battista Ghidoni, her death by Bartolomeo Salvestrini, and her funeral by Filippo Tarchiani), removed from the apse in the 19C, have been returned to their original frames, thus completing the recent restoration of the entire church.

In the canonica of Santa Verdiana a small **museum** has earlier works from the church, including paintings by Taddeo Gaddi, Taddeo di Bartolo, and Francesco Granacci. It also houses paintings and sculptures from the churches of Voltigiano, Cambiano, Ortimino, and Petrazzi, as well as illuminated manuscripts and liturgical objects.

Across the garden in front of Santa Verdiana is the apse of **San Francesco**, a 13C Franciscan church built in brick, which has 14C frescoes by Giovanni del Biondo.

Upper town

Signposts (Affreschi del Gozzoli) indicate the way to the upper town. Here at Via Tilli 41 (named after Michelangelo Tilli, the 17C physician, botanist, and philosopher) the **Biblioteca Comunale** (open Tues, Thur, and Sat 16.00– 19.00; fest. 10.00–12.00, 16.00–19.00) houses detached frescoes by Benozzo Gozzoli. The frescoes came from two chapels in the area. Those of the Tabernacle of the Madonna della Tosse come from Castelnuovo d'Elsa, a few kilometres north of Castelfiorentino. On the tabernacle vault is a figure of *Christ with the four Evangelists* above a trompe-l'oeil altarpiece representing the *Madonna and Child enthroned with Saints Peter, Catherine, Margaret and Paul* surrounded by angels holding up a red curtain. On the two side walls are the *Dormition of the Virgin* and her *Assumption*. The frescoes were painted by Benozzo Gozzoli and his workshop in 1484. The larger *Tabernacle of the Visitation*, dated 1490, was situated in Castelfiorentino, near the river. These frescoes, which had suffered from damp and flooding, were detached in 1965, uncovering the fine *sinopie*. Although in fragmentary condition, the surviving scenes illustrating the *Life of the Virgin* are a typical example of Gozzoli's charming narrative style. The episodes, painted in a rich range of colours, are transformed into scenes of everyday life, full of picturesque details, with architectural and landscape backgrounds. Benozzo Gozzoli, a pupil of Fra Angelico with whom he worked in Orvieto and Rome, is famous for his frescoes in the Medici-Riccardi chapel in Florence (1462). He travelled extensively, working in Pisa and in the Elsa Valley, assisted towards the end of his life by his sons.

Via Tilli leads into **Piazza del Popolo**. The clock tower of the **municipio** (on the left), has a bell which chimes every hour when the little seated soldier, called *Membrino*, strikes it with a hammer.

Steps lead up from the piazza to the Romanesque church of **San Leonardo**, whose interior was rebuilt in the 16C. It has a small dome which comes into view as you climb up the adjacent street leading to the 12C **Pieve di Sant' Ippolito** (originally San Biagio, the parish church of the medieval Castello). It stands at the top of a flight of steps in a beautiful panoramic position dominating the countryside and the towers and rooftops of the old town. The simple brick façade is decorated with a two-light window over the doorway and ceramic dishes. A marble inscription records the creation of the Tuscan League in 1197, the first Treaty between Volterra, Lucca, Siena, San Miniato, and Florence. The simple interior (extensively restored; if closed, the key is available from the old people's home next door) has fine proportions. Over the baptismal font is a frescoed lunette with a half-length figure of the *Dead Christ and two angels* (14C). Over the high altar is a *Crucifix* of the same period. On the left side of the church is a bell-cot with three bells, one of which is dated 1253. The elegant apse is visible from the garden (access from the church sacristy) which is partly enclosed by the old walls with remains of two towers.

North of Castelfiorentino, on the road to Castelnuovo d'Elsa, is the chapel of the **Madonna della Tosse**, where Benozzo Gozzoli's frescoes (see above) will eventually be reinstalled. Nearby is the **Pieve di Coiano** dedicated to Saints Peter and Paul, on a hill (182m). This ancient church, founded in the 11C, has a Pisan-type façade with a two-light window and remains of 14C frescoes.

Montespertoli

Montespertoli is a small market town between Castelfiorentino and San Casciano on the Via Volterrana, at the heart of an important wine-growing area (which produces *Chianti Putto*, *Chianti Colli Fiorentini*, *Montalbano* and *Galestro*, see p 141). The main piazza, forming a triangle with a well at the centre, has an interesting 17C building surrounding the **Oratory of the Misericordia** with two gabled clock-towers surmounted by small bells. Also facing the piazza is the church of **Sant'Andrea** (16C, but rebuilt after the Second World War) which has an early 12C baptismal font, decorated with marble inlay. Over the high altar is a 14C *Crucifix* and there is a damaged triptych by Niccolò Gerini.

South-west of Montespertoli (on the Tresanti road) is the *pieve* of **San Pietro in Mercato** which derived its name from the important market, held here until the late 15C (open Sun 11.00). Probably founded in the 10C, the present church was consecrated in 1057. It has a basilican plan with three apses and a nave and two aisles separated by simple arched piers. Left of the entrance, beneath a lunette with a fresco of the *Baptism of Christ* by the school of Ghirlandaio, is a 12C font, with geometrical motifs inlaid in coloured marble.

The **Museo di Arte Sacra** in the adjacent monastery houses works removed for protection from churches in the neighbourhood, including Sant'Andrea a Botinaccio, San Biagio a Poppiano, Santa Maria a Torri, San Bartolomeo a Tresanti, and San Giusto a Montalbino. There are some interesting gold-ground panels by Cenni di Francesco and Bicci di Lorenzo; a charming early painting of the *Madonna and Child* by Filippo Lippi; another *Madonna* by Andrea di Giusto; and altarpieces by Neri di Bicci. There is a 12C baptismal font, a della Robbia relief of *St Jerome in the desert*, liturgical objects (15C–18C), a 13C Limoges plate, fine processional Crosses, manuscripts and vestments.

In beautiful countryside east of Montespertoli on the road to San Casciano is **Poppiano**, a 13C castle belonging to the Guicciardini family, famous for its wine (*Chianti Colli Fiorentini*).

The Via Volterrana proceeds towards Florence past the **Villa of Montegufoni**, originally a medieval castle of the Accaiuoli family. Its tower, built in 1386, was modelled on that of Palazzo Vecchio in Florence. The story is told that the owner of the castle had taken an oath that if St Anthony answered his prayers he would never live out of sight of the tower of Palazzo Vecchio. When his prayers were granted he decided to build a copy of the tower in order to avoid moving from his country estate. The villa was rebuilt in the 17C, together with the little church of San Lorenzo which contains a fresco of *St Lawrence* by Gian Domenico Ferretti (1764) and a painted *Crucifix* by Taddeo Gaddi. The villa was purchased in 1910 by Sir George Reresby Sitwell (author of *An essay on the making of gardens*, 1909). He was father of the three well-known writers, Edith, Osbert and Sacheverell. Sir George spent 28 years restoring the castle, making pseudo-Gothic alterations, and redesigned the garden. He stayed on during the Second World War when many paintings from the Uffizi were stored here for safety. Osbert, who described the family holidays at the villa in his autobiography, died here in 1969 (it is now a hotel-residence).

Beyond Montagnana and **Cerbaia**, with a famous restaurant (see p 153) is the Romanesque church of **Sant' Alessandro a Giogoli** (12C), beautifully situated on a hill. From the Via Volterrana is a view of **I Collazzi** (private), one of the grandest Renaissance villas on the hills around Florence, built in the mid-16C on a project by Santi di Tito.

Certaldo

Like many other Tuscan towns, Certaldo (population 15,600) is divided between its medieval walled town on a hill and the modern residential and industrial suburb spread out below. Etruscan and Roman in origin, Certaldo was also situated on the Via Francigena.

Lower town

In the lower town is the main square, **Piazza Boccaccio** (car park), with a marble statue by Augusto Passaglia (1879) which was commissioned to mark the fifth centenary of the death of Giovanni Boccaccio.

Giovanni Boccaccio

The birth place of the celebrated author Giovanni Boccaccio (1312–75) is uncertain: Certaldo, Florence, or even Paris, where his Florentine father had mercantile interests. He lived most of his life in Florence and acted as ambassador for the city after 1350. He is famous for his *Decamerone* (1348–58), a brilliant secular work which established him as the father of Italian prose, and which had a great influence on European writers (including Chaucer). His close friends included Petrarch and Dante. He is known to have died at Certaldo.

The pseudo-Romanesque church of **San Tommaso**, patron saint of Certaldo, was founded in 1843.

Certaldo Alto

The charming medieval upper town, reached on foot in c 10min or by cablecar from the station in the main piazza (2min), built almost entirely of brick, is well preserved despite some damage during the Second World War. All the principal buildings, as well as some attractive houses, face onto Via Boccaccio.

Half-way up on the left is the **Casa del Boccaccio** (rebuilt in 1947), with a tower and loggia, which was bought and restored in the early 19C by Marchesa Carlotta dei Medici Lenzoni. Boccaccio is known to have spent part of his later years here (or in the contiguous house), enjoying a peaceful and simple life. He was buried in the nearby church. The house (open daily 09.00–12.00, 15.00–18.00) is now a museum and the *Centro Nazionale di Studi sul Boccaccio*, with a small library containing editions and translations of his writings. On the first floor is a fresco representing Boccaccio in his study which was commissioned from Pietro Benvenuti by the Marchesa Carlotta in 1826.

Facing onto the little piazza is the church of **Santi Michele e Jacopo**. The simple brick façade dates from the 13C and the interior has been restored to its original Romanesque appearance. In a niche is an urn containing the body of Beata Giulia, an Augustianian tertiary who lived thirty years walled up in a cell next to the sacristy in order to devote herself to prayer and meditation. Her death in 1367 was announced by the mysterious tolling of all the bells in Certaldo. The predella by an anonymous Florentine 15C artist on her altar depicts scenes from her life: Giulia saves a child by miraculously passing through a fire unscathed and thanks the children of Certaldo with flowers for having brought her bread. On the wall of the nave is a large glazed terracotta relief of the Madonna with two kneeling saints, and two small della Robbia tabernacles (c 1500), one on either side of the high altar. The marble bust of Giovanni Boccaccio, above an epitaph, is by Giovan Francesco Rustici (1503); his modern tombstone is now in the centre of the nave. To the left of the entrance is a niche with a charming fresco of the *Madonna and Child with Saints* by the 14C Sienese artist Memmo di Filippuccio.

Next to the church is a small cloister which gives access to the **Museo d'arte Sacra** inaugurated in 2001 (open daily 10.00–19.00). The museum has some fine and rare works which include: a monumental 13C **Crucifix;** paintings by Meliore, the Bigallo master, Puccio di Simone, and Ugolino di Nerio, most of them removed from churches in the countryside around Certaldo. The museum also has later paintings and sculptures; a fine collection of liturgical objects from the 12C–19C; vestments; and a silver reliquary head of Beata Giulia by Paolo Laurentini (1653).

At the top of the street is **Palazzo Pretorio**, originally the castle of the Conti Alberti, with its façade decorated with picturesque coats of arms in stone and glazed terracotta which record the Governors (*Vicari*) sent from Florence. The interior is open in summer 09.30–12.30, 16.30–19.30). Around the courtyard are the rooms where justice was administered, dungeons, and a chapel with a fresco of *Doubting Thomas* attributed to Benozzo Gozzoli. Several rooms have fine doorways, fireplaces and some fresco decoration. There is also a small collection of Roman and medieval finds from local excavations. A staircase leads up to the rooms of the former governors where temporary exhibitions are held. Through a garden is the entrance to the church of **San Tommaso** which has some interesting frescoes. Inside is displayed the Tabernacolo dei Giustiziati by Benozzo Gozzoli and Giusto d'Andrea, representing the *Deposition*.

A terraced garden and a walkway overlooking the town walls provide a splendid view stretching from the hills of the Val d'Elsa to San Gimignano.

Environs of Certaldo

Gambassi Terme is a small spa to the west of Certaldo which is known for its springs of *Acqua Pillo.* It has an attractive public garden outside the **Palazzo Civico** which houses a small collection of Etruscan and Roman finds excavated in the area. The town was already known in medieval times for its glass production (still manufactured here). It was the birthplace of Domenico Livi who made some of the stained-glass windows of Florence cathedral in the 1430s.

A short distance north of Gambassi on the road to Castelfiorentino is the **Pieve di Santa Maria a Chianni**, a Pisan-Romanesque church of the late 13C, with three orders of blind arches on the façade. The exterior is built of honey-coloured sandstone. Fine lancet windows and two tall half-columns with nteresting capitals decorate the exterior of the north transept. The Latin-cross interior has a basilican plan and raised chancel with a wide transept and five apses (the central apse was altered in the 16C). The columns dividing the nave from the aisles differ in type and size and have capitals decorated with floral, geometrical, and anthropomorphic motifs. There is a copy by Santi di Tito of Andrea del Sarto's Gambassi altarpiece depicting the *Madonna and Child surrounded by six Saints* (now in the Pitti Gallery in Florence).

Montaione, on a hill, now has an unattractive modern suburb. Etruscan and Roman in origin, the medieval **castle**, which had survived with its walls, towers and gates almost intact, suffered considerable damage in the Second World War. The old town has a simple plan of three parallel streets with a central piazza. The 13C church of **San Regolo**, was rebuilt in 1635 by Scipione Ammirato il Giovane, to a design perhaps by Bartolomeo Ammannati. The imposing bell-tower dates from 1795. In the church is a 13C *Madonna and Child* by a follower of Cimabue. The **Palazzo Pretorio** dates from the 15C and its façade is decorated with numerous coats of arms. It now houses a local **museum** (opened on request at the Comune, ☎ 0571 690 31), which contains an interesting collection of fossils, minerals, and prehistoric stone implements.

San Vivaldo

South of Montaione a road passes the public park of Poggio all'Aglione and continues through woods to San Vivaldo in the Bosco di Camporena. This was originally a hermits' retreat and is associated with Beato Vivaldo Stricchi of San Gimignano, a Franciscan tertiary, who was found dead in a hollow tree in 1320. A chapel was built on the spot under the custody of Franciscan friars. In 1500–15 a friar named Tommaso created here a mystical itinerary or ideal pilgrimage to the Sacro Monte, or Holy Mountain, of Jerusalem, with 30 chapels containing tableaux representing the Life and Passion of Christ. Not all of these survive but 18 have been restored. The sequence comprises the *Annunciation, Flight into Egypt, Supper in the house of Simon the Pharisee, Last Supper, the Prayer in the Garden, House of Pilate, Flagellation and Mocking of Christ, Jesus Condemned, Way to Calvary, Meeting with Mary His Mother, Meeting with the Holy Women, Veronica, Crucifixion, Deposition, Noli me Tangere, Doubting Thomas, Ascension* and *Pentecost*. The terracotta figures are mostly Florentine, from the della Robbia and Buglioni workshops, although a few are attributed to the Sienese sculptors Rustici and Cozzarelli.

The chapels lead to the 15C church of **Santa Maria in Camporena** with a portico. It has a Romanesque *Crucifix* and an altarpiece of the *Madonna and Child with Saints Jerome, Francis, and Vivaldo* by Raffaellino del Garbo.

West of San Vivaldo, in a more open landscape with clay downs and some interesting rock formations, is the hill-top village of **Castelfalfi** which has a little Romanesque church dedicated to St Florian.

The Via Volterrana (*Strada Provinciale* no. 4) passes through **Il Castagno**. There is a fine view of Volterra (see p 280), against a range of hills. The road continues west through wild and sparsely inhabited countryside and, after crossing the river Era, proceeds uphill past woods and olive groves. Volterra is approached from the northwest with the church of Santi Giusto e Clemente forming a prominent landmark. On either side are dramatic views of the precipices and eroded slopes of Le Balze.

Empoli, Vinci, and west of Florence

This area is little visited by tourists, but is easy to reach by public transport from Florence. Empoli has a fine church and museum, and Montelupo ceramics are well illustrated in that village in a museum. The village of Vinci in the lovely hills above the Arno is famous as the birthplace of Leonardo.

Practical information

Getting there
By car

The *superstrada* from Florence to Pisa which begins in the southern suburbs of Florence near Scandicci has exits at Montelupo Fiorentino and Empoli. The old road (N67) is not very attractive as it has been ribbon-developed and is lined with small factories.

By train

On the main line from Florence to Pisa. Frequent service to Empoli (in 20–30 mins; the railway station is 10 mins' walk from the Collegiata). Slow trains on this line also stop at Montelupo. One of the earliest lines in Italy, it was in fact a project by Robert Stephenson for the Tuscan grand-dukes (1838–40; completed in 1844–48). Empoli is also a junction for the Florence–Siena secondary line.

By bus

Lazzi runs services from Florence for Lastra a Signa, Montelupo, Empoli. From Empoli (*Lazzi* and *COPIT*) frequent services for Vinci (in 20mins).

Information offices

APT Florence (☎ 055 290 832). At Vinci, *Ufficio Turistico* (for Vinci, Empoli, Cerreto Guidi, and Montelupo), Via della Torre 11 (☎ 0571 568 012; 🖷 0571 567930; terredelrinascimento@comune.vinci.fi.it). Information office at Montelupo, Via Sinibaldi 74, ☎ 0571 518993; ✉ turismo@montelupoceramica.firenze.it.

Where to stay
Hotels

EMPOLI ☆☆☆ *Tazza d'oro*, Via Giuseppe del Papa 16 (☎ 0571 721 29; 🖷 0571 700 73); *Commercio*, Piazzetta Ristori 16 (☎ 0571 772 47; 🖷 0571 711 681); *Il Sole*, Piazza Don Minzoni 18 (☎ 0571 737 79; 🖷 0571 798 71). **VINCI** ☆☆☆ *Alexandra*, Via Martiri della Libertà 38, ☎ 0571 562 24; 🖷 0571 567 972; *Gina*, Via Lamporecchiana 27, ☎ 0571 562 66; 🖷 0571 567 913; and agriturist accommodation. **CERRETO GUIDI** ☆☆☆ *Il Tegolo*, Via Corliano 16 (☎ 0571 559 011, 🖷 0571 559 038), with restaurant. **MONTELUPO FIORENTINO** ☆☆☆ *Baccio da Montelupo*, Via Don Minzoni 3 (☎ 0571 512 15, 🖷 0571 511 71).

Youth hostel

FUCECCHIO Ponte a Cappiano, ☎ 0571 401 469.

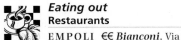

Eating out
Restaurants

EMPOLI €€ *Bianconi*, Via Tosco-Romagnola 70 (2km outside the town on the Florence road); *Il Galeone*, Via Curtatone e Montanara 67. € *Sant'Andrea*, Via Salvagnoli; *Il Petrarca*, Viale Petrarca 122; *Sciabolino*, Via Ormicello 14; *Da Cioffi*, Via Valdorme 333A. **VINCI** € *Il Nicchio* (Bar centrale), Via Fucini 16.

LASTRA A SIGNA €€€ *Antica*
Trattoria Sanesi, Via Arione 33.

Empoli

Empoli, 32km west of Florence, is a pleasant small town spaciously laid out (after damage in the Second World War) around two long parallel shopping streets either side of the small piazza which lies in front of the collegiata. It has long been famous for its glass factories, and is now an important commercial centre of the clothing industry.

History

In 1984 excavations revealed Roman remains in the centre of Empoli. The town grew up around the church of Sant'Andrea after 1119. Here in 1260 the Ghibelline party held their famous parliament after their victory at Montaperti; the proposal to raze Florence to the ground was defeated by Farinata degli Uberti, who is honoured for his protest by Dante (*Divina Commedia*, *Inferno*, X). Jacopo Chimenti, the painter, known as Empoli (1551–1640) was a native of the town.

The **glassworks** of Empoli have long been known for their production of green glass, including the characteristic wine fiasco (protected by straw) which was first produced here in large quantities at the beginning of this century. Glassworks still operating here include: **Consorzio Centrovetro**, Piazza Guido Guerra and **Consorzio Toscanavetro**, Piazza Gramsci; also at Monticiana, 6km outside the town.

From the station, the wide straight Via Roma leads to Piazza della Vittoria and the oratory of the **Madonna del Pozzo**, an unusual building by Andrea Bonistalli (1621). A long nave, surrounded on the exterior by a portico, precedes a pretty octagonal domed sanctuary. At no. 16 in the piazza is the musician **Ferruccio Busoni's House**, in which there is a small museum. As a pianist Busoni (1866–1924) was a child prodigy and he performed all over Europe. and is known also as a composer (his works include a piano concerto and *Doktor Faust*, an opera completed by a pupil in 1925).

From the right of the oratory Via Giuseppe del Papa leads to the Canto del Pretorio and **Piazza Farinata degli Uberti**, the pleasant arcaded central square. Here there is a large fountain with four amusing lions by Luigi Pampaloni (1827). There is also a local **Museum of Paleonthology** (open Thur, Sat & Sun 17.00–20.00) with a well illustrated collection of fossils from the Pliocene period, including numerous shells, found in central Tuscany.

The **Collegiata di Sant'Andrea**, documented as early as 780, was begun in its present form in 1093. The handsome black-and-white marble façade recalls that of San Miniato al Monte in Florence. It was probably begun in the mid-12C, and the upper part is a successful imitation of this style carried out when the church was enlarged in the 18C by Ferdinando Ruggeri. The marble portal dates from 1546.

The interior by Ruggeri has a ceiling painting by Vincenzo Meucci and Giuseppe del Moro which was reconstructed after severe damage in the last War. On the west wall, fresco of *Christ with instruments of the Passion* attributed to Raffaello Botticini.

South side. First chapel, venerated 14C *Crucifix*, and a painting of 1808 symbolising the recovery from the plague. Second chapel, interesting detached 14C Florentine fresco of the *Martyrdom of St Lucy* (with white oxen). On the high altar by Zanobi del Rosso (1785), triptych by Lorenzo di Bicci. On the east wall, fresco of the *Martyrdom of St Andrew* by Ferdinando Folchi (1862). To the left of the presbytery is the entrance to two oratories, the second of which is used as a sacristy. Here are the remains of a della Robbian tiled pavement around the altar. Outside the chapel at the end of the left transept is a very ruined fresco of *St Joseph* attributed to Empoli (right). The statuette of the *Madonna* on the altar (repainted) is attributed to the *bottega* of Buglioni.

North side. Fourth chapel, 17C painting of the *Madonna and Saints*, and (first chapel) reliquary cupboard of c 1724.

Museo della Collegiata di Sant'Andrea

In the courtyard (to the right of the façade) is the entrance to the *Museo della Collegiata di Sant'Andrea, one of the first local museums in Tuscany, founded in 1859. The museum contains fine works of art from the Collegiata and other churches in the area, as well as private donations: it was reopened in 1990 and the sculptures, frescoes, and paintings are beautifully displayed and well labelled Open 09.00–12.00, 16.00–19.00 except Mon. The ticket includes admission to the church of Santo Stefano degli Agostiniani (see below), usually only open 09.00–12.00.

Room 1 was formerly part of the church of San Giovanni Evangelista, transformed into a baptistery in the 15C and connected by a passageway to the Collegiata. Here is a ***font** dated 1447, an exquisite and unusual work attributed to Bernardo Rossellino. The *fresco of *Christ in Pietà* (detached from the window wall in 1946) is a superb work by Masolino (1424–25). Also here are frescoes and *sinopie* of *Saints* by Lo Starnina (1409).

Room 2: stoup of 1557; lectern of English workmanship donated to the Collegiata in 1520; bas-relief of the *Madonna and Child* attributed to Mino da Fiesole; small tondo of the *Madonna and Child*, an early work by Tino da Camaino; terracotta dossal of the *Madonna enthroned with Saints* attributed to Santi di Buglioni.

Room 3 contains 14C and 15C paintings. *Madonna and Child with Saints* by the 'Master of 1336' (Pistoian school), works by Niccolò di Pietro Gerini; *Crucifixion and Virgin of the Holy Girdle* by Lorenzo di Bicci. The early 15C painting for an altar step of the *Miracle of the Almond Tree and the brotherhood of the Compagnia del Crocifisso* depicts a miracle which took place in Empoli in 1399. The brothers (shown in hooded white cloaks) were on their way to Val di Marina to invoke the end of a plague which was afflicting the inhabitants of Empoli. They leant their crucifix against a dead almond tree which miraculously came into flower, signalling the end of the plague. Also here, *Madonna del Latte* attributed to Ambrogio di Baldese; triptych attributed to Agnolo Gaddi; *Saints* by Cenni di Francesco; *Madonna and Child* by Mariotto di Nardo. The polychrome wood statue of *St Stephen is signed and dated 1403 by Francesco di Valdambrino.

Room 4. Triptych by Rossello di Jacopo Franchi; *Saints* by the Maestro di Signa; *Madonna enthroned with Saints* by Lorenzo Monaco; *Madonna enthroned between Angels and Saints*, a very small work by Filippo Lippi; **Madonna of Humility with four Saints* (1404) by Lorenzo Monaco; *Madonna and Saints* by Bicci di Lorenzo. The polychrome wood statue of the penitent

*Magdalene (dated 1455) is attributed to Don Romualdo da Candeli and Neri di Bicci. **Room 5** displays works by Francesco Botticini and his son Raffaello, including an *Annunciation, and angel musicians, Saints Sebastian and Jerome*. The *tabernacle of St Sebastian (c 1475) contains exquisite paintings of two angels by Francesco Botticini and a beautiful statue of *St Sebastian* by Antonio Rossellino.

Room 6. *Incredulity of St Thomas* by Jacopo da Empoli, *Assumption of the Virgin* by a 17C Florentine painter, tabernacle of the *Holy Sacrament*, an elaborate work by Francesco and Raffaello Botticini; *Madonnas* by Jacopo del Sellaio; *St Blaise* by Giovanni Antonio Sogliani (in a splendid frame); *Madonna enthroned with Saints* by Pier Francesco Fiorentino. The upper walk of the cloister (closed in winter) displays della Robbian works in enamelled terracotta, including a tondo of the *Holy Father* by Andrea and dossals by Benedetto Buglioni and his *bottega*. There is also a precious collection of ten illuminated missals (13C–16C).

Santo Stefano degli Agostiniani

Near the museum, in Via dei Neri, is the 14C church of Santo Stefano degli Agostiniani (open with the same ticket as for the Museo della Collegiata, 09.00–12.00 except Monday). The church, with no façade, is important for its remains of frescoes by Masolino.

The organ at the west end, with an elaborate gallery of 1756, dates from 1558. The first chapel on the south side was frescoed with the *Legend of the True Cross* in 1424 by Masolino; the scenes were destroyed in 1792 except for the intrados of the entrance arch, the window frame, and a niche with trompe l'oeil shelves. However the *sinopie have survived here. Beyond the second chapel with a 17C wood dossal, the fourth chapel has remains of frescoes and *sinopie* attributed to the *bottega* of Bicci di Lorenzo. A damaged tomb slab of an Augustinian monk dated 1432 has been placed here. Beyond is the entrance to an **oratory** (1510) with carved benches by Nofri d'Ascanio and a copy of a *Deposition* by Cigoli (the original was removed by Ferdinando II and is now in the Galleria Palatina in Florence), carried out in 1690 by Antonio Domenico Gabbiani.

South transept. Here there are more fresco fragments by Masolino: a group thought to represent the *Pupils of St Ivo*, and a lunette of the *Madonna and Child with two angels*.

To the right of the high altar is the entrance of the **Oratory of the Santissima Annunziata**, with two beautiful *statues of the *Annunciation* by Bernardo Rossellino (c 1447). In the chapel on the left of the high altar, *Adoration of the Shepherds* by Passignano, (1621).

The fourth chapel on the north side has an altarpiece of the *Assumption* by Mario Balassi (1659); the third chapel was decorated in 1759–63 with frescoes by Vincenzo Meucci and Giuseppe del Moro. Second chapel, *Martyrdom of St Catherine* by Rutilio Manetti (1627) and frescoes by Ottavio Vannini. In the first chapel, the *Madonna of the Rosary* by Francesco Furini encloses a painting of *St Nicholas of Tolentino* protecting Empoli from the plague by Bicci di Lorenzo (1445).

At the far end of Via Giuseppe del Papa is Via della Noce, in which are remains of the **Porta Pisana** (1487; damaged in the Second World War), the only part to survive of the once-famous walls of Empoli (demolished in the early 19C).

Churches of interest on the outskirts of Empoli include **Santa Maria a Ripa** (works by the della Robbia, Santi Buglioni, Giovanni Antonio Sogliani), **Pianezzoli** (15C pulpit and a *Madonna and Child with Saints* signed and dated 1593 by Ludovico Cigoli) and **Monterappoli** (fresco attributed to Raffaello Botticini).

Pontorme

On the eastern outskirts of Empoli is the unattractive suburb of Pontorme, birth-place of the painter Jacopo Carucci, called Pontormo (1494–1556; plaque set up in 1956 by Emilio Cecchi on the house at no. 97 on the main road). The small church of **San Michele** (identified by its tall domed campanile; inconspicuous sign off the main road) contains *St John the Evangelist* and *St Michael Archangel* (c 1519) by Pontormo. In a niche with very faded frescoes of the *Baptism of Christ*, also attributed to Pontormo, is a handsome round 15C marble font. On the fine gilded wood high altar is a ciborium and two paintings by Girolamo Macchietti of *St Michael Archangel* and *St John the Baptist*. In the chapel to the left of the high altar, *Immaculate Conception* by Lodovico Cigoli (c 1590).

A short distance from the church, on the outskirts of the village, is the church of **San Martino**, with a brick façade which incorporates a bellcote. The attrac-tive simple interior (if closed, ring at the house on the right) contains (behind the left altar), a good 15C fresco fragment of two saints. On the left of the apse arch is a statuette of the *Madonna and Child* by Michele da Firenze. Above, on either side of the apse arch are two paintings of five saints attributed to Giovanni Toscani.

Vinci

On the southwest slope of Monte Albano, 11km north of Empoli, in beautiful countryside, is the little village of Vinci, famous as the birthplace of Leonardo da Vinci.

The restored 13C **castle** of the Guidi family houses the particularly interesting *Museo Leonardiano* (open daily 09.30–18.00 or 19.00). It contains numer-ous *models* which are interpretations of the drawings of machines invented by Leonardo, exhibited beside facsimiles of his drawings (well labelled, also in English). Next door is the Biblioteca Leonardiana, a library relating to Leonardo. The nearby church of Santa Croce preserves the font in which Leonardo is sup-posed to have been baptised. A 17C painting of *Mary Magdalene* here was restored in 1997 and attributed to Alessandro Rosi.

Above Vinci is the hamlet of **Anchiano** (also approachable on foot by an old path, c 2km long), amidst magnificent olive groves. Here is the house which is traditionally thought to be the actual birthplace of Leonardo. It was restored in 1952 as a humble memorial to him (open as for the castle). In the lower town is the church of the Santissima Annunziata, preceded by a porch, with an *Annunciation* (over the high altar), attributed to Fra Paolino da Pistoia.

A road, with splendid views, connects Vinci and Pistoia (see p 184) crossing Monte Albano.

A short way southeast of Vinci is the **Pieve di Sant'Ansano in Greti** (open on Sat from April–Sept) founded before 998, which preserves interesting sculptures and a painting by Rutilio Manetti.

Leonardo da Vinci

Leonardo da Vinci (1452–1519) was the illegitimate son of a notary. At the age of 17 he went to work in Verrocchio's studio in Florence and stayed there until around 1476. His early works produced at this time are preserved in the Galleria degli Uffizi: the *Annunciation*, *Adoration of the Magi*, and the *Baptism of Christ*. He was in Milan c 1482–99 where he received commissions as a sculptor from Ludovico Sforza and where he painted the *Virgin of the Rocks* (now in the Louvre) and the *Last Supper* (Cenacolo) on the refectory wall at the convent of Santa Maria delle Grazie. When he returned to Florence in 1503 he worked in the Salone dei Cinquecento in Palazzo Vecchio with Michelangelo and his unfinished mural of the *Battle of Anghiari* (now lost) was carefully studied by contemporary artists. He returned to Milan in 1506–13, and after a time in Rome, spent the last two years of his life in France. He died in 1519 at Amboise where he is buried.

Perhaps the most famous Italian of all time, he was not only known as a painter (although only about 30 works by his own hand survive), but also for his 'universal' talents illustrated in his writings and notebooks. He had extraordinary skills as an architect, military engineer, anatomist, botanist, mechanic and hydraulic engineer. The exquisite drawings by Leonardo which have survived in Italy are kept in Florence at the Gabinetto dei Disegni e Stampe in the Uffizi, at the Ambrosiana in Milan, and the Biblioteca Reale in Turin, although the most important collection of his drawings (which number around six hundred) now belong to the Royal Library at Windsor Castle. The models which have been made in this century, some of which are exhibited at Vinci (and others in the Science Museum in Milan) are interpretations of his drawings which illustrated concepts of physics and were studies of machinery and apparatus, including a submarine, an underwater diving suit, a parachute, flying machine, and a tank.

His greatest pictorial work, which was to have a profound influence on generations of artists, the *Last Supper*, survives in Milan (its restoration was completed in 1999). Also in Milan is his *Portrait of a Musician* (in the Ambrosiana), and his mural decoration of the Sala delle Asse in the Castello Sforzesco. Two other paintings by him which are still in Italy are in the Galleria Nazionale in Parma (the *Head of a Girl*) and the Vatican picture gallery (*St Jerome*). All his other known works are in important museums outside Italy, including the portrait of Monna Lisa (*La Gioconda*), a painting begun in Florence, which is now the most famous work in the Louvre.

Between Empoli and Vinci is **Cerreto Guidi**, a centre of wine production (*Chianti Putto*). The **Villa Medici** here can be visited (open 09.00–19.00; except the 2nd and 3rd Mon of the month). It is approached by a splendid double ramp built in brick to a design of Buontalenti. The villa, incorporated in a castle, was begun in 1565. The early Medici grand-dukes used the palace which now contains portraits of the family, and decorations carried out in the early 20C. The small Baroque garden was designed in the 18C by Ferdinando Ruggeri. In the church next door (open only on Sunday) is a *font by Giovanni della Robbia.

Fucecchio on the western border of the province of Florence, was founded before the 11C. Nearby a bridge carried the Via Francigena (a stretch of which can still be seen at Galleno) across the Arno (for a description of this pilgrimage route to Rome, see p 442). The town was beseiged in 1323 by Castruccio Castracani and after 1330 came under Florentine rule.

In the central Piazza Vittorio Veneto a long flight of steps leads up to the large church of **San Giovanni Battista**, founded in the 10C and rebuilt in the 18C. It contains on the north side (first altar) a *Madonna and Saints* (in very poor condition) by the 16C Florentine school beneath a fragment of a *Baptism of Christ*, and (on the last altar) a 16C marble relief of the *Madonna and Child*. On the left side of the church is a terrace with a panoramic view. Here is the church of **San Salvatore** (Misericordia) preceded by a pretty loggia. In the interior (closed order of nuns), on the third south altar, is an *Allegory of the Conception* by Giorgio Vasari (one of several versions of this painting by the artist).

In the piazza, opposite Palazzo del Podestà, another flight of steps leads up to Palazzo Corsini (14C, enlarged in the 15C) which now houses the Biblioteca Comunale. It is being restored and will house the **Museo di Fucecchio**, with some archaeological material, and paintings by Zanobi Machiavelli (*Madonna in Adoration*), the Maestro dei Paesaggi Kress (*Trinity and Evangelists* and *Nativity with Saints*), and Berlinghiero Berlinghieri (*Saints*).

Montelupo Fiorentino

East of Empoli is Montelupo Fiorentino, an attractive village where the Pesa and Arno rivers meet. Its 14C fortifications still determine the layout of the old centre. It was fortified by the Florentines in opposition to the now demolished stronghold of Capraia, beyond the river. Baccio da Montelupo (1469–1535) and his son Raffaello (c 1505–66), both sculptors and architects, were born here.

The approach road passes the fine **Villa dell'Ambrogiana** (now used as a prison), a Medici hunting lodge. It has a square plan with four angle towers and was reconstructed after 1587, possibly to a design by Buontalenti. It once had a garden on the Arno with fountains and grottoes.

Across the river Pesa off the main street of Montelupo, roads lead up towards the castle past the restored **Palazzo Pretorio** with a neo-Gothic loggia. This is now the **Museo Archeologico e della Ceramica** (open 09.00–12.00, 14.30–19.00 exc. Mon). In the 15C and early 16C Montelupo was one of the most important centres of ceramic production in the Mediterranean. The modern display is accompanied by detailed explanations.

Ground floor. The archaeological collection is displayed here. **Room 1** contains Paleolithic finds, and **room 2** Bronze Age weapons. Imported vases from Greece and Southern Italy, and Etruscan and Roman material are displayed in **room 3**. Remains of 15C frescoes, and medieval finds are in **room 4**.

Upper floor. Rooms 5 and **6** contain a didactic display of ceramic manufacture. **Rooms 7–10** contain examples of majolica produced in Montelupo, arranged chronologically. The earliest potteries dating from the late 13C produced

An example of majolica from Montelupo

green and brown ware mostly with geometric designs. By the late 14C cobalt blue was also widely used. The production in the 15C reflected the influence of Hispano-Moresque ware. There was a notable decline in the industry in the late 16C and 17C when the so-called 'arlecchino' or 'harlequin' style was introduced on a yellow ochre ground. The museum also has examples of ceramics produced in the rest of Italy and a room is dedicated to Paolo Azzati who donated his large private collection of ceramics to the museum.

In Via Bartolomeo Sinibaldi, just below the museum, is the church of **San Giovanni Evangelista** with a *Madonna enthroned with Saints Sebastian, Lorenzo, John the Baptist, and Roch* by Botticelli and his workshop. At the top of the castle hill is the church of **San Lorenzo** (the custodian lives nearby) with fresco fragments signed and dated 1284 by a certain Corso di Buono. The tall, square campanile was probably once one of the castle towers.

To the south of Montelupo, is the **Pieve di Sant'Ippolito** of the 11C, with a marble ciborium by a 15C Florentine sculptor.

Across the Arno is Capraia (see above). Excavations at Montereggi alla Castellina have revealed Etruscan and Roman remains. **Limite**, to the west, is well known for its boat builders. To the east of Montereggi, on the hill of **Bibbiani** is a villa with **gardens** laid out in the mid-19C by Cosimo Ridolfi, often visited by Giacomo Puccini (usually open Apr–July, and mid-Sept–Oct on Fri and Sun 09.00 and 11.00; information from the Comune di Capraia e Limite).

Lastra a Signa

East of Montelupo is Lastra a Signa, a large village near the confluence of the Vingone and the Arno, once famous for the production of straw hats. The medieval centre (right of the main road) is remarkable for its walls built in 1380, with three gates, which were strengthened by Brunelleschi c 1424. Here is the **Loggia di Sant'Antonio**, part of a former hospital erected at the expense of the Arte della Seta (silk-weavers' guild) in 1411. The portico of six arches (the seventh is walled up) has traditionally been attributed as an early work to Brunelleschi. Nearby is the ex-Palazzo Pretorio, a little building, with the escutcheons of many podestà. Just out of the main square is the church of **Santa Maria alla Lastra** (for admission ask at the Misericordia), rebuilt in 1904, with a *Madonna and Child* by the school of Cimabue.

Just outside the town, off the main road to Montelupo (signposted), is the church of **San Martino a Gangalandi**, at the end of an attractive row of houses. Founded in the 12C or earlier, it has a restored campanile and a 15C loggia at the side. The baptistery at the west end is decorated on the exterior and in the vault with frescoes by Bicci di Lorenzo and his school (1432). The font (1423) was sculpted by a follower of Ghiberti. Here is hung a painting of *St John the Baptist* attributed to Bernardo Daddi (1346). Over the first south altar is an unusual painting of *Saints Margaret, Catherine of Alexandria, Catherine of Siena, Mary Magdalene and Apollonia*, by Piero Salvestrini, a pupil of Bernardino Poccetti. Over the third south altar, *Immaculate Conception* by Matteo Rosselli (1615). The fine semicircular apse was decorated in *pietra serena* by Leon Battista Alberti, who was rector here from 1432–72. The high altar bears the date 1366. On the north wall is a large detached fresco of *St Christopher*, and fragments of 14C frescoes over the second altar.

A small **museum** is opened by request (preferably by appointment). In a little room with fine capitals the paintings include a *Madonna of Humility* by Lorenzo Monaco (from San Romolo a Settimo), a triptych with the *Assumption and four Saints* by Bicci di Lorenzo and a *Madonna and Child* attributed to Jacopo del Sellaio. Also here is a 15C gilded bronze Cross. Upstairs is 18C church silver.

In the hills to the southwest is **Malmantile** castle (1424), an outpost of Castracani, the military adventurer who died in 1328, against the Florentines, celebrated in a poem by Lorenzo Lippi, *Il Malmantile racquistato*, published 11 years after his death in 1676.

Opposite Lastra a Signa, on the other side of the Arno, is **Signa**, with an old district on the hill where the church has 13C frescoes and a painting attributed to Lorenzo Monaco. In the church of San Giovanni Battista, in the lower town, the body of Beata Giovanna da Signa is preserved. Frescoes of 1441 and 1462 illustrate stories from her life. The **Museo della Paglia e dell'Intreccio** (open Tues & Sat 09.00–13.00; Wed, Thurs & Fri 15.00–19.00) in Via degli Alberti, is a charming little museum illustrating the history of straw plaiting for which Signa first became famous after 1714 when Domenico Michelacci had the idea to cultivate wheat here specifically for this purpose so it could be used in manufacturing hats: these were first sold to the English in Livorno and then exported all over the world. The industry flourished up until about 1953. There is a project to create a park along the Arno, around the small island formed by a mud-bank in the Arno known as the **Isola dei Renai**, where fragments of classical statues have been unearthed.

Campi Bisenzio is now a large industrial suburb of Florence, but of ancient origin. It was granted privileges in 780 by Charlemagne. Situated in low-lying ground, it has often been subject to flooding from the river Bisenzio. In Piazza Matteotti are **Palazzo del Podestà** and the **Pieve di Santo Stefano**, founded in 936. It was restored in neo-Classical style in 1835 and given its façade in 1938. It contains a fresco of the *Annunciation* by Paolo Schiavo, a painting of *St Anthony Abbot and the angel* by Francesco Curradi (c 1650), and an altarpiece of the *Madonna and Child with Saints* attributed to Sebastiano Mainardi. In the adjoining **Teatro della Pieve** (formerly an oratory) is a fresco fragment of the *Annunciation* and *Holy Trinity* attributed to Raffaellino del Garbo. The **Teatro Dante** was built by Falcini in 1871. Across the Bisenzio is the **Rocca Strozzi** rebuilt in 1377 and the church of **Santa Maria** which contains a chapel frescoed by Mariotto di Cristofano in 1420, and a 15C *Crucifix*.

On the Florence road is the suburb of **Brozzi**, where the church of Sant'Andrea has frescoes by Domenico Ghirlandaio and pupils. Nearby is **Peretola** which was the home of the Vespucci family before they moved to Florence. The church of Santa Maria contains a *tabernacle by Luca della Robbia (1441). The airport of Florence, at Peretola (see p 55) is beside the motorway which runs from Florence to the coast. At the Firenze-Nord exit is the church of San Giovanni Battista, built in 1960–64 by Giovanni Michelucci.

Badia di San Salvatore a Settimo

East of Lastra a Signa, on the south bank of the Arno, is the Badia di San Salvatore a Settimo, a 10C abbey, rebuilt for Cistercians in 1236–37, walled and fortified in 1371, and restored after 1944. The church has a rebuilt campanile and a Romanesque façade with a round 15C window (open for services; otherwise ring the inconspicuous bell by the gate to the left of the façade); or ☎ 055 731 0537.

Over the second altar on the south side, *Martyrdom of St Lawrence* by Lodovico Buti (1574). Behind the high altar in *pietre dure* is the choir with a della Robbian enamelled terracotta frieze of cherubim and the Agnus Dei, and two frescoed tondi of the *Annunciation* by the school of Ghirlandaio. On the left of the high altar is a little marble *tabernacle, beautifully carved and attributed to Giuliano da Sangallo. The chapel on the left of the high altar has good *frescoes (in poor condition) by Giovanni da San Giovanni (1629). They depict scenes from the lives of *Saints Stephen, Benedict, Bernard and Lawrence*, with *God the Father* in the dome and the *Evangelists* in the spandrels. The wall-tomb of the Countesses Gardia and Cilla (d. 1096)—a rare example of a pre-Romanesque tomb—on the north side dates from 1096. In the sacristy two paintings which were once in the church are displayed: the *Adoration of the Magi* and an unusual scene of *Christ at the sepulchre*, both attributed to Domenico Ghirlandaio or his school.

The remains of the **monastery** (carefully restored and now privately owned, but sometimes courteously shown; ring at the cloister) include much of the old fortifications, and the chapterhouse and the remarkable vaulted lay brothers' hall.

Near the badia is the church of **Santi Giuliano e Settimo**, an 8C building, altered in subsequent centuries.

South of the main road between Lastra a Signa and Florence is **San Martino alla Palma** (open only for services; at other times ring at the green door under the portico) in a magnificent position among low, rolling hills (easily visible from the main road). It was founded in the 10C, and contains a charming *Madonna* by a follower of Bernardo Daddi known, from this painting, as the Maestro di San Martino alla Palma (1325–30).

On the other side of the motorway, which skirts the west side of Florence, is the huge suburb of **Scandicci** where much new building has taken place since the Second World War. To the south, beyond Vingone, is **San Paolo a Mosciano**. D.H. Lawrence stayed in the Villa Mirenda (next to the little cemetery and church) in 1926–27 while completing *Lady Chatterley's Lover* (first published in Florence in 1928).

Prato and its province

Prato (163,000 inhab.) is a rapidly expanding industrial town, known as the Manchester of Tuscany, and long famous for its wool factories; it is one of the most important centres of the textile industry in Europe. In 1992 it became the capital of a new Province. It is surrounded by extensive suburbs, but it has a peaceful historic centre which preserves some beautiful monuments, all within its medieval walls.

Practical information

Getting there
By car

Prato has two exits from the A11 motorway from Florence to the coast. The centre is closed to traffic: **parking** (with hourly tariff) in Piazza Mercatale, Piazza Santa Maria delle Carceri, and Piazza San Francesco. Free parking in Piazza Macelli.

By train

Centrale, east of the town across the Bisenzio, for all trains on the main Florence–Bologna line. Services on the Florence–Lucca–Viareggio line stop also at **Porta al Serraglio**, 200 metres north of the cathedral.

By bus

Every 15 minutes services via the motorway in c 30 mins from Florence run by *CAP* and *Lazzi* from the right side of the Florence railway station. It stops in Prato in Via Frascati (near Piazza Santa Maria delle Carceri) and in Via de' Tintori (request stop in Via Rinaldesca for the return services from Prato to Florence).

Information office

APT, Via Luigi Muzzi 38 (☎ 0574 351 41), north of the duomo, with information office at Via Cairoli 48 (☎ & 📠 0574 241 12; ✉info@prato.turismo.toscana.it).

Where to stay
Hotels

☆☆☆☆ *President*, Via Simintendi 20 (Map 1; ☎ 0574 302 51, 📠 0574 360 64; www.bestwestern.it). ☆☆☆ *Flora*, Via Cairoli 31 (Map 2; ☎ 0574 335 21, 📠 0574 402 89; hotelflora@textnet.it); *Giardino*, Via Magnolfi 4 (Map 3; ☎ 0574 606 588, 📠 0574 606 591); *San Marco*, Piazza San Marco 48 (Map 4; ☎ 0574 213 21, 📠 0574 223 78;hotelsanmarco@

virgilio.it); *Milano*, Via Tiziano 15 (Map 5; ☎ 0574 233 71, 📠 0574 277 06). ☆☆ *Il Giglio*, Piazza San Marco 14 (Map 6; ☎ 0574 370 49, 📠 0574 604 351).

Rooms to let

Villa Rucellai (Fattoria di Canneto), Via di Canneto 16 (☎ 0574 460 392).

Eating out
Restaurants

€€€ *Baghino*, Via dell' Accademia 9.
€€ *La Cucina di Paola*, Via Banchelli 14; *La Veranda*, Via dell'Arco 10; *Le Anfore*, Via Cambioni 21.
€ *Lapo*, Piazza Mercatale 141; *La Vecchia Cucina*, Via Pomeria 23.

Pasticcerie

Antonio Mattei, Via Ricasoli 22 (opened here in 1858) specialising in biscuits (*biscotti di Prato*). *Nuovo Mondo*, Via Garibaldi 23.

Museums and monuments

There is a combined ticket for the two museums and the castello.

Theatres and annual festivals

Teatro Comunale Metastasio, with a renowned theatre season (October to April). *Teatro il Fabbricone*, Via Targetti 10.
The **Prato Fair** is held in September (with a historical pageant on 8 September).
A big general **market** is held on Mondays at the Mercato Nuovo.

Australian University

Monash University in Prato, Palazzo Vaj, Via Pugliesi 26 (☎ 0574 448073). This Australian university opened a campus here in 2001.

History

Although probably already settled in the Etruscan period, the first recorded mention of Prato is in the 9C. It became a free commune in the 12C and after 1351 came under the influence of Florence. The manufacture of wool in the city had reached European importance by the 13C, and it received further impetus in the following century through the commercial activity of the famous merchant Francesco di Marco Datini. Its textile factories continue to flourish, and it has become the centre of the rag-trade in Europe. As an industrial centre, its population is expanding faster than almost any other city in central Italy.

Piazza del Duomo is a pleasant large square where many streets converge around the cathedral. The attractive fountain, crowned by a laughing fisherboy and decorated with numerous fish, dates from 1863 (by Emanuele Caroni and Ulisse Cambi).

The Duomo

The *Duomo (closed 12.30–15.00 or 15.30) was founded in the 10C, but the present Romanesque building was begun in 1211 by Guidetto da Como. The unusual façade (1385–1457), partly striped in green and white marble, is crowned with a quadrilobe open sculptured frieze. Above the main portal is a *lunette with the *Madonna and Saints Stephen and Laurence* by Andrea della Robbia (1489). The *pulpit of the Sacred Girdle, designed by Donatello and Michelozzo (1434–38), is protected by a charming roof. It has a frieze depicting

dancing putti by Donatello (replaced by casts in 1972—the originals are kept in the Museo dell' Opera del Duomo, see below). The Holy Girdle (see below) is displayed from the pulpit in a traditional ceremony on 1 May, Easter Day, 15 August, 8 September, and Christmas Day (it is processed three times out of one of the little doors and back through the other). The *south side of the cathedral, the oldest part of the building, has beautiful blind arcading and Romanesque inlaid marble decoration, and two fine doorways. The handsome campanile also dates from the early 13C, except for the last storey which was added c 1356 by Niccolò di Cecco del Mercia.

Donatello's pulpit on the exterior of the Duomo at Prato

The nave is supported by massive shiny green marble columns with good capitals, and the deep arcades are decorated with green and white striped marble. Immediately to the left is the *Chapel of the Sacred Girdle**. The splendid bronze *screen was begun in 1438 by Maso di Bartolomeo and continued by Antonio di Ser Cola and Pasquino di Matteo (1467). On the altar is a statuette of the *Madonna and Child*, one of the best works of Giovanni Pisano (1317). The

chapel is entirely frescoed by Agnolo Gaddi and his *bottega* (1392–95) with
*Scenes from the Life of the Virgin and the Story of the Relic of the Sacred
Girdle* (beautifully restored in 2000).

The Sacred Girdle

The chapel was built in 1385–90 to house the greatly revered relic which is
traditionally considered to be the girdle (*cintola*) which the Madonna gave to
St Thomas at her Assumption. Thomas is supposed to have given it for safe-
keeping to a friend before he set out on a long sea voyage. When Michele
Dagomari from Prato married a girl called Maria in Jerusalem, he is meant
to have received it from her mother as a dowry.

The story goes that when he returned to Prato with it in 1141 (his wife
died on the journey) he preserved the relic in secret in the rush basket in
which he had received it, and in order to protect it he is supposed to have,
irreverently, slept on it. Angels, as a sign of their disapproval, placed it on
the floor several times while he slept. On his death bed, Michele presented
the relic to the church where it was solomnly installed after an elaborate
procession in 1174. (St Francis of Assisi came here to see it in 1212.)

After the attempted theft of the girdle in 1312, its custody was disputed
between the church and the Comune, and since its installation in this
chapel, built specially for it, in 1395, both the canons and the rulers of the
city have kept a key. The pulpit (see above) on the façade, connected to the
chapel by an internal corridor, was built for its ostentation in the 15C, when
it was also seen by Pope Alexander V, King Louis of Anjou, St Bernardine,
and the Byzantine emperor John Paleologus. At this time an exquisite
reliquary was made for it by Maso di Bartolomeo (now kept in the Museo
dell'Opera del Duomo), but since 1638 it has been preserved in a crystal
box. The frescoes in the chapel by Gaddi illustrate (on the right wall) the
story of Michele and the relic from the time of his marriage to his donation
of it to the church.

Above the west door, *Assumption of the Virgin* by Ridolfo del Ghirlandaio. In the
south aisle is a wooden *Crucifix* by the *bottega* of Giovanni Pisano. The *pulpit in
the nave is by Mino da Fiesole and Antonio Rossellino. The beautiful transept and
east chapels, thought to have been designed by Giovanni Pisano, were added in
1317–68 (the stained glass dates from the 19C). A balustrade (incorporating
some sculpted marble panels by Francesco di Simone Ferrucci, 1487), by
Bernardino Radi and Gherardo Silvani (1637) precedes the high altar on which
is a bronze *Crucifix* by Ferdinando Tacca (1653).

The **choir** is decorated with celebrated *frescoes by Filippo Lippi (helped by Fra
Diamante). This is one of the most beautiful fresco cycles of the early
Renaissance (1452–66), and the monumental figures demand and reward close
study, but they are covered for restoration until 2004. On the right wall: scenes
from the *Life of St John the Baptist*; the Salome in the *Banquet of Herod* is
supposed to be a portrait of Lucrezia Buti, the nun who was first Lippi's model
and then his wife. On the left wall: scenes from the *Life of St Stephen*. Filippo
Lippi also designed the beautiful stained glass window (except for the lower
register which has been remade).

The fine bronze candelabrum in the south transept is by Maso di Bartolomeo. The tabernacle of the **Madonna dell'Ulivo** (1480), designed by Giuliano da Maiano, contains a statue of the *Madonna and Child* and a bas-relief of the **Pietà** by his brothers Benedetto and Giovanni. The second chapel right of the choir (Cappella Vinaccesi) was frescoed with episodes from the Old Testament by the local painter Alessandro Franchi in 1880. The 13C wooden figure of Christ was part of a Deposition group.

The **Cappella dell'Assunta** (first chapel right of the choir) is decorated with 15C frescoes of the *Life of the Virgin and of St Stephen*. The cycle was begun in 1435 by Paolo Uccello who painted the upper *scenes (the vault, two lunettes with the *Birth of the Virgin and St Stephen*, and the *Stoning of St Stephen*). When Paolo Uccello left the following year to paint the monument to Hawkwood in the Duomo in Florence, the lower scenes were frescoed by Andrea di Giusto.

In the first chapel left of the choir are more early 15C frescoes; and in the second chapel is the *tomb of **Filippo degli Inghirami** (d. 1480) and a fine early 16C stained glass window depicting the Visitation and Nativity. Above the door into the sacristy is a good monument to Carlo dei Medici (d. 1494) by Vincenzo Danti. The Chapel of the Sacrament in the north transept has a carved entrance arch by Giovanni Camilliani (1544), and an altarpiece by Zanobi Poggini (1549).

Museo dell'Opera del Duomo

To the left of the cathedral, is **Palazzo Vescovile** with a 15C loggia, and a little courtyard with a 16C fresco in a tabernacle. Here is the entrance to the Museo dell'Opera del Duomo (open 09.30–12.30, 15.00–18.30; fest. 09.30–12.30; closed Tues).

Room I has a good view of the Romanesque cloister (see below). Here are displayed 14C paintings, including a *Madonna and Child* by the Maestro di San Lucchese, and *Saints* by Giovanni Toscani. The marble relief by Giroldo da Como dates from 1261. **Room II** displays illuminated 15C anthem books, and vestments including two late 16C embroidered copes. **Room III** (the loggia of Palazzo Vescovile) displays unusual high reliefs dating from 1354–60 by Niccolò di Cecco del Mercia, a Sienese sculptor, which used to decorate an external pulpit and an altar dossal of the cathedral.

Stairs lead down to a room where excavations have revealed walls dating from the 8C (the finds, including Etruscan material) are to be exhibited here. Beyond is a room which exhibits the *seven relief panels of dancing putti** by Donatello and his *bottega* from the Pulpit of the Sacred Girdle (outside the cathedral, see above). Dating from 1434–38 these were restored in 2000, but have been irreparably damaged by their exposure to the elements up until 1970 and by poor restorations in the past (some of them still have a brownish red patina, and the surface of others has a *craquelure* effect). It is now thought that probably only the central panel is by Donatello's own hand, and possibly the panel to the left of that and the first one on the right. The gilded mosaic background was added after the crowd of chubby putti had been carved, in imitation of his more famous reliefs of putti made for the cantoria of the Florence Duomo at about the same time.

The *reliquary for the sacred girdle**, an exquisite work by Maso di Bartolomeo (1446), is also displayed here.

Part of the old **cloister** is a unique survival from the 12C, with tiny slender columns with exquisite capitals and green and white marble decoration. From here you can visit the medieval arches (*Le Volte*) beneath the transept of the Duomo, with early 15C frescoes, a small antiquarium, and some remains of the earlier church. A very unusual medieval pavement here is composed of some one hundred pieces of pottery kitchen ware.

Some of the masterpieces in the collection are temporarily housed in the Museo di Pittura Murale (see below).

Piazza del Comune

Opposite the right flank of the Duomo **Via Mazzoni** (called the Corso), the main street of the town, leads to the handsome Piazza del Comune, with a statue (1896) of the Merchant of Prato (see below), and a pretty little fountain by Ferdinando Tacca (1659; the original statue of the young Bacchus and the basin are preserved inside Palazzo Comunale, see below). The main stone façade with its Gothic windows and outside staircase of the splendid **Palazzo Pretorio** was added to a medieval core in the early 14C, and the battlements completed in the 16C. The main hall, with a fine roof, survives from the 14C. The palace houses the *Galleria Comunale** and the **Museo Civico** founded in 1852 which was closed for long-term restoration work in 1998 (not expected to reopen until after 2002). Meanwhile some of the masterpieces are exhibited at the Museo di Pittura Murale (see below).

Also in the piazza is the arcaded late 18C **Palazzo Comunale** (by Giuseppe Valentini). A worn Medici stemma of 1550 survives on the corner, by Battista del Tasso. In 1997 the **Museo del Tessuto** opened in a room on the ground floor (open Mon, Wed, Thur, and Fri 10.30–18.30, Sat 10.30–14.30).

It contains a collection of textiles (kept for conservation reasons in drawers) including pre-Columbian works, Coptic fabrics, medieval fragments, Renaissance velvet, 17C embroideries and lace, 18C damask and brocade, and 19C cloth produced in the Prato textile manufactories. A section is dedicated to material made in Prato since the Second World War, including silk and synthetic fibres. There are also looms, carders, and spinning-machines, a display illustrating natural dyes, a collection of samples, and some costumes. The museum is to be moved to a disused textile factory (Campolmi) near the Castello dell'Imperatore.

At the foot of the stairs of Palazzo Comunale (entrance at no. 2) is the original fountain by Ferdinando Tacca, removed from the piazza. Upstairs the **Sala del Consiglio** (shown by appoinment, ☎ 0574 382 07) has a fine ceiling, two 15C frescoes, and a series of portraits in handsome frames (some by Alessandro Allori) of the grand-dukes of Tuscany, and of Cardinal Niccolò of Prato by Tommaso di Piero Trombetto.

Via Cairoli leads out of the piazza through a little square with the 19C façade of Palazzo Buonamici and its hanging garden. No. 19 is the Baroque Palazzo Gatti and beyond is the 16C **Palazzo Novellucci**, seat of the new province of Prato, which contains 18C stuccoes and painted decoration. At Via Pugliesi 26 is the 18C **Palazzo Vaj**, the first floor of which (used as a gentlemen's club in the 20C) is the Italian centre of Monash University, founded in Victoria, Australia in 1958. Interesting conferences and concerts are held here. Close by, beside a tall medieval tower, is Piazza Santa Maria delle Carceri. Palazzo della Canonica by Giuseppe Valentini adjoins the church of *Santa Maria delle Carceri** (closed 12.00–16.00), a masterpiece of the early Renaissance. It is one of the most important works by Giuliano da Sangallo, begun in 1485 (the exterior was left incomplete in 1506). The Greek-cross plan is derived from the architectural principles of Alberti and Brunelleschi. It was built on the site of a prison wall (hence *Carceri*) on which a painted image of the Virgin was thought to work miracles. The exterior, in green and white marble, recalls the Romanesque buildings of Florence (the last side was completed in the 19C). In the domed centrally-planned interior *pietra serena* is used to emphasise the structural elements. The beautiful enamelled terracotta frieze and tondi of the *Evangelists* are by Andrea della Robbia. The stoup, with a bronze statuette of St John the Baptist, is by Francesco da Sangallo, son of the architect, and the stained glass windows date from the 15C.

On a mound next to the church is the ***Castello dell'Imperatore** (restored). The castle was begun by the son of the Emperor Frederick II to protect the route from Germany to southern Italy, but left unfinished at the death of the Emperor in 1252. It is typical of the simple, austere Hohenstaufen castles of southern Italy.

In the empty interior (open 10.00–16.00 or 17.00; closed Tues) three of the eight vaulted towers can be visited. On the other side of Viale Piave the **Cassero** was restored and opened to the public in 2000. This was a fortified corridor built in 1351 to connect the castle to the city walls, and both the barrel-vaulted interior and the walkway on its summit (with a view of the castle, the dome of Santa Maria delle Carceri, and the campanile of the cathedral and that of San Francesco) have been partly preserved.

From Piazza Santa Maria delle Carceri, Via Cairoli leads to the 19C **Teatro Comunale Metastasio** (admission on request at no. 59). The elegant interior was built in 1827–30 by Luigi Cambray Digny. It has a good theatrical reputation. Via Mazzini continues from the theatre towards Piazza San Marco where there is a sculpture (*Square form with cut*; 1969–70) by Henry Moore, known by the inhabitants of Prato since its installation here in 1974 as Il Buco (the hole).

Via Verdi skirts the theatre building and forms a crossroads with Via Garibaldi. This road leads (right) to the huge **Piazza Mercatale**, surrounded with a medley of pleasant buildings. Here the modern church of **San Bartolomeo** (the 14C church was destroyed in the Second World War) has a 15C marble tabernacle on the high altar with a painted *Crucifix* of the 14C Pistoian school above. The paintings include a tondo (above the west door) in a fine frame by the school of Botticelli, and works by Santi di Tito, Leonardo Mascagni, Livio Mehus (*Rest on the Flight*, at the end of the left wall), and Empoli. In the crypt is a fine wooden *Crucifix* of the 14C.

In the other direction, Via Garibaldi (see above) passes the oratory of the **Madonna del Buon Consiglio** (no. 53; if closed ask at Santa Maria delle Carceri), with a della Robbian lunette (and other works by the della Robbia inside).

Opposite the entrance to the castle (see above) is the east end of the Romanesque church of **San Francesco**, with a handsome striped marble façade. At the foot of the altar steps is the tomb of Francesco di Marco Datini (see below), by Nicolò Lamberti (1412). On the north wall is the tomb of Gimignano Inghirami (d. 1460), attributed to Bernardo Rossellino. The effigy rests on a comfortable damask catafalque and elaborate cushion. From the charming 15C cloister (planted with olive trees), with 19C funerary monuments, or from the sacristy is the entrance to the **chapter house** (or Cappella Migliorati) with good and well-preserved frescoes by Niccolò di Pietro Gerini (c 1395) of the *Crucifixion*, and stories from the life of St Anthony Abbot and St Matthew.

In front of the church (see below) is the **Biblioteca Roncioniana** (1751–66). In the vestibule is a white enamelled terracotta high relief of *Tobias and the Archangel*, attributed to Andrea della Robbia).

Via Santa Trínita leads out of Piazza San Francesco. In Via Silvestri (right) is the church of the **Spirito Santo**. In the nave is a *Presentation in the Temple* by Fra Diamante, possibly to a design of Filippo Lippi, and a *Madonna and Child with St Anne* attributed to Sogliani. The high altarpiece of the *Pentecost* is by Santi di Tito. In the presbytery is a high relief of *St John the Baptist* (15C) and a charming *Annunciation* and a tiny predella by the school of Orcagna. Off the south side there is a pretty little portico with Ionic columns.

Palazzo Datini

Via Rinaldesca leads out of Piazza San Francesco to the huge *Palazzo Datini with unusually large projecting eaves on the corner of Via Ser Lapo Mazzei. This was part of the residence of Francesco di Marco Datini, the famous Merchant of Prato (1330–1410), whose life was described in *The Merchant of Prato* (1957) by Iris Origo. Datini's papers and business documents (including over 140,000 letters), all of which were carefully preserved by him, provide a unique record of medieval life; they are housed in an archive in the palace. During his lifetime the palace was also used by the Comune of Prato to entertain illustrious visitors, among them Leonardo Dandolo, the Venetian ambassador in 1397, Pope Alexander V's representative in 1409, the illegal occupant of the papal chair, the antipope John XXIII, and Louis of Anjou in 1409–10.

The palace was acquired by Datini in 1354 and modifications were made by him between 1387 and 1390 when Niccolò di Pietro Gerini was commissioned to carry out the painted decoration in the courtyard and loggia, part of which survives. Datini left the palace to a charitable institute called the *Ceppo dei Poveri*, and after his death the exterior of the palace was frescoed with scenes from his life by Ambrogio di Baldese, Niccolò di Piero Gerini, and others (some of the *sinopie* of these frescoes are preserved inside the palace). The present frescoes on the exterior by Giuseppe Catani, replaced the originals in 1910. Part of the ground floor, including the courtyard, is open (09.00–12.00, 15.30–18.30 except Sat afternoon and Sun). At the foot of the stairs is a fresco of *St Christopher* by Niccolò di Pietro Gerini and a room with a painted vault and a portrait of Datini, dressed in red. Another room with a frescoed lunette of the *Redeemer* above the door has delightful painted decoration with woods and animals, and another good vault. Other rooms have frescoes detached from the courtyard.

Beyond is **Palazzo degli Alberti**, the headquarters of the Cassa di Risparmio bank, which owns a particularly interesting art collection (open by previous appointment; 08.30–12.30, 15.00–16.00, except Sat and Sun). The works, arranged in a gallery overlooking the banking hall, include: a *Crucifix* (with an interesting landscape), an undocumented work attributed to Giovanni Bellini; a *Madonna and Child* almost certainly by Filippo Lippi; Caravaggio, *Christ crowned with Thorns*. The fine 17C Tuscan paintings are by Matteo Rosselli, Santi di Tito, Alessandro Rosi, Giovanni Battista Vanni, Lorenzo Lippi, Giovanni Bilivert, Carlo Dolci (*Charity*), Cesare, Vincenzo and Pier Dandini, Francesco Furini, Sustermans, and Bernardino Mei. The collection of marble sculptures by Lorenzo Bartolini include *Faith* and some portrait busts. On the stairs are two large paintings by Galileo Chini.

In front of Palazzo Datini, Via Tinaia leads to Via Pellegrino on which is the pretty little 19C church of **San Pier Forelli** (1838). It has a barrel vault and semi-circular apse lit from a semi-dome. Nearby is the huge 18C **Collegio Cicognini**, a well-known school attended by the poet Gabriele d'Annunzio. It has an elaborate façade, and incorporates 18C frescoes, and a theatre built c 1780.

Via Santa Caterina leads up to a little piazza in front of the church and convent of **San Niccolò** (for adm. ring at the convent school). Chamber music **concerts** are sometimes held here. The Dominican convent founded in 1321, was altered in the 18C. In 1785 the school was founded here and a neo-Classical wing was added by Giuseppe Valentini.

The **church** has an 18C interior with frescoes attibuted to Rinaldo Botti. It preserves two 14C frescoes on the right wall, including a fragment of the story of the life of San Nicola by Pietro di Miniato and the high altarpiece of the *Assumption* is by Alessandro Gherardini. In the sacristy is a fine enamelled terracotta lavabo (1520) attributed to Benedetto and Santi Buglioni, and a 15C *Crucifix*.

The interesting **convent** has an 18C nuns' choir, with Rococo decorations by Niccolò Nannetti, and stuccoes, and wooden choirstalls. Two 15C frescoes survive here, including a lunette with the *Madonna of the Holy Girdle* attributed to Pietro di Miniato. The altarpiece of the *Madonna of the Rosary* is by Luigi Crespi (1732). In a corridor is displayed the *Mystical Marriage of St Catherine* by Tommaso di Piero del Trombetto and a 16C *Crucifix*. The delightful **pharmacy**, with its original cupboards painted with blue-and-white landscapes, dates from 1764. There are similar cupboards in the **Stanza dei Padri**. The chapter house has a 14C wooden ceiling and a large fresco (1509) attributed to Girolamo Ristori. The large refectory has a fresco attributed to Tommaso di Piero del Trombetto, and its wood furnishings dating from the late 16C, and the small refectory has a 15C fresco of the *Supper of St Dominic* attributed to Bartolomeo Bocchi. In a chapel on the upper floor is a *Nativity with Saints Stephen and Catherine* attributed to Zanobi Poggini.

From Palazzo Alberti, Via Banchelli leads right and Via Guasti left to the 13C–14C church of **San Domenico**, which has an arcaded flank. Founded in 1283 it was finished by Giovanni Pisano before 1322. It contains a 17C organ, on which the composer Domenico Zipoli (born in Prato in 1688 and died in Argentina in 1726) probably played. Over the high altar is a Baroque baldacchino. South aisle. Second altar, *Crucifix* by Niccolò Gerini; third altar, *St Vincent Ferrer* attributed to Pier Dandini; fifth altar, *Madonna and Saints and Angels* by Camillo Sagrestani. North aisle. Second altar, *Madonna appearing to St Philip Neri*, by Matteo Rosselli; fourth altar, *Crucifix before St Thomas Aquinas*, by Francesco Morandini; fifth altar, *Annunciation*, signed by Matteo Rosselli. In the chapter house (off the cloister) interesting early 15C frescoes of the *Life of St Dominic* attributed to Pietro di Miniato were uncovered in 1984.

Museum of Mural Painting

In the adjoining convent is a Museum of Mural Painting (entered from no. 8 in the piazza) which has a permanent exhibition of detached frescoes from buildings in the town and surrounding area (open 10.00–18.00; fest. 10.00–13.00; closed Tues).

Since 1998 the museum has hosted an exhibition called *I Tesori della Città* with works from the Museo Civico (closed for restoration, see above), and the Museo dell'Opera del Duomo.

At the top of the stairs is a stained glass fragment with the *Annunciation* by Fra Paolo di Mariotto da Gambassi (1509).

First section. *Predella by Bernardo Daddi, illustrating the story of the *Sacred Girdle* (see p 171), and a polyptych of the *Madonna and Saints* by the same artist. A polyptych of the *Madonna and Saints* with a double predella is by Giovanni da Milano. The polyptych, also with a double predella, with the *Coronation of the Virgin and Saints* (two of them missing) was commissioned by the merchant Francesco di Marco Datini from Pietro di Miniato in 1410. Beyond a *Madonna and Four Saints* by Lorenzo Monaco are two works by Andrea di Giusto. On the opposite wall *sinopie* by Paolo Uccello are displayed, detached from the Chapel of the Assunta in the Duomo of Prato in 1964, and *Jacopone da Todi*, a fresco detached in 1871 from the same chapel and also attributed to Paolo Uccello (or the Master of Prato).

Room A displays a detached fresco and a *sinopia* by Agnolo Gaddi, and a fresco of the *Madonna and Child with angels and Saints Catherina of Alexandria and Mary Magdalene* with its *sinopia* commissioned from Niccolò Gerini by Francesco Datini for his garden.

Second section. **Works** by Filippo Lippi, including the *Madonna del Ceppo* (with Francesco di Marco Datini presenting members of the confraternity of the Buonomini del Ceppo to the Madonna), the *Death of St Jerome* and stories from his life (from the Duomo), and a *Nativity* (with the help of assistants). The *Madonna of the Holy Girdle with Saints* was begun by Filippo but probably finished by his assistant Fra Diamante, to whom the predella, also displayed here, is attributed, showing the *Presentation in the Temple*, the *Adoration of the Magi*, and the *Massacre of the Innocents*.

In **room B** is a painting of *St Dominic* attributed to Bernardo Daddi, a choir book with miniatures by Rossello Franchi, works by Domenico di Michelino and the Maestro di Pratovecchio, and two small paintings of the *Annunciation with St Julian* derived from a work by Filippo Lippi.

Third section. 15C works: Francesco Botticini, *Madonna enthroned with four Saints*; Filippino Lippi, *Madonna and Child with Saints Stephen and John the Baptist* (in its original frame); 15C Florentine master (formerly attributed to Filippino Lippi), *St Lucy*. The two tondi are by Raffaellino de' Carli, and Luca Signorelli. In the side corridor are 15C *graffiti decoration of courtly scenes by Girolamo Ristori detached from the garden of Palazzo Vaj in Prato. **Room C** has late 15C works, including a *Crucifix* painted by the *bottega* of Botticelli.

Opposite the façade of San Domenico is the 18C church of **San Vincenzo e Santa Caterina de' Ricci** (open in summer Tues, Wed, & Fri 10.00–12.00; or ring for admission), with a fine interior of 1733. In the Dominican convent are mementoes of St Catherine de' Ricci (1522–90) who lived here from the age of 15. She became prioress and was famous for her visions and saintliness. She was canonised in 1746. In Via San Vincenzo, at no. 24, is the church of San Clemente in another convent (closed order; service at 18.00).

Via Convenevole leads from Piazza San Domenico past the little church of **San Michele** (the church of the Misericordia) with an altarpiece of the *Assumption* by Alessandro Allori (1603) and a Romanesque *Crucifix*.

At the end of Via Convenevole Via della Stufa leads left to a piazza in front of the church of **Sant'Agostino**, erected in 1271, but considerably altered since then.

The interior contains 16C–17C altarpieces, including, in the north aisle (second altar), a *Madonna* designed by Vasari (and executed by Giovanni Battista Naldini), and (third altar) *St Thomas of Villanova*, by Lorenzo Lippi. In the chapel at the end of the north aisle, *Sacred Conversation*, by Empoli (who also painted the *Immaculate Conception and Saints* on the second south altar). A door in the north wall leads into the garden of the cloister; to the left is reached the **Cappella di San Michele** with a damaged frieze of saints (14C) and a relief of a *Madonna and Child* by the school of Ghiberti. The chapter house, beyond, has a fine cross-vault and a 14C fresco of *Christ in Pietà*.

Nearby is the church of **San Fabiano** (entrance on request at Via del Seminario 28; see the Map). Interesting fragments of the pre-Romanesque monochrome mosaic pavement with figures of animals, sirens, and birds, are displayed in the cloister and on the west wall (the façade can be seen from Via Giovanni di Gherardo which skirts the walls).

In front of San Michele (see above), Largo Carducci leads back to Piazza del Duomo.

Over 2km south-east of the centre (bus 7 or 8 from Viale Piave near the Castello dell'Imperatore) between the motorway exit (Prato-est) and Viale della Repubblica, is the **Centro per l'Arte Contemporanea Luigi Pecci**, designed by Italo Gamberini (1907–90), and opened in 1988. The huge, well illuminated galleries are used for contemporary art exhibitions (open 10.00–19.00 except Tues). The permanent collection can only be seen by previous appointment. There is also an open-air theatre, library, auditorium and snack bar.

The province of Prato

Practical information

 ### Getting there
By bus

COPIT or CAP from Florence (Largo Alinari 9) every half hour (in c 30 mins) to Poggio a Caiano. From Poggio a Caiano bus via Comeana to Artimino in 20 mins, and via Seano to Carmignano (in 20mins).

 ### Information office

APT of Prato, Via Cairoli 48, Prato (☎ 0574 24112).

 ### Where to stay
Hotel

ARTIMINO ☆☆☆☆
Paggeria Medicea, Via Papa Giovanni XXIII 3. (☎ 055 8718081 or 055 875141, 📠 055 8718080 or 055 8751470).

 ### Eating out
Restaurants

ARTIMINO
€€ *La Delfina*, Via della Chiesa 1.
BACCHERETO €€ *La Cantina di Toia*, Via Toia 16.

Villa di Poggio a Caiano

The village of Poggio a Caiano at the foot of Monte Albano, is visited for its Medici *villa, rebuilt in 1480 by Giuliano da Sangallo for Lorenzo il Magnifico. It was then used by later members of the Medici dynasty, and in subsequent centuries

PROVINCIA DI PRATO

the Austrians and French rulers, and the kings of Italy all stayed here. Since 1996 work has been in progress to restore the furnishings of the villa to the appearance it had during the Savoy period in 1911. The top floor is now used for exhibitions.

Open every half hour on the half hour 08.15–15.30; March and Oct 08.15–16.30; Apr–Sept 08.15–18.30; closed on the 2nd and 3rd Mon of the month.

The fine rectangular building stands on a broad terrace surrounded by a colonnade. A classical Ionic portico on the first floor with the Medici arms in the tympanum bears a beautiful polychrome enamelled terracotta frieze (a copy of the original, which is now kept inside the villa). The semicircular steps were added by Pasquale Poccianti in 1802–07.

On the **ground floor** is a little **theatre** built in the 17C by Marguerite-Louise of Orléans, wife of Cosimo III. When Elisa Baciocchi, Napeolon's sister, was Grand-duchess of Tuscany at the beginning of the 19C it was restored, and the famous violinist Niccolò Paganini often played here. The theatre was redecorated after 1860. The **billiard room** has charming 19C painted decorations. A room in Bianca Cappello's apartment has a 16C fireplace and stone staircase (closed for restoration).

First floor A room with 19C grisaille decorations by Luigi Catani overlooking the loggia, adjoins another room where the original polychrome enamelled *terracotta frieze*, once on the façade, is displayed. A classical representation of a

Villa di Poggio a Caiano

Medici villas

Villa di Poggio a Caiano is the most important of the **Medici villas** surrounded by parks and gardens in the environs of Florence, nearly all of which are open to the public. There are long-term plans to arrange a museum here, encompassing the history of all the Medici villas. These country houses were used by the Medici to entertain artists and poets and as summer retreats from the heat of Florence. Leading architects of the time, including Michelozzo and Buontalenti were employed to enlarge or design these luxurious residences which were decorated with fine paintings (most of them now dispersed).

In the 15C, Cosimo il Vecchio employed Michelozzo to build **Cafaggiolo** (in 1451) and **Trebbio** (in 1461), both villas in the Mugello valley. Cosimo's grandsons Lorenzo and Giuliano spent their childhood at Cafaggiolo (which was sufficiently far from Florence to be safe during outbreaks of the plague in the city). Cosimo also employed Michelozzo to enlarge the villa of **Careggi**, nearer to Florence, which became the literary and artistic centre of the Medicean court in the 15C and is traditionally taken as the meeting place of the famous **Platonic Academy** which saw the birth of the Renaissance Humanist movement. Among its members, who met in the gardens, were Marsilio Ficino, Angelo Poliziano, Pico della Mirandola, and Greek scholars including Gemisthos Plethon and Argyropoulos, who came to Florence after the fall of Constantinople. Cosimo spent the last years of his life here (both his son, Piero di Cosimo, and Lorenzo il Magnifico also died here). Cosimo also had Michelozzo design the Medici villa outside Fiesole in 1458–61.

Lorenzo il Magnifico enjoyed hunting at Cafaggiolo, and he employed Giuliano da Sangallo to build **Poggio a Caiano**. Surrounded by a large park it became his favourite country residence, and he kept a large stud here. His younger cousins, Giovanni and Lorenzo di Pierfrancesco de' Medici acquired the **Villa di Castello** in about 1477 (and Botticelli's *Birth of Venus* and *Primavera* were hung here until the 18C).

The Medici grand-dukes in the 16C also took an interest in the villas. Cosimo I had Buontalenti design the villa at **Cerreto Guidi**, and he renovated the villas of Careggi and Castello (where he took a particular interest in the garden). Francesco I commissioned Buontalenti to build the villa at **Pratolino** (now Demidoff) and he took up residence with Bianca Cappello at Poggio a Caiano. They both died here on the same day in 1587, apparently of tertian fever (although there were rumours that they had been poisoned). Ferdinando I, who often stayed at Cafaggiolo, ordered Buontalenti to design the **Villa della Petraia**. He also built the hunting lodges of **Artimino** (known as La Ferdinanda) and the **Ambrogiana** (not open to the public).

In the 17C Cosimo III lived at **La Topaia** above the Villa di Castello beneath Monte Morello (now privately owned). After 1696 he commissioned the large paintings from Bartolomeo Bimbi (some of which are now kept at Poggio a Caiano) which document the numerous fruits and vegetables he grew there.

Platonic myth (or philosophical interpretation of the Golden Age with representations of classical heroes and myths; apparently an allusion to the good government of Lorenzo the Magnificent), it was designed to celebrate the Medici dynasty. It is thought by some scholars to be the work of Andrea del Sansovino (c 1490–94), with the help of a collaborator, but others consider it a later work (it is also attributed to Bertoldo di Giovanni). The pretty little 19C living room has wallpaper decorated with the Florentine iris.

The decoration of the *****salone**, was designed by Lorenzo's son Leo X in 1513–21 to celebrate the return of the Medici to Florence (after Lorenzo's eldest son, Piero, had been exiled in 1494 and a Republican government established in Florence). It has a carved and gilded barrel vault with the Medici arms by Andrea Feltrini and Franciabigio. The **frescoes** were begun by Franciabigio, Andrea del Sarto and Pontormo (1519–21) and completed by Alessandro Allori (1579–82). The subjects were designed by Paolo Giovio and illustrate incidents in Roman history paralleled in the lives of Cosimo il Vecchio and Lorenzo il Magnifico, as well as mythological scenes celebrating the return of the Medici dynasty in the 16C as rulers of Florence.

On the left of the entrance: *Julius Caesar receives the Tributes from Egypt* (recalling Lorenzo il Magnifico receiving gifts from the Sultan of Egypt in 1487), by Andrea del Sarto (Allori added the child with the turkey, the figures with the horse on the right-hand side, and the man with the parrot on the left). The numerous animals include a parrot and a giraffe. Opposite, *Scipio received by Syphax, King of Numidia after his victory over Hasdrubal in Spain* (in memory of Lorenzo il Magnifico's visit to Naples where he was entertained by Ferdinand of Aragon) by Alessandro Allori. On the other side of the door, the *Return of Cicero from exile* (alluding to the return of Cosimo il Vecchio to Florence in 1434) is by Franciabigio (the four figures on the right-hand side, and the statue of a river-god, as well as the obelisk and rostrum were added by Allori). On the entrance wall: *The Consul Flaminius at the council of the Achaean league* (alluding to Lorenzo il Magnifico's intervention at the Diet of Cremona which reversed the plans of the Venetian Republic), also by Allori.

The decorative scheme culminates in the remarkable *****lunette** illustrating the story of *Vertumnus and Pomona* as told by Ovid, a very fine work by Pontormo (c 1520). The harmonious idyllic scene was probably intended as a celebration of the new members of the Medici family. On the right are three female figures with white stoles: the splendid figure of Pomona, goddess of fruits, in green, with Ceres seated above her on the wall and Summer dressed in lilac. On the left, on either side of a dog, are Vertumnus in two disguises (as an old man and as a young man), with Bacchus seated above. Above and round the oculus (which looks towards Florence) putti play in the sacred laurel tree, above this idealised rustic scene. Bernard Berenson commented: 'as design, as colour, as fancy, the freshest, the gayest, most appropriate mural decoration now remaining in Italy'. The lunette opposite, illustrating the *Garden of the Hesperides*, and the frescoes above the windows were added by Allori.

Beyond a room with red silk hangings and Medici portraits by Sustermans, is Vittorio Emanuele II's bedroom. Other rooms include an Empire bathroom added by Elisa Baciocchi.

Beneath the loggia on the façade (with a fine barrel-vault) are remains of a fresco by Filippino Lippi, part of Lorenzo's original decoration.

Top floor This was reopened in 1998 for exhibitions. There are also long-term plans to open a museum here to exhibit the numerous still lives collected by the Medici and Lorraine grand-dukes. Of particular interest are those by Bartolomeo Bimbi from the Villa La Topaia (see above), with numerous different types of grapes, lemons, citrons, apples, and cherries (in their splendid original Dutch frames). For the time being this part of the villa is accessible only by appointment. In 1987 a large wooden merry-go-round which dates from 1799 was found in the villa.

The delightful **garden** and **park**, which descend behind the villa to the River Ombrone, contain numerous fine trees. The huge orangery was built by Poccianti in 1825.

Etruscan tombs at Comeana and Montefortini

Southwest of Poggio a Caiano is **Comeana**. Just outside the village, beside the cemetery (signposted), is the Etruscan tomb of **Boschetti** (7C BC), discovered in 1955 and formerly inside a mound or tumulus. It is now covered for protection. Nearby is the **Tumulus of Montefortini** now covered with oak trees, beside the road (entrance gate on the left; open 09.00–14.00 exc. fest.). Inside the mound an **Etruscan chamber tomb** was found in 1962, with an entrance corridor (or dromos) open to the sky. The antechamber and rectangular funerary chamber both have interesting 'false vaults'. The huge monolith which sealed the entrance survives. The stone shelf which runs round the walls of the inner chamber probably served for the illustrious defunct's possessions. The tomb dates from c 620 BC. Next to it excavations have been in progress since 1980 of a second tomb in the same tumulus, with a longer dromos, and a circular inner chamber supported by a central column 6m high. This seems to have been the more important tomb, built some 30 years earlier. The vault may have collapsed in an earthquake.

Villa di Artimino

The beautiful Villa di Artimino (also known as La Ferdinanda), stands in attractive woodland surrounded by superb Tuscan countryside about 2km from Comeana. It was designed by Bernardo Buontalenti (1594) for Ferdinando I.

This is one of the finest Medici villas. A singular feature of this villa are its numerous different chimneys. Galileo was a guest here in 1608. The Paggeria Mediea or service wing, also by Buontalenti, is now a hotel. The empty rooms of the villa are used for conferences and parties (for adm. enquire at the Paggeria, ☎ 055 871 8081).

The basement of Villa di Artimino houses the **Museo Archeologico Comunale** (open 08.30–12.30 exc. Wed), which displays Etruscan finds from excavations (still in progress) of the Etruscan-Roman settlement of Artimino and its necropoli.

The museum is beautifully arranged and well labelled. **Cases 1–8** contain material from Etruscan dwellings including Bucchero vases, ceramics, spindles and weights for looms and cooking pots. The rest of the collection comes from the necropoli. In **case 9** are ointment jars (7C BC). Displayed on its own in **case 10** is a rare *incense burner in Bucchero ware (7C BC) with an elegant stand, found at Prato di Rosello. In **case 11** are ivories (including small winged lions), bronze harnesses, and jewellery from the Boschetti tumulus. In **case 12** are Bucchero and impasto vases from the same tomb.

Cases 13 and **14** contains objects (ivory plaquettes and bronze objects) from the Montefortini tumulus. In **case 15** is a well-preserved bronze service for use at banquets (4C BC), including a splendid bronze situla with two handles. Displayed on its own in **case 16** is a large red-figure crater (4C BC) with dionysiac scenes found at Grumaggio. **Case 17** contains a beautiful Etruscan *amphora found at Prato di Rosello dating from the end of the 6C BC or beginning of the 5C BC. Also displayed here are cippi, a 6C stele, and three Volterra urns. The adjoining room has a fine display of 14C–15C ceramics from Bacchereto.

This hilltop site between the Ombrone and Arno rivers was once occupied by an Etruscan settlement from the 7C BC. Remains of a sacred area, probably part of the acropolis, were excavated in 1972 behind the Paggeria. A huge necropolis, known as **Prato di Rosello**, with some ten tumuli dating from the 7C BC, has come to light on the eastern slopes of the hill above the tumuli of Montefortini and Boschetti.

On the little hill in front of the villa is the charming medieval borgo of **Artimino**, and the fine Romanesque church of San Leonardo (only open for services on fest.). Imbedded in the outer walls of the church are casts of urns (the originals of which are in the Archaeological Museum of Artimino). Near the church, tombs from around 300 BC and later have been found.

At **Carmignano** (reached cross-country from Artimino in about 7km, or direct from Poggio a Caiano in 5km) the church of San Michele (open all day) contains a remarkable altarpiece of the *Visitation* by Pontormo (c 1530) on the second south altar. At the east end are two detached frescoes by Andrea di Giusto. This area has been famous since the 14C for its wine (produced with the addition of cabernet grapes), in particular at Bacchereto and Capezzana.

A few kilometres below Artimino is the little town of **Seano**. Beside the road an attractive sculpture park was opened in 1988 with a fine collection of 36 bronzes by the sculptor Quinto Martini (1908–90), who was born here.

The road continues across Monte Albano, past the Romanesque church of San Giusto to descend to Vinci (see p 163).

The Apennines above Prato

The road from Prato to Bologna (100km; N325) follows the main railway line across the Apennines. It ascends the Bisenzio valley passing through the wide upland basin of **Vaiano**, with its 13C campanile. There is a small archaeological and liturgical collection (15C–19C) in the Badia di San Salvatore, founded by the Benedictines in the 9C–10C, and restored in 1997. Nearby is **Figline di Prato** with the Romanesque Pieve of San Pietro (14C–15C frescoes; and a small museum of 14C–17C paintings and church silver). In the hills to the right of Vaiano is **Savignano**, the birthplace of the painter Fra Bartolomeo della Porta (1475–1517) and the sculptor Lorenzo Bartolini (1777–1850).

Near the ruined 12C–13C castle of **Cerbaia** is **San Quirico di Vernio** (278m), a substantial village with two residences (16C and 18C) belonging to the Conti Bardi family. The Oratory of San Niccolò dates from 1706. The mountain pass is just before **Montepiano** (700m), a summer resort. Here the 11C–12C Badia di Santa Maria contains 13C–14C frescoes. The region of Emilia (see *Blue Guide Northern Italy*) is entered near Castiglione dei Pepoli.

In the other direction, the old road from Prato to Pistoia passes **Montemurlo**, where the medieval Guidi castle was the scene of the last attempt of the partisans of the Florentine Republic to overthrow the Medici dynasty (1537).

Pistoia

Pistoia (93,200 inhab.) is a lively old Tuscan town with an unusual number of beautiful churches, whose character reflects its position between Florence and Pisa. Many of the churches contain good sculptures. It is an important horticultural centre, particularly noted for the cultivation of ornamental plants. There are extensive nurseries on the surrounding plain.

Practical information

Getting there
By car

Pistoia has an exit on the A11 motorway from Florence to the coast. The centre is closed to traffic: car parks at the ex-Officine Meccaniche Breda, off Via Pacinotti, or east of the Fortezza Santa Barbara, between Via del Bastione Mediceo and Via Cellini.

By train

Piazza Dante Alighieri, with services on the Florence–Viareggio line (from Florence, 34km in 35–45 mins).

By bus

From Florence run by *Lazzi* via the motorway in 45mins, to Piazza Dante Alighieri; and by *COPIT* in 1 hour to Piazza San Francesco. *COPIT* services from Pistoia to Abetone, Cutigliano and San Marcello Pistoiese *Lazzi* services to Prato, Montecatini Terme, Lucca and Pisa.

Information office
APT Abetone, Pistoia, Montagna Pistoiese in Palazzo dei Vescovi, Piazza Duomo 4 (☎ 0573 216 22, ▤ 0573 343 27; ✉ aptpistoia@comune.pistoia.it).

Where to stay
Hotels

☆☆☆ *Patria*, Via Crispi 8 (Map 1; ☎ 0573 251 87; ▤ 0573 368 168); *Milano*, Via Pacinotti 12 (Map 2; ☎ 0573 975 700; ▤ 0573 326 57);

Leon Bianco, Via Panciatichi 2, ☎ 0573 266 75; ▤ 0573 267 04. ☆☆ *Firenze*, Via Curtatone 42 (Map 3; ☎ 0573 216 60; ▤ 0573 231 41). 4km east at Pontenuovo, ☆☆☆ *Il Convento*, Via San Quirico 33; (☎ 0573 452 651, ▤ 0573 453 578).

Eating out
Restaurants in the centre

€€ *San Jacopo*, Via Crispi 15; *Corradossi*, Via Frosini 112. € *Trattorio dell'Abbondanza*, Via dell'Abbondanza 10; *Trattoria Lo Storno*, Via del Lastrone 8; *Il Sipario*, Corso Gramsci 159; *Le chiavi d'oro*, Via del Frantoio 3.

Restaurants on the outskirts of the city

€€ *La Cugna*, Località La Cugna, Via Bolognese 238 and *Rafanelli*, Località Sant'Agostino, Via Sant'Agostino 47.

Café

Valiani, Via Cavour (in a 13C oratory next to the church of San Giovanni Fuorcivitas).

Picnics

The public gardens in Piazza della Resistenza and in the Fortezza di Santa Barbara are both pleasant places to eat a snack (although the latter closes at 13.30).

Shopping

There are markets in Piazza Duomo and Piazza Spirito Santo on Wed and Sat mornings.

Annual festival

The *Giostra dell'Orso* is a medieval jousting tournament in which the mounted participants have to hit a wooden bear (the *orso*, the heraldic symbol of the city which supports its coat of arms) with their lance. It is held on 25 July in Piazza del Duomo (at 21.30).

History

Pistoia is first mentioned as the scene of Catiline's defeat in 62 BC. It was a republic in the 12C but was seized by the Florentines in 1306 and in 1315 by Castruccio Castracani, a military and political adventurer who died in 1328. The following year it came under the protection of Florence, whose fortunes it shared, as the Medici arms on the walls testify. As an ironworking town in medieval times, it gave its name to the pistol (originally a dagger, afterwards a small firearm).

The town became well known in the 18C for the organs constructed here by the Tronci and Agati families. The Breda works of Pistoia are famous for the production of railway carriages and buses; a new factory was built in 1973 on the outskirts of the town between the railway and the motorway (the huge old *officine*, off Via Pacinotti, have been abandoned and are at present used as a car park).

Guittone Sinibaldi, called Cino da Pistoia (1270–1337), friend of Dante, was born here; also Clement IX (Giulio Rospigliosi), Pope in 1667–69.

If you are approaching the town from Florence (or from the station) you will enter it on the site of the south gate; from here Via Vannucci and Via Cino lead to Piazza Gavinana.

San Domenico

Corso Fedi, on the right before the piazza, leads to the church of **San Domenico** built c 1280, probably to the design of Fra Sisto and Fra Ristoro, with 14C alterations.

The interior is particularly interesting for its sculptured **funerary monuments**. The fine stained glass in the east window dates from 1930. South side. Tomb of the lawyer and teacher Filippo Lazzari, by Bernardo and Antonio Rossellino; third altar, *St Sebastian* by Giacinto Gimignani. In a niche below 14C fresco fragments is the beautiful sculpted tomb effigy of Beato Lorenzo da Ripafratta (the friar, who was acclaimed for his generosity to those in need, died in the convent in 1457). Beyond the fourth altar, Gothic tomb of Andrea Franchi; fifth altar, *Assumption* by Matteo Rosselli.

South transept. *St Charles Borromeo* with members of the Rospigliosi family by Empoli, and 17C Rospigliosi funerary monuments (the busts are attributed to Bernini). In the chapel to the left of the presbytery, *St Dominic receiving the Rosary* by Cristofano Allori (the artist himself is depicted discussing his payment for the painting with the sacristan of the convent), and more 17C monuments. The organ, by Rovani da Lucca, dates from 1617.

In the **sacristy** (usually shown on request) are some interesting detached frescoes: the *Journey of the Magi*, attributed to the school of Benozzo Gozzoli; *St Jerome kneeling*, thought to be an early work by Verrocchio (also attributed to Domenico Veneziano and Antonio del Pollaiolo); and *St Mary Magdalene* (14C

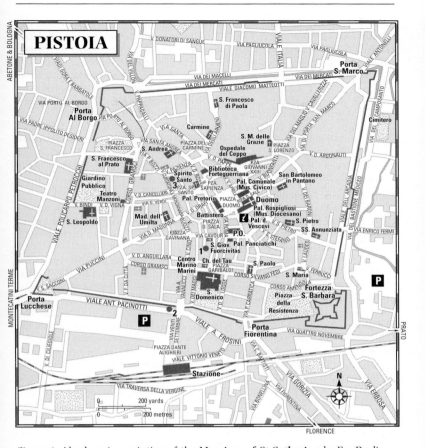

Sienese). Also here is a painting of the *Marriage of St Catherine*, by Fra Paolino.

A door in the south aisle leads into the **cloister** where, in an unknown spot, the body of Benozzo Gozzoli is buried. He died here in 1497 during the plague (commemorative plaque). Some of the lunettes are frescoed with scenes from the *Life of Mary Magdalene* by Giovanni da San Giovanni and Matteo Rosselli. The **chapter house** here has a damaged fresco of the *Crucifixion* by an unknown master of the mid-13C, with its *sinopia*, thought to be the oldest known in Italy.

On the other side of Corso Fedi is a little garden with palm trees, an equestrian statue of Garibaldi (1904) and amusing Art Nouveau lamp-posts. The **Chapel of Sant'Antonio Abate (del Tau)** (open 09.00–14.00 exc. Sun) was built in 1360 by the monks who cured the sick and disabled (they wore a T or Greek *Tau* on their cloaks, probably symbolising a crutch). The fine Gothic vaulted interior is entirely frescoed with *Scenes from the life of St Anthony Abbot* and the *Story of the Sacred Girdle*, and, in the vault, the *Creation*. These are by Niccolò di Tommaso (1372), probably with the help of Antonio Vite.

In the adjoining **Palazzo del Tau** (the former convent) the **Centro Marino Marini** (open 09.00–13.00, 15.00–19.00 except Sun pm and Mon; cumulative ticket with the Museo Civico and Museo Rospigliosi) has graphic works and plaster-casts by the sculptor, who was born in Pistoia (1901–66).

Farther along Corso Fedi, on the left, is the church of **San Paolo**, with a fine façade of 1291–1302. Over the later door are statues of *St Paul between two angels* by Jacopo di Mazzeo, and (high up on the pinnacle) a figure of *St James*, attributed to Orcagna. Inside is a 14C wooden *Crucifix* (left wall).

Via Porta Carratica and Via Campo Marzio lead to Piazza della Resistenza where there is a public park beside the 14C city walls. The impressive **Fortezza di Santa Barbara** is open 09.00–13.30 exc. Mon. Originally a 14C fort, it was strengthened for the grand-duke Cosimo I and protected by bastions designed by Bernardo Buontalenti.

San Giovanni Fuorcivitas

Via Crispi leads north from Piazza Garibaldi to the 12C–14C church of San Giovanni Fuorcivitas. The handsome striped north side, with a blind arcade surmounted by two blind galleries, serves as a **façade**. The fine portal bears a relief of the *Last Supper* by Gruamonte (1162).

In the dark **interior** (light on right side), with stained glass of 1908, the *pulpit is by Fra Guglielmo da Pisa, a follower of Nicola Pisano (1270). The *stoup, with the theological and cardinal Virtues, in the middle of the church is by Giovanni Pisano. On the west wall is a large Cross (13C–14C). Over the altar on the right side, tondo of the *Madonna and Child*, a good work by the 15C Florentine school. The high altar is composed of 12C intarsia panels from the Duomo. On the right wall of the sanctuary, *St John the Evangelist* and stories from his life, by Giovanni di Bartolomeo Cristiani (1370); on the opposite wall, polyptych by Taddeo Gaddi (1353–55), and *St Roch* by Bernardino di Antonio del Signoraccio. On the altar on the north side of the nave, *Visitation* in white glazed terracotta, a particularly moving work by Luca della Robbia (c 1445). Above the door, 15C wooden statue of *St Lucy*.

Near the west end of the church, through the entrance to the Cinema Verdi, the charming cloisters can be seen.

Farther along Via Cavour, Via Roma leads left past (right) the **Palazzo della Cassa di Risparmio**, an interesting building of 1905 by Tito Azzolini (with interior decorations by Galileo Chini) which stands opposite the old **Palazzo del Capitano del Popolo** (1283), on the corner of Via di Stracceria. The low medieval buildings here (which now have interesting old shop fronts) were used by the workmen who constructed the baptistery (see below). Beyond is **Piazza della Sala**, a delightful medieval market square, with the Pozzo del Leoncino, a well (1453) surmounted by the Florentine *Marzocco* (1529).

The large **Piazza del Duomo** has two handsome Gothic public buildings, as well as the Duomo, baptistery, and campanile. Above the far corner rises the tall medieval **Torre di Catilina**.

Duomo

The *Duomo (closed 12.30–15.30; the Chapel of St James is opened by the sacristan) has an arcaded Romanesque Pisan façade. The porch was added in

1311, and the high arch in the barrel vault is beautifully decorated by Andrea della Robbia, as is the *lunette above the central door. The separate *campanile was originally a watch tower, and is thought to have been adapted to its present use, with the addition of the three tiers of arches, in 1266 by Fra Guglielmo of Pisa, or in 1301 by Giovanni Pisano (the clock dates from 1712). In 2001 it was opened to the public: accompanied visits up the stairs on the hour every hour between 10.00–13.00 and 15.00–18.00. If it is a clear day there is a splendid view stretching as far as the Duomo and campanile of Florence.

A cathedral in Pistoia is documented as early as the 5C. The present church, dedicated to the Lombard St Zeno, erected c 1220 was drastically altered at the end of the 16C, but in 1951–66 it was restored as far as possible to its Romanesque form, and the fine wooden ceiling, decorated in 1388, was exposed.

The Benedictine Bishop Atho, known for his unselfish charity in the city as well as his writings, was canonised after his death in 1153. He successfully engineered the removal of the relics of St James the Greater from his famous shrine at Santiago de Compostela to Pistoia in 1144 by a group of pilgrims, and in 1145 he built the **Chapel of St James** in part of the south aisle of the cathedral (with a separate entrance), to conserve the precious relics of the apostle, who became patron saint of the city. For this chapel the silver altar was commissioned in 1287 which since 1953 has been displayed in a chapel in the south aisle. Bishop Atho's chapel was demolished in 1787. Next to the chapel was the sacristy which was robbed by Vanni Fucci in 1293, recorded by Dante in his *Divina Commedia* (*Inferno*, XXIV) as the *Sagrestia dei belli arredi* (the sacristy with beautiful furnishings). This is now incorporated in part of the Cathedral Museum (see below).

The 13C Duomo and campanile of Pistoia

Interior West wall. Funerary monument of St Atho, with reliefs showing the Bishop receiving the reliquary of St James, attributed to Cellino di Nese (1337). When the bishop's body, first buried in the baptistery, was translated to the cathedral in 1337, legend relates that a wonderful scent of roses emanated from his coffin (roses are still blessed in the cathedral on his saint's day). The *font is by Andrea Ferrucci da Fiesole, on a design by Benedetto da Maiano. In the lunette above the door, the fresco of St Zeno may date from the 12C.

South aisle. On the west wall is a Gothic window surrounded by beautiful fragments of 14C frescoes, attributed to Bonaccorso di Cino, all that remains of the famous Chapel of St James (see above). On the aisle wall, *tomb of Cino da Pistoia, thought to be by Agostino di Giovanni on a design by Cellino di Nese (1337). The painted *Crucifix* is by Coppo di Marcovaldo (and his son Salerno, 1275).

The chapel, which since 1953 has contained the ***Altar of St James**, was decorated in 1839. The famous altar is a masterpiece of medieval goldsmiths' work. It is decorated with numerous silver and partially gilded bas-reliefs and statuettes. It was commissioned in 1287, and remodelled and added to during successive generations (up to 1456). It is made up of a dossal—the earliest part—attributed to Pace di Valentino, with a statue of *St James enthroned*, which was added by Maestro Giglio in 1353. The altar frontal below, with fifteen scenes from the New Testament was completed in 1316 by Andrea di Jacopo di Ognabene. The two panels on either side of the altar are the work of Francesco di Niccolò and Leonardo di Ser Giovanni (1361–71). The panel on the left flank, with stories from the life of St James, includes two half figures of prophets which were added in 1400 by Brunelleschi (who may also have executed the standing figure of St Augustine, and the seated figure of an Evangelist). Behind the altar is a charming 15C Flemish tapestry.

Beside the steps down to the crypt, in a Gothic niche, are fine 14C frescoes and a triptych with the *Crucifixion* (1429). Two sides of the Romanesque **crypt** survive, and fragments from the earlier church can be seen here including panels from the pulpit by Guido da Como (1199; dismantled in the 17C). On a lower level is the 17C crypt.

In the chapel at the end of the south aisle is a good altarpiece of the *Coronation of the Virgin with Saints Baronto and Desiderio* by Mattia Preti, and *Moses receiving the tables of the law* by Luigi Sabatelli and the *Entombment* by Giuseppe Bezzuoli (1845–6).

The **choir** was designed in the early 17C by Jacopo Lafri. The frescoes are by Passignano and the high altarpiece of the *Resurrection* is by Cristofano Allori. The colossal statues of *Saints James* and *Zeno* are by a certain Vincenzo (1603), a pupil of Giambologna. To the right, at the top of the sanctuary steps, stands a bronze candelabrum by Tommaso di Bartolomeo (1442). At the entrance to the choir, on the north wall, is a fresco fragment of the *Madonna* attributed to Coppo di Marcovaldo.

North aisle. At the end of the north aisle is the **Chapel of the Sacrament**. Here (south wall) is the ***Madonna di Piazza with Saints John the Baptist and Zeno**, an extremely beautiful painting commissioned from Verrocchio around 1476, but probably painted by Lorenzo di Credi. It is protected by a red curtain, but it is usually possible to see it on request. Opposite is a ***half-length bust** of Archbishop Donato de' Medici, variously attributed to Antonio Rossellino or Verrocchio. The ciborium on the altar dates from 1662.

In the north aisle are a frescoed 14C *Madonna* and a seated statue of *Pope Leo XI*. At the west end of the aisle is the ***tomb of Cardinal Niccolò Forteguerri** projected by Verrocchio (1476–83) with Christ in Glory surrounded by angels and statues of Faith and Hope. The figure of Charity (on the left) was added by Lorenzetto in 1515, and the bust, two putti, and sarcophagus and the frame added in 1753.

The ***baptistery** (open 09.30–12.30, 15.00–18.00; closed Mon) is a beautiful octagonal building entirely decorated on the outside by bands of green and white marble. It was started in 1337 by Cellino di Nese, traditionally thought to be on a design by Andrea Pisano, and finished in 1359. The capitals and reliefs above the main entrance and the Madonna (attributed to Tommaso and Nino Pisano) in the tympanum are particularly fine. On the right is a tiny Gothic pulpit of 1399. The wooden doors are the work of Pier Francesco di Ventura (1523).

In the bare brick interior is a font with fine intarsia panels by Lanfranco da Como (1226). The statue of *St John the Baptist* is by Andrea Vaccà (1724).

Palazzo dei Vescovi

Palazzo dei Vescovi was founded on this site at the end of the 11C. Building continued in the 12C (and it was enlarged in the 14C) and it was well restored in 1982 by a bank (which now owns it and uses part of it as offices). It contains two museums: an archaeological section and the ***Museo della Cattedrale di San Zeno**. Admission to both museums by guided tour on Tues and Thur from 10.00–13.00 and 15.00–17.00.

The **archaeological section** is in the **basement**. Material found during excavations in the area of the palace, from the Roman period onwards, is displayed here. Highlights include two Etruscan cippi used in the foundations, and a hoard of medieval ceramics found in a well. Details of the excavations themselves including a Roman villa and part of a road are shown and explained.

In the **first room** of the **Museo della Cattedrale di San Zeno** there is a Roman cinerary urn (2C AD) with a carriage drawn by four horses, found during excavations in the Duomo. The 15C illuminated choirbooks are displayed in rotation. In the 12C **Sacristy of St James** (which was attached to the Chapel of St James, formerly in the Duomo, see above) is the ***reliquary of St James**, by Lorenzo Ghiberti and his bottega (1407). In the **Sala dell'Udienza** is a fresco of the *Crucifixion* by Giovanni di Bartolomeo Cristiani (1387); two 14C marble statuettes (Sienese or French); the ***reliquary of San Zeno**, made by the local goldsmith Enrico Belandini while in Aix-en-Provence in 1369; the so-called Cross of St Atho (c 1280), and the so-called chalice of St Atho, attributed to Andrea and Tallino d'Ognabene (1286). Two *reliquaries are displayed in the **Corte Vescovile**, one by Rombolus Salvei (1379), and the other by Maestro Gualandi (1444). The octagonal ebony and ivory coffer is by the *bottega* degli Embriachi (late 15C). Here also are a chalice of 1384 signed by the local goldsmith Andrea di Pietro Braccini, and a polychrome wooden statue of an *Angel with the head of the Baptist*, an interesting work thought to be by a French sculptor (c 1361).

A spiral staircase leads up to the **Torre Vescovile** displaying 17C vestments, and 18C church silver. In another room are *tempera murals by Giovanni Boldini (1868), with scenes of pastoral life and of the sea at Castiglioncello. They were detached from the Villa La Falconiera near Pistoia, where the Falconer family entertained Boldini and other painters of the Macchiaioli school, who were at work in Tuscany at this time (the name comes from their characteristic use of *macchie* or 'patches' of colour). Beyond a room with two carved panels by the local sculptor Ventura Vitoni (1442–1522) which survived the fire in 1641 which destroyed the choir in the Duomo, is more 17C church silver. The 12C **Cappella di San Nicolò**, the Bishop's private chapel, contains 14C fresco fragments. Steps lead up to the top of the Romanesque façade of the cathedral (now closed in), above the present loggia. Another room has 17C reliquaries, including the reliquary of St Bartholomew (1663). The **Sala Sinodale** contains fragments of battle scenes, among the oldest medieval frescoes in Tuscany, and a triptych by Giovanni di Bartolomeo Cristiani.

On the west side of the piazza is **Palazzo Pretorio**, a Gothic building of 1367 and later, which has a good courtyard, with painted and sculptured armorial bearings of magistrates.

Museo Civico

On the opposite side of the piazza is **Palazzo del Comune**, another fine Gothic building of 1294, with later additions. On the façade is a curious black basalt head which has probably been here since 1305. The palace houses the Museo Civico. Open 10.00–19.00; fest. 09.00–12.30; closed Mon; combined ticket with Palazzo del Tau and Museo Rospigliosi.

Piano nobile At the top of the stairs on the left is the **Sala dei Donizelli**. 13C ˙panel of *St Francis*, with stories from his life; a lovely 14C painting of *Mourning over the dead Christ* attributed to Lippo di Benivieni; polyptych of the *Madonna and Saints* attributed to the Master of 1310; 14C Tuscan statues; *Madonna enthroned with four angels* by Mariotto di Nardo; chalice by the local goldsmith Andrea di Jacopo d'Ognibene or Piero Braccini; *Angel* by Francesco di Valdambrino; *Annunciation and Saints* by Mariotto di Nardo and Rossello di Jacopo Franchi; three paintings of the *Madonna enthroned and Saints* by Lorenzo di Credi, Ridolfo del Ghirlandaio, and Gerino Gerini; 15C marble relief of the *Madonna and Child*.

Sala dei Priori. *Madonna della Pergola*, a very unusual work full of strange symbols and unusual iconographical references by Bernardino di Antonio Bernardino di Antonio del Signoraccio (Bernardino Detti; 1460–c 1532)Detti; bust of the *Redeemer* by Agnolo di Polo; a 15C and a 16C statue of *St Sebastian; Annunciatory Angel* and *Virgin Annunciate* by Fra' Paolino; and a *Rest on the Flight into Egypt* by the 16C Florentine school.

Stairs lead up past the **Centro Michelucci**, with drawings and models of works by the architect Giovanni Michelucci (1891–1991), born in Pistoia, and a section of 20C Pistoian paintings, to three rooms on the top floor.

Top floor The **Salone** contains late 16C and 17C paintings, including works by Gregorio Pagani, Matteo Rosselli, Il Cigoli, Empoli, Francesco Curradi, Carlo Saraceni (*Madonna and Child*, attributed), Giacinto Gimignani, Antonio Domenico Gabbiani, Lo Spagnoletto (*Portait of Lanfredino Cellesi of Pistoia*), Giuseppe Gambarini, and a contemporary copy of Carlo Maratta's *Portrait of Clement IX*. The decorative arts displayed here include Venetian glass, and Italian majolica.

The **Puccini Collection** was left by the last descendant of this family, Niccolò, in the 19C to a charitable institute, and part of it was acquired by the Museo Civico in 1913 and 1977. It includes: *Madonna enthroned with angel musicians* by Giovanni di Bartolomeo Cristiani, triptych by the Frankfurt Master; *Angels and the Madonna* by the *bottega* of Maso di San Friano; *Holy Family* by Giovanni Battista Naldini; *Marriage of St Catherine* by Il Cigoli; *Susannah and the Elders* by Mattia Preti; portrait of the doctor *Tommaso Puccini* (1669–1727) by Pietro Dandini, and a marble bust of him by Giovanni Battista Foggini.

The last room contains 18C and 19C works by Luigi Sabatelli, Anton Raphael Mengs (portrait of *Cardinal Francesco Saverio de Zelada*), and Gilbert Stuart Newton, and historical canvases by Enrico Pollastrini and Giuseppe Bezzuoli (as well as Puccini portraits).

Palazzo Rospigliosi

A 17C covered passageway links Palazzo Comunale with the Duomo high up above the narrow Ripa del Sale which descends to Palazzo Rospigliosi (no. 3; open Tues–Sat, 10.00–13.00, 16.00–19.00; combined ticket with Palazzo del

Tau and Museo Civico). The **Museo Rospigliosi** and the **Museo Diocesano** can be visited here. The palace was left to the cathedral by the last member of this branch of the Rospigliosi family in 1981. Pope Clement IX (Giulio Rospigliosi) probably stayed in the sumptuous bedroom in the apartment on the piano nobile. The four rooms contain original furnishings and 17C and 18C frescoes. The interesting 17C paintings (with fine frames) include numerous works by Giacinto Gimignani (1606–81, a native of Pistoia) and his son Ludovico, as well as works by Jacopo Vignali, Lorenzo Lippi, and Felice Ficherelli.

The **Museo Diocesano** is well labelled. The first room (which overlooks the hanging garden) contains 12C–13C Crosses, a 14C Cross in silver by a local craftsman, and chalices. The second room has a 14C painting of the *Madonna enthroned*, and reliquary busts and church silver. The third room has 17C–18C church silver. The fourth room has paintings of the *Sacred Conversation*: three of them by Bernardino del Signoraccio and one by Leonardo Malatesta. Beyond the fifth room displaying 18C vestments, the sixth room contains an exquisite small polychrome terracotta figure of the *Kneeling Virgin* (c 1460). The last two rooms contains a series of six paintings by Alessio Gimignani and 17C local works.

Via Pacini (at the end of Ripa del Sale) and Via San Pietro lead to the disused 12C church of **San Pietro**, with a characteristic façade. A relief of Christ giving the keys to St Peter, the Madonna, and the Apostles can be seen over the main portal.

San Bartolomeo in Pantano

Crossing Via Pacini at the bottom of Ripa del Sale, Via San Bartolomeo leads to the eponymous disorderly piazza in front of the church of *San Bartolomeo in Pantano. This was the church of a famous Benedictine monastery founded c 761. Count Ugo of Tuscany died here in 1001. The church was enlarged in 1159 and has a fine **façade** with a relief (1167) over the door of Christ and the Apostles, probably by Gruamonte.

The beautiful basilican interior with large capitals has a 13C Tuscan fresco of *Christ in majesty* in the apse. On the walls other fresco fragments have been exposed. The *pulpit by Guido da Como (1250), still Romanesque in spirit, has one of its columns resting on a crouching figure thought to represent the sculptor. It has four bas-reliefs showing scenes in the life of Christ and at the corners, symbols of the Evangelists. On the wall behind are exhibited four more bas-reliefs from the pulpit with scenes from the life of the Virgin. The altarpieces include (south aisle) works by Ignazio Hugford and Giovanni Maria Butteri, (south transept) Alessio Gemignani, and (north transept) Matteo Rosselli.

Via Pacini leads north to the **Ospedale del Ceppo**, a hospital founded in 1277, and still in use. The fine portico may be by Michelozzo, with modifications by Giovanni Battista di Antonio di Gerino (c 1480). It is decorated with a colourful enamelled terracotta *frieze (1514–25), excellently carved and very well preserved. It depicts the *Seven Works of Mercy* by Giovanni della Robbia, with the help of Santi Viviani Buglioni; the seventh scene was added by Filippo di Lorenzo Paladini in 1584–86. Between the panels are the cardinal and theological Virtues, also by Giovanni della Robbia. Beneath are medallions with the *Annunciation*, *Visitation*, and *Assumption* and the arms of the hospital, of the city, and the Medici, by Benedetto Buglioni and Giovanni della Robbia. To the left of the hospital, above the door of the adjoining church, is a *Coronation of the Virgin* by Benedetto Buglioni (1512), the oldest work of the series.

To the east of the hospital in Piazza San Lorenzo, is the church of **Santa Maria delle Grazie** or del Letto. It was built in 1451 and was formerly attributed to Michelozzo, but the fine presbytery is now generally considered to be the work of the local architect Ventura Vitoni. The high altar has a fine silver tabernacle (1641). The 14C bed, held to be miraculous (legend relates that a patient was miraculously healed when he had a vision of the Madonna while lying in this bed), which gave its name to the church, is preserved in a chapel on the left.

Sant'Andrea

From the Ospedale del Ceppo, Via delle Pappe and Via del Carmine (left) lead to Via Sant'Andrea in which is the church of *Sant'Andrea, with another good 12C **façade** with polychrome marble decoration by Gruamonte and his brother Adeodato who signed the relief of the Journey and Adoration of the Magi (1166).

In the long narrow interior (similar to San Bartolomeo in Pantano) is a 14C font of the Pisan school. The hexagonal *pulpit signed by Giovanni Pisano (1298–1301) is perhaps his masterpiece. Slim porphyry columns, held up by lions, eagles, and a crouching figure support Gothic arches with reliefs and statuettes of prophets and sibyls. Above, five dramatic reliefs show the *Annunciation* and *Nativity; Adoration of the Magi* and *St Joseph being warned to leave Bethlehem; Massacre of the Innocents; Crucifixion; Last Judgement.* Between the scenes are prophets, symbols of the Evangelists and the angels of the Apocalypse. It is probably that Tino da Camaino also worked on the carving. In the apse is a fresco of *God the Father* by Fra Paolino (Bernardino di Antonio del Signoraccio), 1506. In the south aisle, in a 15C tabernacle, a wooden *Crucifix* by Giovanni Pisano and a statuette of *St Andrew* by the school of Giovanni Pisano (formerly on the façade). At the end of the north aisle, *Madonna of Humility*, by Niccolò di Mariano (15C Sienese). The little organ dates from 1888.

At the end of Via Sant'Andrea is Piazza San Francesco, with the church of **San Francesco** (formerly known as *San Francesco al Prato*) begun in 1289, with a façade completed in 1717. The wide open-roofed nave with damaged remains of frescoes (and an altarpiece of the *Raising of Lazarus* by Alessandro Allori on the fourth left altar), ends in a wide vaulted transept with five east chapels. Behind the high altar (lights to right switched on by request) are 14C frescoes showing the influence of Giotto, possibly the work of a pupil, Puccio Capanna. In the chapel to the left is a splended fresco cycle of the *Allegory of the triumph of St Augustine*, by the Sienese school. 14C frescoes also decorate the second chapel to the right of the choir. In the south transept are interesting remains of a huge frescoed *Crucifix*, attributed to the Master of 1310. A door in this transept leads through the **sacristy** to the chapter house (not always open) both of which retain good late 14C frescoes, notably on the east wall of the latter, the *Tree of Life* with a *Crucifixion*, possibly by Pietro Lorenzetti. The 14C cloister is beyond.

In Corso Gramsci, south of the church, is the **Teatro Manzoni**, inaugurated in 1694, and altered in the mid-18C by Il Bibbiena.

From Piazza San Francesco, Via Bozzi and Via Montanara e Curtatone lead back towards the centre of the town. To the left is the church of the **Spirito Santo**, founded by the Jesuits in 1647 with a good Baroque *interior by the Jesuit father Tommaso Ramignani. Cardinal Giulio Rospigliosi, on becoming Pope Clement IX in 1667, commissioned Gian Lorenzo Bernini to design the high altar, and Pietro da Cortona to paint the high altarpiece of the *Apparition of Christ to St Ignatius*. The ciborium in *pietre dure*, ebony, and gilded bronze, also dates from this time. North side. First chapel, *Deposition* by Ottaviano Dandini (who also painted the two small works on either side); second chapel, 17C wooden, robed statuette of the *Madonna of Loreto*, and early 18C paintings of the *Nativity* and *Conception*. The little organ on the left (and its decorative counterpart opposite) are by the Flemish organ-maker Willem Herman (1663). The contemporary carved confessionals have also been preserved.

Nearby in Piazza Sapienza is the **Biblioteca Forteguerriana**. The library occupies a palace completed in 1534 by Giovanni Unghero for the Scuola della Sapienza, the school founded by Cardinal Niccolò Forteguerri in 1473. The library was founded in 1696 as an adjunct to the school. The main room on the first floor was designed for the library in 1776 by Giuliano Gatteschi.

In Via della Madonna, which leads right off Via Montanara e Curtatone, is the 15C basilican sanctuary of the **Madonna dell'Umiltà**, built by Ventura Vitoni (1495), a pupil of Bramante. The **dome**, a conspicuous feature of the city when viewed from the plain, was added by Vasari in 1562. The main portal dates from the 17C. The fine barrel vaulted vestibule contains 18C frescoes illustrating the history of the basilica. The octagonal centrally planned interior is an interesting example of High Renaissance architecture. South side. On the first altar, *Rest on the Flight into Egypt* by Lazzaro Baldi; second altar, *Adoration of the Magi* by Francesco Vanni; third altar, *Assumption* by Il Poppi. On the first altar left of the high altar, *Annunciation* by Lodovico Buti (on a design by Vasari); second chapel on the left, *Adoration of the Shepherds* by Passignano. The marble high altar by Pietro Tacca (with two angels by Leonardo Marcacci) encloses a miraculous 14C fresco of the *Madonna of Humility*, attributed to Bartolomeo Cristiani, around which the sanctuary was built.

The province of Pistoia

The province of Pistoia is very extensive and includes the famous spa town of Montecatini Terme and the gardens of Collodi, as well as the interesting little town of Pescia. Mountain roads lead up from Pistoia into the Apennines on the border with Emilia.

Practical information

Getting there
By car
The A11 motorway from Florence to the sea follows the main road with exits at Montecatini (for Montecatini, Buggiano, and Monsummano) and Chiesina Uzzanese (for Pescia and Collodi).
By train
The Florence–Viareggio line has stops at Montecatini Terme and Pescia. Montecatini has two stations: *Centrale*,

Piazza Italia, and *Succursale*, Piazza Gramsci (the most convenient to visitors, as the nearest to Viale Verdi). All trains on the Florence–Viareggio line stop at both stations; from Florence local trains in 50mins to Montecatini Terme, and in 1hr to Pescia (which has a railway station c 1km south of the town).

By bus

(*Lazzi*) from Florence to Montecatini (Via Toti) and Pescia. From Florence and Pistoia to Abetone. Bus services (*COPIT*) from Pescia to Collodi (in 25mins), and Uzzano, Castelvecchio, and the other small villages in the vicinity.

 Information offices
APT Montecatini Terme–Valdinievole, Viale Verdi, Montecatini 66 (☎ 0572 772 244; ✉ apt@montecatini.turismo. toscana.it) for **Montecatini** and **Pescia**. *Società delle Terme*, Viale Verdi 41 (☎ 0572 778 451) where tickets for the mineral water can be purchased.
APT Abetone-Pistoia-Montagna Pistoiese, Via Marconi 28, San Marcello Pistoiese (☎ 0573 630 145; ✉ aptpistoia@comune.pistoia.it) for the mountain areas above Pistoia. *APT* information offices at **Abetone**, Piazza Piramidi 502 (☎ 0573 602 31) and **Cutigliano**, Via Roma 25 (☎ 0573 680 29).

 Where to stay
Hotels
MONTECATINI TERME There are two ☆☆☆☆☆, thirteen ☆☆☆☆, about seventy ☆☆☆, and over ninety ☆☆ hotels, most of them open only from March or April to October or November. The most famous hotel (with a €€€ restaurant) is the ☆☆☆☆☆ *Grand Hotel e la Pace*, Corso Roma 12 (☎ 0572 758 01, 📠 0572 784 51). Information and booking

service at *Promozione Albergatori Montecatini*, ☎ 0572 753 65.
MONTECATINI ALTO ☆☆☆☆ *Park Hotel-Le Sorgenti* (☎ 0572 951 116, 📠 0572 952 731), at Pieve a Nievole.
MONSUMMANO TERME ☆☆☆☆ *Grotta Giusti*, swimming pool (☎ 0572 511 65, 📠 0572 512 69).
PESCIA ☆☆☆ *Villa delle Rose*, Via del Castellare, near the railway station (☎ 0572 451 301, 📠 0572 444 003).
SAN MARCELLO PISTOIESE ☆☆☆ *Il Cacciatore*, with restaurant (☎ 0573 630 533, 📠 0573 630 134). Cutigliano has numerous ☆☆☆ and ☆☆ hotels. At Abetone two ☆☆☆☆ hotels, and numerous ☆☆☆ and ☆☆ hotels.

Campsite

VICO near Montecatini Alto. ☆☆☆ Belsito (☎/📠 0572 673 73).

 Eating out
Restaurants
ENVIRONS OF PISTOIA € *Bischio*, at La Verginina zoo.
MONTECATINI TERME All categories all over the town including €€€ *Enoteca da Giovanni*, Via Garibaldi 25. €€ *San Francisco*, Corso Roma 112.
MONTECATINI ALTO €€ *Le Pietre Cavate* and *Uno Più* at Pieve a Nievole.
PESCIA €€ *Cecco*, Via Forti 84. € *La Buca*, 4 Piazza Mazzini.
MONTE A PESCIA €€ Monte a Pescia.
CIREGLIO €€ *Da Ildo* at Castagno di Piteccio.
CUTIGLIANO €€ *Fagiolino*, Via Carega 1.
ABETONE €€ *La Capannina*, Via Brennero 254.

Fattoria di Celle

At **La Verginina**, northwest of Pistoia, is a small **zoo** (open daily 09.00–dusk), created in 1970 on a pleasant hillside. In the Valle del Vincio is the pretty village of **Serra Pistoiese**, with an 11C Romanesque *pieve*. A few kilometres east of Pistoia, on the Santomato road, is the **Fattoria di Celle** (adm. May–Sept by written appointment to the Fattoria di Celle, 51030 Santomato, Pistoia, ☎ 0573 479 907). The villa was built at the end of the 17C by Cardinal Carlo Agostino Fabroni, and the huge Romantic *park was enlarged in 1830 by Giovanni Gambini (the delightful aviary and neo-Gothic coffeehaus date from that time). The property has been owned by the Gori since 1970, and here is displayed part of Giuliano Gori's private collection of modern and contemporary art made since the Second World War. From 1982 onwards some 37 sculptures have been set up in the landscape, some of them designed as isolated 'installations' and others forming part of their natural surroundings. The amphitheatre is the work of Beverley Pepper. Celle has become famous in Italy as one of the most successful experiments in providing a fitting setting in the open air for contemporary sculpture.

There is a fine road, in parts lined with pine trees, which leads due south from Pistoia across the Albano hills with spectacular views to Vinci (see p 163).

Montecatini Terme

Montecatini Terme (20,600 inhab.) is the best known of Italian spas, with an international reputation. It became famous at the beginning of the 20C, when the monumental thermal buildings were built. They are spaciously laid out and surrounded by attractive well-kept parks. The warm saline waters are taken, both internally and externally, for digestive troubles. The season runs from May to October.

History

Ugolino Simoni (1348–1425), born in Montecatini, made a fundamental study of the mineral waters of Italy, including those of Montecatini. Although probably known in Roman times, and used by the Medici, they were first developed on a grand scale by the Austrian Grand-duke Pietro Leopoldo in 1773–82. By the beginning of this century, Montecatini was one of the most famous spas in Europe. Giuseppe Verdi often stayed at the *Locanda Maggiore*, and wrote the last act of *Otello* here (1887). Most of the thermal buildings were built in 1928 on a project drawn up in 1915–18 by Ugo Giovannozzi for the Società delle Terme.

The centre of Montecatini is **Viale Verdi** on which are all the most important buildings; at the upper end is a view of Montecatini Alto (or Montecatini Valdinievole). From the unattractive Piazza del Popolo (the church of Santa Maria Assunta was built in 1962) the avenue ascends past the *Gambrinus* café in a piazza with a colonnade and decorative lamp-posts. The monumental **town hall** (and post office) built in 1919, stands opposite the **Società delle Terme** which runs the spas. The spas, used for drinking water and bathing, are all in the fine park beyond. The elaborate *Terme Excelsior* (open all year) was built in 1909 by Giulio Bernardini in a florid mixture of styles. The handsome extension was added in 1968. The *Terme Leopoldine* (which probably cover the most ancient spring) was rebuilt in 1926 by Ugo Giovannozzi in a classical style (the temple bears a dedication to Asculapius, the god of healing).

At the end of the Viale rise the splendid buildings of the *Terme Tettuccio*, the most famous thermal establishment in Montecatini, whose waters were mentioned as early as 1370. It was also rebuilt by Giovannozzi in 1925–28, although it preserves an inner façade by Gaspare Paoletti (1779–81). The café, reading room, and drinking gallery are all sumptuously decorated with ceramics, murals, statuary, and wrought-iron work by Galileo Chini, Ezio Giovannozzi (brother of Ugo), and many others.

Beyond the Terme Regina, on Viale Diaz, is the **Accademia d'Arte Dino Scalabrino** (at present closed) with a gallery containing works by Galileo Chini, Giovanni Fattori, Lorenzo Viani, Pietro Annigoni, and others, and a small historical museum. Also on Viale Diaz is the funicular station for Montecatini Alto (see below). In the extensive well-kept park beyond the Tettuccio are the Terme Tamerici and the Terme Torretta both built at the beginning of the century by Bernardini in a neo-Gothic style. On the hillside above is the Parco delle Panteraie with fine woods (and a swimming pool). The central railway station, with handsome marble decoration, dates from 1937. The huge Kursaal, once the Casinò, was sold in 1989 and again in 1994, and may one day be restored.

Montecatini Alto

Montecatini Alto (or *Montecatini Valdinievole*) is reached from Montecatini Terme by funicular railway from Viale Diaz to Montecatini Alto (usually open May–Oct 10.00–13.00, 15.00–19.30; in Aug 10.00–midnight (services c every half hour) or by road (5km). It is an old hill town (290m) in a spectacular position. Here the men of Lucca were defeated in 1315 by Uguccione della Faggiola, leader of the Ghibellines of Pisa.

The attractive piazza has several cafés and the Teatrino dei Risorti, an amusing building dating from the early 20C. Above it, on a hill planted with cypresses and ilexes, is the Prepositurale of San Pietro (open only for services). Walks may be taken in the pleasant surroundings, especially in the Val di Nievole, to the north.

Monsummano Terme

On the other side of the motorway is the little spa of Monsummano Terme, at the foot of the hill. Its vapour baths were once visited by the wounded Garibaldi. In the large piazza with a statue of the Tuscan poet, Giuseppe Giusti (1809–50), who was born here, is the parish church of **Santa Maria della Fontenuova** (1605). It is surrounded by a portico with frescoed lunettes by Giovanni da San Giovanni (1630). In the pretty interior there is a fine ceiling and organ. In the south transept, *Madonna with St Joachim and Anne* by Piero Dandini. Over the high altar, venerated fresco of the *Madonna and Child*. In the **north transept**, *Adoration of the Magi* by Matteo Rosselli. A delightful **museum** (open on request) contains works by Matteo Rosselli, Cristofano Allori, and a *Cross* in ivory attributed to Giambologna.

At the end of the piazza is the **Osteria dei Pellegrini**, a fine building of 1609–16, with a portico in travertine. Just out of this end of the piazza, at the corner of Viale Martini, is **Casa Giusti**, which houses a fine museum relating to the poet. From the piazza various grotte are signposted; these are caverns in the hillside once used as spas.

A narrow road (also signposted) leads up round the hill with chestnut woods (disfigured by quarries) to **Monsummano Alto**, a fortified medieval village. Its strategic position enabled it to defend the pass between the plain of Lucca and the valley of Pistoia. The road enters the ruined hamlet beside the tallest pentagonal tower. A path leads straight on to the 12C church with its campanile beside a picturesque group of houses, most of them abandoned. Another gate can be seen at the end of the ridge on the hillside below. There is a fine view of the plain stretching towards the sea.

South of Monsummano is **Montevettolini** where the parish church contains an *Assumption* signed and dated 1599 by Santi di Tito and a *Madonna and Saints* by Piero di Cosimo.

Buggiano

West of Montecatini is Borgo a Buggiano, outside which is the huge **Villa di Bellavista**, built at the end of the 17C by Antonio Ferri, with frescoes by Pier Dandini. It is owned by the State and has been partly restored as an exhibition centre (and is also sometimes used for concerts).

The parish church (**Santissimo Crocifisso**) of Borgo a Buggiano was rebuilt in 1771. On the nave pilasters in the interior are four paintings by Fra Felice da Sambuca (1777). On the first altar on the south side, *Madonna enthroned with Saints* by Fra Paolino da Pistoia, and in the south transept, *Madonna of the Rosary with Saints Dominic and Francis* by Bernardino del Signoraccio (1500–10). Behind the high altar, wooden *Crucifix* thought to date from the early 14C and two terracotta statues of the *Madonna and St John the Evangelist* attributed to the workshop of the Buglioni. On the north side (second altar), *Madonna and Saints* by Giacomo Tais, and (first altar), *Martyrdom of St Agatha* by Alessandro Allori. A charming small **museum** (opened on request) contains church silver, vestments, a 14C painted reliquary and numerous Crosses, some from Buggiano Castello.

A by-road leads up through olive groves past a large tabernacle on the right of the road with 15C frescoes of the *Madonna and Child and two angels* to **Buggiano Castello**, a charming old village, extremely well preserved. Many of the handsome houses have attractive red plaster finish. It is best to leave the car on the road below, and walk up through the castellated gateway. The **ex-convent of Santa Scolastica** has a pretty loggia with tiny columns high up on its façade. Beyond is the delightful little piazza with **Palazzo Pretorio** decorated with numerous coats of arms including some in della Robbian enamelled terracotta. Through an arch there is a view of the plain and the church tower of Stignano.

The **pieve** (Madonna della Salute), also in the piazza, was founded in 1038. The wide **interior** has fine capitals. At the west end are a *font and lectern (c 1250). South side, second altar, *Madonna and four Saints* by Giovanni del Brina (1571); third altar, *Annunciation* by Bicci di Lorenzo (or his school). Over the high altar is a small wooden *Crucifix* (possibly dating from the 14C). In the chapel to the left of the sanctuary, the *Madonna and Saints* is in the style of Andrea del Castagno (1498). North side, second altar, *Madonna of the Rosary* by Giovanni del Brina, The terracotta statue of the *Madonna and Child* in the niche is a Tuscan work c 1530. On the first altar, 16C painting of the *Baptism of Christ* (in very poor condition). At the top of the hill are remains of the medieval **Rocca**.

At **Ponte Buggianese**, south of Borgo a Buggiano, in the church of San Michele Arcangelo, are frescoes of the *Passion cycle* by Pietro Annigoni (1910–88), including a striking *Last Supper* in the apse.

Near Borgo a Buggiano is **Stignano**, a hamlet in a fine position where Coluccio Salutati (1331–1406), Chancellor of the Florentine Republic, was born (plaque). The church of Sant'Andrea has a Romanesque campanile.

Pescia

Pescia (18,200 inhab.) is a busy town which has expanded to the south. It has a very unusual plan, laid out longitudinally on both sides of the Pescia river: on the left bank is the cathedral and on the right bank the exceptionally long market square (Piazza Mazzini) with the town hall. The town became established in the Middle Ages when it was governed by a Vicario. As an ally of Florence, it suffered a severe defeat by Lucca and the Guelf party in 1281.

The town expanded in the 16C and 17C, and since the Second World War it has become an important horticultural centre particularly noted for its asparagus, carnations, lilies, and gladioli. The striking **flower market** built in 1951 by

Giuseppe Gori was superseded by an even larger one in 1980 (by Leonardo Savioli) on the southern outskirts of the town where a flower show (the Biennale del Fiore) is held in early September (next in 2002).

Piazza Mazzini, at the centre of the town is a huge, long, narrow square which characterises the general layout of the town. At the upper end is the town hall—**Palazzo del Vicario**—covered with coats of arms (restored in the 19C). In the loggia (seen behind an iron grille) is a war memorial by Libero Andreotti. A neo-Gothic outside staircase connects the palace to the Cancelleria and the Torre Civica. Among the fine palaces in the piazza is Palazzo Della Barba (no. 79) on a design traditionally attributed to Raphael. The Renaissance church of the **Madonna di piè di Piazza** closes the southern end of the square. It was built in the 15C by Buggiano and preserves its exterior, although the interior dates from 1605 (the wood ceiling is by Giovanni Zeti). Over the high altar is a venerated 15C fresco of the *Madonna* in the centre of a painting by Alessandro Tiarini which includes a view of Pescia. The last palace on the west side of the piazza was built c 1530 by Baccio d'Agnolo (it was reduced in size at the beginning of the 20C).

Ruga degli Orlandi runs parallel to the Piazza on its west side. Among the handsome palaces here is the decorative Palazzo Forti (no. 42). Farther north is the church of the **Santissima Annunziata** (closed), built in 1713–20 by Antonio Ferri. It contains a painting of *St Charles Borromeo* by Volterrano. In Piazza Santo Stefano (left) there is a view of the Castello di Bareglia on the hillside (now the convent of San Francesco di Paola).

The church of **Santi Stefano e Niccolao** is approached by a pretty outside staircase (thought to be by Agostino Cornacchini). Founded in 1068 the church was reconstructed in the 18C. In the south aisle, on the first altar, there are two wooden statues of the *Annunciatory Angel* and the *Virgin Annunciate*; the Virgin is attributed to Matteo Civitali. On either side of the second altar are two paintings of *St Sebastian* and *St Michael* by Agostino Ciampelli. In the sanctuary, *Madonna and four Saints* by Ercole Bazzicaluva (17C) and, on the right wall, *Madonna and Child with angel musicians* (and the *Epiphany* below), a fine 15C painting.

In front of the church is the 18C Palazzo Galeotti, seat of the Biblioteca Comunale and the **Museo Civico**. Open Wed, Fri and Sat 10.00–13.00; Thur 16.00–18.00; or by request at the Library.

In **Room 1** on the lower floor: *Annunciation and two Saints* by Neri di Bicci; triptych of the *Madonna and two Saints* attributed to Lorenzo Monaco (1464). **Room 2**: lunette of the *Madonna and Child with a bishop saint and St Dorothy*, attributed to Benedetto Pagni da Brescia (a pupil of Giulio Romano). **Room 3**: *Coronation of the Virgin* by Neri di Bicci; *Christ and St Mary Magdalene* by Santi di Tito. Beyond, a room of the Galeotti palace has been furnished with 18C decorations.

The first room of the **upper floor** displays a garland by the della Robbia; *Resurrection of Christ* by Benedetto Pagni, and *St John the Baptist in the desert* attributed to Giovanni da San Giovanni. Beyond it is a room with mementoes of the musician Giovanni Pacini who lived in Pescia from 1855 to 1867. There is also a library containing the papers of the historian Giovan Carlo de' Sismondi who lived in Pescia in the early 19C. The last room has a collection of local material belonging to the Comune, and a plan of the city dating from 1621.

On the right of Santo Stefano a short road leads up to another quiet little piazza in front of the **Palazzo del Podestà**, a handsome 13C building altered over the centuries. Here is a gallery of plaster casts (a *Gipsoteca*) with the works of the sculptor Libero Andreotti who was born in Pescia (1875–1933).

On the left, by the campanile of Santo Stefano (restored in 1388) Via San Policronio leads up beneath an archway to a bridge over a stream. From here a charming country lane continues uphill, past a tabernacle and skirting the town walls, to the **Castello di Bareglia**. It was converted into the convent of San Francesco di Paola in 1674 and has a pretty loggia. The church (1713) contains paintings by Giacomo Tais. On the other hill (left of the stream), called Colle dei Fabbri, in the church of an ex-convent (now a hospice) is a painting of *St Philip Neri* by Carlo Maratta.

Ponte San Francesco leads across the Pescia torrent to Piazza San Francesco and the **Teatro Pacini**, founded in 1717 (altered in the 19C).

San Francesco

The church was first built in the 13C, but later altered. **Interior. South wall**, frescoed lunette, detached from the exterior; second altar, painting of the eleven thousand martyrs (1577); third altar, **St Francis* with six stories from his life signed and dated 1235 by Bonaventura Berlinghieri. Painted only nine years after the saint's death, it is considered to be one of the most faithful images of him. **South transept**, *St Charles Borromeo* by Rodomonte Pieri and Francesco Nardi.

In the **sacristy** is a large fresco of the *Crucifixion* attributed to Puccio Capanna. In the chapel to the right of the sanctuary are remains of frescoes attributed to Nicolò Gerini or Bicci di Lorenzo, and other frescoes dated 1431. In the **sanctuary** with fresco fragments, on the left wall is an interesting painting of *A Miracle of St Anthony* by Giovanni Martinelli. In the chapel to the left of the sanctuary, triptych of *St Anne* by Angelo Puccinelli (1335), and on the left wall, *Deposition* by Passignano. The altarpiece in the **north transept**, of the *Martyrdom of St Dorothy*, is a fine work by Jacopo Ligozzi. **North wall**, *St Louis of Toulouse*, *St Elizabeth of Hungary*, and *St Anthony before St Francis* attributed to Lodovico Cigoli. In the large Chapel of the Immacolata (early 16C) there is a 15C wooden statue of the *Madonna and Child*, and a *Pietà* attributed to Cristofano Allori. Also off this side is the beautifully designed **Cappella Cardini*, attributed to Buggiano, considered to be an important work of the early Renaissance, its architecture derived from Brunelleschi. It is in urgent need of structural repair and restoration; the 15C *Crucifix* has been temporarily removed to another part of the church. The frescoes are by Neri di Bicci.

Via Battisti leads out of the piazza past the hospital of **Santi Cosma e Damiano**, built in 1762, with a coat of arms on its façade, and modern hospital buildings. Set back from the road on the left is the little church of **Sant'Antonio Abate** (1361; sometimes open on Sat, or by request at the hospital), which contains fine early 15C frescoes with scenes from the *Life of St Anthony Abbot* attributed to Bicci di Lorenzo, and a wood **Deposition* group dating from the 13C. At a crossroads by a bridge (left) **Palazzo Ricci** (1635) can be seen with a pretty little marble fountain at the foot of its façade.

Via Cavour (beware of traffic) leads on to the **Duomo**, with a massive Gothic campanile (the top was added in 1771), once a tower in the walls. Founded in the 10C, it was rebuilt in 1726 and has a façade dating from 1895 in the Renaissance style. The **interior** was designed in 1693 by Antonio Ferri. Off the south side opens the **Cappella Turini** built by Baccio d'Agnolo. The funerary monument of Baldassare Turini has two male figures by Raffaello da Montelupo and an awkward effigy by Pierino da Vinci. The painting of the *Madonna del Baldacchino* by Piero Dandini is a fine copy of the original by Raphael, removed to Palazzo Pitti by Ferdinando dei Medici in 1697. Beside the high altar (by Andrea Vaccà) is a lectern composed of Romanesque sculptures from the ambone of the old church. **North side**, third chapel, altar by Andrea Pozzo and an altarpiece of the *Martyrdom of St Lawrence* by Antonio Domenico Gabbiani; second altar, *Madonna and Saints* by Antonio Franchi.

The little Romanesque church of **San Michelino** is closed.

Beneath the campanile of the Duomo an arch leads into a courtyard. Here is the entrance (at the top of outside stairs) to the **Biblioteca Capitolare**, the cathedral chapter library (open on request in the mornings). In the **Cappella del Vescovado** is a lovely small enamalled terracotta *triptych of the *Madonna between Saints James and Blaise*, a late work of Luca della Robbia, with the help of his nephew Andrea (1455–60). Over the altar is a painting of the *Madonna and Saints* by Domenico Soldini (1592).

In front of the cathedral is the 18C church of **Santa Maria Maddalena** with a pretty dome. A venerated carved *Crucifix* is kept in the sacristy.

Via Giusti continues out of the town, passing beneath the **Porta Fiorentina** erected in 1732 by Bernardo Sgrilli in honour of Gian Gastone dei Medici.

In Piazzale Leonardo da Vinci, in the southern part of the town, is a small civic **Museum of Archaeology and Natural History** (open 09.00–13.00; Tues also 15.00–17.30), with finds from the Valdinievole (the mountain valley north of Montecatini Terme), and a zoological section.

From behind San Francesco (on Piazza San Francesco), a road (unsignposted) leads up through olive groves to **Uzzano**, a charming, quiet little village, extremely well preserved, with pretty gardens and orchards. The entrance is through a narrow medieval archway. It is best to park in Piazza Umberto where the **Palazzo del Capitano del Popolo** has a loggia on the ground floor. From the terrace there is a view of the plain, crowded with greenhouses.

Via Barsanti leads up to the **church** with a decorative little façade and massive campanile. The interior has two vaulted chapels at the west end with worn 15C frescoes, a 13C stoup, a font with a rare 16C wood cover, and (in a niche) a life-size della Robbian statue in polychrome terracotta (in very poor condition) of *St Anthony Abbot*.

In the two attractive green valleys of the River Pescia are numerous old paper mills (interesting monuments of industrial architecture) and picturesque villages: **Pietrabuona**, **Medicina**, **Fibbialla**, above the Val di Torbola, **Aramo**, **San Quirico**, and **Castelvecchio**, with the fine Romanesque pieve of San Tommaso. **Pontito** is the highest village in the valley with an interesting fan-shaped plan. It was the birthplace of Lazzaro Papi (1763–1834) who translated Milton's *Paradise Lost*. Another road from Pietrabuona leads up to **Vellano**, with the pieve di San Martino founded in 910.

Collodi

Collodi is famous for its Baroque gardens and children's park dedicated to Pinocchio.

On the right of the road is the entrance to the spectacular *gardens of Villa Garzoni**, now situated in disappointing surroundings. The gardens are open 09.00–dusk; from Nov–Mar the park closes on weekdays between 12.00 and 14.30; children's park open daily 08.30–dusk.

The grounds, much visited by tourist groups, are administered in a pretentious fashion. The terraced gardens were laid out on this steep hillside c 1650 and embellished in 1786. They are decorated with yew hedges, fountains and statues. From the hemicycle, beyond a sloping parterre, a double staircase leads to an upper terrace at the foot of a theatrical cascade, bordered by two water staircases. At the left end of the terrace is the green theatre laid out with box hedges. At the top is a colossal statue of *Fame*, and, beyond, enclosed by cypresses, an 18C bath-house with separate enclosures for men and women, near a screened gallery intended for an orchestra.

Paths lead up through the ilex woods to the villa or **Castello** (closed indefinitely for restoration), bought by the Garzoni in the early 17C and altered in 1652. It contains frescoed architectural perspectives attributed to Angelo Michele Colonna and 18C furniture.

The peaceful old village of **Collodi** climbs up the hill behind the villa. It is best approached on foot by the stepped lane which leads up beside the wall of the villa. The picturesque hamlet (no cars) has incredibly steep stepped lanes. There are splendid views of the valleys on either side of the ridge.

Across the river is the entrance to the **children's park** commemorating Pinocchio. *Le Avventure di Pinocchio, Storia di un burattino* is the famous book written by Carlo Lorenzini (1826–90) who took his pen-name from Collodi, the birthplace of his mother. It was first published in 1880–83 and later translated into 63 languages. The careful character portrayal and the trying situations in which the boy puppet often finds himself have a universal appeal so that this delightful book is also widely read and acclaimed by adults. Lorenzini was born in Florence where he lived; he took part in the Risorgimento and worked as a journalist and for the Prefecture of Florence.

The children's park, built in 1956 and much visited as a school outing, has a bronze monument to the puppet hero by Emilio Greco and a piazza with mosaics illustrating the life of Pinocchio by Venturino Venturini. The *Osteria del Gambero Rosso* restaurant was designed by Giovanni Michelucci in 1963. A garden was laid out in 1971 with sculptured tableaux recalling episodes from the book, and an exhibition hall, also designed by Michelucci was opened in 1987.

In the valley beyond Collodi a by-road left is signposted for **Villa Basilica**. The ancient *pieve* has a delightful exterior and fine interior (12C–13C). In the apse is an unusual painted *Cross* by Berlinghiero Berlinghieri. The font now serves as a fountain in the piazza outside.

To the south of Collodi is **San Gennaro** on a hill surrounded by olives, pine trees, and cypresses, with open views. The domed campanile (1840) stands between a large villa and the interesting Romanesque façade of San Gennaro. The church (usually locked) contains an ambone of 1162 and two 15C terracotta statues of the *Annunciation*. In front is a little terrace with lime trees.

The Apennines above Pistoia

A road constructed in 1776–78 by Leonardo Ximenes from Pistoia crosses the Montagna Pistoiese or Pistoian Apennines. It climbs steeply through woods and several villages through the small resorts of Cireglio, Maresca and Gavinana. The defeat of the Florentine army by Imperial troops at Gavinana in 1530, in which both commanders, Francesco Ferrucci and Philibert, Prince of Orange were killed, sealed the fate of the Florentine Republic and led to the firm establishment of Medici rule over Florence and Tuscany (a fine equestrian monument of 1920 by Emilio Gallori and the Museo Ferrucciano here both commemorate the battle).

The road reaches a summit level of 820m before descending to **San Marcello Pistoiese** (623m), the most important summer resort on the Pistoian Apennines. There are several old dams across the River Lima.

Cutigliano (670m) is a well-kept little resort. The 14C Palazzo Pretorio is covered with coats of arms. In the nearby church of the Compagnia is an enamelled terracotta high altarpiece of the *Madonna between Saints Anthony and Bernardine of Siena* by the Della Robbia family.

On the edge of the village, beside two horse-chestnut trees is the **parish church**. In the light interior is a high altarpiece of a *Miracle of St Bartholomew* by Sebastiano Vini, and on the left wall of the sanctuary a *Circumcision* by Giovanni da San Giovanni. At the end of the left aisle is a fine wooden altarpiece which encloses the *Birth of the Virgin* by Nicodemo Ferrucci.

Winter sports facilities include a funicular to **Doganaccia** (1540m), another ski resort, and to Croce Arcana (1730m).

Above **Pianosinatico** (948m) a splendid forest still covers the Tuscan slope of the mountains. **Rivoreta**, north of Pianosinatico, has an Ethnographical Museum which illustrates peasant life in the area.

The **Passo dell'Abetone** (1388m) takes its name from a huge fir-tree which

The Palazzo Pretorio at Cutigliano

has long disappeared. Round the road summit, still on the Tuscan side of the boundary with Emilia, is **Abetone**, one of the best-known ski resorts in the Apennines, specially favoured by Florentines. Numerous ski-lifts and chair-lifts ascend to the snow fields. It is also much visited in summer (it has swimming pools and tennis courts). Across the border in Emilia is Monte Cimone, the highest peak in the northern Apennines (2165m).

The main road to Bologna, leads north from Pistoia over the Passo della Porretta (or della Collina; 932m) in the Apennines. Next to it runs the Porrettana railway which until 1934 was the main line across the Apennines. The mountain stretch between Pistoia and Porretta Terme, opened in 1863 is particularly fine. **Pracchia** (616m), above the Reno valley was a summer resort, fashionable between the wars, at the mouth of a long railway tunnel on the border of Emilia.

Lucca

Lucca (86,600 inhab.) is one of the most beautiful small towns in Italy. It is surrounded by magnificent 16C–17C ramparts which are its most remarkable feature. It conserves much of its Roman street plan, and is especially rich in Romanesque churches. There are also an unusual number of private walled gardens within the walls. Lucca produces large quantities of olive oil.

Practical information

Getting there and getting around
By car

Lucca is on the A11 motorway between Florence and the sea. **Car parking** is not allowed inside the walls for longer than 90 mins except with an hourly tariff. Visitors are therefore strongly advised to park outside the walls in one of the free car parks (the most convenient of which is *Le Tagliate*, outside Porta San Donato). Limited space is sometimes available off the Viali Carducci, Margherita, del Prete, and Giusti, or outside the station or Piazza Risorgimento. There is a special car park for caravans (with facilities) in Via Luporini outside Porta Sant'Anna.

By train

The station at Lucca is in Piazzale Ricasoli, a few hundred metres south of the Baluardo di San Colombana. Services on the Florence–Viareggio line, slow trains stopping at numerous stations (from Florence, 78km in 70–90 mins). A footpath leads directly from the station across the lawn at the foot of the walls through the bastion of San Colombano and up over the walls to the piazza beside the apse of the Cathedral.

By bus

Terminus in Piazzale Verdi. *Lazzi* (☎ 0583 584 876) from Florence (direct via the motorway in 1hr). Services also to Bagni di Lucca, Montecatini, the coast, Pisa, and Livorno. *CLAP* (☎

0583 587 897) for numerous places in the province, including the Garfagnana.

By bicycle

Bicycles can be hired at the Casermetta San Donato, near the Comune tourist office.

Information offices
APT, Piazza Guidiccioni 2; Information Office, Piazza Santa Maria 35, ☎ 0583 919 991; ✉ info@luccaturismo.it. Information office of the municipality (Comune), Vecchia Porta di San Donato, Piazzale Verdi (☎ 0583 442 944).

Where to stay
Hotels within the city walls

☆☆☆ *Universo*, Piazza Puccini 1 (also known as Piazza del Giglio; Map 1; ☎ 0583 493 678, 🖷 0583 954 854); *La Luna*, Corte Compagni 12 (Map 2; ☎ 0583 493 634, 🖷 0583 490 021; ✉ laluna@onenet.it); *Piccolo Hotel Puccini*, Via di Poggio 9 (Map 3; ☎ 0583 554 21, 🖷 0583 534 87; ✉ info@hotelpuccini.com).
☆☆ *Diana*, Via del Molinetto 11 (Map 6; ☎ 0583 492 202, 🖷 0583 467 795; ✉ info@albergodiana.com).

Hotels outside the city walls

☆☆☆☆ *Napoleon*, Viale Europa 536 (☎ 0583 316 516, 🖷 0583 418 398).
☆☆☆ *Rex*, Piazza Ricasoli 19 (Map 4; ☎ 0583 955 443, 🖷 0583 954 348;

info@hotelrexlucca.com); *Celide*, Viale Giusti 27 (Map 5; ☎ 0583 954 106, 🖷 0583 954 304; ✉ hotelcelide@arcadiatel.it.

Hotels in the environs

☆☆☆☆ *Villa la Principessa*; swimming pool, at Massa Pisana, 3.5km outside the town on the N12 for Pisa (☎ 0583 370 037, 🖷 0583 379 136; ✉ info@hotelprincipessa.com); *Villa San Michele* at San Michele in Escheto (☎ 0583 370 276, 🖷 0583 370 277; ✉ htlvillas.michele@tin.it).

☆☆ *Villa Casanova*; swimming pool, at Balbano, 10km west of Lucca towards Massaciuccoli(☎ 0583 548 429, 🖷 0583 368 955).

Youth Hostel

San Frediano, Via della Cavallerizza 12, ☎ 0583 469 957; 🖷 0583 461 007.

Eating out
Restaurants within the city walls

€€€ *Antico Caffé delle Mura*, Piazzale Vittorio Emanuele 4; *Buca di Sant'Antonio*, Via della Cervia 1;

Antica Locanda dell'Angelo, Via Pescheria 21.
€€ *Il Giglio*, Piazza del Giglio 3; *All'Olivo*, Piazza San Quirico 1.
€ *Da Giulio*, Via delle Conce 47; *Trattoria Gli Orti*, Via Elisa 17; *Trattoria Leo*, Via Tegrini 1; *Vecchia Trattoria Buralli*, Piazza Sant' Agostino; *Trattoria Baralla*, Piazza Anfiteatro.

Restaurants outside Lucca

€€ *La Mora* at Sesto di Moriano (about 10km north).

Picnics

The ramparts.

Pasticcerie

Taddeucci, Piazza San Michele (for *buccellato*, a delicious simple cake made with fennel and raisins); *Cioccolateria Caniparoli*, Via San Paolino (excellent chocolate).

Shopping

An **antiques market** is held in Piazza San Martino on the third Sunday of every month (and on the preceding Saturday).

History

Stone implements discovered in the plain of Lucca show that it was inhabited some 50,000 years ago. The Roman colony of *Luca* was the scene in 56 BC of the meeting of Caesar, Pompey, and Crassus which led to their political alliance two years later, known as the First Triumvirate. The town is reputed to have been the first place in Tuscany to have accepted Christianity and its first bishop was Paulinus, a disciple of St Peter. In 552 the Goths were besieged here by the Byzantine general Narses who two years later, after the defeat of the Goths, was appointed prefect of Italy by Justinian. In the Middle Ages it was an important city under the Lombard marquesses of Tuscany, and later was constantly at war with Pisa and Florence. Under the rule of Castruccio Castracani, in 1316–28, Lucca achieved supremacy in western Tuscany, but his death was followed by a period of subjection to Pisa (1343–69). Charles IV then gave the Lucchesi a charter of independence, and it maintained its autonomy, often under the suzerainty of noble families, until 1799. In 1805 Napoleon presented the city as a principality to his sister Elisa Baciocchi, and in 1815 it was given to Marie Louise de Bourbon as a duchy.

The Romanesque churches were greatly admired by John Ruskin who spent much time here (at the *Hotel Universo*) studying them. The sculptor Matteo Civitali (1435–1501) was born in Lucca, and nearly all his works remain in the town. Pompeo Batoni (1708–87), also born here, painted fashionable portraits, mainly in Rome. The city also is the birthplace of the musicians Francesco Geminiani (1687–1762), Luigi Boccherini (1743–1805) and Giacomo Puccini (1858–1924).

The city centre

The delightful ***Piazza San Michele**, on the site of the Roman forum, is still the centre of city life. The pavement and columns date from 1699–1705. The statue of Francesco Burlamacchi is by Ulisse Cambi (1863). When podestà of the city in 1546 Burlamacchi (1498–1548) led a rebellion against Medici rule, but was beheaded for his daring. In the portico of **Palazzo Pretorio** (1492; enlarged 1588) is a statue by Arnaldo Fazzi (1893) of Matteo Civitali, traditionally thought to be the architect of the original building.

San Michele in Foro

*San Michele in Foro (closed 12.00–15.00), is typical of the Pisan Romanesque style which developed in Lucca. Mentioned as early as 795, the present church was largely constructed in the 11C and 12C, though work continued until the 14C. The splendid tall ***façade** is richly decorated with coloured marbles, carved columns, and capitals. The upper part and lateral arcading date from the 14C when it was intended to raise the height of the nave (the project was abandoned because of lack of funds). On the tympanum is a huge statue of *St Michael Archangel*. On the southwest corner is a copy of a *Madonna* by Civitali (see below). The façade was often sketched by Ruskin.

The traditional beamed roof has been hidden by a vault built in the early 16C. On the west wall is a 14C fresco of the *Madonna and Child*, the *Madonna* by Civitali (from the façade), and an organ dating from 1804. In the apse hangs a *Crucifix* painted in the late 12C.

South aisle. The white enamelled terracotta relief of the *Madonna and Child* on the first altar is attributed to Luca della Robbia. Beyond a *Martyrdom of St Andrew* by Pietro Paolini, on the second altar is a little sculpted figure of *St Michael* (1658). South transept. Monument by Vincenzo Consani (1876) to Sylvester Giles, Bishop of Worcester, who died in Italy in 1521, and a painting of *St Filomena* (1867). The beautiful painting of *Saints Helena, Jerome, Sebastian, and Roch*, by Filippino Lippi has been removed for restoration.

North transept, *Marriage of the Virgin* by Agostino

The upper façade of San Michele in Foro, Lucca

Marti, and a *Madonna and Child* by Raffaello da Montelupo (1522), a high relief from the tomb of Bishop Sylvester Giles (destroyed in the 19C). In the north aisle, between the second and first altars, *St Catherine*, by Antonio Franchi.

Puccini's birthplace

Opposite the west door, Via di Poggio leads to Corte San Lorenzo and, at no. 9, the birthplace of Giacomo Puccini (open June–Sept 10.00–18.00; other months 10.00–13.00, 15.00–18.00 exc. Mon).

The flat, on the second floor, was owned by Puccini's family, many of whom were also musicians, from the beginning of the 19C. The composer (1858–1924) spent his youth here. His forbears had for four generations been organists of San Martino, though he himself was only a chorister at San Michele. His first great success after he moved to Milan was *Manon Lescaut* (1893). His other famous operas are *La Bohème, Madama Butterfly, Tosca,* and *Turandot,* left unfinished on his death in Brussels in 1924. The house contains interesting mementoes of the composer including portraits of his family, two of his early musical scores composed in 1880–83, letters, and the Steinway piano on which he composed *Turandot.* The Centro Studi Giacomo Puccini was founded in 1996 to promote the study and perfomance of his works, and provide a research centre with a specialised library.

In Piazza Cittadella a monument to Puccini, by Vito Tongiani, was erected in 1994.

Via San Paolino leads west to the church of **San Paolino**, by Baccio da Montelupo and Bastiano Bertolani (1515–36), with a fine façade. The **interior** has small early 16C stained glass windows.

First altar on the south side, *Holy Trinity* (1566) by Il Riccio; third altar, 15C polychrome wooden statue of *St Ansano,* by Francesco di Valdambrino; fourth altar, *St Theodore* by Pietro Testa. The two small cantorie in the nave are by Nicolao and Vincenzo Civitali; Giacomo Puccini often played on the 19C organ.

South transept. In the right chapel is the *Burial of St Paulinus and three other Saints,* a very unusual 14C painting attributed to Angelo Puccinelli. In the chapel opposite, *Miracle of St Paulinus* by Gerolamo Scaglia, and *Madonna and Child with Saints* by Lorenzo Zacchia (1585). In niches on either side of the presbytery, 14C wooden statues of the Angel Gabriel and St Paolino. In the chapel to the left of the presbytery, an unusual 15C painting of the *Coronation of the Virgin,* with a view of Lucca beneath. In the chapel opposite, *St Joseph* by Lorenzo Castellotti, and a 16C *Madonna and Child.*

North side. Fourth altar, *Martyrdom of St Valerio* by Paolo Guidotti, and a rare stone statuette of the *Madonna and Child* dating from the end of the 13C, brought here from Paris by merchants of the city in the Middle Ages. Second altar, *Madonna and Child* by Francesco Vanni; first altar, *Deposition* by Giovanni Domenico Lombardi. The stoup is by Nicolao Civitali.

Museo Nazionale di Palazzo Mansi

Nearby, in Via Galli Tassi, is the Museo Nazionale di Palazzo Mansi (open 09.00–19.00; fest. 09.00–13.00; closed Mon).

The *piano nobile* of the 17C palace has rooms decorated in the 17C–19C and the pinacoteca is especially interesting for its 17C paintings (many with good frames), and Medici portraits. A fine staircase leads up to the impressive loggia with Tuscan columns, and (left) the **Sala da Pranzo** (dining room) with mirrors, and 18C painted decorations by Francesco Antonio Cecchi. The **Salone del Ballo** (ballroom) has late 17C frescoes by Giovanni Gioseffo dal Sole. In the little **chapel** is a copy of a *Madonna* by Mabuse.

The **pinacoteca** is arranged in the four rooms beyond (the pictures are not all labelled but there is a hand-list in each room). **Room I** (the salone) contains works by Leandro Bassano; Paolo Veronese; Luca Giordano; Beccafumi (*Scipio*); Domenichino; Carlo Dolci; Giovanni Battista Naldini; Orazio Marinari; Jacopo Vignali (*Tobias and the angel*); Ventura Salimbeni; Rosa da Tivoli; Salvator Rosa; Federico Zuccari; Rutilio Manetti (**Triumph of David*); Orazio Gentileschi; and Francesco Furini.

Room II contains a fine collection of *portraits: those by Sustermans include *Cardinal Leopoldo* and *Vittoria della Rovere*; *Cosimo I in armour* is one of several versions of this well-known portrait by Bronzino, who also painted *Ferdinando de' Medici as a boy*, and *Don Garzia de' Medici as a child*. The **Portrait of a boy* (once thought to be Alessandro de' Medici) is by Pontormo. *Federico Ubaldo della Rovere at the age of two* is by Federico Barocci, and *Bianca Cappello* by Alessandro Allori.

Room III displays works by Andrea Schiavone, Vincenzo Catena, Sodoma, Jacopo Bassano, and Tintoretto. Also here is a good copy of a *Madonna and Child with St Anne* and the *Young St John* by Andrea del Sarto; and a *Madonna and Child* which is the only known work by the 16C Milanese painter Francesco Avanzi.

Room IV. Battle scenes by Salvator Rosa, Bergognone, and Rosa da Tivoli; landscapes by Paul Brill, and a *Portrait of a boy* by Michel Sweerts.

Off the Salone del Ballo (see above) are three small drawing rooms hung with 17C Flemish tapestries. The pretty **bedroom**, with an alcove, has 18C hangings made in Lucca. Beyond another room with a *Holy Family with St Anne* attributed to Van Dyck, are 19C rooms with 18C still lifes.

Top floor. Works by the native artist Pompeo Batoni (1708–87) include a portrait of *Archbishop Giovan Domenico Mansi*. Also here are paintings by Bernardino and Pietro Nocchi (the *Orsucci family* by Pietro), Stefano and Agostino Tofanelli, Michele Ridolfi, and late 19C paintings by Edoardo Gelli. The court portraits include one of *Elisa Baciocchi* by Marie Guillemine Benoist (1806). The bas-reliefs by Vincenzo Consani were made for the base of the monument to Marie Louise de Bourbon in Piazza Napoleone.

On the **ground floor** three rooms frescoed in 1691 by Giovanni Maria Ciocchi contain paintings from the deposits including works by Stradano and Antonio Franchi.

Via San Paolino ends in **Piazzale Verdi** with the old **Porta San Donato**, described with the ramparts at the end of this chapter.

Piazza San Martino

The attractive Piazza San Martino and the adjoining **Piazza Antelminelli** have a delightful miscellany of buildings from different periods: the Romanesque cathedral, the 14C building of the Opera del Duomo next to a 13C tower house and the 16C Oratory of San Giuseppe (all now restored as the Museo della Cattedrale), the 16C Palazzi Sanminiati (on either side of a little garden with palm trees), and the fine Palazzo Micheletti (1556) with a charming walled

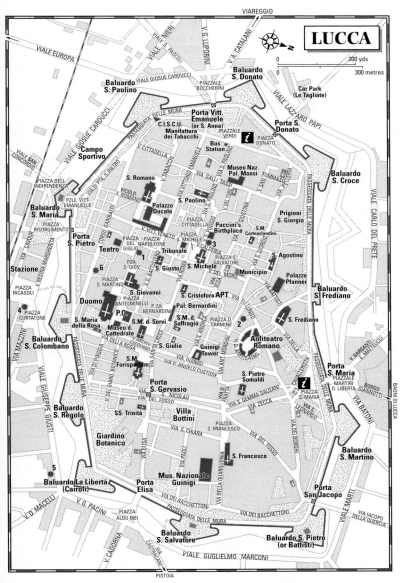

LUCCA

garden, by Bartolomeo Ammannati (above which can be seen the roof of the Baptistery). The circular fountain dates from 1835.

The cathedral of San Martino

The *cathedral was consecrated in 1070 by Pope Alexander II, who had begun the rebuilding while bishop of Lucca. The asymmetrical ***façade** is decorated with delightful sculptures in the Pisan-Lucchese Romanesque style. The statue of St Martin is a copy of the original 13C work, now inside the cathedral. The upper part, with three tiers of arcades, is signed by Guidetto da Como (1204). The columns are beautifully designed. The lower part of the embattled ***campanile** dates from 1060, the upper from 1261.

The three wide Romanesque arches (the one on the right smaller to accommodate the campanile) lead in to the **portico**, again beautifully decorated with sculptures, begun in 1233, and partly the work of Guido Bigarelli da Como. The exquisite decorative details are carried out in pink, green, and white marble. On either side of the central door, bas-reliefs depict the story of *St Martin* and the months of the year. Over the left doorway is a relief of the *Deposition*, and under it an *Adoration of the Magi*, perhaps early works by Nicola Pisano. Over the right doorway, in the architrave, is the *Meeting of St Martin with the Arians*, and in the lunette, the *Beheading of St Regolus*. On the right pier of the portico is a symbolic labyrinth (12C). The sides of the building are also beautiful, as well as the exterior of the ***apse**, with its arcades and carved capitals, surrounded by a green lawn.

The tall ***interior** (open 07.00–17.00 or 19.00) was rebuilt in the 14C–15C in a Gothic style, with a delicate clerestory, and a beautiful inlaid pavement designed by Matteo Civitali. On the entrance wall is the sculpture of ***St Martin dividing his cloak** removed from the façade. It dates from the 13C or possibly the early 14C. The two stoups are by Matteo Civitali (1498).

South aisle. First altar, *Nativity* by Passignano; second altar, *Adoration of the Magi* by Federico Zuccari; third altar, *Last Supper* by Tintoretto (and his school); fourth altar, *Crucifixion* by Passignano; fifth altar, *Resurrection* (1825) by Michele Ridolfi. The pulpit is by Matteo Civitali.

A door leads into the **sacristy** (combined entrance ticket with the Museo della Cattedrale, and San Giovanni). Here is the celebrated ***tomb of Ilaria del Carretto Guinigi**. The serene effigy is the masterpiece of Jacopo della Quercia (1407), and one of the most original works of the very early Renaissance. The sarcophagus may be the work of Francesco di Valdambrino. Ilaria, who died in 1405, was the second wife of Paolo Guinigi (1376–1432) ruler of the city from 1400–30, who built Villa Guinigi (see p 218). The tomb was moved here in 1995 from the north transept where it had been placed in 1842, and it has not yet been decided where it will be definitively installed.

The altar in the sacristy was designed in 1835 and incorporates an early 15C bas-relief of *St Agnello*. The fine painting of the *Madonna and Saints*, with a good predella, is by Domenico Ghirlandaio, and the lunette of the *Dead Christ* attributed to a follower of Filippino Lippi.

South transept. The 17C

The tomb of Ilaria del Carretto Guinigi in the cathedral of Lucca

organ is the work of Domenico Zanobi. The *tomb of Pietro da Noceto (1472) is a beautiful Renaissance Humanist work, by Matteo Civitali, who also sculpted the tomb of Domenico Bertini here. Bertini was papal secretary to Sixtus IV; he commissioned the monument in 1479 before he became podestà of the city in 1487. The two angels flanking the tabernacle in the chapel of the Holy Sacrament, and the altar of St Regulus (1484), right of the sanctuary, are also the work of Civitali. The modern bronze **high altar** was installed in 1987, and part of the marble screen, by the school of Civitali moved to the side chapels, despite local protest. The stained glass in the apse is the work of Pandolfo di Ugolino of Pisa (1485), and the choir stalls by Leonardo Marti (1452). On the high altar is a 14C Sienese triptych.

North transept. The altar with figures of the *Risen Christ* and *Saints Peter and Paul*, is by Giambologna (the predella with a view of Lucca is of slightly later date). In the Cappella del Santuario, *Virgin and Child enthroned with Saints* by Fra Bartolomeo (1509). In the middle of the north aisle is the octagonal marble *tempietto, also by Civitali (1484), built to house the famous *Volto Santo, a wooden likeness of Christ, supposed to have been begun by Nicodemus and miraculously completed. According to tradition, it was brought to Lucca in 782. It was greatly revered for centuries (and many copies made of it); the favourite oath of the English king William Rufus is said to have been *Per Vultum de Lucca*. The effigy is usually assigned stylistically to the 13C, probably a copy of an 11C work (in its turn perhaps modelled on a Syrian image of the 8C). On the outside of the Tempietto is a statue of *St Sebastian* by Civitali.

North aisle. Fifth altar, *Assumption* (1808) by Stefano Tofanelli; fourth altar, *Visitation* by Jacopo Ligozzi; third altar, *Annunciation* (1597) by Giovanni Battista Paggi; second altar, *Presentation of Maria in the Temple* byAlessandro Allori; first altar, *Birth of the Virgin* by Giovanni Battista Paggi.

Museo della Cattedrale

The Museo della Cattedrale in Piazza Antelminelli was reopened in 1992 in modernised rooms on four floors (open daily 10.00–14.00; summer 10.00–18.00; combined ticket with San Giovanni and the sacristy of the Duomo).

To the right of the ticket office is a room with elaborate goldsmiths' work made to decorate the Volto Santo, including a *frieze of 1382–84, a 17C crown, a huge jewel made in France in 1660, and a sceptre of 1852. *The Evangelists* by Domenico Fancelli (1663) are from the tempietto. **Room I** has illuminated codexes, including some by Martino di Bartolomeo. The **Oratory of San Giuseppe** has fine 17C gilded wood decorations.

Upper floor. **Room II** has a tiny wood pyx (1174), a Limoges *reliquary coffer showing the martyrdom of St Thomas Becket, and an ivory diptych from Constantinople (506). The famous *Croce dei Pisani* is an elaborate Crucifix almost certainly commissioned by Paolo Guinigi in 1411 from Vincenzo di Michele da Piacenza. The 15C reliquary of *St Sebastian* is by Francesco Marti.

Room III displays a 15C wood cupboard, part of the marble screen from the Duomo by Matteo Civitali, paintings by Vincenzo Frediani, and an early 16C crozier by Francesco Marti. **Room IV** has three paintings by Leonardo Grazia da Pistoia, Agostino Marti, and Zacchia il Vecchio. The two carved tondi of the head of *John the Baptist* are by Masseo Civitali and Vincenzo Consani. **Room V** has goldsmiths' work of the 16C and 17C.

On the **top floor**, **room VI** has late 17C–early 19C church silver. The sculptures in **room VII** include the head of a bishop or a Pope (late 11C), Fra Fazio, a quaint 14C work, 14C–15C sculpted heads from the cathedral, the head of a man and a colossal statue of *St John the Evangelist* by Jacopo della Quercia, two statuettes of prophets by Francesco di Valdambrino, and two classical female heads dating from c 1480. Also displayed on this floor is a very colourful 17C Sicilian carpet. The **Torre Belevedere** can be visited and the outside walkway with a view of the piazza.

Santi Giovanni e Reparata

In nearby Piazza San Giovanni, with a pretty walled garden, is the church of *Santi Giovanni e Reparata (combined entrance ticket with the sacristy of the Duomo, and the Museo della Cattedrale), whose fine portal of 1187 was preserved when the façade was erected in 1589. The **interior** (1160–87) has Roman columns with Romanesque capitals, a late 16C coffered ceiling, 19C funerary monuments, and frescoes of the *Madonna enthroned with Saints* attributed to Giuliano di Simone. At the east end the 9C crypt of San Pantaleone (which preserves his relics) can be seen.

Off the north side is the **baptistery** with a remarkable roof of 1393. The excavations here show the 12C font above a square 9C font which partially covers the early Christian font. The **excavations** (separate ticket) carried out in 1969–92 below the church revealed five building levels. Here you can see a fragment of the mosaic pavement of a Roman house (1C BC), traces of Roman baths (2C AD), and the remains of the huge geometric mosaic pavement of the first church (4C–5C) on this site which was the cathedral of Lucca until 715. Its nave is occupied by conspicuous round kilns used during the construction of the present church.

From Piazza San Giovanni a short road leads north across Via del Battistero (with numerous antique shops) to the 12C church of **San Giusto** (left), with a pretty façade and finely carved portal.

Adjoining Piazza San Giovanni is **Piazza del Giglio** (also called Piazza Puccini), with the neo-Classical façade of the **Teatro del Giglio**, built in 1817 by the local architect Giovanni Lazzarini. It was one of the most important opera houses in Italy in the early 19C, and here in 1831 was given the first performance of Rossini's *William Tell* (with Niccolò Paganini playing in the orchestra).

Palazzo Ducale

The adjoining **Piazza Napoleone** was laid out in 1806 in front of the Napoleonic residence, and planted with plane trees. The statue of Marie Louise de Bourbon, Duchess of Lucca in 1815–24, is by Lorenzo Bartolini.

Here is the huge Palazzo Ducale, in part designed by Bartolomeo Ammannati in 1578 and enlarged by Filippo Juvarra in 1728. The palace stands on the site of a much bigger castle (which occupied almost a fifth of the town) built for Castruccio Castracani (see p 207), probably by Giotto, in 1322. Most of this was demolished by the populace in 1369 in anger against the Pisans who had occupied it. The palace became the seat of the Lords of Lucca until 1799, and then the ducal residence. The seat of the Province of Lucca and of the Prefecture, it was restored in 2000 and is open to the public for concerts or by appointment (☎ 0583 417 454). The most interesting parts are the monumental neo-Classical staircase (1818), decorated with stuccoes, the long corridor with classical sculpture, and a grand reception room entirely decorated with frescoes of the life of Trajan by Luigi Ademollo dating from the early 19C.

Behind the building (reached through Ammannati's Cortile degli Svizzeri) is the huge Dominican church of **San Romano** (closed many years ago), which contains the tomb of St Romanus by Matteo Civitali (1490). The church was reconstructed before 1281 and enlarged in the 17C. Opposite the façade is a neo-Gothic stable block.

San Frediano

In the northern part of the town is the church of *San Frediano (1112–47), with a conspicuous tall **campanile**, with crenellations, restored in 1853. The façade is unusual for its large mosaic on a gold ground, possibly the work of Berlinghiero Berlinghieri (13C; restored in the 19C). It represents the *Ascension* (with the Apostles below). The church replaced an earlier basilica and has its apse at the west end.

In the splendid basilican *interior the columns of the nave have handsome classical capitals. At the beginning of the south aisle is a magnificent *font (probably dating from the mid-12C), in the form of a fountain covered by a small tempietto, sculpted with reliefs of the *Story of Moses*, the *Good Shepherd*, and the *Apostles*. Behind the font is a lunette of the *Annunciation* by Marco (Fra 'Mattia) della Robbia. Nearby are two interesting frescoes detached from behind the organ on the west wall. In the corner is the *Virgin Annunciate*, a polychrome wooden statue by Matteo Civitali. Above the entrance is the organ, attributed to Domenico di Lorenzo. Beneath it are two framed detached frescoes of the *Madonna and Child with Saints*, and a *Visitation*, both by Amico Aspertini.

Near the font is the 17C **Chapel of Santa Zita** (d. 1278), with paintings of *Miracles of the Saint* by Francesco del Tintore. Outside is a high relief of *St Bartholomew* by the della Robbia, and an altar carved by Matteo Civitali. In the next chapel is an interesting painting of the *Deposition* by Paolo Guidotti. In the last chapel (right) is a wooden relief of the *Assumption* by Masseo Civitali (in a marble frame), and a detached 13C fresco of the *Crucifixion*. On the left wall of the presbytery is a huge marble monolith, probably from the Roman amphitheatre (see p 217).

In the **Cappella Trenta** (fourth chapel in the north aisle) is an elaborately carved *altarpiece by Jacopo della Quercia (1422: assisted by Giovanni da Imola) and two pavement tombs by the same artist. Opposite is an *Immaculate Conception and Saints*, by Francesco Francia. Outside the chapel is a statue of *St Peter* by Vincenzo di Bartolomeo Civitali. The second north chapel contains beautiful early *frescoes by Amico Aspertini (c 1508–09) depicting stories of San Frediano, St Augustine, and the bringing of the Volto Santo to Lucca, with interesting local details and classical ruins in the landscapes.

Southwest of the church Via Cesare Battisti, with 17C–18C palaces, leads to **Palazzo Pfanner**, a privately owned palace (formerly Moriconi-Controni; open from March to Oct 10.00–17.00 or 18.00; ☎ 0583 954 176), built in 1667, with a delightful galleried outside staircase. The little 18C *garden, with a charming fountain and fine statuary, can also be seen from the avenue along the city walls (see below). The piano nobile or first floor of the palace has 17C frescoes and is partly furnished. The charming old kitchen can also be visited beside the dining room where the table is laid. The contents include four engravings by Stefano della Bella, and a polychrome wood statue of *St Michael Archangel and the dragon*, apparently dating from the 14C–15C.

Nearby is the 14C church of **Sant'Agostino**, with a plain unfinished façade, and its small campanile resting on arches of the Roman theatre. Inside, a little Baroque chapel was built in 1620 to house a venerated fresco of the *Madonna del Sasso*.

Across Via San Giorgio, Via del Loreto leads to **Santa Maria Corteorlandini**. The apse and south side of the church reconstructed in 1187 survive; the façade dates from the late 17C.

The pretty **interior** with painted decoration dates from 1715–21. Over the west end is a decorative organ gallery. The east end has painted decoration by Angelo Michele Colonna, and the gilded tabernacle on the high altar, decorated with precious marbles, dates from 1673 (by Giovanni Vambrè. Over the first altar in the south aisle, *Madonna and Saints* attributed to Matteo Rosselli, and over the second altar in the north aisle, *Birth of the Virgin* by Francesco Vanni. A door in this aisle leads to a chapel built as a replica of the Santa Casa of Loreto in 1662. Outside is a fresco by Filippo Gherardi. A precious collection of silk *altar frontals (17C–18C) made in Lucca belongs to the church (some of them are exhibited on the main altar throughout the year, the colours changing according to the liturgical calendar). In December a remarkable Christmas crib is set up in the church, the life-size figures dressed in splendid clothes made in Lucca in the 17C and 18C.

Also south of Via San Giorgio is **San Salvatore**, a 12C church with a charming architrave over its south portal, showing a *Miracle of St Nicholas*: the saint as a baby stands up in the bath in which he is being washed by two women. On either side are observers in towers and domed buildings. On the bath is the signature of the sculptor Biduino. On the façade, the right door has another carved architrave with another story from the *Life of St Nicholas*, showing a royal banquet. In the piazza is a pretty fountain by Lorenzo Nottolini (1842).

Via Buia leads from Piazza San Salvatore to cross the picturesque Via Fillungo with two old towers, one, with a bell, dating from the 13C. Next to it is the 13C church of **San Cristoforo** with a fine interior (now used for exhibitions). It is the burial place of the sculptor, Matteo Civitali (d. 1501) and also serves as a war memorial (the walls are covered with the names of soldiers killed).

The Guinigi Tower

Via Sant'Andrea continues to the Guinigi Tower (open daily 09.00–19.30; winter 10.00–16.30), 41m high, famous because of the trees which grow on its summit (staircase to the top).

During the rule of Castruccio Castracani in the 14C, the Guinigi were one of the richest families in Lucca, many of them involved in the silk trade. The family continued to take an active part in the government of the city up to the 19C. The last descendants of the family left the tower to the Comune of Lucca.

The upper part of the tower is reached by an iron staircase and on the top is a delightful little garden of seven ilex trees. The view offers a panorama of the city and its tree-planted walls, and the hills beyond. To the south is the side of the cathedral and the unusual dome of the baptistery (San Giovanni); farther to the right is the campanile of San Michele, behind the rear of its tall façade (with an outside staircase which can just be seen). Nearer at hand is the high medieval bell-tower in Via Fillungo. To the north is the campanile of San Frediano which stands beside the conspicuous mosaic on the church façade. Nearby, the oval shape of the amphitheatre, and the campanile and white colonnaded façade of San Pietro Somaldi can be seen; farther round is the white façade and rose window of San Francesco, near the castellated roof of Villa Guinigi. To the east, the top of Santa Maria Forisportam with its campanile is visible.

Adjoining the tower on Via Guinigi (nos 20–22 and 29) are the **Case dei Guinigi**, two large brick Gothic palaces facing each other. They were both built in the 14C and remodelled in the 16C.

The Guinigi Tower, Lucca

Via Guinigi leads north to Via Mordini which continues right to Via Fratta. Just beyond is the church of **San Pietro Somaldi**, founded in 763. The church was rebuilt at the end of the 12C, and work continued up to the 14C. The grey and white banded façade dates from 1248, although the relief above the central door by Guido da Como and assistants is a little earlier (1203).

On the first altar in the south aisle, the unusual painting of the *Assumption* dated 1532 by Zacchia da Vezzano has been removed for restoration. On the second altar there is a good 17C painting of the *Annunciation*. The third altarpiece of *St Bona* is by Giovanni Marracci. At the end of the aisle is a 14C frescoed lunette of the *Madonna and Child*. North aisle. On the altar at the east end, *Holy Family* (1840) by Nicolau Landucci; third altar, *St Peter* by Antonio Franchi; second altar, a beautiful and highly venerated *Madonna and Child* by Sebastiano Conca; first altar, *Saints Anthony Abbot, Bartholomew, Francis, Domenic and Andrew*, a good painting attributed to Raffaellino del Garbo.

Via Busdraghi and and Via del Portico lead to the **Roman amphitheatre**. The medieval houses which follow the ellipse of Via dell' Anfiteatro incorporate some of the brick arches of the amphitheatre. Its arena, where public spectacles were held in Roman days now forms a delightful *piazza, created in 1830–39 by the local architect Lorenzo Nottolini.

The eastern district

In the eastern district of the town at a crossroads by Via del Fosso on a pretty canal (formerly the moat outside the medieval walls) is the **Madonna dello Stellario**, a statue set up in 1687 on an ancient column. Carved on its base is an interesting view of Lucca from outside the walls, at Porta San Donato. Nearby is a neo-Classical fountain by Lorenzo Nottolini.

The church of **San Francesco** was rebuilt in the 14C (the upper part of the façade was finished in 1930). **South side**: second altar, *Madonna and Saints* by Sebastiano Conca; between the second and third altars, unusual monument to Giovanni Guidiccioni (1500–41), with a fine statue of the *Madonna and Child* attributed to Vincenzo Civitali. In the chapel to the right of the high altar a detached fresco of remarkably high quality by the 15C Florentine school has been removed for many years.

North side: fifth altar, *Noli me tangere* by Passignano; fourth altar, *Nativity* by Federico Zuccari; between the fourth and third altars, funerary monuments to the musicians Luigi Boccherini (1743–1805) and Francesco Geminiani (1687–1762). In the cloister is the tomb of Bonagiunta Tignosini (1274) with a ruined fresco by Deodato Orlandi.

The Museo Nazionale Guinigi

Nearby, in Via della Quarquonia, is the unusual brick Villa Guinigi, a castellated suburban villa built in 1418. The austere building was restored to house the **Museo Nazionale Guinigi** which contains a fine collection of sculpture and paintings from Lucca and its province, as well as an archaeological collection. In the garden is a Roman mosaic (1C–2C AD), and a group of carved Romanesque lions from the medieval walls (open 09.00–19.00; fest. 09.00–14.00; closed Mon).

Ground floor. The archaeological collection and medieval sculpture is arranged here. **Room I** (left of the portico) displays Bronze Age and Villanovan finds from near Lucca, and material from the Etruscan settlement of Serchio. **Room II**: four Ligurian tombs (reconstructed); Etruscan tomb with gold jewellery and an Attic krater (3C BC). Beyond are Roman finds from the city, including an altar of 40 BC–30 BC found in Piazza San Michele, mosaics and marble heads. **South portico**: medieval architectural fragments. **Room III**: fine examples of Lucchese sculpture (8C–14C) including a transenna with a relief of Samson and the lion; fragment of a statue of *St Martin* (12C–13C) from the Duomo; bas-reliefs from the church of San Jacopo in Altopascio; statuette of the *Madonna and Child* attributed to Biduino (late 13C); finds, including gold jewellery from a Lombard tomb (600 AD–650 AD).

Upper floor. On the upper floor are the paintings and later sculpture, mostly by artists born in Lucca or who worked here. **Room X**: marble statuette of the *Madonna and Child* by Tino da Camaino; **Madonna and Child* and *St John the Evangelist* by 'Ugolino Lorenzetti'; *St Michael Archangel* by Francesco Traini; painted **Crucifix* (from San Cerbone) by Paolo da Siena; *Crucifix* (1288) and *Madonna and Child* by Deodato Orlandi.

In the next part of the room: *Madonna enthroned* and **Mystical marriage of St Catherine and Saints* by Angelo Puccinelli; wooden statue of the *Madonna and Child* by Andrea Pisano; polyptych by Giuliano di Simone; and marble statue of the *Virgin Annunciate* by the early 14C school of Lucca.

In the last part of the room: *Saints* by Gherardo Starnina; polychrome wooden statue of the *Madonna and Child* (early 15C); and, at the end of the room: polyptych (c 1430) by Priamo della Quercia, enclosing marble statuettes. The very damaged pavement tomb of Balduccio degli Antelminelli is by Jacopo della Quercia, and that of Caterina Antelminelli by his *bottega*. The stalls from the Duomo, dating from 1452, are the work of Leonardo Marti.

Room XI: painted Cross by Borghese di Pietro Borghese; *Madonna and Child* *with Saints* by Zanobi Machiavelli; detached fresco of the *Nativity* attributed to Giuliano di Simone; two high reliefs in terracotta of the *Madonna and Child* by the *bottega* of Donatello; wooden statues of *St Ansano* Jacopo della Quercia and of *St Anthony Abbot* by Francesco di Valdambrino.

Room XII: *Annunciation* by a late 15C Flemish painter; *Dormition* and *Assumption of the Virgin* (in polychrome wood) by Vecchietta and Neroccio di Bartolomeo di Landi; intarsie by Cristoforo Canozzi da Lendinara; terracotta relief of the *Madonna and Child* and marble *relief of the *Annunciation*, by Matteo Civitali; wooden intarsia of *St Martin* from the cathedral by Masseo Civitali; *Visitation* by a 15C painter from Lucca; wooden statue of *St Nicholas of Tolentino* (1407) by Francesco di Valdambrino (from the church of Santa Maria Corteorlandini).

Room XIII: late 15C altarpieces of the *Madonna and Child with Saints* by Bernardino del Castelletto, Michele di Pietro Membrini, Vincenzo di Antonio Frediani, and Amico Aspertini. The marble *Ecce Homo* is by Matteo Civitali, and the statue of *Christ in Pietà* (1478) by Masseo Civitali. Also displayed here is a very fine 15C processional Cross in gilded silver, made in Lucca.

Room XIV: *Assumption and Madonna with Saints* by Zacchia il Vecchio; *Madonna della Misericordia* (1515), and *God the Father with Mary Magdalen and Catherine of Siena*, both good works by Fra Bartolomeo. Above the marble tomb of St Silao by Andrea di Giovanni da Carrara are two putti by Marco della Robbia.

Room XV: intarsia views of Lucca by Ambrogio and Nicolao Pucci (1529) from the Cappella degli Anziani in the Duomo. Works by Riccio, Daniele da Volterra (*Deposition*), Francesco del Brina, and Vasari (*Immaculate Conception*). **Room XVI**. Works by Aurelio Lomi, Jacopo Ligozzi, Domenico Passignano, Ludovico Cigoli, and Federico Zuccari. **Room XVII**. Works by Pietro da Cortona, Guido Reni, Giovanni Lanfranco, and Rutilio Manetti. **Room XVIII–XX** contain 17C–18C works by Pietro Paolini and Gerolamo Scaglia.

From Piazza San Francesco, Via del Fosso follows the line of medieval walls leading south between a canal (formerly the moat) and the garden wall of **Villa Bottini** (*Buonvisi*; entrance on Via Elisa). This is a fine building (1566) with two façades, surrounded by a pretty walled garden (open weekdays 09.00–13.00), with beautiful magnolia trees, and a nymphaeum attributed to Buontalenti. The interior, with many rooms frescoed by Ventura Salimbeni, has been restored by the Comune and it is now used for conferences. It also contains a newspaper library. In July and August concerts are usually held in the garden.

Opposite the entrance in Via Elisa is the church of the **Santissima Trinità** (1589; key from the adjoining convent) which contains a sentimental statue of the *Madonna della Tosse*, by Matteo Civitali. **Porta San Gervasio** (1255) is the best of the medieval gates remaining from the earlier fortifications of the city.

To the south of the gate, entered from Via San Micheletto are the **Botanical Gardens** designed in 1820 by Bernardino Orsetti (open 09.00–13.00 except Mon; fest. 09.00–13.00, 15.30–18.30). An extremely interesting garden for specialists, it includes medicinal plants, a huge cedar of Lebanon (1820), a sequoia, a camphor tree, and a three-stemmed ginkgo tree.

Santa Maria Forisportam

Inside Porta San Gervasio Via Santa Croce continues to the piazza in front of *Santa Maria Forisportam, named from having been outside the city gates until

1260. It is another fine church with a marble **façade** in the 13C Pisan style. Above the left door is a fine architrave with a lion and a griffin and a cast of a 12C high relief of the *Madonna enthroned*. In the lunette above the right door is a 13C statuette of a bishop saint. Above the central door is a 17C relief of the *Coronation of the Virgin*.

The pleasant grey **interior** was altered in 1516 when the nave and transepts were raised. On the west wall an early Christian sarcophagus has been adapted as a font. **South aisle**: first altar, *Coronation of the Virgin* by Gerolamo Scaglia (with a 15C fresco fragment below); fourth altar, **St Lucy* by Guercino. The ciborium in *pietre dure* and bronze in the south transept dates from c 1680. The handsome **high altar** was designed by Vincenzo Civitali (and finished in the 18C). In the **north transept** is a neo-Classical monument to Antonio Mazzarosa by Vincenzo Consani (1870) and an altarpiece of the **Assumption* by Guercino.

In the **sacristy**, off the south transept, is a *Dormition* and *Assumption of the Virgin* by Angelo Puccinelli (1386) and a *Madonna and Child* by Pompeo Batoni. There is a charming small **museum** (opened on request) in some adjoining rooms with sculpture (including a 13C wooden statuette of the *Madonna and Child*), church silver, altar frontals, vestments, a missionary museum, fossils and Roman material.

Via della Rosa leads south to the charming little oratory of **Santa Maria della Rosa** (locked), built in 1309–33 in the Pisan Gothic style. Inside are some traces of the original Roman wall.

The ramparts

A walk around the top of the 16C–17C **ramparts (4195m in circumference) which enclose the town completes a visit to Lucca. The road has been completely closed to traffic and some of the bastions have recently been restored. They have been planted with trees since the 16C (although some of these are now diseased and are being replanted) and provide delightful views of the town and of the Apuan Alps. The avenues and parks are beautifully maintained. The earliest circle of walls, of which traces have survived, date from the Roman period; new walls were built in 1198. The present fortifications, extremely well preserved, were carried out in 1544–1650.

The walls are 12m high and 30m wide at the base, and have eleven bastions, on many of which guardhouses survive. The interiors of some of the bastions have complicated defence works, armouries, ammunition stores and passages. Outside the walls are grassy fields on the site of the moat. In medieval times there were only three gates. The walls were never put to use but must have served as an effective deterrent to Lucca's enemies. They were built on a system afterwards developed by Vauban, and recall the ramparts of Berwick-on-Tweed in Scotland and Verona.

The **Baluardo di San Paolino** (see the Plan) dates from 1594–1642. In the delightful park is a monument to the musician Alfredo Catalani by Francesco Petroni. The guardhouse at no. 21 is the seat of *CISCU* (*Centro Internazionale per lo Studio delle Cerchia Urbane*, an International Centre for the Study of Urban Enceintes), founded in 1967 (when the bastion was restored) with a photo archive and library. The bastion has an interesting interior which incorporates the remarkable vaulted central hall of the 15C defensive tower on this site, as well as various corridors, an armoury, and a well and drinking trough for the horses. A small museum is open here in summer (for information, ☎ 0583 442 140).

A splendid double avenue of plane trees planted by Marie Louise de Bourbon in the early 19C leads along the ramparts to the **Baluardo di Santa Maria** designed by Francesco Paciotti and constructed by Matteo Civitali in 1562. Here is a 19C piazzale with a statue of Vittorio Emanuele II by Angelo Passaglia, and two 13C lions from the medieval walls. The *Antico Caffè delle Mura* (now a restaurant; see listing on p 207) was built in 1840 by Cesare Lazzarini.

The avenue passes beneath a loggia above the florid **Porta San Pietro**, the most important entrance to the town (1566; by Alessandro Resta), which preserves its original doors and portcullis (the side gates were added in 1846). From here there is a view of the campanile of San Giovanni and the roof of the baptistery. Beyond can be seen the side and apse of the Duomo beneath a bank planted with magnolia trees.

On the **Baluardo di San Colombano** are two more 13C lions, and the ruins of a medieval tower. From the **Baluardo di San Regolo** there is a view down Via del Fosso with its canal which runs along the line of the walls, built in 1198. On the bastion there is a children's playground and an ilex grove around a bust of Mazzini on a column. The ramparts (here planted with ilexes) now skirt the wall of the Botanical Gardens (see above). The **Baluardo La Libertà** (or Cairoli) is asymmetrically placed at the southeast corner of the fortifications.

There is a view of the Torre Guinigi from the avenue as it crosses above the neo-Classical **Porta Elisa**, opened in 1809. At the end of Via Elisa, Porta San Gervasio can be seen in the medieval walls. Near the **Baluardo di San Salvatore** remains of a medieval fortification (a rectangular enclosure with four wells on the left of the path) can be seen. From the **Baluardo di San Pietro** (or Cesare Battisti) there is a splendid view of the Apuan Alps. The ramparts pass above **Porta San Jacopo** (opened in 1930) to reach the **Baluardo di San Martino**, the foot of which has been disfigured by a car park. The interior was restored in 1967, and ruins of a medieval tower can be seen here. The avenue passes beneath the loggia above **Porta Santa Maria** (1593), one of the three original gates.

The **Baluardo di San Frediano** is a small rectangular bastion protected by grassed earthworks (1554). From the walls there is a splendid view across fields (crossed by paths) and trees to the mountains beyond. Inside the walls stand the campanile and apse of San Frediano, and the pretty garden decorated with statues of Palazzo Pfenner. The viale skirts a prison wall as far as the **Baluardo di Santa Croce** with remains of a medieval tower. The guardhouse here has two columns and is vaulted below.

The walk now passes beneath the loggia of the handsome **Porta San Donato** (1639) with two statues of San Paolino and San Donato by Giovanni Lazzoni. This replaced the old **Porta San Donato**, built in the medieval walls in 1591, which is conspicuous nearby in Piazzale Verdi. This area of the town, formerly called Prato del Marchese, was used from the 18C onwards for football games, horse races and other public spectacles. The gateway, on a design by Ginese Bresciani, was beautifully restored in 1976 and is now the municipal tourist information office. The line of the old walls can also clearly be seen here, and the foundations of the drawbridge outside the gate. A handsome stable block of 1876, at the foot of the ramparts, may one day be used as a conference centre.

The **Baluardo di San Donato** is beautifully planted with trees. The bastions pass above **Porta Sant'Anna** (or Vittorio Emanuele), opened in 1910 to return to the Baluardo di San Paolino.

Environs of Lucca

The environs of Lucca are noted for their fine villas and gardens built between the 16C and 19C, although only a few of them are at present open to the public (many others are being studied and may be restored and opened to the public).

In the foothills, northeast of the town, is the late 17C **Villa Reale** at **Marlia** (8km from Lucca), once the home of Napoleon's sister, Elisa Baciocchi. Niccolò Paganini, Metternich and John Singer Sargent all stayed here. It was bought in 1923 by Anna Laetitia (Mimì) Pecci-Blunt (1885–1971). She opened the Galleria La Cometa in Rome in the 1930s, and became a well-known collector of Italian art. The house is not open to the public, but the 17C Orsetti ***garden**, with notable statuary and a theatre, is (open 1 Mar–30 Nov at 10.00, 11.00, 12.00, 15.00, 16.00, 17.00, 18.00 exc. on Mon).

Nearby at **San Pancrazio** are two more villas: the 16C **Villa Oliva Buonvisi**, built by Matteo Civitali (the park is open from 15 March–15 Nov daily 09.30–18.30); and the neo-Classical **Villa Grabau**, with a large English park and orangery. The ground floor of the villa and the park are open from Apr–Oct 10.00–13.00, 15.00–19.00 exc. Mon and Tues morning.

At **Segromigno** (10km) is the 17C **Villa Mansi** (open 10.00–12.30, 15.00–17.00; summer 09.30–13.00, 15.00–19.00; closed Mon). Part of the garden, altered by Juvarra in 1742 survives near the house, with a pescheria (fish pond), the Bagno di Diana, and fine statues. The English park was created in the 19C. The villa has late 18C decorations, including frescoes of the *Myth of Apollo* in the salone by Stefano Tofanelli.

At **Camigliano**, nearby, is the **Villa Torrigiani** (open Mar–Nov exc. Tues 10.00–12.30, 15.00–dusk) with a Rococo façade, and fine park. It contains 17C and 18C paintings and a collection of porcelain.

A few kilometres south of Lucca, in località Vicopelago (off a by-road to Pozzuolo), is the **Villa Bernardini** built in 1600–15 by Bernardo Bernardini with a (modern) garden which includes an 18C green theatre (open daily exc. Mon morning, 10.00–12.00, 14.30–17.00; summer: 09.30–12.00, 15.00–19.30).

Five kilometres east of Lucca is **Lunata**, with its tall Romanesque campanile, which lies 2km south of **Lammari**, where the parish church contains a tabernacle, Matteo Civitali's last work. Farther east (17km from Lucca) is **Montecarlo**, well known in Tuscany for its production of good wine (red and white, including *Michi* and *Buonamico* and *Montechiari Cabernet*). On the other side of the motorway is **Altopascio**, where Castruccio beat the Florentines in 1325. The Order of the Knights of Altopascio (*del Tau*) ran a hospice for pilgrims here in 1084, and it has since been famous for its hoteliers. It is also well known for its bread.

At **Badia di Cantignana**, south of Lucca, The African explorer Carlo Piaggia (1827–82), was born. Together with Romolo Gessi he was the first to circumnavigate Lake Albert. A camellia festival is held at **Pieve di Compito** on three weekends in March (for information ☎ 0583 906 24).

On the plain to the south of Lucca is a monumental aqueduct built by Lorenzo Nottolini, c 1823, to bring water to the town from Monte Pisano.

The Garfagnana

The beautiful upper valley of the Serchio north of Lucca is known as the Garfagnana. It is well-wooded and richly cultivated. Lying between the Apennines and the Apuan Alps the scenery is spectacular in the side valleys and on the higher ground. In the centre of the valley is Castelnuovo di Garfagnana, situated between the Parco delle Alpi Apuane and the Parco dell'Orecchiella in the Apennines. In the lower valley is the interesting village of Barga.

Practical information

Getting there
By car

A pretty secondary road from Lucca follows the banks of the Serchio up the Garfagnana valley.

By train

A magnificent railway line, with fine scenery, follows the valley from Lucca to Aulla (91km in c 2hrs 15mins). It is served by local trains stopping at all stations including Bagni di Lucca, Barga, and Castelnuovo di Garfagnana (in c 1hr).

By bus

From Piazzale Verdi in Lucca (*CLAP*, ☎ 0583 587 897) to Bagni di Lucca, Barga, Castelnuovo di Garfagnana, Vagli, etc. Services run by *Lazzi* (☎ 0583 584 876) also to Bagni di Lucca.

Information offices
Castelnuovo di Garfagnana. *Comunità Montana della Garfagnana*, Via Vittorio Emanuele 9 (☎ 0583 644 911); *Pro Loco*, Loggiato Porta 10 (☎ 0583 641 007). **Bagni di Lucca**: *Comune*, c/o Anglican Church, ☎ 0583 805 745. **Borgo a Mozzano**: *Comunità Montana della Media Valle del Serchio*, Via Umberto I 100 (☎ 0583 883 46). **Barga**: *Pro Loco*, Piazza Angelio (☎ 0583 723 499).

Where to stay
Hotels

CASTELNUOVO DI GARFAGNANA ☆☆☆ Da Carlino, Via Garibaldi 15 (☎ 0583 644 270, 4 0583 626 16).

CORFINO near the **Parco dell'Orecchiella** (Villa Collemandina) ☆☆☆ *California* (☎ 0583 660 173), *Panoramico* (☎ 0583 660 161, ▤ 0583 660 159), and *La Baita* (☎ 0583 660 084).

SAN ROMANO GARFAGNANO (Villetta). ☆☆☆

Il Grotto (☎ 0583 612 392, 📠 0583 612 243).

PASSO RADICI Casone Profecchia near Castiglione di Garfagnana: ☆☆☆ *Il Casone* (☎ 0583 649 028, 📠 0583 649 048).

PARCO DELLE ALPE APUANE ☆☆☆☆ *Lo Scoiattolo*, Passo Carpinelli (Minucciano) (☎ 0583 611 071; 📠 0583 611 072). ☆☆☆ *Mini Hotel*, Gramolazzo (Minucciano) (☎ 0583 610 153; 📠 0583 610 668); *Belvedere*, Carpinelli (Minucciano) (☎/📠 0583 611 043), and at Vagli Sotto, *Le Alpi* (☎/📠 0583 664 057).

BARGA ☆☆☆ *Villa Libano*, Via del Sasso 6 (☎ 0583 723 059; 📠 0583 724 185); *La Pergola*, Via Sant'Antonio (☎ 0583 711 239, 📠 0583 710 433).

BAGNI DI LUCCA ☆☆☆ *Bridge*, Piazza Ponte a Serraglio (☎ 0583 805 324); *Corona*, Via Serraglio 78 (☎ 0583 805 151; 📠 0583 805 134); *Bernabò*, Bagni Caldi (☎ 0583 805 215). ☆☆ *Svizzero*, Via Casalini 30 (☎ 0583 805 315).

☆ *Roma*, Via Umberto I 110 (☎ 0583 872 78).

Campsites

GIUNCUGNANO ☆☆ *Argegna* (☎ 0583 611 154).
MINUCCIANO ☆☆ *Lago Paradiso* (☎ 0583 610 662). Open May–Sept.

Eating out

There are numerous *trattorie* in the Garfagnana, especially good in the mountain areas around the Parco dell'Orecchiella, including Casone di Profecchia, and Castelnuovo di Garfagnana.

Rsetaurants

BAGNI DI LUCCA €€ *Vinicio*, Via del Casinò 8 and *Circolo Forestieri*, Piazza Jean Varraud (Villa).
PONTE A MORIANO €€ *La Mora*, Via Sesto di Moriano 1748.

Sports
Hiking and horse riding

These are organised along some 350km of nature trails in the Apuan Alps and the Apennines (with overnight stays in mountain refuges). Information from the *Comunità Montana* in Castelnuovo di Garfagnana.

The lower Serchio Valley

At the southern end of the Serchio valley, some ten kilometres north of Lucca (reached from Vinchiana) is **San Giorgio di Brancoli**, in beautiful countryside, where the Romanesque church has an *ambone and a font, both 12C, a *St George* by Andrea della Robbia, and a 14C painted *Crucifixion*. On the west bank of the Serchio is **Diecimo** (at the tenth Roman mile from Lucca), with its 13C Romanesque church. To the west, on the by-road for **Pescaglia** is **Celle dei Puccini**, the home of Puccini's ancestors (their house can be visited by appointment, ☎ 0583 359 154). Near Pescaglia is the tiny village of **Vetriano** where a theatre, built in 1890 and reputed to be the smallest public theatre in the world, was donated to the *FAI* (*Fondo per l'Ambiente Italiano*, founded in 1975 modelled on the British National Trust) in 1998 and has been restored.

Borgo a Mozzano on the bank of the Serchio, a few kilometres north of Diecimo, has a church which contains expressive 16C sculptures and a wooden figure of *St Bernardine* by Matteo Civitali. The conspicuous **Ponte della Maddalena** is a remarkable ancient footbridge over the Serchio. There are many Romanesque churches in the vicinity.

Bagni di Lucca

A by-road on the east bank of the river leads to Bagni di Lucca, a little spa with warm sulphur and saline waters (open to the public), somewhat off the main valley. It is divided into several districts including Bagni Caldi and Bagno alla Villa. Noted for its waters since the 12C, it was particularly fashionable as a residence of the nobility of Lucca and foreigners from the 17C up until the end of the 19C. Its famous visitors have included Shelley, Byron, Browning (who advised Tennyson, Poet Laureate, to stay here in 1851), and Walter Savage Landor. The novelist Francis Marion Crawford (1854–1909) was born here, and in the little Protestant cemetery the romantic novelist Ouida (Marie Louise de la Ramée, born in England in 1839) was buried in 1908.

The town is entered by **Ponte a Serraglio**, from which the lower road leads left along the river overhung with pretty trees to the **Casinò** built by Giuseppe Pardini and founded in 1837 as the first licensed gaming house in Europe. A plaque on the house beside it records Alphonse de Lamartine's stay here in 1825.

The upper road leads through woods to the pretty spa of **Bagni Caldi**, with the **Stabilimento Jean Verraud** (early 20C). The thermal building next door is open from around 15 Apr–15 Nov).

In the other direction a road leads from the bridge to **La Villa**, a typical little spa. The **Palazzo del Circolo dei Forestieri** here was built in 1923–24, and the **Teatro Accademico** in 1790. The old English Chemist still has the royal coat of arms. Here, in the public gardens, is the neo-Gothic **English Church** built in 1839 by Giuseppe Pardini and on the hillside above the royal stables built in 1811.

A road leads up to the tiny hamlet of **Bagno alla Villa**, once an elegant residential district, but which now has an air of decadence. **Villa Buonvisi** was built in Piazza di Sopra in 1570, and Montaigne stayed here in 1581. The village was restored in 1669 for the visit of the grand-duchess Vittoria della Rovere, and more houses, including the **Casa Mansi** were built at that time. In 1722 James Stuart, the Old Pretender, came here with his wife Clementina Sobieska and stayed at the Villa Buonvisi. In 1811 Elisa Baciocchi, having received the principality of Lucca from her brother Napoleon, transformed **Palazzo Orsetti** into her summer residence, and this period of splendour for Bagno alla Villa continued during the Bourbon duchy. In 1818 Shelley and Mary Wollstonecraft lived in the Casa del Chiappa, and in 1822 Byron stayed with his friend John Webb who owned the Villa Buonvisi. The baths here were rebuilt in the 17C (but are now closed).

The by-road continues up the Lima river to **San Cassiano di Controne**. The church owns a remarkable polychrome wood sculpture of *San Cassiano* (or San Martino) on horseback, now attributed to Francesco di Valdambrino, which is one of the earliest equestrian groups produced in the Renaissance (c 1406–07).

In the main valley of the Serchio is the village of **Ghivizzano** with the castle and tombs of the Castracani family who were lords of this district. The village of **Coreglia Antelminelli**, reached by a by-road, contains an interesting church and a museum of 18C–20C figurines (open weekdays 08.00–13.00; fest. in summer, 08.00–13.00, 16.00–19.00) for which the locality is famous. Traditionally made in plaster, the statuettes include animals, Greek gods, works by Canova, peasants, and figures for a crib. There are also numerous busts of the famous including Garibaldi, Napoleon, Wellington and Franklin. Although local artisans still practice this craft, they now usually use alabaster or plastic.

Barga

Barga (11,000 inhab.) is the most important place in the lower Serchio valley. It has expanded at the foot of its hill (410m) leaving the little old village remarkably peaceful. Cars can be parked by the bastion, where there is a war memorial, a monument to Antonio Mordini (1819–1902) and a huge cedar of Lebanon. Beyond the old **Porta Reale** (or Mancianella) the narrow **Via di Mezzo** winds up and down through the centre of the village. It passes the church of the **Santissima Annunziata** built in 1595 with decorative stuccoes, beside Palazzo Mordini.

Beyond Palazzo Cordati which follows the curve of the street, is a little piazza in front of the **Teatro dell'Accademia dei Differenti**. A theatre was first built here in 1689 and the present building dates from 1795. Above the piazza is a view of the Duomo and its campanile (described below). Piazza Angeli is named after the Humanist, Pietro Angeli (1517–96), whose bust is on the corner of his house here. Concerts are often held in this attractive piazza. Via di Mezzo continues to **Piazza del Comune** (or Salvi) with a picturesque loggia (once a market place), with a stone lion, the heraldic *Marzocco*, symbol of the political domination of Florence. Palazzo Pancrazi houses the town hall. In the adjacent Piazza Garibaldi is the handsome 16C **Palazzo Balduini**, perhaps on

Barga

a design by Bartolomeo Ammannati.

From Piazza Comune a steep flight of steps leads up to the church of **Santissimo Crocifisso** with a pleasant façade. It contains wooden stalls and a decorative gilded wood high altar. Via della Speranza leads out of the village through Porta Machiaia and over the interesting old **Ponte dell' Acquedotto**. Steps continue up from the Santissimo Crocifisso to the grassy terrace in front of the Duomo. From here there is a splendid view which takes in the snow-capped Apuan Alps and the Apennines.

The Romanesque *Duomo (restored in 1920 after earthquake damage) has a fine exterior built in the local white stone (*alberese*), and an embattled campanile. It dates from the 9C–14C with later alterations. The side of the earliest church serves as the façade which has an interesting main door. The north doorway has a carved architrave.

In the dark **interior** is a handsome stoup beneath a 14C fresco of *St Lucy*. The painting of *St Christopher* dates from the 18C (probably by Stefano Tofanelli). The sculpted 13C *pulpit is attributed to Guido Bigarelli of Como (or his pupil). In the main apse is a huge imposing figure of *St Christopher* in polychrome wood (early 12C). The stained glass tondo above is on a cartoon attributed to Lorenzo di Credi. In the chapel to the right of the high altar is a terracotta altarpiece of the *Madonna with Saints Sebastian and Roch*, and della Robbian works. In the chapel to the left of the high altar is a large painted *Crucifix* (15C), and a 16C painting of *St Joseph* with a view of Barga (in an elaborate frame), with a Byzantine *Madonna and Child* inserted into the top part of the painting. The contents of the rich treasury, which include a chalice by Francesco Vanni, are at present kept in the Canonica.

Across the grass is the **Palazzo Pretorio** with a loggia and a small museum. Steps lead down past a pretty garden to the **Conservatorio di Sant'Elisabetta** (ring for admission). In the church is a fine high altarpiece in enamelled terracotta attributed to Benedetto Buglioni. A large 15C *Crucifix* has been removed for restoration.

Via del Pretorio returns to the Porta Reale. Outside the gate, below Via Marconi by the hospital, is the church of **San Francesco**, with fine polychrome enamelled terracottas: the *Nativity and Saints* is attributed to Luca della Robbia 'il giovane', great nephew of Luca, and *St Francis receiving the Stigmata* to his brother Giorolamo.

The by-road which leads south from Barga to Fornaci di Barga passes a farm and cemetery next to the *pieve* of **Loppia**, founded in the 9C, with a worn Romanesque façade. A pretty road continues east beyond Barga to **Tiglio Alto** where the church contains 14C statues of the *Annunciation*, reminiscent of those in the cathedral of Carrara (see p 240).

On the west bank of the Serchio, opposite Barga, is **Gallicano**, where a by-road leads up to the hermitage of **Calomini**, excavated from the rock in the 12C (the double loggia dates from the 18C). To visit, ☎ 0583 767 003.

Another road continues along the river Turrite from Gallicano to the **Grotta del Vento**, above **Fornovolasco**, a huge **cave** extending for hundreds of metres below the Apuan Alps (guided tours every hour, 10.00–12.00, 15.00–18.00; ☎ 0583 722 024).

In the main valley above Barga is **Castelvecchio Pascoli**. Nearby, on the hill of Caprona is the house where Giovanni Pascoli (1855–1912) lived from 1895 until his death (for opening times, ☎ 0583 766 147).

Giovanni Pascoli

One of the best known Italian poets, Pascoli was born in Romagna and had a sad childhood. When he bought this house with his sister Maria he was known as a poet and Latinist. He succeeded Giosuè Carducci in the chair of Italian literature at Bologna University. His *I Canti di Castelvecchio* were published in 1903. One of his last public appearances was in 1911 when he talked at the theatre in Barga about the war in Libya.

The house has remained as it was at the time of his death with its original furnishings carefully preserved by his sister who survived him by many years and left their house to the Comune of Barga. It contains mementoes and some of the poet's manuscripts. Pascoli and his sister are buried in the chapel in the garden (the tomb was designed by Leonardo Bistolfi).

Castelnuovo di Garfagnana

Castelnuovo di Garfagnana (6500 inhab.) is at the centre of the Garfagnana, situated where the Turrite river meets the Serchio. In Piazza Umberto I are remains of the 13C **Rocca** or governor's palace (now used as the town hall), the residence in 1522–25 and in 1640–42 of the poets Ludovico Ariosto and Fulvio Testi when they were governors of the district.

Via Fulvio Testi leads up past a little piazza—where you can see the recently restored façade of the Rocca—past the local tourist office to the **Duomo**, rebuilt in 1504. In the interior (left wall), *St Joseph and angels, a beautiful enamelled terracotta altarpiece (attributed to Verrocchio, or the della Robbia); *Madonna and two Saints* attributed to Michele di Ridolfo Ghirlandaio and an *Assumption* by Santi di Tito. In the chapel to the right of the sanctuary, 14C *Crucifix*.

Via Castracani leads down to the old **Porta Miccia** with a bridge (1324) over the Serchio. On the other side of the river, in Via Marconi, is the **Teatro Alfieri**, dating from 1860, by Giovanni Carli), now used as a cinema. There is a street market in Castelnuovo on Thursdays. Near the village is the **Fortezza di Monte Alfonso** (1579). From Castelnuovo a spectacular mountain road leads over the Apuan Alps via Arni (where the road passes through an unpaved tunnel under Monte Altissimo; 1589m) to Massa on the coast (see p 240).

The Parco Regionale delle Alpi Apuane

Castelnuovo is the starting point for excursions to the **regional park of the Apuan Alps**, a protected area since 1985 and interesting for its spectacular mountain scenery between the Versilia and the Serchio valley. You can also go hiking and horseback riding (map and information from the park office in Castelnuovo di Garfagnana, ☎ 0583 644 242). Most of the hotels are in the comune of Minucciano in the northern part of the park (see listings above). On both sides of the mountain chain are marble quarries. The fauna include wild boar, deer and mountain goats. The highest peak is Monte Pisanino (1946m).

At **Vagli** (about 18km from Castelnuovo) is a large lake formed by the dam of a hydro-electrical plant (1946). Every 10 years or so when the lake is drained (last time in 1994) the borgo of **Fabbriche di Careggine**, founded in the 13C, re-emerges. Near **Campocatino** are interesting shepherds' huts built with dry-stone walls and slate roofs, once characteristic of this area. Some of them date from the 17C and are being restored. An oasis here is run by the *LIPU* wildlife office, ☎ 0583 664 103. The hermitage of **San Viviano** is perched on an isolated rock nearby.

The Parco dell'Orecchiella

On the other side of the valley is the Parco dell'Orecchiella in the Apennines with meadows in the green upland plains and extensive woods. For hiking and horse-back riding, information and map from the *Comunità Montana* in Castelnuovo di Garfagnana. There are some hotels near **Corfino** (see listings, above).

A road from Castelnuovo follows the left bank of the Serchio past **Sambuca**. Beyond San Romano in Garfagnana is **Verrucole** with the spectacular ruins of a castle which belonged to the Gherardenghi. The walls and a tower survive and are being restored. From **Vibbiana** the road continues up to Orecchiella where there is a visitor's centre. From here a path leads to a little **botanical garden** with Alpine plants on the **Pania di Corfino** (1300m) (guided tours May–Sept, or by appointment, ☎ 0583 644 911).

From Castelnuovo a road leads north across the Apennines towards Modena and Pievepelago (see *Blue Guide Northern Italy*). It passes **Pieve Fosciana** with a 14C church which contains an enamelled terracotta *Annunciation* by Benedetto Buglioni and **Castiglione di Garfagnana** with its 14C walls. The church preserves a *Madonna* (1389), the only signed work by Giuliano di Simone of Lucca. **Villa Collemandina** has a Romanesque church with two altars by Matteo Civitali.

Another mountain road leads north from Castelnuovo to **San Pellegrino in Alpe** with an interesting local ethnographical **museum**. It occupies 14 rooms of the 12C hospice which served travellers crossing the Apennines, and illustrates peasant life in the area (open 09.30–13.00, 14.30–19.00; Oct–May 08.00–14.00; closed Mon). The church has more fine works by Matteo Civitali. A few kilometres above San Pellegrino is the **Foce delle Radici Pass** (1529m), with winter sports facilities.

Higher up the main valley (10km north of Castelnuovo) is **Camporgiano**. The 15C castle contains a museum with an archaeological section and a collection of medieval and Renaissance ceramics (open by appointment, ☎ 0583 618 888).

A picturesque road continues past **Giuncugnano** beside the pretty upland plain of **Argegna** to the Foce di Carpinelli Pass (842m). It enters the Aulella Valley at Casola in Lunigiana which, with Aulla, is in the province of Massa-Carrara (described on p 243).

Versilia

Versilia, in the province of Lucca, is the name given to the narrow coastal plain at the foot of the splendid Apuan Alps, famous for its beaches which stretch north from the well-known resort of Viareggio all the way to Forte dei Marmi. In summer the coast is crowded with holiday-makers, many of them from Florence. The little inland town of Pietrasanta, as well as Camaiore and Seravezza are attractive and have buildings of interest.

Practical information

Getting there
By car

The A12 **motorway** follows the coast from Viareggio with the exits Viareggio-Camaiore and Versilia for Pietrasanta, Forte dei Marmi, and Seravezza.

By train

The area is on the main Pisa–Genoa line with stations at Viareggio and Pietrasanta (slow trains only). In Viareggio the railway station is in Piazza Dante.

By bus

A comprehensive network (run by *Lazzi* and *CLAP*) serves all the towns in the area. In Viareggio buses from the station along the sea-front (Viale Carducci) to Forte dei Marmi, and circular bus service to Torre del Lago; also inland to Camaiore; from Piazza d'Azeglio to Pisa; to Lucca and Florence.

Information offices
APT Versilia, Viale Carducci 10, Viareggio (☎ 0584 962 233; ✉ Viareggio@versilia.turismo.toscana.it), with information offices at Forte dei Marmi, Lido di Camaiore, and Marina di Pietrasanta, and the railway station of Viareggio (open in summer). The *Comunità Montana Alta Versilia* has its headquarters at Seravezza, where a *Pro Loco* office is also open in summer.

Where to stay
Hotels

VIAREGGIO has eight ☆☆☆☆, twenty-four ☆☆☆, and about forty ☆☆ and ☆ hotels (some of them seasonal). Numerous hotels of all categories in the coastal resorts of Versilia. Information from *APT* offices and *Associazione Albergatori Viareggio*, Via Leonardo da Vinci 1, Viareggio (☎ 0584 483 85).

PIETRASANTA ☆☆☆ *Palagi*, Piazza Carducci 23 (☎ 0584 702 49; 📠 0584 711 98); and numerous hotels of all categories at the coastal resort of Marina di Pietrasanta.

Campsites

Several near Torre del Lago Puccini.

 Eating out

VIAREGGIO There are restaurants in and around Viareggio of all categories, including € *La Darsena*, Via Virgilio 150.

FORTE DI MARMI €€ *Lorenzo*, Via Carducci 61 and *Tre Stelle*, Via Montauti 6.

CAMAIORE €€ restaurants in the environs include: *Emilio e Bona* at Lombrici; *La Dogana* and *Cavallino*

Bianco at Capezzano Pianore, Via Lorenzi 13 and *Il Vignaccio* at Santa Lucia.

PIETRASANTA €€ *Il Gatto Nero*, Piazza Carducci 32.

Dasci, Vicolo Porta a Lucca 5.

Festivals

The **Carnival**, held in the Lenten period preceding Easter (usually at the end of January or in February) is one of the most famous in Italy. The parade of allegorical floats (many of them topical) takes place on four consecutive Sundays and on Shrove Tuesday. The first three parades usually start at 15.00, on Shrove Tuesday and the last Sunday they start at 17.00 followed by a display of fireworks.

Sports

Golf

18-hole *Versilia* at Pietrasanta.

Viareggio

Viareggio (60,000 inhab.) is the main town of Versilia, and the most popular seaside resort on the west coast of Italy. It first became fashionable in the early 19C and it retains an old-fashioned air with its esplanade planted with palm trees, Art Nouveau houses, and huge old grand hotels and cafés.

Shelley drowned offshore near Viareggio in 1822 (see p 301). In the last century regular visitors to Viareggio have included the poet D'Annunzio and the great actress Eleonora Duse, Isadora Duncan, the American dancer, the painters Carlo Carrà and Felice Carena, the writer and philosopher Giovanni Papini, the playwright Luigi Pirandello, and the art historian Roberto Longhi. Since 1929 the **Premio Viareggio** has been awarded annually here for a work of Italian literature.

The town retains its regular plan from the early 19C when it was laid out by Lorenzo Nottolini on a chessboard pattern with long avenues parallel to the seafront and numerous parks. After Paolina Bonaparte built her villa (now the Villa Paolina, see below) on the edge of the sea in 1820 it became one of the first seaside resorts in Europe. Numerous decorative buildings (in Viale Carducci, Via Michelangelo Buonarroti, Via Ugo Foscolo, Via Antonio Fratti) survive from the Art Nouveau and Art Deco periods, many with frescoes and graffiti as well as external ceramic decoration (much of it by Galileo Chini). Among the architects who worked here were Giovanni Lazzarini, Alfredo Belluomini, and Roberto Narducci.

A splendid double promenade, with a road and a footway, leads along the shore from **Piazza d'Azeglio** to **Piazza Puccini**. Some old *bagni* (bathing establishments) survive here. At the inner corner of Piazza d'Azeglio is Piazza Shelley, with a bust of the poet by Urbano Lucchesi (1894). At Via Machiavelli 2, in the 19C **Villa Paolina** (see above) is the **Museo A.C. Blanc and Pinacoteca Lorenzo Viani** (closed for restoration; ☎ 0584 961 076). It contains a prehistoric and archaeological collection, paintings by Lorenzo Viani (1882–1936), born in Viareggio, and the Lucarelli collection of 20C Italian artists, including De Pisis, De Chirico, Guttuso and Carrà.

In Piazza Mazzini the first **Ospizio Marino** survives, built in 1854–61 by Giuseppe Barellai as a model hospital. Beautiful pine-woods extend along the shore in either direction from the town, and there is a distant view of the Apuan Alps. The outer harbour is busy with boat-yards and a 16C tower guards the inner basins where there is a port.

Coastal resorts north of Viareggio
On the coast to the north is **Lido di Camaiore**, another extended bathing resort. It is the first of a series of more or less exclusive resorts which stretch for some thirty kilometres all the way along the coast to Marina di Carrara. They are extremely crowded (mostly with Florentines) in summer. They are laid out on regular plans with long straight roads parallel to the shore and consist of elegant villas and hotels surrounded by gardens. The sea is not as clean as it once was, but the sand, separated from the road by colourful beach huts, is kept clean by the various bathing clubs and hotels along the shore. All the resorts have spectacular views inland to the Apuan Alps (often snow-capped in winter) and white marble quarries.

The most elegant bathing resorts along this stretch of coast are **Forte dei Marmi** and **I Ronchi**, with numerous villas and small hotels set in thick vegetation including pine-woods. The beaches are mostly private and have splendid views of the mountains.

In Forte dei Marmi Aldous Huxley wrote *Crome Yellow* in 1921, and two years later, *Antic Hay*. The Molo, a low pier, is the scene of the evening passeggiata.

Lago di Massaciuccoli
Torre del Lago Puccini, on the Lago di Massaciuccoli has been developed as a holiday resort with numerous campsites. It can be reached from Viareggio along the Viale dei Tigli, a fine avenue of lime trees which borders the **Macchia Lucchese**, a protected area of woods. It can also be reached from Piazza d'Azeglio by bus, or, in summer by boat from Largo Risorgimento.

Torre del Lago Puccini adopted Giacomo Puccini's name because he made his bohemian home on the lake here where he enjoyed shooting waterfowl. On the waterfront, surrounded by a garden, is the **villa** which Puccini built (guided tours every half hour, 10.00–12.30, 15.00–18.30; winter 10.00–12.30, 14.30–17.00; closed Mon). All his operas except the last, *Turandot*, were, to a great extent, written here. The house preserves mementoes of Puccini (1858–1924) and his tomb is in the chapel. An **opera festival** is held on the lakeside in summer in an open-air theatre. Outside is a bronze statue of Puccini by Paul Troubetzkoy (1925).

It is possible to take **boat trips** (60 minutes; enquire locally) on the lake to visit the marshes, either from the landing in front of Villa Puccini or from Viareggio. Since 1979 the lake has been part of the **Parco Naturale Migliarino-San**

Rossore-Massaciuccoli which protects the coast from Viareggio to Livorno (information from the *Ente Parco Regionale*, Via Aurelia Nord 4, Pisa, ☎ 050 522 111; visitor centre: ☎ 050 530 101 or 050 989 084; see also p 271).

The other side of the lake, which is prettier, is reached by the road from Viareggio for Lucca via **Massarosa**. At Quiesa a by-road leads right for the village of **Massaciuccoli**. By the right side of the road, marked by two cedars of Lebanon (yellow signpost) are the remains of a **Roman villa** discovered in 1935. It belonged to the Venulei, a Pisan family, in the 2C AD. There is a small antiquarium in the former school building in Via Pietra a Padule, which contains a mosaic pavement with fantastic animals made of stone tesserae lifted and restored in 1987 (for adm. ☎ 0584 937 311). On the other side of the road a path (sign-posted) leads up through olive groves (five minutes' walk) to remains of small **Roman baths** (unenclosed) on the hillside below the church (which can also be reached by car from the Lucca road). There is a fine view of the lake from here.

At the entrance to the village (a few hundred metres from the Roman villa) a road (signposted Oasi Lipu) leads down to a canal from the lake beside two picturesque old houses. Beyond two bridges a walkway raised on stilts continues across the marshes to the bird sanctuary on the lakeside where there are hides and fishing huts, as well as a small museum (for adm. ☎ 0584 975 567).

From Massaciuccoli a road signposted to Lucca crosses a hill with some disused quarries, and then descends through woods. It passes the conspicuous 14C castle of **Nozzano** (see p 273). Nearby is **Arliano**, with a very ancient *pieve*, possibly dating from the 8C.

Camaiore

Inland from Viareggio (reached by a road alongside a canal) is Camaiore, a pleasant little town in a fine position, surrounded by the foothills of the Apuan Alps. It is built on a regular plan with long straight streets, crossed by the ancient Francigena pilgrim route (see p 442). The **Collegiata** (1278) has been much altered. In the presbytery is an *Assumption with Saints Peter and Paul* by Benedetto Brandimarti (late 16C). At the end of the left aisle, *Communion of the Apostles* by Piero Dandini, and on the third left altar, 14C wooden *Crucifix*. In the baptistery the font dates from 1387.

Next to the tiny little Romanesque church of **San Michele** are the 17C premises of the Confraternità del Santissimo Sacramento which now houses a **Museo di Arte Sacra** (open in winter on Thur & Sat 15.30–18.00; fest. 10.00–12.00; in summer, Tues, Thur & Sat 16.00–19.30, and fest. 10.00–12.00; if closed ring at no. 71). It contains a Flemish *tapestry with the Last Supper and scenes of the Passion*, dated 1516, on a cartoon by Pieter Pannemaker; fine vestments, church silver, and a wooden statue of the *Virgin Annunciate* (restored) attributed to the 15C Lucchese school (Matteo Civitali?).

Off the Corso is the **Badia di San Pietro**, founded by the Benedictines in the 8C, and rebuilt in the 11C. Outside, a 14C portal survives from the convent walls. The church contains a Baroque altar and remains of a 14C fresco. The approach road from the sea passes the prominent church of the **Francescani**, with an 18C choir and a marble statue over the high altar dating from 1689.

In the environs of Camaiore is the Romanesque **Pieve di San Giovanni Battista e Santo Stefano** which contains a Roman sarcophagus (2C AD), used as a font, and a triptych by Battista da Pisa (1443). In the village of **Nocchi** the church contains a 15C wooden *Crucifix* and a painting of the *Nativity* attributed to Piero Dandini. Other churches worth a visit in the environs towards Viareggio include **Mommio**, **Corsanico** (with a precious organ built by the Venetian Vincenzo Colonna in 1602–06), **Conca di Sotto**, and **Stiava**.

Towards the sea on the road to Massarosa is **Pieve a Elici**. The restored 11C church stands in a beautiful position and contains a sculpted high altar, a stoup and ciborium attributed to Lorenzo Stagi, and a 13C fresco of the *Madonna and Child*.

Pietrasanta

Pietrasanta is the main inland town of Versilia (25,000 inhab.), which has long been famous for its highly skilled marble workers, and for its bronze foundries. Numerous artists come here to study the techniques of sculpture. A pleasant small town, it has retained its interesting plan with four long straight parallel streets which run at right angles through Piazza Duomo. On the outskirts of the town are some old marble works (some dating from the Art Nouveau period).

History

The town was founded by Guiscardo da Pietrasanta, the Podestà of Lucca in 1255, and thrived under the lordship of Castruccio Castracani in 1316–28. In the following centuries its possession was disputed between Genoa, Lucca, Pisa and Florence. From the 16C up until c 1820 it declined because of the presence of malaria in the surrounding marshes. Famous natives include the sculptors Lorenzo and Stagio Stagi (1455–1506 and 1496–1563) and Eugenio Barsanti (1821–64), inventor (with Felice Matteucci) of the internal combustion engine.

***Piazza Duomo** has a fine group of buildings and a splendid view of the castle and town walls climbing a wooded hillside. Behind the monument to the Grand-duke Leopoldo II (by Vincenzo Santini, 1843) is a column bearing the Florentine *Marzocco* by Donato Benti, and a wall fountain.

The **Duomo** (or Collegiata di San Martino), first built in 1256 and enlarged in 1330, has a white marble **façade** with a beautiful rose *window by the Riccomanni, a local family of sculptors. Above the three portals are unusual sculpted lunettes. The 16C bas-relief of *St John the Baptist* is by Stagio Stagi, and the coat of arms (1513) is that of the Medici Pope, Leo X. The unfinished brick campanile is attributed to Donato Benti.

The **interior** has fine marble altars and confessionals. The frescoes in grisaille are by Luigi Ademollo (1825). The two stoups are by Stagio Stagi, and the ***pulpit** is by Lorenzo Stagi (1504), with a staircase by Andrea Baratta. The interesting 17C altarpieces in the aisle have recently been restored. At the end of the south aisle, 15C statue of the *Virgin Annunciate*. In the south transept, *Nativity* by Piero Dandini. In the handsome chapel to the right of the sanctuary a late Gothic painting of the *Madonna and Child with Saints John the Evangelist and John the Baptist* (exhibited only on certain religious festivals) is preserved. On either side of the sanctuary are two candelabra by Sergio Stagi and two bronze angels by Ferdinando Tacca. Over the high altar is a *Crucifix*, also by Tacca. The carved marble ***stalls** are also by Stagi. In the north transept, *Madonna of the Rosary*, by Matteo Rosselli. At the end of the north aisle is an unfinished statuette of *St John the Baptist* by Stagio Stagi, who also carved the two capitals on the pilasters of the crossing. The sacristy and baptistery, with an 18C interior (opened by the sacristan) are also interesting: one font is by Donato Benti (1509), the other dates from 1389; a processional Cross dating from 1509 is kept in the sacristy.

Beyond the campanile is the 16C **Palazzo Moroni** with a pretty staircase. It houses the **Museo Archeologico Versiliese** which has been closed for a number of years (☎ 0584 795500). The 14C church of **Sant'Agostino**, with a handsome façade, has been deconsecrated and restored as a hall for concerts and exhibitions.

The ex-convent and cloisters (entrance to the right) have been restored as a cultural centre and the seat of the Biblioteca Comunale. Here is the **Museo dei Bozzetti** (open in summer 18.00–20.00, 21.00–24.00 except Mon; winter Tues–Fri 09.00–12.00, 14.30–19.00), with plaster models by various sculptors, notably Leone Tommasi (1903–65).

Via della Rocca leads up past a few palm trees and the domed bell tower of Sant'Agostino to the **Rocca di Sala**, on a hillside planted with olive trees. The fortress was originally built by the Longobards, and reconstructed in 1324 by Castruccio Castracani. It contains a 15C palace built by Paolo Guinigi. On the other side of the square is the 18C **theatre**, and at the far end of the square the **Rocca Arrighina** can be seen inside the Porta Pisana, near the Torre delle Ore. A house here has a plaque recording Michelangelo's stay in 1518.

In Via Mazzini (where a plaque marks the house of Stagio Stagi) is the **Misericordia**, next to the church of Sant'Antonio Abate or San Biagio. It contains an altarpiece of the *Madonna enthroned* by the local painter Lorenzo Cellini. A statue of *San Biagio* by Francesco da Valdambrino has been removed for restoration. The two large frescoes by the Columbian artist Fernando Botero date from 1993.

On the outskirts of Pietrasanta, near the hospital, is the church of **San Salvatore**, founded in 1523. In the cloister are lunettes of the *Life of St Francis* by Luigi Ademollo. The long straight Viale Apua leads directly to the sea at Marina di Pietrasanta. It passes the park (right) of **La Versiliana** in Fiumetto, where D'Annunzio stayed at the beginning of the century. Built in 1886, it is now used for exhibitions, and plays and concerts are held in the open-air theatre in summer.

On the southern outskirts of the town (signposted off the Lucca road by the cemetery) is the by-road for **Valdicastello Carducci**. It passes the **Pieve di Santi Giovanni e Felicità** a very ancient church amid olive trees. It has a fine rose window, and contains an early sarcophagus and 14C frescoes. In the courtyard is a well by Giuseppe Stagi (1559). Valdicastello was the birthplace of the poet Giosuè Carducci (1835–1907). The house can be visited (open Tues 09.00–12.00; Sat 09.00–12.00, 15.00–18.00; fest. 15.00–18.00; in summer: Tues–Sun 17.00–20.00). The church contains a marble tabernacle by Stagio Stagi.

Seravezza

Seravezza is attractively situated in a narrow ravine surrounded by high mountains, with numerous quarries and marble works. Michelangelo stayed here while looking for marble suitable for his sculptures in 1517. The tree-lined streets are built along the Versilia river (its waters white from marble) between two bridges.

The **Duomo** (1503; finished in the 17C), on the right bank of the river beside a group of handsome houses, has a castellated campanile and a dome. The wide

interior has fine marble altars and confessionals. The high altar has a picture of *St Laurence* on the grille in marble inlay. Behind and above it is a marble reliquary and a Cross. In the chapel to the left of the high altar is a font by Stagio Stagi.

On the left bank of the river, some way upstream, is ***Palazzo Mediceo** built for Cosimo I in 1555 by Ammannati where exhibitions are held. It is also the seat of the **Museo del Lavoro e delle Tradizioni popolari** (open in winter 15.00–19.30 exc. Mon; in summer 16.00–22.00 exc. Mon), with a collection illustrating local crafts, including the extraction and working of marble. The courtyard has a well with a charming fish above it. Opposite the palace is an old marble works.

On the road which leads to the coast is **Vallecchia** with the *pieve* of Santo Stefano, another ancient church with interesting sculptures including a pulpit by Andrea Baratta (1681), a bas-relief attributed to Donato Benti, and a 14C *Madonna and Child*.

A road leads east from Seravezza along the floor of the Vezza valley past numerous small quarries and some waterfalls. At Ponte Stazzemese a road leads right and climbs through Mulina for **Stazzema**, a climbing centre, in a splendid position at the foot of oddly-shaped mountains. Reconstruction work is in progress in the vicinity after disastrous flooding and landslides occurred in 1996.

Just before reaching the village, the road passes the church of **Santa Maria Assunta** (if closed ring at the canonica) on the edge of the hill, preceded by a charming paved forecourt with a porch overlooking the valley. The first church on this site dates from the 9C; it was enlarged in the 13C and 14C. The façade has a pretty 15C rose window and interesting old carvings around the door.

The columns in the interior have fine capitals, Gothic on the left, and Renaissance on the right. The wood ceiling dates from after 1630. The organ at the west end is attributed to Filippo Tronci (1775). On the west wall is a 16C bas-relief of the *Baptism of Christ*. At the end of the right aisle is a marble statue of *St Anthony Abbot*, attributed to Nicolao Civitali or Leonardo Riccomanni. The high altar dates from 1649 and bears an altarpiece of the *Assumption* attributed to Matteo Rosselli. The tabernacle on the right wall of the sanctuary and fine portal of the sacristy are both attributed to Lorenzo Stagi. On the left wall of the sanctuary is a very unusual painting of the *Assumption*, with angels, saints, and apostles, attributed to a Catalan painter of the 14C–15C.

From outside the church a cobbled path (300m) leads down through woods to the **Santuario del Piastraio** (open only for occasional services, but visible through an open window), with an 18C interior and a painting of the *Madonna del Bell'Amore* (Madonna and Child with the Host and two Evangelists) attributed to a certain Guglielmo Tommasi (1772).

The road ends at the quiet little village of Stazzema, situated on a ridge, with a clock tower of 1739. The people of Stazzema showed particular courage during the German occupation in the last war when 561 civilians were killed by German soldiers in 1944 in the nearby village of **Sant'Anna** (most easily reached from Camaiore). Here the **Museo Storico della Resistenza** (usually open 09.00–12.30, 15.00–19.00) is both a memorial to them and a documentation of the Italian Resistance movement.

A by-road leads north from Seravezza via Fabbiano for the hamlet of **Azzano**, passing the 13C *pieve* of the **Cappella**, in a panoramic position, with a fine rose window on its façade, and an hexagonal ciborium inside. From the terrace there is a view of the marble quarries and Monte Altissimo. Michelangelo is known to have used marble from quarries in this area, and a road and bridge believed to have been constructed in 1518 by the sculptor for the transportation of the marble from the Valle del Serra have been identified.

A by-road off the Stazzema road leads to **Retignano**, where there is another ancient church which contains a font attributed to Donato Benti and carved altars by Lorenzo Stagi (1486) and Benti (1532). The road continues to **Levigliani**, an ancient village and a centre for climbing in the Apuan Alps.

The province of Massa Carrara

The marble quarries above Carrara are world famous. The inhabitants of the small towns of Massa and Carrara, although they live only a few kilometres apart, are proudly independent of each other. Their province incorporates the whole of the northeast corner of Tuscany, and includes the Lunigiana district in the Magra river valley, with a number of castles (many of them being restored) built to defend the Apennine passes and the Via Francigena, as well as the interesting town of Pontremoli, although this area has perhaps more in common with Liguria than with Tuscany.

Practical information

Getting there
By car
The A12 motorway follows the coast north from Viareggio with exits at Massa and Carrara. It continues through a corner of Liguria to a junction with the motorway spur to La Spezia and the A15 motorway which branches right up the Magra valley in Tuscany for Parma (exits at Aulla and Pontremoli). **Car parking** in Carrara off Via Cavatore, or (with an hourly tariff) in the main squares.
By train
On the main Pisa–Genoa line with stations at Massa and Carrara (and Sarzana). From Sarzana a secondary line diverges up the Magra valley via Aulla and Pontremoli.
By bus
(*CAT*) **from Carrara** (Via del Cavatore) to Marina di Carrara and the railway station (every 10mins); to the Fantiscritti quarries and Colonnata; and to Massa, Fosdinovo, and Pontremoli.

Information office
APT Massa-Carrara, Lungomare Vespucci 24, Marina di Massa (☎ 0585 240 046; ✉ apt@massacarrara.turismo. toscana.it), with an information office at Marina di Massa, Via delle Pinete 77, località Partaccia (☎ 0585 631 115), and at Carrara, Viale XX Settembre,

località Stadio (☎ 0585 844 403).

Where to stay
Hotels

CARRARA ☆☆☆
Michelangelo, Corso Fratelli Rosselli 3
(☎ 0585 777 161; 🖷 0585 745 45).
☆☆ *Da Roberto*, Via Apuana 5
(☎ 0585 706 34); and many more at
Marina di Carrara.
FIVIZZANO ☆☆ *Il Giardinetto*
(with restaurant), Via Roma 151
(☎ 0585 920 60).

Eating out
Restaurants

CARRARA € *Roma di Prioreschi*, Piazza Cesare Battisti 1.
COLONNATA €€ *Locandapuana*
and *Venanzio*, Piazza Palestro 3.
CANIPAROLA € *Trattoria dell'Arca*.
PONTREMOLI € *Da Bussè*, 31
Piazza Duomo.

Massa

Massa is a provincial capital at the foot of the narrow Frigido valley, below the Apuan foothills. It has greatly expanded since the Second World War and now has a largely modern aspect (68,000 inhab.). Founded in the Middle Ages, it was the capital of the duchy of Massa-Carrara from 1442 to 1790 ruled by the Malaspina.

Numerous orange and lemon trees were planted here in the early 19C, notably in the central **Piazza degli Aranci**. Here also is a grandiose marble monument with lions and an obelisk dating from 1861, and the huge **Palazzo Cybo Malaspina** with a delightful red façade by Alessandro Bergamini (1701). The courtyard is by Gian Francesco Bergamini (1665).

The Duomo

The Duomo, reached by Via Dante Alighieri, has an imposing marble façade of 1936. The 18C **interior** was decorated at the end of the 19C. Right aisle. The baptistery has an early 15C font by Riccomanni. First altar, *Coronation of the Virgin* attributed to Matteo Rosselli; third altar, *Saints John the Evangelist, John the Baptist, Peter, and James* by Luigi Garzi.

Stairs lead down from the right aisle to the funerary **Chapel of the Cybo Malaspina** with tomb-slabs of the ducal family and two funerary monuments. The tomb of *Eleonora Malaspina (d. 1515) by Pietro Aprili (influenced by the monument to Ilaria del Carretto by Jacopo della Quercia in the Duomo of Lucca) was beautifully restored by local craftsmen. The monument to Lorenzo Cybo is by the school of Stagio Stagi.

Right transept. Marble altarpiece in high relief by Andrea and Tommaso Lazzoni (1672). The **Chapel of the Holy Sacrament** (by Giovanni Francesco Bergamini) dates from 1675–94. The fine *altar (1694) was designed by Bergamini to preserve the fresco fragment of the *Madonna and Child* by Pinturicchio (from the Cybo chapel in Santa Maria del Popolo in Rome). Also here is a triptych attributed to Filippo Lippi and a *Nativity* in enamelled terracotta by Benedetto Buglioni. On the **high altar**, bronze Crucifix and six candlesticks by Ferdinando Tacca. In the left transept is a highly venerated wood *Crucifix* of the early 13C. Left aisle, third altar, *Immaculate Conception* by Carlo Maratta. There is also an interesting **museum** containing vestments, church silver and a *Crucifix* by Ferdinando Tacca (open only by appointment, ☎ 0585 426 43).

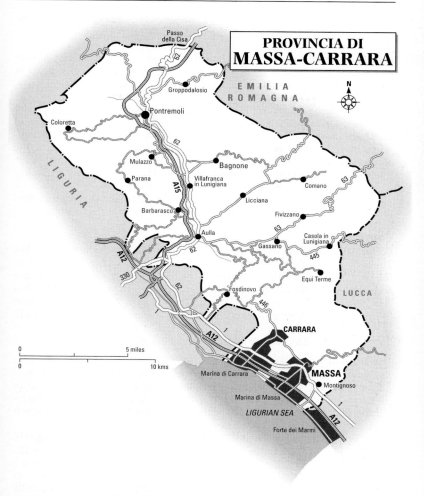

PROVINCIA DI MASSA-CARRARA

The **Rocca** or **Castello Malaspina**, on a high hill, is reached by a narrow (signposted) road. It was first built in the 11C–12C, and the Renaissance palace of the Malaspina family was enlarged in the 16C–17C. A building of the highest architectural interest it has been partially reopened on holidays (☎ 0585 447 74). At its foot, Rocca is the oldest district of Massa, with very narrow streets (but few old houses) and the church of **San Rocco** which has an interesting 16C *Crucifix*, attributed to the local sculptor Felice Palma.

In the modern part of town, towards the sea is the church of **Santa Maria degli Uliveti**. A wooden sculpture of *St Leonard* by Jacopo della Quercia has been removed to the canonica. There is an **Ethnological Museum** illustrating peasant life over the centuries in the Apuan Alps at no. 85 Via Uliveti (☎ 0585 251 330). The church of **San Giacomo Maggiore** in Via Piastronata contains an interesting 15C painting of the *Madonna del Carmine* by the Lombard School. In the church of **San Sebastiano** (1957) there is a 17C *Pietà* by Felice Palma.

From Massa, a spectacular mountain road leads over the Apuan Alps via Antona and Arni to Castelnuovo di Garfagnana (see p 229). This was constructed in 1880 to provide access to the quarries on Monte Altissimo.

Just to the south of Massa is the village of **Montignoso** with fine views. Higher up is **Sant'Eustachio** where the church contains a fine small seated statue of the *Madonna and Child* (in wood) attributed to Tino da Camaino, and a beautiful painting by the Florentine school (dated 1424) at the east end of the *Madonna and four saints* and the story of the patron saint in the predella. A marble statue of *St Eustachio* dates from 1906. The marble mosaic high altar and confessionals were made by local craftsmen in the 1950s.

A pretty secondary road (the Strada del Foce) connects Massa to Carrara across the hills. It crosses woods and quarries and has good views of the mountains.

Carrara

Carrara (67,700 inhab.) is a flourishing town, world famous for its white marble. The earliest record of Carrara's existence dates from 963 when it was given to the bishops of Luni. It then passed into the hands of Lucca and Genoa before becoming part of the duchy of the Malaspina family with Massa in 1442. It has been known for its marble since Roman times, and is now one of the main centres in the world for marble production. Carrara has also been well known in Italy since the 19C as a centre of the Anarchist movement. A number of interesting old-fashioned shop fronts are preserved in Carrara.

The Duomo

The most interesting part of town is around the good Romanesque *Duomo, altered in the 13C when the attractive Gothic storey was added to its façade. In the handsome south wall is a 13C portal; this is the usual entrance. The charming apse and campanile can be seen in the courtyard of the canonica from which there is a view of the marble quarries in the Apuan Alps.

The well proportioned interior has rough marble walls and huge capitals. There are 13C–16C fresco fragments all over the church. South aisle. Beyond the first altar is the Arca di San Ceccardo, supported by two 17C putti. Farther on are two charming 14C *statues of the *Annunciation* showing French influence. At the end of the aisle is the altar of the Holy Sacrament, with a *Madonna and Child* by Clemente da Reggio (16C) and in niches on either side, two statues (in very high relief) of *Saints John and Thomas*. The vault is frescoed by Acquilio Bernardino (1518).

On either side of the **presbytery** are fine carved screens. Over the high altar is a painted 14C *Cross* by Angelo Puccinelli. The pulpit, decorated with local coloured marbles, dates from 1541. At the end of the north aisle the altar of the Assumption has a statue of the *Madonna* attributed to Moschino (17C) and two statues of *Saints Catherine and Jerome*. On the north wall, recomposed marble ancona with seated statues of the *Madonna and Child with four saints*, and an interesting 15C bas-relief beneath. Beyond is a small bas-relief which may represent *Countess Matilda of Canossa* crowned as marquis of Tuscany by Pope Gregory VII.

A door leads into the **baptistery** (if closed, admission on request through the sacristy) which contains a large 16C hexagonal font for total immersion, with an unusual little cupola in polychrome marble on top. The other font is another good work of the 16C. At the west end of the north aisle is a fine carved arch over the altar (perhaps by Giroldo da Como) and a *Crucifix* made as a model by Pietro Tacca flanked by two Baroque statues of the *Annunciation*. At the west end of the south aisle is an altar carved in 1869 by Pietro Lazzerini di Tommaso.

The fountain in the piazza with a statue of Andrea Doria was left unfinished by Baccio Bandinelli. Also in the square is a red house (plaque) believed to have sheltered Michelangelo on his visits to buy marble.

The pretty, narrow **Via Santa Maria** leads away from the Duomo passing some interesting old doorways; at no. 14, the unusual **Casa Repetti** has animal reliefs and little slender columns. It ends in front of the 17C church of the **Carmine** by a monument to Mazzini (1892) and the pink 17C façade of a palace, now the seat of the **Accademia di Belle Arti**, entered from the other side, where it incorporates the medieval Malaspina castle (restored). On the lawn outside is a small statue of Pietro Tacca by Carlo Fontana (1900). A carved Roman marble relief (now very worn) found in the quarries of Fantiscritti with the signatures of Giambologna (1598) and Canova (1800) is at present in the courtyard (adm. sometimes on request). The pleasant Piazza Gramsci, adjoining the Accademia, has trees (including palms) and views of the hills and quarries.

Via Giorgi leads down to the handsome **Piazza Alberica** with some fine red 17C palaces, and a white marble pavement. An interesting old road runs along the Carrione stream, just out of the square. In the nearby Piazza Garibaldi is the neo-Classical **Teatro degli Animosi** by Giuseppe Pardini (1840).

From Piazza Gramsci, Via Roma leads straight down to the 19C **Piazza Matteotti** with evergreen trees, and the monumental **Politeama Verdi** (1892). In Via Verdi, on the corner of Via Pelliccia, is an amusing mushroom-coloured Art Nouveau building (no. 16). In Via Mazzini is the delightful marble **post office** designed in 1932 by the local architect Giuseppe Boni (with decorations by Sergio Vatteroni).

A long straight avenue (Viale XX Settembre) connects Carrara with **Marina di Carrara** a marble shipping port and resort. It passes a modern building which houses the **Museo Civico del Marmo** (open 08.30–13.30; 10.00–17.00 or 20.00 in summer), an exhibition illustrating marble quarrying and craftsmanship. Outside the cemetery of Turigliano, in a pleasant little garden, a colossal white marble monolith by Sergio Signori (left unfinished at the sculptor's death in 1990) bears a dedication to Gaetano Bresci from the Anarchists. Bresci assassinated King Umberto I in 1900 and died a year later in prison.

The famous marble quarries in the Apuan Alps which have been worked for over 2000 years are well worth a visit (information from the Carrara *APT* office, ☎ 0585 844 403). They produce about one-and-a-half million tons of white marble a year, and over 95 quarries are now in use. They are situated in three valleys: **Colonnata**, **Fantiscritti** and **Ravaccione**. They can all be reached by road (signposted from Carrara). There is a bus from Carrara to Colonnata six times a day (three on fest.), and to Fantiscritti (Ponte di Vara) on weekdays (four times a day). The quarries of Fantiscritti are perhaps the most interesting, since they are approached past the Ponte di Vara, the old railway bridge, and there is a good museum (see below).

The marble quarries ~ Carrara marble

Up until the end of the 19C marble was extracted from the mountainside by hand. Wooden wedges were inserted along the natural fissures in the marble: these were kept wet so that they would swell and eventually the block of marble would fracture. Another method was a handsaw operated by two workers, with the help of water and sand, but they could only cut into the marble at a rate of about 5cm a day. A radical change in quarrying methods occurred at the end of the 19C when steel wire, several hundred metres long, was introduced. This, still with the help of sand and water, can cut into the marble at a rate of c 10–20cm an hour. Diamond wire and diamond point saws are now also widely used. The dangerous quarrying techniques used in the last twenty years, which pay little attention to the geological structure of the mountains, have been criticised, and fatal accidents caused by landslides occur every year.

In the past, once the blocks were extracted, they used to be sent down the mountainside on a slide using ropes and wooden rollers, and then transported by wagons drawn by up to ten bullocks in pairs. A railway was constructed between 1876 and 1891 from the quarries to Marina di Carrara. This is no longer used, but the track which traverses tunnels and the high Ponte di Vara has been converted into a road which is now used by the lorries which climb up into the quarries on rough roads to pick up the marble. It is then transported either to Marina di Carrara for shipping, or to one of the numerous saw mills in and around the town which cut up the marble into slabs and polish it before exportation.

There is a delightful private outdoor **museum** (open daily) by the Fantiscritti quarries which illustrates the history of marble quarrying by means of instruments and tools and remarkable life-size sculptures in marble. From here rough roads lead up through the quarry, and another road follows the old railway tunnel to the Ravaccione quarries.

A beautiful minor road connects Carrara with Fosdinovo, traversing wooded hillsides with views towards the Apuan Alps, and then towards the sea. A by-road leads further inland to **Campo Cecina** (1300m), in the Apuan Alps with a fine panorama of the marble quarries.

Fosdinovo

Fosdinovo is a medieval fortified borgo on the border between Tuscany and Liguria. It is in a beautiful position on a hill top with views of the Apuan Alps, the valley of the Magra, and the gulf of La Spezia. It became a feudal stronghold of the Malaspina family in 1340 and they remained here until 1820.

Since 1867 the **castle** has been owned by the Malaspina-Torrigiani family. It probably dates from before the 13C, and was well restored in 1997 (usually open for a guided tour of c 30 mins 10.00–12.00, 15.00–17.00 exc. Tues ☎ 0187 688 91). In 1981 much of the furniture was stolen. The most interesting rooms are the tiny **Camera di Dante** where the poet is supposed to have stayed as a guest in 1306, which has a frescoed niche of *Christ in Pietà* with the kneeling figure of a Malatesta crusader, and the **great hall** with frescoes illustrating Dante's visit by Gaetano Bianchi (1882). From the enclosed loggia there is a fine view of the village and the plain which extends towards the sea. The **battlements** can also be visited. Exhibited in various rooms of the castle are 16C–19C arms and armour, a peacock from a 17C merry-go-round, Montelupo ceramics, and coins minted in Fosdinovo in 1661–69.

From the castle a narrow paved street runs through the borgo to the parish church of **San Remigio**, which has a pleasant grey-and-white interior with colourful Baroque marble altars. On the right side, *Madonna* (second altar) and a bas-relief of the *Liberation of Souls from Purgatory* (last altar), both by Giovanni Baratta. The choir has carved wooden stalls, and on the east wall, high up in a niche, is a seated *statue of *St Remigio* (c 1300). At the end of the left side, funerary monument to Galeotto Malaspina (d. 1367) with his effigy (fully armed) beneath a Gothic canopy. On the west wall are two interesting small bas-reliefs, and near the door the 16C font. A few steps lead down from the east end to the **Oratorio del Santissimo Sacramento**, with more elaborate, well-carved marble altars and a 17C wooden *Crucifix*.

Just beyond San Remigio, preceded by a marble balustrade and pavement, is the unusual white marble façade (1666) of the **Oratorio dei Bianchi**. The 14C polychrome wood statue of the *Virgin Annunciate* which belongs to the church is at present shown in San Remigio only on 25 March and 8 September.

The road which winds down past olive groves from Fosdinovo towards the sea passes through an ancient archway at **Caniparola** where the handsome Villa Malaspina, with a pretty garden, dates in its present form from 1724. Places of great interest nearby which form part of Lunigiana, include Castelnuovo Magra, Luni, and Santo Stefano di Magra, all described, together with Sarzana, the gulf of La Spezia and the rest of Liguria, in *Blue Guide Northern Italy*.

Northeast of Fosdinovo is the valley of the Aulella with the ancient **Pieve di Codiponte**, **Casola in Lunigiana** with a local ethnographical museum (open 09.00–12.00, 16.00–19.00 except Mon; winter 09.00–13.00), and the little spa of **Equi**. Beyond **Giuncugnano** is the valley of the Garfagnana, described on p 230.

Farther north is **Fivizzano** a small town enclosed in ramparts by Cosimo I de' Medici. Nearby is the 14C castle of Verrucola. It is on the road via the Passo del Cerreto (1261m) which leads to Reggio Emilia (see *Blue Guide Northern Italy*).

Aulla is in the Magra valley, in the district known as the **Lunigiana**, named after the Roman city of Luni, in Liguria (it now covers the province of Massa Carrara and most of that of La Spezia). The town lies at the foot of the picturesque 16C fort of **Brunella**. At the beginning of this century the castle was bought by Lina Duff Gordon, the journalist, and her husband Aubrey Waterfield, painter and gardener. Waterfield created a remarkable roof-garden on the ramparts. They were visited here by D.H. Lawrence and Rex Whistler. They had to restore the castle after its occupation in the Second World War by German forces. A vivid description of life at the castle is given by Kinta Beevor, the Waterfields' daughter, in *A Tuscan Childhood* (1993). The ground floor now contains a natural history museum and botanical garden related to the Lunigiana (open 09.00–12.00, 15.00 or 16.00–18.00 or 19.00, except Mon). **Villafranca in Lunigiana** has a local ethnographical museum in an old mill (open 09.00–12.00, 15.00 or 16.00–18.00 or 19.00 except Mon).

Pontremoli

Pontremoli, a pleasant little town with some 17C and 18C palaces, lies in a strategic position among the chestnut-clad foothills of the Apennines. There was a castle here in 990, and a medieval borgo grew up between the Magra and Verde rivers.

Via Cavour and Via Mazzini cross the town from the Porta Parma to the Porta Fiorentina on the line of the ancient Via Francigena to Rome (see p 442). The central **Piazza della Repubblica** is separated from Piazza Duomo by a clock tower. Here is the municipio with a portico (and the tourist information office in the courtyard), and the fine **Palazzo Pavesi** (no. 1; 1734–43) attributed to Giambattista Natali. Opposite the town hall is the 18C pretura (local magistrate's court).

The **Duomo** was built by Alessandro Capra in 1636–87. The façade by Vincenzo Micheli dates from 1881, with a lunette mosaic by Annibale Gatti and two statues by Antonio Bucci of Seravezza. The bronze doors are by Riccardo Rossi of Carrara (1965).

The elaborate interior, hung with chandeliers, has gilding and stuccowork, and marble altars and confessionals. The first north chapel has a 17C altarpiece and a 16C painting of the *Madonna enthroned*. In the sanctuary are four 18C paintings by Giuseppe Bottani, Giuseppe Peroni, Giovanni Domenico Ferretti, and Vincenzo Meucci. In the south transept is an elaborate carved altar by Lorenzo Franzoni (1808) and in the north transept, an altar dating from 1654 and a painting by Pierre Subleyras (in very poor condition). On the left wall is a 19C *Deposition* by Giuseppe Collignon. In the spandrels of the dome are 19C frescoes of the *Evangelists* by Giovanni Gaibazzi. The chapel of the Holy Sacrament, on the right of the presbytery, is a fine work of 1828.

Opposite the Duomo is the neo-Classical **Palazzo del Vescovo** (bishop's palace), with an outside staircase. The winding Via Garibaldi leads gently up to Porta Parma past a series of handsome doorways and several Baroque palaces. On the left, Vicolo del Piagnaro, a lovely old lane, continues up past some old

houses to the **Castello del Piagnaro** with the **Museo delle Statue-Stele** (open 09.00–12.00, 14.00–17.00; summer 09.00–12.00, 16.00–19.00; closed Mon), a museum of menhirs found in the Lunigiana. The castle, founded in the 10C was enlarged in the 14C and destroyed several times. In the Middle Ages it was of fundamental importance to the defence of the Via Francigena (or Strada della Cisa; see p 442) on the stretch of the road across the Apennines from Emilia into Tuscany. It contains a collection of remarkable menhirs of the Lunigiana cult found over the last two centuries in the Magra valley. Fifty-nine of these megaliths, which date from prehistoric times up to the Roman era (but mostly from the Bronze Age), have been found in

A menhir in the museum at Pontremoli

Lunigiana in the last 100 years or so, and the museum provides a complete documentation of them all. These stone cult images, most in the form of warriors with arms or female figures, were found scattered over a large area, not in stone circles nor alignments, nor near burials, and their origins are still being studied. The original ones are displayed in room III, while rooms V and VI contain casts of the others.

Just out of Piazza Duomo (see above), off Via Garibaldi, Via della Cresa leads beneath some arches to the narrow old **Ponte della Cresa** across the Verde river. Via Ricci Armani continues from Piazza della Repubblica past (left) **Palazzo Dosi** dating from the early 18C by Giovanni Battista Natali, with a courtyard, to Via Cavour with a Baroque palace at no. 15. At the end are some fortifications by the Ponte del Casotto. The bridge leads across the Verde river to a lane which continues to the church of **San Francesco** (marked by its Romanesque campanile). The unusual and attractive entrance portico is by Giovanni Battista Natali (1740). The church contains a fine painting of the *Ecstasy of St Francis* by Gianbettino Cignaroli (18C) on the east wall, and a lovely relief on the second left altar attributed to Agostino di Duccio. The unusual composition shows a half-figure of the *Madonna* with the Child lying in front of her, and a frame of cherubs' heads.

From the end of Via Cavour, opposite a palace with a pretty double loggia in the courtyard and a palm tree, Ponte Battisti (rebuilt after the war) leads across the Magra beneath an arch which connects the old stone **Castelnuovo** (12C–14C) to the bright orange church of **Nostra Donna**, a fine Rococo build-ing built by Giovanni Battista Natali (1738). It contains frescoes by Sebastiano Galeotti, and altarpieces by Alessandro Gherardini and Giuseppe Galeotti. In the piazzetta is the Teatro della Rosa.

Via Mazzini runs parallel to the Magra past a pink palazzo with statuary on the balconies. At no. 30 is the office of the *Comunità Montana della Lunigiana*.

Beyond Piazza Dodi begins Via Pietro Cocchi where at no. 7 is Palazzo Damiani (18C; in very poor repair) and at no. 24 is a neo-Classical palace (1807).

On the southern outskirts of the little town is the church of the **Annunziata** (for adm. ring at priest's house nearby), with an unusual tall façade (1937). It contains an octagonal tabernacle attributed to Jacopo Sansovino (1527), and paintings by Luca Cambiaso. The chapel of San Niccolò is decorated by Giovanni Battista Natali, and the sacristy has a vault painted by Francesco Natali and carved benches and cupboards by Francesco Battaglia (1676).

Pisa

Pisa (104,300 inhab.), standing on the Arno a few miles from its mouth, is famous for its beautiful Piazza del Duomo, with the Duomo, Leaning Tower, and Baptistery. The building of these splendid monuments was begun in the 11C and 12C when Pisa was a great maritime Republic. In the 13C and early 14C Nicola Pisano and his son Giovanni decorated both the inside and outside of the Duomo and Baptistery with their remarkable sculptures. Pisa has a flourishing university (founded in the 14C) as well as the renowned Scuola Normale university college. The Lungarni along the two banks of the river, lined with some fine palaces, are still a special feature of the town (and the seagulls on the Arno are a reminder of its proximity to the sea).

Practical information

Getting there and getting around
By air

Galileo Galilei airport, 3km south of the centre of the city, for flights to London Gatwick, Manchester, Glasgow, Dublin, Munich, Barcelona, and Paris (and, since 1999, New York via Venice) and internal flights to Rome, Milan, Naples, Sardinia, Sicily, and Elba (☎ 050 500 707).

Airport railway station (Pisa Aeroporto) with express **train** services (1 hr) via Pisa Centrale station to Florence (where there is an air terminal in the station).

SITA **bus services** also from the airport to Florence in 1 hr. Bus no. 3 from the airport via Pisa Centrale station to Via Bonanno Pisano a few metres from Piazza del Duomo (services every 20–30 min.).

By car

From Florence, Pisa is normally approached by the superstrada which leaves Florence south of the Arno (and one branch of which runs to Livorno). However, this is a poorly engineered road without service stations. An alternative (longer, and with a toll) is the A11 motorway via Lucca. Pisa also has an exit in the A12 motorway along the coast between Livorno and Viareggio.

There is a free **car park** in Via Pietrasantina northwest of Piazza del Duomo, served by two shuttle buses (A and C, see above).

By train

Railway stations. Centrale (just

beyond **Map 15**), Viale Gramsci for all services, one of the main railway junctions in central Italy, with services to Florence, Genoa, Turin, and Milan, and to Grosseto and Rome. For buses to the centre of the city, see below. Pisa Aeroporto with services via Pisa Centrale to Florence. San Rossore (**Map 1**) served by all trains on the Lucca line and a few slow trains on the La Spezia line.

By bus

Town buses run by *CPT*. **A** a shuttle bus which connects the central railway station with Via Bonanno Pisano (a few metres west of Piazza del Duomo), and the free car park of Pietrasantina north of the Duomo. **C** a shuttle bus between the free car park of Pietrasantina and largo Cocco Griffi just west of the Duomo. **No. 3**, see above.

From the railway station, the most pleasant route **on foot** through the centre of Pisa north to Piazza del Duomo (a walk of about 30 minutes) is via Viale Gramsci, Corso Italia, Ponte di Mezzo, Borgo Stretto, Via Ulisse Dini, Piazza Cavalieri, Via dei Mille, and Via Santa Maria.

Country buses run by the *CPT* (☎ 050 505 511) from Piazza Sant'Antonio (**Map 14**) for Volterra, the coast, and places within the province of Pisa. *Lazzi* (☎ 050 462 88) from Piazza Vittorio Emanuele for places outside the province including Lucca, Florence, Livorno, Versilia.

Bicycles can be hired from the *CPT* bus station in Piazza Manin (see **Map 1**).

Information offices

APT, Via Pietro Nenni 24 (☎ 050 929 777; ✉ info@pisa.turismo.toscana.it). Information offices beside Piazza del Duomo (Via C. Cammeo 2; **Map 2:** ☎ 050 560 464; open all day every day), and at the main railway station, and the airport.

Where to stay
Hotels

For hotel bookings, *Consorzio Turistico* in the **APT** information office in Via Carlo Cammeo (**Map 2**), ☎ 050 830 253; ✉ pisa.turismo@ traveleurope.it

☆☆☆☆ *Grand Hotel Duomo*, Via Santa Maria 94 (**Map 2**,*1*: ☎ 050 561 894, 📠 050 560 418); *Jolly Hotel Cavalieri*, Piazza della Stazione 2 (south of **Map 15**: ☎ 050 432 90, 📠 050 502 242); *D'Azeglio*, Piazza Vittorio Emanuele 18 (**Map 14**,*3*: ☎ 050 500 310, 📠 050 280 17).

☆☆☆ *Villa Kinzica*, Piazza Arcivescovado 4 (**Map 3**; *4*: ☎ 050 560 419, 📠 050 551 204); *Royal Victoria*, Lungarno Pacinotti 12 (**Map**11;*2*: ☎ 050 940 111, 📠 050 940 180).

☆☆ *Amalfitana*, Via Roma 44 (**Map 6**;*6*: ☎ 050 290 00, 📠 050 252 18); *Villa Primavera*, Via Bonanno Pisano 43 (**Map 5**;*7*: ☎ 050 235 37, 📠 050 270 20).

Campsite

☆*Torre Pendente*, Viale delle Cascine 86 (☎ 050 561 704; beyond **Map 1**: open Apr–Oct).

Eating out
Restaurants

€€€ *Il Ristoro della Faggiola*, Via della Faggiola 1 (☎ 050 552 725); *Al Ristoro dei Vecchi Macelli*, Via Volturno 49 (☎ 050 204 24).

€€ *Taverna Kostas*, Via del Borghetto 39 (Greek food), (☎ 050 571 467);

Osteria dei Cavalieri, Via San Frediano 16 (☎ 050 580 858); *Alle Bandierine*, Via Mercanti 4 (☎ 050 500 000); *Osteria La Mescita*, Via Cavalca 2 (☎ 050 544 294); *Turiddo*, Piazza S. Frediano 12 (☎ 050 580 600); *Salza*, Borgo Stretto 44 (☎ 050 580 144); *La Grotta*, Via S. Francesco 103 (☎ 050 578 105).

€ (including self-service restaurants and pizzerie): *Ambarabà*, Via Cavalca; *Il Montino*, Vicolo del Monte 1 (☎ 050 598 695); *Da Matteo*, Via l'Arancio 46 (☎ 050 410 57).

Cafès

Salza, Borgo Stretto 44 (**Map 7**;*11*); *Caffè dell'Ussero*, Lungarno Paccinotti 26 (**Map 10**), and several with tables outside in Piazza delle Vettovaglie (**Map 7**;*11*).

Picnics

Places to picnic include the Giardino Scotto in the Fortezza Nuova (**Map 16**), Piazza San Paolo a Ripa d'Arno (**Map 14**), the area near the Cittadella and Arsenal (**Map 9**), and Piazza Martiri della Libertà (**Map 7**).

Festivals

In June, the *Festa di San Ranieri*, commemorating the patron saint of the city, St Ranieri (1117–60), is celebrated with candle-light festivities on the Arno and the *Gioco del Ponte*, a sham fight on the Ponte di Mezzo between the people living on either side of the Arno (the *Tramontana* and *Mezzogiorno*). Formerly the contestants were protected in armour for the fight to gain possession of the bridge, but since 1947 it has become a battle of strength with a cart in the centre of the bridge which is pushed from one side to the other. The combatants wear 16C–17C costumes and the day ends with a procession of both parties. As one of the historic Italian Marine Republics, together with Genoa, Venice, and Amalfi, a *Regatta* is held here every four years.

History

The origins of the city are uncertain, but the site near the sea seems to have been settled by at least 1000 BC. An Etruscan town, it expanded in the 4C BC and became a Roman colony from the 2C BC, when, situated on a lagoon, it was a naval and commercial port (some ancient boats have been excavated since 1999 near the station of San Rossore; see p 268). It continued to flourish under the Lombards in the 7C and 8C. By the 11C Pisa had become a maritime republic, rivalling Genoa, Amalfi, and Venice. Constantly at war with the Saracens, Pisa captured from them Corsica, Sardinia, and the Balearic Isles (1050–1100), and at the same time combined war and trade in the East. The wealth of the Pisans was proverbial. In 1135, assisting Pope Innocent II against Roger of Sicily, Pisa destroyed Amalfi. It subsequently joined the Ghibelline party, and remained proudly faithful to it, even though surrounded by Guelf republics such as Florence, Lucca and Genoa. The 12C was the period of her greatest splendour when she was one of the most important cities in Europe.

But in 1284 Pisa was defeated by the Genoese in the naval battle of Meloria and lost her maritime supremacy; from then onwards the city had to submit to a succession of lordships, including those of the Gherardesca family (1316–41) and of Gian Galeazzo Visconti of Milan (1396–1405). The Florentines gained possession of Pisa in 1406, and after one or two unsuccessful efforts at rebellion it became a quiet refuge of scholars and artists, a university having been established in the city in 1343 by Pope Clement VI. When Charles VIII entered Italy in 1494 he was expected to restore Pisa's liberty, but he broke his promise, and Florence took final possession of the city in 1509.

In 1944 the town was bombarded by both German and Allied artillery; the Camposanto and the area near the station suffered worst, and further damage was caused when all the bridges were blown up. Disappointing and disorderly reconstruction work resulted in an unusually high number of unattractive buildings in various parts of the town.

The most illustrious native of Pisa is Galileo Galileo (1564–1642), physicist and astronomer. The mathematician Leonardo Fibonacci (1165–1235) and Titta Ruffo (1877–1953), the famous baritone, were also born here.

British writers in 19C Pisa

In the 19C, the mild marine climate of the town was thought to have been good for those suffering from tuberculosis, and a small English colony was established here. In 1814 Margaret Jane King (Lady Mountcashell) from Ireland, settled here with George William Tighe whom she had met in Rome on the Grand Tour, and they lived for the rest of their lives under the assumed names of Mr and Mrs Mason. Her governess had been Mary Wollstonecraft (1759–97), author of *Vindication of the Rights of Woman* (1792) and mother of Mary Godwin, future wife of Shelley, and she became known for her educational and childrens' books. She also founded the *Accademia dei Lunatici* in Pisa, which was attended in 1927 by the famous Italian poet Giacomo Leopardi when he spent a happy year in the town. Mrs Mason saw much of the Shelleys when they were staying in Pisa at Palazzo

Scotto in 1820–22. Shelley wrote *Epipsychidion*, inspired by the Contessa Emilia Viviani, and *Adonais* during his stay here. A descendent of the Tighes discovered an unknown manuscript by Mary Shelley in the attic of her house in 1998 (*Maurice or the Fisher's Cot*, published in the same year).

Mary Wollstonecraft's husband, William Godwin, subsequently married Mrs Clairmont whose daughter Claire, by her first marriage, bore a daughter, Allegra, to Lord Byron in 1817. In 1821 Byron also took up residence in Pisa, in the Palazzo Lanfranchi, with his last mistress Countess Teresa Gamba Guiccioli. In 1822 Leigh Hunt brought his family to stay at Palazzo Lanfranchi and together with Byron and Shelley they published the radical journal called *The Liberal*. An English literary periodical called *The Ausonian* was issued in Pisa in 1827–28 (but was soon repressed because of its radical social views). In 1846 Browning brought his bride, Elizabeth Barrett, to Pisa, before they settled in Florence.

Piazza del Duomo

Piazza del Duomo, or Campo dei Miracoli (Map** 2), with its bright marble monuments, is one of the most remarkable sights in Italy. The splendid Romanesque buildings of the Cathedral, Baptistery, and Campanile (Leaning Tower) are spaciously laid out in a rational arrangement and superbly set off by the green lawns between them. They are enclosed to the north by the Camposanto and the crenellated city walls in an almost rural setting. The piazza lies well northwest of the centre of the city and, unlike most other Italian cathedral towns, it does not provide the focus of city life.

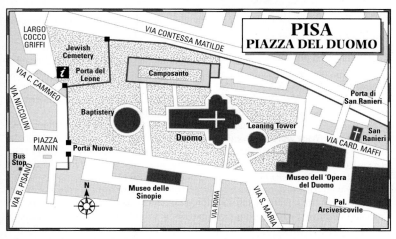

• Admission. The **Baptistery**, **Camposanto**, **Museo delle Sinopie** and **Museo dell'Opera del Duomo** remain open throughout the day, 09.00–dusk (16.40, 17.40, or 19.40; April–Sept: 08.00–19.40). The **Duomo** is open 10.00–12.45, 15.00–16.45 in winter; and from March–September from 10.00 to dusk. There are admission charges for all of the above (except for the Duomo in Nov–Feb, when it is free), and there are **inclusive tickets** for 5, 3 or 2 of them. Children under 10 are free. The ticket has to be bought in one of the museums or at the offices of the Opera del Duomo, just north of the Duomo. The **Campanile** in open 09.00–16.30; insummer 08.00–19.40. Pre-booked guided tours of 30 people every 40 minutes. Booking service at ✉ www.duomo.pisa.it; ☎ 050 560 547). Tickets at the offices of the Opera del Duomo.

In the vicinity of the piazza are a tourist information office, WCs, and numerous souvenir stalls.

The Duomo

The *Duomo (**Map** 2) is one of the most celebrated Romanesque buildings in Italy, and the prototype of the Pisan style of architecture in which a strong classicism survives. It was begun by a certain Buscheto in 1063, and continued by Rainaldo (both architects known only from their work on this building). It was restored in 1602–16 after a serious fire in 1595.

The building stands on a white marble pavement and is covered inside and out with black-and-white marble, toned on the exterior to a delicate grey and russet.

Detail of the portal of San Ranieri, Pisa Duomo

The *façade shows four tiers of columns with open galleries, with a row of seven tall arches below. In the left-hand arch is the tomb of Buscheto. The bronze doors were remodelled after the fire by sculptors of the school of Giambologna. The **entrance** is now always at the east end near the Leaning Tower through the **Portal of San Ranieri** which has superb bronze *doors by Bonanno da Pisa (1180). Above is a lunette with a 15C *Madonna and Child and two angels* by Andrea di Francesco Guardi.

The cruciform interior (admission, see above) is over 94.5m long and 32m wide (72m across the exceptionally deep transepts). The 68 pillars have 11C capitals in imitation of classical ones. The coffered, gilded ceiling of the nave was remodelled after 1596. Some of the small stained glass windows (restored in 1947–48) in the aisles are attributed to Alesso Baldovinetti.

The two stoups (1) bear statues by Felice Palma (1621), perhaps on a design by Giambologna. West wall. The tomb of Archbishop Matteo Rinuccini (d. 1852; 2) incorporates a *Crucifix* by Pietro Tacca. The 14C fresco of the *Crucifixion* (3) is attributed to Bernardo Falconi. The Frosini funerary monument (4) has a bas-relief of the *Deposition* by Giovanni Battista Vaccà (1702).

On the walls of the south aisle, between the altars, are hung a series of large 18C canvases, all of them labelled. First altar (5) *Madonna and Saints* by Cristofano Allori (1610; perhaps completed by Zanobi Rosi in 1626); second altar (6) *Disputation of the Holy Sacrament* by Francesco Vanni (with a figure on the left attributed to Annibale Carracci); third altar (7) *Madonna delle Grazie* by Andrea del Sarto and Giovanni Antonio Sogliani. Beyond a historical painting (8) by Sebastiano Conca, the fourth altar (9) has a carved lunette of *God the Father* by Bartolomeo Ammannati.

South transept. On the first altar (10), carved by Stagio Stagi, *Madonna and Child with Saints* by Giovanni Antonio Sogliani and Perin del Vaga. The two

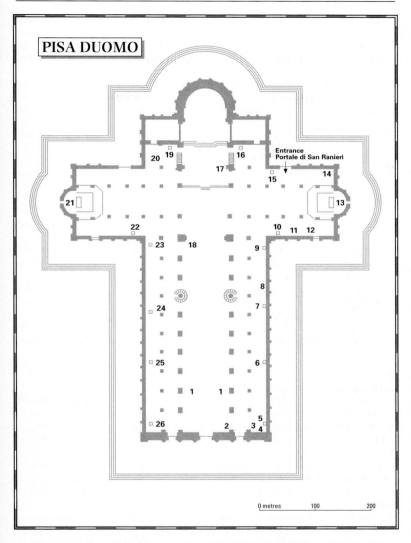

PISA DUOMO

Entrance
Portale di San Ranieri

0 metres   100   200

early 18C paintings (11, 12) are by Domenico Muratori and Benedetto Luti. The **Chapel of San Ranieri** (13) Pisa's patron saint (1117–60) has 17C sculptures by Francesco Mosca, and a marble and bronze coffer by Giovanni Battista Foggini which contains the remains of the saint. The *tomb of the Emperor Henry VII (14) was sculpted by Tino da Camaino (1315) with a fine effigy (it has been partly reassembled here; other statues are in the Museo dell'Opera del Duomo). The Renaissance altar (15) was carved by Pandolfo Fancelli. On the altar right of the choir (16), *Christ on the Cross* by Giovanni Bilivert.

Beneath the oval dome, frescoed by Orazio Riminaldi (1627) are remains of a Cosmatesque pavement with marble inlay; another fragment near the high altar may date from the end of the 11C. In the centre of the outside face of the triumphal arch is a large 14C fresco of the *Madonna and Child* attributed to the Master of San Torpè. The balustrade at the entrance to the choir bears two bronze angels by Giambologna and assistants (1602). A new altar and pulpit by Giuliano Vangi were installed here in 2001, but there are, thankfully, plans to remove them. The wooden throne and benches have good marquetry work. The stalls (15C) were reconstructed in 1616 from what survived of the fire. On the entrance piers, in rich frames, are a delightful *St Agnes* (17) by Andrea del Sarto and a *Madonna* by Giovanni Antonio Sogliani. The marble lectern and candelabra are by Matteo Civitali. On the walls beneath the cantoria are paintings by Andrea Del Sarto: *Saints John, Peter, Margaret and Catherine*. The *Crucifix* on the high altar is by Giambologna; the angel on the column to the left is by Stoldo Lorenzi (1483).

The paintings in the apse include: *Descent from the Cross* (1540) and *Sacrifice of Abraham* (1542), both by Sodoma, and works by Sogliani and Beccafumi. On the intrados of the apse arch are frescoed angels by Domenico Ghirlandaio (restored). In the apse is a fine mosaic, the *Redeemer enthroned between the Madonna and St John the Evangelist*, a 13C work completed by Cimabue in 1302.

The *pulpit* in the nave (18) by Giovanni Pisano (1302–11; perhaps with the assistance of Tino da Camaino), removed in 1599 after the fire, was reconstructed in 1926. It is a masterpiece of Gothic sculpture. The columns, on plain bases, resting on lions, or carved into figure sculpture, have statues of sibyls above the capitals, and florid architraves. Above, deeply carved relief panels representing scenes from the New Testament are separated by figures of prophets.

13C and 14C sculptors of Pisa

Nicola Pisano (c 1200–80) had a profound influence on the development of sculpture in Italy. His works mark a break with medieval art and contain a new Gothic realism and narrative style which point the way forward to the Renaissance.

Nicola was probably a native of Puglia in southern Italy but lived most of his life in Pisa where his first known work is the Baptistery pulpit. The only other two sculptures certainly by his hand are the pulpit in Siena cathedral (1268) and the Fontana Maggiore (the fountain outside the cathedral) in Perugia (1278).

For these last two commissions he was assisted by his son **Giovanni Pisano** who later carved two more splendid pulpits of exquisite workmanship, one in the church of Sant'Andrea in Pistoia (1301), and the other, the most sumptuous of all, in the Duomo of Pisa (1302–11). Giovanni, who worked for some ten years as a sculptor for Siena cathedral, is also recognised as having had a fundamental influence on Italian sculpture.

Later in the 14C two more important sculptors were at work, also called Pisano (but no relation to Nicola and Giovanni): **Andrea Pisano** (1290/95–1349) who produced masterpieces for the Campanile and Baptistery of Florence, and his son **Nino Pisano** (d. 1368) who worked mostly in Pisa.

The bronze *lamp hanging over the nave, supposed to have suggested to Galileo the principle of the pendulum, was in fact cast by Battista Lorenzi in 1587, six years after the discovery.

On the altar to the left of the presbytery (19) is a much venerated 13C painting of the *Madonna* to which the Pisans are traditionally supposed to have turned in times of trouble since 1225. The large painting nearby of the *Birth of the Virgin* (20) is by Corrado Giaquinto.

North transept. Funerary monument of Archbishop d'Elci by Vaccà (1742). In the Cappella del Sacramento (21) there is a bronze and silver ciborium by Giovanni Battista Foggini (1685), and sculptures by Chiarissimo Fancelli (1625) and Francesco Mosca (c 1563). In the arch high above is a mosaic of the *Annunciation* attributed to Gaddo Gaddi. On the altar (22), carved by Stagio Stagi is a *Miracle of Christ* by Aurelio Lomi.

The north aisle is hung with more large 18C paintings (all labelled). Fourth altar (23), 16C bas-relief in the lunette of the *Madonna appearing to St Ranieri*; third altar (24) *God the Father and Saints* by Ventura Salimbeni; second altar (25) *Holy Spirit and martyrs* by Passignano; first altar (26) *Christ on the Cross and Saints*, by Giovanni Battista Paggi.

Outside the Portale di San Ranieri is a copy made in 1930 of a beautiful Greek vase (2C–1C BC), with dancing nymphs and satyrs and Dionysiac scenes carved in low relief, a superb work which was studied by sculptors of the Renaissance. The original, not at present on view, is kept in the Camposanto.

The Campanile

Superbly sited at the east end of the cathedral rises the *Campanile, the famous **Leaning Tower** (Map 2). It is a beautiful work, circular in plan with eight storeys of round arches, six open galleries, and a bell-chamber of smaller diameter. The tower, 54.5m high, leans over 4 metres out of the perpendicular. It is one of the most original bell-towers in Italy, apart from its marked inclination which has accounted for its world-wide fame. It was reopened to the public at the end of 2001 (see p 250).

Begun in 1173, the tower was only 10.5m high when a subsidence of the soil threw it out of the perpendicular. During the 13C the architect in charge appears to have been Giovanni di Simone, who endeavoured to rectify the inclination as the building proceeded. By 1301 the building had risen as far as the bellchamber, and Tommaso di Andrea da Pontedera completed the tower in the late 14C as it now stands. A spiral staircase (294 steps) leads to the top (splendid *view). In the 1980s it was found that the lean was increasing by about 1mm a year, so in 1990 it was closed to the public, and in 1992 steel cables were inserted around the base of the tower, and between the first and second galleries. Then from 1998–2001 the tower was 'anchored' with two steel cables and a complicated operation on the subsoil was carried out to stabilise the foundations. The result of these measures has been that by 2001 the lean had been reduced by some 40 centimetres, thus returning to the same position it had some 300 years ago. Excavations at the foot of the tower since 1980 have revealed remains of Etruscan and Roman buildings.

Galileo, according to his pupil Vincenzio Viviani, carried out experiments from the tower to provide an ocular demonstration to members of Pisa university that all falling bodies independent of their size, descend with equal velocity.

The Baptistery

The *Baptistery (**Map** 2), west of the Duomo, is a very fine circular building begun in 1152 by Diotisalvi. The Gothic decoration was added to the Romanesque building in the 13C by Nicola Pisano (1270–84) and his son Giovanni (1297).

The Gothic dome and cusped arches were added in the 14C by Cellino di Nese. There are four portals, of which the most elaborate, facing the Duomo, has foliated columns and a Madonna by Giovanni Pisano (copy; original in the Museo dell' Opera).

The handsome interior (admission, see above) has a two-storeyed ambulatory, and is decorated with bands of black-and-white marble.

The Baptistery, Pisa

A staircase leads up to the gallery, and another flight continues up to the top of the dome where the vaulting can be seen. The beautiful octagonal *font of white marble, carved and inlaid in mosaic, is by Guido da Como (1246). The statue of *St John the Baptist* is by a local artist, Italo Griselli (1880–1958). The 13C altar stands on a raised mosaic pavement. The *pulpit, by Nicola Pisano, is signed and dated 1260. Resting on slender pillars bearing figures of the *Virtues*, it bears panels sculptured in bold relief (*Nativity, Adoration of the Magi, Presentation, Crucifixion*, and *Last Judgement*).

The Camposanto

The *Campostanto (**Map** 2), or cemetery, (adm., see above) was begun in 1278 by Giovanni di Simone, and completed in the 15C. The bright marble exterior wall has handsome blind arcading and a Gothic tabernacle over one door with statues attributed to the bottega of Giovanni Pisano.

The interior is in the form of an oblong cloister, lit by graceful traceried windows (never filled with glass), around a lawn. Tradition has it that this is the site of an earlier burial ground for which Archbishop Ubaldo Lanfranchi (1108–78) brought five shiploads of earth from the Holy Land. It was used as a cemetery for illustrious Pisan citizens up to 1779. It was decorated with extremely important **frescoes** in the 14C and 15C by Taddeo Gaddi (1300), Andrea Bonaiuti, Antonio Veneziano, Spinello Aretino, Piero di Puccio (1377–90), and Benozzo Gozzoli (1468–84).

From the 14C onwards Roman sculptures were brought here, including a huge collection of sarcophagi. All these works were severely damaged in the Second World War, when the roof fell in. The frescoes (also ruined by exposure to the elements) have now all been detached for reasons of conservation, and some are displayed in a gallery here. The *sinopie* are preserved in the Museo delle Sinopie (see below). In the walks, bitterly cold in winter, are numerous pavement tombs.

The **Roman sculpture and sarcophagi** in the Campostanto made up one of the most important classical collections in Europe in the early Renaissance. Many of these have been destroyed or removed, but a remarkable series of 84 sarcophagi, most of them dating from the 3C AD, remain (although many of them are very damaged). Some of them were re-used by Pisan citizens in the Middle Ages. Over the centuries funerary monuments were also erected here, some of which were later removed. The monuments have been in the process of cleaning and re-arrangement for a number of years.

South walk To the left of the entrance there are 2C and 3C sarcophagi on the outer wall and neo-Classical monuments and two Roman statues on the inner wall. The large wall tomb at the end is that of the physicist, Francesco Algarotti (d. 1764).

West walk The oval sarcophagus with two male figures in togas, dating from the mid-3C AD, was re-used in the 14C by the Falconi family. On the wall, funerary monument of Francesco Vegio by Francesco Ferrucci (Il Tadda) with remains of 16C frescoes by Agostino Ghirlanda around it. Behind a Roman sarcophagus with figures of Genii (3C) is the wall tomb of Counts Bonifazio and Gherardo della Gherardesca attributed to a Pisan sculptor and dated 1330–40. The sarcophagus is decorated with arcaded niches with the *Pietà and Saints*, and the figure of the defunct is flanked by the *Annunciatory angel* and the *Virgin Annunciate*. Beyond the small funerary monument of Selvaggia Borghini with her profile by Enrico Van Lint (1829), in the centre of this walk is the large wall monument to Bartolomeo Medici (1573), with a bust and an obelisk attributed to Niccolò Tribolo.

The harbour chains of the ancient port of Pisa, displayed here, were carried off by the Genoese in 1342 (and returned by them in 1860). On two plinths, busts of *Carlo Metteucci* by Giovanni Duprè (1869) and of *Giorgio Regnoli* by Reginaldo Bilancini (1860). On the wall is a bust of *Amedeo of Savoy* by Cesare Zocchi (1897). The sarcophagus with festoons (one of the earliest in the Camposanto) was the tomb of Bellicus Natalis, Consul in AD 87. On the wall is the funerary monument of the painter Giovanni Battista Tempesti, with a seated female figure by Tommaso Masi (1804), and at the end of the north walk is the large monument to Francesco Sanseverino Murci by Francesco Mosca decorated with coloured marbles. At the end of the wall, funerary monument of the physicist, Lorenzo Pignotti (d. 1817), with a good relief by Stefano Ricci. A granite column serves as a base for a marble crater of the 1C BC. The frescoes (late 16C–early 17C) are by Aurelio Lomi (*Esther and Assuero*) and Paolo Guidotti (*Story of Judith and Holofernes*).

North walk On the outer wall are two 3C sarcophagi, and that of Larcius Sabinus (mid-2C AD); on the inner wall, the tomb of Rafidia, a freedwoman (1C AD). In the Cappella Ligo degli Ammannati is the tomb of a Pisan doctor who died in 1359.

On the left is a huge room built in 1952 to house some of the frescoes detached from the south walk of the Campostanto, including **Triumph of Death, Last Judgement*, and *Stories of the Anchorites*. These have been variously attributed to Orcagna, Francesco Traini, Vitale da Bologna, and Buffalmacco, but are now generally held to be by an unknown 14C master named from these frescoes the Master of the Triumph of Death (1360–80). In 1839 Franz Liszt, the pianist and composer, was inspired by these scenes to create his *Totentanz* (he lived for a period with his mistress Countess d'Agoult near Pisa on the sea at Il Gombo).

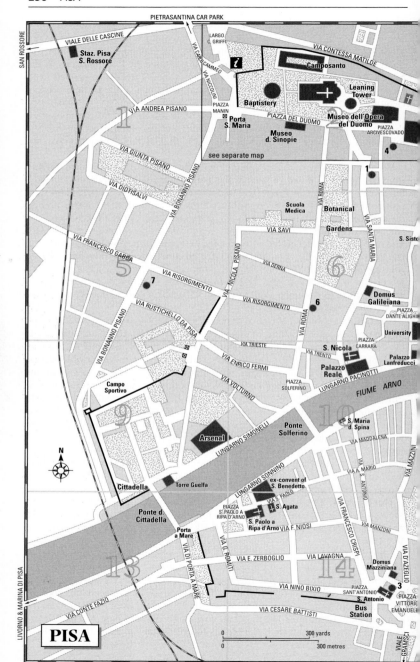

PISA

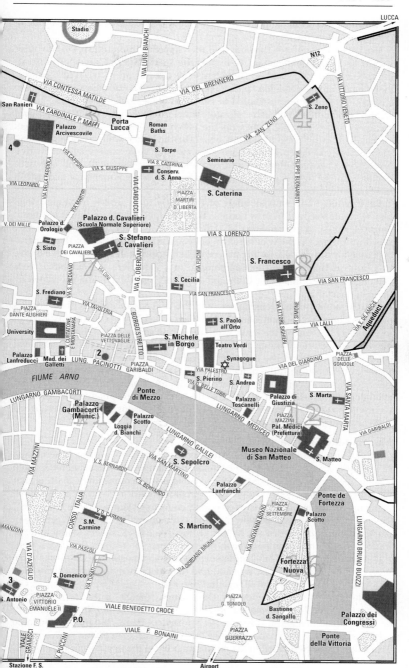

Also here is a scene of the *Crucifixion* by the Maestro della Crocifissione di Camposanto (c 1380).

North walk (right of the door into the Cappella Ammannati). On the outer wall are 2C and 3C sarcophagi, re-used in the Middle Ages. A large one illustrating the myth of Phaedra and Hippolytus was used again in 1076 for Beatrice, mother of Countess Matilda of Canossa. The Cappella Aulla has a polychrome terracotta *Assumption* attributed to Giovanni della Robbia (damaged). To the right of the door, beyond three 3C sarcophagi is one decorated with Satyrs and Meanads and Dionysiac scenes on the cover, and one showing the myth of Meleager hunting the Caledonian boar. On the inner wall are several small sarcophagi for children. Beyond two steps, two fine large sarcophagi, one with a battle scene between Romans and barbarians (very damaged), and one with niches with the figures of the Muses (and on the cover a marriage bed with a husband and wife).

East walk Tomb with an effigy of Filippo Decio (d. 1535) by Stagio Stagi; seated female statue (1842) by Lorenzo Bartolini for the tomb of Count Mastiani; tomb of the scientist Mossotti (d. 1863), with a reclining female figure by Giovanni Duprè. On the wall here can be seen the nails and part of the preparation used for the *intonaco* for the frescoes. The **Cappella del Pozzo** with a dome, was built at this end of the Camposanto in 1594. Here are exhibited more detached frescoes, including *Cain and Abel* and *Noah's Ark* and the *Flood* by Piero di Puccio.

South walk (being rearranged). On the outer wall are inscribed decrees ordaining honours for Gaius and Lucius Caesar, nephews of Augustus; Roman milestones (2C), and on the inner wall, the second sarcophagus right of the door has winged Victories holding a medallion (on which was later carved a medieval coat of arms). Beyond the door, on the outer wall: sarcophagus with winged Victories inscribed with the name of Aelius Lucifer, a Roman freedman (former slave); two oval sarcophagi with lions attacking their prey; sarcophagus with an open door symbolising the entrance to the after-life; sarcophagus with hunting scenes illustrating the myth of Meleager and the Seasons, with a marriage bed and husband and wife on the cover.

Museo delle Sinopie

On the south side of the lawn is the former Ospedale Nuovo di Misericordia (13C–14C), where the Museo delle Sinopie del Camposanto Monumentale (**Map** 2; adm. see above) was opened in 1979. A *sinopia* is the name given to the sketch for a fresco made on the rough wall (prepared with *arriccio*) in a red earth pigment (called *sinopia* because it originally came from Sinope on the Black Sea). The *sinopia* was then gradually covered with *grassello*, another type of wet plaster, as work proceeded day by day on the fresco itself. By detaching a fresco from the wall it has been possible in many instances to recover the *sinopia* from the inner surface. The 14C–15C frescoes of the Campostanto (see above) were severely damaged in the last war and had to be detached: the *sinopie* were then restored and are now displayed together here.

A platform provides a view of three huge *panels with *Stories of the Anchorites*, the *Last Judgement and Hell*, and the *Triumph of Death*, all generally attributed to the Master of the Triumph of Death (but thought by some scholars to be by Buffalmacco). On the far (end) wall, *Crucifixion* by Francesco Traini and *Ascension*, attributed to Buffalmacco. On the north wall, *Theological*

Cosmograph by Piero di Puccio. On the last wall are smaller *sinopie* (very damaged) by Spinello Aretino, Antonio Veneziano, Andrea Bonaiuti, and Taddeo Gaddi. On the upper level are frescoes and *sinopia* fragments by Buffalmacco (including *Incredulity of St Thomas* and *Resurrection*). On the ground floor the *sinopie* are by Piero di Puccio and Benozzo di Lese.

Museo dell'Opera del Duomo

The *Museo dell'Opera del Duomo (adm. see above), in Piazza dell'Arcivescovado, is a very fine museum opened in 1986, using the latest methods of security and display, in the former chapter house of the Cathedral behind the Leaning Tower. The collection includes works of art from the Duomo, Baptistery, and Camposanto. The fine building, with a double loggia, overlooking a little garden, has good views of the Leaning Tower.

Ground floor Room 1 displays 19C models in wood and alabaster of the monuments in Campo dei Miracoli, and casts of their foundation stones. **Room 2** contains casts of the first pulpit made for the Duomo by Guglielmo Pisano in 1162.

Room 3: 12C sculpture from the Duomo, showing Islamic and French influences. The intricately carved transenna (probably an altar frontal) is attributed to Rainaldo. On the left wall are capitals and inlaid marble panels from the façade of the Duomo (their original postitions are shown on a diagram). In front is a long transenna from the presbytery by the school of Guglielmo Pisano, carved on the back of a Roman panel with a frieze of dolphins. The polychrome wood figure of *Christ descending from the Cross* is a remarkable work attributed to a 12C Burgundian artist. The splendid bronze *griffin (11C) and the basin and capital (10C) are Islamic works brought from the East as war booty. The statue of *St Michael* is attributed to Biduino, and the seated statue of David playing the cithern shows the influence of Provence sculptors.

The small **room 4** displays a late 12C *capital from the Campanile. **Room 5** contains 13C heads from the exterior of the Baptistery (their original positions are shown on a diagram) and fragments from the transenna. **Room 6**, a pretty barrel vaulted room with wall paintings, displays the Gothic statues (very worn) from the summits of the triangular tympanums on the exterior of the Baptistery. They are by Nicola and Giovanni Pisano, and assistants. Facing them are busts of *Christ blessing*, by Nicola Pisano, between the *Madonna and St John the Evangelist*, originally above the main entrance of the Baptistery facing the Duomo.

In the **corridor** and room 7 are parts of the late 13C frieze with carved rectangles which ran round the base of the exterior of the Duomo. **Room 7** displays sculptures by Giovanni Pisano, including a (headless) *Madonna and kneeling figure* representing Pisa, formerly part of an allegorical group with the Emperor Henry VII. The *Madonna and Child and Saints John the Evangelist and John the Baptist* were removed from the main door of the Baptistery. The half-length *Madonna del Colloquio* is a beautiful composition.

Room 8 contains works by Tino da Camaino: fragments of the font from the Duomo; statues of the *Annunciation* and two deacons from the tomb of the Emperor Henry VII in the south transept of the Duomo; the tomb of St Ranieri (his first work, 1301–06); and the seated Henry VII between dignitaries of the state. **Room 9**. Funerary monuments of two archbishops by Nino Pisano. **Room 10**. Funerary monument of Archbishop Pietro Ricci by the Florentine sculptor

Andrea di Francesco Guardi; architectural fragments by Matteo Civitali, and the workshop of Lorenzo and Stagio Stagi.

The **cathedral *treasury** is displayed in **rooms 11 and 12**: 12C Cross, known as the Croce dei Pisani in bronze and silver; two 12C Limoges enamelled caskets; Tuscan embroidered altar-frontal (1325); and a cope, also dating from the 14C. The *girdle with five reliefs decorated with enamels and precious stones dates from the end of the 13C or beginning of the 14C. Also displayed here: 15C reliquary of St Clement, and an 11C ivory casket. The ivory statuette of the ***Madonna and Child**, is a superb work by Giovanni Pisano (1299–1300), originally over the main altar in the Duomo. The *Crucifix* is also by Giovanni Pisano. In the 17C chapel (room 12) are displayed 17C reliquaries and the service of gilded church silver (French, 1616–17) given by Maria de' Medici to Archbishop Bonciani.

First floor Stairs lead up to **room 13**: paintings by a follower of Benozzo Gozzoli (*Madonna and Child, four Saints, and patrons*), and by Battista Franco and Aurelio Lomi. Marble angels by Tribolo and Silvio Cosini. **Room 14**: 18C paintings by Giuseppe and Francesco Melani and Giovanni Domenico Ferretti.

Room 15 displays wood intarsia (fragments from furnishings made for the Duomo); allegories of Faith, Hope, and Charity, by Baccio and Piero Pontelli (1475) are displayed opposite two works by Cristoforo da Lendinara. Also here are panels from choir-stalls by Guido da Seravallino. **Room 16**: two liturgical parchment scrolls, known as *Exultets* (12C and 13C), with illuminations, 14C illuminated choirbooks, and a 16C wooden lectern.

Rooms 17–19 retain their neo-Classical decorations (including a charming alcove) from the time when the palace was the home of Giovanni Rosini (1776–1855), writer and publisher, and curator of the Campostanto. He befriended Giacomo Leopardi when the poet was staying in Pisa in 1827. The church vestments now displayed here date from the 16C–19C. **Room 21**: engravings and watercolours by Carlo Lasinio (1759–1838) responsible for the restoration of the Campostanto. The delightful copies in watercolour of the frescoes of the Campostanto provide a precious record of them before their almost total destruction in the Second World War.

Rooms 22–24 contains an archaeological collection displayed by Lasinio in the Camposanto in 1807: cinerary urns, sarcophagi, busts, including one of Julius Caesar, Etruscan urns, and Egyptian antiquities.

The exit from the museum is along the **portico** on the **ground floor** where the colossal *half-figures of *Evangelists*, *Prophets*, and the *Madonna and Child*, by Nicola and Giovanni Pisano from the exterior of the Baptistery (1269–79) are displayed.

The handsome Renaissance **Palazzo Arcivescovile**, also in Piazza Arcivescovado, has a bright yellow façade and an attractive 16C courtyard (with a statue of *Moses* by Andrea Vaccà, 1709). A flying bridge connects the palace with its walled garden across Via Capponi. At the end of Via Corta is the church of **San Ranieri** (often closed) which contains a fine painting of the *Madonna and Saints* by Aurelio Lomi.

The 12C castellated walls which enclose the north and west side of Piazza del Duomo were pierced by the **Porta del Leone** (opposite the west end of the Campostanto) in the 13C. The gate was named after the Romanesque lion which survives here. Through the closed wooden gates can be seen part of the **Jewish Cemetery** which was moved here in the 16C, and surrounded in 1801 by a high wall. The **Porta Nuova**, the present exit from the piazza, replaced the Porta del Leone in 1562.

From Piazza del Duomo, Via Santa Maria runs south. Opposite the end of Via dei Mille the short Via Luca Ghini leads to the entrance of the **Botanical Gardens** (**Map** 6; open 08.00–13.00, 14.00–17.30; Sat 08.00–13.00; fest. closed; ring at the door on the left). Founded in 1543 by Luca Ghini, and on this site since 1591, this is the oldest university botanic garden in Europe. The large building which houses the Botanic Institute was built in 1890, and in the same year the two fine palm trees from Chile were planted here. The old garden is laid out in rectangular beds (well labelled) in front of the Institute. At the end on the left is the original building which housed the Botanic Insitute, its façade decorated in imitation of a grotto with shells and pebbles. The gardens (damaged in a hurricane in 1994) contain notable examples of palm trees, ginkgos, magnolias, and camphor trees.

Via dei Mille continues left, passing the end of Via della Faggiola where (on the corner of Via dei Preti, now called Via Leopardi) the Italian poet Giacomo Leopardi took lodgings in 1827–28. The pretty Romanesque church of **San Sisto** has a fine interior, with beautiful old columns and capitals. The high altar was designed by Giuseppe Vaccà in 1730. The aisles are decorated with banners and in the corners of the west wall are 14C–15C ships' masts, and a 14C Arab inscription from the Koran.

Piazza dei Cavalieri

Once the centre of the city, (**Map** 7), the piazza was named after the Knights of St Stephen, an order founded by Cosimo I in 1561 to combat the Turkish infidel, in imitation of the Knights of Malta.

Santo Stefano dei Cavalieri (**Map** 7; open 09.00–12.30; also Sat and Sun pm), their church, has a handsome façade by Giovanni de' Medici (1594–1606), son of Cosimo I, and an unusual campanile by Vasari (1572).

The fine **interior** by Vasari (1565–69) is decorated with the banners captured from the infidel. The ceiling (1604–13) has six scenes of *Cosimo I as Grand Master of the Order*; the *Return of the fleet after the battle of Lepanto*; *Maria de'Medici setting out to marry Henri IV of France*; and three naval battles (1602–13) over the Turks in which the Knights were victorious. These are good paintings by Cigoli, Jacopo Ligozzi, Cristofano Allori, and Empoli. 17C carved wooden ornaments (attributed to Santucci) and lanterns (also removed for restoration) from the Knights' galleys are displayed in various parts of the church. The two fine organs date from 1734 and 1569. The high altar, with a statue of the patron saint, is by Giovanni Battista Foggini.

The two stoups were designed by Vasari and carved by Fancelli. The five tempera paintings (late 16C) of scenes from the life of St Stephen in grisaille (on the north, south, and west walls) are attributed to Empoli, Alessandro Allori, Vasari, and Ligozzi (or Stradano). The pretty pulpit by Chiarissimo Fancelli (1627; restored in 1930) has *pietre dure* inlay. At the end of the south side is a painting of the *Madonna and Child* by Aurelio Lomi, in an elaborate frame.

In the monumental side aisles are white marble confessionals. On the south side: first altar, *Stoning of St Stephen* by Vasari; second altar, Crucifix attributed to Tacca. On the north side: second altar, *Nativity* by Bronzino; first altar, *Miracle of the Loaves and Fishes* by Lodovico Buti.

To the left of the church is **Palazzo dei Cavalieri**, formerly della Carovana, modernised in 1562 by Vasari, with spectacular graffiti decoration, designed by him (much restored). It is now the seat of the **Scuola Normale Superiore**, a university college of extremely high standing, founded by Napoleon in 1810, and modelled on the Ecole Normale Supérieure in Paris. It incorporates a large medieval hall of the old Palazzo del Popolo, now used as a lecture hall. Concerts are given here from December to May. Outside is a statue of Cosimo I by Francavilla (1596).

The **Palazzo dell'Orologio**, closing the north side of the square, occupies the site of the old Torre dei Gualandi also called the Torre della Mula when it was used as a mews for eagles (emblems of the city as incorporated into the Pisan coat of arms) which were confined here at moulting time. The tower continued its function as a small prison when in 1288 Count Ugolino della Gherardesca, who was suspected of treachery at the battle of Meloria, and his sons and grandsons were starved to death here. The episode is described by Dante (*La Divina Commedia, Inferno*, XXXII) who notes that since that time the tower came to be known as the Torre della Fame (the Tower of Famine). The building is now used as a library by the Scuola Normale, and the tower can be seen from the entrance, incorporated in the structure.

Borgo Stretto

Via Ulisse Dini leads down to Borgo Stretto (**Map 7**), a pretty arcaded shopping street in the centre of the town (closed to private traffic), with wide pavements. Some of the porticoes date from the 14C–15C. Off the narrow old Via Notari (parallel to the right) a daily **market** is held in **Piazza delle Vettovaglie**, with porticoes dating from 1544 (but damaged in the War).

In Borgo Stretto is the church of **San Michele in Borgo**, built in the 11C, with a lovely 14C façade by Fra Guglielmo Agnelli, follower of Nicola Pisano and typical of the Pisan Gothic style. Over the central door are statues of the *Madonna and Child with two Saints* in a Gothic tabernacle. The curious red lettering dates from the 16C–17C when the lower part of the façade was used for propoganda in the elections for a rector of a local school. Above is pretty arcading with a great variety of capitals and masques in the spandrels between the arches. In the **interior** (damaged in the last war) are high arcades with good capitals. Over a door on the west wall (at the end of the north aisle) is a detached 13C fresco of *St Michael*. At the end of the south aisle are four paintings of the *Virtues* by Aurelio Lomi (1605; restored in 1997), and a *Presentation in the Temple* also painted by him (1611). The high altarpiece of the *Madonna and Saints* is by Baccio Lomi. At the end of the north aisle are two paintings by Matteo Rosselli (1627), and, over an altar, a 14C Pisan *Crucifix*.

Borgo Stretto ends at the central Piazza Garibaldi on the Arno (described below). From Borgo Stretto, opposite Via Ulisse Dini (see above), the narrow Via San Francesco leads to the church of **Santa Cecilia** (1103) with a façade and campanile decorated with majolica plaques (replaced by copies). Inside, a handsome Romanesque column at the west end supports a corner of the campanile. Over the high altar, *Martyrdom of St Cecilia* by Ventura Salimbeni.

Santa Caterina

To the north, across the huge Piazza Martiri (planted with plane trees), stands the large church of Santa Caterina (**Map** 4), built for the Dominicans in the 13C, with a façade of 1330. The interior has a colourful east window (1925). On the south side is the tomb of Gherardo di Compagno (1419), and *St Catherine of Alexandria* by Aurelio Lomi. A chapel off this side, which serves as a war memorial, contains a *Pietà* by Santi di Tito.

In the chapel to the right of the high altar there is a polychrome 15C relief of the *Madonna and Saints*. On either side of the **presbytery** are *statues of the *Annunciation* by Nino Pisano. In the north transept, *Madonna and Saints* by Fra Bartolomeo.

North side. *Apotheosis of St Thomas Aquinas* by Francesco Traini; second altar, *St Vincent Ferrer* by Cesare Dandini; tomb of Archbishop Simone Saltarelli (d. 1342) by Nino Pisano; and first altar, *St Catherine of Siena receiving the stigmata* by Raffaello Vanni.

To the northeast of the church (see the **Map**) are vestiges of **Roman baths**, uncovered in 1942. From Via Cardinale Maffi there is a dramatic view of the Leaning Tower. In the other direction, Via San Zeno leads northeast to (c 400m) the little Romanesque chapel of **San Zeno** (**Map** 4). Of ancient foundation it shows various architectural styles from the 10C and incorporates a few Roman fragments in its façade. It has been deconsecrated and is now sometimes used for exhibitions and concerts. There are plans to open a research centre and small museum here called the *Giardino di Archimede*, dedicated to mathematics. Outside Porta San Zeno, Via Vittorio Veneto skirts a fine stretch of the city walls.

San Francesco

Via San Francesco (see above) continues east to the Gothic church of San Francesco (**Map** 8), with an elegant Gothic campanile. The handsome plain façade was finished in 1603. The well illuminated interior is typical of Franciscan churches, with a wide aisleless nave and Gothic chapels at the east end. South side: first altar, *Baptism of Christ* by Empoli; second altar, *Resurrection* by Giovanni Battista Paggi; third altar, *St Peter receiving the keys from Christ* by Passignano; fourth altar, *St Francis receiving the stigmata* by Santi di Tito. In the Gothic chapel of St Filomena is a tomb of 1414.

On the **high altar** is a large marble reredos by Tommaso Pisano. In the vault, frescoes of the Apostles, friars and monastic virtues by Taddeo Gaddi (1342). The east window has good stained glass dating in part from the 14C; the other windows at the east end also have pretty stained glass. In the second chapel to the right of the high altar, *Crucifixion and Saints* by Spinello Aretino. In the third chapel left of the high altar are remains of 14C frescoes. The vaulting in the north transept bears the weight of the campanile.

In the **sacristy** a chapel is frescoed by Taddeo di Bartolo, and on the walls are *sinopie* by Niccolò di Pietro Gerini of the frescoes by him in the chapter house. North side: fifth altar, *St Francis*; by Francesco Vanni, and third altar, *Assumption* by Ventura Salimbeni.

On the south side of Via San Francesco is Piazza San Paolo, with the deconsecrated church of **San Paolo all'Orto**. It retains the lower part of its beautiful, delicately carved façade with polychrome marble inlay and sculptures by Biduino (c 1180), carefully restored in 1992. Farther south is **San Pierino** (1072–1119; closed), which has a large crypt (seen from the outside). Via Palestro, with the **Teatro Verdi** (1867; small museum), and **synagogue** (1648; restored in 1865 by Marco Treves), leads east to **Sant'Andrea**, another good 12C church (closed; used by a theatrical society). Beyond the huge **Palazzo di Giustizia** (1938–58) Via Giusti and Via del Giardino lead to Piazza delle Gondole, built on a canal, with a 16C fountain. Here is the end of the **aqueduct** built by the Medici in 1601–13 to bring water to the city from Asciano (c 6km away). The low brick arches are very well preserved. South of the piazza, in Via Santa Marta, is the church of **Santa Marta**, with a harmonious 18C interior.

Several streets lead south from San Francesco to the Lungarno Mediceo, on which is the Museo Nazionale di San Matteo.

Museo Nazionale di San Matteo

The ex-convent of San Matteo (used as a prison in the 19C) has been occupied since 1947 by the Museo Nazionale di San Matteo (**Map** 12; open 09.00–18.00; fest. 09.00–13.00; closed Mon), which contains works of art from Pisan churches and convents. The later works belonging to the city collections are now exhibited in Palazzo Reale (see below). Important exhibitions are held on the ground floor.

In the entrance hall, sarcophagus with the Good Shepherd (4C AD). Off the attractive brick **cloister**, with sculptural fragments, are four rooms which display 16C pottery and the Tongiorgi *collection of majolica tondi from Pisan church façades and ceramics (10C–18C), including numerous Islamic pieces. Another room contains 14C and 15C sculptures from Pisan churches including works by Lupo di Francesco.

First floor Room 1 (left) has a fine collection of early Tuscan painted *Crucifixes* (13C), including one signed by Giunta Pisano (believed to be the earliest painter whose name is inscribed on any extant Italian work), and one signed by Berlinghiero. The 13C Pisan panel paintings include: *St Francis with stories from his life*; the *Madonna enthroned with stories from the lives of St Joachim and Anna*; and (on the balcony) *St Catherine with stories from her life*. A Bible dated 1168 (from Calci) is also displayed here. **Room 2** displays early 14C works: panels by Deodato Orlandi and the Maestro di San Torpè; *polyptych of *St Dominic* with stories from his life (signed) and *Madonna and Child with Saints* both by Francesco Traini; and a polyptych by Lippo Memmi. At the end of the room is a *polyptych signed and dated 1319–21 by Simone Martini. Also here are works by Giovanni di Nicola, and a wooden statue of the *Virgin Annunciate* by Agostino di Giovanni.

Room 3 (right) contains 14C and 15C Pisan wooden sculptures, including works by Francesco di Valdambrino. The *Madonna del Latte*, a half-length polychrome marble gilded statue from Santa Maria della Spina and the *Annunciatory angel*, a wooden statue from San Matteo, are both by Andrea and Nino Pisano. The *Christ in pietà*, a wooden high relief of the *Madonna and Child*, and a marble statuette of the *Madonna and Child* (the last two also from Santa Maria della Spina) are all by Nino Pisano.

In the **long gallery** (**room 4**) overlooking the cloister are sculptural fragments, which were arranged in the 19C in the Campostanto. They include French and Pisan statuettes (including two by Tino da Camaino and Nicola Pisano) and capitals carved by Giovanni di Balduccio.

Room 5 displays 14C paintings: *Madonnas* by Barnaba da Modena; processional standards by Antonio Veneziano, Taddeo di Bartolo, and the Maestro di Barga; polyptychs by Martino di Bartolomeo; *Madonna and Saints and two angels* by Taddeo di Bartolo; *Coronation of the Virgin* by Spinello Aretino; as well as works by Jacopo di Michele, Agnolo Gaddi, Luca di Tommè, Cecco di Pietro, and Francesco Neri da Volterra.

In the short gallery (**room 6**), are four delightful polychrome wooden statues by Francesco di Valdambrino. **Room 7** contains works by Turino di Vanni. In **room 8** are some of the most precious works in the collection; *St Paul* by Masaccio; a stucco relief of the *Madonna and Child* by Michelozzo; *Madonna of Humility* by Fra Angelico; reliquary *bust of *St Rossore* (or St Luxorious), a splendid work in gilded bronze (1424–27) from Santo Stefano dei Cavalieri by Donatello; *Madonnas* by the Maestro della Castello Nativity and Zanobi Machiavelli; and *Coronation of the Virgin* by Neri di Bicci. **Room 9** contains three paintings by Benozzo Gozzoli.

In the last long gallery (**10**): *Madonna of Humility* by Gentile da Fabriano and two altarpieces of the *Madonna and Saints* by Domenico Ghirlandaio. The painted terracotta bust of the *Redeemer* is by the circle of Verrocchio, and the bronze bust of a saint attributed to Michelozzo. Also here are an enamelled terracotta tondo by Benedetto Buglioni, and a *Madonna in Adoration* by Andrea della Robbia.

In the little piazza outside the museum is the church of **San Matteo**, founded in 1027. The pretty blind arcading and the east end of the Romanesque church can be seen along the Lungarno. The church (and façade) was reconstructed after a fire in 1607. The handsome Baroque interior has fine 17C and 18C paintings in marble frames, and marble stoups and confessionals. The 18C vault fresco of the *Glory of St Matthew* is by the local painters Giuseppe and Francesco Melani. On the south side are stories from the *Life of St Matthew* by Jacopo Zoboli and Marco Benefial on either side of the altarpiece of *Christ in Judgement with the Madonna and Saints* by Clemente Bocciardi. The high altarpiece of the *Calling of St Matthew* by Francesco Romanelli is flanked by two oval paintings by Giuseppe Melani. On the **north side** are stories from the *Life of St Matthew* by Sebastiano Conca and Francesco Trevisani on either side of the altar which has a 13C Pisan painted *Crucifix* (the head is ruined) and the *Madonna and St John the Evangelist and angels* painted by Stefano Marucelli. Beneath the nuns' choir, *Madonna and Child with angels and Saints*, by the 16C Florentine school.

Palazzo Medici (now the prefecture), on the left of the piazzetta, was built in the 13C–14C and owned by the Medici from 1446. Lorenzo il Magnifico often stayed here with his friend Politian. It was restored to its medieval aspect in 1879 by Ranieri Simonelli. In Piazza Mazzini is a statue of Mazzini by Giuseppe Andreoni (1883).

The attractive **Lungarno Mediceo** continues along the river. Next to **Palazzo Roncioni** (no. 16) with a handsome façade by Giovanni Stefano Marucelli (1630), where Madame de Stael stayed in 1815–16, is **Palazzo Toscanelli** (formerly Lanfranchi), with a fine 16C façade. It was occupied by Lord Byron in 1821–22, and is now the seat of the State Archives. Via delle Belle Torri runs parallel to the Lungarno here; fragments of some of the 12C–13C tower houses survive incorporated into unattractive new buildings. In Piazzetta Cairoli is a column surmounted by a pretty statue of *Abundance* by Pierino da Vinci (1550).

The small but busy **Piazza Garibaldi** (**Map** 11), at the end of Ponte di Mezzo, is at the centre of the city. The bronze statue of Garibaldi is by Ettore Ferrari (1892). The 18C Palazzo del Casino dei Nobili has three high arches. The arcaded Borgo Stretto (described above) leads north from the piazza. **Ponte di Mezzo** (**Map** 11), rebuilt in 1950, is on the site of the Roman bridge over the Arno. It has been the scene of the annual *Gioco del Ponte* (in June) since it was first celebrated under the Medici in 1596 (see practical information, above).

Lungarno Pacinotti

Lungarno Pacinotti continues along the river past the Hotel Victoria opened in 1842 (where Charles Dickens stayed in 1845). **Palazzo Agostini** (or dell'Ussero; no. 26) has early 15C terracotta decoration on its façade. Here is the opened in 1794, and famous as the meeting place of writers during the Risorgimento (it preserves mementoes of its famous patrons, including Giuseppe Giusti, and Renato Fucini).

Via Curtatone e Monatanara leads away from the river to the **university**, on this site since 1473. The present façade dates from 1907–11. The splendid courtyard survives from 1550. A studio existed in Pisa as early as the 12C, and the university was founded in 1343. It has a high reputation. Beyond the university, in Via Cavalca (right) the high Torre del Campano (13C) can be seen.

On the opposite side of Via San Frediano is the 11C church of **San Frediano** (**Map** 7), with a good façade. It preserves columns and capitals in its altered interior which has delightful 17C confessionals. In the first chapel in the south aisle is a 13C painted *Crucifix*, and on the right wall, an *Adoration of the Magi* by Aurelio Lomi. In the chapel to the right of the high altar is an amusing Baroque altar. In the chapel to the left of the high altar are three paintings by Alessandro Tiarini illustrating stories from the *Life of Santa Brigida*. On the north wall, *Saints Paul and Bartholomew* by Ranieri Borghetti, and in the third and first chapels, paintings by Ventura Salimbeni.

On Lungarno Pacinotti (see above) the tiny church of the **Madonna dei Galletti** has an attractive 17C–18C interior and a fresco of the *Madonna and Child* by Taddeo di Bartolo over the high altar, flanked by two wooden 18C angels. At no. 43 is **Palazzo Lanfreducci** (or Upezzinghi), also known as the **Palazzo alla Giornata**, with a fine white marble façade by Cosimo Pugliani (1594). **Palazzo Mazzarosa** (no. 45) dates from the 19C. In Piazza Francesco Carrara is a good statue of the Grand-duke Ferdinando I by Pietro Francavilla (1594).

Museo di Palazzo Reale

At no. 46 is the huge **Palazzo Reale** (**Map** 10), built in 1583–87 by Bernardo Buontalenti for Francesco I de' Medici. It is on the site of a medieval building and incorporates an old tower house, but it was severely damaged in the last war. It now houses the Museo di Palazzo Reale (open 09.00–14.00, except fest).

The museum contains part of the city's art collections, illustrating the period of the Medici and Lorraine grand-dukes of Tuscany, as well as the Royal House of Savoy, and important private donations made to the city by Pisan citizens in the 19C. The contents of the rest of the civic museum, with works of art from Pisan churches and convents, is housed in the Museo di San Matteo (see above).

On the stairs is an 18C bust of the Lorraine grand-duke Pietro Leopoldo I by Giovanni Antonio Cybei and paintings of the last grand-dukes wearing the uniform of the Knights of Santo Stefano, the order founded by Cosimo I.

The important **Ceci collection** donated to the town by the surgeon Antonio Ceci (1852–1920) is displayed in four rooms. The main room has numerous paintings from his collection by Valerio Castello, Francesco Francia (*Madonna and Child*), Andrea Boscoli, Michele di Matteo (*Coronation of the Virgin*), Magnasco, Bernardo Strozzi, and Frans Francken. The exquisite little *Holy Family* is thought to be a 16C copy of a work by Jan Brueghel, and the small painting of the *Crucifixion* is attributed to Herri met de Bles. The drawings and watercolours include works by Elisa Toscanelli and a *bozzetto* is attributed to Canova. Another room contains 18C–19C ivory miniatures, part of the most important private collection of its kind in Italy. In the adjoining room is a painting by Guido Reni of *Sacred and Profane Love*, small bronzes, and medals. Ceci's collection of porcelain includes fine examples from France and the far East.

On the other side of the room with the miniatures is a room with red furnishings. The paintings here include: *Rebecca at the well* attributed to Rosso Fiorentino; a tiny early work by Raphael (part of a predella); and a *Madonna* signed by Giusto de' Menabuoi. In a room decorated with yellow damask are more court portraits, three of them by Giuseppe Maria Crespi, and oval paintings in pretty frames of ladies of the court commissioned in the late 17C by Vittoria della Rovere from Antonio Franchi. Beyond a room which contains the *bozzetti* for the large 18C paintings in the aisles of the Duomo, two rooms display more Medici portraits, including *Ferdinando I as Cardinal* (before he became grand-duke) by Alessandro Allori, and Cosimo III and his family (some by Tiberio Titi).

In a room where the early 18C grisaille decoration by the workshop of Luigi Ademollo dating from the period of the Lorraine grand-dukes survives, there is a display from the huge collection of armour (dating from the 15C onwards) originally kept in the Cittadella della Rocca and afterwards adapted for use in the Gioco del Ponte (see above). A small adjoining corridor exhibits part of the Del Testa family collection. Near the ticket office a large room at present displays a rare velvet dress which belonged to the grand-duchess Eleonora di Toledo, exhibited next to her *portrait (with her son Francesco) by Bronzino. There are plans to exhibit at least some of the 35 precious 16C tapestries made in the Medici workshops here. There is also a gipsoteca, with works by the local sculptor Italo Griselli (1880–1958).

Behind the palace, in Via Santa Maria, is the church of **San Nicola** (Map 10), founded c 1000, but much altered over subsequent centuries. In the 13C *campanile is a remarkable spiral staircase on which Bramante (according to Vasari) modelled his Belvedere staircase in the Vatican.

Interior. South side. In the first chapel is a beautiful *Madonna and Child* by Francesco Traini, and a polychrome wooden *Madonna Annunciate* by Francesco di Valdambrino. On the wall of the second chapel, *St Charles Borromeo* by Giovanni Bilivert; and in the fourth chapel, *St Nicholas of Tolentino* protecting Pisa (clearly depicted) from the plague, c 1400. The 17C chapel to the right of the high altar was decorated by Matteo Nigetti, who also designed the high altar (flanked by two statues by Felice Palma). In the chapel to the left of the high altar, *Crucifix* by Giovanni Pisano (c 1300). North side. Fourth chapel, *Madonna and Child*, a statue by Nino Pisano; second chapel, altarpiece of the *Annunciation* by Giovanni Bilivert (in very poor condition).

At Via Santa Maria 26 is the **Domus Galileiana**, opened in 1942 to commemorate the famous scientist Galileo, born in Pisa. It has a fine library (admission granted to scholars). Next door is the birthplace of the scientist Antonio Pacinotti (1841–1912). Farther on, the modern Palazzo Da Scorno incorporates a large Romanesque capital into its unattractive façade.

Lungarno Pacinotti ends at **Ponte Solferino**, rebuilt in 1974 after its collapse in the flood of 1966. Lungarno Simonelli continues to the **Arsenal** (open 10.00–13.00; 14.00–18.00), a boatyard built by the Medici grand-dukes in 1548–88. On the façade are marble masques and five inscriptions. The buildings were used until recently as stables, but one of the splendid huge vaulted brick halls has recently been restored for an exhibition relating to the sixteen **ships** dating from between the 5C BC and the 5C AD which, since 1999, have been unearthed near the station of San Rossore (**Map** 1) where traces of an old port have been discovered. Finds from the excavations are displayed here including remains of cargo such as amphorae, objects in glass, bronze, terracotta and leather, as well as ropes, baskets, and mats, and skeletons of sailors and animals. There are long-term plans to exhibit some of the boats themselves here. Beyond rises the tall medieval **Cittadella** or Fortezza Vecchia (**Map** 9), with the **Torre Guelfa**, enlarged in the 15C. The tower can now be climbed (200 steps; open 10.00–14.00; summer 10.00 or 11.00–13.20, 14.30–18.00/20.00). And there is a very fine view from the top. Ponte della Cittadella (1957; first built in the 13C) leads to the south bank of the Arno.

The south bank of the Arno

At the south end of Ponte della Cittadella is the 13C **Porta a Mare** (**Map** 13), and abandoned ruins of a bastion in the walls. On the river the old gate of the Navicelli canal (now covered over) which was begun by Cosimo I in 1541 to connect Pisa with Livorno can be seen. Inside the Porta a Mare is a large Art Nouveau villa with a tower (no. 12), with good wrought-iron work and palm trees in its garden.

In this quiet part of the city a spacious piazza with trees (and an excellent view of the tall Cittadella across the river) opens out in front of the church of ***San Paolo a Ripa d'Arno** (**Map** 14), founded in 805. The splendid **façade** (restored in 1944) probably dates from the 13C and the north flank has fine blind arcading. The solemn bare interior has been closed for many years. Behind the east end, surrounded by a lawn with a few trees, is the unusual Romanesque chapel of **Sant'Agata**, a tiny octagonal brick building (after 1063). On the other side of Via San Paolo is the wall of the **ex-Convent of San Benedetto** (1393), the courtyard of which has been restored in an incongruous style by a bank. The façade on the Lungarno, beyond the little church (closed) has terracotta decoration carried out in 1850 by Domenico Santini.

Lungarno Sonnino leads along the river to Ponte Solferino, just beyond which is the charming little church of ***Santa Maria della Spina** (**Map** 10), named after a thorn of the Saviour's crown, is a gem of Pisan Gothic architecture (1230, finished in 1323), the gift of a Pisan merchant. It was restored after war damage (open 10.00–14.00). In the light interior there is a statue of the *Madonna and Child* by Andrea and Nino Pisano, and two statues of saints also by them. On the left wall there is a marble tabernacle carved by Stagio Stagi in 1534. At the opposite end of the church in a carved niche dating from 1524 there is a copy made in 1996 of the beautiful *Madonna del latte* by Andrea and Nino Pisano now kept in the Museo Nazionale di San Matteo.

From the bridge Via Crispi leads south towards Piazza Vittorio Emanuele II and the station. It ends in front of the church of **Sant'Antonio** (1341; reconstructed after the Second World War).

Nearby, at Via Mazzini 71, is the **Domus Mazziniana** (open 08.00–13.00 exc. Sun), built in 1952 on the site of a house (destroyed in the war) where Giuseppe Mazzini died in 1872, while visiting his friends the Rosselli under the false name of John Brown. It contains mementoes of Mazzini and a library specialising in the Risorgimento. In Piazza Sant'Antonio is a mock-Gothic tram station (now used as a bus station) near a stretch of the city walls.

Across Piazza Vittorio Emanuele II, with a bronze statue of the king by Cesare Zocchi (1892) is the church of San Domenico (closed) in Corso Italia.

Corso Italia (**Map 11, 15**; closed to traffic), the main street on the south bank of the Arno, returns north towards the river and Ponte di Mezzo past the church of **Santa Maria del Carmine** (**Map 15**). It was founded in 1325 and enlarged in 1612 (restored). In the pretty **interior** with attractive confessionals, on the right of the entrance is a painting of *St Teresa* by Crescenzio Gamberelli. On the south side, *Annunciation* by Andrea Boscoli, *Madonna and Child with two Saints* by Antonio Sogliani (and beyond a pretty pulpit of 1705, *Madonna and Saints* by Baccio Lomi. The altarpieces on the north side are by Alessandro Allori (*Ascension*), and the school of Aurelio Lomi (*Saints*).

Lungarno Gambacorti continues to the handsome **Palazzo Gambacorti** (no. 1), built by Pietro Gambacorti in 1370–80, and now the town hall. In Piazza XX Settembre, at the south end of Ponte di Mezzo, is the **Loggia dei Banchi** built by Cosimo Pugliani (1603–05), on a design by Bernardo Buontalenti, as a market place. From here Corso Italia leads due south to Piazza Vittorio Emanuele II.

Lungarno Galileo continues along the river to **San Sepolcro** (**Map 11**), an octagonal church with a very unusual pyramidal roof built in the 12C by Diotisalvi, probably for the Knight Templars, now below the level of the road. The striking interior lit by small windows, has tall pilasters forming a high Gothic arcade around the brick pyramidal roof. The font has stone reliefs by Mario Bertini (1956).

Lungarno Galileo continues to **Palazzo Lanfranchi** (now owned by the Comune) dating from the Middle Ages but rebuilt in the 16C. It has recently been drastically restored (only two rooms with 19C ceilings have been preserved) and is used for exhibitions.

Via Lanfranchi leads south to **Via San Martino**, a handsome street with a number of 16C–18C palaces, and one of the best preserved in the city. Here is the church of **San Martino** (**Map 16**), begun in 1332 and consecrated in 1477. On the façade is a copy of a relief of St Martin (the original is now inside the church). The **interior** has an open timber roof. At the west end are detached frescoes of the *Life of Mary* by Giovanni di Nicola. **South side**. The 13C painted *Crucifix* with stories of the Passion is by Enrico di Tedice. First altar, *St Andrew* by Aurelio Lomi. Above the entrance into the side chapel, 14C relief of *St Martin and the beggar* by Andrea da Pontedera. The chapel, with a pretty barrel vault, has two detached frescoes and *sinopie* attributed to Antonio Veneziano. Second altar, *St Benedict* by Palma Giovane; third altar, *Madonna and Child* by Passignano. **North Side**. Second altar, *Mary Magdalene in front of the Crucifix* by Jacopo Ligozzi; first altar, *Annunciation* by Giovanni Sordo (Mone).

At Via San Martino 19 is a Roman relief of a female figure, a fragment of a 3C sarcophagus. Known as *Kinzica*, it is named after a legendary Pisan heroine who saved Pisa from the Saracens in 1004.

At the end of Ponte della Fortezza (1959; first built in 1286) is **Palazzo Scotto** to the right of which is the 17C Palazzo Chiesa. Shelley lived here in 1820–22 (plaque). Lungarno Fibonacci follows the wall of the ruined **Fortezza Nuova** built in 1512 by Giuliano da Sangallo. It now encloses a public garden known as the **Giardino Scotto**.

The province of Pisa

The province of Pisa is very extensive and takes in part of the coast as well as a large area south as far as Volterra and the metalliferous hills (both described in p 292), and localities along the Arno towards Florence. On the plain just outside Pisa is the huge Certosa di Pisa with its 18C monastic buildings. Towards the sea is the Romanesque basilica of San Piero in Grado. The coastline is protected by the nature reserve of San Rossore. The most interesting town inland is San Miniato with some fine churches and a diocesan museum. In the attractive countryside to the south are the pretty little-known villages of Montopoli in Val d'Arno, Palaia, Peccioli, Casciana Alta, and Lari.

Practical information

Getting there
By car

A secondary road follows the Arno to the sea for San Piero a Grado and San Rossore. The Certosa di Pisa and the villages north of the Arno are best reached by N67, while the places in the province south of the Arno, with San Miniato, have exits from the Florence–Pisa– Livorno superstrada.

By train

On the Florence–Pisa line to *San Miniato-Fucecchio* in San Miniato Basso for San Miniato (slow trains only in 40 mins from Florence).

By bus

From Pisa, the *CPT* (☎ 050 505 511) runs buses from Piazza Sant'Antonio (**Map** 14) to towns in the province.

Information offices
APT Pisa, ☎ 050 560 464 or 050 929 777; local offices at **San Miniato**, Piazza del Popolo (☎ 0571 427 45); at **Casciana Terme**, Via Cavour 9, ☎ 0587 646 258; at **Montopoli in Val d'Arno**, ☎ 0571 466 501; and in summer) at **San Giuliano Terme**, ☎ 050 815 064, **Tirrenia**, ☎ 050 325 10 and **Marina di Pisa**.

Where to stay
Hotels

Of all categories at the resorts of **Marina di Pisa** and **Tirrenia,** and at the spa town of **Casciana Terme**. SAN GIULIANO TERME ☆☆☆ *Villa di Corliano*, at Rigoli (☎ 050 818 193, 📠 050 818 897).

SAN MINIATO ☆☆☆ *Miravalle*, with first-class restaurant, Prato del Duomo 3 (☎ 0571 418 074, 🖷 0571 419 681).

Campsites

Campsites at Marina di Pisa and Tirrenia.

Eating out
Restaurants

MARINA DI PISA €€
Da Gino, Via delle Curzolari 2 (☎ 050 354 08)
SAN MINIATO €€ *Canapone*, Piazza Bonaparte (☎ 0571 418 121); *Collebrunacchi*, Via Collebrunacchi 12 (in the environs; ☎ 0571 409 601).

The coast near the mouth of the Arno

A road from Pisa, lined by a long straight avenue of plane trees, follows the Arno to its mouth, past boat building yards and fishing huts.

San Piero a Grado

The church of *San Piero a Grado was built on the site where St Peter is said to have landed on his journey from Antioch to Rome. Excavations have confirmed the existence of a building here in the 1C AD. In Roman times this was the site of the last ferry across the Arno. The present Romanesque basilica dates from the 10C–12C.

The pretty **exterior** has blind arcading and incorporates Roman and medieval architectural fragments and friezes. The 11C ceramic basins (some of them from Tunisia, Morocco, and Spain) have been replaced by copies (the originals are displayed in the Museo Nazionale di San Matteo in Pisa). The 13C campanile was destroyed in 1944. The entrance is through a central lateral door.

The interior (open all day) is unusual in having apses at both the east and the west ends. The re-used columns have a great variety of Roman capitals. At the west end a ciborium covers an area of excavations of earlier churches on this site including two apses, one dating from the 3C–4C and one from the 8C–9C. Here a granite half-column (which formerly supported the ancient altar) marks the spot where St Peter is supposed to have preached. The 16C loggia was built in the apse at the west end to support a cantoria. Against the walls of the church are numerous ancient architectural fragments found in the excavations, and four inscriptions in *pietra serena* (formerly part of the 17C high altar) which recount the story of St Peter. Also here is an interesting carved wood 16C confessional. The *fresco cycle in the nave is attributed to Deodato Orlandi (1300–12; restored in 2000). Above portraits of popes from St Peter to John XVII (1003) are scenes from the life of St Peter and St Paul.

Marina di Pisa is a pleasant old-fashioned bathing resort (with several Art Nouveau houses) at the mouth of the Arno, first developed in 1869. It is backed by dense pinewoods, whose seeds are used in making confectionery.

The nature reserve of San Rossore

The coast to the north and south has been protected since 1979 as the **Parco Naturale Migliarino–San Rossore–Massaciuccoli**, although there are still problems over the administration of the park. Between the Arno and the Serchio

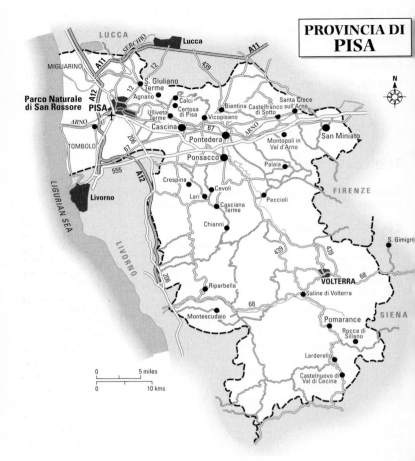

PROVINCIA DI
PISA

rivers is the **Tenuta di San Rossore**, a summer estate of the President of the Republic was donated to the State in 1988. Camels were kept here in the 19C but its bird and animal sanctuaries now house less exotic animals including wild boar and deer which were first introduced for hunting. To the south is the **Tenuta di Tombolo**, and to the north (beyond the Serchio) **Migliarino** and **Massaciuccoli** (see p 233). Although the area has fine pinewoods, wetlands, and birdlife, in some parts of the park the trees are threatened with disease, the rivers are still polluted, and the coastline has been eroded.

● Information on the nature reserves from the *Ente Parco Regionale*, Via Aurelia Nord 4 (☎ 050 525 211 or 050 530 101). Part of the Tenuta di San Rossore is open on Sat & fest. 08.30–17.30 or 19.30. The entrance for those with cars is from Ponte alle Trombe on the Gombo road which also passes the Cascine Vecchie. **Guided tours** (for information, ☎ 050 989 084 or 050 523 019) are organised from the Cascine Vecchie near the restaurant called *Da Poldino* for those on foot, with bicycles, or on horseback. These provide access to areas of the park not otherwise open, including the River Arno, Gombo (north of the mouth of the Arno), and the rivers Morto Nuovo and Serchio. Bicycles can be hired from the *CPT* bus company in Pisa in Piazza Manin (☎ 050 505 511).

Shelley's body was washed ashore on the beach of Gombo in 1822 (see p 301). Allan Ramsay, the painter, was more fortunate and escaped with his life from a shipwreck here in 1736 on his first jouney to Rome. The mouth of the Serchio at **Marina di Vecchiano** is one of the most beautiful parts of the coastline with interesting bird life.

To the south of Marina di Pisa the modern resort of **Tirrenia** extends towards Livorno (see p 293). **Stagno** in the midst of the former marshes of the Arno, drained (c 1620) by Sir Robert Dudley, is now occupied by a huge oil refinery.

The province north of the Arno

The road to Lucca from Pisa, which follows a canal constructed by Cosimo I lined with ancient plane trees, passes **San Giuliano Terme**, a small spa at the foot of Monte Pisano, whose spring waters have been known since ancient times. New thermal buildings were constructed here in 1744 by Francesco Pecci for the grand-duke Francesco I. A bust and plaque mark the Casa Prinni where Shelley stayed in the summer of 1820.

A road continues up Monte San Giuliano past olive groves (with a view back of Pisa), through a tunnel, and then descends towards Lucca (see p 206). The old road to Lucca, slightly longer, passes between the 14C castle of **Nozzano**, a Luccan outpost and the Pisan castle of **Ripafratta**.

To the east is the straggling unattractive village of **Calci**. From the piazza with four palm trees a road leads shortly to the **pieve**, founded in 1088–98, marked by its massive, square, unfinished campanile. The attractive façade in the Pisan style has decorations in two shades of grey. The basilican interior has fine columns and capitals. The large monolithic rectangular *font has an interesting sculpted front (mid-12C) by an artist influenced by Biduino. Beside the unusual robed figure of Christ in the centre is a gnome, symbolising the river Jordan. On the right is *St John the Baptist*; the other figures represent the Madonna and two angels. The pretty marble confessionals date from 1757. On a pilaster of the church is a 13C head of Christ which has been adapted as a copy of the Volto Santo of Lucca (see p 213). On the altar right of the high altar, *Madonna and Child with Saints* signed by Aurelio Lomi (who may also have painted the *Adoration of the Shepherds* in a chapel off the right side of the church). In the sacristy is kept a beautiful late 14C painting of the *Madonna and Child*.

The Certosa di Pisa

Nearby is the huge *Certosa di Pisa on low ground, now in a disappointing setting. This is one of the largest monumental monasteries in the country. The Charterhouse was founded in 1366 and reconstructed in the 18C. It was built to house 60 Carthusian monks, but the monastery was closed in 1973.

Guided tours are given every hour: 08.30–18.00; fest. 08.30–12.30; closed Mon. In the **first courtyard** is the monumental façade (1718) of the church and the two wings of the monastery. To the right, an elaborate gateway (1768),

The Certosa di Pisa

decorated in the form of a grotto with shells and pebbles, leads into the garden. The **church** has colourful frescoes by Giuseppe and Pietro Rolli and a marble lectern in the form of an angel by the school of Bernini. The east end has a high altarpiece by Volterrano. The side chapels contain altarpieces including a *Crucifix* by Bernardino Poccetti, and *St Bruno* by Jacopo Vignali. The Cappella del Rosario and Cappella della Sacra Famiglia have decorations by Giuseppe Maria Terreni.

The large **cloister** has an elaborate fountain and white marble porticoes by Giovanni Battista Cartoni (1636–51). It is surrounded by the spacious monks' cells, one of which is shown. The smaller **chapter cloister** survives from the 15C (the well dates from 1614). Beyond the Cappella del Capitolo is the **refectory** with a *Last Supper* by Bernardino Poccetti and 18C frescoes of *Supper at Emaus* and the *Marriage at Cana* by Pietro Giarrè. The elaborate **grand-ducal apartments** where distinguished guests stayed in the 18C, have period furniture and stuccoes by Angelo Maria Somazzi and more frescoes of a pilgrim on his way to the Certosa and other scenes by Pietro Giarrè. The 17C **prior's cloister** has an unusual double well. A **terrace** looks out over the monastery garden and fish tanks (and to the right, in the distance, can be seen the Leaning Tower and baptistery of Pisa). A grand staircase (by Michele Fossi) leads down to the courtyard and vestibule.

In a wing of the monastery (and in a covered loggia, once used by the monks to take their exercise) the University of Pisa has recently arranged the **Museo di Storia Naturale e del Territorio**, a collection founded at the university in 1591 by Ferdinando I and enlarged in the 18C and 19C (open 09.00–18.00; fest. 10.00–19.00; closed Mon). The natural history collections are extremely interesting and some are still displayed in showcases dating from 1752. The zoological section includes mammals, cetaceans, molluscs and birds, and there is a comparative anatomy display. Another section is dedicated to Tuscan minerals and marble from the Apuan Alps, and ammonites and Triassic fossils from the Veneto.

Nearby is the little spa of **Uliveto Terme** (well known for its mineral water) and the conspicuous Torre degli Uperrighi at Caprona on the very edge of a quarry.

The little town of **Cascina**, a centre of the furniture trade, lies beneath Monte Verruca (563m), a prominent peak of Monte Pisano. In 1364 it was the scene of a Florentine victory over the Pisans. The environs are no longer attractive, with numerous small factories, but the main street of the town, **Corso Matteotti**, is lined with porticoes.

At the beginning on the left, behind a railing, is the little 14C **Oratory of San Giovanni** (if closed, ring at the convent school next door at no. 9). The Gothic vaulted interior contains a cycle of frescoes by Martino di Bartolomeo (1398), including saints in Gothic niches and scenes from the Old Testament above.

Farther along the main street, between the town hall and a palace with an attractive balcony, Via Palestra leads to **Piazza della Chiesa** with three churches and a 15C tower. Only the 12C **Pieve di Santa Maria** is open regularly. It has a fine basilican interior with handsome columns and a seated terracotta statue of the *Madonna and Child* (early 16C; in the chapel to the right of the apse).

The church of **San Benedetto**, a short distance west of Cascina on the main road, has a splendid English alabaster relief (14C).

To the north of Cascina is **Vicopisano**, a village built on a little hill which still has a number of towers and part of its fortifications, restored by Brunelleschi after it was taken by the Florentines in 1407. It is bordered on the south by a canal built by the Medici grand-dukes to deviate the course of the Arno which now flows 2km south.

At the foot of the hill is the **Torre del Brunelleschi** (c 1406) in the walls which mount the hillside. Near it is the **Torre delle Quattro Porte** resting on a vault which once had four open arches. These fortifications are sometimes open at weekends. On the other side of the hill, a narrow road can be followed up on foot past the municipio, with a tower, to the 14C **Palazzo Pretorio**, with numerous coats of arms. It can be visited on a guided tour on Sunday afternoon from April to Oct. Above, on top of the hill, is the castle tower (now enclosed in a private garden) and a number of other towers can be seen below.

Outside the village (near Piazza Cavalca) on flat ground by the main road is the fine 12C Romanesque *pieve*. It contains a sculptured wood group of the *Deposition* (12C–13C) and (in a niche on the left side) a large statue of *St John the Baptist*, a fine work dating from before 1390 attributed to Nino Pisano (although the arms and head probably date from the 17C). The little baptismal font dates from the 15C.

Farther east is the village of **Santa Maria a Monte** which has an interesting circular plan—all its streets are curved. Its castle was of strategic importance in the Middle Ages and was contested by Florence, Lucca, and Pisa. From Piazza della Vittoria, where a large yellow palace houses the town hall, Via Carducci leads down and continues right round the village. It passes a terrace with a view of the built-up plain of the Arno beside a fine palace and the church of **San Giovanni Evangelista**. In the interior the baptismal font has fine sculptures by Domenico di Giovanni Rosselli (1468). On the right of the high altar (behind glass; difficult to see) is a *statue of the *Madonna and Child* enthroned in polychrome wood of 1255. At the east end is a 14C *Crucifix*. Over the side door is an unusual dark stone ambone supported by two lions, with carvings and (unfinished) inlaid marble decoration. Above the attractive east end are worn frescoes by Luigi Ademollo. The **canonica** next door has a large (but damaged) della Robbian tondo over the door. Via Carducci continues back to Piazza della Vittoria past another pretty curving street with a nice row of little houses. Various winding streets lead up around the top of the hill and the site of the castle which was never repaired after severe damage in the Second World War.

Farther east is **Castelfranco di Sotto**, on low ground beside the Arno, severely damaged in the Second World War, and by the Arno flood of 1966. It preserves its rectangular plan. Beyond an old gate, a road leads to the main piazza with the 15C Palazzo Comunale with a portico facing the flank of the church of **San Pietro**, which contains a painting by Alessandro Allori, a fine 13C statue of *St Peter*, and a 14C *Annunciation* group.

On the eastern border of the province is **Santa Croce sull'Arno** with some 430 tanneries which produce 35 per cent of Italian leather. The parish church contains a wood figure of Christ (*Volto Santo*) dating from the 13C–14C. Fucecchio and the towns further east are in the province of Florence (see p 164).

The province south of the Arno

San Miniato

San Miniato is an interesting little town in a fine position, formerly known as San Miniato al Tedesco. It is roughly equidistant between Pisa and Florence (45km from both). On the site of an 8C church dedicated to the Florentine martyr St Minias, the Lombard town became the seat of the Imperial Vicariate in Tuscany. Here Countess Matilda was born in 1046. Its name 'al Tedesco' is supposed to have been derived from the fact that is was often visited by emperors in the 12C and 13C. From 1369 San Miniato came under Florentine dominion.

At the highest point of the town was the **Rocca** (open 10.00–17.00) built by Frederick II in 1240 and used by him as a prison for Pier delle Vigne in 1247. Vigne, formerly his most trusted minister ('*io sono colui, che tenni ambo le chiavi del cor di Federico*'—'I am he who kept both the keys of Federico's heart'; Dante *La Divina Commedia, Inferno*, 31–108) fell into disgrace in 1247 (perhaps because he had plotted against the Emperor with Pope Innocent IV) and was blinded and held here. He is supposed to have committed suicide by throwing himself from the tower in 1249. Only two towers remain of the castle; the highest one, conspicuous for miles around, was rebuilt after its destruction in the Second World War. Paths lead up to the gardens around it. The second massive square tower now serves as the belfry for the Duomo, in the **Prato del Duomo** with pretty trees.

The **Duomo** was built c 1195, but later altered and restored in 1860. The Romanesque brick façade was decorated, like a number of other Pisan church façades at this time, with blue and brown ceramic bowls, probably manufactured in North Africa. Some of these, which numbered 31, are now exhibited in the Museo Diocesano.

The pulpit and funerary monuments in the aisles are by Amalia Duprè. On the first altar in the south aisle is a *Nativity* by Aurelio Lomi. Over the high altar is a 17C wooden *Crucifix*. In the north transept, *Deposition* (1528), by Francesco di Angelo Lanfranchi. Over the first altar in the north aisle, *Raising of Lazarus* by Cosimo Gamberucci.

Next to the Duomo is the **Museo Diocesano** which displays works of art that have been collected from churches in the region. The works are all labelled (open 09.00–12.00, 15.00–18.00, except Mon; in winter open only on Sat and Sun 09.00–12.00, 14.30–17.00; combined ticket with the other buildings open to the public in the little town).

Room 1: sculptural fragments; detached fresco fragment of a *Maestà* by the Maestro degli Ordini. **Room 2**: *Madonna and Child with Saints*, by Neri di Bicci; *St Catherine of Alexandria* by Rossello di Iacopo Franchi, and a scene of her martyrdom; *St Jerome translating the Bible*, signed and dated 1411 by Cenni di Francesco di Ser Cenni (the predella scene shows the saint being fed by the angel); *St Michael Archangel* (and a scene of his fight with the devils) by the school of Orcagna; detached fresco of the *Annunciation and prophets* attributed to Giovanni da San Giovanni. Cases display liturgical objects and church silver. **Room 3**: two drawings by Lodovico Cigoli; small *Crucifixion* (c 1430) attributed to the Master of Santi Quirico e Giulitta; *Madonna enthroned with Saints* by Francesco Granacci; processional standard by Jacopo di Michele; wooden model of the church of the Crocifisso (see below) by Antonio Maria Ferri ; *Madonna of the Holy Girdle* an early work by Andrea del Castagno or his circle; *Circumcision* by Fra Bartolomeo and assistants. The terracotta bust (with traces of polychrome) of the **Redeemer* is attributed to Andrea del Verrocchio.

The two rooms upstairs display paintings by Matteo Rosselli, Il Poppi, and Lodovico Cigoli (including the *Sacrifice of Isaac*). The two large paintings of the *Deposition* and the *Way to Calvary* are unusual 17C works by the Tuscan-Flemish school.

Opposite the Duomo is the 12C **Palazzo dei Vicari dell'Imperatore**, and the handsome 17C **Palazzo Vescovile** with an angled façade. Three flights of steps lead down beneath the palace to Piazza della Repubblica where the big 17C **Seminario** has a fine façade, with painted decoration above restored medieval shop-fronts. Via Vittime del Duomo leads out of the piazza beneath an arch down to the old **Palazzo Comunale**, the town hall. The Council Chamber on the first floor (admission on request) has a fresco of the *Madonna and Child between Saints* by Cenni di Francesco di Ser Cenni. On the ground floor (entered from the street; unlocked on request at the town hall) is the 15C **Oratory of the Madonna di Loreto** with delightful frescoes probably dating from 1413 and attributed to Arrigo di Niccolò and others, and a fine wood ancona with 16C Florentine paintings. A theatrical staircase leads up the **Sanctuary of the Crocifisso**, an unusual builing on a Greek-cross plan by Antonio Maria Ferri (1705–18, open Sat & Sun). It contains 18C frescoes by Antonio Domenico Bamberini. The statues outside include (in a niche) the *Risen Christ* by Francesco Baratta.

Farther on a road climbs left to the huge church of **San Francesco** built in 1276 on the hillside below the Rocca (and completed in 1480). In the interior on the left wall is a fresco fragment of *St Christopher* by the school of Masolino.

From Piazza della Repubblica (see above) Via Conti descends to **Piazza del Popolo**, the centre of San Miniato, with the church of **San Domenico**. Of ancient foundation, the **interior** has 18C frescoes depicting the *Life of St Dominic* on the upper walls attributed to Antonio Domenico Bamberini. In a chapel at the end of the right side (left of the door into the sacristy) is the tomb of Giovanni Chellini, a Florentine doctor who died in 1461, with a fine effigy, now attributed to Pagno di Lapo Portigiani (on a model by Donatello, who was Chellini's patient). It was recomposed here in the 19C. The altarpiece of the *Madonna and Child* is by Domenico di Michelino and the Master of the Johnson Nativity. In the adjacent chapel (right of the sanctuary) are restored 14C frescoes of the *Life of the Virgin* and (on the pilaster) *St Lawrence*, a fragment attributed to the *bottega* of Masolino. The *Madonna and Child* is by the Master of San Miniato. The sanctuary was frescoed in 1900 by Galileo Chini. In the chapel opposite the one with the Chellini monument is a *Deposition and two Saints* in a fine ancona by Il Poppi. In other parts of the church are interesting frescoes by the 15C Florentine school and altarpieces by Francesco Curradi, Giovanni Battista Vanni, and Antoniazzo Romano.

Via IV Novembre continues past a number of handsome palaces. In a little piazza the 16C **Palazzo Grifoni** (with a loggia), attributed to Giuliano di Baccio d'Agnolo, is the seat of the Accademia degli Euteleti (open 15.00–18.00) Via Carducci continues past the church of the **Santissima Annunziata** (1522), centrally planned, with an octagonal cupola (over the altar is a worn 14C fresco of the *Annunciation*), and farther on (left; no. 15 Via Roma) is the Conservatorio and church of **Santa Chiara** (usually open at the same time as the Museo Diocesano) which contains a *Crucifix* by Deodato Orlandi and a *Noli me tangere* by Lodovico Cigoli.

West of San Miniato, close to the Arno, is **San Romano**, scene of the indecisive battle of 1432 between the Florentines and the Sienese. The Florentines, led by the condottiere Nicolò da Tolentino, considered it their victory, and a painting of it in three episodes was commissioned by the Medici c 1456 from Paolo Uccello. Considered his masterpiece, the three scenes are now divided between the Uffizi Gallery, the Louvre and the National Gallery in London. There is a good collection of old pharmacy jars in the Farmacia Mannelli in San Romano.

Nearby is **Montopoli in Val d'Arno** in San Romano in pleasant farming coun-tryside. There was a fortress here by the 8C. On the approach road (preceded by a portico and a palm tree) is the church of **Santa Marta** (usually closed) which contains a *Raising of Lazarus* by Lodovico Cigoli and a *Madonna with Souls* in Purgatory by Santi di Tito.

The road leads up past the large church and campanile (formerly a tower of the castle) of **Santo Stefano** (if closed; ring at no. 5). In the pleasant interior (south side) the baptistery has a large 16C oval font, and a chapel containing a 14C *Crucifix*. Beyond the second altar, with a *Madonna of the Rosary* by Francesco Curradi, is a *Resurrection* by Orazio Fidani. North side. *Prayer in the Garden* attributed to Ludovico Cigoli; second altar, *Madonna with Adam and Eve*, a striking painting, signed and dated 1664 by Jacopo Vignali. On the wall is an interesting small painting of the *Annunciation* (1513), and, above, a lunette with *God the Father*. On the first altar, fresco of the *Holy Family* (1519).

The road leads on to Piazza Michele da Montopoli from which a short road leads to a remarkably high and wide arch at the foot of a hill on which the castle was built. The road continues to ascend, and beyond the town hall facing a little piazza with a view and an old tower, it narrows into a track.

From Montopoli a pretty country road leads south up through woods to **Palaia**, first mentioned in 980. There are views of the distant hills to the south towards Volterra and north towards the Apennines. The approach road leads left around the little hill, with a view of the large 13C **Pieve di San Martino** outside the village. It is approached by a signposted road but is usually closed (it was over-restored in the 19C). Porta Fiorentina leads into the long Piazza della Repubblica (closed at the far end by another gate). Above Porta Fiorentina is the campanile of the little 12C church of **Santa Maria** (closed) with a plain façade. Via del Popolo leads out of the piazza under a gate with a clock and up past (left) the inconspicuous church of **Sant'Andrea** with a brick façade and small tower. In the interior are two fine statues of the *Madonna and Child* on the right and left of the high altar: the one on the right in painted wood is signed and dated

1403 by Francesco da Valdambrino and the one on the left in terracotta has recently been attributed to Luca della Robbia (c 1435). On the left wall are parts of a terracotta ciborium with figures of saints, by Andrea della Robbia. On the east wall is a *Crucifix* attributed to the school of Giovanni Pisano. There is a fine view from the Rocca at the top of the village.

To the southwest is **Peccioli**, a pleasant little village in the Era valley. A road leads up from the market square in front of the church of the Carmine (closed) to the central piazza. Here is the unusual east end of **San Verano**, next to an amusing bell-tower crowned with circular battlements. The church is entered by the side door. It was founded in the 12C, but later altered and restored after the Second World War. The Romanesque Pisan façade looks out over the plain. In the interior on the right side is a 13C Madonna and Child attributed to Enrico di Tedice. The oratory (1580) off the left side has a fine carved wood ceiling and paintings by Jacopo Vignali. Here is hung a *Madonna and four saints* by Neri di Bicci. A 14C *Crucifix* and a 13C painting of *St Nicholas of Bari* also belong to the church. In the piazza, opposite the east end of the church, is the restored **Palazzo Pretorio** (no. 5) with coats of arms high up on the façade, some in enamelled terracotta. It contains a collection of 60 Russian icons (mostly 19C and 20C) donated to the town in 2000 (open Wed, Sat & Sun 10.00–13.00, 16.00–20.00).

Outside the village (well signposted) is a small park with life-size models of dinosaurs and a children's playground (open daily).

To the west is **Casciana Terme**, an attractive little spa town surrounded by low hills planted with olives and vineyards. It has tree-lined streets and some Art Nouveau houses. It was known for its curative waters in Roman times and in the Middle Ages (when they were taken by Countess Matilda). In 1311, the Pisans built baths here and it became well known again in the 18C. It has warm anti-rheumatic waters used for both bathing and drinking. The season runs from April to November.

In the central Piazza Garibaldi is the handsome neo-classical façade of the **Terme** by Giuseppe Poggi (1870). Behind are the new spa buildings (being enlarged) and a park. Just off the piazza is the tourist information office (called the Ritrovo del Forestiero). There are numerous small furniture factories in the area.

A pretty by-road leads up to **Casciana Alta**, a hamlet with a spacious piazza with plane trees, and a terrace overlooking lovely countryside. Here the church of **San Niccolò**, with a cupola, has a heavily decorated neo-Classical interior with orange-painted Corinthian columns. The painting of the *Hospitality of St Julian* is by Orazio Fidani.

To the north is **Crespina**. The Macchiaioli artist Silvestro Lega often stayed and painted in this area. Above the village is the church of **San Michele** with a statue of the saint on the façade. A painting of *St Michael Archangel* by Bernardo Daddi belongs to the church.

From the church, Via Montegrappa (signposted La Guardia), Via San Rocco, and Via Belvedere lead to the beautiful 18C **Villa di Belvedere**, with a monumental flight of steps on the façade, approached by an ancient cypress avenue and preceded by a handsome garden (not open to the public). The elegant little 18C domed chapel was built by Mattia Tarocchi in 1775–84 and decorated by Giovanni Battista Tempesti. It contains a painted *Cross* by the Master of San Torpè. The countryside here is particularly lovely.

A narrow road which crosses pretty countryside where the vineyards produce good wine, passes a neo-Classical oratory on its way east to **Lari**. A little village of Etruscan origins, it was built in a circle around the foot of a huge Medici fortress with splendid brick bastions designed by Francesco da Sangallo in 1530. A gate leads through the outer walls and then steps (signposted) lead up round the bastion to the entrance to the **castle** (open Oct–Apr on fest. 15.00–18.00; May–Sept on fest. 15.30–19.30; or ☎ 0587 684 126). Founded in the 11C the castle became the property of the Pisan family of Upezzinghi in the 13C and in the 15C of the governors of Florence. Inside is a little paved courtyard with a well and numerous coats of arms on three walls including many in enamelled polychrome terracotta. The ground floor can be visited. There is a *Madonna and Child* by the bottega of Andrea della Robbia, as well as the prisons, and it is possible to walk around the ramparts.

The **church** at the foot of the castle was restored in 1910. On either side of the choir, the two marble statues of the *Annunciation* are attributed to Andrea Guardi. On the left wall is a beautiful tabernacle with a *Madonna and Child* in enamelled terracotta surrounded by a garland, by Giovanni della Robbia (1524). In a niche off the right side is a painting of the *Madonna* by Francesco Melani, highly decorated.

Cevoli, nearby, has a conspicuous church beside a cemetery with a large semicircular apse which contains the only known painting signed by Andrea de Pisis (who helped Benozzo Gozzoli with the frescoes in the Camposanto in Pisa), dated 1490.

Due north, on the south bank of the Arno is Pontedera, a busy market well known for its large *Piaggio* motor-scooter factory. In 1998 a museum (open Wed–Sat 10.00–18.00) dedicated to the *Vespa* was opened here in one of the factory warehouses erected in the 1920s. The exhibits include the first model designed in 1946 (some 20 million Vespas were manufactured by the end of the 20C), and other vehicles produced by *Piaggio* since 1884. The church of the Cappuccini has an early 14C Crucifix by the 'Maestro di Trecolli'.

Volterra and environs

Volterra lies in a magnificent position on a precipitous hill (531m) with open views in every direction across a splendid yellow and grey landscape of rolling clay hills. It is an austere medieval walled town (12,600 inhab.), the successor to an Etruscan city of much greater extent. Almost all the buildings are constructed from *panchina*, a kind of limestone which is the matrix of alabaster, and which is found here in abundance. The town has for long been famous for the traditional skill of its craftsmen in working alabaster, and some two hundred workshops here still produce objets-d'art.

Practical information

Getting there
By car

The fastest route by road to Volterra from Florence is via the Florence–Siena superstrada as far as the exit Colle Val d'Elsa Nord. Here N68 continues west past Colle Val d'Elsa (described on p 413). The beautiful road runs along a pretty ridge of hills with distant views, including the towers of San Gimignano to the north (see p 405). The road then climbs through magnificent countryside to reach the distinctive open landscape around Volterra. Large underground **car park** at the entrance to the town just before Piazza Martiri della Libertà. Other car parks outside the walls.

By train

The nearest station for Volterra is Volterra–Saline–Pomarance, 11km southwest in the valley. It is on a branch line to Cecina (in 30 mins; some trains are substituted by buses), which is on the main line from Pisa to Rome (slow trains only). Bus connection with trains runs to Piazza XX Settembre in Volterra.

By bus

Services run by **SITA** from Florence via Castelfiorentino in 2hrs 40mins. Other services from Florence and Siena via Colle Val d'Elsa, where a change is necessary. There are also buses to Volterra from Pisa, Massa Marittima, and San Gimignano.

Information office

IAT, Via Turazza 2 (☎ 0588 861 50; ✉ provolterra@libero.it).

Where to stay
Hotels

VOLTERRA ☆☆☆☆ *San Lino*, Via San Lino 26 (☎ 0588 852 50; 📠 0588 806 20).
☆☆☆ *Villa Nencini*, Borgo Santo Stefano 55 (outside Porta San

Francesco; ☎ 0588 863 86; 📠 0588 806 01); *Etruria*, Via Matteotti 32 (☎/📠 0588 873 77); Sole, Via dei Cappuccin 10 (☎/📠 0588 840 00).

Hotels in the environs

POMARANCE ☆☆☆ *Pomarancio*, Via Roncalli 18, ☎ 0588 646 16.
LARDERELLO ☆☆☆ *La Perla*, località La Perla, ☎ 0588 672 87.

Youth hostel

Ostello della Gioventù, Via del Poggetto 3 (☎ 0588 855 77).

Campsite

☆☆ *Le Balze*, Via Mandringa, open Apr–Oct (☎ 0588 878 80).

Eating out
Restaurants

VOLTERRA €€ *Etruria*, Piazza dei Priori 8.
€: *Il Pozzo degli Etruschi*, Via delle Prigioni 28; *La Pace*, Via Don Minzoni 29; *Pizzeria il Rifugio*, Piazza XX Settembre; *Da Badò*, Borgo San Lazzaro 9; *Lo Sgherro*, Borgo San Giusto (beyond Porta San Francesco).

Picnics

Lovely places to picnic include the Parco Archeologico and the outskirts of the town, near San Giusto or overlooking the Balze.

Festivals

Astiludio on 1st Sun in September, with flag-throwing and processions. Theatre festival in July.

Shopping

A large **market** is held in the town on Saturday mornings (near the Roman theatre in summer).

Museums

There is a **combined ticket for the three museums** in the town.

History

Velathri was the northernmost of the 12 cities of the Confederation of Etruria Propria and one of the most prominent. In the 3C BC it became the Roman Volaterrae. In the late 2C BC it supported the cause of the democratic consul Marius against the dictator Sulla during the Civil Wars which preceded the collapse of the Roman Republic. Volterra was besieged for two years before falling to Sulla's troops. It gained some importance under the Lombards and was for a time the residence of the Lombard kings.

After bitter struggles, it was subdued by Florence in 1361, and again in 1472 in the the **War of Volterra**, waged by Lorenzo il Magnifico for control of its alum deposits, which culminated in the sacking of the city by the Florentines under the command of Federico da Montefeltro. Lorenzo is said to have asked for forgiveness on his deathbed for this brutal act. Another rebellion was crushed by Francesco Ferrucci in 1530 and from then on Volterra remained under Florentine dominion, and later under the grand-duchy of Tuscany, until the unification of Italy in 1860.

Natives of Volterra include the satirist Persius Flaccus (AD 34–62), St Linus, the reputed successor of St Peter in the papal chair, Pope Leo the Great (440–461), and the painter Daniele Ricciarelli da Volterra (1509–66).

Piazza dei Priori

Piazza Martiri della Libertà forms the southern entrance to the town; at the north end of the piazza, Via Marchesi leads left to Piazza dei Priori, bordered by some medieval buildings and others built in the medieval style. Immediately to the left is the austere Palazzo dei Priori (open 10.00–13.00; Sat & Sun also 14.30–18.00), with its battlemented tower, now the town hall, the oldest building of its kind in Tuscany. It was begun in 1208 and completed in 1257 by Riccardo da Como; the windows on the first floor were altered later and the upper part of the tower was rebuilt and modified in 1846.

The vestibule is decorated with coats of arms, and steps lead up to the first floor and the **Sala del Consiglio Comunale** (admission when not in use), the town council chamber since 1257. The original timber ceiling was replaced by the present double cross-vault in 1516. On the end wall is a fresco of the *Annunciation* by Jacopo di Cione (1383), and to the right, the *Marriage Feast at Cana* by Donato Mascagni. In the **Saletta della Giunta**, are several paintings: *Job and his wife* by Donato Mascagni, the *Birth of the Virgin* by Ignazio Hugford, and the *Adoration of the Magi* by Giovanni Domenico Ferretti.

To the right of Palazzo dei Priori is **Palazzo Vescovile**, originally the town granary, which was begun in the 14C. In between, set back from the piazza, is the north transept of the cathedral, decorated with horizontal bands of black-and-white marble.

Across the piazza are some remarkable 13C buildings. On the right is **Palazzo Pretorio**, surmounted by the Torre del Porcellino, which derives its name from the sculpted boar on a bracket to the right of the top window. The vertical emphasis of the building is underlined by the narrow windows flanking the tower. The adjacent **Palazzo del Podestà** has three large rounded arches on the ground floor and two-light windows on the three upper storeys. The crenellated tower to the left, formerly a prison, has a variety of architectural elements in various different materials. At the end of the piazza is the former **Palazzo Incontri**, now used as a bank, which has been considerably modified through

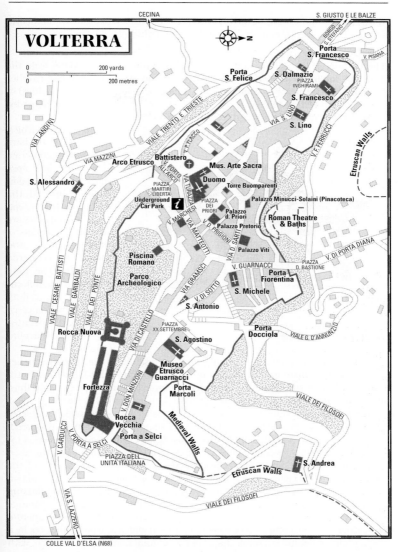

VOLTERRA

CECINA

S. GIUSTO E LE BALZE

0   200 yards
0   200 metres

Etruscan Walls

the centuries. Facing it, at the opposite end of the piazza, is the modern **Palazzo Demaniale**, designed to harmonise with the older buildings.

Via Turazza leads out of the piazza to the left of Palazzo dei Priori. It passes the remains of the Romanesque transept and nave of the cathedral, and the late 18C **Oratorio della Misericordia**. This chapel contains a *Crucifixion* by Donato Mascagni (1602) over the altar, and paintings by Giovanna Forzoni (*Agony in the Garden*, 19C), Giuseppe Nicola Nasini (*Birth of the Virgin*), and Giuseppe Arrighi (*St Anthony of Padua*).

In the beautiful **Piazza San Giovanni** is the Baptistery, opposite the cathedral façade, and, at the far end, the Hospital of Santa Maria Maddalena.

The Duomo

The Duomo, or Basilica of Santa Maria Assunta (open all day), dates from the 12C. The **façade** is a fine example of 13C Pisan architecture, with blind arches beneath the roof and three small round windows. The lower part was modified in the 16C with the addition of the three larger windows and the doorway, decorated in the lunette with green and white marble.

The interior, which was rebuilt in the later 16C, has a Latin-cross plan with five apse chapels and an additional chapel at the end of each transept. The nave and aisles are divided by columns of painted stucco and capitals by Leonardo Ricciarelli. The long nave has a magnificent coffered ceiling designed by Francesco Capriani, and executed by Jacopo Pavolini (1580).

The Duomo, Volterra

South aisle. First altar, the *City of Volterra presented to the Madonna by her patron Saints Giusto and Ottaviano* by Pieter de Witte (also known as Pietro Candido; 1578); second altar, *Birth of the Virgin* by Francesco Curradi; third altar, *Presentation of the Virgin* by Giovanni Battista Naldini (1590).

South transept. Outside the Chapel of San Carlo Borromeo, which preserves the wall of its Romanesque structure, is a *Crucifixion* by Francesco Curradi (1611). Inside are paintings by Matteo Rosselli (*St Carlo*), Camillo Incontri (*St Mary Magdalen*), Alessandro Gherardini (*St Francis of Paola*) and Francesco Brini (*Immaculate Conception*). The Holy Sacrament chapel at the end of the transept has a fine ceiling with stucco decoration by Lionello Ricciarelli and two scenes from the life of Christ by Giovanni Balducci; the altarpiece of the *Raising of Lazarus* is by Santi di Tito (1592) and the painted niches have 18C frescoes of saints by Agostino Veracini. The Chapel of the Deposition has a monumental *Deposition* (1228), composed of life-size figures in gilded and painted wood, by a Pisan sculptor. Behind is a small chapel of the original Romanesque church, with fresco fragments representing Christ's Passion, attributed to Taddeo di Bartolo.

To the right of the choir is the **Chapel of St Ottaviano**, whose body is preserved in a marble urn by Raffaello Cioli of Settignano (1522–25). St Ottaviano, a 6C hermit and one of Volterra's venerated patron saints, saved the city from a terrible plague in 1522.

The **choir** has fine choirstalls behind the high altar by Andreuccio di Bartolomeo and Antonio del Tinghio (1404). Over the early 19C altar is a magnificent **tabernacle** carved by Mino da Fiesole (1471): the *Infant Christ* stands above the chalice and pairs of adoring angels kneel beside the tabernacle door. Below, on the pedestal, are the ***Theological Virtues and four Saints***. The two kneeling angels holding candlesticks are by Andrea Ferrucci, also from Fiesole. Flanking the high altar are two angels by Mino da Fiesole, kneeling on two elegant Gothic columns. The fresco of ***God the Father*** in the vault is by Niccolò Cercignani.

The first chapel off the **north transept** contains the marble tomb of St Ugo (1644), bishop of Volterra. In the next chapel is a polychrome statue of the ***Madonna*** by Francesco di Valdambrino. The end chapel, dedicated to St Paul, has frescoes in the vault depicting the ***Life of St Paul***, by Giovanni da San Giovanni. The altarpiece of the ***Conversion of St Paul*** is by Domenichino, the ***Decapitation*** by Francesco Curradi, and ***Paul's mission to Damascus*** by Matteo Rosselli.

Outside the sacristy is a holy water stoup by Andrea Sansovino and, over the door, the ***Immaculate Conception*** by Cosimo Daddi. The **sacristy** has 15C choir-books and cupboards. An impressive Baroque reliquary cupboard contains fine silver busts of the patron saints of Volterra.

North aisle. Third altar, ***Immaculate Conception*** (1586) by Niccolò Cercignani. The 13C Pisan pulpit supported on columns borne by lions was assembled in 1584 using various sculptural fragments. The reliefs represent the ***Sacrifice of Isaac***, the ***Annunciation*** and ***Visitation***, and the ***Last Supper***. Second altar, ***Annunciation***, a painting of great harmony and beauty, full of light and space, with a landscape extending far into the distance, by Fra Bartolomeo (1497). First altar, ***Martyrdom of St Sebastian*** (1588) by Francesco Cungi.

A little chapel, dedicated to Our Lady of Sorrows, has two niches containing painted terracotta scenes of the ***Adoration of the Magi*** and the ***Nativity***, attributed to Luca and Andrea della Robbia c 1474) the latter with a charming frescoed background by Benozzo Gozzoli. On the west wall is the tomb of Monsignor Mario Maffei attributed to Giovanni Angelo Montorsoli (1537) and a Romanesque altar frontal.

The Baptistery

Facing the cathedral is the elegant, octagonal Baptistery. It is built in the local stone with a façade decorated with horizontal bands of black-and-white marble. The doorway is framed with clusters of slender columns supporting a rounded arch above the architrave, which is carved with heads of Christ and the Madonna and the twelve apostles, and inscribed with the date 1283. The dome was added in the 16C when the walls had to be heightened to counteract the thrust.

The interior is simple and unadorned. Inside the entrance is a holy water stoup made from an Etruscan funerary stone. The large octagonal font in the centre is by Giuseppe Covo, and the statue of ***St John the Baptist*** by Giovanni Cybo (1759). Above the altar is an altarpiece representing the ***Ascension*** by Niccolò Cercignani (1591) the upper part of which was destroyed in the Second World War. To the right of the altar is the original baptismal **font** by Andrea Sansovino (1502), with marble bas-reliefs of the ***Baptism of Christ*** and four seated figures of ***Faith, Hope, Charity***, and ***Justice***.

To the left of the cathedral façade is a lunette containing statues of ***Saints Giusto, Lino***, and ***Ottaviano*** by the contemporary sculptor Raffaello Consortini. Beyond is the tall, square **campanile**, dated 1493, which towers over the piazza.

Closing the piazza on the left is the ex-hospital of **Santa Maria Maddalena** (now a study centre), with an elegant Renaissance portico. The **Oratorio** in Via Franceschini has 17C frescoes.

Museo Diocesano d'Arte Sacra

The **Palazzo Vescovile** in Via Roma houses the Museo d'Arte Sacra (open summer 09.00–13.00, 15.00–18.00; winter 09.00–13.00). The collection comprises works of art and objects from the cathedral and from other churches of the diocese. In the vestibule are bells (11C–15C) and bas-reliefs with scenes from the life of St Vittore attributed to Giovanni di Agostino, Roman and Romanesque reliefs and four 14C Pisan sculpted angels.

In **room 1**: sculptures by Giovanni di Agostino; a bust of *St Lino* by Andrea della Robbia; a silver reliquary bust of *St Ottaviano* by Antonio del Pollaiolo; a painted wooden tabernacle attributed to Bartolomeo della Gatta; paintings by Taddeo di Bartolo and Neri di Bicci; and a fine Pisan 13C *Crucifix*. There are numerous liturgical objects, inlaid wood panels and reliquaries. The most precious painting is a small panel of the *Madonna and Child with St John the Baptist and St John the Evangelist* (1521) by Rosso Fiorentino.

In **room 2** is a gilded bronze *Crucifix* attributed to Giambologna and church silver and several paintings including a *Madonna and Child with Saints* by Daniele da Volterra of (1545), a *Madonna* attributed to Giusto d'Andrea, and an *Annunciation* by Benvenuto di Giovanni and two *Saints* by Cosimo Daddi. **Room 3** contains illuminated choir books and vestments.

The Pinacoteca and Museo Civico

Via Roma crosses Via Ricciarelli, off Piazza dei Priori, and passes under the lofty archway of the 13C Buomparenti and Buonaguidi tower houses. The medieval Via Buomparenti leads into Via Sarti. On the corner (no. 1) is **Palazzo Minucci Solaini** which houses the Pinacoteca e Museo Civico (open 09.00–19.00; winter 09.00–14.00).

The small, elegant Renaissance palace with a loggia surrounding the courtyard is traditionally attributed to Antonio da Sangallo il Vecchio. The collection, consisting mainly of paintings by Tuscan artists, is small but choice. The works are arranged chronologically.

First floor. Room 1: 13C Tuscan *Crucifix*; Romanesque capitals and a sculptured lunette. **Room 2**: 14C and early 15C works and a chapel with a small altarpiece, attributed to Francesco Conti. **Room 3** displays a magnificent polyptych, signed and dated 1411 (from the Palazzo dei Priori), and the *Madonna of the Rose*, both by Taddeo di Bartolo. **Room 4**: polyptych by Cenni di Francesco (1408) and works by Francesco Neri da Volterra and Jacopo di Michele. **Room 5** contains a triptych by the Portuguese painter Alvaro Pirez (c 1423). **Room 6**: two polychrome wood statues of the *Virgin* and the *Angel Gabriel* by Francesco di Valdambrino (c 1410), from the cathedral. **Room 7**: several paintings by Priamo della Quercia. **Room 8**: altarpiece by Neri di Bicci. **Room 9**: *Nativity* and predella scenes, signed and dated 1470, by Benvenuto di Giovanni. In **room 10** there is an impressive altarpiece representing *Christ in glory worshipped by Saints Benedict, Romualdo, Attinia, and Greciniana*, in a beautiful landscape (1492), by Domenico del Ghirlandaio, as well as two *Madonna and Saints* by the brothers Agnolo and Donnino di Domenico Mazziere, and Leonardo Malatesta. **Room 11** displays the gallery's most famous work, the *Deposition* by **Rosso Fiorentino**, signed and dated 1521, one of the masterpieces of Florentine Mannerist art. Also here are two fine works by Luca Signorelli, both dated 1491, an *Annunciation* and *Madonna and Child enthroned with Saints John the Baptist, Francis, Anthony of Padua,*

Bonaventura, and Jerome. **Room 12**: two paintings by Pieter de Witte (Pietro Candido) and a *Nativity* by Domenico Mascagni and three works by Pomarancio. **Room 13**: fragments including a *Head of the Madonna* by Giuliano Bugiardini, and some small 15C–16C Florentine and Flemish paintings. **Room 14**: Baldassare Franceschini (called Il Volterrano), *Madonna and Child in glory with Saints Francis, Clare, John the Evangelist, Stephen, Mary Magdalen, and Paul* (1639). There is also a collection of 17C and 18C silver, and coins and medals. The loggia provides beautiful views over the valley.

Via Sarti

In the spacious Via Sarti are several fine palaces including Palazzo Tortora Salvetti (on the left) and Palazzo Ruggieri Buzzaglia with two balconies (on the right).

Farther down is the fine 16C façade of **Palazzo Incontri Viti** (open March–Nov 09.00–13.00, 14.30–18.00 exc. Tues morning), attributed to Bartolomeo Ammannati. In the early 19C the ground floor and courtyard, which had remained unfinished, were bought by the Accademia dei Riuniti and rebuilt as a **theatre** (now a cinema). The palace was acquired in 1850 by Benedetto Giuseppe Viti, an alabaster merchant, who had the interior redecorated for a visit of Vittorio Emanuele II in 1860. The entrance staircase (at no. 41) by Giovanni Caccini was decorated with a bust of the king and a plaque commemorating his visit. The **piano nobile** has elegant period furniture and a unique collection of works in alabaster, as well as Indian and Chinese objects acquired by Viti during his trading expeditions in the East.

Via Sarti leads into the small Piazza San Michele. Here is a 13C medieval tower and the church of **San Michele Arcangelo** which has a fine Pisan-Romanesque façade decorated with blind arches on two levels, divided by striped black-and-white marble decoration. In the lunette over the doorway is a 14C statue of the *Madonna and Child*. The interior was altered in 1827. To the left of the altar is a glazed terracotta *Madonna and Child* attributed to Giovanni della Robbia in a marble tabernacle. The church also has an unglazed terracotta statue of *St Michael Archangel* by Andrea della Robbia.

Via Guarnacci leads north from the piazza to **Porta Fiorentina**, which preserves its old wooden doors. Just outside the gate is the entrance to the ***Roman theatre** (open March–Oct 11.00–17.00, but closed if it is raining), built at the end of the 1C BC and one of the best preserved in Italy. Excavations, begun in 1952 by Enrico Fiumi, revealed part of the cavea and scena, with Corinthian columns over 5m high. Numerous coins (3C BC–4C AD) found here are now in the Museo Guarnacci (see below). Inside the portico, which was added a century later, are remains of Roman baths. When closed, the theatre can be viewed from above.

From Piazza San Michele, Via di Sotto passes the Romanesque flank of San Michele and Via Docciola, a picturesque street with steps leading down between cypress trees to the **Fonti di Docciola**, a fountain protected by a brick vault supported on two large Gothic arches, dating from 1245. Nearby is the 13C **Porta di Docciola**. Via di Sotto broadens as it reaches Piazza XX Settembre. To the right is the 15C **Oratory of Sant'Antonio Abate**, inside which is a painting of the titular saint by Priamo della Quercia (1442).

On the left is a war memorial and the church of **Sant'Agostino**, founded in the late 13C, but rebuilt in 1728. It has a basilican plan with a nave and two aisles divided by Corinthian columns. Inside, on the right, is the tomb of

Alessandro Riccobaldi (d. 1523), decorated with skulls and cross-bones. In the south aisle is a 13C painted *Crucifix* (damaged) and a 14C fresco of the *Madonna and Child* in a marble tabernacle. A chapel to the right has mono-chrome frescoes, all copies after famous paintings, dating from 1912, and over the altar is a 14C fresco of the *Madonna* and beneath it is a painted terracotta *Pietà*. In the chapel to the left of the high altar is a *Madonna with Saints Thomas of Villanova and Clare of Montefalco* by Volterrano (1669), and, in the north aisle, the *Madonna del Soccorso* by Ulisse Giocchi (1614). On the entrance wall are fresco fragments of a large *Crucifixion*, detached from the Badia, attributed to a follower of Giotto.

The Guarnacci Etruscan Museum

The lovely building, with a garden, at no. 15 Via Don Minzoni houses the *Museo Etrusco Guarnacci, one of the most interesting Etruscan collections in Italy, and extremely well displayed (open 09.00–19.00; winter, 09.00–14.00).

The nucleus of the collection was donated in 1732 by Canon Pietro Franceschini who was the first to discover Etruscan urns in the area. It was subsequently enriched by the important bequest of Monsignor Mario Guarnacci (1701–85), a wealthy prelate of Volterra who financed local excavations and bequeathed his archaeological collection and library to his native city.

The arrangement begins on the **ground floor** with a prehistoric section demonstrating the existence of primitive communities in this territory, with finds from excavations, and maps. The Roman section includes portrait heads, reliefs, fragments of murals, and several mosaic floors from the theatre and baths.

The Etruscan civilisation, from the 10C BC onwards, is magnificently documented. Entire finds from local tombs dating from the 8C–7C BC are exhibited, with arms, household objects, fibulae and bronzes. From the 6C BC there are stele and fragments with inscriptions. The collection is particularly famous for its **Etruscan cinerary urns**, in alabaster or terra-cotta, mostly dating from the 3C BC, found locally and numbering over 600. The terracotta urns are probably the oldest. Many are sculpted with fine reliefs and the lids generally bear the recumbent figures of the dead, with the cup of life reversed.

An Etruscan urn in the Guarnacci Etruscan Museum, Volterra

On the staircase walls are Roman inscriptions and Romanesque fragments. **First floor**. Rooms XIII–XIX contain cinerary urns arranged according to the subjects of the reliefs: Theban and Trojan cycles, Amazons, Ulysses, mythological themes. Room XX: terracotta *tomb cover with strikingly realistic portraits of a husband and wife (early 1C BC). Room XXII contains lamps and works in bronze, including the famous bronze votive figure of the early 3C BC, known as the 'Shadow of the Evening' on account of its immensely elongated proportions. Room XXIII displays coins. Room XXIV: bronze figurines, bone and ivory objects, and jewellery.

Second floor. Room XXVII: fragments of a pediment. Room XXIX contains examples of tools used for sculpting marble and alabaster. Room XXX (with a fine view) has chosen examples of alabaster urns dating from the 3C–2C BC. Room XXXI has examples of urns, illustrating various themes. Room XXXII: portraits and large-scale reclining figures. Room XXXIII: mirrors. Room XXXIV: bronze objects. Room XXXV: marble statues, stele, and inscriptions. Room XXXVI: contains Etruscan pottery.

Opposite the museum, Vicolo Marchi leads to Via di Castello, which has a magnificent view of the **Fortezza**. This massive structure is composed of the Rocca Vecchia to the left, built by the Duke of Athens in 1343, joined by a double rampart to the Rocca Nuova on the right, which was added by Lorenzo il Magnifico in 1472–75. The Rocca Nuova forms a square, with circular towers at each corner, surrounding the battlemented tower known as *Il Maschio*. The Rocca Vecchia has a semicircular tower called *La Femmina*, and another tower next to the Porta a Selci beside the entrance. The Fortezza has always been a prison, and is still used as such. A remarkable theatre group gives performances here.

Via di Castello leads back to the town centre via the **Parco Archeologico Fiumi**, a beautiful public garden (ideal for picnics) on the site of the Etruscan and Roman acropolis. There are fine views from the park which overlooks excavations of a Roman piscina or reservoir.

From Piazza San Giovanni (see p 284) Via Persio Flacco (beside the Baptistery) leads to Via Lungo Le Mura which continues downhill overlooking the valley to the south, ending at the famous **Porta all'Arco**, the main gateway to the Etruscan town, dating from the 4C–3C BC, partly rebuilt by the Romans in the 1C BC.

The splendid, impressive round arch is decorated with three monumental heads, supposed to be of Etruscan divinities. It has miraculously survived despite sieges and modern warfare. A plaque to the right records how the citizens of Volterra saved it from destruction in 1944 by undertaking to fill it with paving stones overnight: *Ospite, quest'opera grande dei nostri maggiori minacciata dal furore di una barbara guerra fu serbata alla tua ammirazione soltanto da noi Volterrani* (Know, O Visitor, that this arch, one of the greatest of our monuments, was preserved for your admiration from the threat of a barbarous war by citizens of Volterra singlehanded).

From beneath the arch the pretty Via Porta all'Arco winds back uphill to Piazza dei Priori.

The historic centre

The centre of the old town has a maze of winding streets which run up and downhill, with narrow alleys, many of which are arched. From Piazza dei Priori, Via Ricciarelli leads west past the Buomparenti and Buonaguidi tower-houses (see above), and other interesting houses including a fine rusticated palace, to the little **Oratory of San Cristofano**, inside which is a fresco of the *Madonna* attributed to Mariotto d'Andrea da Volterra. Via San Lino continues downhill. On the right is the church of **San Lino**, with a façade of 1513. The interior has a series of lunettes with scenes from the *Life of Christ* by Cosimo Daddi (1618). On the south altar, *Birth of the Virgin* by Cesare Dandini. The high altarpiece of the *Madonna in Glory with St Lino and other Saints* is by Francesco Curradi. On the north altar is a *Visitation* by Cosimo Daddi. The tomb of Beato Raffaele Maffei, the founder of the church, is by Silvio Cosini (1522) and the statues of

Beato Gherardo and the archangel *Raphael* in the side niches are by Stagio Stagi.

The street ends at Piazza Inghirami, inside Porta San Francesco. To the left is the small church of **San Dalmazio**, which is still owned by the Inghirami family, with a Renaissance doorway (1516). It contains an altarpiece of the *Deposition* signed and dated 1551 by Giovan Paolo Rossetti, a native of Volterra. The ceiling fresco of the *Glory of St Dalmazio* is by Ranieri del Pace. The two ovals with stories of *St Benedict* are by Giovanni Camillo Sagrestani, the *Vision of St Dominic* by Jacopo Vignali and the *Noli me Tangere* by Giovanni Balducci.

San Francesco

Opposite, above a slope, is the 13C church of San Francesco, which has been extensively rebuilt. On the south side of the nave: *Immaculate Conception* (1585) by Giovanni Battista Naldini; fresco of the *Pietà* by Niccolò Circignani; and *Hermits* (1748) by Alessandro Gherardini.

A door leads into the **Cappella della Croce di Giorno**, built in 1315 next to the church by the Tedicinghi family, with its own entrance facing the piazza. The chapel was entirely painted with **frescoes** by Cenni di Francesco in 1410, representing the *Legend of the True Cross* and the *Infancy of Christ*, commissioned by the subsequent owners, the Conti Guidi. This is not only a rare and fascinating example of a narrative cycle, but it is also a description, in countless details, of the architecture and costumes of the period.

On the main entrance wall, in a lunette: *Seth receives the branch of the Tree of Sin and plants it on Adam's grave*; and below: *the Queen of Sheba predicts the future of the miraculous wood*; left wall: *the wood is used to make the Cross*; next bay: *St Helena identifies the True Cross*; below: *St Helena carries away the Cross*; to the left: on the pilaster, *St Francis receiving the stigmata*; *Chosroes, King of Persia, steals the Cross*; *Vision of the Emperor Constantine*, and the *Battle of Maxentius at the Milvian bridge*; left of the door: *the idolatry of Chosroes*; right wall: *Chosroes beheaded, and Heraclius, barefoot, brings the Cross back to Jerusalem*; on the right pilaster: *St John the Baptist*. The second bay of the right wall represents *the Nativity and Adoration of the Shepherds* in the lunette, and a large, dramatic scene of the *Massacre of the Innocents* below. In the apse, from left to right, the *Holy Sepulchre*, above the *Flight into Egypt*; *Death of the Virgin* (damaged); *Annunciation*, above the *Circumcision*. The spandrels of the vault are frescoed by Jacopo da Firenze with figures of the *Evangelists and Saints* standing on clouds against a blue sky. On the altar a *Crucifixion* attributed to Bartolomeo Neroni replaces Rosso Fiorentino's *Deposition*, now in the Pinacoteca.

Outside the chapel, over the doorway, there is a tomb (1719) of a member of the Guidi family.

The marble Baroque **high altar** contains a 15C image of the *Madonna*. In the crossing (left) is the tomb of Bishop Jacopo Guidi who died in 1588. On the left side of the nave is a *Madonna and Child with Saints* by Vincenzo Meucci. At the entrance to the sacristy there is a holy water stoup in the form of a marble, prow-like, female figure of the vestal virgin Tuccia, holding a sieve, dated 1522. In the **sacristy** is a group of terracotta figures by Zaccaria Zacchi, representing the *Pietà*. Farther down the nave are a *Crucifixion* by Cosimo Daddi, the tomb of Mario Guarnacci (see p 288) in yellow and white marble with reclining figures of *Justice* and *Contemplation* beside his portrait bust, and a *Nativity* by Giovanni Balducci.

Outside the 14C **Porta San Francesco**, one of the grandest and best preserved gateways of the town, Via del Borgo di Santo Stefano leads down past the ruined church of that name to the church and convent of **Santa Chiara**, which has a portico attributed to Ammannati. Nearby is an impressive stretch of **Etruscan walls**.

Borgo San Giusto continues downhill to (c 15 minutes) the church of **Santi Giusto e Clemente**, its eccentric tall façade rising above a grassy slope planted with cypresses. It was founded in 1627 to replace an earlier church which disappeared into the Balze (see below), but only completed in 1775. In front of the **façade** are terracotta figures of the patrons and protectors of Volterra, *Saints Giusto* and *Clemente* (right), the titular saints (brother missionaries who came from Africa in the 6C), and (left) *Saints Ottaviano* and *Lino*. They stand on monolithic stone columns with Romanesque capitals.

The grandiose interior has a Latin-cross plan with a single nave. South side: *Visitation* by Cosimo Daddi and *St Francis Xavier preaching; Martyrdom of Saints Attinia and Greciniana* (1642) by Giovanni Domenico Ferretti. In the south transept there is a photographic reproduction of a *Madonna and Child* by Neri di Bicci. The Cappella della Compagnia has a ceiling fresco of *Elisha and the angel* by Volterrano (1631). On the north side is a painting of the *Martyrdom of St Ursula, and Saints surrounding the Madonna* by Pietro Dandini.

The road continues past a small gate (view) and ends beside the restored Etruscan walls overlooking the formidable precipice of **Le Balze**, formed by the natural erosion of the Pleistocene clay. Erosion and several earthquakes have not only engulfed the greater part of the earliest necropolis of Volterra and buildings of subsequent periods, but continues to be a threat. Off Via Pisana, on a hill, are the ruins of the **Badia** which was abandoned after the earthquake of 1846 and subsequent landslides.

Environs of Volterra

Below the Fortezza (see above) Viale dei Ponti, a beautiful panoramic road built by the grand-duke Leopoldo II, runs beneath the medieval walls overlooking the Cecina valley. It passes close to the 15C church and monastery of **San Girolamo**, possibly designed by Michelozzo. Beneath the portico are two chapels with reliefs, representing *St Francis giving the Tertiary Rule to St Louis of France* and the *Last Judgement*, both by Giovanni della Robbia, and dated 1501. In a chapel to the right of the entrance is the *Immaculate Conception* by Santi di Tito. Flanking the high altar are a *Madonna enthroned with Saints* by Domenico di Michelino and the *Annunciation with Saints Michael and Catherine of Alexandria* signed and dated 1466 by Benvenuto di Giovanni, a work of great charm and refinement. The two statues representing *St Francis* and *St Jerome* are by a follower of Cieco da Gambassi. In the four niches on the sides are stucco figures of saints by Mazzuoli. Not far from the church are remains of the few surviving Etruscan ipogee tombs (their contents are in the Museo Guarnacci).

West of Volterra is the medieval castellated village of **Montecatini Val di Cecina** (416m) surrounding a monumental castle tower. It commands a beautiful view above the Cecina valley. On the opposite side of the valley is **Montegemoli**, another medieval castle in a fine position, which was partially rebuilt in the Renaissance period.

South of Volterra the main road descends through rolling hills and white chalk hillocks (*crete*), to **Saline di Volterra**, a small industrial town, named after its underground salt deposits which have been systematically mined since the 9C. Here a beautiful winding road diverges left (there is a spectacular view of Volterra in the distance).

Pomarance

The road follows a ridge overlooking the Cecina valley, characterised by the *crete*, and then climbs towards the medieval town of Pomarance (370m). Of Etruscan and Roman origin, it owed its prosperity to the wealth of minerals mined locally and later to the exploitation of vapour jets. In 1472 it came under the dominion of Florence and exercised control over a vast area comprising the upper Cecina valley and most of the surrounding metalliferous hills. It was the birthplace of two painters called Pomarancio: Niccolò Cercignani (c 1517–96) and Cristoforo Roncalli (1552–1626).

Parts of the old walls survive and the **Porta Volterrana**, on the north side of the town, dates from 1326. In the central piazza is the clock tower and the **Palazzo Pretorio**, first built in the 12C, with a Florentine *Marzocco* lion on the corner and numerous coats of arms.

Beyond an archway is the parish church of **San Giovanni Battista** which was rebuilt in the 18C but preserves its Romanesque façade with blind arches. Inside are frescoes covering the nave and apse, by Luigi Ademollo including a large *Last Supper* behind the altar, and altarpieces by Roncalli *(Annunciation)* and Cercignani (*Madonna of the Rosary*). In the south transept chapel is a *Madonna and Saints* by Vincenzo Tamagni (1525). The baptistery chapel has a charming Nativity group of painted terracotta figures attributed to Zaccaria Zacchi with a background fresco of the *Magi* by Tamagni. The church also owns a *Madonna and Child enthroned* and scenes of the *Infancy of Christ* by a 13C artist and a *Madonna* by a Sienese painter, dated 1329.

There are several palaces belonging to the Larderel and other local families and some medieval houses and towers in the older part of the town. On the south side is a natural rocky terrace.

South of Pomarance is **San Dalmazio**, an attractive little town on a hill, which was originally a monastery before being transformed into a fortified castle, parts of which still survive. A little beyond San Dalmazio is a turning, past the ruins of a Romanesque church, for the **Rocca di Sillano** (530m), reached by a steep climb on foot. This 12C castle, which was a stronghold of Volterra, preserves ruins of three circles of walls around a polygonal tower. A short distance further on is another hill-top town, **Montecastelli** (494m) which still has its medieval walls, two towers and a Romanesque church. Inside are interesting, carved capitals and an altarpiece by Cosimo Daddi.

The main road to the south (N439) continues uphill past chimneys and pipelines, with a distinct smell of sulphurous springs, to **Montecerboli** (386m), with some medieval houses and a Romanesque church built in brick. In the new parish church is a 13C triptych of the *Madonna and Child* flanked by the two St Johns and a 14C Sienese *Crucifix*.

The industrial town of **Larderello** (390m) is noted for the production of boric acid. François De Larderel began to extract boric acid from the nearby natural vapour jets (known as *lagoni* or *soffioni*) in 1818. A German scientist, Franz Hoefer, discovered its presence here in 1777. The small town built for the workers near the original industrial plant was named Larderello in 1846 by Grandduke Leopoldo II.

The National Electrical Company (*ENEL*) has opened the **Museo della Geotermia** (open daily exc. Sat & fest. in winter) on its premises. It documents the scientific exploitation of the steam jets which was continued by Larderel's son and grandson, initially for the production of boric acid and later for electricity. Guided tours also include a visit to a boric acid spring and a power station. Today there are 14 power stations fed by over 60 kilometres of pipelines. The museum will eventually be housed in the De Larderel palace. In front of the palace are busts of François de Larderel and his wife on two columns. Another column commemorates a prize received at the Paris Exhibition of 1867.

The residential area, rebuilt after damage from bombing in 1945, has a church by Giovanni Michelucci. There is also a late Renaissance church dedicated to the *Madonna of Montenero* with a Gothic bronze pulpit. The bare landscape, with its pipelines, furnaces, and power stations covering some 170 sq km, with clouds of steam bursting from the ground, has been called the 'Valley of Hell'.

After a steep climb, the road descends to **La Perla** where there are baths recommended for the treatment of rheumatism, and continues to **Castelnuovo di Val di Cecina** (612m). This is a small industrial and agricultural town, also popular as a summer resort on account of its location near ancient chestnut woods. The town was extended beyond the medieval castle in the 16C. A pretty by-road diverges left towards Radicondoli (see p 419).

Livorno

Livorno is a busy and lively town with a maritime air, which, since the 1970s has become one of the biggest container ports in Italy (169,000 inhab.). As well as a commercial port with important ship repair yards it also has numerous car ferry services to Sardinia and Corsica. It was laid out on a polygonal plan in 1576 by Bernardo Buontalenti for the Medici who constructed the fortifications and surrounded it by a deep moat (the Fosso Reale). In the 19C the city expanded on open symmetrical lines. Although it suffered systematic destruction from bombing in 1943, part of the Medici defence works survive, as well as numerous monumental 19C buildings, and the town was well reconstructed. The spacious seaboard is particularly attractive. It has a well-known street market where American goods are sold (Camp Darby, a US army base is nearby). In the 17C and 18C the town, as a free port, was much frequented by British merchants and sailors who called it *Leghorn*. On the first Sunday of every month museums and churches are often specially opened and street markets and boat excursions organised.

Practical information

Getting there
By car

Livorno is about 15km south of Pisa, reached by the A12 motorway. **Car parking**. Much of the centre of the city has restricted access for motorists (except residents) from 07.30–19.30. Car parking best off Viale Carducci (and bus no. 1 to the centre). Car park (with hourly fee and reduction for long-term parking), Scali Bettarini 5.

By train

The station is in Piazza Dante, c 1km east of Piazza Grande (bus no. 1). Frequent train service to Pisa in 10–20 mins, and local trains to Florence via Pisa and Empoli in 1hr 20 mins. Express services to Rome and Genoa on the main line along the coast. Local trains on this line serve Castiglioncello, Cecina, San Vincenzo, and Piombino.

By bus

Town buses. No. 1 from the railway station to Piazza della Repubblica, Piazza Grande, the Darsena Vecchia, and Viale Italia (for the Museo Civico; Bagni Pancaldi stop); several other buses (including no. 2) from the station to Piazza Grande (some going on to Antignano and Montenero).

Country buses. Although most places in the province, and Florence and Pisa are best reached by train from Livorno, there are also *Lazzi* bus services from Piazza Manin to Empoli, Florence, Pisa, Viareggio, and Lucca; and *ATL* services from Piazza Grande to Bibbona and Castagneto Carducci (as well as Castiglioncello, Cecina, and Piombino).

Maritime services

Boats from Porto Mediceo run by *Toremar* (☎ 0586 896 113) to **Capraia**, daily in 3 hrs (once a week via Gorgona in 3½ hrs), and in summer to **Elba**. In summer *Fratelli Rossignoli* (☎ 0336 582 413) also run a boat service to **Capraia**, **Elba**, and the **Cinque Terre**.

Car ferries from Calata Carrara for **Corsica** (Bastia) run by *Corsica Ferries* (☎ 0586 881 380) and *Corsica Marittima* (☎ 0586 210 507). For **Sardinia**. *Sardinia Ferries* (☎ 0586 881 380) to Golfo Aranci and *Moby Lynes* (☎ 0586 826 823) to Olbia. Services to Olbia and Cagliari from Calata Assab, Porto Nuovo run by *Lloyd Sardegna Compagnia di Navigazione* (☎ 0565 222 300). For **Palermo** *Grandi Navi Veloci (Grandi Traghetti*; ☎ 010 589 331*)* from Calata Tripoli.

Information offices

APT, Piazza Cavour 6 (☎ 0586 898 111); information offices open in summer at the Molo Mediceo, and at the passenger terminal (Calata Carrara), near the Stazione Marittima.

Where to stay
Hotels

☆☆☆ *Gran Duca*, Piazza Micheli 16 (☎ 0586 891 024; 📠 0586 891 153); *Gennarino*, Viale Italia 301 (☎ 0586 803 109, 📠 0586 803 450); *Atleti*, Via dei Pensieri 50, near the Hippodrome, off Viale Italia, towards Antignano (☎/📠 0586 502 409). **ANTIGNANO** on the sea (6km south): ☆☆ *La Capinera*, Via del Castello 32 (☎ 0586 580 508, 📠 0586 580 814).

Campsite

☆☆ *Miramare*, Via del Littorale 220 (open April–Sept; ☎ 0586 580 402).

Youth hostel

Villa Morazzana, Via di Collinet 68 (☎ 0586 500 076, 📠 0586 502 426).

Eating out

Livorno is famous for its fish restaurants (fish is always

more expensive than meat).

€€ *La Barcarola*, Viale Carducci 63;
Il Sottomarino, Via Terrazzini 48.
€ *Carlo*, Via Caprera 43; *Da Galileo*,
Via della Campana (off Via Garibaldi);
Enoteca Doc, Via Goldoni 42.
ANTIGNANO €€ *La Capinera*,
Via del Castello 32.
MONTENERO €€ *Montallegro*,
Piazza di Montenero 3.
Local speciality. The characteristic
torta, a delicious and cheap savoury

snack made from chick peas, is sold
from small snack bars called *pizzerie* all
over the town (customers usually eat it
standing up).

Sports
Swimming
Sea-bathing south of the town
beyond Antignano at Il Romito (rocks)
or at Quercianella (private beaches; fee),
or further south along the coast
between Cecina and Piombino.

History

Though a fortress here was the subject of a dispute between Pisan, Genoese,
and Florentine overlords from the early Middle Ages, Livorno's rise dates from
1571, when the new port was begun by decree from Cosimo de' Medici.
Numerous British sailors came to the town during this period.

Ferdinando I (1587–1609) continued the work and employed Sir Robert
Dudley (see p 299) to construct the great mole (1607–21) as a breakwater,
build warships, and administer the port. Ferdinando, by his proclamation of
religious liberty, made the town a refuge for persecuted Jews, Greeks who had
fled from the Turks, converted Moslems expelled from Spain and Portugal
under Philip III in 1609, and Roman Catholics driven from England under
the penal laws against papists (1606) proclaimed by James I. They were
joined by many Italians fleeing from the oppression of their own states, and
by exiles from Marseilles and Provence. During the 17C the port was used to
import large quantities of red herring from Great Yarmouth and wheat from
King's Lynn. In the 18C the 'British Factory' was established in Livorno by a
group of British merchants and factors to assist the numerous British families
in the town. Ferdinando's policy was pursued by his successors, and Livorno
became a great port, now the third largest in Italy.

As a neutral port it was able to supply numerous ships for the naval battles
against Napoleon, and Lord Nelson came here in 1793. In 1749 Sir Joshua
Reynolds landed here on his only visit to Italy, and Tobias Smollett, Byron,
and Shelley all lived for a time at Montenero on the outskirts of the town (see
below). In the mid-19C Livorno became a well-known bathing resort. Robert
Stephenson built the railway line from Pisa to Livorno which was opened in
1844; it terminated at the neo-Classical Stazione Ferroviaria Leopoldo (San
Marco; see the Map), now closed. A regular steam-ship service was
introduced in 1872 between Livorno and Great Britain.

Giovanni Fattori (1825–1908), the Macchiaioli painter and Pietro
Mascagni (1863–1945), composer of *Cavalleria Rusticana* were both born
here. Another native was the artist Amedeo Modigliani (1884–1920). In
1984 two sculptures were dredged up from the Fosso Reale and acclaimed by
numerous art critics to be lost masterpieces by Modigliani. They were soon
proved to be fakes made by a group of young students, and the incident was
recognised as one of the most successful hoaxes of recent years.

The reef of Meloria rises nearly 5km off Livorno, where the maritime power of Pisa was crushed by the Genoese in 1284. An English trading fleet was also routed hereabouts by the Dutch in 1653.

The **railway station** is a fine Art Nouveau building (1910) by Pietro Via. Beside it, in Piazza Dante, are the remains of a spa hotel built in 1905 by Angelo Badaloni. The long, wide **Viale Carducci**, with an avenue of trees and pretty lamp posts, leads due west towards the centre of the city. Beyond an old factory building of 1906 are the **public gardens** laid out in 1854, and the monumental **Cisternone**, a water cistern built in 1829–32 by Pasquale Poccianti, with a classical portico and exedra (the semi-dome recalls the Pantheon in Rome).

Via de Larderel continues past the large neo-Classical **Palazzo De Larderel** (1832–50). The French Larderel family came to live in Livorno in 1799 and became wealthy through the extraction of boric acid south of Volterra (see Larderello, p 292). Inside are plaster casts of the statues of illustrious Tuscans which can be seen in the niches of the loggia of the Galleria degli Uffizi in Florence. Beyond is the huge **Piazza della Repubblica**, known as the Voltone since it rests on a wide vault over the Fosso Reale (which still flows beneath it; see below). It was laid out in 1834 by Luigi Bettarini: on the great expanse of pavement rise well-designed lamp-posts and two statues, one of Ferdinando III by Francesco Pozzi (1837), and one of Leopoldo II by Emilio Santarelli (1885). To the north is a good view of the moated Fortezza Nuova (described below).

Via Grande continues past the handsome **Cisternino**, another fine neo-Classical building designed by Poccianti in 1827. In Via Madonna (right) three Baroque façades survive among the unattractive modern buildings: the former churches of the **Annunziata** (1605), and of the **Concezione** (1599), both by Alessandro Pieroni, and the 18C façade of **San Giorgio degli Armeni**.

Piazza Grande, in the centre of the city, was a huge square laid out in the 16C–17C and formerly surrounded by porticoes by Alessandro Pieroni (only a fragment survives at the southwest corner). It was greatly reduced in size when a much criticised modern building was built in the centre, so that it is now divided from Largo Municipio to the north.

The **Duomo** was begun in 1587, modified in 1606 by Alessandro Pieroni, and completed in 1609 by Antonio Cantagallina. It had to be virtually rebuilt in 1954–59, after severe damage in 1944, when only the south wall was left standing. The Doric portico which precedes the façade (and which was an integral part of the design of Piazza Grande) is also probably by Pieroni. Although the traditional attribution of the piazza and portico to Inigo Jones is now discredited, it may be that the famous architect saw the square if he docked at the port of Livorno on the second of his two trips to Italy when he accompanied the Earl and Countess of Arundel on their Grand Tour in 1613–14. The huge square with porticoes and the church of St Paul, which he designed for Covent Garden, London in 1631–39 are certainly reminiscent of an Italian piazza.

Although the ceiling was destroyed the paintings were salvaged and were reinstalled here after restoration: *Assumption* by Passignano; *Madonna and Child with St Francis of Assisi* by Empoli; and *Triumph of St Giulia* by Jacopo Ligozzi. Among the funerary monuments on the south wall, the most notable is that of Alessandro del Borro by Giovanni Battista Foggini. On either side of the high altar are two small heads of angels by François Duquesnoy, killed in Livorno by

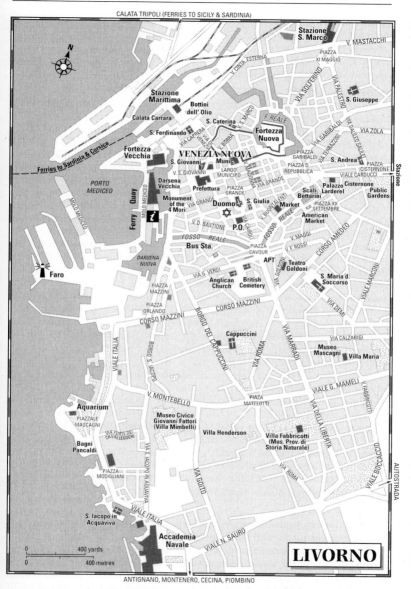

his brother in 1643. On the right wall, *Translation of the body of St Giulia* by the local painter Tommaso Gazzarrini (1834) opposite a *Miracle of St Francis* by Giuseppe Bezzuoli. The transepts were added in the 18C (reconstructed after the Second World War).

In Largo Municipio, north of Piazza Grande, is **Palazzo Municipio** by

Giovanni del Fantasia (1720), with a bell tower and a double staircase added by Bernardino Ciurini. On the left is the 17C **Palazzo di Camera di Commercio**, designed with three large arches by Annibale Cecchi. On the corner of Via della Posta is **Palazzo Granducale** (now Palazzo della Provincia) designed in the 17C by Antonio Cantagallina (and reconstructed after the war).

Nuova Venezia

Via San Giovanni (once the main street of the old town, but now without character) leads out of the west side of the piazza past the 17C church of **San Giovanni** (restructured) which contains a handsome ciborium by Ferdinando Tacca incorporated in the high altar. Behind the church a road leads across a bridge to an area, laid out in 1629–44, and known as **Nuova Venezia**, because of its numerous canals used as moorings for small boats. **Via Borra** was one of the most important streets in the city in the 18C (the most interesting palace here is Palazzo delle Colonne at no. 29, designed by Giovanni Battista Foggini). Beyond the next pretty bridge is the 18C octagonal church of **Santa Caterina**, with interesting *trompe l'oeil* frescoes and a *Coronation of the Virgin* behind the high altar by Vasari.

There is a good view from the bridge of the wall of the **Fortezza Nuova** built in 1590 on a design by Giovanni de' Medici, Vincenzo Bonanni, and Bernardo Buontalenti (altered in 1696). It is surrounded by a moat, and the interior has been laid out as a pleasant **public park** (the entrance is near a palm tree). It is sometimes used for exhibitions.

Just beyond the church of Santa Caterina, Via San Marco crosses the interesting Via dei Floridi with houses built above the old bastions, to the façade of the former **Teatro di San Marco**. A worn plaque here records the founding of the Italian Communist Party in 1921. A modern school building has recently been built behind the façade.

On the other side of Santa Caterina the Scali del Rifugio skirts the canal past the ex-convent of Santa Caterina where Sandro Pertini (1896–1990; elected President of the Republic in 1978) was held as a political prisoner during the Fascist regime (plaque set up in 1977). To the right a roadway leads down over an archway giving access to the canal to the **Bottini dell'Olio** (1705–31) which were the last important buildings constructed in Livorno by the Medici, on a project by Giovanni Battista Foggini. The warehouse could store some 24,000 barrels of oil; the fine vaulted hall is now used for exhibitions. Amidst evident signs of bombing from the last War is the church of **San Ferdinando**, with a good 18C interior (also by Foggini) and excellent marble sculptures by Giovanni Baratta.

The port

Via della Venezia leads back from San Ferdinando to Via San Giovanni which continues right to the **Darsena Vecchia** (1591), the main harbour for the fishing fleet. In the harbour is the wall of the crumbling **Fortezza Vecchia**, the most important of the Medici defence works in the city. It was built to the design of Antonio da Sangallo in 1521–34, and embodies part of a small Roman fortress, the so-called Matilda Tower (11C), and remains of a Pisan fort of 1377. The road skirts the Darsena Vecchia past a theatrical piazza with a colossal equestrian statue of Vittorio Emanuele II by Augusto Rivalta (1882) facing the huge **Palazzo del Governo** (now the Prefecture), a Fascist building of 1942 with monumental white marble bas-reliefs (1954). In Piazza Micheli, is the famous ***Monumento dei Quattro Mori**, a monument to Ferdinando I with a statue of him by Giovanni Bandini (1595), and four colossal Moorish slaves in bronze (1623–26), the masterpieces of Pietro Tacca chained to the pedestal. On the wall of the Medici fortifications here (restored as part of a hotel) is a plaque which Sir Robert Dudley's biographer, John Temple Leader, placed here in 1896.

Sir Robert Dudley

Sir Robert Dudley (1574–1649) was the son of Sir Robert Dudley, Earl of Leicester, Elizabeth I's favourite. Famous as a navigator and mapmaker, he sailed to the West Indies and was knighted by Elizabeth I. However in 1605 when he failed to prove he was Dudley's legitimate son he decided to move to Italy and lived in Tuscany for the rest of his life. Although he had already married three times, he took with him to Italy his cousin Elizabeth Southwell, Elizabeth I's lady-in-waiting and after their conversion to Roman Catholicism he gained a dispensation from the Pope to marry her (and they went on to have twelve children).

He became a naval engineer and administered the port of Livorno for the Medici grand-dukes. He also built warships, the first of which he launched in 1608 armed with 64 large cannon, and he supervised the draining of the marshes between Livorno and Pisa. In 1608 he was recognised as the Duke of Northumberland by the Habsburg emperor. Some of his nautical instruments and gauges to measure the ebb and flow of tides are preserved in the Museo della Storia della Scienza in Florence. He was lent Villa Corsini on the outskirts of Florence near the Villa della Petraia by the Medici grand-dukes and died there.

From Piazza Micheli a bridge leads to the ferry quay in the Porto Mediceo, and on the other side of the Fortezza Vecchia is another ferry quay (Calata Carrara) near the Stazione Marittima. Some way farther north, at the entrance to the port, is the tall **Torre del Marzocco**, attributed to Lorenzo Ghiberti (1439).

From Piazza Micheli the ugly **Via Grande**, with monotonous square arcades, leads past two copies of the fountains made by Tacca for the monument to Ferdinando I (see above) but instead installed in Piazza Santissima Annunziata in Florence, back to Piazza Grande (described above).

The apse of the Duomo faces **Via Cairoli** which leads south towards Piazza Cavour. At the beginning on the left is the church of **Santa Giulia** (1603) with attractive benches and confessionals in the interior. Over the high altar is a painting of the patron saint with stories from her life, attributed to the Maestro di Varlungo. Beyond an 18C courtyard is the Cappella di San Ranieri (1696–1701), with interesting pavement tombs.

Off Via Cairoli, behind the post office, in Via del Tempio is the **Synagogue**, built in 1962 on a design by Angelo Di Castro, after the destruction of the old synagogue in the Second World War.

The Fosso Reale

Via Cairoli ends in **Piazza Cavour** (statue by Vincenzo Cerri, 1871) across two branches of the attractive Fosso Reale, built as a defensive moat around the town by the Medici c 1559. In the centre of the Scali Aurelio Saffi which skirts the left-hand canal, is the huge russet-coloured building of the **central market** set up in 1894 by Angelo Badaloni. It has eight caryatids by Lorenzo Gori in its impressive interior. On the opposite side of the canal is the large Benci school building in a similar colour, also by Badaloni, and the neo-Gothic façade of the **Dutch Church** (1864). Off this side of the canal (see the Map) is Piazza XX Settembre, laid out in 1819 by Poccianti around the neo-Classical portico of the church of **San Benedetto** built in 1819 on a design by Angelo Pampaloni. Since 1944 the piazza has been the site of the famous **Mercatino** where American goods are sold (open all day except Mon morning) in iron sheds.

Via Verdi leads to the right out of Piazza Cavour, past the neo-Gothic **Waldensian Church**, built in 1845 by Rumball as the Presbyterian Church of Scotland. Beyond the entrance (No. 59) to the **Old British Cemetery** (for the key to the gate apply at the offices of the Misericordia, open 09.00–12.00, 15.00–18.30; fest. 09.00–12.00). Probably opened in the 16C, this was for many years the only Protestant cemetery in Italy. Numerous British merchants, sea captains, and Anglican clergymen, with their families, were buried here. Also some Swiss and French Huguenots and Americans, including Elizabeth Seton, a Roman Catholic convert who became a missionary in America and was canonised in 1977. Many of the monumental tombs, pyramidal in form, date from the 1660s. Tobias Smollett (see below) was buried here in 1773 (the tomb, with an obelisk and Latin inscription, is to the right of the centre). The cemetery was visited by Shelley, Longfellow, and Fenimore Cooper and was closed in 1840 when the new cemetery was opened in the northern suburbs. The **Anglican church** outside, with a classical temple façade, was built by Angiolo della Valle in 1840. It is now used by the Misericordia as a chapel.

The southern part of town

Off Via Rossi, the other side of Piazza Cavour, Via Goldini leads to the **Teatro Goldoni** (1843–47 by Giuseppe Cappellini) where in 1921, at a Congress of the Socialist Party, a schism resulted in the founding of the Italian Communist Party (see above). A short way further east, across Corso Amedeo, is the church of **Santa Maria del Soccorso** (1835) by Gaetano Gherardi, with a painting of *St Lawrence* by Enrico Pollastrini (1862) in the first south chapel.

In Via Calzabigi (see Map) is the entrance (no. 54) to the **Museo Mascagnano**, opened in 1985 in a 19C Castelletto to commemorate Pietro Mascagni (1863–1945), the Livornese musician (open 10.00–13.00 except Mon; Thur and Sat also 16.30–19.30). Among numerous mementoes are Mascagni's musical scores, his piano, photographs and manuscripts. In the park of Villa Maria (entered from no. 22 Via Redi) is a modern art gallery.

The 19C **Villa Fabbricotti**, over 1km south of Piazza Cavour, approached along the unattractive, straight Via Marradi and Via della Libertà (best reached by bus no. 2 from Piazza Cavour) is surrounded by a public park (open daily 08.00–dusk). A new building in the park houses the **Museo Provinciale di Storia Naturale** (usually open 09.00–12.30, 16.00–19.00 exc. Sat afternoon & fest.). Founded in 1929 it has sections dedicated to geology, botany and zoology, and a large collection of finds from the district of Livorno dating from the Palaeolithic era onwards. There is an exit from the park on Via Roma, where, at no. 234, is the **Villa Henderson**. This was built in 1780 by John Webb and purchased from the Webbs in 1917 by George Henderson (it now belongs to the Province). The Hendersons founded a sailors' mission (known as The Bethel) in Livorno and George built a Seamen's Institute with funds provided by British merchants.

The Shelleys in Italy

The poet **Percy Bysshe Shelley** sailed to Leghorn in 1818 with his second wife, Mary Wollstonecraft (author of *Frankenstein*, and daugher of his friend the philosopher William Godwin) and their two children William and Clara. While in Italy they stayed in Milan, Bagni di Lucca, Venice, Padua, Este, Pisa (see p 248), Florence, and Rome (where William died in 1819). They then settled at Villa Valsovona in Montenero where Shelley finished his tragedy *The Cenci*. While in Livorno he bought a little schooner, the *Ariel*, which he used to sail up the Arno to Pisa with his friend Lieutenant Edward Williams.

In 1822 the Shelleys moved to the Casa Magni at Lerici, on the Gulf of La Spezia in Liguria with Williams and his wife, where they continued to enjoy sailing in the *Ariel*. Byron, who spent a holiday at the 18C Casa Dupuy in Montenero, may have sailed from Livorno in his boat, the *Bolivar*, to visit them at the Casa Magni. In the same year Shelley and Williams sailed from Lerici back to Livorno to meet the essayist, poet and philosopher Leigh Hunt on his arrival from England. It was on their return to the Casa Magni on 8 July 1822 that they were drowned when the *Ariel* sank off Viareggio. Their bodies, washed ashore ten days later on the beach of Gombo, north of the mouth of the Arno, were cremated there in the presence of Byron and Leigh Hunt. Shelley's ashes were collected and buried in the Protestant cemetery in Rome. He was 30 years old.

As both his prose and poetry show, Shelley was deeply inspired by Italy and the cause of Italian liberty. He wrote *Lines written among the Euganean Hills* in Este in 1818, and *Ode to the West Wind* in Florence in 1819. *Prometheus Unbound* was completed in Rome in 1820. When in Pisa in 1821, a year before his tragic death, he wrote *Epipsychidion*, inspired by Contessina Emilia Viviani whom he had met at the Terme di San Giuliano the previous summer, and *Adonais*.

Villa Mimbelli

Towards the sea, in Via San Iacopo in Acquaviva, the remarkable 19C Villa Mimbelli surrounded by a fine park (open daily) houses the **Museo Civico Giovanni Fattori**.

- The museum is usually open 10.00–13.00, 17.00–23.00; winter 10.00–19.00; closed Mon. It is best reached by bus no. 1 from the station or Piazza Grande to Viale Italia (Bagni Pancaldi stop), from which it is a 5 minute walk along Via Forte dei Cavalleggeri to Via San Jacopo in Acquaviva.

The villa, completely restored in 1994, was built in 1865–70 for Francesco Mimbelli, a rich merchant, by Giuseppe Micheli and decorated in elaborate neo-Renaissance style. It includes an unusual staircase with the bannister supported by majolica putti, exotic fireplaces, trick mirrors, stencilling and frescoes (some by Annibale Gatti), and a domed 'cabinet' (or fumoir) in Moorish style. At present (while the stable block in the park is being restored) exhibitions are also held here so the arrangement is subject to change.

A modern staircase (with busts of Byron by Pietro Tenerani and Vittorio Alfieri by Luigi Pampaloni, and a bronze statuette by Ettore Ximenes) leads up to the

second floor where a selection of the collection of 135 *paintings by the Macchiaioli painter Giovanni Fattori born in Livorno are usually on display. These include battle scenes at Montebello and the *Madonna della Scoperta*, country scenes in the Maremma and Roman Campagna, and portraits (including a *Peasant Woman* and *Signora Martelli at Castiglioncello*).

Other Macchiaioli painters represented include Silvestro Lega (*Peasant Girl*), Vincenzo Cabianca, Telemaco Signorini, Serafino da Tivoli, Giovanni Boldini (including a portrait of Cabianca), Cristiano Banti, and Angiolo Tommasi. There are also good works (not always exhibited) by Enrico Pollastrini (1871–76) and Plinio Nomellini.

The civic collection also includes important earlier works not at present exhibited: *Adoration of the Child* by the Maestro della Natività di Castello; *Battle scene* by Borgognone; *Madonna and Child* by the circle of Botticelli; *Crucifixion* by Neri di Bicci, *Deposition* by Carlo Cignani; and *Head of the Redeemer crowned with thorns*, an unusual and striking work by Beato Angelico. There are also Greek and Russian icons with interesting examples of the Cretan School (16C–17C).

The pleasant **Viale Italia** (see Map) skirts the shore with a wide promenade passing ship-building yards, then gardens and elegant seaside houses, and 19C hotels and bathing establishments, including the Bagni Pancaldi. On Piazzale Mascagni, a pretty terrace built out into the sea with a Doric gazebo (recently restored), is the **aquarium** (open 10.00–12.00, 16.00–19.00 or 14.00–17.00 in winter; closed Mon) and, farther on, the huge **Naval Academy**, founded in 1879. Next to it is the 17C church of **San Jacopo in Acquaviva**, sited where St James the Greater is supposed to have landed on his way to Spain; St Augustine also is said to have stayed here after his baptism. The Viale continues past Art Nouveau houses and the attractive suburbs of **Ardenza** (with a neo-Classical crescent, built in 1840, overlooking the sea), and **Antignano**, built as bathing resorts.

Montenero

Above Antignano is Montenero (193m). A funicular railway opened in 1909 (or a winding road) ascends the hill. The little village, with fine views of the coast, is built round a sanctuary. Tobias Smollett (born in 1721) lived here for the last two years of his life (he died in 1771) and finished *Humphrey Clinker*. The villa where he died, surrounded by a large garden towards Antignano, has a plaque (Villa del Giardino, now Villa Niccolai Gamba). He described it then as being in 'a most romantic and solitary situation'. Shelley (see above) took up residence here in 1819.

The pilgrimage **church** (1676) contains a miraculous painting of the *Madonna*, supposed to have sailed by itself in 1345 from the island of Negropont (Euboea) to the shore at Ardenza. The painting was formerly attributed to Margaritone di Arezzo, but is now thought to be by Il Gera of the Pisan school. Beneath the loggia (1866) are the funerary monuments of illustrious natives of Livorno including Enrico Pollastrini, Giovanni Fattori and Pietro Mascagni. In the **interior** the ceiling is frescoed by Filippo Galletti and the dome by Giuliano Traballesi. The high altar is a fine work in *pietre dure*. In rooms near the sacristy is a huge collection of 19C and 20C ex votos including some charming seascapes, and the Turkish costume of a little girl who was saved by her brother in 1800 after she had been carried off to a harem from Livorno by the Turks (the story was the inspiration for Rossini's opera *L'Italiana in Algeri*).

The coast south of Livorno

The name Maremma was originally given to the marshy coastal plain which stretched from Cecina, some 35km south of Livorno, to the Argentario and beyond to the border with Lazio. It has come to refer to much of south-west Tuscany: the Maremma Pisana, which includes the coast between Pisa and Piombino and the metalliferous hills *(colline metallifere;* p 292) further inland, and the Maremma Grossetana (see p 310) covering the area between Piombino to the north, the promontories of the Uccellina (p 329) and Monte Argentario (p 334) to the west and Monte Amiata to the east.

The typical vegetation in this area, known as *macchia mediterranea,* comprises a variety of evergreen plants, shrubs and trees. Along the coast, growing out of the sand, are lilies, honeysuckle, rosemary, heather, juniper, myrtle and wild olive, backed by maritime and domestic pine trees. Further inland are thick woods of cork, ilex and oak trees with bushes of broom, arbutus, gorse and briar spreading over the hilly slopes. The fertile plains have extensive stretches of wheat and oat crops, sunflowers and corn. Fruit trees, especially peach trees abound and, of course, the traditional vines and olive trees.

There has been increasing awareness in recent years of the need to protect the natural, archaeological and wildlife environment of the Maremma. The Parco Naturale della Maremma was created in 1975 (see p 329), followed by the bird sanctuaries along the coast (Bolgheri, Orbetello, Lake Burano). Other sites, combined with archaeological and walking itineraries have been opened in the Val di Cornia (see below).

The swamplands were for centuries abandoned until the development of modern industrial towns along the coast (Vada, Rosignano Solvay, Cecina) as a result of the building of the railway, connecting Pisa to Rome, the rebuilding of the Via Aurelia and the draining of the marshland.

Practical information

Getting there
By car

Via Aurelia (N1) is now a busy road, recently realigned and made into dual carriageway. It still follows the line of the ancient **Via Aurelia** built c 241 BC to link Rome with the Etruscan towns on the Tyrrhenian coast. It left Rome at Porta Aurelia (now Porta San Pancrazio) and reached the shore at Alsium (Palo Laziale), a port of the Etruscan city of Caere (Cerveteri), then followed the coastline to Cosa. In c 109 BC it was extended to Populonia, Pisa and Genoa. It ended in Gaul at Forum Julia (Fréjus, on the French Riviera). The modern road follows roughly the same line, although in places it now runs further inland and by-passes the towns.

By train

The main railway line from Pisa to Rome follows the above route. Only slow trains stop at the coastal towns: Castiglioncello, Rosignano, Vada, Cecina, Bolgheri, Castagneto Carducci, San Vincenzo, Campiglia Marittima. A branch railway runs from Piombino to Campiglia in 20mins.

By bus

Buses run by *ATL* from Livorno along the coast to Castiglioncello, Cecina, and Piombino.

Information offices

APT Livorno, Piazza Cavour 6 (☎ 0586 898 111).
Information offices open in summer at **Castiglioncello**, Via Aurelia 967 (☎ 0586 752 017); **San Vincenzo**, Via B. Alliata (☎ 0565 701 533); **Cecina**, Piazza Carducci (☎ 0565 611 111); **Piombino**, località Fiorentina (☎ 0565 276 478); and **Suvereto**, Via Matteotti (☎ 0565 829 304).

Where to stay
Hotels on the coast

The coast south of Livorno has numerous seaside resorts, which are extremely crowded in summer. Detailed up-to-date information about hotels, apartments, and campsites is available from the *APT* of Livorno (☎ 0586 898 111).
CASTIGLIONCELLO Numerous hotels of all categories (most of them closed in winter), including ☆☆☆ *Atlantico*, Via Diego Martelli 12 (☎ 0586 752 440; 🖷 0586 752 494) and *Martini*, Via Diego Martelli 3 (☎/🖷 0586 752 140). Hotel residences: ☆☆☆☆ *Villa Godilonda*, Via Biagi 12 (☎ 0586 752 032; 🖷 0586 751 177); ☆☆☆ *San Domenico*, Via Diego Martelli 22 (☎ 0586 752 116).
QUERCIANELLA ☆☆☆ *Villa Margherita*, Via M. Puccini 44 (☎ 0586 491 023; 🖷 0586 491 622).
DONORATICO (ROSIGNANO MARITTIMA) Near the Aurelia. ☆☆☆ *Nuovo Hotel Bambolo* (☎ 0565 775 206; 🖷 0565 775 346) with restaurant.
SAN VINCENZO Numerous hotels of all categories include the ☆☆☆☆ *Park Hotel I Lecci*, Via della Principessa 116 (☎ 0565 704 111; 🖷 0565 703 224).
CECINA ☆☆☆ *Palazzaccio*, on the Aurelia (☎ 0586 682 510; 🖷 0586 686 221).
CECINA MARE has numerous ☆☆☆

hotels, including *Il Gabbiano*, Viale della Vittorio 109 (☎ 0586 620 183; 🖷 0586 620 867) and ☆☆ hotels, including *Azzurra*, Viale della Vittorio 3 (☎/🖷 0586 620 595).
MARINA DI BIBBONA and **FORTE DI BIBBONA** have numerous ☆☆☆ and ☆☆ hotels.
PIOMBINO ☆☆☆☆ *Centrale*, Piazza Verdi 2 (☎ 0565 220 188; 🖷 0565 220 220); and ☆☆☆ *Collodi*, Via Collodi 7 (☎ 0565 224 272; 🖷 0565 224 382).

Campsites

SAN VINCENZO sites include ☆☆ *Park Albatros* (☎ 0565 701 018) and **CECINA MARE** ☆☆☆☆ and ☆☆☆ sites.
MARINA DI BIBBONA, **VADA**, and **FORTE DI BIBBONA** ☆☆☆ sites.
PIOMBINO all category sites.

Eating out
Restaurants

CASTIGLIONCELLO
€ *La Baracchina*, Punta Righini; €€ *Nonna Isola*, Via Aurelia 556.
ROSIGNANO MARITTIMO € *La Gattabuia*, Via Gramsci 32; €€ *San Marco* in località San Marco; €€ *Bagnoli*, at *Bagnoli*; €€ *Il Cacciatore* at Castagneto.
SAN VINCENZO Famous luxury-class restaurant €€€ *Gambero Rosso*, Piazza della Vittoria 13, one of the best places to eat in Italy. €€ *Il Bucaniere*.
CECINA €€€ *Scacciapensieri*, Via Verdi 22; € *Antica Cecina*, Via Cavour 17.
CASALE MARITTIMO €€ *Le Volte*; € *Vecchio Frantoio*, Via Marconi 28.
SUVERETO €€ *Ghigo*, Via Matteotti 45.
CAMPIGLIA MARITTIMA € *Il Canovaccio*, Via Vecchio Asilo 1.
PIOMBINO €€ *Osteria Carugi*, Via Francesco Ferrer 10.

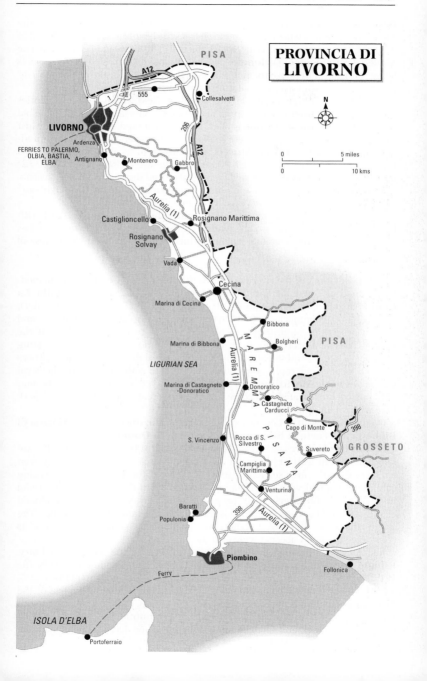

PROVINCIA DI
LIVORNO

PISA

A12

555

Collesalvetti

206

A12

LIVORNO

Ardenza

FERRIES TO PALERMO,
OLBIA, BASTIA,
ELBA

Antignano   Montenero   Gabbro

Aurelia (1)

Castiglioncello   Rosignano Marittima

Rosignano
Solvay

Vada

Cecina

Marina di Cecina

Bibbona

Bolgheri   PISA

Marina di Bibbona

Aurelia (1)

LIGURIAN SEA

M
A
R
E
M
M
A

Marina di Castagneto
-Donoratico

Donoratico

Castagneto
Carducci

Capo di Monte   398

S. Vincenzo   Rocca di S.
Silvestro

Suvereto   GROSSETO

P
I
S
A
N
A

Campiglia
Marittima

Venturina

Baratti   398

Aurelia (1)

Populonia

Piombino

Ferry   Follonica

ISOLA D'ELBA

Portoferraio

Castiglioncello is a large resort on a promontory. It was a favourite place of the *Macchiaioli* painters who drew inspiration from the beautiful scenery and used to stay with the writer and art critic, Diego Martelli (1838–96) in his villa here. The **Museo Archeologico Nazionale**, designed to look like an Etruscan temple, is being rearranged to house the rich finds, excavated at the beginning of the 20C in a nearby Etruscan necropolis dating from the 4C–1C BC.

Just beyond Castiglioncello to the south at **Rosignano Solvay** factories process the soda from the salt-works of Saline di Volterra (see p 292). The old town of **Rosignano Marittimo** is a few kilometres inland. It was originally just a castle and its medieval walls were reinforced with towers in the 17C by grand-duke Cosimo II. The **Civico Museo Archeologico**, in Palazzo Bombardieri (open 09.00–13.00, 16.00–19.00, excluding Mon; ☎ 0586 799 232) documents the history of the lower Cecina Valley and the coast south of Livorno. It has a collection of Etruscan and Roman material excavated in the neighbour-hood. This area is known for its excellent wine (*Montescudaio*).

To the north of Castiglioncello is **Quercianella**, a little seaside resort with beaches backed by pine woods. **Vada**, to the south of Castiglioncello has numerous campsites near the beaches, which are less crowded than those of Castiglioncello.

On the north bank of the river Cecina, on the outskirts of **Cecina**, a small mod-ern industrial town, at San Pietro in Palazzi, is the early 18C **Villa La Cinquantina** (open Sat & Sun 10.00–19.00; Tues–Fri 15.00–19.00 (winter); 10.00–19.00 (summer), ☎ 0586 680 145). On display is an Etruscan and Roman collection comprising objects discovered in two ships wrecked off the nearby coast. A necropolis near Casale Marittimo has yielded interesting weapons, a helmet and shield, and objects in bronze dating from the 6C BC. There is also a local ethnographical museum here. Inland is the pretty little medieval village of **Casale Marittimo**. Just south of Cecina, at San Vincenzino, a Roman villa has been excavated and there are plans to create an archaeological park here with an antiquarium.

On the coast south of Cecina are the resorts of **Marina di Cecina**, **Marina di Bibbona** and **Forte di Bibbona**, and **Castagneto-Donoratico**.

At **San Guido** there is a splendid avenue of some 3000 cypresses, nearly 5km long, planted in 1801 by Camillo della Gherardesca, whose family had been feudal lords in this area since the early 13C (some of the diseased trees are being carefully replanted with adult plants). It leads up to the castle (restored) and little village of **Bolgheri**. Here the poet Giosuè Carducci spent his childhood (1838–49) and the cypress avenue is the subject of a famous poem by him. The white and rosé wines of Bolgheri are particularly good, and *Sassicaia* is considered the best Cabernet wine of Italy.

Just south of the road to Bolgheri is a turning for the wildlife sanctuary, **Rifugio faunistico padule di Bolgheri** (2100 hectares), administered by the *WWF* (open 15 Oct–15 Apr, Fri and 1st and 3rd Sat of the month, 09.00–12.00, 14.00–16.30; *bookings only*, ☎ 0565 777 125). The landscape, typical of the Maremma, includes umbrella pines, ilexes, cork trees, and dunes covered with vegetation known as the *macchia*. This was once a hunting reserve of the Della Gherardesca family, and the wild animals here include deer and wild boar. The marshland attracts a great variety of migratory birds.

A few kilometres further south, there is a turning inland for the medieval village of **Castagneto Carducci**, dominated by the Gherardesca castle. The little 17C oratory of the SS Crocifisso has a Pisan *Crucifix* above the high altar. The road winds uphill to Sassetta, another picturesque village. Nearby, the wooded slopes of **Poggio Neri** have been equipped for trekking, cycling and horseriding. Nearer the coast are the remains of the 10C castle of **Donoratico**.

San Vincenzo and Rocca San Silvestro

San Vincenzo is a well known large seaside resort extended to the south by the **Riva degli Etruschi**, a vast bungalow colony. Around San Vincenzo are six protected areas, of archaeological, historical and naturalistic interest, that have been grouped together to form the **Parchi della Val di Cornia**. They include Poggio Neri, San Silvestro and Montioni inland, and the coastal parks of Rimigliano, Populonia and Baratti and La Sterpaia. All have parking facilities (info. Piombino 57025, via G. Lerario 90, ☎ 0565 494 30; 🗐 0565 497 33, also for public transport). East of San Vincenzo is the **Parco archeologico-minerario di San Silvestro**. This area has been mined for almost three thousand years, and is one of the most important medieval mining sites in Europe.

• There are various itineraries for visiting the Rocca San Silvestro, the mining areas, the Temperino underground gallery (360m long) and the museum (open Sat and Sun 11 May–16 June, 09.00–19.00; 22 June–29 Sept, Tues–Sun 09.00–20.00; **guided tours only in certain areas**, ☎ 0565 494 30). **Car parks** (Madonna di Fucinaia and Il Temperino, off SP 20, about 6km from San Vincenzo on the road to Campiglia Marittima) and information office.

The **Rocca San Silvestro**, a medieval fortified village and castle in a striking position, now in ruins, was still inhabited well into the 15C by the miners who extracted silver, copper and lead for the mints of Lucca and Pisa. The park has been called an 'open-air archive' which documents mining in the Etruscan, medieval and Renaissance periods. The mines were closed down in the mid-15C when they ceased to be viable. An attempt on the part of Cosimo I to reactivate the mines and furnaces was soon abandoned and the last to exploit the mines were some English and French companies in the 19C.

Campiglia Marittima (231m) is an attractive little town, about 10km inland, spread over two hills with wide views. The medieval district round the **Rocca** preserves parts of its walls including several of its city gates. At the centre is the **Palazzo Pretorio** which displays numerous coats of arms of the 15C–16C governors, or *podestà*, on the façade. The surrounding streets and alleyways offer charming vistas. Outside the Porta Fiorentina gate is the cemetery and the **Pieve di San Giovanni**, a fine example of Pisan Romanesque architecture of the 11C–12C. It is built of beautifully cut stone and the doorways are decorated with geometrical and animal carvings. A boar hunt is represented in the architrave over the side door. The interior has a timber roof and a single apse with a stone vault. An **annual festival**, the *Maggio Campigliese*, with a procession and joust, is held in the town in May.

Due west of Campiglia is the coastal nature reserve of Rimigliano stretching along 4km of coast, with beautiful walks in ilex and pine woods.

Inland is the charming little town of **Suvereto**, one of the first medieval towns in the area to become a free commune. Much of the castle survives and the circle of walls, though restored, is almost intact. The Romanesque church of **San Giusto** dates from the 12C and has columns and figures of lions decorating the doorway. Many of the medieval buildings and winding streets are well preserved, as is the **Palazzo Comunale** with its 12C tower, loggia and staircase. The church of **Santa Maria** has a relief of *Christ blessing* over the doorway, attributed to Vittorio Ghiberti.

Continuing south over the hills (approximately 12km) you reach Montioni and the nearby **Parco di Montioni** which may be explored on mapped footpaths.

Populonia

The ancient Etruscan town of *Populonia* is situated high on the Massoncello promontory, originally an island, from which there is a magnificent view stretching from the Apuan Hills to Punt'Ala and the islands of Elba, Corsica and Capraia. It is reached from the little port of **Baratti**, on the south side of the Gulf of Baratti near a beautiful beach, backed by pine trees.

Populonia was one of the most important ports of ancient Etruria. Iron from Elba and perfumes, amulets and objects from Syria, Egypt, and Greece were traded here as early as the 8C BC in exchange for tin and copper mined in the nearby hills known as the *Colline Metallifere* (metalliferous hills). Its importance was also due to its furnaces for smelting metals. In 1974 the wreck of a Roman ship, 20m long, was discovered at a depth of 18 metres. It was carrying goods from the Middle East, and the finds are now exhibited in the new Archaeological Museum in Piombino.

The **necropolis** of Populonia and the archaeological sites document settlements in the area from the Iron Age to Roman times (information office and car park; open daily 09.00–dusk; guided tours also available, ☎ 0565 290 02). Excavations of the necropoli of **San Cerbone**, **Casone** and **Poggio della Porcareccia** were begun in 1919 and in certain areas are still taking place. There are several interesting large tumulus tombs dating from the 7C–5C BC as well as one in the form of an edicola. Remains found here of two iron chariots, and bronze figurines are now in the Archaeological Museum in Florence. Some tombs were discovered under enormous slag heaps.

Further uphill, on the south-eastern slope of **Poggio della Guardiola** is the extensive necropolis of **Le Grotte** (mid-4C–2C BC) with numerous underground tombs, two of which have simple painted decoration. There are two marked itineraries in the woods: an archaeological walk among the tombs and stone quarries, and a nature tour illustrating the different species of trees and plants. Off the main road, about half way up the hill to Populonia, is another necropolis known as **Bucche delle Fate** (3C–1C BC), reached from a footpath through the woods. The path terminates in a beautiful cove (Cala San Quirico) with rocks and a small beach. There are footpaths continuing along the south side of the promontory towards Salivoli, with a beach and car park, which may also be reached from Piombino.

Continuing up the road to Populonia there is a splendid view over the bay of Baratti. Enormous blocks of stone forming the outer walls of the Etruscan acropolis are visible. Today, Populonia is a typical medieval hill-top town, encircled by its walls and dominated by its castle. In the 5C it had its own coinage but with the Roman conquest and the siege of Sulla the town began to decline. In 546 it was sacked by Totila and given by Charlemagne to Pope Hadrian I c 780.

The **castle** (open 09.30–12.30, 14.30–dusk, except Mon), which has two impressive towers and ramparts, commands a magnificent view. Outside the circle of the medieval walls on the west side excavations, begun in 1980, have brought to light the foundations of a temple of the 2C BC. There are plans to create an Archaeological Museum near the site. The medieval town has three parallel streets. Near the castle is the little church of Santa Maria della Croce, remodelled in the 18C. There is a little private museum, **Museo Archeologico Gasparri** (open daily ☎ 0565 295 12). Objects in bronze and terracotta from the surrounding necropoli and a number of Attic, Apulian and Etruscan vases are exhibited here. Photographs record the most interesting finds, which are kept in Florence.

Piombino

On the other side of the Massoncello promontory is Piombino (39,600 inhabitants). It is an important seaport and one of the major steelworks in Italy. It is also the port for Elba (see p 529).

Piombino, the Roman port of *Falesia* was fortified by the Pisans in the 12C–13C. It came under the dominion of the Appiani family and was extensively rebuilt by the Florentine architect and sculptor Andrea Guardi. Parts of its city walls still survive including the towered gateway and oval fortification known as the **Rivellino** in the main piazza.

Corso Vittorio Emanuele II leads down to the 13C **Palazzo Comunale** (restored) and late-16C clock tower in the old town which is now a picturesque pedestrian zone with numerous restaurants. A road leads uphill to the left to the 14C church of **Sant'Antimo**, which has a Renaissance cloister. Inside tombs of the Appiani family, a baptismal font by Andrea Guardi (1470), and an altarpiece by Francesco Vanni.

Continuing uphill you reach a parapet beyond which is the **castle** built by Cosimo I, with a little museum illustrating the history of Piombino.

A short distance from Palazzo Comunale, towards the sea is **Piazza Bovio**, with Palazzo Appiani (the future Museo del Mare) and the aquarium at Via Mazzini 5. The road along the coast continues above the little **habour** with fishing boats and reaches an arched recess with a medieval fountain called the **Fonti dei Canali** composed of four zoomorphic heads attributed to Nicola Pisano and dated 1248. Uphill is Piazza Manzoni with the church of the **Misericordia** (restorations have brought to light fragments and inscriptions of the earlier medieval church) and a public garden overlooking the sea. Beyond, is the **citadel** where the Appiani established themselves in 1465. Although much transformed, the Renaissance chapel survives, with a charming façade by Andrea Guardi, and a stretch of walls and three round towers at the back, allegedly designed by Leonardo da Vinci. Here is the new **Museo Archeologico** (open Tues and Thur 09.00–13.00, Wed & Fri 15.00–19.00; weekends 10.00–13.00, 15.00–19.00) housing finds from the Populonia and Baratti area. Steps lead down to a small beach with a beautiful view.

The road from Piombino to Follonica passes (left) the *WWF* bird sanctuary of **Orti-Bottagone** and (right) turnings for **Perelli** and **Sterpaia** where there are pinewoods and extensive sandy beaches along the gulf of Follonica.

Grosseto and its northern province

Grosseto, although little visited by tourists, has fine ramparts, an interesting cathedral, and a museum with a good archaeological collection. The province covers a wide area of the Maremma known as the *Maremma Grossetana*. In the northern part are the important Etruscan sites of Roselle and Vetulonia, and a number of lovely little villages in beautiful countryside, including Montepescali and Roccatederighi, and the medieval town of Paganico.

On the coast there is the attractive resort of Castiglione della Pescaia, and other stretches of sea which are easily accessible from Grosseto include some very pretty bays with sandy beaches.

The Maremma Grossetana

The numerous rivers and streams in this area attracted settlements long before the Etruscans, who arrived in the 8C BC and founded the cities of Vetulonia, Populonia, Marsiliana and Roselle. Necropoli, traces of houses and remains of walls composed of huge blocks of stone dating from this time are a constant and evocative presence. Following the destruction of the Etruscan settlements and their colonisation by the Romans, the population declined, the consular roads fell into disrepair, and canals and land were neglected. The few inhabitants withdrew to the towns and villages in the hills. After the Lombard invasions in the 10C the area came under the dominion of the Aldobrandeschi family and other feudal lords, who erected strongholds in defence against attacks, mostly from Siena and Orvieto.

From the 13C onwards sieges, conflicts, pirate raids and malaria caused destruction and depopulation until the final capitulation to Sienese rule. When Siena in turn fell to the Medici of Florence in 1555, becoming part of the Grand Duchy of Tuscany, Cosimo I was obliged to cede parts of the Sienese territory to Spain and these were provided with impressive fortifications (these can still be seen at Orbetello and Porto Ercole). The poverty was such that many villages were all but totally abandoned.

Radical reforms did not begin until the 19C under grand-duke Leopoldo II, who improved living conditions by draining the marshes, promoting an agricultural programme and introducing a few industries. However, it was only in the 20C, after the First World War, with land development, the introduction of industries along the railway and the building of the acqueduct which supplied water from the Fiora river to the Argentario, that modernisation was achieved. Today, with the disappearance of malaria, the increased ownership of cars and the development of tourism, there has been a real transformation in the standard of living. This explains why so many of these villages survive almost intact and why the landscape preserves its wild and mysterious character.

Practical information

Getting there
By car

Grosseto is reached from Siena by a fast road (N223), or from Pisa and Livorno by the Via Aurelia (N1) down the coast. **Parking** in Grosseto outside the ramparts.

By train

Grosseto railway station (☎ 0564 223 31) is on the Pisa–Rome main line (services from Pisa in 1hr 30mins). **Follonica** also has a station on this line (slow trains only).

By bus

Buses from Grosseto run by *RAMA* (☎ 0564 252 15) from all places of importance in the province. **Buses** run by *TRA-IN* from Siena (Piazza San Domenico) via Paganico to Grosseto.

Information offices

Grosseto. *APT*, Viale Monterosa 206 (☎ 0564 462 611), with information office in Via Fucini (☎ 0564 414 303). *APT* information offices also at **Castiglione della Pescaia**, Piazza Garibaldi (☎ 0564 933 678) and Follonica, Via Roma (☎ 0566 520 12).

Where to stay
Hotels

GROSSETO ☆☆☆☆
Bastiani Grand Hotel Piazza Gioberti, 64 (☎ 0564 200 47; ▤ 0564 293 21). ☆☆☆ *Leon d'Oro*, Via San Martino 46 (☎ 0564 22 128; ▤ 0564 225 78) and *San Lorenzo*, Via Piave 22 (☎ 0564 279 18; ▤ 0564 253 38).
MARINA DI GROSSETO ☆☆☆
Lola Piccolo, Via XXIV Maggio 39 (☎ 0564 344 02; ▤ 0564 340 11).
CASTIGLIONE DELLA PESCAIA has numerous hotels of all categories, including ☆☆☆ *Miramare*, Via Vittorio Veneto 35 (☎ 0564 933 524; ▤ 0564 933 695), with restaurant, and ☆☆☆

Corallo, Via N. Sauro 1 (☎ 0564 933 668; ▤ 0564 936 268), both with restaurants.
PUNTA ALA ☆☆☆☆ *Hotel Alleluja*, Via del Porto (☎ 0564 922 050; ▤ 0564 920 734) and *Gallia Palace*, Via delle Sughere 70 (☎ 0564 922 022; ▤ 0564 920 229), both with restaurants. ☆☆☆ *Punta Ala*, Via del Pozzino 5 (☎ 0564 922 646; ▤ 0564 922 636).
TIRLI ☆☆ *Tana del Cinghiale*, Via del Deposito 10 (☎ 0564 945 810; ▤ 0566 343 56), with restaurant.
FOLLONICA has numerous ☆☆☆ and ☆☆ hotels on its popular sandy beach, including ☆☆☆ *Piccolo Mondo*, Lungomare Carducci 2 (☎ 0566 403 61) and ☆☆ *Miramare*, Viale Italia 84 (☎/▤ 0566 415 21) .
PAGANICO ☆☆ *La Pace*, Via della Madonnina 1 (☎ 0564 905 046; ▤ 0564 903 629).
BAGNI DI PETRIOLO ☆☆☆☆ *Grand Hotel Terme di Petriolo*, with sulphur pools (☎ 0564 908 871; ▤ 0564 908 712).
GAVORRANO *Finoria*, Via Monticello 66, ☎ 0566 846 248, is a nature park with a hotel, cabins to rent, and a campsite. It has a swimming pool and restaurant, and is often used for conferences.

Campsites

MARINA DI GROSSETO, CASTIGLIONE DELLA PESCAIA and LE ROCCHETTE Sites of all categories
FOLLONICA ☆ *Pineta del Golfo*, Via delle Collacchie 3 (☎ 0566 533 69; ▤ 0566 844 381).

Eating out
Restaurants

GROSSETO €€€ *La Buca di San Lorenzo*, Via Manetti 1.
MACCHIASCANDONA, near Badiola € *Macchiascandona*.

FOLLONICA €€ *Leonardo Cappelli (da Paolino)*, Piazza XXV Aprile.
PORTIGLIONE € *Vittorio*.
CASTIGLIONE DELLA PESCAIA € *Taverna Osteria nel Buco*, Via del Recinto 11.

TIRLI €€ *Tana del Cinghiale*.
VETULONIA € *Taverna Etrusca*.

Festivals
An **opera festival** is held every summer at Battignano.

Grosseto

Grosseto (72,000 inhab.) is capital of the province of the same name. It is the chief town of the Tuscan Maremma, a district ravaged by malaria throughout the Middle Ages. Reclamation work was begun by the Lorraine grand-dukes of Tuscany, and the marshes were gradually drained. A drainage scheme (*bonifica*) on a large scale was undertaken after 1930 and Grosseto is now the centre of a rich agricultural zone. The town suffered considerable damage in the Second World War.

PROVINCIA DI GROSSETO

History

Grosseto probably had Etruscan origins. In the 10C it was a castle ruled by the Aldobrandeschi and strategically situated where the Ombrone river was bridged. The seat of the Bishop of Roselle was transferred here in 1138 following a Saracen raid on Roselle. After a century of conflicts, Grosseto was subjected to Siena in the 14C, and eventually came under the dominion of the Medici in 1559. The town derived its wealth from its port on the Ombrone, and the nearby salt deposits.

The old town, which has a few medieval remains, is entirely enclosed in hexagonal brick **ramparts**, incorporating the 14C Sienese keep or *cassero*. These fortifications were built by the Medici in 1564–93, and also served as a defence against pirate attacks from the nearby coast. The Sienese keep, originally a tower and courtyard with a gateway, was later roofed over and transformed into the governor's headquarters. It is now used for exhibitions. Five of the bastions were laid out as public gardens by Leopoldo II in 1835.

The main road which enters Grosseto from the north passes the railway station on the right, and terminates at the circular Piazza Fratelli Rosselli. Here are the prefettura, with a classical colonnade, and the **Palazzo delle Poste** (1930), a fine example of Fascist architecture. From **Porta Nuova** Corso Carducci leads through the old town past the 11C façade of **San Pietro**, to Piazza Duomo, onto which face the **Palazzo Comunale** (1870) and the cathedral.

The **Duomo**, dedicated to St Lawrence, was founded, probably on the site of an earlier church, in 1294 (the date is recorded in the curious circular palindrome to the right of the main entrance). After Grosseto fell to Siena in 1336 Sienese craftsmen were employed here under the architect Sozzo di Rustichino, recorded in an inscription on a pilaster.

The sculpture on the **façade**, including the symbols of the Evangelists, and a number of the capitals and columns of the unusual arched gallery, date from the mid-14C and are by Giovanni di Agostino. The same sculptor was responsible for the first two windows and the carvings on the jambs of the doorway on the south side. The lunette and remaining decoration were added by Leopoldo Maccari in 1897. The exterior of the cathedral underwent modifications in the 16C and was completed in neo-Gothic style in the 19C, using the same Carrara marble.

The interior was also considerably remodelled: the transept, side chapels and vault in the 16C, the high altar and choirstalls in the 17C and an overall restoration was carried out in the mid-19C. The baptismal font and marble frame surrounding the *Madonna delle Grazie* by Matteo di Giovanni are by Antonio Ghini (1470) and the holy-water stoup is the work of a Sienese sculptor close to Antonio Federighi (1506). On the west wall is a lunette with Christ blessing attributed to Giovanni di Agostino and two 15C stained glass windows. The large altarpiece in the choir is attributed to Ventura Salimbeni.

To the right of the cathedral is **Piazza Dante**. It has a portico running along two of the sides and at the centre a monument to Leopoldo II by Luigi Magi (1846). **Palazzo della Provincia**, in neo-Gothic Sienese style, dates from the beginning of this century and probably stands on the site of the original Aldobrandeschi castle. Beyond is the Piazza del Mercato off which is Via Mazzini. At no. 61 is the **Museo di Storia Naturale** (open daily exc. Mon 09.30–12.30, 14.30– 19.30; fest. 09.30–12.30). It contains an interesting collection of mammals, birds and insects native to the region, as well as prehistoric remains and Neolithic finds, and a large collection of shells.

The town centre is small and easy to explore. Off Piazza Indipendenza is the late 13C church of **San Francesco**, which has a simple Gothic façade with a rose window and a modern lunette over the doorway. The interior has a single nave with a timber roof and rectangular apse. There are remains of 14C–15C frescoes, including a *Madonna*, *St Anthony Abbot* and a large *St Christopher*. The large painted *Crucifix* hanging above the high altar is attributed to Duccio, an early work strongly influenced by Cimabue. To the right of the choir is the chapel of St Anthony with a fresco cycle illustrating the saint's life and virtues, by Francesco and Antonio Nasini (1683). The sacristy has an *Annunciation* by Francesco Curradi. To the left of the church is the cloister (much restored) with 14C fresco fragments. The fine well in travertine was built by Ferdinando I dei Medici in 1590.

The Archaeological and Art Museum of the Maremma
In the contiguous Piazza Baccarini is the **Museo Archeologico e d'Arte della Maremma** and the **Museo d'Arte Sacra della Diocesi di Grosseto**, reopened in 1999 and beautifully arranged on three floors (open daily 09.00/10.00–13.00; weekends and in summer also 16.00/17.00–18.00/

20.00, closed Mon; ☎ 0564 458751). The fine archaeological collection, founded in 1860 by Canon Giovanni Chelli, has objects ranging from prehistoric to the Etruscan and Roman eras. The Chelli collection (**room 1**) comprises mostly objects from the districts of Chiusi and Volterra, including cinerary urns and early Etruscan pottery. **Rooms 2–12** document the history and excavations of Roselle, the Etruscan city situated on the east side of Lake Prile, from the archaic to the medieval period. Of particular interest are the monumental statues of Claudius and his family, dating from the time when Roselle became a Roman colony, and other statues of the Bassus family recently discovered in their private basilica. Excavations from the Grosseto district (**rooms 13–23**) are arranged systematically according to sites and are well labelled. The exhibits range from votive offerings to objects of daily use, with a good collection of Etruscan pottery and examples from Greece, and the cargo of a Roman ship discovered off the island of Giglio.

The section covering the diocese of Grosseto (**rooms 24–34**) comprises many paintings and liturgical objects removed from the cathedral. The final section (**rooms 35–40**) covers the medieval and later periods and the history of the city of Grosseto. There are several interesting early Sienese paintings including a *Last Judgement* by Guido da Siena, a *Madonna and Archangel Michael* by Segna di Bonaventura and works by Ugolino di Nerio and the Master of Ovile. There is a charming *Madonna of the Cherries* by Sassetta and other 15C paintings by Pietro di Domenico, Girolamo di Benvenuto and a *Madonna and Child* by Sano di Pietro. Among the later paintings is an altarpiece of the *Madonna in Glory* above a view of Grosseto by Alessandro Casolani of 1631. There are also sculpture fragments from the cathedral façade, sculptures and illuminated choirbooks.

Environs of Grosseto

Roselle

Northeast of Grosseto are the excavations of Roselle, reached by a well-signposted by-road. One of the most important Etruscan cities in northern Etruria, probably founded in the 7C BC on the southeastern side of Lake Prile (see below), it came under Roman dominion in 294 BC and most of its major buildings dated from the Imperial era. A bishopric was founded here in the Middle Ages. In 935 it was pillaged by the Saracens, and abandoned after 1138 when it became a quarry for the nearby villages.

The pretty drive up Poggio Moscona through a wood passes several tombs (car park at the top). A footpath to the right continues along a stretch of the impressive cyclopean walls (6C BC), reaching 5m in height, which formed a ring over 3km long around the Etruscan town. Open to the public daily (summer 07.30–19.30; winter 09.00–17.30) and leaflets are provided in English.

The footpath leading uphill overlooks the Roman road (formed of large flagstones) and the area comprising the Roman forum and basilica. Nearby are remains of a house with mosaic floors, a paved street, and drains. Towards the hill on the right, large statues of the Emperor Claudius and the Imperial family were discovered in a rectangular chamber; they are now in the museum of Grosseto. Beyond further excavations (still in progress) is the amphitheatre, 37m x 27m, with four entrances, in *opus reticulatum* of the 1C AD. On the adjacent hill traces of the earlier Etruscan settlement have been brought to light, together with remains of household objects, pottery, tiles and unbaked bricks. There is evidence from wells found here that the Etruscans used a system of collecting rain water similar to the Roman *impluvium*. The view over the plain (formerly Lago Prile) is particularly beautiful.

Near the modern village of Roselle were thermal baths known since Roman times and still in use until the early 20C.

On the other side of the main road to Siena is **Nomadelfia**, a Christian community, founded in 1947 by Don Zeno Saltini (d. 1981) for young people in need. On the hillside is the medieval village of **Battignano**. In the 1980s the remains of the nearby abbey were partially restored and transformed into a centre for opera by a group of English musicians. A festival is held here every summer.

East of Grosseto in the Ombrone valley is **Istia d'Ombrone**, a pretty village situated on a bend of the river. Parts of its walls survive, and an arched gateway leads to the interesting 14C church of **San Salvatore**. It has a simple brick façade in the Sienese style. The interior has a late medieval capital transformed into a holy-water stoup; a 14C fresco fragment of *St Anthony Abbot* worshipped by three women; the *Meeting at the Golden Gate* by Vincenzo Tamagni (1528); a charming *Madonna and Child*, by Giovanni di Paolo, and a statue of the *Madonna and Child* in polychrome wood by Domenico di Niccolò dei Cori, dating from the early 15C.

The coast near Grosseto

The nearest places to the provincial capital on the sea, both with extensive beaches, numerous hotels and camping sites are **Marina di Grosseto** and **Principina a Mare**, a resort in pine woods, which was extensively developed in the last decades of the 20C.

Along the coast to the north is an extensive wood of umbrella pines known as the Pineta del Tombolo off a beautiful sandy beach. Inland is a marshy area called **Le Marse**, privately owned but protected by the *WWF*, which may be visited on request (☎ 0564 26148). A short distance to the north is **Castiglione della Pescaia**, the most famous and attractive resort on the Maremma coast. It is very crowded in summer, but extremely pleasant in other seasons. Its small harbour, which was strategically important in Etruscan and Roman times, is now crowded with yachts and boats. It belonged to Pisa in the 12C and later came under the rule of Alfonso of Aragon, Siena, and Florence. The Medici grand-duke Ferdinando I rebuilt its walls in 1608 around the Aragonese fort on the hill overlooking the harbour.

The old town, restored in recent years, is entered through an arched gateway and a street leads up to the **castle** (private) from which there are extensive views along the coast and inland across the plain to the hills. A pretty street winds round inside the walls which are well preserved. The church of **San Giovanni Battista**, originally Romanesque but remodelled in the 16C, has a large belltower added in the 19C, which dominates the sky-line. There is a medieval relief on the architrave over the doorway and a carved stone font. The paintings are of the Baroque period. A silver reliquary containing relics of the local saint Guglielmo (see below) dates from 1668. In the cemetery is the tomb of the writer

Italo Calvino (1923–85) who lived at Roccamare from 1972 until his death.

Just outside Castiglione, beyond the Giorgini bridge, a road leads along the canal to the **Casa Rossa** (car park). This interesting building in brick and travertine, with three arched sluices, was designed in 1767 by Leonardo Ximenes, a Spanish Jesuit and an expert in hydraulics, for grand-duke Pietro Leopoldo of Lorraine. It was part of one of the earliest projects to reclaim the Grosseto plain and it served as a dam to control the waters between the Ombrone and Bruna rivers. The bridge was added in the 1830s. At the entrance is a map of walks in the surrounding marshland for the exploration of the beautiful natural setting and birdlife. The building houses a small museum which documents the local fauna and flora.

A road runs inland from Castiglione to Grosseto alongside the Bruna river, which marks the northern boundary of the former **Lago Prile**, the salt lake of Etruscan and Roman times which gave access to the harbours of Vetulonia and Roselle. At **Ponti di Badia** an unsurfaced road crosses the Bruna and leads to a hillock with remains of the **Badia al Fango**, a Benedictine monastery on the site of the Roman Villa Clodia, where Catullus' beloved Lesbia is said to have resided. Formerly a small island or peninsula, it served as the port of the Lake of Castiglione during the Medici period. It commands an extensive view over the plain of Grosseto (standing out across the marshes to the west is the Casa Rossa, described above). Further along the main road, beside an avenue of cypress and pine trees which leads to the estate of **La Badiola**, is a simple stone with a Cross erected in 1989 to commemorate Leopoldo II who used to stay here, and whose love and concern for the Maremma were fundamental in bringing this area back to life after it had suffered centuries of neglect.

Along the coast known as Riva del Sole, to the north of Castiglione, there are numerous beaches and resorts. Exclusive holiday villas at **Roccamare** are set among pine trees, with private beaches beyond low sand dunes.

On the point at the southern end of the gulf of Follonica, is **Punta Ala**, surrounded by thick pine woods. Formerly a natural beauty spot, with only a watch tower, in 1929 it became the property of Italo Balbo, the Fascist politician and pilot, and since the Second World War it has been transformed into a luxury holiday resort equipped with its own harbour, a golf course (18 holes) and other sports facilities.

To the north of Punta Ala a road runs inland along the Alma river and uphill to the village of **Tirli** (410m), first recorded in the 9C. The parish church (17C) has altars and stucco decoration by Andrea Ferrari of Lugano (1674). The high altar contains various relics of San Guglielmo (St William of Aquitaine) who died here in 1157 and who, together with St George, is traditionally venerated in the Maremma. At the north end of the village is a beautiful chestnut wood. On the opposite side is a path which leads to the ruins of the Guglielmite hermitage of **Malavalle**, which may also be reached from a country road on the outskirts of Castiglione. A procession is traditionally held at Tirli on Good Friday.

Follonica, 20km north of of Punta Ala, now an unattractive industrial town on the coast, has popular sandy beaches. From here there are good views of Elba and the promontory of Piombino.

Iron furnaces, supplied from the iron mines of Elba, have existed here since ancient times. Under the Medici the furnaces became a state monopoly for the production of arms and ammunition (cannon balls). The iron foundry created by Leopoldo II in 1834 was bombed in 1947 and abandoned in 1962: only the impressive iron entrance gate by Carlo Reishammer survives. The same architect also built the parish church of San Leopoldo, in an interesting combination of cast iron, stone, plaster, and wood. Across the piazza, past the car park, is the area of the former foundry which is now a public garden where various objects such as cast-iron columns, anchors and machinery are displayed. Some of the buildings have been restored and the main one houses the municipal library and a small museum relating to the foundry and its history as well as an Etruscan collection (open Wed & Fri afternoons, and Sat morning). The Pinacoteca Civica at no. 2 Piazza del Popolo overlooking the sea has a small collection of paintings and holds temporary exhibitions.

South of Follonica is the little harbour of **Portiglione**. A footpath just off the main road leads through beautiful evergreen vegetation, known as *macchia mediterranea* along the cliffs and down to the little bay of **Cala Martina**. It was from here that Garibaldi, following his defeat in Rome and subsequent flight across Italy, escaped by boat in 1849 (commemorated by a bronze bust on a column). A little further on is **Cala Violina**, a small bay famous for its clear water and sandy beach. Another road to these beaches is from a turning off the Collacchie SS 322 on the north side of Pian d'Alma towards the Torre della Civetta.

From Portiglione a road goes inland to **Scarlino** (229m), a particularly attractive hill-top town in a beautiful position overlooking the sea and the surrounding countryside. Parts of the 13C fortress, including an impressive round tower and some of the defence walls, are well preserved, as are many of the medieval streets and houses. The Palazzo Comunale (partially rebuilt) also dates from the 13C, the tower is a 17C addition. In the main square in the upper town is a marble monument to Garibaldi, represented half-length in a declamatory pose, with an inscription recording how five young men of Scarlino courageously helped the hero at the time of his escape.

The church of **San Donato** and its cloister, at the lower end of the town, date from the late Romanesque period but have been greatly altered over the centuries. In the chancel are carved choirstalls dating from 1713. There is also the fine tomb of Vanni and Emanuele Appiani, sons of Jacopo III Lord of Piombino, who died in 1471, by a Tuscan sculptor influenced by the great humanist tombs in Florence. A number of paintings and frescoes, some fragmentary, of various dates and varying in quality are also of interest.

Vetulonia and environs

The little hill-top town of Vetulonia (335m), northwest of Grosseto, is built on the site of the city of Vetulonia or Vetluna, one of the richest and most flourishing of Etruscan cities. The discovery of several necropoli has confirmed the documented description of Vetulonia as an important member of the Etruscan Confederation. Its identification was officially established in 1888 when the name was changed from Poggio Colonna. The earliest tombs date from the late 9C BC. The period of greatest prosperity was in the 8C–7C BC and the numerous tombs excavated at the end of the last century, some of them outstanding in size, were particularly rich in terracotta vases and objects in bronze, silver, and gold.

The Romans defeated the Gauls here in 224 BC, and are said to have borrowed from Vetulonia the insignia of their magistrates—the fasces, curule chair, and toga praetexta—and the use of the brazen trumpet in war.

Before entering Vetulonia, after the turning for the Via dei Sepolcri, are the ruins of a Romanesque abbey. Outside the town is an excavated area with interesting Roman remains of streets, houses and other buildings, drains and cisterns. The archaeological areas and the tombs are open daily, summer 08.00–19.30, winter 09.00–16.30; ☎ 0564 949 587).

The remains of the **citadel walls**, visible in various stretches, originally made a 5km circuit. At the top of the town is another stretch of walls probably dating from the 6C–5C BC and there are several medieval houses built out of older stones. The parish church, originally Romanesque, has an impressive bell-tower. There are several points around the town which offer splendid views.

Off the main street is the **Museo Archeologico**, named after Isidoro Falchi, a doctor and amateur archaeologist who excavated and identified Vetulonia. The museum, which opened in 2000, is well displayed (open daily 10.00–16.00; ☎ 0564 927 432). The collection comprises objects from the neighbouring necropoli and the Etruscan town, dating from the 9C–3C BC. Panels explain finds in detail and supplement with photographs those items which are still kept in the museums in Florence and Grosseto. The inscription Vetl (Vetluna) on some coins shows that the town enjoyed a short period of independence in the 3C BC.

The Via dei Sepolcri leads down to the domed **Tumulo della Pietrera** and the **Tumulo del Diavolino**, the most remarkable tombs in the necropolis, dating from 630–600 BC.

At the foot of the hill of Vetulonia, the road to the south passes another necropolis, and then branches right to the picturesque village of **Buriano** (239m), which is dominated by the massive ruins of its 10C Rocca. The church, built in 1302, has a fine tower. Inside is a 15C stained glass window representing the *Birth and Assumption of the Virgin*, a fresco fragment of an *Epiphany* dated 1524, and a wooden statue of *St Guglielmo*. A road encircles the whole village and there are beautiful views in all directions.

North of Vetulonia, across the Rigo valley, is **Caldana**, a village in a beautiful natural setting which preserves its medieval walls. The church of San Biagio (16C) has a travertine façade in the style of Antonio da Sangallo il Vecchio. The simple interior has arched bays, windows and cornices picked out in grey stone against the white plaster. The fresco of St Biagio (Blaise) and St Guglielmo is by Giuseppe Nicola Nasini and the 17C baptismal font is carved out of the locally quarried *portasanta* marble.

Nearby is **Ravi**, a fascinating little village, formerly a castle in a fine position on a slope of Monte Calvo. This mountain which rises to 469m can be explored on foot, and offers spectacular views stretching from Massa Marittima to Monte Amiata and the Argentario.

Gavorrano (273m) is another small fortified town in lovely surroundings. There was originally a double circle of elliptical walls with towers—now incorporated into the houses—and an arched gateway. The Palazzo Comunale was largely reconstructed in the 19C. Nearby is the parish church, of Romanesque origin but later enlarged and provided with a façade in 1927. It preserves an exquisite statue of the *Madonna del Carmine* by Giovanni di Agostino (c 1336).

Beyond the modern Aurelia (5km and then a turning to the right) are the ruins of **Castel di Pietra** (172m) where Pia de' Tolomei was allegedly murdered by her husband, Nello de'Pannocchieschi (Dante, *Divina Commedia*, 'Purgatorio' V, 130–136). Dante's story became a favourite theme with poets, playwrights and artists in the Romantic period and was also used by Donizetti in his opera *Pia de'Tolomei* of 1837. Situated on private property, it may be reached via a footpath by previous request at the nearby *Azienda agricola di Castel di Pietra*.

Roccastrada and environs

Roccastrada (475m), originally a small walled town built round its castle, has expanded considerably in recent years thanks to various industries. The old medieval district has picturesque streets, many of which are joined by steps and archways. The old castle, built onto a spur of rock and the two churches preserve very little of their original character and are much restored.

The road from Roccastrada to the Aurelia by-passes the village of **Sticciano**, nestling on the top of a hill behind which rises Monte Leoni (614m). A pretty road leads up to the former medieval castle, which was demolished when it was taken by Siena in the 14C. The Romanesque church is well preserved and has an altarpiece of the *Madonna del Rosario* by a local painter, Giovan Giuseppe Mattei, dated 1700. There are beautiful views across the plain towards the hills round Vetulonia and the sea. The nearby woods have good footpaths.

Farther south is **Montepescali** perched high up above the plain which, in Etruscan times, was filled with the salt Lake Prile. It is a small medieval town surrounded by olive groves. The old walls survive in part and there are terraces with panoramic views towards the sea and towards Monte Leoni.

The small 14C church of **San Lorenzo**, at the entrance to the town, has a fresco of the *Assumption* by the school of Bartolo di Fredi on the left wall. Picturesque streets lead up to the castle tower, with a large clock, and the pretty stone façade of the Romanesque church of San Niccolò. Inside are numerous fragmentary frescoes and four charming scenes of the *Life of the Virgin* dated 1389, by a close follower of Bartolo di Fredi. *The Madonna and Child enthroned with Saints and Angels* by Matteo di Giovanni was originally in San Lorenzo. Over the high altar is a fine 14C painted *Crucifix* of the Sienese school.

To the northwest of Roccastrada is the village of Sassofortino from which a

Roccatederighi

road leads into the woods of **Monte Sassoforte** (787m). A footpath, signposted to the Castello, crosses a wild wood with enormous rocks and age-old trees. There is a splendid view from the impressive castle ruins at the summit. **Roccatederighi** (520m) is a picturesque town situated on a rocky spur of Monte Sassoforte. The castle was extensively rebuilt at the beginning of this century. The parish church of **San Martino** was given a new façade in the late 15C and was modified inside over the centuries. It contains a little *Madonna with St Augustine* by a Sienese artist and a finely carved reliquary, both dating from the 17C. The streets and houses still preserve their medieval character and offer picturesque views.

To the south is the impressive castle of **Montemassi**. The village, with its towering ruins, dominates a cone-shaped hill surrounded by olive groves. The castle, a stronghold of the Aldobrandeschi, fell to Guidoriccio da Fogliano commander of the Sienese troops in 1328, a victory celebrated by Simone Martini in his famous fresco in the Palazzo Pubblico in Siena (see p 361). There is a particularly fine view from the castle ruins. The church of **Sant'Andrea Apostolo** contains a few paintings, including a fragmentary *Madonna* close in style to Matteo di Giovanni and various furnishings and liturgical objects. The little church of **Santa Maria delle Grazie** is surrounded on three sides by a portico; inside is a 19C copy of a Madonna by Matteo di Giovanni. The medieval village and parts of the walls are still partially preserved.

The road leading north from Roccastrada winds through woods of oaks and chestnut trees passing beneath the fortified village of **Torniella** (441m), from which there are fine views. Steps lead past the church of San Giovanni Battista to the castle overlooking a small piazza.

Just north of Torniella is a footpath (approx. 10km) along the Farma Valley which leads to Bagni di Petriolo (see below).

Paganico and environs

Paganico is the principal town on the fast, busy road between Grosseto and Siena. Although called a superstrada the road is not dual-carriageway. It passes through beautiful and varied scenery, perhaps at its most lovely in spring when the yellow broom is in flower. The little medieval town of **Paganico**, on a loop of the river Ombrone, was in a strategic position for defending Siena from the south. Its walls and gates which survive almost intact were built in the mid-14C by Lando di Pietro, the architect of Siena cathedral.

The church of **San Michele**, in the piazza, dates from the same period. On the right wall of the nave is a giant figure of *St Christopher*. On the left, is an altarpiece of the *Madonna and Child with Saints* by Andrea di Niccolò (c 1480). The *Madonna and Child enthroned worshipped by Saints* over the high altar is by Guidoccio Cozzarelli, and there is also a very expressive *Crucifix* of the late 15C.

The **frescoes** in the choir are a masterpiece of 14C Sienese painting. When they were restored, the name of the artist, Biagio di Goro Ghezzi and the date (1368) were discovered. On the soffit of the arch are half-length figures of *Saints* and in the vault, the *Evangelists*. On the end wall, around the window, is the *Annunciation*. The artist has made use of the window jambs to make the perspective of his composition more convincing (note the presence of the Infant Jesus and the Dove on the left). On the north wall is the *Nativity*, with angel choirs, and other charming details. Below are three scenes from the *Legend of*

St Michael. On the opposite wall is the *Epiphany* above a scene with *St Michael dividing the Damned from the Blessed*, who are received by the Queen of Heaven.

North of Paganico, the main road passes close to **Civitella Marittima** (329m). On the other side of the main road an unsurfaced road winds down to a cypress avenue and the Romanesque abbey church of **San Lorenzo al Lanzo**, in a particularly beautiful position in the Lanzo valley. The only authentic part of the church is the façade. The doorway is flanked by two half-columns supporting capitals with strange animal heads, similar in style to those of Sant'Antimo (see p 429). The interior is heavily restored and the former monastic buildings are now private.

The road runs along a viaduct high above the Farma valley. A by-road branches off towards the hill-top village of **Pari** again in a beautiful position. Far below the main road is **Bagni di Petriolo**, a rare example of a medieval fortified spa. A little loggia on the edge of the river, a chapel and parts of the peripheral 15C walls still survive from the time when Pope Pius II came here to benefit from the sulphurous water springs. The modern baths are open in summer on weekdays (06.30–13.30, 15.30–20.00).

To the south of Paganico, on the other side of the Ombrone, is **Sasso di Ombrone**. A very pretty road climbs up to the picturesque village which is beautifully situated overlooking the valley. The church of San Michele, dating from the early 20C, has a fine early 15C polychrome wooden *Crucifix* by a Sienese sculptor.

Further south is **Campagnatico** (275m), a pretty village on a ridge with remains of its old castle. At the entrance to the village on the left is the church of the Misericordia (closed for restoration). The main street leads to a small piazza onto which faces the former church of Sant'Antonio, now transformed into a public hall and containing some 14C and 15C frescoes. Further up is the Romanesque church of **San Giovanni Battista**. It has an elegant façade with a perforated rose window. The bell-tower is built onto the earlier fortifications. The interior has a single nave and three apses with some frescoes. Other frescoes representing the *Life of the Virgin* (temporarily exhibited here from the Misericordia) are signed and dated 1393 by Meo di Piero and Cristoforo di Bindoccio.

In the 19C, horse breeding was encouraged here and several elegant houses have stables decorated with horses' heads. A *palio* or donkey race is held every summer. There is a particularly pretty road from Campagnatico via Istia d'Ombrone to Grosseto which runs through beautiful countryside.

Opposite Campagnatico, on the other side of the superstrada, is the hill-top village of **Montorsaio** (384m), on the edge of thick woods. The parish church has a copy of a *Madonna* by Sano di Pietro (now exhibited in the museum of Grosseto) and a late Renaissance sacristy cupboard. In the nearby confraternity chapel of Santa Croce is a fine *Crucifix* (1629). From Montorsaio a footpath leads (in 1 hr, or 1hr 30min.) to the summit of **Monte Leoni** (614m), passing remains of the convent of San Bernardino (suppressed in 1751), with panoramic views. Roselle, further south on the outskirts of Grosseto, is described above.

Massa Marittima

Massa Marittima is an ancient mining town in beautiful countryside. Mining has taken place in the surrounding metalliferous hills (rich in iron, copper, and lead ores) since Etruscan times. It was a flourishing industry in the Middle Ages (when the earliest known Mining Code was drawn up here), and again in the last century. The town's period of greatest glory was from 1225 to 1335 when it was an independent Republic: its splendid Duomo, with its remarkable sculptural works, dates from this time. Massa Marittima remains one of the most fascinating and enchanting towns in southern Tuscany.

Practical information

Getting there
By car
Massa Marittima is about 12km north of the Via Aurelia (N1), north of Grosseto. It can also be reached by a pretty secondary road from Siena (N73 and N441) via San Galgano, or by another lovely road from Volterra (N439). **Parking**. Outside the old town.

By train
The nearest railway station is at Follonica, 17km southwest on the main line from Pisa to Grosseto.

By bus
Buses run by *Autolinee Società Ferrovia Massa-Follonica* (☎ 0566 902 016) from Follonica. Services also from Grosseto (*RAMA*), and Volterra.

Information office
Via Ximenes 14 (☎ 0566 901 255).

Where to stay
Hotels
☆☆☆ *Il Sole*, Corso della Libertà 43 (☎ 0566 901 971; 📠 0566 901 959).
☆☆ *Duca del Mare*, with restaurant, Piazza Dante Alighieri (☎ 0566 902 284; 📠 0566 901 905).

Eating out
Restaurants
Taverna del Vecchio Borgo, Via Parenti 12. *Osteria Da Tronco*, Vicolo Porte 5

Bar
Le Logge, Piazza Garibaldi (specialising in *panforte*).

Festivals
Il Girifalco, a cross-bow contest between the districts (or *Terzieri*) of the town, in traditional costume, takes place twice a year on the **Feast of St Bernardine** (20 May or the following Sunday), and on the second Sunday in August.

History

Massa Marittima flourished as an independent republic from 1225–1335, before falling under Sienese rule. From 1317 it minted its own silver coin, the *grosso*, which bore the figure of St Cerbone. The famous Mining Code drawn up at this time is one of the most important legislative documents to have survived from the Middle Ages in Italy. **St Bernardine of Siena** (1380–1444) was born in Massa, and it was here that he preached his last

Lenten Sermons. His family, the Albizzeschi, were nobles. He became a Franciscan friar and was famous as a preacher throughout northern and central Italy. Many of his sermons and writings have survived. He had a particular devotion to the Name of Jesus and he is represented as an old, ascetic friar holding a tablet with rays surrounding the letters IHS and a cross.

The town is divided into two distinct parts, the **Città Vecchia** around the cathedral, and the **Città Nuova** on a hill above. Both districts were enclosed in the 13C circuit of walls, the extent of which reflects the prosperity of the medieval town prior to Sienese dominion in 1335. The Città Nuova and the Città Vecchia were then divided by the Sienese who erected an immense fortified wall which incorporated Porta alle Silici.

The Città Vecchia

You can enter the Città Vecchia either through the 13C Porta Salnitro, from which a road leads steeply up along the side of the Duomo, or from Porta dell'Abbondanza (or delle Formiche), behind the Duomo. The main square, **Piazza Garibaldi** (usually called Piazza del Duomo), is triangular in shape and presents beautiful and varied views in every direction.

The Duomo

The Duomo was begun in the early 13C and is magnificently positioned at a strange angle above an irregular flight of steps with the north side creating a monumental perspective, counterbalanced by the bishop's palace, and the towering campanile at the centre. Dedicated to St Cerbone, whose relics were transferred to Massa from Populonia in the 9C, the cathedral has a splendid Romanesque **exterior** in travertine with blind arcading. The upper part of the façade, with exquisitely carved arches and capitals, symbols of the Evangelists, and a kneeling telamon, was added in the Pisan Gothic style in 1287–1314. Bas-reliefs sculpted above the main doorway in a single marble block, probably by a 12C Pisan sculptor, illustrate stories from the life of St Cerbone (see below): the saint is miraculously saved from shipwreck; he is thrown into the bears' den; he performs a miracle with two deer; he presents the Pope with a flock of geese; and he celebrates Mass in the presence of the Pope.

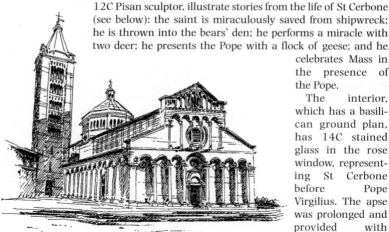

The Duomo of Massa Marittima

The interior, which has a basilican ground plan, has 14C stained glass in the rose window, representing St Cerbone before Pope Virgilius. The apse was prolonged and provided with slender Gothic windows in the late

13C and the octagonal dome was added in the 15C. The nave and aisles are divided by travertine columns with magnificent capitals. The nave vault dates from 1626.

To the right of the entrance is a series of reliefs, thought to be pre-Romanesque, representing **Christ with angels**, the **Apostles**, and the **Massacre of the Innocents**. The splendid rectangular font, carved in a single square block of travertine resting on three lions and a lioness, with reliefs of the **Life of the Baptist and Christ Blessing**, is by Giroldo da Como (1267). The 15C tabernacle which rises from its centre, with carved figures of prophets in niches and crowned by a marble statue of the Baptist is dated 1447 but the sculptor is not known. The paintings in the south aisle include the **Virgin in glory with Saints** by Giuseppe Nicola Nasini and the **Birth of the Virgin** by Rutilio Manetti. Beyond is a side chapel with a 14C Sienese fresco of **Saints Lucy, Margaret and Agatha**, and some illuminated choirbooks in a showcase. The Chapel of the Crucifix has a painted **Crucifix**, attributed to Segna di Bonaventura, and an **Immaculate Conception** by Rutilio Manetti.

The high altar, designed as a triumphal arch, is by Flaminio di Girolamo del Turco (1623) and its polychrome wooden **Crucifix**, is now recognised as an autograph work by Giovanni Pisano.

Behind the high altar is the **Arca di San Cerbone**, a marble urn signed and dated 1324 by Goro di Gregorio, a masterpiece of Sienese Gothic sculpture. The sculptor reveals great gifts as a storyteller and his reliefs are full of charming details, spontaneity and poetry.

St Cerbone

The story of St Cerbone, who was probably born in Africa in 493, is illustrated in the scenes on the Arca di San Cerbone: he escapes from vandals to the Maremma, where he leads a hermit's life; he is condemned by Totila to be devoured by bears for giving shelter to enemy soldiers, but instead the bears only lick his feet; after becoming Bishop of Populonia, his parishioners object to his saying Mass before dawn and, since he will not change his ways, denounce him to Pope Virgilius; the Pope sends a delegation summoning the bishop to Rome; the envoys refuse Communion from Cerbone and are overcome by thirst; in answer to the saint's prayers two female deer allow themselves to be milked; three sick men he meets on the way to Rome are miraculously cured; at the gates of Rome, Cerbone summons a flock of geese to accompany him, as a gift for the Pope; he is received by Virgilius whom he invites to assist at Mass before dawn; at the service the Gloria is sung by angels which is the reason why he insisted on saying Mass so early, a fact that his humility prevented him from divulging.

Along the walls of the choir are eleven small marble statues of the Apostles by the Sienese sculptor Gano di Fazio (early 14C).

In the chapel to the left of the high altar is the **Madonna delle Grazie**, a majestic icon of the **Madonna and Child** (1316), by a close follower of Duccio and probably executed in his workshop, but which has been attributed also to the young Simone Martini. The panel, which has been cut down, also has the Crucifixion and Passion scenes painted on the back by the same hand. Fragments of a *Presentation in the Temple* by Sano di Pietro, which was sawn into pieces and stolen in 1922, are on the adjacent wall.

Steps lead down to the **undercroft** in which are displayed a silver-gilt reliquary *Cross* decorated with enamels by Andrea Pisano, a reliquary of two thorns of Christ's crown in crystal, silver and enamels by Goro di Ser Neroccio, and two wooden angels attributed to Vecchietta. The fresco of the *Crucifixion* in a lunette is by a 15C Sienese artist.

In the **north aisle** of the church are an *Annunciation* by Raffaello Vanni (1643); a fragmentary fresco of the *Adoration of the Magi* by Biagio di Goro and some 14C frescoes. Beside the entrance is a 14C frescoed triptych above a 3C Roman sarcophagus relief.

The tall bell-tower is probably contemporary with the church, but the upper part is restored. Beside it is Palazzo Vescovile, the Bishop's Palace.

Palazzo del Podestà ~ the Archaeological Museum

Opposite the cathedral to the left of the piazza is the 13C **Palazzo del Podestà**, with steps leading up to the entrance. Its austere façade in travertine has four double windows on two levels and numerous coats of arms recording the governors of the town from 1426 to 1633. The palace houses the **Museo Archeologico** and the **Pinacoteca** (open 10.00–12.30, 15.30–19.00, in winter 15.00–17.00; closed Mon). The collection documents the various settlements in the district from prehistoric times to the Roman era and has a particularly rich Etruscan section.

The Pinacoteca comprises a small collection of paintings from the 14C to the 17C. The most important painting is the famous *Maestà* by Ambrogio Lorenzetti of c 1330, showing the *Madonna and Child enthroned surrounded by saints, angels, and the theological virtues*. Other fine works include a small *Madonna* by Sano di Pietro, and the *Angel Gabriel* by Sassetta (the companion panel with the *Virgin* is in New Haven, USA).

Much of the interesting archaeological material was excavated in the vicinity of Massa Marittima. The earliest dates from the Paleolithic age. Of particular interest are the unusual funerary stele carved in stylised human form, reminiscent of those of Luni (see p 244), dating from the 3rd millenium BC. There is pottery from the early Bronze Age. The **Etruscan section** documents the excavations in recent years of the necropoli and settlements near Lake Accesa which have brought to light objects ranging from the 9C–6C BC. There is a fine collection of ceramics, including imported Hellenistic works. The 19C Galli collection comprises interesting Etruscan pieces from Tarquinia and Vulci.

To the right of Palazzo del Podestà is the small 13C palace of the Conti di Biserno (the first-floor windows were added in the 16C), beside Palazzo Comunale with two robust crenellated towers (extensively restored). From the corner of Palazzo Vescovile, Via Ximenes leads to **Palazzo dell'Abbondanza**, a former granary built above a 13C public fountain in an arched loggia with remains of frescoes. From Piazzale Mazzini there is a fine view of the cathedral apse and tower.

In Via Corridoni, a short distance away, is the **Museo della Miniera** (guided visits every half hour, 10.15–12.00, 15.30–17.00; closed Mon). Situated in an abandoned mine, it demonstrates mining techniques and exhibits equipment, machinery and mineral specimens.

The Città Nuova

From Porta dell'Abbondanza two streets lead uphill to Piazza Matteotti in the Città Nuova. Here parallel intersecting streets create a quite different plan to the lower town. **Porta alle Silici**, part of the vast and impressive fortifications erected by the Sienese after their conquest of Massa in 1335, is connected to the older **Torre del Candeliere** by an immense flying arch. The clock tower, which was reduced to two-thirds of its original height by the Sienese, may be climbed (open 11.00–12.30, 17.00–19.00; closed Mon; open in winter only on request). The Sienese **fortress** (on the site of the former Bishop's Palace) was partly destroyed in the 18C–19C to make room for the hospital. From the adjoining parapet there is a splendid view over the roofs of Massa and the surrounding countryside.

Downhill from Piazza Matteotti is the **Porta San Francesco**, near the 13C Franciscan church, which was reduced in length after a landslide. On the north side of the Piazza is Palazzo delle Armi, with an arched portico, where ammunition was stored. It now contains the **Museo di Storia e Arte delle Miniere** (closed for restoration). The museum documents excavations in the district, with reliefs, diagrams and photographs illustrating the development of mining from Etruscan to modern times. The **Mining Code** document of 1310 is also kept here. On the upper floor are a selection of minerals, instruments, and tools, and a cast of an ape skeleton (*Oreopithecus Bambolii*), discovered in a lignite mine.

Sant' Agostino

Corso Diaz leads to the church of Sant'Agostino, founded in 1299. The simple **façade** has an oculus above an elegant doorway. The polygonal apse, pierced by arched Gothic windows (with modern glass), was designed by Domenico di Agostino (1348), who completed the cathedral of Siena.

The interior has a single nave, divided into bays by grandiose pointed arches. The paintings include: *St Guglielmo* attributed to Antonio Nasini; *Flight into Egypt* by Lorenzo Lippi; *Madonna and Saints* by Rutilio Manetti; *Annunciation* by Jacopo da Empoli. The tomb of the Augustinian theologian Michele Bellucci (d. 1479) is by Urbano da Cortona. In the **St Lucy Chapel**, right of the choir, is a reclining effigy of *St Lucy* (the 15C original is in the Musée des Arts Decoratifs in Paris) and frescoes, one of them representing the presentation of the Mining Code of Massa, attributed to Vincenzo Tamagni. In the **choir** is a *Nativity* by Bartolomeo Ponti (1627) and frescoed angels on the left wall flanking a 15C marble tabernacle.

The *Adoration of the Shepherds with Saints Bernardine and Anthony of Padua*, behind the high altar, is by Pietro di Francesco Orioli (c 1480). In the chapel on the left is a painted terracotta *Madonna and Child* by Zaccaria Zacchi. The *Visitation* is by Rutilio Manetti (1639). The **sacristy** has showcases with liturgical objects and choirbooks. A door opens from the church into the elegant cloister. The tall slender bell-tower which rises behind was built onto one of the towers of the city walls in 1627.

Next to Sant'Agostino is the façade of the former church of **San Pietro all'Orto**, now the premises of the Terziere della Città Nuova, which houses the paraphernalia for the annual Girifalco contest (see above). The rooms also contain a small collection of pottery and coins found locally, and some 14C frescoes recently discovered under whitewash. The beautiful stepped Via Moncini returns downhill from Porta alle Silici to the cathedral.

Environs of Massa Marittima

South of the town is the **Lago dell'Accesa**, a small lake (580m long, 400m wide), set in a beautiful, tranquil landscape. It is next to the source of the river Bruna. Nothing remains of the Medici and Lorena iron foundry (another one was in the nearby village of **Valpiana**), but there is evidence that the fusion of metals here dates back to Etruscan times. The area around the lake, which has been excavated over the past 20 years, has recently been opened to the public as an archaeological park. It is the earliest known settlement with necropoli dating from the Archaic period (late 7C–mid 6C BC), and the finds are exhibited in the Archaeological Museum of Massa Marittima.

A road leads north of Massa Marittima towards the metalliferous hills (see p 292). It winds up through oak and chestnut woods onto a high ridge above the Pavone valley through very wild countryside. **Monterotondo Marittimo** is built on a hill in a natural ravine. It preserves part of its 13C castle, a crenellated tower (restored) of the Palazzo Comunale and picturesque medieval streets and alleyways. A *Madonna and Child* by the so-called Master of Monterotondo, an artist close to Duccio, has been removed from the parish church of San Lorenzo to the Pinacoteca in Siena. This was the birthplace of the writer Renato Fucini (1843–1921) who wrote stories set in the Maremma, charmingly told but mostly very sad. The hills around are covered with thick chestnut woods and there is a splendid view towards the sea.

To the west are the **Terme di Bagnolo** (550m) a spa, with hot springs (43°C). Towards the sea, on the road for Piombino, is the village of **Frassine** which has ruins dating from the Lombard (early medieval) period. It has a Sanctuary of the Madonna (restored) containing a carved wood *Madonna and Child* of the 14C Pisan school, and an interesting collection of painted ex-votos (16C–19C).

Suvereto, and the coastal area beyond are described on p 307.

East of Monterotondo, in the heart of the metalliferous hills, is the little town of **Montieri** (704m), important for its silver mines. In the medieval village, which is well preserved, is the church of **Santi Paolo e Michele** and an impressive Romanesque bell-tower. It has a number of 16C–17C paintings and an 18C terracotta *Via Crucis*. Above the high altar are the remains of Beato Giacomo Papocchi of Montieri, a 13C hermit whose saintly life is illustrated in the surrounding paintings. Opposite the church is a medieval tower-house and other interesting buildings. A short rise leads up to the 13C **castle** beyond which is the church of **San Giacomo** and the cell inhabited by Beato Giacomo. Off Via Roma is the church of **San Francesco** which has 17C paintings and furnishings.

There are plans to map itineraries for walking tours in the neighbourhood, which is rich in areas of archaeological and mining interest, in beautiful natural surroundings.

South of Montieri is a turning for **Boccheggiano** (664m), reached by a winding road through woods. It was important for its pyrite mines. Although the village has been completely changed over the centuries, it has a certain charm and is beautifully situated. In the church of **San Sebastiano** is a marble statue of the saint by Bartolomeo Cennini of 1650, a gift of the 17C antiquarian, Leonardo Agostini, who was born here.

The Parco Naturale della Maremma

The Parco Naturale della Maremma, a coastal area of some 70 sq. km just south of Grosseto, was designated a national park in 1975. It extends from Alberese south across the beautiful wooded and roadless *Monti dell'Uccellina* (417m) to Talamone. The fifteen kilometres of coastline here are perhaps the best preserved in Italy.

Practical information

Getting there
By car

At the **northern entrance** of the park cars have to be left at Alberese, where a bus takes visitors to the entrance. The **southern entrance** to the park (car park) is on the Talamone road from Fonteblanda. The coast can be explored along the beach from the car park at Marina di Alberese.
By bus

There is a *RAMA* bus service from Grosseto to Alberese (☎ 0564 252 15).

Park information office
Alberese (☎ 0564 407 098). *Tourist information, APT* Grosseto (☎ 0564 414 303).

Where to stay
Hotels
TALAMONE ☆☆☆☆ *Talamonio*, Via Garibaldi 4 (☎ 0564 887 008; 🖷 0564 887 380). ☆☆☆ *Capo d'Uomo*, Via Cala di Forno 7

(☎ 0564 887 077; 🖷 0564 887 298).
Agriturismo accommodation

ALBERESE There are no hotels here, but some 26 farms offer generally excellent Agriturist accommodation (all listed in the Grosseto *APT* hotel list): information about these can also be had by enquiring locally.
Campsite

TALAMONE ☆☆ *Talamone International Camping* (☎ 0564 887 026, 🖷 0564 887 170).

Eating out
Restaurants
ALBERESE €€ *Da Remo*, at Rispescia (Via Stazione 5) TALAMONE €€ *La Buca di Nonno Ghigo*, Piazza Garibaldi 1 and *Da Flavia*, Piazza IV Novembre.

Special events
Rodeo at Alberese in August when cattle and horses are herded into the village.

North of Alberese a road leads to the coast, past farms where the Maremma white long-horned cattle are grazed and then through pine woods to **Marina di Alberese**; a beach with a car park. This unspoilt stretch of coast (although suffering from erosion) with sand dunes, and backed by thick pinewoods planted in the mid-19C, begins at the estuary of the Ombrone river (the Classical *Umbro*, one of the chief rivers of Etruria). This marks the northern limit of the park. On the right bank of the river is the remarkably well preserved **Palude della Trappola**, a marsh area and bird sanctuary. The beach extends south as far as **Cala di Forno**, at the foot of the Monti dell'Uccellina, where there are natural grottoes. Farther on, the rocky slopes of the Uccellina plunge straight into the sea: here the beautiful coastline and distinctive vegetation, which includes dwarf palm trees, can only be seen from the sea.

Alberese

Alberese is a small pleasant village built on a spacious plan in 1951 near the northern entrance to the park. **Tickets** must be purchased here at the information office in order to visit the park. A bus leaves on the hour every hour (09.00–dusk) on Wed, Sat, and Sun (numbers are limited during the summer months) for the entrance to the park (10mins) from which various itineraries are indicated along marked footpaths (most of them require a minimum of three hours; children are welcome).

The vegetation in the park varies from woods of pine trees, ilexes, elms, and oaks to marshlands, and the typical Mediterranean *macchia* of myrtle and juniper bushes. Animals which run wild here include the famous white long-horned cattle, deer, foxes, goats, wild cats, horses, and wild boar. The cattle and horses are herded by cowboys known as *butteri* (rodeo at Alberese in August). Migratory birds and numerous aquatic species abound.

Behind the church is the entrance (pedestrians only; open daily) to the *Itinerario Faunistico*, a beautiful walk of less than an hour through a protected area, where deer and other wild animals can usually be seen.

The **Monti dell'Uccellina** offer splendid views and walks through a natural setting of great variety and beauty, with a few towers and romantic ruins. The **Torre della Bella Marsilia** is the lonely remnant of the castle of Collecchio, home of the Marsili family of Siena. In 1543 the castle was destroyed by the corsair Barbarossa and the entire household murdered except for the lovely Margherita, who was carried off to the harem of the Sultan Suleiman the Magnificent, soon to become his legitimate sultana and the mother of Selim II.

Nearby are the ruins of **San Rabano**, an 11C Benedictine abbey later occupied by the Knights of St John of Jerusalem. The apse of the Romanesque church survives in part with some of its original decoration. The octagonal dome was probably a 14C addition and the tall tower is still standing. There are also remains of the walls built around the monastery.

The towers of **Castelmarino** and **Collelungo** are near some natural caves and rocks, facing onto the beach. The walk to **Cala di Forno** and its tower, at the far end of the beach, ends in a charming little bay.

The Via Aurelia skirts the park as far as **Fonteblanda** where a road leads towards Talamone, at the southern boundary of the park. The road passes olive groves and the cemetery, on the right. A short way beyond, an unsurfaced road to the right (500m; signposted Parco Naturale della Maremma) leads past the site of a Roman villa and baths, to the south entrance to the park.

Cars may be parked outside an enclosure with a stile. No ticket is required but visitors must leave the park before dusk.

There are two footpaths (the longer walk takes approximately 2–2.5 hrs) which lead through the thick *macchia* vegetation and woods and emerge on the coast overlooking the sea. These walks are especially beautiful towards sunset.

Talamone

The approach to Talamone, a summer resort, is particularly striking with the castle silhouetted against the sky. The original Etruscan city and port, said to have been founded by the Argonaut Telamon c 1300 BC stood on the south side of the bay, but was abandoned for its present position by the Romans in the Imperial era. The medieval town developed on the rocky promontory overlooking the bay and in the 14C Talamone became the port for Siena. Here also Garibaldi and the Thousand put in on their way to Sicily in 1860 to collect arms and ammunition and to land a party for a feigned attack on the Papal States.

The picturesque harbour with yachts and fishing boats at their moorings, lies at the foot of the steep village. Although damaged in the Second World War, Talamone retains its charm and the walk up along the walls to the Rocca offers splendid views of the Argentario and island of Giglio. The 15C **Rocca**, an impressive block-like construction with tower, was rebuilt by the Sienese on the site of an Aldobrandeschi family castle. Lower down is Piazza Garibaldi (with a bronze bust of the hero) and the parish church (1953) which contains modern paintings and stained glass windows. A terrace overlooking the harbour dominates the entrance to the village, with the war memorial at the centre of a parapet.

The origins of Talamone go back to the late Bronze Age. The Etruscan settlement occupied the nearby hill of **Talamonaccio**, north of the Osa estuary, and excavations have identified the acropolis and necropolis. The temple (4C BC) was later rebuilt and provided with a splendid pediment (150 BC), which was recently restored and is now exhibited in Orbetello (see below).

Orbetello and Monte Argentario

Orbetello was the most important harbour south of Livorno, protected by one of the many fortresses along the coast. The town is situated on the central strip of land linking the Argentario promontory to the mainland, with a lagoon on either side enclosed by two sand bars (or *tomboli*), the Tombolo di Giannella and the Tombolo di Feniglia, both of which have extensive beaches. The Monte Argentario is very beautiful, especially in the wilder southwestern parts and there is a magnificent view from Monte Telegrafo (635m). There are two important WWF sanctuaries, one in the lagoon of Orbetello and the other further south, near the station of Capalbio, on Lake Burano. Although the Argentario is known for its rather exclusive and fashionable summer resorts, there are also campsites along the Tombolo della Giannella. The islands of Giglio and Giannutri can be reached by regular boat services from Porto Santo Stefano. The mild climate of the promontory is not only ideal for the winter quarters of numerous migratory birds but it also favours a luxuriant and unusual flora, including wild orchids and dwarf palm trees. As well as the typical *macchia mediterranea* (see p 303), there are also citrus fruit trees, olive groves and vineyards. The archaeological site of Cosa combines the fascination of ruins with a beautiful natural setting.

Practical information

Getting there
By car

The Via Aurelia between Pisa and Rome skirts the lagoon of Orbetello.

By train

There is a railway station at Orbetello Scalo on the main line between Pisa and Rome (slow trains only).

By bus

Bus services (*RAMA*) from Grosseto and Follonica to Orbetello.

Information offices

APT Grosseto (☎ 0564 414 303); **Orbetello**, Piazza della Repubblica (☎ 0564 860 447); **Porto Santo Stefano**, Corso Umberto 55 (☎ 0564 814 208).

Where to stay
Hotels

ORBETELLO ☆☆☆
I Presidi, Via Mura di Levante 34 (☎ 0564 867 601, 📠 0564 860 432) and *Sole*, Via Colombo (☎ 0564 860 410; 📠 0564 860 475). ☆ *Piccolo*

Parigi, Corso Italia 169 (☎ 0564 867 233; 📠 0564 867 211).
PORTO ERCOLE ☆☆☆☆
Il Pellicano, località Sbarcatello (☎ 0564 833 801; 📠 0564 833 418).
PORTO SANTO STEFANO ☆☆☆
and ☆☆ hotels, including ☆☆☆ *Villa Domizia* at Santa Liberata (☎ 0564 812 735, 📠 0564 811 119).

Campsites

On the **Tombolo di Feniglia**.
☆*Feniglia* (☎ 0564 831 090), and on the Tombolo di Giannella ☆☆☆ and ☆☆ sites.

Eating out
Restaurants

ORBETELLO €€ *Il Nocchino*, Via dei Mille 64; € pizzeria *Da Gennaro*, Corso Italia 106. On the Tombolo di Giannella € *Il Tramonto*.
CAPALBIO €€ *Da Maria*, Via Comunale 3 and *Da Carla*, Via Emanuele 3; and € *Trattoria La Toscana*, Via Emanuele 2.

The extensive **Lagoon of Orbetello** is enclosed between the Tombolo di Giannella and the Tombolo di Feniglia, two tongues of sand which extend to the Argentario promontory. At the centre of the lagoon, on another isthmus, is the small town and harbour of Orbetello. The **Laguna di Orbetello bird sanctuary** in the Laguna di Ponente for some 200 species, is protected by the *World Wide Fund for Nature* (*WWF*; guided tours in winter, ☎ 0564 820 297). Access is from Cariolo on the Via Aurelia, two kilometres south of the railway station of Albinia. There are several walks, nine bird-watching stations and two towers. The next turning after the *WWF* oasis goes to the **Bosco di Patanella**, a beautiful pine wood, open daily, stretching along the lagoon.

Orbetello

Orbetello, on a sandy isthmus, is an old-fashioned resort (considerably damaged in the Second Word War) in a beautiful site in the middle of the lagoon with palm trees on the waterfront.

The position of Orbetello favoured settlements in ancient times. It was an Etruscan colony (remains of the town walls are still visible) and a place of importance in the Middle Ages. It became the capital of the *Stato dei Presidi* (or garrison state), comprising Ansedonia, Porto Ercole, Porto Santo Stefano, and

Talamone along the Maremma coast which came under the control of Philip II of Spain after his alliance with Cosimo I in 1555 following the defeat of Siena and her territories. Later, in 1646, the town held out against a two-month siege by the French. After the war of Spanish Succession the area came under Austrian control, and was part of Napoleon's Kingdom of Etruria in the early 19C. All these coastal towns were incorporated into the grand duchy of Tuscany after the Congress of Vienna (1815).

On the approach to the town the road passes the former airfield from which Italo Balbo (see p 317) led a formation flight of seaplanes across the Atlantic to celebrate the tenth anniversary of Fascism at the World Fair of Chicago in 1933.

The road leads through one of the elegant gateways, built by the Spaniards when they fortified the town, to a piazza with a large public garden, partly surrounded by fortifications. There is a large car park on the waterfront to the right. Via Dante leads to the **cathedral** (Santa Maria Assunta). The beautiful **façade** of travertine stone has an upper triangular section containing a rose-window, above which is a niche with a statue of Christ blessing. The arched doorway, dated 1376, has finely carved decoration. The church was almost entirely rebuilt in the 17C, incorporating the original façade. Inside, the decoration and floor tiles are Spanish in taste. The pretty chapel of St Biagio has an early Romanesque marble altar-frontal carved with Biblical symbols, peacocks, and vine branches.

On the opposite side of the piazza is the former **convent of the Clarisse** which houses the municipal library (it contains a well documented section on the Maremma and its history) and the tourist information office. The celebrated Etruscan **Pediment of the Temple of Talamone**, of the 2C BC, is exhibited here (open daily in summer 10.00–12.30, 16.00 or 17.00–19.00 or 20.00; in winter afternoons only Thur–Sun, ☎ 0564 860 447). The pediment is a grandiose relief in terracotta, with figures modelled partly in the round. Although fragmentary, it is a moving representation of the story of Oedipus and the death of his two sons, Polynices and Eteocles. The foundations of the temple may be visited on the site of the Etruscan city excavated on the hill of Talamonaccio (see p 331).

Via Solferino, to the right of the cathedral, leads to Piazza Garibaldi. Here is the **Palace of the Spanish Governor** with a porticoed façade and clock-tower, at the foot of which is a bust of Garibaldi. Left of the palace the corso leads to Piazza del Plebiscito onto which faces the Palazzo del Municipio, decorated with coats of arms. Along the sea front are impressive walls of Etruscan origin. On the south side is the **Polveriera Guzman**, a rectangular building with three defence towers, built in 1692 by the architect Ferdinando de Grunenbergh. Inside are two spacious rooms which will house the Archaeological Museum.

In the lagoon around Orbetello are various towers and one surviving windmill. To the south of Orbetello the **Tombolo di Feniglia**, a beautiful sandy isthmus, 6km long and 1km wide, joins the peninsula to the mainland. The woods felled here at the beginning of the 19C have been replaced by a forest of pine trees, planted at the beginning of the 20C. It is now one of the most beautiful stretches of pine trees along the coast and is a protected area. It is crossed by a footpath (also open to cyclists) some 7km long. A port for private boats constructed at Cala Galera nearby has eroded the coastline.

The Monte Argentario peninsula

A dyke, 1.5km long, built by Leopoldo II in 1842, joins Orbetello to **Monte Argentario** (635m), usually known simply as the Argentario, a roughly circular peninsula once covered with thick woods of ilexes and oaks and still beautiful despite deforestation and extensive building in some areas. It is covered with wild flowers in spring. The beauty of the promontory can best be appreciated from the sea. Porto Santo Stefano and the smaller Porto Ercole are now famous as holiday resorts with harbours for yachts and lively fish markets.

Porto Ercole

Porto Ercole is a well-known resort. It has a particularly sheltered port above which are situated impressive fortifications of the Spanish period (16C). Etruscan in origin, it was known as *Portus Herculis* by the Romans, and thrived until the 15C when, through poor administration and the threats of pirates, it fell into decline. Porto Ercole then became an important military and naval base of the Spanish *Stato dei Presidi* (see p 332).

At the entrance to the old town, surrounded by walls, is an elegant gate with a plaque commemorating the painter Caravaggio who died offshore here in 1610. Steep steps lead up to the Piazza Santa Barbara with the parish church of **Sant'Erasmo**. Inside are interesting tombstones of some of the governors and a fine marble altar. The nearby **Palazzo Consani**, built for Agostino Chigi in the early 16C, was the residence of the Spanish governors. It is attributed to the architect Baldassare Peruzzi.

The towering **Rocca Spagnola** (privately owned, but open April–Dec 10.00–13.00, 16.00–dusk exc. Wed; ☎ 0564 831 019; free ticket obtainable from the Comune, 78 Viale Caravaggio) is a vast citadel with powerful fortifications and moats. Its earliest parts date from the 13C but it was considerably rebuilt in the 15C and 16C. There is a little Renaissance church with a portico designed by Bernardo Buontalenti. A passage connects the fort to the bastion of Santa Barbara by the harbour.

On the hill facing the Rocca is the **Forte Filippo**, built in 1558 to a design by Giovanni Camerini. The fort has four enormous bastions with defences on various levels. Below, by the coast, is the **Forte Santa Caterina** surrounded by tall defence walls and a moat with a drawbridge. Both these forts are private.

South of the town, opposite the small island of Isolotto, a footpath leads up to the **Forte Stella**, the third fortress surrounding Porto Ercole. It was built by Florentine architects sent by the Medici grand-duke Cosimo I and financed by King Philip II of Spain. It derives its name from the star-shaped fort surrounded by high walls with four projecting bastions.

On the north side of the Argentario peninsula, the road skirts the lagoon and meets the road from Albinia which runs along the Tombolo di Giannella. At Santa Liberata there are excavations of a large Roman villa and fish farm. The road winds along the coast down to the harbour of **Porto Santo Stefano**. Originally a fishing village, the port was first developed in the 15C and the massive Spanish fort dates from 1560. It is now a popular summer resort but its charm has been greatly impaired by War damage and excessive rebuilding. This is the port for the Isola del Giglio (see below).

A strada panoramica, beginning at the harbour encircles the promontory through beautiful and varied scenery with splendid views. From Porto Santo Stefano it passes along the coast high above cliffs planted with vineyards, olive groves, and orange and lemon trees. The Cala Grande is one of the most beautiful bays along the coast. A parapet faces the island of Giglio and provides an ideal point from which to enjoy the sunset. The road becomes more tortuous (there is an unsurfaced stretch of c 4km) on the south side of the promontory and passes through wilder areas overlooking steep cliffs, rocky bays and grottoes, rocks emerging from the sea and two small islands. As it approaches Porto Ercole the road passes the bays and sandy beaches of villas and hotels.

Near the turning for the Tombolo della Giannella a road climbs inland to the summit of **Monte Telegrafo** (635m). It passes the mother-house of the Passionist Order, founded by St Paul of the Cross (Paolo Danei, 1694–1775). Eight monks now live here; the small church (1735) has altarpieces by Sebastiano Conca and Pietro Aldi. The road continues through thick vegetation, characteristic of the *macchia mediterranea*, to the peak where there is a splendid view.

Isola del Giglio

Practical information

Getting there
Navigation services. Frequent service (car ferries and hydrofoils) in c 1hr run by *Toremar*, at Porto Santo Stefano, (☎ 0564 810 803); on Giglio (☎ 0564 809 349) and *Maregiglio*, at Porto Santo Stefano (☎ 0564 812 920); on Giglio, ☎ 0564 809 309).

Information office
Isola del Giglio, ☎ 0564 809 400; *APT* Porto Santo Stefano (☎ 0564 814 208).

Where to stay
Hotels
☆☆☆ and ☆☆ hotels at Campese and Giglio Porto, including ☆☆ *Pardini's Hermitage*, Cala degli Alberi (☎ 0564 809 034; 🖷 0564 809 177).
Campsite
☆ *Baia del Sole*, at Campesi (☎ 0564 804 036; 🖷 0564 804 101
Rooms to let
Campese, Castello and Giglio Porto.

The pretty island of Giglio, 17.5km west of Porto Santo Stefano, has an area of 21 sq. km and a little grey granite fortess-village (bus from the port), and vineyards. Pathways lead down to the sandy beach from the village. The island is crowded at weekends in summer, and new buildings are spoiling its natural beauty, although about half of the island has been protected since 1996 as part of the *Parco Nazionale dell'Arcipelago Toscano* (see p 529).

In 1961 a boat was discovered offshore in the bay of Campese some 50m below the surface, shipwrecked c 600 BC. Its cargo of Greek and Etruscan ceramics, including numerous aryballos and Corinthian ware, wooden flutes, and a rare bronze Corinthian helmet, has mostly been recovered, and in 1985 part of its keel, 3m long, was salvaged. Oxford University has been in charge of the project.

The **island of Giannutri**, to the southeast, was also threatened with tourist development, but became part of the *Parco Nazionale dell'Arcipelago Toscano* in 1996. It has ruins of a Roman villa belonging to the Domizi Enobardi family. A **boat service** from Porto Santo Stefano via the Isola del Giglio in summer is run by *Maregiglio* (see above).

Ansedonia and Cosa

At the southern end of the Orbetello lagoon is the modern fashionable resort of Ansedonia with elegant villas surrounded by pines and oak trees on the slopes of a beautiful promontory. On the top of the hill (114m) are the ruins of the Roman town of Cosa. There are two turnings off the Via Aurelia for Ansedonia: the one to the north leads to Cosa, the one further south to the harbour.

Excavations in the area have revealed that there have been settlements here since prehistoric times. The Etruscan settlement became a Roman colony in 273 BC. By the 2C BC, Cosa was a flourishing town with its capitol and forum, and the city gates and walls are still partially preserved. Beneath the cliffs on the south side, was a small harbour, the *Portus Cosanus*.

Extending south was an extensive lagoon rich in fish, separated from the sea by sand dunes, with a canal leading to a deep natural passage, 260m long, linking the lagoon to the sea, called the **Spacco della Regina**. This passage provided for the ebb and flow of the tides and prevented the harbour from silting up. When parts of the passage collapsed causing it to block up, another shorter passage, the **Tagliata**, was cut through the cliffs nearer the harbour. The hewing out of this passage, with walls some 15–20m high and other parts tunnelled through the rock, was an amazing feat and it was also engineered to control the waters and the catching and farming of fish. There are steps and a walkway on the cliffs from which one may see the Tagliata. Some remains of the Roman harbour are still visible in the little bay and there is a fine view of the promontory and cliffs from the beach.

The particularly interesting excavated site of **Cosa** extends over a considerable area amidst magnificent olive trees and ilexes (open daily 09.00–sunset; explanatory panels, also in English. The little museum is open daily 09.00–19.00, Oct–Apr 09.00–14.00).

The site includes several stretches of walls constructed of enormous stone blocks. On a slight rise are remains of two temples and the forum, from which there is a splendid view stretching from the Orbetello lagoon and Monte Argentario to the lake of Burano. More excavations are in progress on another slope on the south side of the promontory.

The little **Museo Archeologico**, in a reconstructed house, contains interesting pieces of sculpture, terracotta ornaments from the temples, pottery, oil jars, glass, bronze objects and coins. There are texts (also in English) explaining the history and excavations of Cosa and its port. There is also a section on the medieval monastery on the site and the later castle of Ansedonia which was raised to the ground by Siena in 1328.

On the beach is a house and a medieval defence tower built on the site of a Roman villa. Puccini composed part of his opera *Tosca* here. There were several large Roman villas in the area on estates which produced wine and oil.

On the other side of the Aurelia a by-road (signposted Villa Romana) leads inland past the ruins of a Roman villa (**Villa delle Colonne**) whose interesting perimeter wall has unusual cylindrical towers. The road continues to the overgrown ruins of the Roman villa (1C BC–mid 2C AD) of **Settefinestre** in a romantic setting, with farm buildings attached, excavated in the 1970s and now abandoned.

Capalbio

Inland, at the southernmost end of Tuscany, is Capalbio, a charming little medieval village, visible from the main road, which has become fashionable as an exclusive summer resort in the last few decades. It is in a beautiful position on a low hill above thick ilex, cork, and oak woods once typical of the vegetation in the Maremma, in the centre of a game reserve. The area is famous for its wild boar (*cinghiale*; fair in September).

The double circle of medieval walls and the entrance gateway and tower are well preserved. The **castello** has a tall tower which dominates the village. The streets are picturesque and there are charming views from the walkways above the walls overlooking houses and gardens. The church of **San Nicola**, remodelled in the 15C, has some Romanesque capitals and remains of 15C–16C frescoes. The little oratory of the **Madonna della Providenza** has an interesting chapel decorated with frescoes in the style of Perugino (c1500).

Domenico Tiburzi, the most famous brigand of the Maremma, died here. A legendary figure, and the terror of upper Lazio and the Maremma, he was finally caught and shot in 1896 aged 60, having been on the run for 24 years.

At **Pescia Fiorentina**, to the east on the border with Lazio, an old iron foundry survives, of great interest to industrial archaeologists (there are long-term plans to restore it). It also has a modern sculpture garden known as the **Giardino dei Tarocchi** (for admission, ☎ 0564 895 122) by Niki de Saint-Phalle, containing gigantic compositions of glass, ceramics and coloured enamels.

On the other side of the Via Aurelia is Capalbio station, and across the railway line, a short distance along a by-road to the left, is the entrance to the lovely **bird sanctuary** of the **Lago di Burano**, a marshy lagoon 4km long administered by the *Word Wide Fund for Nature* (*WWF*) (open Sept–Apr for guided tours of 2–3 hours on Sun, at 10.00 and 14.30; ☎ 0564 898 829).

Standing above the lake is the Torre di Buranaccio (private), a small well-preserved fort similar to that of Porto Santo Stefano. Visitors may walk down as far as the lake on a path between tall rushes. There are posters illustrating the variety of local fauna and flora, including butterflies.

There is a fine beach at **Chiarone** to the east.

Pitigliano and Saturnia

This is an area of great natural beauty in the south eastern corner of Tuscany near the border with Lazio. The landscape is immensely varied: at times dramatic and austere, at others inviting and serene. Dense woods and coppices alternate with rolling hills and fertile valleys scattered with farmhouses. Characteristic are the ruined castles and hill-top villages, built out of the underlying rock or stone, many of them still enclosed in their medieval walls. Important Etruscan necropoli have been found in the area (especially around Sovana and Saturnia) and excavations continue. The finds are exhibited in the local museums of Pitigliano, Manciano and Scansano.

Practical information

Getting there
By car

Pitigliano, Manciano, Sorano and Sovana are reached from the Via Aurelia (N1) south of the Parco dell'Uccellina by the secondary road N74. The other places described are on lovely by-roads north of the N74.

By bus

Buses run from the railway station in Grosseto (run by *RAMA*) to Scansano, Saturnia, Manciano, Pitigliano and other towns.

Information office

APT of **Grosseto** (☎ 0564 414 303). Local information office in **Sovana** in Palazzo Pretorio (☎ 0564 614 074). **Pitigliano**, Via Roma 6 (☎ 0564 614 433). **Scansano**, ☎ 0564 509 411.

Where to stay
Hotels

PITIGLIANO ☆☆ *Guastini*, Piazza Petruccioli 4 (☎ 0564 616 065; 🖷 0564 616 652). **SEMPRONIANO** ☆☆ *Locanda La Pieve*, Via della Società Operaia 3 (☎/🖷 0564 982 52).

SOVANA ☆☆☆ *Taverna Etrusca*, with restaurant (☎ 0564 616 183; 🖷 0564 614 193). **SATURNIA** ☆☆☆☆ *Terme di Saturnia*, Via della Follonata (☎ 0564 601 061; 🖷 0564 601 266); ☆☆☆ *Villa Clodia*, Via Italia 43 (☎ 0564 601 212; 🖷 0564 601 305). **SCANSANO** ☆☆☆☆ *Antico Casale*, at Castagneta (☎ 0564 507 219; 🖷 0564 507 805). **MANCIANO** ☆☆☆ and ☆ hotels.

Eating out
Restaurants

SORANO € *Da Fidalma*, Via Busatti 6. **SATURNIA** €€ *I Due Cippi*, Villa Pensiero, Piazza Vittorio Veneto 26. **SEMPRONIANO** € *La Posta*, 6km south at Catabbio. **MANCIANO** € *Da Paolino*, Via Marsala 41. **MONTEMERANO** € *Locanda Laudomia*, località Poderi di Montemerano. **MONTORGIALI** € *Franco e Silvana*. **PERETA** € *Da Wilma*. **MAGLIANO IN TOSCANA** €€ *Da Guido*, 18 Via Roma.

Pitigliano

Pitigliano (4500 inhab.) is spectacularly situated on a rocky spur overlooking a gorge on all sides, excavated by three torrents (the Lente, Meleta, and Prochio). Its clustered medieval stone houses, dominated by the cathedral bell-tower and two other towers, give the impression that they are growing out of the rocks amongst the wild vegetation. The area is known for its excellent white wine (*Bianco di Pitigliano*).

History

Etruscan in origin, Pitigliano later came under Roman rule and was subsequently a feud of the Aldobrandeschi family of Sovana. In 1293 it passed by marriage to the Orsini who enlarged the fortress in the first half of the 16C and rebuilt the city defence walls. When the Orsini family became extinct, Pitigliano passed to Cosimo I Medici and became part of the grand duchy of Tuscany in 1608. A Jewish colony, protected by the Medici, was established in Pitigliano in 1570. Leopoldo II, commemorated by a bust on an obelisk in the piazza, restored the town and built the church of Santa Maria Assunta and the bridge over the Meleta.

The arched aqueduct was built in 1545 by Gian Francesco Orsini, who also commissioned Giuliano da Sangallo to enlarge the 13C castle. **Palazzo Orsini** is partly a medieval castle and partly a Renaissance palace. Sangallo added the fine entrance doorway and the elegant courtyard with a well, bearing the family arms. It houses the **Museo Diocesano di Arte Sacra** (open daily, 10.00–13.00, 15.00–18.00, closed Mon, ☎ 0564 616 322). The collection comprises fine liturgical objects from the local cathedral and other churches and includes some 15C sculptures, a *Madonna and Child* enthroned by Guidoccio Cozzarelli and two altarpieces by Francesco Zuccarelli (1702–88) who was born here. There is also a 15C wooden ceiling and fragments of a frescoed frieze of the same period representing members of the Orsini family and famous historical figures, as well as a precious reliquary of St Flora and St Lucilla.

There is also a small **Museo Civico e Archeologico** (open as for the Museo Diocesano) containing an interesting collection, mostly of objects excavated in the nearby necropoli of Poggio Buco with some fine examples of Etruscan pottery. The palace faces onto Piazza della Repubblica, which is decorated with two 18C fountains and overlooks at either end the surrounding countryside.

Via Roma leads into the old town whose narrow streets and darkened stone houses, with their outside staircases, preserve its medieval character. **Piazza del Duomo** has an impressive monument, erected in 1490 to celebrate the Orsini family (the bear, or *orso* is the family emblem). The **cathedral**, medieval in origin, has a Baroque façade, but the interior has been modernised. There is a *Madonna of the Rosary* by Francesco Vanni (1609). Two other paintings commemorating *Pope Gregory VII* are by Pietro Aldi (1885). The massive bell-tower has a bell weighing three tones.

In Via Orsini is the Renaissance church of **Santa Maria**, built to a strange trapezoidal ground plan. A Romanesque sculptural relief of a figure with two winged animals is inserted in the wall under the tower. A small piazza here has a fine view over the Meleta valley. Steps lead down to the **Porta di Sovana**, built into an Etruscan section of the walls (4C BC). Via Zuccarelli leads back to Piazza della Repubblica through the old Ghetto. The **Synagogue** dates from 1589 and has been restored (open May–Oct 10.00–13.00, 15.00–18.00). It documents the presence of a large Jewish community in the town from the 15C (their cemetery was on the road to Sovana).

Outside the town, near the ruins of the monastery of San Francesco, on the road to Sorano, is a gateway which formed the entrance to **Poggio Sterzoni**, once a famous park, similar to that of Bomarzo, near Viterbo in Lazio, with gigantic sculptures of monsters and animals. It is now a wilderness containing remains of carved statues, steps and niches carved out of the tufo rock.

Sovana

Sovana, 8km north of Pitigliano, is now a village with little more than a single street running from the castle ruins to the cathedral. It is in a beautiful position on a ridge overlooking a wide panorama. It is traditionally reputed to be the birthplace of Hildebrand, later Pope Gregory VII (1026/8–85).

History

An important Etruscan settlement and later a Roman *municipium*, Sovana became a bishopric in the 5C. Its period of greatest importance was in the 13C when it was the seat of the Sovana branch of the Aldobrandeschi family, after it had separated from the Santa Fiora branch. It then passed under the Orsini and was conquered by Siena in 1410. Attempts to repopulate the village under subsequent Medici rule were doomed on account of malaria.

At the entrance to the village are the impressive ruins of the Aldobrandeschi **castle** (13C–14C) and remains of the Etruscan walls. Facing onto the small brick piazza is the former Palazzo del Comune, dating from the 12C, with a clock and bell-cot, which has been the local archive since the 17C. To the right is the **Palazzo Pretorio**, which was largely rebuilt by Siena in the 15C and has nine coats of arms of the Sienese governors on the façade. It now houses a **Museo Comunale Etrusco e Medievale** (open 10.00–13.00, 15.00–17.00 or 19.00 exc. Mon; ☎ 0564 614 074). On the adjacent Loggia del Capitano is a large Medici coat of arms carved in marble.

On the opposite side of the piazza is the church of **Santa Maria Maggiore**. The interior has large round arches dividing the nave from the aisles and frescoes of the Umbrian or Sienese school of the late 15C or early 16C have been discovered under the whitewash. The high altar stands beneath a carved marble **ciborium** of the 9C, which was probably removed from the cathedral in the 18C. The workmanship is superb and it is a unique example of its kind in Tuscany: the elegantly carved baldacchino, terminating in an octagonal spire, rests on four slender columns with elaborate capitals. Beside the church is the **Palazzo Bourbon del Monte** which dates from the mid-16C when the Medici restored the town.

At the end of the village, in a stone-flagged piazza surrounded by cypresses, is the Romanesque **cathedral** of Santi Pietro e Paolo. The original church was probably begun during the papacy of Gregory VII, but its present structure is thought to date from the 12C–13C. It has a semicircular apse and a polygonal dome. The doorway on the south side, probably removed from the façade and put together with pre-Romanesque fragments, is decorated with stylised figures, animals, and plants.

Compound piers divide the nave from the aisles and some of the capitals are finely carved, several of them with biblical scenes. The paintings include a *Martyrdom of St Peter* by Domenico Manenti. The 15C urn, possibly Sienese, has a carved image of *St Mamiliano*, whose body it contains. He was long venerated as the evangeliser of the district in the 6C. There are remains of 15C frescoes in the crossing and the baptismal font is dated 1494. The small crypt (11C) has seven simple columns. The nearby **canonica** was the bishop's palace until the bishopric was officially transferred to Pitigliano in 1843, together with reliquaries and an altarpiece by Cozzarelli (now in the museum of Pitigliano).

At 47 Via del Duomo there is a private Museum of Shells (closed Tues).

Near Sovana are many interesting **Etruscan necropoli** (maps obtainable locally, for information, ☎ 0564 633 767), mostly rock tombs of the 3C–2C BC, which were first excavated by George Dennis in 1844. Some, of impressive dimensions among thick vegetation, are visible from the road, such as the arched niche of the Tomba della Sirena.

Off the road heading out of Sovana to the west are the necropoli of **San Sebastiano** (reached by an Etruscan passage through rock) and **Poggio Felceto** where you can see the **Tomba Ildebranda** (3C BC), originally an impressive temple-like structure named after Hildebrand, and the Pola tomb, with remains of columns which supported a pediment. Another passageway connects this necropolis to that of **Poggio Starziale** containing the Tifone tomb, a large niche with a pediment, and the Cavone, an Etruscan passage with wall tombs and inscriptions.

Sorano

Sorano (374m), to the east, is in an area well known for its white wine. This small medieval town, largely derelict but beautiful nonetheless, has a modern suburb. The approach from Sovana, passing Etruscan rock tombs, is particularly spectacular. The town is dominated by the old Orsini fortress called the **Masso Leopoldino** (guided tours only). The district below it is the oldest part of the town and the buildings, many of them in ruin, are intricately wedged together and built into the rock. On the south side of the town is the **Fortezza Orsini e Museo** (open 10.00–13.00, 14.00–18.00, ☎ 0564 633 767). There are guided tours around the bastions and defences of the fortress which was built by Anton Maria Lari in 1552 onto the earlier fortress. It is a fine example of Renaissance military architecture. There is a small collection of medieval and Renaissance ceramics and glass.

There are several ruined castles in panoramic positions, in the area, including **Montorio** and **Ottieri**, which were also strongholds of the Aldobrandeschi and Orsini families.

Saturnia

The **Terme di Saturnia** is a well-known spa of sulphurous water (37°C), known since Roman times. Nearby are the **Cascate del Gorello** next to an old mill, where hot water falls in cascades over whitened rocks, creating natural pools. This uniquely beautiful spot has unfortunately suffered from neglect, and the waters have been partially diverted in recent years.

The village of **Saturnia**, west of Pitigliano and Sovana, was built on a travertine spur overlooking the Albegna valley. It was an Etruscan town of some importance, and there are several necropoli nearby (at Pian di Palma and Puntone). In the 3C BC it became a Roman colony. The Porta Romana, through which ran the Via Clodia, and the adjacent walls are well preserved (the arch is medieval). There are still remains of foundations and floors in the village dating from the 2C–1C BC. In 1299 Saturnia was sacked by the Sienese, who later built the fortifications and rebuilt the medieval castle. There is a large pleasant piazza with a public garden off which is the church of S. Maria Maddalena. The church (of Romanesque origin) has a *Madonna and Child* attributed to Benvenuto di Giovanni. An antiquarium of excavated Etruscan and Roman objects has been transferred to the Archaeological Museum of Grosseto.

A short distance north of Saturnia is the excavated site of **Puntone** which may be visited.

About 15km north of Saturnia is **Semproniano**, a small hill-top town situated high up (600m) and clustered around the ruins of its castle. From here a by-road leads to the picturesque village of **Rocchette di Fazio**. Built on a rock overhanging the Albegna valley it commands a magnificent view. At its centre, surrounded by trees, are the ruins of the 12C castle. The small Chiesa della Madonna on the village square has a 14C–15C wooden statue of the *Madonna*. There are a number of interesting medieval buildings including the Romanesque Pieve di Santa Cristina, reached by a flight of steps, which has some damaged early 15C frescoes.

Manciano

Manciano (444m), south of Saturnia, dominates the surrounding countryside. Largely modern in aspect, it nevertheless preserves its medieval centre. Picturesque streets and houses surround the 15C **Rocca** and its impressive tower, which, like the town walls, has been considerably restored. In Piazza Garibaldi is a monument to the local painter, Pietro Aldi (1852–88), who designed the fountain (only built in 1913). The clock tower was erected by the Sienese in the 15C.

In Via Corsini is the **Museo di Preistoria e Protostoria della Valle del Fiora** (open 09.00–15.30; fest. 9.30–13.00; closed Mon; ☎ 0564 625 327). It contains a well organised arrangement of material from excavated sites in the Fiora valley north-east of Manciano and adjacent areas, including prehistoric finds (it is particularly rich in artefacts from the Bronze Age). The collection of paintings by the two artists born in Manciano, Pietro Aldi and Paride Pascucci (1866–1954), has been transferred to the Comune next to the museum and may be seen on request. There are also works by these painters in the local churches.

In the neighbourhood of Manciano are a number of ruined castles in romantic settings.

North of Manciano is **Montemerano** (303m), a picturesque walled village on a hill of ancient olive trees. On the north side of the hill is a gateway, opening onto a beautiful view, and part of the old walls enclosing a small piazza with the church of **San Giorgio** with a simple late 14C stone façade. Inside are several important works: a monumental polyptych by Sano di Pietro of 1458, complete with its predella and pinnacles; a painted wooden statue of *St Peter* by Vecchietta; a *Virgin of the Annunciation* by the Master of Montemerano; a carved relief of the *Assumption* attributed to Vecchietta and various frescoes of the 15C Sienese school. It is worth exploring the village to enjoy its charming vistas.

Scansano

Scansano (500m) is an agricultural town with a well-preserved medieval district at its centre. Today it is well-known for its red wine, *Morellino di Scansano*. There is a large **car park** at the entrance to the town.

Via XX Settembre leads into Piazza Garibaldi, which has a marble statue of Garibaldi. Opposite the two cast-iron fountains, an arched gateway with a clock-tower leads to the picturesque old town.

From the path which skirts the outside of the walls, overlooking the country-side, there is a striking view of the tower and apse of the church of **San Giovanni Battista**, soaring high above the walls. The church, which was extensively remodelled in the 17C, has several attractive altarpieces and minor works of the 16C Sienese school.

In the Comune in Via XX Settembre there is a small antiquarium, the **Museo Archeologico della Media Valle dell'Albegna** (open Sat, Sun & fest.). Here are objects from the excavated sites in the neighbourhood of Scansano, notably at Ghiaccioforte, a hill on the right bank of the Albegna, and the remains of the Roman Villa Degli Anili. The same building also houses a Wine Museum.

The road north of Scansano towards Roccalbegna by-passes **Poggioferro**, where there is a *Madonna* by Giovanni di Paolo in the parish church, and **Murci** (572m), overlooking an extensive landscape.

On the road to Grosseto, which winds through beautiful, hilly countryside, there is a turning at Pancole for the castle of **Montepò** (451m), an early 16C fortress (private) with four corner towers, in a splendid position, and the ruined medieval castle of **Cotone**. The road also passes near **Montorgiali**, a grey stone village with a castle at its centre, perched on a hill.

South of Scansano another scenic road passes **Pereta**, a charming little medieval village, which preserves its walls and a very tall tower. The entrance is through a gateway with battlements, and the main street is lined with pic-turesque houses. The square tower stands on its own near the former castle. There is a Romanesque church, Santa Maria, with a rose window and frieze on the façade.

Magliano in Toscana

Further south (on the same road) is Magliano in Toscana which has splendid 14C and 15C fortifications with seven semi-circular towers and three gates. Originally this was an Etruscan and later a Roman town. In the Middle Ages it became a stronghold of the Aldobrandeschi and was subsequently conquered by Siena.

Inside Porta San Martino is the Romanesque **church** of the same name dating from the 11C. It has a fine façade of travertine stone and the side entrance has carvings of a figure and dragons. In Corso Garibaldi on the left is **Palazzo dei Priori**, built in 1425, decorated with coats of arms. A little further on to the right is the church of **San Giovanni Battista**, Romanesque in origin but with an elegant Renaissance façade, dated 1471. Inside are frescoes and paintings from the 15C–17C and four Baroque altars. There is a fine baptismal font inscribed with the date 1493.

Further along the Corso is the Gothic Palazzo di Checco il Bello and at various points there are views over the surrounding countryside.

Outside the walls is the church of the **Annunziata** in which there is a charming *Madonna and Child* by Neroccio, unfortunately cut out of a larger altarpiece. The interior of the church is largely covered with 15C frescoes of the Sienese school, some of them in fragmentary state.

In the olive grove beyond the church is a remarkable, ancient, gnarled olive tree, known as the 'witch's olive tree', which is alleged to be well over a thousand years old.

Outside the town, just past the cemetery, a by-road (signposted for Sant' Andrea) leads to the imposing ruins of the 11C church of **San Bruzio**, among olive trees. Originally the church of a Benedictine monastery, now only the apse and the great arches opening towards the transepts and nave survive. There are beautifully carved capitals supporting the arches, on which rests an octagonal drum with squinches, open to the sky. The force conveyed by the structure and the luminous quality of the stone enhance the romantic effect of this extraordinarily beautiful ruin.

The 11C ruins of San Bruzio

Monte Amiata

Monte Amiata, the highest mountain in Tuscany (1738m), was originally a volcano. This explains its interesting geological formation, rocky spurs and ravines, mineral deposits and sulphurous springs. The rich mercury (cinnabar) deposits were known to the Etruscans and they have been systematically mined since 1860.

The mountain is encircled by a road which runs through magnificent woods of chestnuts, beeches, oaks, and fir trees, which are at their most beautiful in autumn. The peak is marked by an enormous iron Cross by Luciano Zalaffi (1910). The view embraces the Orcia, Fiora, and Paglia valleys, and, on a fine day, it is possible to see the Tyrrhenian coast and the islands of Elba and Corsica, as well as the towns of Siena, Cortona, and Orvieto, and the lakes of Trasimene and Bolsena.

All the roads towards the mountain are inviting and varied: those from the south are perhaps the most spectacular. Picturesque small towns and villages are prettily situated on the slopes. Modern suburbs, which have developed conspicuously in recent years, testify to the growing importance of the area as a summer and winter resort. There are numerous ski lifts, hotels and restaurants.

Practical information

Getting there
By car

Monte Amiata is close to the Via Cassia (N2), and approximately one hour's drive from the Siena–Grosseto road (turning at Paganico).

By bus

Buses to **Abbadia San Salvatore** from Siena, Grosseto, Buonconvento, and Chiusi. Abbadia San Salvatore is connected by bus to Santa Fiora and Arcidosso.

Information offices

APT dell'Amiata, Via Adua 25, **Abbadia San Salvatore** (☎ 0577 775 811). *Pro-Loco* offices at Santa Fiora, Piancastagnaio, Arcidosso, and Castel del Piano. *Comunità Montana del Monte Amiata*, località Colonia, **Arcidosso** and Via Grossetana 1, **Piancastagnaio**.

Where to stay
Hotels

CASTEL DEL PIANO
☆☆☆ *Impero*, Via Roma 7 (☎ 0564 955 337; ▯ 0564 955 025), with restaurant.
SEGGIANO ☆☆☆ *Silene* (with restaurant), Via Capo Vetra 8, località Pescina (☎/▯ 0564 950 805).
MONTE AMIATA ☆☆☆☆ *Contessa*, Prato della Contessa, **Castel del Piano** (☎ 0564 959 000; ▯ 0564 959 002); ☆☆ *Lo Scoiattolo*, Prato della Contessa (☎ 0564 959 003) and *Le Macinaie*, Prato delle Macinaie (☎ 0564 959 001; ▯ 0564 959 013).
ABBADIA SAN SALVATORE
☆☆☆ *Adriana*, Via Serdini 76 (☎ 0577 778 116); *Giardino*, Via Primo Maggio 63 (☎ 0577 778 106); and *Kappadue*, Via del Laghetto 15 (☎ 0577 778 609). ☆☆ *San Marco*, Via Matteotti 19 (☎ 0577 778 089) and numerous others.
PIANCASTAGNAIO ☆☆☆ *Del Bosco*, Via Grossetana 41 (☎ 0577 786 090).
BAGNOLO ☆☆ hotels including *Il Fungo*, Via dei Minatori 10 (☎ 0564 953 025).
SANTA FIORA ☆☆ *Eden*, Via Roma 1 (☎/▯ 0564 977 033).
ARCIDOSSO ☆☆☆ *Toscana*, Via Lazzaretti 47 (☎ 0564 967 486; ▯ 0564 967 000); ☆☆ *Gatto d'Oro*, Aia dei Venti (☎/▯ 0564 967 074).

Campsite

Campsite at Castel del Piano ☆☆☆ *Amiata*, località Montoto (☎ 0564 955 107).

Sports

Skiing. There are facilities at Abbadia San Salvatore, Castel del Piano and, località Macinaie, Contessa.

Festivals

Annual fair at Piancastagnaio, celebrating the chestnut harvest, takes place at the beginning of November.

The approach to Monte Amiata from Paganico, along the Orcia valley, passes a turning to the left for **Montenero**, a medieval village situated on a hill (338m). Behind the little church of the Madonna, a narrow street leads up through an arched gateway to a piazzetta with a 16C well built by the Medici. Opposite, in the parish church of Santa Lucia, is a large *Crucifix* attributed to Ambrogio Lorenzetti behind a Baroque altar supporting a graceful glazed terracotta statue of *St Lucy*. Outside the old walls is a public park from which the view opens to the west.

Off the main road is **Montegiovi**, another typical medieval village built in grey stone, with remains of a polygonal tower and parts of the walls. At the foot of the village is the church of San Martino with an early 14C façade flanked by a tall square tower. Inside there are elegant Baroque altars.

A road to the south leads to **Monticello Amiata** (734m) a fortified village with picturesque streets, in a splendid position surrounded by hills. The church of San Michele has a tall tower silhouetted against the sky. The 13C interior, rebuilt in the 19C, contains an altarpiece by Riccio. A 17C house at no. 21 Via Grande has a small museum devoted to local traditions and peasant life.

Montelaterone (685m) is also perched in a panoramic position facing Castel del Piano and Arcidosso across a narrow valley. This village is composed of a network of steps and alleys on various levels within its walls, dominated by a castle. There are many remains of its medieval past in the steep streets and stepped alleyways climbing up to the Romanesque church of San Clemente and the ruins of the Rocca. The Chiesa della Misericordia, the façade of which was rebuilt in 1907, has frescoes by Francesco Nasini (see below). There are beautiful views in all directions.

Castel del Piano

Castel del Piano, on the west side of the mountain, is one of the largest towns (4300 inhab.) on the slopes of Monte Amiata, and shares the history of most of the neighbouring towns and villages. In the late medieval period it came under the dominion of Abbadia San Salvatore, and subsequently passed to the Aldobrandeschi and Siena before becoming part of the grand duchy of Tuscany under the Medici in the mid-16C. It was the birthplace of the Nasini family which produced three generations of painters, the most important being Francesco (1621–95) and his son Giuseppe Nicola (1657–1736). In the 15C Pope Pius II admired Castel del Piano for its situation and charm. It is in a beautiful position overlooking the Orcia and Ombrone valleys and surrounded by woods. It is well organised as a holiday resort in all seasons.

The main road leads to Piazza Garibaldi (car park) which was created in the 19C around a fountain and a monument to Garibaldi. Corso Nasini, the main street, divides the medieval town on the north side from the modern suburb, which is spacious and attractive.

In Piazza Madonna is the church of **Santi Niccolò e Lucia**, with an elegant bell-tower and 18C façade. Inside are four Baroque altars on either side of the nave. The neo-Gothic ceiling was painted by Francesco Notari, a local 19C artist. The second altar on the right has a *Miracle of St Cerbone* by Domenico Manetti (c 1642). In the right transept, the Cappella del Crocifisso has carved wood figures and an altar by Amato and Benedetto Amati of Arcidosso (1670). In the same chapel is a *Pietà* by Giuseppe Nicola Nasini, who also painted the *Agony in the Garden* and *St Francis receiving the stigmata*. The high altar is attributed to the Mazzuoli brothers of Siena; the *Birth of the Virgin* is by Giuseppe Nicola Nasini, who also painted the *Mystic Marriage of St Catherine of Alexandria* and the *Martyrdom of St Agnes* (second and first altars on the left).

The nearby **Oratory of the Madonna delle Grazie** has a fine stone façade (19C). The altarpiece of the *Madonna del Carmine* is by Francesco Nasini (1652). The elaborate Baroque high altar contains a venerated image of the *Madonna and Child* in the manner of Sano di Pietro.

Further down is the **town hall**, in a palace formerly owned by the Ginanneschi family, some fine houses and the **Oratory of the Misericordia**.

Opening onto Corso Nasini are three gateways leading into the picturesque, walled medieval town. The first is under the clock-tower, beyond which is a 16C loggia on the corner of the Piazzetta degli Ortaggi. The medieval streets also have several Renaissance houses. Via delle Chiese leads from the church of San Leonardo (with a few remains of 15C frescoes inside) to the small church of the Santissimo Sacramento. The 18C interior houses a polychrome wood statue of the *Madonna of Loreto*. At the end of Corso Nasini is Piazza Panorama. Here a road leads up to the Parco dei Daini (deer park).

To the northwest is **Seggiano** surrounded by chestnut woods and pretty scenery. Just outside the village is the **Santuario della Madonna della Carità**, a small church with a Greek-cross plan crowned by a dome and an elegant façade, which was built by the inhabitants of Seggiano after a terrible famine in 1603. The interior is also simple and elegant. Since all the original altarpieces were stolen they have been replaced by modern works. The road winds uphill outside the medieval walls, some built on impressive rocks, to a piazzetta with fine views and the church of Corpus Domini. From the main piazza a street leads downhill to the church of **San Bartolomeo** with a simple Romanesque façade (restored). Inside is a polyptych representing *Saints Bartholomew, Michael, and John the Evangelist*, attributed to Bartolomeo Bulgarini.

On the outskirts of the village, in a picturesque position, is the small **Oratory of San Rocco**, dating from 1486. The choir has frescoes representing the *Deposition* and the *Madonna enthroned with Saints* by Girolamo di Domenico (1493).

Pescina (747m) is a modern resort in chestnut woods (beautiful walks). There is a charming *Madonna and Child* by Luca di Tommè in the parish church.

Abbadia San Salvatore

Abbadia San Salvatore (8500 inhabitants) lies on the edge of extensive chestnut woods covering the eastern side of Monte Amiata. The **abbey** is one of the oldest monasteries in Tuscany and had control over a vast area. It was an important station in the Middle Ages on the Via Francigena, the pilgrim route from northern Europe to Rome (see p 442). The modern suburb which has developed round the monastery, has become a popular summer and winter resort.

The picturesque medieval borgo or **village** preserves its outer walls and streets intact, with medieval and Renaissance houses of local grey stone. San Leonardo is a small Gothic church, and Santa Croce retains part of its Romanesque façade, although it was rebuilt in the 18C.

The Benedictine abbey, which was immensely rich and powerful, enjoyed numerous privileges under the protection of popes and emperors, and exercised feudal jurisdiction over much of southern Tuscany. It was founded, according to tradition, in 743 by the Lombard king, Ratchis, on the spot where he saw a vision. At the peak of its temporal and spiritual powers in 1035 the abbey was rebuilt and reconsecrated by Abbot Winizzo. There followed a period of decline when it came under the dominion of Siena in 1347, and eventually was incorporated into the Medici state in 1559. The monastery was suppressed by grand-duke Leopoldo II in 1783, and most of its treasury and archives were removed to Florence. A Benedictine community was reinstalled here in 1939.

A gateway leads into the piazza, with a fountain at the centre, opposite the abbey **church**, restored c 1930, when the Baroque altars were demolished, and again in the 1960s and 1980s when an attempt was made to reconstruct its 11C appearance. The narrow **façade**, with its three-light window over the arched entrance, is flanked by two towers, a tall square crenellated bell-tower on the left, and an unfinished tower on the right; it is a rare example of Romanesque west-work in Italian architecture.

The interior is one of the earliest churches to have a Latin-cross plan. The nave has a timber roof and the elevated choir is framed by three rounded arches spanning its entire width. A late 12C carved wooden *Crucifix* (right) shows *Christ Triumphant* (with open eyes). On the opposite wall is a fresco of the *Martyrdom of St Bartholomew* by Francesco Nasini (1694).

Steps lead up to the **choir** which was decorated with frescoes in the 17C by Francesco and Antonio Annibale Nasini. The same artists painted the right-hand chapel with frescoes illustrating the legend of King Ratchis and his vision of Christ above fir trees during a hunt, allegorical figures and saints, and the *Pietà* with angels beneath the altar. The corresponding chapel on the left, dedicated to the Madonna, has stories of the *Life of the Virgin* and the contiguous chapel has scenes of *Christ's Infancy* (damaged), also by the Nasini brothers.

The **crypt,** which probably dates from the 10C–11C, is one of the largest and earliest in Tuscany. There are 32 columns with beautifully carved capitals supporting a stone vault. The capitals present a variety of leaf, figure, and animal motifs comparable to early Lombard sculpture in northern Italy.

The **monastery**, on the left of the church, has a cloister dating from the 16C (restored), with a well. The **Museo di Oggetti Sacri** (open in summer 10.00–12.00, 16.00–19.00 or on request) contains the precious monastic **treasury,** which includes a tiny 8C Irish reliquary and a copper-gilt reliquary bust of Pope St Mark, decorated with enamels and dated 1381 attributed to Mariano d'Agnolo Romanelli. The unique 8C–9C **red silk cope**, probably of Persian origin, is woven with a pattern of simurghs (legendary birds) in roundels. This was for long associated with the cult of the 4C Pope St Mark, but during its restoration an inscription was discovered relating to Pope John VIII (872–82). The hem was lined with strips of silk which are extraordinarily rare 8C Byzantine textiles, woven in four colours, with pairs of ballerinas in roundels.

The road northwest to the summit of Monte Amiata passes a deer park on the right and on the left the former mercury mine, now a museum (open 09.00–13.00, 15.00–20.00).

Piancastagnaio

Piancastagnaio (872m), overlooks the Paglia valley. Outside the village, on a hill, is the church of **San Bartolomeo**, which was part of a Franciscan monastery. The simple stone façade is half covered by a large porch. Inside are various frescoes of the 14C–15C and works by members of the Nasini family. In the chapter house, off the cloister, frescoes of the *Life of the Virgin* have been discovered under whitewash.

At the entrance to the village, which has narrow picturesque streets, is a fortified gateway beside the impressive Aldobrandeschi **fortress**, one of the best preserved examples of 14C military architecture in the district, with a great tower. It now houses a small local museum. Beyond is the Romanesque church of **Santa Maria Assunta**, which contains some 17C paintings. Dominating the main square is **Palazzo Bourbon del Monte**, built by the Perugian architect Valentino Martelli (1611) in a sadly neglected state. An annual fair is held in the piazza at the beginning of November coinciding with the chestnut harvest. On the road encircling the village to the left of the gateway is the church of **Santa Maria delle Grazie** with a recently discovered fresco cycle attributed to Nanni di Pietro (15C).

On the Santa Fiora road, a short distance from Piancastagnaio, is the sanctuary of the **Madonna di San Pietro**, with an elegant 17C façade and bell-tower. The interior, recently restored, is covered with frescoes by Francesco Nasini, illustrating the *Four Last Things* (1640), in a lively and personal style.The fresco with the venerated image of the *Madonna* is by Martino d'Urbano da Celia (1583). The road which winds across the southern slopes of Monte Amiata has splendid views.

Santa Fiora

Santa Fiora is named after its patron saint. It originally belonged to Abbadia San Salvatore but subsequently came under the dominion of the Aldobrandeschi who ruled over much of southern Tuscany. In 1274 their territorial possessions were divided between two branches of the family: the Santa Fiora branch ruled over Monte Amiata and the northern part of the Maremma and the Sovana branch over southern Maremma and the coastal area. Santa Fiora then passed through the female line to the Sforza Cesarini, until it was incorporated in the Grand Duchy of Tuscany under Pietro Leopoldo in the late 18C.

The entrance to this picturesque little town is by an archway through **Palazzo Sforza Cesarini**, a grandiose, late Renaissance palace (now the town hall) with the family arms of a lion rampant and a quince tree. Only the clock tower dominating the rectangular Piazza Garibaldi and a small stretch of the fortifications survive from the original Aldobrandeschi castle.

Via Carolina leads down past the Misericordia and Piazza XII Giugno (which commemorates an air-raid during the Second World War) to the **Pieve delle Sante Fiora e Lucilla**, dedicated to the two saints, whose relics were brought here in the 11C. The **façade** preserves a fine Romanesque rose-window, but the doorway dates from the 15C–16C when the church was renovated. The interior has rounded arches on piers dividing the nave from the aisles and the simple whitewashed structure, outlined in grey stone, is filled with light from the large windows. The altarpieces and pulpit in glazed terracotta are by Andrea della Robbia and his workshop (c 1480–90). On the right wall is a triptych representing the *Coronation of the Virgin* between *St Francis receiving the Stigmata*, and the *Penitent St Jerome*, with a predella showing the *Annunciation*, the *Nativity*, and the *Adoration of the Magi*, in a frame decorated with fruit, flowers, and classical motifs. Beyond is a *Crucifix* in a niche, also in glazed terracotta, decorated with geometrical and floral designs and a frieze of quinces. The pulpit represents the *Last Supper*, *Resurrection*, and *Ascension*. The largest and most elaborate work is the altarpiece, complete with lunette, predella and ornate frame, representing the *Assumption of the Virgin with Angels and Saints*, in which the white figures are set against a simple blue ground. Above the baptismal font is a lunette in polychrome glazed terracotta representing the *Baptism of Christ*, and the *Last Supper* beneath the altar.

A steep road, terminating in steps, leads down from the medieval district to the church of **Sant'Agostino**, which preserves its fine 14C bell-tower. The church contains a number of interesting polychrome wood statues, in particular a fine *Madonna and Child* by Jacopo della Quercia, and a few paintings.

The road continues through a gateway, past gardens with vines and roses, to a large public fountain, to the right of which is the little oratory of the **Madonna delle Nevi**. Over the entrance is a della Robbia relief representing Fiora and Lucilla. The interior has a rather damaged series of saints frescoed in oval frames by Francesco Nasini. Next to the chapel is a public fountain fed from the Fiora spring.

Behind the chapel is the entrance to the garden of **La Peschiera** (open weekends June–Sept 10.00–13.00, 15.30–18.00, or by appointment, ☎ 0564 977 571). This delightful garden was created in the Renaissance, but later suffered from neglect until it was restored by Lorenzo Sforza in 1851. Wonderfully cool in summer, the garden surrounds a large rectangular fishpond and bubbling rivulets which collect the spring waters of the river Fiora. Further uphill is a public park with a chestnut wood and a children's playground. The Fiora provides the water supply for much of the province of Grosseto.

Arcidosso

Arcidosso (661m) lies on a ridge between Monte Amiata and Monte Labbro. It is now primarily a holiday resort, with a large modern district which has developed towards the southeast. From the car park it is a short walk to Corso Toscana, leading to the old town. The cast-iron fountain, known as the **Fonte del Poggiolo**, was made in Follonica in 1833 and transferred here from Piazza del Duomo in Grosseto.

The **Porta di Mezzo**, a triple-arched gateway surmounted by a clock-tower, was largely rebuilt in the mid-19C. The gateway leads uphill to the winding streets of the old fortified town and downhill to the little piazza and church of San Leonardo. Inside is a holy-water stoup by a local 17C sculptor, Pietro Amati, who also carved the frame surrounding the altarpiece (1589) by Francesco Vanni, representing the *Beheading of John the Baptist*.

Another gateway, the **Porta di Castello**, with the Medici arms, leads steeply up to the Aldobrandeschi **Rocca**, a severe block-like construction with an impressive tower. Nearby is the church of San Niccolò which overlooks a vast panorama. At the far end of the medieval town is the Romanesque church of Sant'Andrea built against the walls beside another arched gateway.

On a hill, facing Arcidosso from the west, above a flight of steps, is the sanctuary of the **Madonna delle Grazie** (also known as **L'Incoronata**). The church was first built to house a venerated image of the Madonna after the plague of 1348 and was rebuilt and enlarged over the centuries and provided with a portico and a bell-tower. The interior has a rich Baroque high-altar containing an oval *Madonna*, of the early 15C Sienese school, and other paintings. On the terrace outside the church is a fountain in local stone, with the Medici arms.

On the road to Montelaterone, just over 2 kilometres from Arcidosso, is the church of **Santa Maria ad Lamulas**, recorded since the 9C. Although largely rebuilt in imitation Romanesque style, it preserves some fine Lombard capitals and its three original apses. The painted and gilt wooden statue of the *Madonna and Child* is by a mid-15C Sienese sculptor.

On the road between Arcidosso and Castel del Piano is the monastery and church of the **Cappuccini**, founded by Ferdinando I de'Medici in 1590. Over the high altar is the *Madonna enthroned with Saints Bernardine, Francis and Leonard* by Francesco Vanni (1593), one of the Sienese artist's finest works. The *Annunciation*, on the right-hand altar, is attributed to Giuseppe Nicola Nasini.

Monte Amiata Wildlife Park

On the road leading south from Arcidosso to Roccalbegna, at l'Aiole is a turning signposted for the **Parco Faunistico del Monte Amiata** (open daily, exc. Mon 07.15–sunset, ☎ 0564 966 867), a wildlife reserve which extends over the northeast slopes of **Monte Labbro**. Wild animals and birds live in protected areas which are equipped with footpaths and hides for visitors. At the summit of the mountain (1193m) are the ruins of the tower and church built by Davide Lazzaretti and his followers. In 1868 Lazzaretti, the 'Messiah of Monte Amiata', founded a Christian community on Monte Labbro which aimed at instructing and helping the poor. A prophet and visionary, he was regarded with suspicion and condemned by the Church, and his republican ideals were interpreted as a threat by the local authorities. He was shot by carabinieri as he led a throng of followers down from Monte Labbro to Arcidosso in 1878.

Roccalbegna

Near the picturesque castle of **Triana** is the turning for the small town of Roccalbegna (522m) which is perched on the southern slopes of Monte Labbro, high above the Albegna valley. It is dominated by a tall, cone-shaped rock 40 metres high, known as **Il Sasso**, on top of which are the remains of an Aldobrandeschi castle. The view from here is worth the climb up the steep steps. Remains of the town walls incorporating the Porta Maremma formerly connected the castle with a fortress on the south side, now an overgrown ruin.

The streets of Roccalbegna are laid out on a regular grid plan with the church of **Santi Pietro e Paolo** at the centre. Its **façade** of beautifully cut stone has a large oculus above a richly carved arched doorway, flanked by spiral columns.

The interior has been restored to its medieval appearance. On the high altar is a triptych by Ambrogio Lorenzetti (c 1340), which has unfortunately been reduced in size. The central panel of the *Madonna and Child* is a very beautiful work. Typical of the artist is the meditative, slightly sad expression of the Madonna and the refined attention to detail. On either side are two stately seated figures of *St Peter* and *St Paul* with their attributes. Other works include a *Deposition* attributed to Casolani, besides a few frescoes and a late 14C *Crucifix*.

Behind the church steps lead up to the **Oratorio del Crocifisso** (open on request), which has been converted into a museum for works of art and liturgical objects from the local churches. The contents include a fine large painted *Crucifix* by Luca di Tommè (c 1360), a number of paintings by 17C Sienese artists and several by Francesco Nasini.

Beyond the Porta di Maremma is a pleasant public park with tall trees. Steps lead down to the bank of the Albegna river which flows amongst huge boulders and acquatic plants.

From the Grosseto road, which winds uphill, there is a particularly spectacular view over Roccalbegna and the surrounding countryside.

Siena

Siena (59,000 inhabitants), is not only one of the most fascinating towns in Tuscany but is also in a particularly beautiful position, with lovely environs. The town is the capital of the Tuscan province of the same name. It preserves its medieval character to a remarkable degree, and has been largely unspoilt by new buildings. Its beautiful Gothic buildings include the Cathedral and Palazzo Pubblico, as well as numerous churches. The delightful Sienese school of painting produced, in the first half of the 14C, masterpieces by Duccio di Buoninsegna, Simone Martini, and Pietro and Ambrogio Lorenzetti, all of whose work is well represented in the Pinacoteca, Palazzo Pubblico, and Museo dell'Opera del Duomo. The Campo is one of the most remarkable squares in Italy. The seventeen *Contrade* or wards into which the town is divided still manage to play an active part in the life of the city, culminating in the famous Palio horserace which has survived as perhaps the most spectacular annual festival in Italy, in which the whole city participates.

The town is built on a Y-shaped ridge and spreads into the adjacent valleys; the streets are consequently often steep, and to pass from one part of the city to another it is often necessary to cross a deep valley. For this reason, and also because its treasures are unusually scattered, several days are needed for an adequate visit. From the town there is an extensive and varied panorama which includes Monte Amiata and the metalliferous hills, as well as the clay downs of Asciano and the wooded district of Montagnola. To the north, the scenery changes once again, with the densely cultivated hills of the Chianti. The particularly beautiful environs of the town are described on p 399.

Practical information

Getting there
By car

From Florence, there is a fast superstrada to Siena, but it is poorly engineered and can be very busy. A much more beautiful approach is along the Via Chiantigiana (N222) through the Chianti countryside, or by the Via Cassia (N2) via Tavarnelle.

Parking The centre is entirely closed to traffic. Parking areas are clearly indicated at the entrances to the town. For access to hotels and garages, permission to enter the centre of the city can be obtained from the Vigili Urbani (town police) at San Domenico or no. 7 Viale Tozzi. Sometimes free parking space can be found near the Fortezza and La Lizza (**Map** II;5), except on market day (Wednesday) and on Sunday (when football matches are held). Car parks with an hourly tariff in Via Fontanella, near Porta Tufi (**Map** II;14) called Il Campo, and near Porta San Marco (**Map** II;13) called Il Duomo and by San Domenico in Viale dello Stadio (**Map** I; 1), called Lo Stadio.

Park and ride

There is a car park at **Fontebranda** (**Map** II; 9), with a mini-bus service to the centre. Free car parking (with minibus service every 15mins) on the outskirts of the town at: **Due Ponti** (beyond Porta Pispini; **Map** II; 12; bus to Logge del Papa, **Map** I; 7), and at **Coroncina** (beyond Porta Romana, **Map** II; 15; bus to Piazza del Mercato **Map** I; 11).

By train

The station (beyond **Map** I;1) is c 1.5km north of the town at the
bottom of the hill. Buses connect from the piazza opposite the station to Piazza Gramsci (**Map** II;6) in 7mins.

By bus

Long-distance buses run by *SITA* from Florence (Piazza Stazione) to Piazza Gramsci (**Map** I I;2) at least every hour in 1hr 15mins (via the superstrada). Also to Grosseto, Lucca, and Arezzo. *TRA-IN* town buses (for the environs) from La Lizza (**Map** II;5).

 Information offices
APT, 43 Via di Città (**Map** I; 6); Information office at Piazza del Campo 56 (**Map** I; 6; ☎ 0577 280 551).

Web sites

APT: ✉ www.siena.turismo.toscana.it
Comune: ✉ www.comune.siena.it
Duomo and Museo dell'Opera:
✉ www.operaduomo.it
Santa Maria della Scala:
✉ www.santamaria.comune.siena.it

 Where to stay
Hotels

☆☆☆☆ *Park Hotel*, Via Marciano 18 (beyond **Map** II; 1; towards the Florence superstrada), with swimming pool (☎ 0577 448 03, 🖷 0577 490 20); *Athena*, Via Mascagni 55 (**Map** II; 13; *1*: ☎ 0577 286 313, 🖷 0577 481 53); *Jolly Hotel Excelsior*, Piazza La Lizza 1 (**Map** II; 6; *2*; ☎ 0577 288 448, 🖷 0577 412 72). ☆☆☆ *Santa Caterina*, Via Piccolomini 7 (**Map** II; 15, 16; 8: ☎ 0577 221 105, 🖷 0577 271 087); *Pensione Palazzo Ravizza*, Pian dei Mantellini 34 (**Map** I; 13; *3*; ☎ 0577 280 462, 🖷 0577 221 597); *Minerva*, Via Garibaldi 72 (**Map** II; 2; 4; ☎ 0577 284 474, 🖷 0577 433 43); *Duomo*, Via Stalloreggi 38 (**Map** I; 13; 5; ☎ 0577 289 088, 🖷 0577 430

43); *Chiusarelli*, Via Curtatone 9 (**Map** I; 1; 6; ☎ 0577 280 562, 🖷 0577 271 177).

☆☆: *Lea*, Viale XXIV Maggio 10 (**Map** II;9;*7*; ☎ 0577 283 207, 🖷 0577 283 207).

Hotels on the outskirts

☆☆☆☆ (all with swimming pools): *Certosa di Maggiano*, Via Certosa 82 (beyond **Map** II; 16; ☎ 0577 288 180, 🖷 0577 288 189); *Villa Patrizia*, Via Fiorentina 58 (beyond **Map** II; 9; ☎ 0577 504 31, 🖷 0577 504 42); *Villa Scacciapensieri*, Via di Scacciapensieri 10 (near the Osservanza; beyond **Map** II; 4; ☎ 0577 414 41, 🖷 0577 270 854). ☆☆☆ *Castagneto*, Via dei Cappuccini 39 (beyond **Map** II; 9; ☎ 0577 451 03, 🖷 0577 283 266).

Youth hostel

Guidoriccio, Via Fiorentina 89, località Stellino (on the northern outskirts towards the Florence superstrada; bus no. 15 from La Lizza; ☎ 0577 522 12).

Campsite

☆☆☆ *Siena Colleverde*, Via di Scacciapensieri 47 (open mid-March–mid-Nov; bus no. 8 from Piazza del Sale; **Map** I;6; ☎ 0577 280 044, 🖷 0577 333 298).

 Eating out
Restaurants

€€€: *Alla Speranza*, Piazza del Campo 33 (**Map** I; 6); *Da Enzo*, Via Camollia 49 (**Map** II; 2).

€€: *Da Mugolone*, Via dei Pellegrini 8 (**Map** I; 6); *Medioevo*, Via dei Rossi 40 (**Map** I; 2); *Grotta del Gallo Nero*, Via del Porrione 67 (**Map** I; 7, 11); *Grotta Santa Caterina*, Via Galluzza 26 (**Map** I; 5, 6); *L'Angolo*, Via Garibaldi 13 (**Map** II; 2); *Renzo*, Via delle Terme 14 (**Map** II; 6,10); *Spadaforte*, Piazza del Campo 13 (**Map** I; 6); *Il Ghiottone*, Via Massetana 68 (**Map** I; 13, 14).

€: *La Vecchia Osteria*, Via San Marco 8 (beyond **Map** II; 13); *Il Carroccio*, Via

Casato di Sotto 32 (**Map** I; 10);
La Speranza, Piazza del Campo 35
(attached to a luxury-class restaurant;
see above; **Map** I; 6); *Pizzeria il Riccio*,
Via Malta 44 (**Map** II; 1); *Pizzeria
O'Pazzariello*, Via Curtatone 22 (**Map**
II; 6); *Pizzeria Roberto*, Via Calzoleria
26 (**Map** I; 6); *Quattro Venti*, Via San
Pietro 68 (**Map** I; 14).

Restaurants in the outskirts

€€€: *Antica Trattoria Botteganova*,
Via Chiantigiana 29 (beyond **Map** II; 4).
€: *La Colombaia*, Strada Chiantigiana
99, località Malafrasca.

Pasticcerie

Panforte and other traditional Sienese
sweets are sold in *pasticcerie* and cafés all
over the town, including **Nannini**, Via
Banchi di Sopra 24 (**Map** I; 6).

Picnic places

The Botanical Gardens (**Map** II; 14); the
Orti del Tolomei public park below
Sant'Agostino (**Map** I; 14); in front of
the Basilica of Santa Maria dei Servi
(**Map** I; 16); below San Domenico (Via
Camporegio) and near Fontebranda
(**Map** I; 1, 5); the Fortezza (**Map** II; 5);
outside Porta San Marco (**Map** II; 13)
and Porta Tufi (**Map** II: 14).

Museums and galleries
Combined entrance tickets

There is a 2-day combined ticket for the
Museo Civico (Palazzo Pubblico),
Palazzo delle Papesse, and Santa Maria
della Scala, or a ticket valid one week for
the Museo Civico, Santa Maria della
Scala, Palazzo delle Papesse, the Museo
dell'Opera del Duomo, Libreria
Piccolomini, Baptistery, Oratorio di San
Bernardino (and Museo Diocesano), and
Sant'Agostino.

Entertainment
Theatres

Dei Rinnovati, Palazzo
Pubblico. Chamber music concerts in
the *Accademia Musicale Chigiana*,
Via di Città 89 (**Map** I; 10). **Music
week** in August.

History

Siena appears in history as *Saena Julia*, a Roman colony founded by Augustus.
Although it was not an important Roman centre, the Roman she-wolf feeding Romulus and Remus was adapted as an emblem of the city in the Middle
Ages when her rulers wished to increase her prestige by emphasising her
glorious past. In the early Middle Ages the Lombards took control of the town
which was then on the the pilgrimage route from France to Rome (the Via
Francigena, see p 442). Under Charlemagne the town was governed by
counts, but during the 12C it became a self-governing commune and the
noble families and bishops became less powerful. From this time began the
rivalry with Florence which was to last for centuries, and there were frequent
wars between the two cities for control of their neighbouring territory.

In the 13C Siena expanded and became an important centre of banking
in Europe. Rivalry with Florence reached a peak in 1260 when Siena,
now head of the Tuscan Ghibellines who supported the Emperor
(including Florentine exiles from the Guelf or pro-papal regime of the
Primo Popolo), defeated Florence at the battle of Montaperti, which remained
a celebrated victory in Sienese history and a constant source of pride for
the smaller town. However, when Manfred was killed and his Imperial
German army defeated at Benevento in southern Italy by Charles of Anjou in
1266, the merchant families and bankers of Siena decided it was in their
interest to support the Pope instead (since their support of the Ghibelline

cause and subsequent excommunication had damaged their trade in Europe).

In 1287 a Guelf middle class (*popolo grasso*) oligarchy, ruled by a Council of Nine, was established in Siena. These councillors, often rich merchants, held office for only two months, and provided an exceptionally stable form of government for over half a century. They accepted the supremacy of the Guelf city of Florence, and, deciding on a policy of peace with their neighbours, created a climate in which the town could prosper. It was at this time that the greatest works of art were executed by the famous Sienese school of painting. However, in 1348, the town was devastated by the Black Death and over three-quarters of the population died.

The government of the Council of Nine was overthrown by Charles IV of Bohemia in 1355. There followed a long period of instability, with a revolt by the wool workers in 1371. In 1399 Siena came under the power of Gian Galeazzo Visconti of Milan for a few years (as part of an alliance against Florence). The period of unrest continued throughout the 15C although the commune survived despite an attempt by the nobleman Pandolfo Petrucci in 1487 to take over autocratic control of the government.

In the 16C the town made an alliance with the Habsburg Emperor Charles V, but when he sent a Spanish garrison to occupy it the Sienese revolted and switched their allegiance to France. As a result the Emperor combined forces with the Medici Duke Cosimo I of Florence and Siena was taken in 1555 after a disastrous 18-month siege. The Sienese showed great courage, and some 700 families, refusing to live beneath the Medici yoke, migrated to Montalcino, where they maintained a Sienese republic until 1559 when that too was handed over to Florence by the Treaty of Cateau-Cambresis. From then on Siena shared the history of Florence and Tuscany. The town suffered little damage in the Second World War since it was entered unopposed by French Expeditionary Forces in 1944.

Sienese art

The architecture of the town is chiefly memorable for its superb Gothic buildings including the Palazzo Pubblico, the cathedral, and numerous palaces. The Renaissance period is represented by several fine palaces by Bernardo Rossellino and Giuliano da Maiano. The native architect Baldassarre Peruzzi also worked here.

The sculptors **Nicola Pisano** and his son **Giovanni** carried out numerous works for the Duomo in the late 13C: Nicola was involved in its design as well as carving the splendid pulpit, and Giovanni was responsible for the façade and its superb Gothic statues (the originals are preserved in the Museo dell'Opera del Duomo). Tino da Camaino also produced sculptures for the Duomo. The most important Sienese sculptor of the early Renaissance was **Jacopo della Quercia**, although little is known about his early life and where he trained. His masterpiece in Siena was the monumental Fonte Gaia in the Campo (replaced by a copy in the 19C), the damaged fragments of which are being slowly restored and they are now exhibited in the Ospedale di Santa Maria della Scala. He also made an important contribution to the exquisite font in the Baptistery, and there are more works by him or his pupils in Palazzo Pubblico and the Museo dell'Opera del Duomo (although he carried out many other works outside Siena, notably in Bologna and

Lucca). From the 13C to the 15C many Sienese sculptors, including Francesco di Valdambrino produced delightful polychrome wooden statues, although many of these are now to be found outside Siena itself.

Other sculptors active in the town in the later 15C and early 16C included Giacomo Cozzarelli (also an architect), Marrina, and Riccio (also a painter and architect).

The splendid early Sienese school of painting, which flourished from the second half of the 13C to the first half of the 14C, began with Guido da Siena, whose *Maestà* can be seen in San Domenico. Other panels by him and his followers are kept in the Pinacoteca. But the first great Sienese painter was **Duccio di Buoninsegna** (c 1260–1319), who painted his celebrated *Maestà* in 1311 for the Duomo (see p 373). His most important follower was **Simone Martini** (1284–1344), who frescoed the *Maestà* in the Palazzo Pubblico, although only two other paintings certainly by his hand remain in Siena (in the Pinacoteca). His brother-in-law Lippo Memmi (fl. 1317–47) produced some beautiful Madonnas, some of which are preserved in the Pinacoteca, and others are to be found elsewhere in Tuscany (and he also painted a *Maestà* for San Gimignano). The brothers **Pietro** and **Ambrogio Lorenzetti** (fl. 1306–50) produced numerous beautiful frescoes and paintings throughout Tuscany. In Siena Ambrogio painted the famous fresco cycle of Wise and Evil Government in Palazzo Pubblico, and a remarkable Madonna (from Lecceto) by him is now in the Museo Diocesano. There are numerous panel paintings by both brothers in the Pinacoteca, and a painting by Pietro in the Museo dell'Opera del Duomo (although he is particularly remembered for his frescoes in the lower church of San Francesco in Assisi). Their followers included Domenico di Bartolo whose works can be seen at the Ospedale di Santa Maria della Scala, as well as the Pinacoteca.

Sassetta and his pupil, known as the Maestro dell'Osservanza, were elegant late-Gothic Sienese painters, some of whose works are preserved in the Pinacoteca.

15C artists at work in the city included the sculptor and painter **Vecchietta** (who carried out frescoes at the Ospedale di Santa Maria della Scala and the Baptistery). The versatile artist **Francesco di Giorgio Martini** produced sculptures in bronze for the Duomo as well as frescoes for Sant'Agostino, and some of his paintings are preserved in the Pinacoteca (although his most important architectural work is the church of Santa Maria del Calcinaio in Cortona). Neroccio di Bartolomeo Landi was another good painter and sculptor who sometimes worked with Francesco di Giorgio (his works can be seen in the Duomo, the Pinacoteca, and the oratory of the Casa di Santa Caterina).

Matteo di Giovanni was a very original painter, as can be seen in his works depicting the *Massacre of the Innocents* (two paintings in Palazzo Pubblico and Santa Maria dei Servi, and a panel in the pavement of the Duomo). He was a prolific painter and numerous altarpieces and *Madonnas* by him can still be seen in Siena (the Pinacoteca, Museo Diocesano, San Domenico), and throughout Tuscany. **Sano di Pietro** produced numerous similar small devotional panels of the *Madonna and Child* in Tuscany (one of the most beautiful of which is in the Oratorio di San Bernardino in Siena), and other works by him are kept in the Museo dell'Opera del Duomo and the Pinacoteca.

At the beginning of the 16C **Sodoma**, born in Lombardy, came to live in Siena, and there are a number of frescoes and paintings by him in the town (in Palazzo Pubblico, the Pinacoteca, San Domenico, Sant'Agostino, and the Oratorio di San Bernardino). **Domenico Beccafumi** was one of the most original artists of the century, as can be seen from the ceiling he painted in the Sala del Concistoro in Palazzo Pubblico, his designs for the pavement of the Duomo, and his remarkable paintings in the Pinacoteca, the Museo del Opera del Duomo, and in San Niccolò al Carmine. In the later 16C and early 17C Francesco Vanni, Ventura Salimbeni, Rutilio Manetti, and Bernardino Mei produced numerous fine altarpieces for Sienese churches. Artists born in Siena in the 19C include the painter Cesare Maccari, and the sculptor Giovanni Duprè.

The skill of Sienese artists over the centuries can be fully appreciated by examining the superb marble pavement of the Duomo, and the delightful 'tavolette di Biccherna', the painted covers of the municipal account-books preserved in the Archivio di Stato.

Siena's **city walls** survive almost entire (good views from Via Girolamo Gigli, Via Peruzzi, **Map** II; 16, 12, 8, and 7) but of the original 38 gates, only eight are extant. These are (from the northwest clockwise): *Porta Camollia, Porta Ovile, Porta Pispini, Porta Romana, Porta Tufi, Porta San Marco, Porta Laterina*, and *Porta Fontebranda*.

The Campo

Steep alleys lead down from the main streets of the town, Via di Città and Via Banchi di Sotto, to the ****Campo** (**Map** I; 6), the main piazza of Siena and centre of civic life, laid out in the 12C. First paved in red brick and marble in 1327–49, it has the remarkable form of a fan or scallop-shell and slopes down to the Palazzo Pubblico on the flat southeast side. Occupying the site of the Roman forum, it is the scene in summer of the famous Palio. It is enclosed by a picturesque medley of palaces (with restaurants, cafés, and shops); the only survivor of the original 14C buildings, besides the splendid Palazzo Pubblico, is Palazzo Sansedoni which follows the curve of the piazza at the northeast end of the semicircle. Although it was reconstructed in 1767, it dates from 1340, with three stories of Gothic windows and a tower asymmetrically placed. The huge **Fonte Gaia** is a free copy made in 1858 by Tito Sarrocchi of the famous original fountain by Jacopo della Quercia (see p 377). This was the main fountain in Siena, at the centre of the system of underground acqueducts which provided water for the citizens.

Palazzo Pubblico ~ The Museo Civico

The *Palazzo Pubblico (**Map** I; 6, 10), or Palazzo Comunale, is a very fine Gothic town hall built in 1297–1310 to house the Council of Nine, government offices and council chambers. The ground floor is still used as municipal offices, while the top floor, with its splendid frescoes, is open to the public.

Restoration of the exterior began in 1998, and is expected to be completed by the end of 2002. The higher central block was the first to be built, with characteristic Sienese stone arches at ground level and brick upper storeys. The two wings on either side were heightened with a third storey in Gothic style only in 1681. But the most remarkable feature is the slim, tall tower (102m high), known as the ***Torre del Mangia**, which can be seen from many miles around. It was built by Muccio and Francesco di Rinaldo in 1338–48 in ruddy brown brick. The beautiful stone cresting, probably designed by Lippo Memmi, is thought to have been constructed by Agostino di Giovanni. The tower may be climbed (see below). At its base is the **Cappella di Piazza** (1352–76), an open loggia built to commemorate the deliverance of the city from the plague in 1348. Most of the statues are by Mariano d'Agnolo Romanelli (1376–80). The chapel was heightened above the four pilasters with arches and a beautiful carved architrave by Antonio Federighi in 1463–68.

The door beside the loggia leads into the **Cortile del Podestà** (14C) with the **ticket office** and the entrance to the tower (see below). On the right an iron staircase (1979) leads to the **upper floor**. On the landing is a case of Sienese ceramics, mostly 17C–18C. The museum is **open** daily 10.00–18.30 or 19.00; July & Aug 10.00–23.00. Separate ticket for the tower (open in mid-March–Oct 10.00–19.00, Nov–early March 10.00–16.00; July & Aug 10.00–23.00.

The upper floor, now the Museo Civico, is remarkable for its superb frescoes by the Sienese school dating from the early 14C to the 16C (by Simone Martini, Ambrogio Lorenzetti, Sodoma and others).

The first four rooms of the museum usually display paintings from the municipal collections (diagrams are provided in each room), but are also used for temporary exhibitions. **Room 1**: 16C–18C non-Sienese and foreign schools, including works by Felice Brusasorci, Johann Heinrich Schonfeld, and Il Bamboccio. **Room 2** (right) and **room 3** contain 16C–17C Sienese paintings including works by Alessandro Casolani, Il Pomarancio, Ventura Salimbeni, and frescoes and sinopie by Sodoma detached from the Cappella di Piazza. **Room 4**: 17C–18C Sienese paintings (Domenico and Rutilio Manetti) and a case of church silver.

The **Sala del Risorgimento** was designed in 1878–90 and decorated under the direction of Giuseppe Partini to celebrate the life of the first king of Italy, Vittorio Emanuele II. It illustrates the most important episodes of the Risorgimento in which the king had been involved and which led to Italian unification: the *Battle of San Martino*, by Amos Cassioli and his son Giuseppe; the *Meeting between Vittorio Emanuele and Garibaldi at Teano* by Pietro Aldi; the *Presentation of the plebiscite in favour of unification in Rome* by Cesare Maccari; an *Allegory of united Italy* by Alessandro Franchi; and the *Funeral of Vittorio Emanuele in the Pantheon in 1888*, also by Maccari. In the vault is an allegory of national unity. Here are 19C busts of famous Sienese, and sculptures by Tito Sarrocchi (Flora) and Giovanni Duprè (reclining figure of a child).

A flight of stairs leads up to the spacious **loggia** with a view of the covered market building and orchards beyond. It has a restored timber ceiling. The **Sala della Signoria** is the seat of the Consiglio Comunale. The 16C lunettes are decorated with frescoes illustrating events in Sienese history.

The **Sala di Balia** is entirely frescoed with *scenes from the life of Pope Alexander III by Spinello Aretino and his son Parri (1407–08), including a splendid naval battle. The entrance wall is being restored. Also here is an inlaid seat by Barna di Turino.

The **Anticamera del Concistoro** contains some detached frescoes (one attributed to Ambrogio Lorenzetti) and a *Madonna and Child* attributed to Matteo di Giovanni.

The **Sala del Concistoro** has a marble doorway by Bernardo Rossellino

The Palio

Every year 10 Contrade (see p 360) are selected to compete in the famous *Corsa del Palio*, a horserace which takes place twice a year in the Campo: on 2 July (Visitation) and 16 August (the day after the Assumption). The later and more important contest was first run in 1310; the earlier race was established in 1659. Rivalry between the Contrade is strong, and provides an extraordinary atmosphere of excitement in the city throughout the summer. The prize is the *Palio* (also known as the *drappellone* or *cencio*), a banner designed anew each year which goes to the winning Contrada, not an individual, and celebrations continue for many weeks after the victory, in which the horse is the main protagonist.

Three days before the *Palio* the horses are drawn by lot by each Contrada. Jockeys are chosen in advance (and paid for) by each Contrada. There are six dress rehearsals, the last one on the morning of the race called the *provaccia*. At 14.30 or 15.00 the horse and jockey are blessed in the church of each Contrada, a remarkable ceremony in which everyone is invited to keep silent (and flash photography forbidden) in order not to disturb the horse; not until it is well outside the church does the cheering and singing erupt. At 16.30 or 17.00 in Piazza Duomo (well seen from Via del Capitano) a parade forms, led by the dignatories of Siena and members of each Contrada in Renaissance costume, drummers, knights, and horses. It then proceeds round the Campo to the accompaniment of the tolling bell from the Torre del Mangia, and with two flag throwers performing the *sbandierata* for each Contrada. At the end of the procession a triumphal chariot drawn by four white oxen bearing the *Palio*, with eight buglers and three Sienese dignatories enters the Campo from Casato di Sotto, ringing a bell. The crowds wave flags as it passes. The *Palio* is hung up at the corner of the Campo near Via dei Pellegrini (beside the starting posts).

The horses and jockeys (riding bare back) enter from the courtyard of Palazzo Pubblico, lining up behind a rope. Another horse (drawn by lot) canters up from behind *outside* the rope: when he is level with the rope the *mossiere* (or race official) lets the rope fall so that they all start together (*la mossa*). The timing is extremely difficult so there are usually a number of false starts (which are signalled by a loud *bombarda* or cannonshot which recalls the jockeys to the starting point). It can take some 40 minutes to start the race (after three false starts the order of horses is changed). The *mossiere* is rushed out of the Campo as soon as the race starts as his decision is often contested. The race consists of three laps of the Campo, and it is the horse that wins (even if it is riderless).

Celebrations by the winning Contrada last all night (and the horse eats at the head of the table at the banquet held in its honour). The following morning the Captain, flag throwers, drummers, and horse of the winning Contrada parade around the city with the Palio visiting the headquarters of each Contrada (except that of their traditional enemies). Each Contrada honours the winners by joining them in flag throwing. The banner of the winning Contrada is flown from Palazzo Pubblico. There has been criticism in recent years that the Palio is too dangerous for the horses; it is quite common for one of the horses to be put down after breaking a leg.

Siena is closed to traffic for several days before the Palio. Tickets (not cheap) are sold in advance for the stands or terraces or for the area inside the railings of the fountain, but they are very difficult to find (enquire at the APT). The most exciting way to see the race is from the centre of the Campo (free standing room only) which is crowded with spectators. All entrances to the Campo are closed some time before the ceremony begins; the last one to close is at Via Duprè. The Campo can hold about 30,000 people.

The Contrade

Aquila (eagle)
Bruco (caterpillar)
Chiocciola (snail)
Civetta (owl)
Drago (dragon)
Giraffa (giraffe)
Istrice (porcupine)
Leocorno (unicorn)
Lupa (she-wolf)

Nicchio (scallop shell)
Oca (goose)
Onda (wave)
Pantera (panther)
Selva (wood)
Tartuca (tortoise)
Torre (tower)
Valdimontone (*montone*, mountain goat)

Since the 13C the city has been divided into three **Terzi**: *di Città*, *di San Martino*, and *di Camollia*, and each Terzo subdivided into wards, or **Contrade** by the Comune for administrative purposes. In the 14C there were 42 Contrade, reduced in the 16C to 23. Since 1675 there have been 17, each with a headquarters and small museum beside its oratory, run by an assembly elected by all those born in the Contrada over 18 years old. Children are baptised at an open-air font in the Contrada. The oratories and museums are only open on certain days of the year (enquire at the *APT* office) or by appointment in advance.

(1448). The *vault is frescoed by Beccafumi (1529–35), illustrating heroic deeds of ancient Greece and Rome.

In the **vestibule** is a ruined fresco of the *Madonna* from the loggia by Ambrogio Lorenzetti, and the gilded bronze she-wolf (part of the arms of Siena, evincing pride in her Roman origin), by Giovanni di Turino (c 1429), removed from the exterior of the palace.

The **Anticappella** is decorated with frescoes by Taddeo di Bartolo illustrating the Virtues and famous Roman and Greek heroes and divinities, and a colossal *St Christopher*. Two 15C intarsia panels and a case of goldsmiths' work (12C–17C) are also displayed here.

The **Cappella** has a fine wrought-iron screen (1435–45) on a design attributed to Jacopo della Quercia. It is also frescoed by Taddeo di Bartolo, with scenes from the *Life of the Virgin* (1407–08). The altarpiece is by Sodoma. The 15C chandelier in wrought iron and gilded polychrome wood is by Domenico di Niccolò dei Cori (1420–30) who also carved the *stalls (1415–28).

Sala del Mappamondo

The Sala del Mappamondo was named after a circular map of the Sienese state painted for this room by Ambrogio Lorenzetti, now lost (see below). The Council met here before 1342. Here is the famous *Maestà, the earliest work of **Simone Martini**

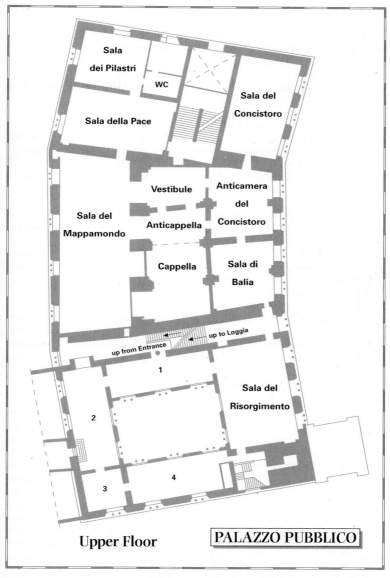

Sala dei Pilastri

WC

Sala della Pace

Sala del Concistoro

Vestibule

Anticamera del Concistoro

Sala del Mappamondo

Anticappella

Cappella

Sala di Balia

up to Loggia

up from Entrance

1

2

3

4

Sala del Risorgimento

Upper Floor

PALAZZO PUBBLICO

(1315; partly repainted by him in 1321), depicting a beautiful Madonna seated beneath a baldacchino borne by apostles and surrounded by angels and saints.

On the opposite wall is the famous fresco of **Guidoriccio da Fogliano*, Captain of the Sienese army, setting out for the victorious siege of Montemassi, a delightful work (partly repainted, but cleaned in 1981), traditionally attributed to

Simone Martini (1330). Since 1977 it has been the subject of a heated debate among art historians, some of whom suggest it may be a later 14C work, and therefore no longer attributable to Simone Martini. The fresco beneath, discovered in 1980, and thought to date from 1315–20, which represents the deliverance of a borgo (with the castle of Giuncarico) to a representative of the Sienese Republic has been variously attributed to Duccio di Buoninsegna, Pietro Lorenzetti, or Memmo di Filippuccio. The traces of a circular composition here are thought to mark the position of the lost fresco of the Sienese state which gave its name to the room (see above). On either side are *Saints Victor* and *Ansanus*, by Sodoma.

On the long wall: *Victory of the Sienese at Poggio Imperiale* by Giovanni di Cristoforo Ghini and Francesco d'Andrea (1480), and *Victory at Val di Chiana*, by Lippo Vanni, both predominantly in burnt sienna. On the pilasters below (left to right) *Blessed Bernardo Tolomei* by Sodoma (1533); *St Bernardine* by Sano di Pietro (1450), and *St Catherine of Siena* by Vecchietta (1461). The painting of the *Massacre of the Innocents* is by Matteo di Giovanni (1482; from the church of Sant'Agostino).

The *Sala della Pace* was the room of the Council of Nine who ruled Siena from 1287 until 1355. The remarkable allegorical *frescoes* by **Ambrogio Lorenzetti** (1338) are considered the most important cycle of secular paintings left in Italy from the Middle Ages. On the wall opposite the window is an *Allegory of Wise Government*: on the entrance wall are illustrated the effects of *Good Government* in the town and countryside. The city represents Siena. Opposite is an *Allegory of Evil Government* (very damaged) with its effect on the town and countryside.

The **Sala dei Pilastri** contains 13C–15C paintings including a 13C *Crucifix*, part of a polyptych by Martino di Bartolomeo, a stained glass window with *St Michael Archangel* by Ambrogio Lorenzetti; an *Annunciation* by Niccolò di Ser Sozzo; two statues of Saints by Jacopo della Quercia and his bottega, and some carved wooden painted and inlaid coffers.

The Torre del Mangia

The entrance to the tower, the *Torre del Mangia is on the left-hand side of the courtyard.

Stairs lead up to the ticket office, and then out onto a little roof terrace at the foot of the tower. A stone staircase continues up past the mechanism of the clock. Higher up there is a view of the church of Santa Maria dei Servi, before the two bells are reached. Narrow wooden stairs continue right up to the top of the lantern with another bell. There is a splendid view: to the northwest are the Campo and San Domenico with the tree-covered Fortezza; to the northeast in the foreground the domed church of Santa Maria

The Torre del Mangia, Siena

Provenzano and San Francesco, and a stretch of walls enclosing fields beyond. On the hill behind is the Osservanza. To the southeast can be seen the church of Santa Maria dei Servi with its tall brick campanile, and orchards, and to the southwest the church of Sant'Agostino and the Duomo, with the tall nave of the Duomo Nuovo.

From the Campo to Piazza del Duomo

From the west side of the Campo *Via di Città (Map I; 10, 6), bordered by handsome mansions, winds upwards to the south. To the left (no. 89) is the 14C **Palazzo Chigi-Saracini** (Map I; 10), a characteristic Sienese Gothic fortified palace with splendid three-light windows, partly rebuilt in 1791. The charming courtyard is usually open. It houses the renowned **Accademia Musicale Chigiana**, founded in 1932 by Count Guido Chigi Saracini. The academy holds international courses in July and August and concerts are given in the theatre built in 1923 in 18C style.

Exhibitions are held in the palace periodically of parts of the famous *Chigi-Saracini Art Collection**. The huge collection was formed at the end of the 18C by Galgano Saracini, and opened to the public in 1806 as Siena's first important museum. It is particularly important for its Sienese works, ranging from the 13C–17C, including an *Adoration of the Magi* by Sassetta. Most of it is now owned by the Monte dei Paschi bank (for information, enquire at the head office of the Monte dei Paschi bank in Piazza Salimbeni).

To the right (no. 128) is the splendid Renaissance **Palazzo Piccolomini delle Papesse**, built by Caterina Piccolomini, sister of Pius II, from the plans of Bernardo Rossellino (1460–95). In 1998 a Contemporary Art Centre was opened here where exhibtions are held (open 12.00–19.00). Then comes **Palazzo Marsili** built in brick in 1444–50. Next to it is the 15C **Palazzo Marsilli-Libelli**, restored by Giuseppe Partini in 1872–73 in medieval style, which bears the Piccolomini coat of arms, attributed to Urbano da Cortona or Vecchietta.

The Duomo

Via di Città ends in **Piazza Postierla** (or I Quattro Cantoni; **Map I**; 10). Here a column with a fine iron standard-holder is surmounted by a she-wolf (1487; recently replaced by a disappointing copy). The chemist's shop here preserves its cupboards dating from c 1830. Via del Capitano leads past the 16C Palazzo Piccolomini Adami and the late 13C Palazzo del Capitano (no. 15) to **Piazza del Duomo**, with the Duomo (inside which is the Piccolomini Library), the Museo dell'Opera del Duomo, the Baptistery, and the Ospedale di Santa Maria della Scala.

- The **Duomo** is open 07.30–13.00, 14.30–17.00; mid-March–Oct 07.30–19.30 (the floor is totally uncovered in Sept). Throughout the year it is open on fest. only from 14.30 onwards. The **Piccolomini Library** is open 10.00–13.00, 14.30–16.45; mid March-Oct, 09.00–19.30. The **Baptistery** is open March–Sept. 09.00–19.30; winter 10.00–13.00, 14.30–17.00. The **Museo dell'Opera del Duomo** is open 09.00–13.15; mid-March–Sept 09.00–19.15; Oct 09.00–18.00. For combined tickets, see p 354.

The *Duomo (**Map** I; 9), dedicated to the *Assumption*, is the earliest of the great Tuscan Gothic churches, despite certain Romanesque elements. It is known that Nicola Pisano was involved as architect in the 13C.

The first church on this site probably dates from the 9C, and a second building is traditionally thought to have been consecrated in 1179. The present cathedral was under construction from c 1215 and the cupola was completed in 1263. In 1316 it was enlarged under the direction of Camaino di Crescentino. After 1285 the façade, designed by Giovanni Pisano was begun and in 1339 there was a scheme to build an even bigger cathedral: an immense nave was to be constructed south of the original church, which was to be turned into a transept (see plan on p 366). Lando di Pietro and Giovanni di Agostino began this herculean task, but the plague of 1348 and the political misfortunes of the city compelled its abandonment. The original plan was resumed, leaving the huge unfinished nave to record the ambition of the Sienese. The building measures 89m by 24m (52.5m across the transepts). The apse was completed in 1382. The upper part of the façade, in the style of the Cathedral of Orvieto, was added by Giovanni di Cecco after 1376. The whole building was carefully restored in 1865-69 under the direction of Giuseppe Partini.

Exterior

Marble steps, flanked by columns bearing the she-wolf of Siena (the originals, attributed to the workshops of Giovanni Pisano and of Urbano da Cortona are now in the Museo dell' Opera del Duomo) ascend to a plinth of white marble inlaid with

The Duomo and Campanile of Siena

black, on which the cathedral stands. The *façade, in polychrome marble, is remarkable for its magnificent statuary, mostly replaced by copies in the 19C made in the workshop of Tito Sarrocchi (originals in the Museo dell'Opera). The lower part, with three richly decorated portals of equal height and size, with triangular pediments, was designed by Giovanni Pisano in 1284–85 and 1296–97 who, together with his pupils, was responsible for the sculptures of prophets, philosophers, and patriarchs. The architrave of the main portal bears stories from the *Life of the Virgin*, an early work by Tino da Camaino. The two carved columns on either side of the main door were removed in 1970 to the museum. The upper part of the façade, with a great rose window, was added in the second half of the 14C in a less harmonious design; in the three gables are bright mosaics, designed by Alessandro Franchi and Leopoldo Maccari and made in Venice in the 19C.

On the east side the *campanile (1313) rises from the transept (on the base of an earlier tower). Its six storeys, banded in black and white, are pierced by windows whose openings increase in progression from single to sixfold. The **Porta del Perdono** which leads into the south transept bears the cast of a tondo of the *Madonna and Child*, almost certainly by Donatello (original in the museum). On the roof of the nave and south transept are copies of 14C statues of the Apostles (originals in the museum). On the left flank of the cathedral is the lapidary stone of Giovanni Pisano who was buried here.

Interior

The dichromatic style of the exterior, familiar from many Tuscan Romanesque churches, is repeated with greater emphasis in the *interior (for opening times, see above). Here the elaborate use of bands of black and white marble on the walls and columns provides a magnificent effect. The round arches of the nave support a pointed vaulting. The interior contains numerous important sculptural works.

The pavement The floor of the whole church is ornamented with a remarkable series of over 50 exquisite marble figures, designs and scenes. The oldest (1373) were carried out in simple graffiti, with black outlines on the white marble. Others were inlaid with black and white, or coloured marble, or (in the 16C) marbles of different tones. More than 40 artists, most of them Sienese, worked on the pavement over the centuries: the most original and productive was Domenico Beccafumi who, from 1519 to 1547, carried out many of the scenes in the central hexagon and at the east end of the church (the cartoons for which can be seen in the Pinacoteca). Many of the panels have been restored or remade over the centuries, particularly in the 1860s, and some original fragments are kept in the Museo dell'Opera del Duomo.

Those in the nave and south aisle, and some in the north transept and sanctuary can usually be seen, but many of them are covered by protective flooring. However the entire pavement is usually visible from around 28 August to 2 October. The letters below refer to the plan of the Duomo on p 366.

The complicated iconographical scheme, apparently worked out by members of the Opera del Duomo, includes the Sibyls (female prophets), allegories, symbolic references to Sienese history, and biblical scenes, mostly stories from the Old Testament.

In the **nave** are five square panels: *Hermes Trismegistus* (A), an Egyptian sage (also known as Thoth), renowned for his wisdom, by Giovanni di Stefano (1488); *She-wolf of Siena surrounded by her allies* (B), a tondo in mosaic of 1373 (remade in 1864–65). The cities are represented by animal symbols: Arezzo (horse); Orvieto (goose); Rome (elephant); Perugia (stork); Viterbo (unicorn); Pisa (hare); Lucca (panther) and Florence (lion). In the four corners are Massa Marittima (lion), Grosseto (griffin), Pistoia (dragon) and Volterra (eagle). The next panel (C) has the design of a rose window, with the Imperial eagle in the centre (alluding to the Roman origins of the city). This also dates from the 14C but was remade in the 19C. The *Allegory of the Hill of Virtue or Knowledge* (D) is by Pinturicchio (1505). The nude, unstable figure of Fortune is shown conducting a group of wise men to the summit of a rock on which are seated a female figure symbolising knowledge, with Socrates on her right. Crates, the Cynic philopher, on her left, is emptying a basket-full of jewels, symbol of earthly riches, into the tempestuous sea below. The *Wheel of Fortune* (E) shows a king and four Greek philosophers. It dates from 1372 (attributed to Domenico di Niccolò dei Cori), but was remade in 1864–65.

SIENA DUOMO

In the **side aisles** are ten white marble figures of Sibyls (each identified with an inscription) against a black ground with a square black-and-white chequered border. They date from 1482–83, and most of them were restored in 1864–65. The *Delphic Sibyl* (F) is attributed to Giovanni di Stefano or Antonio Federighi; the *Cumaean Sibyl* (G) and the *Cimmerian Sibyl* (H) are both by Giovanni di Stefano. The *Erythraean Sibyl* (J) is by Antonio Federighi and the *Persian Sibyl* (K) is by Benvenuto di Giovanni. The *Libyan Sibyl* (L; made in black marble since she came from Africa) is by Guidoccio Cozzarelli, and the *Hellespontic Sibyl* (M) by Neroccio di Bartolomeo Landi. The *Phrygian Sibyl* (N) and the *Tiburtine Sibyl* (P; or *Albunea*) are by Benvenuto di Giovanni, and the *Samian Sibyl* (O) by Matteo di Giovanni.

In the **north transept** are oblong biblical scenes. The *Expulsion of Herod* (Q) by Benvenuto di Giovanni (1485, restored in 1869–78), shows a battle scene framed with winged lions, and the story is told in a cartouche held up by four putti. On the skyline is a hill town which recalls Siena. The eagle on its nest attacked by a serpent at the top of a tall dead tree is thought to be an allusion to the expulsion from Siena of the autocrat Pandolfo Petrucci in 1482 (see p 355).

The *Massacre of the Innocents* (R) is presumed to be by Matteo di Giovanni (1482) since there are analogies in style to the paintings by him of the same subject in the Sienese churches of Santa Maria dei Servi and Sant'Agostino (now in Palazzo Pubblico). The dramatic scene takes place beneath a portico in the presence of Herod. The *Story of Judith* (S) is attributed to Francesco di Giorgio Martini (1473). Above a battle scene is the figure of Judith with her serving girl carrying the head of Holofernes on a hill outside a walled city with numerous towers.

In front of the altar steps is a tondo with *David composing the psalms* (T) flanked by the figures of *David and Goliath*, by Domenico di Niccolò dei Cori, capomaestro of the Duomo from 1413–23. On either side, in a poor state of preservation, are two scenes (U) from the life of Joshua and Samson, both attributed to Sassetta.

In the **south transept** are two rectangles (V), one with *Emperor Sigismondo and his ministers* by Domenico di Bartolo (1434). The emperor, shown seated on a throne beneath a canopy, visited Siena in 1431 on his way to be crowned in Rome. The other scene shows the *Death of Absolom* (who is hanging from a tree by his hair), by Piero del Minella (1447). Beneath these two panels is an oblong scene with the *Story of Jephthah* (W), showing a battle taking place in front of a hilly landsdcape and a town on a hilltop. This is attributed to Neroccio di Bartolomeo Landi (1485).

The hexagon beneath the dome encloses seven smaller hexagons and six lozenge-shaped scenes, illustrating the *Story of Elijah* (X). The most beautiful (the central scene and the three hexagons and two lozenges nearest to the altar) are by Domencio Beccafumi (1519–24) who here introduced a new technique of marble inlay. All the others, which replaced earlier works, were made by Alessandro Franchi in 1878.

In 1525–31 Beccafumi also carried out the two splendid scenes (Y) beside the pulpit illustrating the Story of Moses. A long narrow panel shows *Moses striking water from the rock*, and the larger rectangle depicts *Moses on Mount Sinai*. In the **choir**, now between the two altars, is the *Sacrifice of Isaac* (Z), the last beautiful work for the pavement made by Beccafumi in 1547.

The nave The carved columns of the main west door are attributed to Giovanni di Stefano (1483). The reliefs of the pedestals are by Urbano da Cortona. The glass in the rose window represents the *Last Supper* (1549; by Pastorino de' Pastorini, a pupil of Guglielmo de Marcillat). The monument (1) to Paul V (Camillo Borghese) in a fine niche by Flaminio del Turco has a statue by Domenico Cafaggi (1592). The two stoups (2, 3) are beautifully carved by Antonio Federighi. Above the nave arches are a monotonous series of busts of popes produced from 1495 onwards by means of terracotta moulds.

South aisle. First altar (4) Domenico Maria Canuti, St Gaetano (1681); second altar (5) Annibale Mazzuoli, *Ecstasy of St Jerome* (1725); third altar (6) Raffaello Vanni, *St Francis of Sales* (1654); fourth altar (7) Pietro Dandini, *Mystical Marriage of St Catherine* (1671). Above the doorway to the campanile (8) is the tomb of Bishop Tommaso Piccolomini, a fine work (1484–85) by Neroccio di Bartolomeo Landi. Beneath it are six bas-reliefs by Urbano da Cortona. The hexagon of the **dome** was decorated at the end of the 15C with gilded statues of saints attributed to Giovanni di Stefano, and figures of patriarchs and prophets in chiaroscuro, by Guidoccio Cozzarelli and Benvenuto di Giovanni.

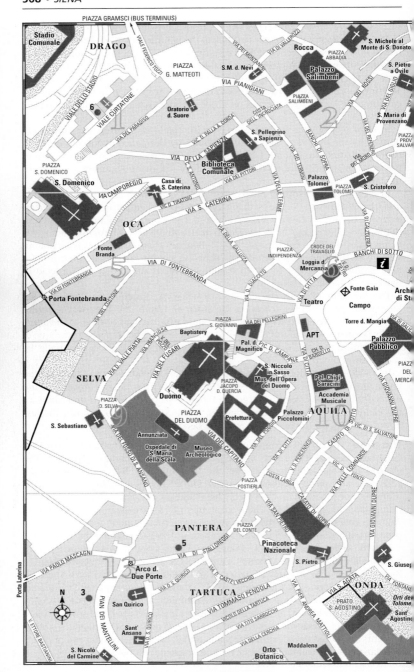

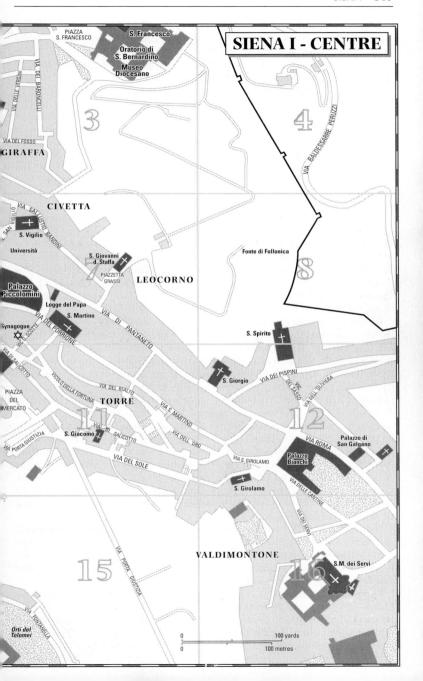

SIENA I - CENTRE

PIAZZA
S. FRANCESCO

S. Francesco

**Oratorio di
S. Bernardino**

**Museo
Diocesano**

VIA DEL BARONCELLI

VIA DELLE VERGINI

3

4

VIA BALDASSARRE. PERUZZI

VIA DEL FOSSO

GIRAFFA

VIA SALICISTIO BANDINI

VIA SAN VIGILIO

CIVETTA

S. Vigilio

Università

**S. Giovanni
d. Staffa**

PIAZZETTA
GRASSI

7

LEOCORNO

Fonte di Follonica

8

**Palazzo
Piccolomini**

Logge del Papa

S. Martino

VIA DI PANTANETO

VIA DEL PORRIONE

Synagogue

VIC. SCOTTE

VIA DI SALICOTTO

S. Spirito

S. Giorgio

VIA DEI PISPINI

VIA DEL SASSO

VIA DELL'OLIVIERA

PIAZZA
DEL
MERCATO

VICOLO DELLA FORTUNA

VIA DEL RIALTO

TORRE

VIA S. MARTINO

VIA PORTA GIUSTIZIA

S. Giacomo

VIA DI SALICOTTO

VIA DELL'ORO

VIA S. GIROLAMO

12

VIA ROMA

**Palazzo di
San Galgano**

VIA DEL SOLE

**Palazzo
Bianchi**

VIA DELLE CANTINE

S. Girolamo

VIA DEI SERVI

11

VIA DI PORTA GIUSTIZIA

15

VALDIMONTONE

16

S.M. dei Servi

VIA PONTANELLA

**Orti del
Tolomei**

0   100 yards

0   100 metres

South transept The circular Baroque **Cappella Chigi** (9) was built for Alexander VII in 1659–62, almost certainly on a design by Bernini to house the Madonna del Voto. The statues are by Antonio Raggi (*St Bernardine*), Ercole Ferrata (*St Catherine*), and Bernini: *St Jerome* (10) and *St Mary Magdalene* (11). Above the statues are marble bas-reliefs of 1748. Maratta painted the *Visitation* (in very poor condition) and the *Flight into Egypt* is a mosaic after a painting by the same artist.

The *Madonna del Voto*, a fragment of a larger painting, is by a follower of Guido da Siena. This venerated painting has been the traditional focus of entreaty for the Sienese in times of crisis. On six occasions in their history the inhabitants have placed the keys of their threatened city before it and prayed for deliverance. The first occasion was before the battle of Montaperti in 1260; the latest on 18 June 1944, a fortnight before the liberation of Siena. It is surrounded by gilded bronze angels by Ercole Ferrata. The bronze statue in the chapel is by Arturo Viligiardi (1918).

The organ (12) was designed by Bernini. The Roman Baroque monument to Alexander III (13) was completed by Ercole Ferrata. On the altars: (14) Luigi Mussini, *St Crescenzio* (1867) and (15) Mattia Preti, *St Bernardine* (1670). On the wall, monument to Alexander VII (16) by Antonio Raggi, on a model by Bernini. The marble pavement tomb of Bishop Carlo Bartoli (d. 1444) was designed by Pietro del Minella and carved by Federighi. The **Chapel of the Sacrament** (17) has a fine altar by Flaminio del Turco (1585) and an altarpiece of the *Adoration of the Shepherds* by Alessandro Casolani.

Choir The marble high altar (18) is by Baldassarre Peruzzi (1532); the huge bronze *ciborium is by Vecchietta (1467–72). At the sides, the uppermost angels carrying candles are by Giovanni di Stefano (1489), the lower two are by Francesco di Giorgio Martini (1490). The Cross and candelabra are to a design of Riccio (1570). The eight candelabra in the form of angels (19) on brackets against the pillars of the presbytery are fine works by Domenico Beccafumi (1548–51). In the apse (20), is a fresco of the *Ascension* by Beccafumi (altered in 1812), and, on either side (21) frescoes by Ventura Salimbeni. The round window in the apse contains splendid 13C *stained glass (1288) from cartoons by Duccio, who was also responsible for the painted decoration. This is probably the oldest existing stained glass of Italian manufacture. It shows the *Burial*, *Assumption*, and *Coronation of the Virgin*, together with the four patron saints of the town, and the four Evangelists. The glass has still not been returned here since its restoration. The intarsia *choir-stalls are of varying dates: 1362–97, by several artists under Francesco del Tonghio; 1503, by Giovanni da Verona; and those by Riccio and his school, 1567–70.

To the left of the altar is the entrance to the **sacristy** and **chapter house** (22; sometimes shown on request). The sacristry contains frescoes (1412) now attributed to Benedetto di Bindo. Beyond a vestibule with a fine bust of *Alexander VII* by Melchiorre Caffà, a follower of Bernini, is the chapter house, with a *Madonna and Saints* by Pietro di Francesco Orioli.

The octagonal *pulpit (23) is a remarkable Gothic work by Nicola Pisano (1265–68), completed six years after his famous pulpit in the Baptistery of Pisa. He was assisted by his son Giovanni, and by Arnolfo di Cambio. Around the base of the central column are the figures of Philosophy and the seven Liberal Arts, and at the top of the columns, the Christian Virtues, Evangelists, and Prophets.

The seven panels beautifully carved in high relief symbolise the Redemption, with scenes from the life of Christ and two scenes of the Last Judgement. They are divided by another series of carved figures, including a beautiful Madonna and Child. The elegant staircase was added in 1543 to a design of Riccio.

North transept The altar (24) has an altarpiece by Francesco Vanni. The *tomb of Cardinal Riccardo Petroni (25; d. 1313) is by Tino da Camaino, the design of which was frequently copied throughout the 14C. In front (26) is the bronze pavement *tomb of Bishop Giovanni Pecci, signed by Donatello (1426). The monument to Pius II(27) is by Giuseppe Mazzuoli (1694); that of Pius III (28) is by Pietro Balestra (1703).

The *Cappella di San Giovanni Battista** (29) is a graceful Renaissance structure probably by Giovanni di Stefano (1492). The elegant portal is by Marrina (and the classical bases to the columns by Antonio Federighi); the wrought-iron gate is the work of Sallustio Barili. In the interior are frescoes by Pinturicchio including three scenes from the *Life of St John the Baptist*, and portraits of two kneeling figures (the one shown in the robes of the Order of St John is Alberto Aringhieri, the founder). They were restored in 1865 (when the stained glass window was made), and one of them (*St John leaving prison*) replaced by Cesare Maccari. The statue of *St Ansanus* is by Giovanni di Stefano; that of *St Catherine* is by Neroccio. The bronze statue of *St John the Baptist* is one of Donatello's later works (1457) which is similar, in some ways, to his *St Mary Magdalene* (now in the Museo dell'Opera del Duomo in Florence). The font (c 1460) is beautifully carved by Antonio Federighi. Outside the chapel (30) is the monument to Marcantonio Zondadari by Giuseppe and Bartolomeo Mazzuoli.

The Piccolomini Library

In the **north aisle** is the entrance to the *Libreria Piccolomini (31) one of the most delightful creations of the Renaissance. It was founded in 1495 by Cardinal Francesco Piccolomini (afterwards Pius III) to receive the library of his uncle Aeneas Silvius Piccolomini (Pius II). Its marble façade is by Marrina (1497). Above the altar (right) was placed a relief of *St John the Evangelist* attributed to Giovanni di Stefano. The large fresco above it, by Pinturicchio, shows the *Coronation of Pius III*.

The bright interior consists of a hall decorated with colourful and highly decorative *frescoes** by Pinturicchio and his pupils (1502–09) in an excellent state of preservation. Raphael is thought to have contributed to the design of some of the scenes. They represent ten episodes from the life of Pius II (beginning at the right of the window): 1. *Aeneas Silvius goes to the Council of Basle*; 2. *He presents himself as envoy to James II of Scotland*; 3. *He is crowned as poet by Frederick III* (1442); 4. *He is sent by the Emperor to Eugenius IV* (1445); 5. *As Bishop of Siena, he is present at the meeting in 1451 of the Emperor Frederick and his betrothed Eleonora of Portugal outside the Porta Camollia*; 6. *He is made Cardinal by Calixtus III* (1456); 7. *He becomes Pope* (1458); 8. *He proclaims a crusade at Mantua* (1459); 9. *He canonises St Catherine of Siena* (1461); 10. *He arrives, dying, at Ancona* (1464).

The beautiful vault decoration is also by Pinturicchio and his pupils. In the centre is the celebrated group of the *Three Graces*, a Roman copy of an original by Praxiteles, acquired in Rome by Cardinal Francesco Piccolomini. It served as model to Pinturicchio, Raphael, and Canova. Here are exhibited the 15C *choir**

books of the cathedral and the Scala hospital, illuminated by Liberale da Verona, Girolamo da Cremona, Sano di Pietro, and others. The ceramic floor has a beautiful design.

The great *Piccolomini altar* (32) in the north aisle, is by Andrea Bregno (c 1480). The statuettes in the four lower niches of *St Peter, St Pius, St Gregory*, and *St Paul* are documented early works by Michelangelo (1501–04), who may also have worked on the figure of *St Francis* above, which was begun by Pietro Torrigiani. The *Madonna and Child* at the top, traditionally attributed to Giovanni di Cecco, is thought by some scholars to be Jacopo della Quercia's earliest work (c 1397–1400). The painted *Madonna and Child* over the altar (framed by marble reliefs) is attributed to Paolo di Giovanni Fei (c 1385). Third altar (33) Pietro Sorri, *Epiphany* (1588); second altar (34) Francesco Trevisani, *Christ between Saints James and Philip*; first altar (35) Francesco Trevisani, *Martyrdom of the Four Soldier Saints*.

Museo dell'Opera del Duomo

Piazza Jacopo della Quercia occupies the site of the unfinished nave of the Duomo Nuovo (see p 364): the marble arcades survive as well as the façade and side portal which give some idea of the size and beauty of the projected building. Its south aisle has been converted into the *Museo dell'Opera del Duomo (**Map** I; 10). This is a beautifully kept museum with important works of art from the cathedral (for admission, see p 363).

Top floor The **Sala della Madonna dagli Occhi Grossi** is named after the *Madonna dagli Occhi Grossi*, by a Sienese painter known as the Maestro di Tressa (1220–30). It adorned the high altar of the cathedral before Duccio's *Maestà*. The other paintings here include: Ambrogio Lorenzetti, *Four Saints*; Giovanni di Paolo, *St Jerome*; and four small works by Sodoma. The painting of *St Bernardino of Siena* by Sano di Pietro is flanked by two paintings showing the Saint preaching in the Campo and in Piazza San Francesco; Gregorio di Cecco, polyptych; Sano di Pietro, *Madonna and Child with Saints*.

The **Sala dei Conversari** (so called because Vittorio Alfieri read his tragedies to the public here in 1777) displays works by Matteo di Giovanni; Beccafumi, *St Paul* and two statues of the *Annunciation*; Il Pomerancio, *Madonna and Child with Saints*; altar frontals. The **Sala dei Parati** contains vestments and a marble statue of a child by Giovanni Duprè. From here can be reached the **Scala del Falciatore**, a stair which winds up to the façade of the new cathedral (extensive views of the city and countryside).

On a mezzanine floor below is the **Sala del Tesoro** which contains the *treasury of the cathedral including croziers, reliquaries (including the reliquary of St Galganus from the end of the 13C), and paxes. The Crucifixes include *Christ on the Cross* (in wood) by Giovanni Pisano, an early masterpiece (c 1280). Sculptural works include three busts (from statues) of saints, by Francesco di Valdambrino in polychrome wood (1409), and 12 statuettes of saints attributed to Giuseppe Mazzuoli (models for the marble statues now in the Brompton Oratory, London). In a small room off the treasury is displayed the *treasury from the Chigi chapel which has beautiful Roman and French works of the early 17C.

First floor The **Sala di Duccio** is filled with the celebrated *Maestà* by Duccio di Buoninsegna, one of the most beautiful and important works of art in Italy. The main panel depicts the *Virgin and Child enthroned surrounded by angels* *and saints* (the four patron saints of Siena are shown kneeling in the foreground). The Latin inscription on the throne is an invocation: 'Oh Holy Mother of God bring peace to Siena and life to Duccio since he has painted you thus'! On the opposite wall is the *Story of Christ's Passion* in 26 scenes, formerly on the back of the main panel, and along the wall between them are panels from the predella and cimasa with *Scenes from the life of Christ* and the *Last days and death of the Virgin*. This huge painting was commissioned for the high altar of the Duomo in 1308 (the contract is preserved in the Archivio di Stato, see p 385) where it remained until 1505, but it was dismantled in 1771 when the original frame was destroyed and a few of the panels from the predella and cimasa were dispersed (some of them are now in the Washington and London National Galleries) or lost at this time so that it is still not known exactly how the great painting was composed.

Duccio took some three years to paint it and it was at once recognised as a masterpiece by the Sienese who were so pleased with it that they declared a public holiday and processed it through the streets from his studio in Via di Stalloreggi and round the Campo accompanied by the Council of Nine, prelates, and the populace to the accompaniment of the ringing of the church bells and a municipal fanfare. It shows numerous Byzantine influences endowed with a new Gothic spirit which was to be developed from this work by the great Sienese school of painters. It is embued with a calm beauty and rich colour and extraordinary narrative power.

Duccio di Buoninsegna

Duccio di Buoninsegna (c 1260–1319) was greatly admired by his contemporaries, although little else is known about his life, and very few works definitely by his hand have survived. His *bottega* was in Via di Stalloreggi just inside the Arco delle Due Porte, where from 1313 he lived with his wife Taviana and eight children. He is recorded as having worked as a young man for the Commune of Siena decorating their statute-books and store chests, but his earliest surviving painting is the Madonna di Crevole, also exhibited in this room, from the church of Santa Cecilia in Crevole. His first important commission was in 1285 when the Laudesi confraternity in Florence ordered a Madonna from him for their chapel in Santa Maria Novella. This *Maestà*, known as the Rucellai Madonna (and for long attributed to Cimabue), is now exhibited in the Galleria degli Uffizi. His masterpiece was the *Siena Maestà* which established him as the greatest painter of his time. Another exquisite work by him is preserved in Siena, the Madonna 'dei Francescani' which is a tiny painting (now in the Pinacoteca Nazionale). The cartoon for the round stained glass window in the Duomo is also attributed to his hand. Nothing is known of his life after 1313, and it seems that he never worked in fresco. There are works, mostly Madonnas and Child, all over Tuscany attributed to his school. Simone Martini was his greatest follower. Although Lorenzo Ghiberti mentions him with great admiration he was later forgotten and his importance ignored in the 18C when the *Maestà* was divided up.

Also exhibited in this room are the *Madonna di Crevole* by Duccio, and the *Birth of the Virgin* by Pietro Lorenzetti.

A room to the right displays gilded wood statuettes of the *Madonna and Child and four Saints* (from the church of San Martino), generally attributed to Jacopo della Quercia and Giovanni da Imola, but possibly by Antonio Federighi (who probably carved the statue of St Nicholas of Bari). The statue of *St John the Baptist* from the church of San Giovanni is attributed to Jacopo della Quercia or his *bottega*. In the small room beyond are polychrome wood statues: beside a late 14C carved *Crucifix* is the *Madonna and St John the Evangelist* by Domenico di Niccolò dei Cori (1415). The statue of *St John the Baptist* is by Francesco di Giorgio Martini (1464) and that of *St Savino* is by Guido di Giovanni (1393–95), painted by Paolo di Giovanni Fei.

A room to the left of the Sala di Duccio contains illuminated manuscripts, drawing projects related to the cathedral and Piazza del Campo, and a drawing of the cathedral pavement by Giovanni Paciarelli (1884).

Ground floor The **Sala delle Statue** contains the original *statues of prophets, philosophers, and patriarchs and symbolic animals from the façade of the cathedral, by Giovanni Pisano and his school, constituting one of the most important groups of Italian Gothic sculpture in existence. Also displayed here (near the entrance) are two wolves nursing twins, from the columns outside the Duomo, one attributed to the workshop of Giovanni Pisano and one to the workshop of Urbano da Cortona. In the centre is a bas-relief of the *Madonna and Child with St Anthony Abbot and Cardinal Antonio Casini*, by Jacopo della Quercia, and a tondo of the *Madonna and Child*, almost certainly by Donatello (from the Porta del Perdono of the Duomo). In the floor are fragments of the original Duomo pavement.

Off the gallery, steps lead down to the **Sala del portale centrale del Duomo**. The two columns and lions carved c 1290 by Giovanni Pisano and an assistant for either side of the main door of the Duomo (and removed from there in 1970), are displayed here. The statues of the twelve apostles by the school of Giovanni Pisano were originally inside the Duomo where they were replaced by statues by Giuseppe Mazzuoli in 1680–89 and 1717–21 and put on the roof of the cathedral. The statues by Mazzuoli are now in the Brompton Oratory in London. Three of the statues are attributed to Tino da Camaino (1317–18). The seated statue of the *Redeemer and two angels in adoration* by Giovanni di Agostino (c 1345) come from the lunette of the side door of the Duomo Nuovo.

Another door leads out of the gallery to a flight of stairs (decorated with gargoyles from the Baptistery) which leads down to the church of **San Niccolò in Sasso** which retains its early 17C interior virtually intact. The delightful barrel vault was decorated in 1622 with stuccoes and paintings by Ludovico di Antonio Chiappini and Il Francesino. The high altarpiece of the *Madonna enthroned with Saints* is by Francesco Vanni (1608). The gilded statues at the east end of angels and the *Annunciation* are by Domenico Cavedon and Lodovico Chiappini. The altarpiece on the south side of the *Crucifix* is by Niccolò Tornioli, and on the left of it is a *Resurrection* by Rutilio Manetti and on the right of it a *Nativity* by Astolfo Petrazzi. North side. The altarpiece of the *Pentecost* is by Rutilio Manetti and the *Ascension* on the right of it is by Astolfo Petrazzi. On the left is the *Last Judgement* by Raffaello Vanni. At the west end are two stucco statues, *Augustus* (?) and a *Sibyl* by Chiappini.

The museum can be left by the main door of the church which emerges on Via del Poggio.

The side door of the Duomo Nuovo, between the incomplete nave and the cathedral, is a beautiful Gothic *portal (with casts of the original sculptures by Giovanni di Agostino). From here a steep flight of steps, constructed in 1451 descends to the Baptistery. Half-way down is the entrance to the **Duomo crypt** (no admission) where extremely important frescoes were discovered in 2000 dating from c 1270, the earliest known works of the Sienese school (still being restored).

The Baptistery

At the bottom of the steps is the *Baptistery (**Map** I; 5; beneath part of the cathedral) with a noble but unfinished Gothic façade by Domenico di Agostino (1355). The interior (for admission, see p 363), finished c 1325 probably by Camaino di Crescentino has a beautiful hexagonal *font, one of the most interesting sculptural works of the early Renaissance (1417–30). The gilded bronze panels in relief illustrate the Life of St John the Baptist: the *Angel announcing the birth of the Baptist to Zacharias*, by Jacopo della Quercia; *Birth of the Baptist*, and his preaching, by Turino di Sano and Giovanni di Turino; *Baptism of Christ* and *St John in prison*, both by Lorenzo Ghiberti; *Herod's Feast* by Donatello. The six statues at the angles are by Donatello (Faith and Hope), Giovanni di Turino (Justice, Charity, and Prudence), and Goro di Ser Neroccio (Fortitude). The marble tabernacle above was designed by Jacopo della Quercia who carved the five statues of prophets in niches and the crowning statue of the Baptist. The four bronze angels are by Donatello and Giovanni di Turino.

The 15C *frescoes were restored in 1993. On the two lateral vaults nearest the entrance are figures of the *Apostles and Saints* attributed to Agostino di Marsiglio. The four *Apostles* in the central bay are by Vecchietta, who also frescoed the three vaults nearest the altar with the *Articles of the Creed*, the apsidal arch with the *Assumption of the Virgin and a glory of angels*, and the three lowest scenes in the apse of the *Annunciation*, *Flagellation*, and *Way to Calvary*. The three Passion scenes above in the apse are by Michele di Matteo Lambertini (c 1451–55). In the large lunette to the left of the apse are scenes of the *Miracles of St Anthony of Padua* by Benvenuto di Giovanni (c 1460) and in the large lunette right of the apse, *Washing of the Feet* by Pietro di Francesco Orioli (1489). Some paintings (by Andrea Vanni, Giovanni di Paolo and Rutilio Manetti) from the church of Santo Stefano alla Lizza are also kept here as well as some 14C statues from the Duomo. The triptych of the Immaculate Conception is by Giuseppe Catani Chiti (1897).

Near the Baptistery is the **Palazzo del Magnifico**, built for Pandolfo Petrucci from the plans of Cozzarelli, who also designed the bronze ornaments on the façade (1504–08).

Opposite the south flank of the Duomo is Palazzo del Governatore dei Medici (Palazzo Reale), now the prefecture, rebuilt in 1593. Beside the façade of the Duomo is the long Gothic façade of **Palazzo Arcivescovile** (Archbishop's Palace), with marble black-and-white decoration on the ground floor and brick-work above (probably reconstructed in 1665).

Ospedale di Santa Maria della Scala

Opposite the façade of the Duomo is the irregular Gothic façade (modified over the centuries) of the Ospedale di Santa Maria della Scala (**Map** I; 9), a hospital founded in the 9C for pilgrims travelling down the Via Francigena (see p 442) on their way to Rome (the oldest document to have survived which mentions the hospital dates from 1090). Its name Scala comes from its position in front of the 'steps' which lead up to the cathedral. It was at first administered by the cathedral but after 1195 became progressively a lay institution. Up until a few years ago it was still a hospital, but this has now been transferred and the huge group of buildings is slowly being restored. It will be transformed into an important cultural centre and museum (and the Pinacoteca will one day be transferred here). Only a small part is so far open to the public but in the next few years more and more will become accessible. Temporary exhibitions are also held here. The areas at present open, described below, are **open** 10.30–16.30; mid-March–Oct 10.00–18.00.

The **Cappella del Manto** (named after a fresco of the Madonna della Misericordia, protecting the Sienese with her mantle ('manto'; see below), preserves a lovely frescoed lunette by Domenico Beccafumi showing the *Meeting at the Golden Gate*.

The **Sala del Pellegrinaio**, the 14C pilgrims' hall, has delightful *****frescoes** illustrating the history of the hospital and life within it, carried out in 1440–44.

The first two bays are ruined. Over the two doors: *Story of the Blessed Sorore*, the mythical founder of the hospital, by Vecchietta, and, opposite, *Feeding the poor in the hospital* by Domenico di Bartolo. In the third two bays: *Reception and education of orphans in the hospital* and the *Marriage of an orphan*, and (opposite) *Building work to enlarge the hospital*, both by Domenico di Bartolo. Fourth two bays: *Investiture of the Rector of the hospital by the Blessed Agostino Novello* by Priamo della Quercia, and (opposite) *Distribution of Alms* by Domenico di Bartolo. In the fourth two bays: *Healing of the sick*, and (opposite) *Celestine III granting rights to laymen for running the hospital*, both by Domenico di Bartolo. In the last two bays, *Payment of the wet nurses of the hospital* painted in the 16C by Giovanni di Raffaello Navesi and Pietro d'Achille Crogi.

Beyond several rooms with a collection of 13C–18C Sienese majolica, a restoration laboratory where Duccio's superb stained glass window from the Duomo is being restored, and a collection of 19C plaster casts by Tito Sarrocchi, is the **Cappella del Sacro Chiodo** (the Chapel of the Holy Nail), built before 1444 for the precious hospital treasury (not at present on view) most of which was acquired in 1359 in Constantinople. It included the relic of the Holy Nail (for which a reliquary was made in Siena in the 14C), and an exquisite Greek Evangelistery with late 11C Byzantine miniatures and a gilded silver cover, probably made in Venice in the late 13C and incorporating cloisonné enamels, many of them from Constantinople. Later pieces include an arm reliquary signed by Goro di Ser Neroccio, and three 15C reliquary busts.

The chapel was entirely decorated by Vecchietta in 1446–49, illustrating the *Articles of the Creed*. The scenes are particularly interesting for their iconography but are unfortunately very ruined. Beneath a handsome marble tabernacle is a fresco of the *Madonna del Manto* by Domenico di Bartolo (1444), with the *Madonna of the Misericordia* (detached from the Manto chapel in 1610).

Beyond is the **Cappella della Madonna** with frescoes by Giuseppe Nicola Nasini, and a painting of the *Madonna* over the altar by Paolo di Giovanni Fei. The church can be seen at the end of the visit.

Stairs lead to the floor below. A long vaulted corridor with pretty paving leads to the charming **Oratorio di Santa Caterina della Notte**, the oratory of a confraternity which survives with its 17C furnishings virtually in tact. It contains paintings by the school of Rutilio Mannetti and Francesco Rustici, late 17C stuccoes, a marble statuette of the *Madonna and Child* dating from the late 14C (on the altar), and, in the last room, a painting of the *Madonna and Child with angels, and Saints John the Baptist and Andrew* by Taddeo di Bartolo, and four small early 16C paintings used to decorate coffins.

Nearby are the old storerooms used for grain and other supplies in which are exhibited parts of the damaged **Fonte Gaia**, one of the masterpieces of Jacopo della Quercia (see p 355) a fountain made in 1414–19 for the centre of the Campo. Made from a fragile local marble from Montagnola, it weathered very badly and was damaged by the water, so in 1844 it was decided to remove it from the Campo (see p 357) and in 1869 it was replaced by a copy commissioned from Tito Sarrocchi. However some parts of it were lost, and others suffered further damage after the fountain was taken to pieces: the 78 pieces which have survived have been undergoing restoration in an adjoining laboratory here since 1990. The original pieces already restored include two beautiful female allegorical statues, thought to represent the obscure Roman goddess, Acca Larentia and one of the founders of Rome, Rea Silvia, and three relief panels. Here, too, are displayed the casts of the original marble panels depicting two stories from Genesis, the Theological and Cardinal Virtues, the allegorical figure of Justice, and the Madonna with two angels, taken by Sarrocchi before he started work on his copy, as well as casts of Sarrocchi's works.

Another flight of steps leads down to the **Oratory of the Società di Esecutori di Pie Disposizioni** (see p 389), which preserves its furnishings and has a collection of 19C paintings, including one by Cesare Maccari. The early 14C frescoes which have recently been discovered beneath the vault above the stairs, with scenes of the *Thebaids*, are attributed to Andrea Vanni and Luca di Tommè.

From the courtyard above is the entrance to a series of more storerooms, and then a flight of steps leads down to the **Museo Archeologico**, rearranged in 2001 in dark vaulted underground rooms, also once used as stores. Founded in 1933, it contains Etruscan and Roman material. The first corridor has finds from Siena, including a late Hellenistic head known as Seneca. Another corridor has a series of small hand-made urns from Chiusi (3C–1C BC). To the left are finds from the district of Siena, including Murlo (note the terracotta frieze of horses in bas-relief). A small room has finds from the Elsa valley (Colle, Casole d'Elsa, and Monteriggioni) and the Chianti region. Beyond is a collection of bronzes and stele and finds from a tumulus tomb at Asciano. The large **Bargagli Petrucci collection**, mostly displayed in a wide corridor, has finds from Sarteano (including numerous cinerary urns and ceramics). In the last part of the corridor is displayed the **Bonci Casuccini collection** of material from Chiusi, including a terracotta canopic vase and throne (6C BC). On the right is the **Mieli collection** with material found near La Foce (7C BC to the Hellenistic period), and the last rooms display the large **Chigi Zondadori collection** of vases, Bucchero ware, bronzes, the Chigi Muse relief (a Roman sarcophagus front dating from the 2C AD), and a small Hellenistic marble head.

On the way out the **hospital church**, dedicated to the Annunziata, can be visited. It was rebuilt in 1466, and the fine hall interior has been attributed to Guidoccio d'Andrea, Vecchietta, or even Francesco di Giorgio Martini. The carved and painted wooden ceiling is by Benvenuto di Giovanni, Pellegrino di Mariano, Agostino d'Andrea and Domenico di Cristofano. On the south wall, on the first altar, is an *Assumption* by Pietro Locatelli, and on the second altar is a painted *Crucifix* of c 1330. The organ was built by Piffaro of Siena (1514–19); the organ case is thought to be by Peruzzi and is decorated with two polychrome reliefs in roundels attributed to Ventura Turapilli. Raised high above a flight of steps is the main altar, with a relief on the altar frontal of the *Dead Christ* by Giuseppe Mazzuoli, on top of which is a bronze statue of the *Risen Christ* by Vecchietta (1476). Two candle-bearing angels are by Accursio Baldi (1585). In the huge apse is a fresco by Sebastiano Conca (1732). On the north wall (second altar) is a *Vision of St Teresa* by Ciro Ferri, and (first altar) an *Annunciation* attributed to Giovanni Maria Morandi. By the door is a stoup by Urbano and Bartolomeo da Cortona (1453).

From Piazza del Duomo at the right end of the hospital building the stepped Vicolo di San Girolamo leads down to Piazza della Selva in the **Contrada della Selva** (Map I; 9). Here is **San Sebastiano (in Valle Piatta)**, the oratory of the Contrada. This small church is attributed to Domenico Ponsi (1507) or Baldassarre Peruzzi. It contains a *Madonna and Child with Saints* by Benvenuto di Giovanni, and two paintings of c 1630 by Astolfo Petrazzi (*Epiphany*) and Rutilio Manetti (*Crucifixion*).

Via del Fosso di Sant'Ansano, a narrow pretty road, curves south beneath the hill on which the huge Ospedale di Santa Maria della Scala is built. Beyond the low wall on the right are fields planted with olives and vines. It ends at the Arco delle Due Porte (described on p 384).

From the Campo to the Pinacoteca and Sant'Agostino

From the south side of the Campo **Casato di Sotto** (Map I; 10) leads gently uphill past a number of fine palaces. On the left is **Palazzo Chigi** (no. 15), constructed in the early 16C, and the birthplace of Alexander VII (plaque). Palazzo dei Conti della Ciaia (no. 23) has a façade designed by Francesco Brandini (1715). From Vicolo del Salvatore (left) there is a fine view of the Basilica dei Servi di Maria. Beyond is the beige-coloured **Palazzo Ugurgeri** (no. 39) with graffiti decoration. On the right, Vicolo di Tone leads up to Via dei Percennesi, a very narrow street with flying arches and tall medieval houses in the heart of the **Contrada dell'Aquila** (Map I; 10). Off the left side of Casato di Sotto two flights of steps in Vicolo della Fonte lead down to a handsome public fountain beneath the road, protected by a high arch (1359). Near the end of Casato di Sotto is the **Oratorio dei Tredicini**, the oratory of the Contrada, built in 1630. The high altarpiece is by Bernardino Mei. The old Casato di Sopra continues and winds round to join Via San Pietro which we follow right to the church of **San Pietro alle Scale** (Map I; 14), rebuilt in the 18C with a pleasant interior (usually closed). It contains a fresco fragment attributed to Liberale da Verona, five panels by Ambrogio Lorenzetti, and a high altarpiece by Rutilio Manetti. Next to the church is the Pinacoteca.

The Pinacoteca Nazionale

The **Pinacoteca Nazionale (Map I; 14) is the most important gallery for the study of the great Sienese masters, including Duccio di Buoninsegna, Ambrogio and Pietro Lorenzetti, and Sassetta, all of whom are well represented. The collection also includes fine works by Sodoma and Beccafumi. The Pinacoteca has been housed since 1932 in the handsome *14C Palazzo Buonsignori restored in 1848. The display is strictly chronological (open Tues–Sat 08.15–19.15; Mon 08.30–13.30; fest. 08.15–13.15)

Many of the paintings have been restored; others are in the course of restoration. There are long-term plans to move the collection to the ex-Ospedale di Santa Maria della Scala (see above), and a number of rooms have a provisional arrangement, and are not very well kept.

Second floor The first two rooms illustrate the origins of the Sienese school of painting. **Room 1**: *altar frontal, partly in relief, representing *Christ blessing* between symbols of the Evangelists, and scenes from the *Legend of the True Cross*, the first securely dated work (1215) of the Sienese school, attributed to the Maestro di Tressa; *St Francis* attributed to Margarito d'Arezzo (c 1270–80); *Crucifix*, with Passion scenes dating from the first years of the 13C; three scenes from the *Life of Christ*, one of the first paintings known on canvas by **Guido da Siena**. **Room 2** has works by or attributed to Guido da Siena or a follower of the late 13C (known as the Maestro del Dossale di San Pietro), including a *Madonna and Child* (dated 1262), and *St Peter enthroned* with stories from his life, scenes from the *Life of Christ*, and *St Francis* and stories from his life (from the church of San Francesco in Colle Val d'Elsa).

Rooms 3 and **4** contain works by **Duccio di Buoninsegna** and his followers. **Room 3** has two polyptychs of the *Madonna and Saints* by Duccio and assistants; a dossal attributed to Ugolino di Nerio; and *Four Saints* and a *Crucifix* (1345) by Niccolò di Segna; another *Crucifix* is by the circle of Segna di Bonaventura. **Room 4**: the *Madonna dei Francescani*, a tiny work of jewel-like luminosity is considered one of Duccio's masterpieces (c 1285; much ruined). Also here are works by the school of Duccio (some attributed to the Maestro di Città di Castello and some to Ugolino di Nerio), and *Four Saints* by Segna di Bonaventura.

Room 5 has 14C works by Bartolo di Fredi and Luca di Tommé. **Room 6** displays two important works by **Simone Martini**: *Madonna and Child* (from the *pieve* of San Giovanni Battista in Lucignano d'Arbia) and the *Pala di Beato Agostino Novello* (from the church of Sant'Agostino). Also here are Madonnas by his contemporary Lippo Memmi.

Room 7 has some very fine *works by the famous brothers **Pietro and Ambrogio Lorenzetti** who were at work in the city in the first half of the 14C. In the side **room 7A** there is a *Madonna and Child between Saints Mary Magdalene and Dorothy*, another *Madonna*, a *Lamentation*, and an *Allegory of the Redemption*, all by Ambrogio, and a *Crucifixion* by Pietro. In the other side room (**7B**) are two charming small *landscapes* (a city by the sea, and a castle on the edge of a lake), perhaps part of a larger decoration for a cupboard door by Ambrogio, as well as his last dated work, an *Annunciation* (commissioned in 1344). Other works from this room are removed for restoration. In the main part of room 7 are works by followers of the Lorenzetti, such as the Maestro di Ovile (represented by an *Assumption* and *St Peter enthroned between Saints*) and

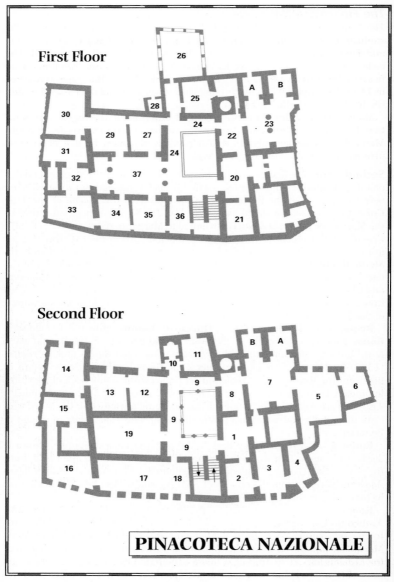

First Floor

Second Floor

PINACOTECA NAZIONALE

Paolo di Giovanni Fei (*Birth of the Virgin and Saints*). In **room 8** there is a *Madonna and Child with Saints* by Pietro Lorenzetti.

The first side of the loggia (**room 9**) has three 14C works by Niccolò di Pietro Gerini, Angelo Puccinelli, and Spinello Aretino.

Beyond the chapel (**10**), with 18C stuccoes, is **room 11** which displays *works by the Sienese painter **Taddeo di Bartolo**: a large *Crucifix*, a tiny portable *Triptych*, and an *Annunciation, Dormition, and Saints Cosmas and Damian* (signed and dated 1409).

The last two sides of the loggia (**room 9**) display two exquisite small triptychs by Bernardo Daddi (dated 1336) and Lorenzo Monaco, and a *Madonna with angel musicians* by Domenico di Bartolo (dated 1433). The *Marriage of St Catherine* is the only signed work known by Michelino da Besozzo.

Rooms 12–19. 15C Sienese painting. **Room 12** displays three large polyptychs by Giovanni di Paolo: *St Nicholas of Bari and other Saints* (signed and dated 1453); *San Galgano* with a *Crucifixion* (signed and dated 1440), and a charming predella; and an *Assumption*. There is also a tiny portable triptych by the same artist. The *Madonna and Child with angels and Saints* is by Sano di Pietro. **Room 13** has more works by Giovanni di Paolo, and small panels by Sassetta (all from an altarpiece painted in 1423–26). **Room 14** has three paintings of the *Madonna and Child with Saints*: by Neroccio di Bartolomeo; a *Madonna and Child with an angel*, by Francesco di Giorgio Martini and a *Madonna and Child with an angel* signed and dated 1470 by Matteo di Giovanni. On the window wall (with a fine view) there is another *Madonna and Child with Saints* signed and dated 1492 by Neroccio. On the next wall three *Madonnas* by Matteo di Giovanni and a triptych by Neroccio, and on the last wall a *Maestà* by Matteo di Giovanni and three very damaged panels with the *Story of St Joseph* by Francesco di Giorgio Martini.

Room 15 displays an *Adoration of the Shepherds*: by Matteo di Giovanni, the *Triumph of David* by Benvenuto di Giovanni, and a *Madonna and Child with Saints* by Pietro di Domenico. **Rooms 16–18** are closed. They contain numerous important works by Sano di Pietro and by the Maestro dell'Osservanza. **Room 19**: *Madonna and Child with Saints* (very damaged) and a painted *cupboard for reliquaries (from Santa Maria della Scala) with scenes from the Passion and lives of the saints, both by Vecchietta; and a *Coronation of the Virgin*, and a detached fresco of the *Madonna enthroned with angels*, both by Francesco di Giorgio Martini.

In a room on the **third floor** the small paintings of the **Collezione Spannocchi,** formed in the 17C, are arranged. Dürer, *St Jerome* (a signed work); Lorenzo Lotto, *Nativity*; Francesco Furini, *Mary Magdalene*; Giovanni Battista Moroni, two portraits of gentlemen; Bernardo Strozzi, *St Francis*; Paris Bordone, *Annunciation, Holy Family*; Bartolomeo Montagna, *Madonna and the Redeemer* (two fragments of a larger work); Palma Giovane, the *Bronze serpent* (signed and dated 1598); Padovanino, *Rape of Europa*; 16C Flemish school, *Portrait of a jeweller*; Girolamo Mazzola Bedoli, *Portrait of a young man*.

On the **stairs** down to the first floor are fresco fragments by Domenico di Bartolo from the Ospedale di Santa Maria della Scala.

First floor Room 20 has an *Annunciation* by Girolamo da Cremona and **room 22** two paintings by the Maestro di Volterra. **Room 23**: **15C** Umbrian and Umbrian-Sienese schools. In the main room are large altarpieces by Pietro di Francesco Orioli (including two of the *Visitation*) and Bernardino Fungai. In the small room (**23A**) is a tondo of the *Holy Family* by Pinturicchio, and in **23B** are two frescoes detached from Palazzo del Magnifico of classical subjects by Girolamo Genga.

Room 26 is an enclosed loggia with a splendid view of the Torre della Mangia, the cathedral bell tower and Duomo Nuovo and the open countryside. Sculptured panels are exhibited here including 14C marble reliefs, some by Gano di Fazio from the church of Santa Maria dei Servi, a relief of *San Galgano*, and six reliefs in *pietra serena* by a Sienese sculptor from Jacopo della Quercia's circle.

Room 27–37 display 16C and 17C Sienese works. **Room 27** has paintings by **Beccafumi** including *St Catherine receiving the Stigmata*, a tondo of the *Madonna and Child*, a triptych with the *Trinity and Saints*, and three panels of *Charity*, *Hope*, and *Fortitude*. Also here are some paintings by Brescianino. **Room 29**. Works by Marco Pino and Beccafumi (*Birth of the Virgin*, and *Coronation of the Virgin from Santo Spirito*). **Room 30** contains the splendid large *cartoons by Beccafumi for the Duomo pavement (restored). **Room 31**. *Annunciation* and *Visitation* (from Santo Spirito) by Girolamo della Pacchia and *Scourging of Christ*, a superb work (1511–14) by Sodoma. **Room 32** has more works by Sodoma, including a *Deposition and a tondo of the Madonna*, and another tondo by Girolamo Genga.

Rooms 33–35 display early 17C paintings by Bernardino Mei, Rutilio Manetti, and Raffaello Vanni. **Room 36** has works by Francesco and Vincenzo Rustici. **Room 37** has two masterpieces by Beccafumi (*Descent into Hell* and *St Michael and the rebel angels*), as well as *Christ carrying the Cross* and a *Holy Family*, also by him. Also here are *Christ in limbo* and *Deposition* by Sodoma. The statues of the *Annunciation, Madonna in Adoration*, and the *Risen Christ* are by Marrina.

The church of Sant'Agostino

Via San Pietro returns downhill past the church to the Arco di Sant'Agostino, beyond which is the church of Sant'Agostino (**Map** I; 14), dating from 1258. From the terrace there is a good view of the town and countryside. The church is open mid-March–end Oct 10.30–13.30, 15.00–17.30 (entrance fee). It is also sometimes used for concerts.

The attractive bright interior was remodelled in 1749 by Vanvitelli. It has particularly interesting early 17C altarpieces. South side. First altar, *Communion of St Jerome* by Astolfo Petrazzi; second altar, *Crucifixion* by Perugino; fourth altar, *Calvary* by Ventura Salimbeni.

The **Piccolomini Chapel** was founded in 1596 by Ascanio Piccolomini, Archbishop of Siena, in the chapter house of the Augustinian convent. It preserves an altarpiece of the *Epiphany* by Sodoma (c 1530), and a lunette fresco of the *Madonna seated among Saints* by Ambrogio Lorenzetti. The statue of the Piccolomini *Pope Pius II* is by Giovanni Duprè.

The altarpiece in the south transept is by Raffaello Vanni. The **Cappella Bichi** has two *frescoes in grisaille of the *Birth of the Virgin* and the *Nativity*, attributed to Francesco di Giorgio Martini (discovered in 1978). Above are two monochrome lunettes with tondoes by Signorelli. The majolica pavement dates from 1488. The high altar is by Flaminio del Turco. Beneath it is a reliquary of the Beato Agostino Novello.

The second chapel in the north transept has an elegant fresco fragment by Riccio of a funerary monument; and *Temptations of St Anthony* by Rutilio Manetti. The tomb of Agostino Chigi (d. 1639) has statues by Tommaso Redi.

Three very fine 15C wooden statues have not yet been returned to the church since their restoration. North aisle. Third altar, *Baptism of Constantine* by

Francesco Vanni; (beyond the door), *Immaculate Conception* by Carlo Maratta (in very poor condition); and *Adoration of the Shepherds* by Giovanni Francesco Romanelli.

In the Prato di Sant'Agostino is the entrance (no. 4) to the **Accademia dei Fisiocritici**, a science academy of physio-chemistry and natural philosophy founded in 1691 by Pirro Maria Gabrielli. It has geological, mineralogical, and zoological collections (open weekdays Mon–Fri 09.00–13.00, 15.00–18.00, except Thur afternoon).

From Sant'Agostino, Via Sant'Agata leads to the church of **San Giuseppe**, the oratory of the **Contrada del Capitano dell'Onda**. The brick façade dates from 1653 and the marble bust of *St Joseph* is by Tommaso Redi. The octagonal cupola was probably designed by a follower of Baldassarre Peruzzi, and it has a centrally planned 16C interior. Beside it is a public fountain. Beyond the Arco di San Giuseppe the picturesque Via Giovanni Duprè descends through the Contrada towards Piazza del Mercato from which Palazzo Pubblico with its loggia and tower is seen from the rear. Below the apse of Sant'Agostino is the entrance to a little public park, known as the **Orti del Tolomei**, on the site of orchards which once belonged to the Tolomei family. It has splendid wide views of the Sienese countryside, and a paved path leads to Via Mattioli beside a pleasant new brick university faculty building (the lower path leads down to the covered car park 'Il Campo').

To the southeast of Sant'Agostino, on a steep slope, are the **botanical gardens** (**Map** I; 14), transferred here in 1856. Via Pier Andrea Mattioli leads past the entrance (no. 4; open 08.00–12.30, 14.30–17.30; Sat 08.00–12.00; closed fest.). There are tropical greenhouses, and well labelled and carefully tended plants. Beyond is the neo-Classical façade (1839) of the church of the **Maddalena** which contains paintings by Antonio Bonfigli and Raffaello Vanni. Via Mattioli ends at **Porta Tufi** (**Map** II; 14), a fine gateway erected c 1326. Outside the gate is the **Misericordia Cemetery** (1843–74), with tombs decorated by Tito Sarrocchi, Cesare Maccari, Amos Cassioli, Giovanni Duprè, and Luigi Mussini.

From the Prato di Sant'Agostino, Via della Cerchia leads southwest towards Pian dei Mantellini. It ends beside the church of **Santi Niccolò e Lucia** (**Map** II; 14), with 17C vault frescoes by Sebastiano Folli and Francesco Bertini and carved benches in the interior. On the south altar is an old painting of the *Madonna* in an 18C frame. The high altarpiece of the *Martyrdom of St Lucy* is by Francesco Vanni (1606); in the vault is a fresco by Ventura Salimbeni. On either side of the presbytery, two 15C polychrome statues: *St Lucy* attributed to a Sienese sculptor close to Francesco di Giorgio Martini and *St Nicola* (with an unusual head), attributed to a follower of Giovanni di Stefano.

San Niccolò al Carmine

Beyond, in the wide Pian dei Mantellini is the Carmelite convent and church of San Niccolò al Carmine (**Map** I; 13; also called Santa Maria del Carmine), founded in the 13C, with a huge campanile.

Interior. South side. *Adoration of the Shepherds* by Riccio and Arcangelo Salimbeni; in the niche, *Assumption* with angels playing musical instruments, and saints, a damaged fresco attributed to Benedetto di Bindo. Over the altar, *St Michael, a superb work by Domenico Beccafumi. In the Chapel of the Sacrament, off the south side, in a fine 16C marble frame, *Birth of the Virgin and the Redeemer* by Sodoma. At the end of the south side a painting of *Saints, signed and dated 1593 by Francesco Vanni, surrounds the 13C *Madonna dei Mantellini* (replaced by a photograph while it is being restored). The 17C high altar attributed to Tommaso Redi bears an earlier ciborium.

On the north side, *Martyrdom of St Bartholomew* by Alessandro Casolani, and, over the altar, *Ascension* by Girolamo del Pacchia. At the west end of the wall, Giuseppe Collignon, *Holy Family appearing to Saints* (1825). On the west wall, Stefano Volpi, *Crucifixion*. In the **sacristy** (admission on request), formerly a private chapel, is a statue of *St Sigismondo* by Giacomo Cozzarelli (in polychrome terracotta) and a painting of the *Annunciation* by Raffaello Vanni. Part of the Convent is now used by the university; the 16C **cloister** with frescoes by Giuseppe Nicola Nasini (1710) can be seen at no. 44.

Pian dei Mantellini has several handsome buildings which follow its curved shape. To the right of the church, at no. 40, is **Palazzo Incontri** (or Palazzo Piccolomini Bellanti al Carmine), a good neo-Classical palace by Serafino Belli (1799–1804) with pilasters and roundels with busts (copies of classical master-pieces). Beyond, at no. 28 is the façade of the former church of the **Conservatorio delle Derelitte** (by Riccio, c 1554). Opposite the flank of the Carmine is **Palazzo del Vescovo** (later Celsi Pollini Neri) attributed to Baldassarre Peruzzi. It has a second façade in the narrow lane which leads up to a fine medieval tower next to the little church of **Sant'Ansano** (Map I; 13; usually closed), built in 1441 by Pietro del Minella, Antonio Federighi, and others. It contains a precious stained glass tondo of *St Ansano* attributed to Cozzarelli, a high altarpiece by Rustichino, signed and dated 1617, and two 15C frescoes of the *Adoration of the Magi* and *St Ansano*. To the right of the church a religious institute occupies a building erected in 1877–81 in Renaissance style.

In front of Sant'Ansano, Via Tommaso Pendola leads through the **Contrada della Tartuca** (Map I; 13, 14), with its oratory, built by members of the Contrada in 1682–85. The stucco relief on the high altar is by Giovanni Antonio Mazzuoli. The panel in the pavement, in imitation of that of the Duomo, was designed by Arturo Viligiardi (1891). The two paintings of *Miracles of St Anthony* are by Giuseppe Nicola Nasini. Parallel to the south is Vicolo della Tartuca, a medieval blind alley with a flying bridge, and Via Tito Sarrocchi, with the house (no. 35) where the artist Beccafumi lived from 1516.

Off the other side of Pian dei Mantellini, Via San Marco leads down through the **Contrada della Chiocciola** (Map II; 14). At the beginning of the street, on the left, is the façade of the former church of San Marco next to a relief of the *Lion of St Mark* (1954). Farther on, at no. 37, in a courtyard behind an iron gateway is the 17C church dedicated to **Santi Pietro e Paolo** which serves as the oratory of the Contrada della Chiocciola. Built in 1645 on a design by Flaminio del Turco, it has a high altarpiece by Andrea del Brescianino. Farther down, at the fork with Via della Diana is the delightful 18C chapel of the **Madonna del Rosario**. In front is a Renaissance well. On the right side of Via San Marco is the huge convent of **Santa Marta** with a long façade probably by Il Tozzo, follower of Peruzzi (1535). On the opposite side, at no. 149, is a taber-nacle with *Christ on the Cross* by Ventura Salimbeni. Outside **Porta San Marco** (c 1326) there is a fine view of the countryside.

Pian dei Mantellini ends at a gate in the walls called the **Arco delle Due Porte** (Map I; 13). High up on the wall of a house (no. 7) is a tabernacle with an early

14C fresco, thought to be the oldest tabernacle in the town. Just inside the gate is a house (on the right; plaque) where Duccio di Buoninsegna lived. The 16C tabernacle has a fresco attributed to Baldassarre Peruzzi (or Bartolomeo di Davide).Via del Fosso di Sant'Ansano, outside the gate, is described on p 378.

From the gate Via Paolo Mascagni leads downhill to **Porta Laterina** (**Map** II; 13) which preserves its wooden doors. Near it is a huge bastion in the walls designed by Baldassarre Peruzzi. Outside the gate is a delightful view of the walls as far as Porta San Marco with olive groves and orchards outside them and unspoilt countryside beyond.

From the Arco delle Due Porte Via di Stalloreggi leads up towards Piazza Postierla through the **Contrada della Pantera** (**Map** I; 13, 14), the oldest part of the city, with numerous medieval houses. The ex-**Palazzo dei Bisdomini** (no. 43) is one of the best Gothic palaces to survive in the city. It stands on the corner of Via di Castelvecchio, at the beginning of which is a pretty tabernacle protecting a fresco of the *Pietà* (called the Madonna del Corvo) by Sodoma. Via di Castelvecchio branches right through an interesting medieval part of the town. Some way along on the left, two arches lead to a little fortified piazza on a hill. Via di San Quirico is wider and ends at the little church of San Quirico. Off Via di Stalloreggi, in Piazza del Conte is the fountain used for baptisms in the Contrada. Via di Stalloreggi ends in Piazza Postierla, described on p 363, and Via di Città returns to the Campo.

From the Campo to Santa Maria dei Servi

From the southeast angle of the Campo, Via Rinaldini leads to ***Palazzo Piccolomini** (**Map** I; 7; which faces Via Banchi di Sotto), a handsome building and good example of Florentine Renaissance architecture, probably designed by Bernardo Rossellino and begun by Porrina in 1469. In the courtyard are good suspended capitals by Marrina (1509). The palace contains the **Archivio di Stato**, one of the finest extant collections of archives in Italy (well catalogued). The study room is open to students in the morning (except 15–30 August).

The fascinating little **museum** (closed for restoration but usually open in the mornings) has important medieval documents (the oldest dated 736), particularly well preserved. The unique series of book bindings known as the ***Tavolette di Biccherna**, the painted covers of the municipal account-books, date from 1258 onwards, and some of them give a fascinating picture of medieval life. The most famous artists of the day were employed to decorate them, including (in the 14C) Ambrogio Lorenzetti, Paolo di Giovanni Fei, and Luca di Tommè, and (in the 15C) Giovanni di Paolo, Vecchietta, Sano di Pietro, Benvenuto di Giovanni, Francesco di Giorgio Martini, Bernardino Fungai, Guidoccio Cozzarelli, and (in the 16C) Domenico Beccafumi.

The collection includes illuminated statute books, the contract between the Commune and Jacopo della Quercia for the Fonte Gaia in the Campo, the contract drawn up by the Opera del Duomo for Duccio's *Maestà*, a pergamene signed by Frederick I Barbarossa, Boccaccio's will, and the Imperial charter (with its seal intact) by which Montepulciano was ceded to Siena after their victory over the Florentines at Montaperti (20 November 1260).

Opposite are the administrative offices of the **university**, founded c 1240, at the side of which Via San Vigilio leads to the university church of **San Vigilio** (**Map** I; 7). The fine ceiling has paintings by Raffaello Vanni. The third chapel on

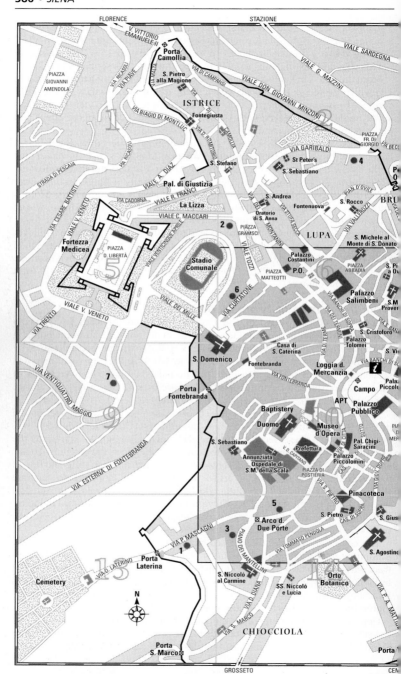

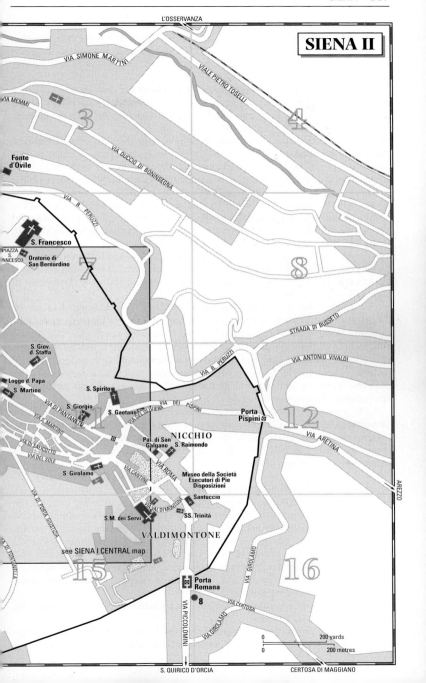

SIENA II

L'OSSERVANZA

VIA SIMONE MARTINI

VIALE PIETRO TOSELLI

VIA MEMMI

3

4

VIA DUCCIO DI BONINSEGNA

Fonte d'Ovile

VIA B. PERUZZI

S. Francesco

PIAZZA S. ANCESCO

Oratorio di San Bernardino

7

8

STRADA DI BUSSETO

VIA ANTONIO VIVALDI

S. Giov. d. Staffa

Logge d. Papa

S. Martino

S. Spirito

VIA DI PANTANETO

S. Giorgio

S. Gaetano

VIA DEI PISPINI

VIA DELL'OLIVIERA

Porta Pispini

12

VIA ARETINA

VIA S. MARTINO

NICCHIO

Pal. di San Galgano

S. Raimondo

VIA DI SALICOTTO

VIA DEL SOLE

VIA ROMA

S. Girolamo

VIA CANTINE

Museo della Società Esecutori di Pie Disposizioni

VIA DI PORTA GIUSTIZIA

VIA VAL DI MONTONE

Santuccio

S.M. dei Servi

SS. Trinità

VALDIMONTONE

see SIENA I CENTRAL map

15

16

VIA GIROLAMO

Porta Romana

8

VIA CERTOSA

VIA PICCOLOMINI

VIA GIROLAMO

AREZZO

0   200 yards

0   200 metres

S. QUIRICO D'ORCIA

CERTOSA DI MAGGIANO

the south side has a marble altar by Tommaso Redi and Dionisio Mazzuoli and reliefs attributed to Mazzuoli. The high altar dates from 1688; the two paintings on either side are by Francesco Vanni. The third altar on the north side has a bronze *Crucifix* attributed to Pietro Tacca and two sculpted half-figures attributed to Giuseppe Mazzuoli.

This area is part of the **Contrada della Civetta** whose oratory is in Via Cecco Angiolieri, and whose headquarters is in the restored **Castellare degli Ugurgieri**, reached by the Vicolo del Castellare, a dark alley opposite the church, in a fascinating old irregular piazza on a tiny hill.

Via San Vigilio ends at Via Sallustio Bandini opposite the Renaissance **Palazzo Bandini Piccolomini**, built c 1465 by Antonio Federighi, in brick with a handsome portal and first floor windows (now used by the university). This characteristic street descends past two more interesting Bandini palaces on the bend of the road, opposite a high wall with two stone 13C lions (perhaps formerly bearing columns on a church façade), and ends in Piazzetta Grassi. Here is the church of **San Giovannino della Staffa**, now the oratory of the **Contrada del Leocorno** (Map I; 7). It contains works by Raffaello Vanni and Rutilio Manetti, and a 14C *Madonna and Child* by Francesco di Vannuccio.

We now follow Via di Pantaneto a short way back towards the Campo to see the elegant **Logge del Papa** (Map I; 7; restored in 2000). It was built for Pius II by Antonio Federighi (1462). The decorations are attributed to Francesco di Giorgio Martini.

Next to it is the church of **San Martino** (Map I; 7) mentioned in an 8C document, with a façade by Giovanni Fontana (1613). The pleasant interior by Giovanni Battista Pelori dates from after 1537. On the south side, the second altarpiece of the *Circumcision* is a lovely work by Guido Reni, and on the fourth altar there is a marble statue of *St Thomas of Villanova* attributed to Giovanni Antonio Mazzuoli. The Baroque **high altar**, with a ciborium, is attributed to Giuseppe Mazzuoli. On the wall of the choir are two sepulchral monuments attributed to Bartolomeo Mazzuoli.

North side. On the fourth altar is a statue of the *Madonna and Child* by Giuseppe Mazzuoli, and on the third altar, a **Nativity* by Domenico Beccafumi. On the west wall is a painting of the *Madonna protecting Siena* (1528). In the chapel beneath the bell-tower frescoes, recently restored, date from 1333 (attributed to Francesco di Segna).

Via di Pantaneto returns downhill to the church of **San Giorgio** (Map I; 12) which has a good marble façade (1738) and a much older campanile (1260). The interior has white stucco decoration. On the west wall is the tomb of the painter Francesco Vanni (1656), with his bust in bronze by his sons Raffaello and Michele, the last of whom carried out the exquisite and very unusual marble panel. On the south side, the first altar has the *Calling of St Peter* by Placido Costanzi. In the south transept, *Pietà with St Carlo* by Vincenzo Meucci, and *Pietà with St Catherine*, by Francesco Vanni, and there are two funerary monuments by Giovanni Janssens (1748) in the transepts. The **high altarpiece** is attributed to Sebastiano Conca.

On the north side are altarpieces of the *Crucifixion*, and *Way to Calvary* by Francesco and Raffaello Vanni.

Beyond the church, Via dei Pispini leads left to a piazza with an attractive fountain. Here is the 16C church of **Santo Spirito** (Map I; 8, 12). The cupola is attributed to Giacomo Cozzarelli (1508) and the portal to Baldassarre Peruzzi (1519). It has been closed for many years.

Via dei Pispini descends to a fork with Via dell'Oliviera. Here is the pretty façade of **San Gaetano** (1683), the oratory of the **Contrada del Nicchio**. Via dei Pispini continues down to the splendid **Porta Pispini** (or Porta San Viene; **Map II**; 12), dating from c 1326–28. The fresco painted by Sodoma above the gate has been detached and removed to the church of San Francesco. To the left of the gate, at an angle of the city walls, is the only surviving bastion of the seven designed by Peruzzi in the 16C to strengthen the earlier defences. On the right of the gate steps lead down to a public fountain.

Opposite Santo Spirito (see above) Vicolo del Sasso leads shortly to Via Roma which we now follow left past the huge **Palazzo Bianchi** (1796–1804), half of which has been restored. The neo-Classical façade is by Giovanni Bartalucci. Opposite is the Renaissance **Palazzo di San Galgano**, built in the style of Giuliano da Maiano (1474; in poor condition) and the church of **San Raimondo al Rifugio** (closed many years ago) which has a marble façade of 1660. It contains interesting 17C paintings, including works by Francesco Vanni and Rutilio Manetti. On the long garden wall of Palazzo Bianchi, opposite, there is a carved tabernacle, dated 1477 by Giovanni di Stefano.

At no. 71 Via Roma are the premises of the **Società Esecutori di Pie Disposizioni** (Map II; 12). This 'society of executors of benevolent legacies' is the successor to the medieval lay brotherhood of the Compagnia della Madonna, suppressed by the grand-duke of Tuscany in 1785. The society's **museum** is open on request (ring on the first floor) Mon and Fri 09.00–12.00, Tues and Thur 15.00–17.00. It includes a painted lunette showing *St Catherine of Siena leading Pope Gregory XI back to Rome*, by Girolamo di Benvenuto; a *Crucifix* by the school of Duccio; *Madonna and Child* by Sano di Pietro; *Madonna and Child, Saints Peter and Paul*, by Niccolò di Ser Sozzo, and *Holy Family* by Sodoma. The custodian conducts visitors across the road to another museum opened in 1981, donated by the Bologna-Buonsignori families, which contains an eclectic collection of prehistoric material, Etruscan and Roman ceramics and glass, jewellery, Deruta majolica, Chinese porcelain, a *Portait of a Lady* by Gino Severini, and arms.

Via Roma ends at **Porta Romana** (Map II; 15, 16), Siena's largest gate (1328), defended with a barbican.

From Via Roma (opposite no. 71) Via Val di Montone (partly stepped) leads up past the ex-church of San Leonardo, now the headquarters of the **Contrada di Valdimontone** (Map II; 15). The Contrada's church is the **Oratorio della Santissima Trinità**, which has a good 16C–17C Mannerist interior. The vault is frescoed by Ventura Salimbeni and the stuccoes are by Brescianino and Lorenzo and Cristoforo Rustici. In the **sacristy** is a *Madonna and Child* by Neroccio di Bartolomeo who also painted the beautiful frame.

Santa Maria dei Servi

Via Val di Montone ends at the church of *Santa Maria dei Servi (**Map** I; 16), a large church with a massive brick campanile in a peaceful corner of the town. From the top of the steps there is an unusual view of the Duomo Nuovo, the campanile and the Duomo, and Palazzo Pubblico.

The spacious interior, with lovely capitals, has numerous interesting works of art from different periods. South aisle. Above the first chapel: remains of 14C frescoes; second chapel: *Madonna del Bordone* by Coppo di Marcovaldo, signed and dated 1261, partly repainted by a pupil of Duccio (and now in very poor conditon). Third chapel: *Birth of the Virgin* by Rutilio Manetti; fourth chapel: *Madonna and Saints* by Alessandro Franchi (19C); fifth chapel: *Massacre of the Innocents* by Matteo di Giovanni (1491; in very poor condition).

South transept. On the right wall, *Annunciatory Angel* by Francesco Vanni. In the chapel, painted *Cross* attributed to Niccolò di Segna; the *Madonna and Child* by Segna di Bonaventura, dates from 1319. The chapels at the east end have late 19C decorations, with some neo-Gothic altarpieces by Alessandro Franchi and the stained glass is by Ulisse De Matteis (1894). In the second chapel to the right of the sanctuary, especially interesting remains of frescoes (including the *Massacre of the Innocents*) attributed to Francesco di Segna, with the help of Niccolò di Segna and Pietro Lorenzetti. On the **high altar**, *Coronation of the Virgin* by Bernardino Fungai. In the first chapel to the left of the sanctuary, frescoed in the 19C, on either side of the altar are small frescoed tondi attributed to Giuseppe Nasini. The second chapel to the left of the sanctuary contains more good frescoes (scenes from the *Life of St John the Baptist*) attributed to Francesco and Niccolò di Segna and Pietro Lorenzetti. The altarpiece of the *Nativity* is by Taddeo di Bartolo (1404).

North transept. In the chapel, *Madonna of the Misericordia* by Giovanni di Paolo (signed and dated 1431). On the wall, *Miracle of the Blessed Gioacchino Piccolomini*, a good work by Rutilio Manetti (1633). Opposite is a painting of the *Madonna and the plague in Siena* by Astolfo Petrazzi painted to frame a painting of the *Madonna del Popolo* by Lippo Memmi (c 1325; now in the Pinacoteca Nazionale).

In the second chapel in the **north aisle** there is a *Madonna di Belvedere* attributed to Jacopo di Mino del Pelliccciaio and Taddeo di Bartolo.

The walk back to the Campo may be made along Via dei Servi, Via San Girolamo (left) and Via di Salicotto (left again). Via di Salicotto runs through the **Contrada della Torre** (Map I; 11) whose **Oratorio di San Giacomo** is on the left of the road beside no. 76 (ring for the custodian, 10.00–12.00, exc. Thur). It contains a *Crucifixion* by Rutilio Manetti. In the last lane on the right before the Campo, Vicolo delle Scotte (off Via di Salicotto), is the **Synagogue** (open on fest. 10.00–13.00, 14.00–16.00 or 17.00), a neo-Classical building (1756). There was a Jewish community in Siena from 1229 onwards. They were confined to a ghetto in this area by Cosimo dei Medici in 1571, the doors of which were burnt down by French troops in 1796. However, it was not until 1895 that the Jews were given complete freedom to reside in the city.

North of the Campo

From the Campo, Vicolo di San Pietro leads up to the **Croce del Travaglio** where the three main streets of Siena, the Banchi di Sopra, the Banchi di Sotto, and Via di Città, meet. Here is the **Loggia della Mercanzia** (Map I; 6), begun in 1417 on a design by Sano di Matteo; the upper story was added in the 18C, and the screen in the late 19C. The five statues of saints (1456–63) are by Antonio Federighi and Vecchietta, the former of whom carved the marble bench (right) beneath the portico. The merchants' guild held a commercial tribunal here, famous for its impartiality, to which even foreign States resorted.

Via Banchi di Sopra (Map I; 2, 6) leads north to Piazza Tolomei, where from the 11C the Sienese parliament used to assemble. *Palazzo Tolomei** (Map I; 2, 6) is one of the oldest Gothic palaces in Siena (now owned by a bank), begun c 1208 and restored some 50 years later.

Opposite is the church of **San Cristoforo** (Map I; 2) where the magistrates of the Republic officiated. Dating from the 11C–12C, it is one of the oldest churches in Siena. The classical Palladian façade by Tommaso and Francesco Paccagnini, dates from 1800, and the two statues are by Giuseppe Silini (1802).

On the first altar on the north side, *Madonna enthroned and Saints* by Girolamo del Pacchia (c 1508). In the north transept is an unusual 15C fresco of the *Pietà* and *Allegory of the Passion* (in very poor condition). In the pretty domed east end, on the high altar, is a statuary group of the *Translation of St Benedict*, attributed to Giovanni Antonio Mazzuoli (1693). In the south transept is a fine statuette of *St Galgano* in terracotta and white glazed enamel, by the della Robbia school, and on the south wall a polychrome terracotta relief of the *Madonna and Child*.

Santa Maria di Provenzano

Via del Moro, flanking San Cristoforo, descends past an archway into the 13C cloister (restored in 1921) to the quiet Piazza Provenzano Salvani (**Map** I; 2). There is a good view of a stretch of the city walls. Here is **Santa Maria di Provenzano** (1594) with a pretty exterior, being restored. The Mannerist **façade** is by Flaminio del Turco (1604) with four terracotta statues of the patron saints of Siena (1816, attributed to a little known artist, Antonio Zini) and the dome was designed by Don Giovanni de' Medici.

The interior (at present closed) has neo-Classical furniture by Agostino Fantastici (1838). On the west wall, monochrome painting by Bernardino Mei. South wall. *Birth of the Virgin* by Giovanni Bruni (c 1837). The first elaborate marble altar by Flaminio del Turco encloses an altarpiece of the *Mass of San Cerbone* by Rutilio Manetti (signed and dated 1630). In the spandrels of the dome are 18C frescoes and the marble pavement beneath it dates from 1685. South transept. Altarpiece by Francesco Rustici (1612) and, in the centre, *Madonna* by a pupil of Raffaello Vanni. On the **high altar**, designed by Flaminio del Turco, is a highly venerated little 15C terracotta bust of the *Madonna* in honour of which the Palio (see p 359) of 2 July is run. The prize banner is kept in the church before the race. On either side are two silver statues by Francesco and Giovanni Antonio Mazzuoli. The ciborium dates from 1734. The two organs are by Sebastiano Montese (1728).

North transept. 17C *Crucifix* and three statues by Antonio Manetti (1837–38) and a 17C ciborium. North wall. *Circumcision* and *Coronation of the Virgin*, both by Giovanni Bruni (1837); on the altar, *Vision of St Catherine* and *Martyrdom of St Lawrence* by Dionisio Montorselli. On the west wall, *Mass of St Gregory the Great* by Bernardino Mei.

To the right of the church, in Via delle Vergini, is the oratory and headquarters of the **Contrada Imperiale della Giraffa** (Map I; 3). Via Provenzano Salvani leads along the left side of Santa Maria to Via del Giglio in which (left) is the church of **San Pietro a Ovile** (Map I; 2), probably of ancient foundation but rebuilt in the 18C, now used for lectures and in poor repair.

San Francesco

Via Provenzano continues to Via dei Rossi, and (right) to Piazza San Francesco (good view of the Osservanza) and the large Gothic church of San Francesco (**Map** II; 7). It was built in 1326–1475, all but destroyed by fire in 1655, and afterwards used as a barracks for a long period. In 1885–92 it was radically restored by Giuseppe Partini in neo-Gothic style; the façade is by Vittorio Mariani and Gaetano Ceccarelli (1894–1913), but the pretty campanile survives from 1763.

The interior has late 19C stained glass by Ulisse de Matteis. High up on the west wall are two detached frescoes from the Porta Romana by Sassetta and Sano di Pietro, and from Porta Pispini by Sodoma. The incongruous scaffolding side altars were installed in 1997 in order to exhibit the fine 16C–17C altarpieces which were painted for the church (the Baroque side altars were destroyed in the 19C). South wall. Beyond a beautiful frescoed lunette with the *Visitation* and a frescoed niche with *Saints*, the three altarpieces are by Giuseppe Nicola Nasini, Giovanni Battista Ramacciotti, and Alessandro Casolani. An ancient wooden *Crucifix* has been placed in a 14C carved tabernacle.

South transept. In the chapel, fresco of a polyptych with the *Madonna enthroned and Saints* by Lippo Vanni. The marble statue of *St Francis* (against the wall of the transept) is by a 15C sculptor close in style to Francesco di Valdambrino. **Choir chapels**. Outside the fourth chapel to the right of the choir, the pavement tomb of 1541 has graffiti decoration on a cartoon attributed to Beccafumi. In the second chapel right of the choir: funerary monument of Cristoforo Felici, with a very unusual carved effigy by Urbano da Cortona (1462–87); and in the first chapel, 14C Sienese *Madonna and Child* (attributed to Andrea Vanni). On the left wall of the choir, two busts of *Silvio Piccolomini* and *Vittoria Forteguerri* (father and mother of Pius II), made for their tomb and probably dating from the 15C. To the left of the choir, first chapel, detached fresco of the *Crucifixion* by Pietro Lorenzetti; third chapel: two fine *frescoes by Ambrogio Lorenzetti, one with the *Martyrdom of Franciscan monks* and one with a scene of *St Louis of Toulouse before Pope Boniface VIII*. Fourth chapel, *Madonna and Child enthroned*, attributed to Jacopo di Mino.

In the north transept is a chapel with a fine marble pavement by Marrina. North wall. Detached fresco of the *Crucifix and St Jerome*, and altarpieces by Alessandro Casolani, Jacopo Zucchi, Pietro Sorri, Pietro da Cortona (*Martyrdom of Santa Martina*), and Dionisio Montorselli. At the end of the wall is the huge monumental doorway by Francesco di Giorgio Martini removed in the early 20C from the façade of the church. The Renaissance **cloisters** house part of the university.

Oratorio di San Bernardino and Museo Diocesano di Arte Sacra

To the right of San Francesco, the 15C Oratorio di San Bernardino (**Map** II; 7) stands on the spot where St Bernard preached (open mid March–Oct 10.30–13.30, 15.00–17.30). The **lower chapel** has lunettes frescoed with scenes representing the saint's life by 17C Sienese artists including Francesco Vanni, Domenico Manetti, Ventura Salimbeni, and Rutilio Manetti. The painting in the ceiling with a view of Siena (1580) is by Francesco Vanni. On a table is a charming little *Madonna and Child* by Sano di Pietro. On the stairs are paintings by Bernardino Mei, and *St Anna and the Virgin* by Alessandro Franchi (19C). In the little chapel, *Saints Bernard and Catherine* by Luigi Ademollo (late 18C), and a bas-relief signed by Giovanni di Agostino (1341).

The *oratory*, beautifully decorated by Ventura Turapilli (after 1496), with a lovely ceiling contains fine frescoes of 1518 by Sodoma (*Presentation, Visitation, Assumption* and *Coronation of the Virgin*), Beccafumi (*Marriage of the Virgin, Transition of the Virgin*), and Girolamo del Pacchia. The 14C antiphonal is illuminated by Lippo Vanni.

The **Museo Diocesano di Arte Sacra**, a delightful little museum with works of art from Sienese churches which have been closed or from churches in the diocese, is exhibited in five small rooms here, some of which have pretty views of Siena and the countryside.

Room 4 contains the front of a marriage-chest (*cassone*) by a follower of Giovanni di Paolo; a *Madonna and Child with Saints* by Neroccio di Bartolomeo, in a lovely wood tabernacle; a painted *Cross* by Giovanni di Paolo; a statuette of *St Paul* by Domenico di Niccolò dei Cori; a late 15C marble relief of the *Madonna and Child*; and a relief of *Christ in pietà* by Urbano da Cortona. Displayed one above the other are two interesting works by Vecchietta: one a fresco of the *Lamentation*, and the other a small polychrome wooden group of the *Pietà*, a very unusual work showing close stylistic similarities to the fresco. The *Annunciation and Saints* by Matteo di Giovanni and Giovanni di Pietro is derived from Simone Martini's famous work of the same subject now in the Galleria degli Uffizi in Florence. The *Madonna and Child with Saints and angels* is one of the finest works of Matteo di Giovanni.

Room 5. *Madonna and Child* by the Maestro di Tressa (early 13C) and a *Madonna and Child* by Segna di Bonaventura. The *Madonna del Latte* (from Lecceto) is one of the best works of Ambrogio Lorenzetti. The *Madonna enthroned and four angels* is by Bartolomeo Bulgarini; and the *Madonna and Child* by Andrea di Bartolo. In the case are small works by Ambrogio Lorenzetti and Taddeo di Bartolo. On the wall, *St Christopher* by Sano di Pietro; *St George and the Dragon*, a delightful work by the 'Maestro dell'Osservanza'; two *Madonnas* by Andrea Vanni; and *St Peter* by Luca di Tommè.

Stairs lead up to **room 6**. The *Christ carrying the Cross* (in a beautiful carved frame) is by Domenico Beccafumi and Giovanni Barili; the *Madonna and Child* is by Lorenzo Brazzi. The little room beneath the roof exhibits 16C–17C works by Rutilio Manetti, Sodoma (two small diptychs with the *Trinity*), three small works by Sano di Pietro, works by Andrea Casolani, and four small works by Riccio. In the last room on the **ground floor** is a late 14C polychrome wood statue of *St Paul* by the 'Maestro del Crocifisso dei Disciplinati', and a *Pietà* by Santi di Tito.

Via dei Rossi, arched at either end (**Map** I; 2), returns to Via Banchi di Sopra which ends (right) at **Piazza Salimbeni** (**Map** I; 2), laid out in 1876–79 when the three palaces here were enlarged or restored. In the centre is **Palazzo Salimbeni**, enlarged in neo-Gothic style in 1866 by Giuseppe Partini. On the left is **Palazzo Tantucci** by Riccio (1548), restored by Partini, and, opposite, **Palazzo Spannocchi** which has two fine façades; one by Giuliano da Maiano in Via Banchi di Sopra (some of the busts of Roman emperors and of Ambrogio Spannocchi high up beneath the roof are also by Giuliano), the other by Giuseppe Partini in imitation of the Renaissance style (1881), facing the piazza. These three palaces form the seat of the **Monte dei Paschi di Siena**, a banking establishment founded in 1624, which owns an interesting collection of Sienese works of art (admission only with special permission), as well as most of the Chigi Saracini Collection, see p 363. The statue of Sallustio Bandini is by Tito Sarrocchi (1880).

Costa dell'Incrociata descends from Piazza Salimbeni to Via della Sapienza. Here is the church of **San Pellegrino a Sapienza** (Map I; 2; usually closed). The vault was frescoed in the 18C by Giuliano Traballesi. On the **south side** (behind glass) is a tiny ivory portable altar known as the *Madonna delle Grazie*, a precious work probably by a French craftsman, and a rare survival from the 14C. On the wall beside it is a small incised marble *Crucifix*, a very unusual work (removed for restoration), recently attributed to Guccio di Mannaia (c 1310). On the south altar, Lorenzo Feliciati, *Madonna of the Misericordia* (1772). On the **high altar**, Giuseppe Nasini, *Birth of the Virgin*. The six stucco statues in niches are by Giuseppe Mazzuoli the Younger. The church also owns a beautiful painting, attributed to the bottega of Simone Martini, of the *Blessed Andrea Gallerani* (founder of the Misericordia).

Parallel to Via della Sapienza is the interesting medieval Vicolo della Palla a corda. The **Biblioteca Comunale** (Map I; 1, 2; open weekdays 09.00–20.00; Sat 09.00–14.00) contains over 100,000 volumes and 5000 MSS, as well as illuminated missals, breviaries, and Books of Hours, St Catherine's letters, a 7C papyrus from Ravenna, drawings by Peruzzi and Beccafumi, a book with illustrations by Botticelli, and fine examples of bookbinding (including an 11C Byzantine work).

Casa di Santa Caterina

Costa Sant'Antonio descends from Via della Sapienza to the Casa di Santa Caterina (**Map** I; 1; open 09.00–12.30, 15.30–18.00), the house where St Catherine of Siena was born. It was converted into a sanctuary after its purchase by the Comune in 1466.

St Catherine of Siena

Caterina Benincasa (1347–80), or Catherine of Siena, was the daughter of a dyer and took the veil at the age of eight. Her visions of the Redeemer, from whom she received the stigmata and, like her Alexandrian namesake, a marriage ring, have been the subject of countless paintings. Her eloquence persuaded Gregory XI to return from Avignon to Rome, and her letters (preserved in the Biblioteca Comunale; see above) are models of style as well as of devotion. She died in Rome, where she is buried in Santa Maria sopra Minerva, was canonised in 1461, and in 1939 was proclaimed a patron saint of Italy. She was made a doctor of the Church in 1970, the first female saint, with St Teresa of Avila, to be given this distinction, and in 1999 was proclaimed a patron saint of Europe. The only authentic portrait of Catherine can be seen in the nearby church of San Domenico, in the chapel in which she became a Dominican. Another chapel in the same church was built in 1460 to preserve the relic of her head brought back to Siena from Rome in 1383. The chapel is frescoed with scenes from her life by Sodoma.

The present entrance is through a **portico** erected in 1941. Beyond, the charming little **loggia** was built perhaps by Peruzzi or by his follower Giovanni Battista Pelori (1533). Here is (left) the **Oratorio della Cucina**, the family kitchen converted in the 16C into an oratory, which has the most interesting decorations. On the wall to the left of the entrance: paintings by Alessandro Casolani, Pietro Sorri (*St Catherine liberating a woman possessed of the devil*), Pomarancio, Lattanzio Bonastri and Gaetano Marinelli (1872). The altarpiece is by Bernardino Fungai, and on either side are two paintings by Riccio. On the wall to the right of the altar: paintings by Pietro Aldi (1872), Riccio and Arcangelo Salimbeni (1578), Pomarancio, and Alessandro Casolani. On the wall opposite the altar, is a curved painting in a niche by Francesco Vanni, and on either side, works by Pietro Sorri, Rutilio Manetti, and Francesco Vanni. The wood stalls date from 1518 and 1555, and the majolica pavement from the 16C.

Opposite is the **Church of the Crocifisso** built in 1623 on the site of the saint's orchard to house the *Crucifixion* (by the late 12C Pisan school) before which St Catherine received the stigmata at Pisa in 1375, now over the high altar. It is preserved in a cupboard decorated by Riccio. The marble high altar is by Tommaso Redi (1649). In the south transept is an altarpiece by Sebastiano Conca and in the north transept an altarpiece by Rutilio and Domenico Manetti. Stairs lead down to the **Camera della Santa**, St Catherine's cell, frescoed by Alessandro Franchi and Gaetano Marinelli in 1896. It preserves a small painting of *St Catherine receiving the stigmata* by Girolamo di Benvenuto.

Below is the **Oratorio della Tintoria** or Santa Caterina in Fontebranda, now the oratory of the **Contrada dell'Oca** and only open on special occasions. It was built in 1465 on the site of the dyer's workshop (*tintoria*). It contains frescoes of five *Angels* by Sodoma, and *St Catherine receiving the stigmata* and other scenes from her life, by Girolamo del Pacchia and Ventura Salimbeni. The splendid poly-chrome *wooden statue of *St Catherine* is by Neroccio di Bartolomeo, sculpted for this oratory in 1475.

Vicolo del Tiratoio passes under the house of St Catherine and a pretty little lane leads downhill to the **Fonte Branda** (**Map** I; 5), the oldest and most abundant spring in Siena. It was mentioned as early as 1081 and covered over in 1248 with brick vaults by Giovanni di Stefano. The water for the public fountain is channelled from a large reservoir. The church of San Domenico is conspicuous on the hill above.

San Domenico can be reached either by Via della Sapienza (see above) or from Costa Sant'Antonio, by taking Vicolo del Campaccio through the first archway on the left, a lane which climbs up above St Catherine's house to Via Camporegio.

San Domenico

At the top of Camporegio hill stands the austere Gothic church of San Domenico (**Map** I; 1, 5), begun in 1226, enlarged, damaged, and altered in successive centuries. The campanile dates from 1340 (altered in 1798). From the edge of the hill there is a view of the Duomo and Palazzo Pubblico above old houses on a hillside. The interior has the typical Dominican plan, with a wide aisleless nave, transepts, and a shallow choir with side chapels. The **Cappella delle Volte**, a chapel at the west end, contains the only authentic portrait of *St Catherine*, by her contemporary and friend, Andrea Vanni. St Catherine (see p 394) assumed the Dominican habit in this chapel. The other paintings here are by Mattia Preti and Crescenzio Gambarelli.

South side. First altar, *Birth of the Virgin* by Alessandro Casolani (1584). Beyond it is the **Cappella di Santa Caterina**. On the entrance arch, *Saints Luke and Jerome*, by Sodoma. The tabernacle on the altar, by Giovanni di Stefano (1466) encloses a reliquary containing St Catherine's head, a very fine early 19C work by Giuseppe Coppini.

On the right and left of the altar are celebrated *frescoes by Sodoma* (1526), representing the *Saint in ecstasy and swooning*. The pilasters have good grotesques. On the left wall, the *Saint interceding for the life of a young man brought to repentance*, also by Sodoma; on the right wall, the *Saint liberating a man possessed* by Francesco Vanni. The beautiful pavement is attributed to Giovanni di Stefano.

Above the steps down to the huge **crypt** (usually closed), begun in the 14C, is a painting of *God the Father and Saints* which surrounds a 14C *Madonna and Child*. The **Nativity* is by Francesco di Giorgio Martini and an assistant. The *Pietà* in the lunette above is by Matteo di Giovanni and the predella by Bernardino Fungai.

Over the **high altar** is a fine **tabernacle* with two angels, by Benedetto da Maiano (c 1475; difficult to appreciate because of the incongruous stained glass inserted into the east windows in 1982). In the first chapel to the right of the altar are fragmentary remains of frescoes by Andrea Vanni and Lippo Memmi, and there is a triptych of the *Madonna and Child with Saints Jerome and John the Baptist* by Matteo di Giovanni. In the first chapel to the left of the sanctuary, polychrome wood statue of *St Anthony Abbot* attributed to Giovanni di Turino, and a detached fresco of the Madonna and two saints by Pietro Lorenzetti. In the second chapel to the left of the high altar is a **Maestà*, a splendid huge painting by Guido da Siena (second half of the 13C, but dated 1221). On the side walls 18C frescoes by Giuseppe Nasini surround **St Barbara enthroned between angels and Saints Mary Magdalene and Catherine* by Matteo di Giovanni, opposite a *Madonna and Child with four Saints* by Benvenuto di Giovanni.

On the north side, the third altar has a 16C painting of the *Mysteries of the Rosary*, and remains of frescoes, and the second altar, *Miracle of St Anthony Abbot* by Rutilio Manetti.

From Piazza San Domenico Viale dei Mille leads above the stadium (**Map** II; 5) on the valley floor, to the huge **Fortezza Medicea** (Map II; 5), or Forte di Santa Barbara, built for Cosimo I by Baldassarre Lanci in 1560. On the bastions are avenues with delightful views. In the vaults is the *Enoteca Italica*, a cellar specialising in Tuscan wines (open 12.00–midnight for wine tasting and buying).

From San Domenico the unattractive Viale Curtatone (**Map** I; 1) leads past the neo-Classical **Evangelical Church** (1882) to the undistinguished **Piazza Matteotti** with its huge post office, built in 1910 (by Vittorio Mariani). Here, the little **Oratorio delle Suore** (or del Paradiso) is approached by a double staircase. This is the oratory of the **Contrada del Drago**. The interior, decorated in 1693, has paintings by Francesco Rustici, Domenico Manetti, and Raffaello Vanni. The bust of *St Catherine* in polychrome terracotta is by Marrina (1517).

Via Pianigiani leads east out of Piazza Matteotti to the little **Oratorio di Santa Maria delle Nevi** (**Map** I; 2; usually locked), an elegant Renaissance building (1471) attributed to Francesco di Giorgio Martini. The **altarpiece* (*Madonna delle Nevi*) is by Matteo di Giovanni (1477).

Just beyond the church, Via di Vallerozzi descends steeply towards Porta Ovile (**Map** I; 2). Halfway down on the right Via dell'Abbadia leads up to Piazza Abbadia (**Map** I; 2) with the **Rocca di Palazzo Salimbeni** (14C; restored in the Gothic style in the 19C). The Medici coat of arms by Domenico Cafaggi (1570) can just be seen high up above the courtyard wall.

Also in Piazza Abbadia is the church of **San Michele al Monte di San Donato** (**Map** I; 2), consecrated in 1147, but transformed in 1691 and heavily restored. The inner door dates from 1918. South wall. *Madonna of the Rosary* attributed to Antonio Buonfigli, and (above) 13C fresco fragments including the *Raising of Lazarus*; first altar, *Madonna and St Apollonia* by Annibale Mazzuoli. Beyond the second altar, in a stucco frame, *Crucifix and Saints* attributed to Antonio Buonfigli or Francesco Nasini. The south transept has 18C paintings by Giovanni Battista Sorbi. The **choir**, with frescoes of the *Fall of the rebel angels* is an innovative work by Luigi Ademollo (1794), is hung with paintings by Benedetto di Bindo and Sodoma. The north transept has paintings by Antonio Nasini (1693).

Via di Vallerozzi continues down to the church of **San Rocco**, the oratory of the **Contrada della Lupa** (Map II; 6). A classical column outside bears a bronze copy of the she-wolf of Rome. The interior has fine 17C Sienese paintings by Raffaello Vanni, Rutilio Manetti, and Ventura Salimbeni.

From here it is a short way left, off Via Pian d'Ovile, to the brick **Fonte Nuova di Ovile** (Map II; 2; 1303) with two fine Gothic arches, reached by steps below the road. Via Vallerozzi ends at **Porta Ovile** (Map II; 2); on the left is a tabernacle with a fresco of the *Madonna and Child with Saints* by Sano di Pietro. The fine gate dates from the 14C; outside there is a view of a stretch of the city walls with orchards and old houses and the side of the church of San Francesco. Steps go down to the picturesque **Fonte d'Ovile** (1262). Just inside the gate, in Via del Comune is the headquarters of the **Contrada del Bruco** (Map II; 6). The inhabitants of this district are known for their independent character and spirit of fierce allegience to the contrada. In the oratory is a *Madonna and Child* by Luca di Tommè. One of the poorest parts of the town in the Middle Ages, there was a revolt here in 1371 of the wool-workers belonging to the contrada. This was one of the first workers' revolts in medieval Italy (preceding the famous Ciompi insurrection in Florence by seven years). Three hundred members of the contrada, with a rag-merchant called Domenico di Lano at their head, took up arms against the Council of Nine and a faction of nobles belonging to the Salimbeni family. After heavy losses, the workers finally gained the upper hand and obtained some benefits and a partial change in the government of the town.

Via Montanini leads north from the Oratorio di Santa Maria delle Nevi (see above) past (no. 92) **Palazzo Ottieri (Costantini)**, with a 15C façade attributed to Francesco di Giorgio Martini, with fine ironwork. On the right, is the church of **Sant'Andrea** (Map II; 6), approached by steps added in 1755. It was founded in the 12C, transformed in the 18C, and restored in the 20C. In the interior on the south side are (first altar), fine 15C frescoes of the *Madonna and Child with St Anne*, and (second altar) a pretty stucco frame enclosing a fresco by Apollonio Nasini. Over the **high altar**, *Coronation of the Virgin*, signed and dated by Giovanni di Paolo (1445). On the north side (second altar), another fresco of a saint by Nasini enclosed in a stucco frame, and (first altar) fragments of 15C frescoes. On the west wall is a stucco bas-relief of the *Madonna and Child* by the 15C Sienese school.

Beside the church is the **Oratorio di Sant'Anna in Sant' Onofrio**. Inside is a half-length figure in terracotta of *St Bernardine* (right of the high altar) dating from the end of the 15C (in the style of Cozzarelli). The stucco statues in the niches date from 1769.

Via Montanini ends at a fork with Via di Camollia and the unattractive Via Garibaldi. On the curve of Via Garibaldi (and considerably below the level of the road) is the church of **San Sebastiano** (locked), which contains early 17C frescoes.

Near San Sebastiano is the Anglican church of **St Peter's**, the building of which was financed by Mrs Georgina Allinson Hignetti in 1908 and it was erected in medieval style in the following year. It is open for occasional services. Via Camollia continues north and Via dei Gazzani diverges left for the church of **Santo Stefano** (closed for restoration), rebuilt in 1671–75.

Santo Stefano is on the corner of **La Lizza** (**Map** II; 5), a small attractive public park laid out in 1778 by Antonio Matteucci and Leopoldo Prucher with two diverging avenues of horse-chestnuts and Cedars of Lebanon beside the Fortezza Medicea (see above). The fine statue of Garibaldi is by Raffaello Romanelli. A general street market is held in this area on Wednesdays. The Palazzo di Giustizia was built here in 1986.

Via del Romitorio leads down from the church of Santo Stefano, under a tunnel and past a little garden, to the church of **Santa Maria in Portico a Fontegiusta** (**Map** II; 1), an elegant little Renaissance church. On the brick façade is a fine marble portal (1489) with a frieze attributed to Giovanni di Stefano. The interior is in the form of a vaulted hall. The tiny round window on the west wall has restored 15C stained glass. The fresco on the right of the *Visitation* (1522) is attributed to Scalabrino. On the south altar, *Coronation of the Virgin with Saints* by Bernardino Fungai. On the east wall (right of the high altar), *Intercession of the Blessed Ambrogio Sansedoni for the protection of Siena* (Siena is portrayed below), by Francesco Vanni. The *high altar is a splendid work in marble in the form of a classical edicola by Marrina (c 1517) with a lunette of *Christ in Pietà* (by Michele Cioli da Settignano) and two winged Victories. It surrounds the highly venerated *Madonna di Fontegiusta*, a late 14C fresco attributed to Cristoforo di Bindoccio (called Malabarba) and Meo di Piero. On either side of the altar are faded frescoes by Ventura Salimbeni and the large lunette above has a fine fresco of the *Virgin in Glory* by Girolamo di Benvenuto (1515). By the door on the north side is a tiny stoup in bronze, signed and dated 1480 by Giovanni delle Bombarde. On the north wall is a fresco (partly repainted) of the *Sibyl announcing to Augustus the Birth of Christ*, attributed to Baldassarre Peruzzi or Daniele da Volterra.

A small **museum** in an old tower of the medieval walls, now incorporated in the church, has an interesting bronze ciborium and a terracotta bust of *St Bernardine*, both attributed to Vecchietta, and a polychrome wooden statue of *St Sebastian*, attributed to Giovanni di Stefano.

From the front of the church of Fontegiusta the short Via Fontegiusta leads up beneath a pretty arch to Via di Camollia. On the right is the headquarters and oratory of the **Contrada dell'Istrice** (**Map** II; 2). Via di Camollia continues left to the church of **San Pietro alla Magione** (**Map** II; 1) with a rebuilt façade and a Gothic portal. In the **interior** are numerous remains of detached 14C frescoes, and (in a niche on the right wall) a 15C sinopia of the *Madonna and Child*. The little marble tabernacle on the right of the sanctuary is modelled on the façade of the Duomo. The adjoining 16C chapel contains a fresco of the *Madonna and Child* by Riccio.

Surrounding the church are the restored buildings of the **Magione**, the house which served as a medieval pilgrims' hospice founded by the Knights Templar.

Via di Camollia ends at the **Porta Camollia** (**Map** II; 1), rebuilt in 1604 and inscribed *Cor magis tibi sena pandit*—'To you Siena opens her heart (wider than this gate)'—to commemorate a visit of the grand-duke Ferdinando I. A few steps beyond is a column recalling the meeting on this spot of Frederick III and Eleanora of Portugal in March 1451 (depicted in the frescoes in the Libreria Piccolomini, see above). Beyond the column in Viale Vittorio Emanuele II, is the Antiporto or barbican (1675), in imitation of the Porta Romana. In Via Cavour, c 500m from the antiporta, is the brick **Palazzo dei Diavoli** or dei Turchi attributed to Antonio Federighi (1460).

The environs of Siena

In the countryside which surrounds Siena there are often splendid views of the hill-town, from the south in particular. At a short distance from the town on all sides there are many charming country roads and a vast choice of places to visit, often in panoramic positions, including monasteries, villas, formal or romantic gardens, little villages, ruined castles, and country churches in a landscape which varies from farmland and woods to river valleys and the unique clay downs known as *Le Crete* towards Asciano. This district lends itself to exploration, and only some of the most interesting places are mentioned below.

Practical information

 Getting around
By car
All the other places described have to be reached by car from Siena (directions given in the text).
By bus
For the Osservanza, bus no. 3 from Piazza del Sale.

 Information office
APT Siena, Piazza dell Campo 56, Siena (☎ 0577 280 551, 🖷 270 676).

 Where to stay
Hotels
Near the **Osservanza**:
☆☆☆☆ *Villa Scaccia pensieri*, Via di Scaccia-pensieri 10 (☎ 0577 414 41; 🖷 0577 270 854). *Certosa di Maggiano*, Via di Certosa 82 (☎ 0577 288 180; 🖷 0577 288 189).
Sovicille: ☆☆☆☆ *Borgo Pretale* (☎ 0577 345 401; 🖷 0577 345 625).

Eating out
Restaurant
TORRI € *Le Torri di Stigliano* at Stigliano, 2km south.

L'Osservanza church and convent
The convent and church of l'Osservanza is the most important Sienese church outside the city walls. About 2.5km from Porta Ovile (see p 394; Map II; 2), it is reached by car along Via Simone Martini and the 16C Madonnina Rossa (beyond the railway crossing).

The basilica (open 09.00–13.00, 16.00–19.00) was founded in 1423 by St Bernardine (see p 323). Its aim was to restore the observance of the original

Franciscan rule, relaxed by papal dispensations. The convent was enlarged in 1476–90 probably by Francesco di Giorgio Martini and Giacomo Cozzarelli. It was confiscated by the city in 1874, restored in Renaissance style in 1932 but then well rebuilt in 1949 after severe war damage.

The stucco and terracotta roundels in the vaults and in the sanctuary are attributed to Giacomo Cozzarelli. On the west wall the two roundels with saints surrounded by garlands of fruit are attributed to Andrea della Robbia. On either

PROVINCIA DI SIENA

N

AREZZO

equanda Sinalunga

Montisi

Torrita
di Siena

MONTEPULCIANO

za

Chianciano   Chianciano
Terme

Chiusi

La Foce

Sarteano

Contignano

Campiglia
d'Orcia

Cetona

Bagni S. Filippo M. CETONA

Abbadia   Radicofani
S. Salvatore

S. Casciano
dei Bagni

Piancastagnaio

LAZIO

2

side of the entrance to the sanctuary are white glazed figures of the *Annunciatory Angel* and the *Virgin* in tabernacles also by Andrea. North side: first altar, *Madonna and Child*, with four angels by Sano di Pietro; second altar, enamelled terracotta altarpiece of the *Coronation of the Virgin* by Andrea della Robbia; fourth altar, *Four Saints* by Andrea di Bartolo (1413). In the sanctuary is a fresco with its sinopia by Pietro di Francesco Orioli.

South side: detached fresco of the *Crucifixion* by Bartolomeo Neroni; third altar, *Madonna and Child with Saints* by Sano di Pietro. On the right wall, *St Elizabeth of Hungary* by Girolamo di Benvenuto, and, on the left wall, *St Bernardine* by Pietro di Giovanni d'Ambrogio; fourth altar, triptych attributed to the Maestro dell' Osservanza, who acquired his name from this painting.

In the **sacristy** is a group of seven polychrome terracotta figures mourning over the dead Christ, by Giacomo Cozzarelli. A small **museum** contains a *Head of Christ* by Lando di Pietro (1338), all that remains of a wood *Crucifix* destroyed in 1944, and a reliquary of St Bernardine by Francesco d'Antonio (1454).

The **Certosa di Pontignano**, also reached from Porta Ovile, is described on p 144.

Near Porta Pispini (see p 389; Map II; 12) the Strada di Busseto leads east out of Siena, and beyond the railway is the pretty little hamlet of **Sant'Agnese a Vignano**. The villa of the art historian, Cesare Brandi (1906–88), with a library and art collection, is used by the University of Siena as a fine arts institute.

Outside Porta Romana (see p 389; **Map** II; 16), on the southern outskirts of Siena, is the **Certosa di Maggiano**, probably the first charterhouse to be founded in Tuscany. It was built in 1315 and suppressed in 1782; it is now restored as a hotel. The church has an interesting 18C interior with (frescoes by the Nasini and sculptures by the Mazzuoli brothers.

Farmhouses near Siena

Outside Porta Camollia (see p 398; Map II; 1), Via Caduti di Vicobello and the Strada di Vico Alto lead north towards the **Villa di Vicobello** built on a hill for the Chigi family by Baldassarre Peruzzi. It is surrounded by a large garden, the best preserved private 16C garden near Siena (adm. by appointment, ☎ 0577 377 184).

West of Siena, outside Porta San Marco (p 384; Map II; 13) is the village of Volte Alte (244m), with the **Ville delle Volte**, another 16C villa attributed to Baldassarre Peruzzi. Also outside Porta San Marco (on the N73 signposted for Roccastrada and Grosseto) is the battlemented **Villa di Monastero**, formerly the Benedictine abbey of Sant'Eugenio (suppressed in 1810 and now a home for the elderly) surrounded by a large park. There are two cloisters, one of which is fortified. The church has a dome with frescoes in the spandrels by Ventura Salimbeni and Francesco Vanni. There are paintings by Rutilio Manetti, Riccio, Benvenuto di Giovanni and Sodoma (attributed).

Nearby is the 12C **Castello di Belcaro**, in a lovely position (adm. weekdays 14.00–16.00 by appointment, ☎ 0577 394 237), enlarged in the 16C by Peruzzi.

Lecceto, west of Siena, is a magnificent fortified monastery in dense ilex woods. It was founded on the site of an ancient hermitage by the Augustinians and is still inhabited by Augustinian nuns (Mass on fest. at 17.00). The **church** has a simple Romanesque façade, partly covered by a portico with remains of 15C frescoes.

The interior was transformed in the late Baroque period when a marble screen was placed behind the altar to separate the nave from the choir. In the nave are the two fine pavement tombs of Niccolò Saracini (1350) and Jacopo Magistri Martini (1499). On the nave wall are some interesting fresco fragments: a figure of *St Michael* is attributed to Ambrogio Lorenzetti, whose famous *Madonna of Lecceto* is now in the Diocesan Museum in Siena. A rare series of twenty **choir-books** (14C–15C), with miniatures by Giovanni di Paolo and others, which belong to the monastery, are now preserved in the Biblioteca Comunale in Siena. Next to the church is the entrance to the elegant cloister on two storeys, from which there is a good view of the massive battlemented tower.

A short distance north of Lecceto is the little church of **San Leonardo al Lago** (reached by a narrow path from the road) on a small hill overlooking a valley which was once a lake. Originally a hermitage founded in the 12C, the present church with its fine façade and rose window dates from the mid 14C. In the early 15C it was provided with fortifications which still survive in part. The interior is decorated with a number of frescoes, in particular the apse, which is covered with scenes of the *Life of the Virgin* (with angels singing and playing musical instruments in the vault), by Lippo Vanni (1360–70), a follower of Pietro Lorenzetti. To the right of the church (ring the bell) are remains of the former monastery. In the refectory is a *Crucifixion* frescoed by Giovanni di Paolo.

The area further west and southwest of Siena is known as the **Montagnola Senese**. Here are extensive woods of oaks, ilexes and chestnut trees, and picturesque villages and isolated farmhouses and villas.

Castello di Celsa

The Castello di Celsa, about 15km west of Siena, owned by the Aldobrandini family, is in a beautiful position, approached by an avenue of umbrella pines. The **garden** can be visited by appointment (☎ 0577 317 002) or apply to the Aldobrandini administration in Rome (☎ 06 686 1138; 📠 06 683 073 26). Standing on a remote hilltop, surrounded by oak forests, it has a superb unspoilt view of Siena and beyond.

Dating back to at least the 13C the castle was sacked by the Spaniards in 1554 and restored in the 17C. One of the two wings on the triangular courtyard was rebuilt in the Gothic style in the last century. Baldassarre Peruzzi is said to have designed the circular chapel as well as the original garden in the early 16C. The garden now consists of a terrace which overhangs the valley below between two simple pavilions, and a semicircular pool. A modern parterre of box and gravel represents the arms of the Aldobrandini. Another semicircular pool is approached from a staircase decorated with reliefs of river gods and dolphins. Beyond is an evergreen wood.

Villa Cetinale

Close by is Cetinale, the most spectacular villa in the area. The grand villa has a 16C core (including the outside stair and portico). It was built in 1680 for Cardinal Flavio Chigi, nephew of Pope Alexander VII, by Carlo Fontana. The **garden** is open to the public by appointment in the mornings (☎ 0577 311 147; fee). After many years of neglect the villa and garden were sold by the Chigi family in 1978. Both are now beautifully maintained and the garden has been carefully restored.

In front of the house is a formal garden with topiary and yew hedges, landscaped in the early 20C. Under the loggia are two Roman statues (4C AD) and an inscription 'welcoming' visitors. On the left side of the villa is another lovely garden, now planted with numerous varieties of rose. The other façade of the house, with an outside staircase, looks towards a densely wooded hill near the top of which is the conspicuous early 18C Romitorio or hermitage.

A broad grassy path runs between two walls decorated with busts and statues (including colossal figures of Dacian prisoners, copies of antique originals). Cypresses planted at the beginning of the 20C line the path leading up to the stone '**theatre**', now surrounded by terracotta urns. The colossal bust on the left is a portrait of *Napoleon*, placed here in his honour when he visited the villa. A gate, flanked by the Chigi arms, admits to a long flight of some 250 steps which leads straight up through dense woods to the **Romitorio** (1717), a five storeyed building, recently carefully restored which has a Cross of Lorraine on the exterior (with reliefs of Christ and the four evangelists). There is a church on the ground floor, used by the hermit monks who once lived here, and a delightful little walled garden (recently replanted). From the highest room there is a wonderful view through the little window down to the villa and (on a clear day) to Monte Amiata in the distance. The woods, no longer all part of the estate, stretch from here more or less continuously all the way to the sea.

On the right of the villa is another wood (enclosed by a wall with two gates) known as **La Tebaide** (Thebaid), also created by Cardinal Chigi in the late 17C. The seven little chapels in the woods dedicated to the Sorrows of the Virgin and the statues of hermits by Giuseppe Mazzuoli were intended to evoke an atmosphere of prayer and contemplation for the visitor. Along the winding paths are tortoises, dragons, and various monsters, carved out of the living rock, and the little lake is overgrown with white water lilies.

Ancaiano, just south of Cetinale, is a charming village which has an unexpectedly large and elegant parish church, built in the 17C, by Pope Alexander VII Chigi. The interior has a few 16C–17C paintings and two earlier frescoes.

The nearby village of **Sovicille** preserves parts of its medieval walls and some picturesque houses. Facing the main square is the much restored church of San Lorenzo, with an old campanile. Inside, on the right of the nave, is a fresco of the *Madonna and Child with Saints* attributed to Alessandro Casolani.

Outside the village is the Pieve di San Giovanni Battista, better known as **Pieve di Ponte allo Spino**. This small 12C–13C Romanesque church is built of evenly-cut stone that has acquired a beautiful patina over the centuries. Its simple **façade** is dominated by a bell-tower built on to a massive earlier tower. The east end, with its three apses and raised crossing decorated with blind arches may be seen from the footpath along the side of the church.

The interior has a basilican plan with pilasters dividing the nave from the aisles, which are of equal height and covered by a timber roof. The transept and crossing are vaulted. The capitals are richly carved with both realistic and symbolic figures, geometrical and plant motifs, showing Lombard and possibly also French influences. An archway to the right of the façade leads into the courtyard which preserves part of the cloister and remains of the canon's house, with two fine Gothic windows.

Rosia, another village on a nearby hill, has a 13C Romanesque church with a tall bell-tower. Steps lead up to the entrance, an arched doorway in an unusually broad façade with three narrow windows. Inside, the nave and two aisles support a timber roof. To the right of the entrance is a triptych of the *Madonna and Child with Saints Sebastian and Anthony Abbot* by Guidoccio Cozzarelli, and a rectangular marble baptismal font, carved with a bas-relief of *Christ and six angels* (15C).

Continuing eastwards, along the Torrente Rosia with wooded slopes on either side, the road passes by an old bridge (the Ponte della Pia) and reaches a cross-roads marked by a column erected by Leopoldo II. Above, on a hill, are the ruined walls and towers of the castle of **Montarrenti**.

Across the Torrente Rosia a cypress avenue climbs uphill to **Torri**, a tiny medieval village surrounded by its old walls. Beyond an archway in the walls is a pretty piazza, leading to an enclosure onto which faces the south side of the Romanesque-Gothic church of **Santissima Trinità e Santa Mustiola**. Built in beautifully hewn stone, it has a fine carved doorway and three arched windows decorated with human and animal heads. The interior, which was heavily restored in the 19C, has a *Madonna and Child* by Luca di Tommè. To the left, under the arms of Pope Pius II with the date 1462, is the entrance to the **cloister** (open Mon and Fri 09.00–12.00) of the former Vallombrosan monastery, now a private villa. This small cloister has loggias on three levels: the lowest arches are decorated with black-and-white marble and supported by a variety of columns with fine capitals. The middle loggia has octagonal brick columns, and the top loggia has slender wood columns. There are extensive woods above Torri, with fine views of Siena in the distance.

To the south is the village of **Orgia** on a hill. The little **Museo del Bosco** (open Fri and Sat 09.30–12.30, ☎ 0577 342 097) has traditional farm implements and objects used in this district. Maps of the footpaths in the surrounding area may be obtained from the Comune in the village (☎ 582 336; for a guide (fee) ☎ 0577 342 053).

San Gimignano

San Gimignano is a charming hill town of 7000 inhabitants, which has pre-served its medieval appearance more completely than any other town in Tuscany. It can, however, be uncomfortably crowded with tourists (mostly on day trips from Florence or Siena) in spring and summer. The town is famous for its numerous towers which make it conspicuous from a great distance and provide one of the most remarkable sights in Italy. It is possible to walk along the 13C walls from which there are fine views of the rich agricultural farm land which surrounds the town, famous for its wine (notably the white *Vernaccia*) which was already renowned in the 14C. The countryside nearby is remarkably unspoilt and exploring the by-roads at random can be particularly rewarding.

Practical information

Getting there
By car
The quickest route from Florence is via the superstrada, taking the exit for Poggibonsi, but a slower and more attractive route is via the Via Cassia.
Car parks Free parking on Via Roma, south of Piazza Martiri di Montemaggio, otherwise Montemaggio car park a few metres from Porta San Giovanni (limited space; with an hourly tariff), and other pay car parks off the approach roads to the north and south (signposted P3 and P4).

By train
There are trains to Poggibonsi (on the line from Empoli to Siena, with some through trains from Florence). Frequent bus services from Poggibonsi station to San Gimignano.

By bus
There is a frequent service from Florence to Poggibonsi in 50 mins (run by *SITA*), and from there services to San Gimignano in 20 mins run by *TRA-IN*.

Information office
Pro Loco, Piazza Duomo 1 (☎ 0577 940 008; 🖾 : prolo-cosg@tin.it). Accommodation can be booked here in person.

Where to stay
Hotels in the centre
☆☆☆ *Bel Soggiorno*, Via San Giovanni 91 (☎ 0577 940 375; 📠 0577 907 521), with a good restaurant; *La Cisterna*, Piazza della Cisterna 24 (☎ 0577 940 328; 📠 0577 942 080); *Leon Bianco*, Piazza della Cisterna 13 (☎ 0577 941 294; 📠 0577 942 123); *L'Antico Pozzo*, Via San Matteo 87 (☎ 0577 942 014; 📠 0577 942 117).

Hotels in the environs
☆☆☆☆ *La Collegiata* at Strada, about 3km below the town off the Via Volterrano (☎ 0577 943 201; 📠 0577 940 566; 🖾 collegia@tin.it); ☆☆☆ *Le Renaie* at Pancole, 6km north (☎ 0577 955 044; 📠 0577 955 126) and *Pescille* at Pescille (☎ 0577 940 186; 📠 0577 943 165).

Campsite
☆ *Il Boschetto di Piemma*, 3km east at Santa Lucia (closed in winter; ☎ 0577 940 352).
Hostel
Monastero San Girolamo, Via Folgore, ☎ 0577 940 573.

Numerous **rooms to let** and **accommodation in farmhouses**, offering agriturism. (Information from Hotels Promotion in San Gimignano at Via San Giovanni, ☎ 0577 940 809).

Eating out
Restaurants
€€ *Dorandò*, Vicolo dell'Oro 2; *La Stella*, Via San Matteo 75. Numerous trattorie and pizzerie on or near Via San Giovanni.

Pasticceria
Armando e Marcella in Via San Giovanni.

Picnics
Beautiful places to picnic can be found in the surrounding countryside or near the Rocca behind the Collegiata.

History

The town derives its name from St Gimignano, a 4C bishop of Modena, traditionally venerated here. It was long known as San Gimignano delle belle Torri from the noble towers of its palaces, most of which were constructed in the 12C–13C. Thirteen still survive out of the 76 traditionally thought to have existed. The town has Etruscan origins and was later inhabited by the Romans. In medieval times it owed its prosperity to its position on the Via Francigena, an important road for commerce and the main pilgrim route to Rome from northern and central Europe (see p 442). Dante was sent here in 1299 as an ambassador of Florence to try to attach the smaller town to the Guelf League. After the devastation caused by the Black Death in 1348 San Gimignano came under the protection of Florence and there was an artistic revival in the 15C. However, the town declined commercially as a result of the deviation of the pilgrim route further northeast to the Elsa valley. The town suffered some damage in the Second World War.

The entrance to the town is through **Porta San Giovanni** (1262), the finest of the town gates. Via San Giovanni, with a good view of the tall tower of Palazzo del Popolo at the end, continues past the little Pisan-Romanesque façade of the deconsecrated church of **San Francesco**. Beyond Palazzo Pratellesi (14C), now

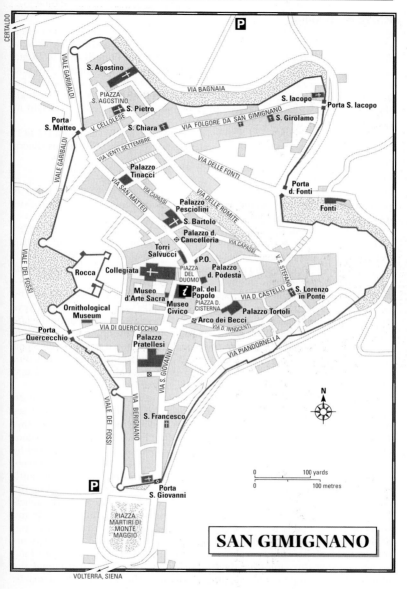

SAN GIMIGNANO

the Biblioteca Comunale, is the **Arco dei Becci**, another ancient gate beside several tall towers, forming part of the first circle of walls (12C). Beyond is the charming triangular **Piazza della Cisterna**, with a well dating from 1287. It is built on a slight slope and is surrounded by 13C–14C palaces, houses and towers.

Piazza del Duomo

Adjoining Piazza della Cisterna is Piazza del Duomo, another handsome medieval square with several spectacular towers. The **Collegiata** stands above a flight of steps. To the left is the crenellated **Palazzo del Popolo** with its loggia and massive tower; to the right is **Palazzo del Podestà** built in 1239 and enlarged a century later. Above the wide archway, which served as a passage for loading and unloading grain, rises the **Torre della Rognosa** which is 51m high (in 1255 the town council decreed that no tower was to exceed this height in order to diminish rivalry in tower building).

To the left of the church is an archway, with a statue of San Gimignano (1342) in a niche. Beyond is **Piazza Pecori,** and the entrance to the Museo d'Arte Sacra and the Collegiata.

The Collegiata

Open 09.30–17.00; in summer 9.30–19.30; fest. 13.00–17.00. A ticket is required which you buy at the Museo d'Arte Sacra; a combined ticket gives admission to all the town's museums.

Beneath an elegant loggia is the baptismal font by Girolamo di Cecco (1378) and a fresco of the *Annunciation* by the *bottega* of Domenico Ghirlandaio (1482). The prophet frescoed in the vault is by Lippo and Federico Memmi.

The Romanesque Collegiata was solemnly consecrated by Pope Eugenius III in 1148 and enlarged in 1466–68 by Giuliano da Maiano.

The interior is decorated with important fresco cycles, which were scarred by war damage but are mainly well restored. South wall: the beautiful **New Testament cycle** composed of 22 episodes on three levels, representing the *Life and Passion of Christ* with a large *Crucifixion* scene in the fifth bay, is one of the great works of Italian Gothic painting. For long attributed to Barna da Siena (c 1381) and Giovanni d'Asciano, it is now thought to have been executed in 1333–41 by a master from the workshop of Simone Martini; possibly Lippo Memmi assisted by Federico Memmi and Donato Martini.

North wall: the **Old Testament cycle**, again on three levels, comprising 26 episodes from the Book of Genesis and relating to Noah, Abraham, Joseph, Moses and Job, are signed and dated 1367 by Bartolo di Fredi. On the west wall are the *Last Judgement, Paradise* and *Hell* by Taddeo di Bartolo (c 1410). Flanking the west door are two fine wooden statues of the *Virgin Annunciate* and the *Angel Gabriel* by Jacopo della Quercia (1421) which were painted in 1426 by Martino di Bartolomeo.

The beautifully preserved Renaissance **Cappella di Santa Fina**, off the south aisle, was commissioned from Giuliano da Maiano (1468) to honour Fina, the patron saint of the town. The altar and marble shrine with exquisite bas-reliefs are by Benedetto da Maiano (1472–77). The frescoes decorating the vault and walls of the chapel are by Domenico Ghirlandaio (c 1475): (right lunette) *St Gregory announcing to Santa Fina her imminent death*, and the *miraculous flowering of violets on her wooden bed*; (left lunette) *Funeral of Santa Fina* accompanied by three miracles: the *healing of her nurse's paralysed hand*, the *blind choir boy's sight regained*, and the *ringing of the church bells by angels*. The *saints* and *prophets* are also by Ghirlandaio, possibly assisted by Sebastiano Mainardi. A very rare early 14C reliquary bust of gilded and painted leather decorated with coloured glass inlay, attributed to the Sienese sculptor Manno di Bandino, is preserved in the shrine (but not always on view).

Benedetto da Maiano also made the marble **tabernacle** over the high altar.

The choir stalls, pulpit and lectern are by Antonio da Colle (1490) who also made the inlaid wooden door leading to the **sacristy**, which has two paintings of the *Deposition* by Jacopo Ligozzi and by Domenico Passignano, both dating from the 1590s. In the second chapel left of the high altar there is a wooden figure of *Christ*, similar to the *Volto Santo* of Lucca, probably an early 13C Sienese work.

The Museo d'Arte Sacra

This small museum has paintings, sculptures, and liturgical objects mostly from the Collegiata, and an Etruscan collection (open daily in summer, 09.30–20.00; in winter 09.30–13.30, 14.30–16.30, except Mon).

In the little chapel on the **ground floor** are tomb-slabs, and other sculptural works and fragments. In the adjoining room are paintings by Fra Paolino, Tamagni, Matteo Rosselli, a few *sinopie* by Benozzo Gozzoli and some very fine illuminated 14C choir books by Niccolò di Ser Sozzo and Lippo Vanni.

First floor. In the room to the right is a detached fresco of the *Crucifixion and Saints* by Benozzo Gozzoli and a *Madonna and Child with Saints* (fresco and *sinopia*) by Tamagni. The room to the left contains 14C polychrome wooden statues of the *Virgin* and *Angel Gabriel*. A marble portrait bust of *Onofrio di Pietro* by Benedetto da Maiano, was commissioned by the Commune of San Gimignano in 1493 to honour this distinguished citizen and scholar. There is also a marble bust of the *Redeemer* by Pietro Torrigiani. In the next room is a *Madonna and Child* signed by Bartolo di Fredi, a red velvet antependium, with doves and the monogram of Christ embroidered in gold, made in Florence in 1449, and a wooden *Crucifix* by Benedetto da Maiano. There is also a collection of 15C–18C church silver, and a statue of *St Anthony Abbot* by Francesco di Valdambrino. In the Loggia is a small collection of Etruscan artefacts excavated locally.

Behind the Collegiata is the ruined **Rocca**, forming part of the fortifications built by the Florentines from 1353, surrounded by a public garden and partly enclosed by old walls. The surviving tower commands a remarkable view of the town and of the countryside beyond. Steps lead down to Via Quercecchio (with a fine view of Colle Val d'Elsa, Casole d'Elsa, Radicondoli, and Monte Maggio in the distance). A small deconsecrated church now houses an **Ornithological Museum** (same ticket and admission times as the other museums, see p 408).

Palazzo del Popolo (1288–1323), also called Palazzo Nuovo del Podestà over-looking Piazza del Duomo, which still serves as the town hall, was restored after war damage. The splendid tower, known as the Torre Grossa (54m) was begun in 1300. Under the loggia is a fresco of the *Madonna and Saints* by a 14C master.

The Museo Civico

A passageway leads into a pretty courtyard with fresco fragments (two by Sodoma) and an outdoor staircase, leading to the Museo Civico (open daily in summer 09.30–19.30; in winter 10.00–17.30).

The **Sala del Consiglio**, where Dante is supposed to have delivered his appeal (see p 406), contains a large fresco of the *Maestà* by Lippo Memmi (signed and dated 1317). This superb work, showing the Madonna enthroned beneath a canopy surrounded by angels and saints, with the podestà Mino de' Tolomei kneeling in adoration, recalls the famous work by Simone Martini in the Palazzo Pubblico in Siena. The fresco was subsequently enlarged in the mid-1350s by Bartolo di Fredi who added two saints on each side and Benozzo Gozzoli is known to have repainted and restored parts of the fresco in 1466. The other walls are decorated with Sienese frescoes of hunting and tournament scenes (late 13C) and, on the end wall, the people of San Gimignano swearing allegiance to Charles of Anjou (ante 1292).

The small adjoining room contains a fine polychrome marble bust of *Santa Fina* (c 1498) and a terracotta bust of *St Gregory*, both by Pietro Torrigiani.

The **chapel** has a fresco of the *Holy Trinity* by Pier Franceso Fiorentino, a *Pietà* with symbols of the Passion by a follower of Neri di Bicci, and a *Madonna and Child with five Saints* by Leonardo Malatesta da Pistoia (early 16C).

Stairs lead up to the **pinacoteca**, with fine views over the town. In the **Camera del Podestà**, a small room off the stair landing (left), are charming frescoes of domestic scenes warning against the wiles of women, including *Aristotle ridden by Campaspe*, by Memmo di Filippuccio (early 14C). The fine reliquary bust of *St Ursula* in polychrome and gilded wood is by the Sienese sculptor Mariano d'Agnolo Romanelli (late 14C), and the painted terracotta bust of Beato Bartolo is attributed to Torrigiani.

The gallery (pinacoteca) contains an important collection of Sienese and Florentine painting from the 13C–15C. Among the earlier works: a *Crucifix with Passion scenes* by Coppo di Marcovaldo, one of the masterpieces of 13C painting in Tuscany; another *Crucifix* attributed to the Maestro delle Clarisse (c 1280–85); a *Madonna and Child enthroned* (c 1280; damaged) by Guido da Siena. The group of 15C works includes a *Madonna and Saints* by Sebastiano Mainardi, a *Madonna of Humility worshipped by two Saints* with a charming predella (1466) by Benozzo Gozzoli, two large circular panels representing the *Annunciation*, early works by Filippino Lippi of 1482, a *Madonna in glory with Saints Gregory and Benedict in a landscape* (1512) by Pinturicchio, one of the artist's last works, a *Madonna and Child with four Saints* by Domenico di Michelino, and a *Madonna and Child with four Saints*, signed and dated 1466, by Benozzo Gozzoli.

Leading off the main hall are two small rooms containing: a *Crucifix* of the Sienese school (c 1290), polyptych of the *Madonna and Child with eight Saints* (c 1310) by Memmo di Filippuccio and female heads by Bartolo di Fredi. The reliquary tabernacle of *Santa Fina* is a charming work painted in brilliant colours on both sides with stories of her life and miracles (c 1402) by Lorenzo di Niccolò. Other paintings include a tondo with the *Madonna and Child and two angels* by Sebastiano Mainardi, a polyptych by Taddeo di Bartolo (1394), a *Madonna and Child, Saints and angels* by Neri di Bicci, and *St Gimignano and stories from his life* (from the high altar of the Collegiata) by Taddeo di Bartolo.

There is also a polyptych with the *Assumption and Saints* (c 1345) by Niccolò di Ser Sozzo, a polyptych of *St Julian* by the Master of 1419, and a triptych of *St Bartholomew* by Lorenzo di Niccolò (1401).

In the passage are various sculptural fragments and reliefs. The **Torre Grossa** (Great Tower) may be climbed (combined ticket with the Museo Civico) for the splendid view.

Beyond the twin Salvucci Towers, the picturesque **Via San Matteo**, lined with medieval buildings, leads towards the 13C Porta San Matteo. It passes Palazzo della Cancelleria, the Romanesque façade of the church of San Bartolo and the 13C Pesciolini tower house, all grouped outside a double arch from an earlier circuit of walls, with Palazzo Tinacci just beyond.

Sant'Agostino

Inside Porta San Matteo, Via Cellolese leads to Sant'Agostino, a large Latin-cross church with three apsidal chapels, consecrated in 1298. The entrance is by a side door. To the right of the main door is the **Cappella di San Bartolo** with the splendid tomb of Blessed Bartolo (1228–1300), another patron of San Gimignano. This elaborate monument was made by Benedetto da Maiano in 1495. It is set in a niche with a marble curtain drawn back on either side. The shrine is composed of an urn with reliefs of two flying angels, above which are the three Theological Virtues seated in niches. At the base of the shrine are three predella scenes representing episodes from the saint's life. Crowning the shrine is a roundel with a beautiful relief of the *Madonna and Child*, surrounded by cherubs and adored by two angels. On the left wall of the chapel are frescoes of *Saints Gimignano, Lucy, and Nicholas of Bari* by Sebastiano Mainardi, who also painted the four doctors of the Church in the vault.

On the **south wall** of the nave are a *Madonna and Child with eight Saints*, predella scenes and saints on the pilasters by Pier Francesco Fiorentino (1494); and above, a fresco of the *Pietà* by Vincenzo Tamagni. Beyond the side entrance is a fresco of *Christ and symbols of the Passion* by Bartolo di Fredi. The same artist also painted the frescoes (c 1374) in the **south apse** of scenes from the *Life of the Virgin (Nativity, Presentation in the Temple, Marriage of the Virgin, and Dormition)*. Over the altar, is the *Nativity of the Virgin* with the donatrix and *St Anthony Abbot* on the right by Vincenzo Tamagni (1523).

The large altarpiece above the **high altar** depicting the *Coronation of the Virgin* worshipped by Saints Fina, Augustine, Bartolo, Gimignano, Jerome, and Nicholas of Tolentino is signed and dated 1483 by Piero del Pollaiolo.

The **choir** is entirely covered with **frescoes** by Benozzo Gozzoli and assistants (1464–65) illustrating the *Life of St Augustine* from his childhood to his death, in 17 scenes on three levels, full of charming details.

The sequence begins on the left from below. **First row**: 1. *Augustine is sent to school in his native town Thagaste*; 2. *at nineteen he goes to Carthage university*; 3. *St Monica prays for her son* (repainted in the 18C); 4. *Augustine sails to Italy*; 5. *his arrival in Italy*; 6. *he studies rhetoric and philosophy in Rome*; 7. *his departure for Milan* (inscribed and dated 1465 by Benozzo Gozzoli who included his self-portrait in this scene—last figure on the right). **Second row**: 8. *Augustine is received by St Ambrose and the Emperor Theodosius*; 9. (left) *he listens to St Ambrose preaching*, (centre) *Monica implores the conversion of her son*, (right) *Augustine discusses Manichaeism with St Ambrose*; 10. *Augustine reads the Epistles of St Paul*; 11. *he is baptised by St Ambrose*; 12. (left) *Augustine and the Infant Jesus on the seashore*, (right) *Augustine explains the rule to his monks*, (centre) *he visits the hermits at Montepisano*; 13. *death of his mother Monica*. **Third row**: 14. *Augustine, a consecrated bishop, blesses the people of Hippo*; 15. *he converts the heretic Fortunato*; 16. *Augustine in ecstasy is inspired by St Jerome*; 17. *Augustine's funeral. The vault and pilasters are decorated with evangelists and saints, by Gozzoli's workshop.*

On the **north wall** is a *Mystic marriage of St Catherine* by Giovanni Balducci, and a *Madonna and Child with Saints* by Fra Paolino of Pistoia (1530). Beyond a door which leads into the sacristy and a pretty Renaissance **cloister**, is Sebastiano Mainardi's, fresco of *St Gimignano blessing three dignitaries of the city* (1487), above an effigy of *Fra Domenico Strambi*, the patron who commissioned the paintings for the high altar and choir. The marble relief, with four half-length bishops in roundels, has recently been identified as part of the original shrine of San Bartolo and attributed to Tino da Camaino (c 1318). Beyond is a fragmentary fresco of the *Madonna delle Grazie* by Lippo Memmi, a marble pulpit of 1524, a large fresco of *St Sebastian interceding for the citizens of San Gimignano*, painted by Benozzo Gozzoli in 1464 after the plague of that year, and a *Deposition and Saints* by Vincenzo Tamagni.

In Piazza Sant'Agostino is the Romanesque church of **San Pietro** which contains frescoes by Memmo di Filippuccio.

Nearby in Via Folgore in the large ex convent of **Santa Chiara**, with a pretty garden, is the **Museo Archeologico and Spezieria di Santa Fina** (open mid June–mid-Nov 11.00–18.00), part of the civic museums. The archaeological collection, well displayed in six rooms has Etruscan, Roman and medieval finds from the city and district. Ceramic jars and glass from the pharmacy of Santa Fina (1507) are arranged in 19C showcases. Also here is a painted terracotta bust of Guido Marabottini dating from the late 15C. Exhibitions are also held in this fine building, and there is a collection of good paintings by Raffaelle De Grada (1885–1957) who lived and worked in San Gimignano after his marriage since his wife was born here.

From Piazza della Cisterna (see above) Via del Castello leads down to the church of **San Lorenzo**, which has a Romanesque façade in brick (1240). Inside are frescoes by Cenni di Francesco who also frescoed the contiguous oratory (1413). All the minor churches of San Gimignano are of interest for their architecture or paintings (or both), but nearly all of them are kept locked. Especially noteworthy are **San Girolamo**, in Via San Gimignano, which has an altarpiece by Vincenzo Tamagni (1522), and nearby **San Jacopo**, a charming little Pisan-Romanesque building, which has frescoes by Lippo Memmi and Memmo di Filippuccio and an altarpiece representing *St James* by Pier Francesco Fiorentino.

Outside Porta delle Fonte, just to the south, is an arcaded medieval public fountain, known as **Le Fonti**.

Environs of San Gimignano

The **Pieve di Cellole**, one of the finest Romanesque churches of the Val d'Elsa, is reached from Porta San Matteo along the Certaldo road (left; signposted for Gambassi) and then the second turning right. This charming church, which gave Puccini the setting for his *Suor Angelica*, is situated on a hill (395m) among cypress trees. It was completed in 1238 and the **façade** of beautifully cut travertine blocks has a simple doorway decorated with two stylised capitals of different shape. Above the lunette is an elegant two-light window.

Broad stone columns with stylised capitals support the arches separating the nave from the aisles. The apse is decorated with blind arches and a narrow window. The hexagonal baptismal font is carved out of a single block of travertine. In the sacristy are two altarpieces (c 1500) and an impressive life-size *Crucifix* of polychrome wood. An Etruscan necropolis has been excavated in the area.

Off the pretty road to Poggibonsi is the **Villa di Pietrafitta** reached by an unsurfaced road which winds steeply up along a cypress avenue. The villa, which once belonged to Cardinal Mazarin, has been extensively altered over the centuries. There is a small octagonal chapel next to the house dated 1584. The view extends over vineyards and olive groves to the surrounding hills.

Colle di Val d'Elsa and environs

Colle di Val d'Elsa is a small town built high up on a rocky spur and a lower town which extends along the river Elsa. Although less well known than many other small towns in Tuscany, it is a delightful place with many interesting art treasures. The medieval upper town is particularly well preserved and its position offers magnificent views on all sides. The environs of Colle are also well worth visiting: Badia a Coneo, Casole d'Elsa, Mensano, Radicondoli, Monteriggioni and Abbadia Isola.

Practical information

Getting there
By car

Colle can be reached by road direct from Florence by the *superstrada* to the exit Colle Val d'Elsa Nord which is 3km from the town centre. **Car park** beneath the walls with access by a flight of steps to the upper town.

By train

Train services to Poggibonsi (on the line from Empoli to Siena, with some through trains from Florence). Frequent bus services from Poggibonsi station to Colle Val d'Elsa.

By bus

From Florence via Poggibonsi in 1hr (run by *SITA*).

Information office
Via Campana 43 (☎ 0577 922 791, ▤ 0577 922 621) Apr–Oct 09.30–13.30, 15.30–19.00, Nov–Mar 10.00–13.00, 15.30–17.30 (closed Sun). *Pro-Loco*: Piazza Arnolfo 5 (☎ 0577 920 389).

Where to stay
Hotels

COLLE DI VAL D'ELSA ☆☆☆ *Villa Belvedere* (☎ 0577 920 966, ▤ 924 128), with restaurant. 2km outside the town at **località Belvedere**; *La Vecchia Cartiera*, Via Oberdan 5

(☎ 0577 921 207; ▤ 0577 923 688). CASOLE D'ELSA ☆☆☆☆ *Relais La Suvera*, at Pievescola (☎ 0577 960 300; ▤ 0577 960 220). MONTERIGGIONI (località Strove): ☆☆☆☆ *Residence San Luigi* (☎ 0577 301 055; ▤ 0577 301 167); ☆☆☆ *Casalta* (☎ 0577 301 002), both with restaurant.
Near POGGIBONSI ☆☆☆ *Hotel Europa* on the Via Senese at Calcinaia, 2km south (☎ 0577 933 402; ▤ 0577 936 069).

Eating out
Restaurants and cafés

COLLE DI VAL D'ELSA €€ *L'Antica Trattoria*, Piazza Arnolfo di Cambio 23 and *Arnolfo*, Piazza Santa Caterina 2. Café: *Lido*, Piazza Santa Caterina 4, for ice-creams. MONTERIGGIONI €€ *Il Pozzo*; restaurants in the hotel *San Luigi* and hotel *Casalta at Strove*; €€ *Il Piccolo Castello* at Castello di Monteriggioni. POGGIBONSI € *Italia*, Via Trento 34 and *La Galleria*, Galleria Cavalieri di Vittorio Veneto 20.

Festivals
Summer festival at Radicondoli, with concerts.

History

In the Middle Ages the exploitation of the river Elsa through a system of canals gave rise to flourishing wool and paper industries. In the 12C Colle was an independent commune. It was repeatedly disputed between Siena and Florence: at the **Battle of Colle**, which was fought on the plain below the town in 1269, the Florentines routed the Sienese, thereby avenging the terrible Battle of Montaperti of 1260. Provenzano Salvani, the valiant veteran of Montaperti, but hated nephew of Sapa (Dante, *Divina Commedia*, *Purgatorio*, xiii, 100–138), met his end here. The town eventually came under Florentine dominion in 1333. Colle received the title of city in 1592. It is also associated with the manufacture of glass which is still produced here, employing over 800 people. Arnolfo di Cambio (1232–1302), the famous sculptor and architect who built Palazzo Vecchio in Florence was born here.

The Volterra road passes beneath the walls beside a car park, from which a short flight of steps leads to the **upper town** (or *Colle alto*), divided into two districts: Borgo Santa Caterina to the west and the Castello, the oldest part, to the east. A street runs along a parapet at the back of the houses following the horse-shoe shape of the hill, with a fine view of the valley and countryside beyond.

San Francesco

To the right, across the slopes of the public gardens, is an old stone bridge with irregular arches which leads to the **monastery of San Francesco** from which there is a fine view of the upper town. The adjacent **church**, founded in 1229, is one of the earliest Franciscan churches in Tuscany. It has a Romanesque façade in sandstone with brick mouldings decorating the two-light window above the doorway.

To the left is the entrance to the **monastery** (now a seminary; ring the bell for admission), with a fine Renaissance **cloister**. It has some interesting frescoes: a charming *Madonna and Child* enthroned by Domenico Ghirlandaio's workshop and fresco fragments by an artist close to Duccio.

From the cloister you enter the church, which was rebuilt inside in the 17C–18C. The nave is decorated with elegant plasterwork and its large windows fill the church with light. Over the high altar is a polyptych, signed and dated 1479 by Sano di Pietro. It shows the *Madonna and Child enthroned with Saints Benedict, Cyrinus, Donatus, and Justina*; and the *Annunciation* above. Behind the altar is an early 16C Florentine *Crucifix*. The frame also includes saints on the pilasters and predella scenes. There are various fresco fragments which have emerged from under the 18C decoration, including a 14C *Madonna and Child with an apostle* (on the first altar to the right of the main entrance), attributed to Cennino Cennini. On the next altar is a copy of the altarpiece of *St Francis* in Santa Croce in Florence. The *Concert of Angels* is a fragment of a larger work by Astolfo Petrazzi. The Baroque tomb of the organist Antonio Giacobbi is dated 1740. The *Madonna and Child appearing to St Philip Neri* is by Simone Pignoni.

Borgo Santa Caterina

Via di San Francesco leads into Borgo Santa Caterina, the western district of the old town, past a squat, circular brick tower (once a fresh water cistern). To the right is the **Porta Nuova**, an impressive gateway attributed to Giuliano da Sangallo. It has two powerful round towers and battlements on the outside. From here the main street, **Via Gracco del Secco**, leads towards the upper town past numerous interesting medieval and Renaissance houses. Opposite the hospital of San Lorenzo is the 17C church of **San Pietro** which has an *Assumption* by Pier Dandini on the main altar. The conventual buildings are used for exhibitions. In a little piazza on the left is the church of **Santa Caterina** inside which is a fine stained glass window representing *St Catherine*, attributed to Sebastiano Mainardi. The adjacent oratory has an impressive group of lifesize figures in painted terracotta, representing the *Lamentation* by Zaccaria Zacchi (early 16C). Via Campana continues past (left) **Palazzo del Municipio** with the Medici arms, to a splendid **bridge** (originally a drawbridge), with a fine panorama on either side. The bridge links Borgo Santa Caterina to the Castello, the eastern (and oldest) district of the upper town, which has very beautiful paving (carefully restored a few years ago).

At the far end of the bridge the road passes beneath an archway incorporated in the fine **Palazzo Campana** (1539) by Giuliano di Baccio d'Agnolo, a stately building with handsome windows, and continues past several picturesque medieval houses.

The Castello

In the pretty **Piazza del Duomo** (which retains its herringbone brick paving) is **Palazzo Pretorio** (1335), decorated with coats of arms. It has recently been restored to house the **Museo Archeologico 'R.Bianchi Bandinelli'**.

Open April–Sept, Tues–Fri 10.00–12.00, 17.00–19.00; Sat & fest. 10.00–12.00, 16.30–19.30; closed Mon; Oct–March: Tues–Fri 15.30–17.30; Sat & fest. 10.00–12.00, 15.30–18.30; closed Mon.

Remains of 15C–16C frescoes discovered under whitewash inside include an *Annunciation* by Giovanni Maria Tolosani (1514) and coats of arms by Pier Francesco Fiorentino. The museum has a section of Etruscan pottery and bronze objects excavated in the Elsa valley, and other material dating from prehistoric to medieval times. Also exhibited here are a fine well-head with reliefs illustrating rural scenes, and capitals and others Romanesque fragments, and ceramics.

The **Terrosi Collection**, acquired in 1971 and arranged on the first floor, contains fine vases and other objects discovered in the Calisna Sepu tomb, one of the most important Etruscan necropoli of the Hellenistic period.

On the second floor is a section devoted to excavations in the area over the last few decades. The most important finds, dating from the archaic period, come from the Pierini tomb. There is a large quantity of material from the later Hellenistic period, including a collection of cinerary urns from the necropolis of Le Ville.

Duomo

The Duomo was originally Romanesque, as can be seen from the series of blind arcades along its north flank. It was rebuilt in 1603–19 and the façade was completed in 1815. The fine campanile (unfinished) dates from the early 17C.

The elegant and dignified interior has a Latin-cross plan. In the nave is a marble pulpit, resting on earlier capitals and supporting columns, decorated with bas-reliefs dated 1465 which are attributed to Giuliano da Maiano.

The nave altarpieces are interesting 17C works. **South side**, first chapel: *Miracle of the St Marziale* and side paintings by Giovanni Paolo Melchiorri (1694); second chapel: *Adoration of the Magi* by Vincenzo Dandini (1673), *Baptism of Christ* and *Marriage at Cana* by Deifebo Burbarini; fourth chapel:

Nativity (1635) by Rutilio Manetti, *Conversion of St Paul and Martyrdom of St Peter* by Astolfo Petrazzi. In the **south transept**, behind a wrought-iron railing, is the **Cappella del Santo Chiodo** (Holy Nail) which was built by Pius II for the relic of one of the nails supposed to have been used at the Crucifixion. The marble tabernacle is attributed to Mino da Fiesole and the bronze lectern with a palm branch and eagle is by Pietro Tacca. Hanging on the transept wall, to the left of the chapel, is a *Nativity* by Francesco Poppi (1567).

Over the **high altar** is a bronze *Crucifix*, which was presented to the cathedral by the Grand-duchess Maria Maddalena of Austria in 1629. It was designed by Giambologna and cast after his death by Pietro Tacca.

In the **north transept** is the **Chapel of the Holy Sacrament** which has a fine altarpiece of the *Last Supper* by Ottavio Vannini, signed and dated 1636. In the adjacent **baptistery** is an *Annunciation* by Cosimo Gamberucci (1618).

North side. Fourth chapel, *Resurrection*, the *Immaculate Conception*, and *Madonna and Child with Saints* by Filippo Tarchiani (1635–42); third chapel, *St Gregory interceding for the plague-stricken in Rome* (1643) by Niccolò Tornioli and side paintings of saints by Giovanni Rosi; second chapel, *Ascension, Noli me tangere*, and *Doubting Thomas* by Giuseppe Chiari; first chapel, *Marriage of the Virgin* by Giovanni Odazzi and *Dream of St Joseph* and *Flight into Egypt* by Paolo de' Matteis.

Also in Piazza del Duomo is **Palazzo Vescovile**, which has a room decorated with frescoes by Bartolo di Fredi. Via di Castello continues alongside the palace, past a large tabernacle on the corner.

Museo Civico d'Arte Sacra

This is next to the former **Palazzo dei Priori**, the façade of which is decorated with graffiti. An outside stairway here leads up to the interesting little **Museo Civico e d'Arte Sacra** (open Apr–Oct 10.00–12.00, 16.00–19.00 except Mon; in winter only on weekends).

Room 1. *Madonna and Child* by Girolamo Genga; 16C–17C paintings by Bachiacca, Giovanni Battista Naldini, Francesco Rosselli, and Francesco and Giovanni Brini. The *Pietà* by Cigoli is a particularly good example of the artist's work. The Medici coat of arms was painted by Poppi. The marble bust of Lorenzo Usimbardi is attributed to Felice Palma or Ferdinando Tacca. Also here, *St Sylvester baptising the Emperor Constantine* by Giovanni Antonio Galli, and *St Cecilia* by Mario Balassi. In the centre of the room are displayed local 19C paintings by Niccolò Cannicci, Antonio Salvetti, Vittorio Meoni and Ferruccio Manganelli.

Room 2 contains earlier paintings. 15C–16C works by Ventura di Moro, Giovan Maria Tolosani (a follower of Ghirlandaio), and Pier Francesco Fiorentino. The beautiful **Maestà* is attributed to the so-called Master of Badia a Isola, a late 13C or early 14C painter very close to Duccio. It comes from the Abbadia Isola (see p 421). The *Madonna and Child* by Segna di Bonaventura is another precious early work of the same period. The *Birth of the Virgin* is by the local 15C painter Cennino Cennini, and the remarkable polychrome wood *Crucifix* (the arms are missing) is by Marco Romano (late 13C or early 14C). The early 16C fresco of the *Adoration of the Magi* from a tabernacle in Colle is by Giovan Maria Tolosani. Also displayed here are illuminated choirbooks once used in the cathedral.

Room 3. The *treasury of Galognano* is composed of four rare silver chalices in four different sizes and a patten, thought to date from the late 6C AD, found in a field near Colle in 1963. The two cases of 14C–19C liturgical objects include a 15C chalice and patten decorated with enamels from Colle cathedral. The 17C works include paintings by Pier Dandini, and a wooden horse's head. At the end of the room is an altarpiece of the *Madonna and Saints* by Simone Ferri (1581) and frescoes by Francesco Rosselli. Also displayed here are a 15C Sienese reliquary of the arm of St Philip Apostle, a carved wooden head of *St John the Baptist*, attributed to the circle of Giambologna, and an *Ecce Homo* by the della Robbia workshop. The large 19C paintings are by Antonio Salvetti, Antonio Puccinelli, and Gennaro Landi.

Opposite the museum is the **Teatro dei Varii**, in a 14C building, formerly the seat of the *Accademia dei Varii*, a literary and theatrical society. The theatre was built to a design by Antonio Galli Bibiena (1760) and reconstructed in 1826. In 1926 Antonio Salvetti restored the façade which has a loggia. The little theatre, which seats just over 200 people, was restored and reopened in 1991.

The street broadens into a charming small square. On the right is the Romanesque church of **Santa Maria in Canonica** with a simple bell-tower. The stone façade has a rose-window and decoration in brick, with small blind arches under the roof. The interior, altered in the 17C, has a large tabernacle of the *Madonna and Child with Saints* by Pier Francesco Fiorentino.

At the end of the street are more interesting medieval houses and the **Tower-house of Arnolfo** dating from the early 13C. A long vaulted alley (**Via delle Volte**) returns from here towards Palazzo Campana and the former drawbridge through the oldest part of the town.

The lower town

A steep footpath (La Costa) paved with bricks descends to the lower town. It meets Via Garibaldi at the Quattro Cantoni with fine palaces of the Beltramini, Palazzuoli, Tommasi, and Sabolini families. In a niche on Palazzo Beltramini is a marble relief of the *Madonna and Child* attributed to Tommaso Fiamberti.

Sant'Agostino

Lower downhill beyond an archway is the church of Sant'Agostino. The façade (unfinished) dates from the 13C but the bell-tower is modern. The interior has beautiful proportions, with columns separating the nave from the aisles. It was rebuilt by Antonio da Sangallo il Vecchio (1521). South aisle: *Immaculate Conception* by Francesco Curradi, *Madonna and Child* by Taddeo di Bartolo, *Deposition with Saints* by Ridolfo del Ghirlandaio (1518), and *Martyrdom of St Catherine* by Giovanni Battista Pozzo(1589).

In the **Cappella Bertini** (1598), to the right of the choir, is a very fine *Pietà with Saints* by Cigoli, a *Nativity* by Giuliano Biagi (1591), and two marble busts, one of *Cosimo I* by Francesco Bordoni, and the other of *Francesco Bertini* by Giovan Battista Caccini. In the north aisle, *St Andrew and other Saints worshipped by the donor Andrea Albertani* by Giovan Battista Paggi (1586), and a fresco of the *Pietà with Saints Anthony and Francis*, known as the '*Madonna di Piano*', surrounded by a marble tabernacle attributed to Baccio da Montelupo.

Beyond the church is the chimney of a former glass factory and a 15C paper factory (now a hotel). The attractive main square, **Piazza Arnolfo**, has an obelisk-like war memorial at the centre, porticoes on two sides and the obsolete railway station at one end. To the northeast is the Banca del Lavoro, a 20C building in orange-painted steel and glass by Giovanni Michelucci. Beyond the former railway station, in Via di Spugna, is the **Cappella del Renaio**, with a Giottesque fresco of the *Pietà* over the altar, and, opposite, the 10C church of **Santa Maria a Spugna**, which has a Romanesque façade. Behind the church is the river Elsa, with remains of the Ponte di Arnolfo and a view towards the former abbey of San Salvatore, now transformed into a farmhouse.

Environs of Colle di Val d'Elsa

On the Volterra road (which passes the impressive Porta Nuova, described above) is the pretty little Renaissance church of **Le Grazie**. The round window on the façade is surrounded by a glazed terracotta garland. The interior has frescoes by Giovanni Maria Tolosani. To the right of the church is a small cloister built of brick.

At a short distance further on to the left is a turning for Casole d'Elsa. A by road leads off to **Badia a Conéo** (open for Mass on Sun at 09.15, or on request), in a beautiful position with panoramic views. This superb 12C Romanesque **church**, once part of a Vallombrosan abbey suppressed in the 16C, combines grandeur and simplicity. Entirely built in light grey stone, it has a plain **façade** with four blind arches and half-columns and two capitals decorated with foliate and animal motifs. The exterior of the apse has blind arcading with small stylised human heads. A wide arch to the right opens on to a courtyard with picturesque farm buildings on the site of the former cloister.

The beautiful interior, entirely faced with stone, has a Latin-cross plan with a single nave and three apses, of which only the central apse is visible from the outside. Over the crossing is a dome. The transept and apse are vaulted, while the nave has a timber roof. A transversal arch divides the nave from the transept; another arch has carved capitals. The apse is decorated with small blind arches and carved capitals.

Casole d'Elsa

In pretty countryside further south is the old hill town of Casole d'Elsa (417m) still partially enclosed by its medieval walls. The fortifications were reinforced by the Sienese in the 15C, allegedly by Francesco di Giorgio, who is also believed to have remodelled the Palazzo Pretorio and the Rocca. The town suffered considerably from bombing in the Second World War.

The Romanesque **collegiata**, which was rebuilt in the later 15C and again in the last century, has been painstakingly restored after war damage. On the arch over the choir, which is divided into five chapels framed by Gothic arches, are remains of 14C frescoes of the *Last Judgement* attributed to Giacomo di Mino del Pelicciaio. To the left of the side entrance is the baptismal font over which is a small statue of the *Baptist* (1485). Along the right wall of the nave are a terracotta relief of the *Nativity* by Benedetto and Santi Buglioni, the tomb of Bishop Tommaso Andrei (d. 1303) by Gano da Siena, and several altarpieces (well labelled). In the south transept is a *Madonna and Child with four standing Saints* by Girolamo del Pacchia. The last chapel to the left of the choir has 15C Florentine frescoes on the vault. In the north transept is a large detached fresco lunette of the *Madonna and Child enthroned with angels* by a close follower of Duccio.

A door leads to a large chapel known as the **Chiesa di Santa Croce**, which has a number of paintings including (flanking the altar) the *Virgin annunciate and angel Gabriel* by Rutilio Manetti. In the nave, against the north wall is the fine cenotaph of Ranieri del Porrina (d. 1315), by Marco Romano, with a full length effigy in a marble niche and two beautiful figures of *Virtues*. Steps lead down to the crypt with remains of the earlier church. The other altarpieces in the nave include the *Immaculate Conception and two Saints* by Amos Cassioli, and *St Augustine washing Christ's feet* by Rutilio Manetti.

To the right of the church is the **canonica**, an interesting structure in stone and brick, with remains of a cloister, dating from c1500. It is now the **Museo Archeologico e della Collegiata** (open daily except Mon 10.00–12.00, 16.00–18.00). The collection includes: a *Maestà with Bishop Ranieri of Cremona and his brother Messer Porrina Aringhieri, Lord of Casole*, a detached fresco of the early 14C by a close follower of Duccio; *Madonna and Child* attributed to Segna di Bonaventura; a triptych by the Master of Sant'Ansano; *Madonna and Child enthroned and Saints and angels* by Andrea di Niccolò (1498), *Visitation* by Girolamo del Pacchia, *Madonna and Child and Saints* (detached fresco) by Giacomo Pacchiarotti (1520); a ciborium by Alessandro Casolani; and illuminated manuscripts and liturgical objects. In 2001 an additional section of 15C–17C paintings was opened on deposit from the Pinacoteca in Siena. An archaeological section comprises finds from excavations of necropoli in the neighbourhood dating from the 4C BC and later.

Via Casolani passes the 14C **Palazzo Pretorio** (right), alleged to have been redesigned by Francesco di Giorgio Martini in 1487. The 14C **Rocca** dominates the far end of the little town, overlooking an extensive landscape, with hills in the distance. On the outskirts of Casole, on a hillock, is the little Romanesque church of **San Niccolò** next to the cemetery. The frescoes inside are by Alessandro Casolani and Francesco Rustici.

Farther south is the little village of **Mensano** (499m) with its walls and castle still in part extant. The 12C Romanesque church of **San Giovanni Battista** has a simple oblique façade with an oculus and a fine portal. The noble interior (restored in the 1950s) has a basilican plan with impressive monolithic stone columns dividing the nave from the aisles, and three apses. The lovely capitals, unusually large in size, and carved with an intricate assemblage of acanthus and other leaves, heads and fantastic animals, are by Bonamico, whose name is carved on a marble slab on the left side of the altar.

Still farther south, beyond Casone, in a beautiful position (509m), is **Radicondoli**. This little town preserves parts of its medieval fortifications, as well as picturesque streets and a few Renaissance palaces. The 16C **Collegiata** has a very fine altarpiece of the *Assumption and Nativity* by Pietro di Domenico and a *Madonna* attributed to Niccolò di Ser Sozzo in a side chapel. The cemetery has a late 12C funerary chapel (the **Pieve Vecchia**) dedicated to San Simone. It has a Latin-cross plan with a single apse and a projecting transept. In the interior brick and stone are used to obtain a decorative effect. It contains some interesting pre-Romanesque carving.

There is an annual summer festival at Radicondoli, during which concerts and theatre performances are held in the cloister of the Convento dell' Osservanza.

Poggibonsi

North of Colle di Val d'Elsa is Poggibonsi, an unattractive commercial town of 25,000 inhabitants which has developed considerably since the last war (with furniture manufactories). Excavations have ascertained the existence of a village on this site from the 6C until the early 10C. Fortifications were built in the 12C by the Conti Guidi, thus creating the foundations of *Podium Bonizi*, which developed into a small town in the early 13C, soon to be destroyed by the Florentines. By the 13C the town was no longer governed by a feudal system but a free Commune and grew rapidly thanks also to its position on the Via Francigena. In 1220 it was granted the title of Imperial city by Frederick II.

Little remains of the old town except for the restored church of **San Lorenzo** in Piazza Savonarola which has a 14C *Crucifix* attributed to Giovanni di Agostino. The Gothic **Palazzo Pretorio**, on the corner of Via Repubblica beside a crenellated medieval tower, has coats of arms on the façade. The **collegiata**, opposite, rebuilt in 1860, has a marble baptismal font of 1341 and, in the apse, a painting of the *Resurrection*, attributed to Vincenzo Tamagni. Dominating the town on a hill is the castle of **Poggio Imperiale** begun in 1488 for Lorenzo il Magnifico by Giuliano da Sangallo and continued by Antonio da Sangallo il Vecchio in the first half of the 16C. From the Colle Val d'Elsa road it is possible to get a good view of the fortifications and of parts of the medieval walls. At the foot of the steep hill is a fountain known as the **Fonte delle Fate**, beneath an arched portico dating from the 13C.

South of Poggibonsi a by-road leads uphill to the monastery of **San Lucchese**, rebuilt and enlarged in the 14C (and damaged in the last war). Parts of the original Romanesque church are visible in the façade and along the left side. The plan follows the style of early Franciscan churches with a nave and three apsidal chapels. On the right wall is a copy of a *Noli me Tangere* by Raffaellino del Garbo (destroyed in the Second World War), a fresco of the *Madonna and Child with Saints* of the Sienese school and another fresco by Bartolo di Fredi of the *Martyrdom of St Andrew*. A door opens onto the cloister with 16C frescoes depicting the story of *St Lucchese*, a holy layman (d. 1260) who spent his life helping the poor. In the sacristy is a 14C cupboard decorated with painted figures of apostles and saints by Memmo di Filippuccio. The apse window is by Rodolfo Margheri (1945). To the left of the transept above the arch of the Chapel of San Lucchese are frescoes (1388) illustrating the *Life of St Stephen* by the Master of San Lucchese who has recently been identified with Cennino Cennini. On the left wall of the transept, *Miracle of St Lucchese* by an anonymous 14C painter. The vault and walls of the chapel were frescoed in the 19C. To the left of the nave is another frescoed lunette with *St Nicholas of Bari* by Bartolo di Fredi and a large della Robbia polyptych dated 1514. From outside the church is a fine view of the surrounding countryside.

To the east of Poggibonsi is **Luco** a picturesque little village and the nearby 14C castle of **Strozzavolpe** (open on the third Sunday in October for the festival of San Luco). Situated in a romantic position above a deep gorge, it is enclosed by high defence walls with a drawbridge beneath a tall square tower. The view embraces Siena, San Gimignano, and Castellina in Chianti. Nearby, on higher ground, is **Talciona** and the little Romanesque church of Santa Maria. It has an interesting carved relief of the *Magi* over the doorway, dated 1234.

On the Cassia road south of Poggibonsi, near Staggia, is a turning (left) for **La Magione**, a medieval hospice consisting of a charming group of buildings beside the small church of San Giovanni al Ponte (11C–12C). This is one of the best preserved of the many hospices for pilgrims which existed along the Via Francigena (see p 442).

The little fortified town of **Staggia** still has several of its defence towers and ruined castle. Beside the Romanesque church of Santa Maria Assunta (restored) is a small **museum** (☎ 0577 930 901 or ring at the priest's house for the key). It houses an important altarpiece by Antonio del Pollaiolo representing the *Communion of St Mary Magdalen*; a 14C Sienese *Madonna and Child*; and other paintings by Arcangelo Salimbeni and Giovanni Maria Butteri. There are some fresco fragments and liturgical objects.

Monteriggioni is a beautifully preserved medieval fortified village, built on a hillock. The circle of walls, dating from the 13C and the largest of its kind in Tuscany to have survived practically intact, has fourteen towers. Monteriggioni is mentioned by Dante: *Divina Commedia, Inferno*, xxxi, 41–44 '...*come in su la cerchia tonda Monteriggion di torri si corona*' ('like Monteriggioni, whose round circle of walls are crowned with towers'). A main street crosses the village, joining the two gates. A few houses and a pretty Romanesque church face onto the piazza, and other houses surround a small public garden. Inside the walls are other private gardens.

A short distance west is the Cistercian abbey of San Salvatore founded in 1001, traditionally known as **Abbadia Isola** on account of its position in the middle of marshland. In the 14C it was fortified by the Sienese. A small village surrounds the abbey church. The church was largely rebuilt after the octagonal cupola collapsed in the 18C. The basilican interior, beautifully proportioned, has alternating piers and columns and three apses, with a simple crypt beneath the raised choir. Two detached fresco lunettes on the right of the nave are by Taddeo di Bartolo and Vincenzo Tamagni. On the left wall is a large fresco of the *Assumption* by Tamagni and a baptismal font with a carved relief representing the *Baptism of Christ* (1419). The beautiful *Maestà* by the so-called Master of Badia a Isola has been removed to the museum of Colle Val d'Elsa. The abbey is recorded in Bishop Sigeric's journey on the Via Francigena (see p 442).

San Galgano and environs

This wild, unspoilt area southwest of Siena has beautiful woods and river valleys. The ruined abbey of San Galgano, in the open countryside a few kilometres northwest of Monticiano, with its grassy nave open to the sky is one of the most remarkable sites in Tuscany, and the chapel of San Galgano on the hill nearby is exceptionally interesting for its architecture. The little neighbouring villages of Monticiano, San Lorenzo a Merse, Frosini, and Chiusdino, although rarely visited, are particularly delightful.

Practical information

 Getting there
By car

N73 leads south of Siena for 30km, and then N441 diverges right for San Galgano.

By bus

Buses (several times a day) run by *TRA-IN* from Siena (Piazza San Domenico) to Massa Marittima via Palazzetto stop at San Galgano.

 Information office
APT Siena (☎ 0577 280 551). Information office at the Comune of Chiusdino (☎ 0577 751 055).

 Where to stay
Hotels

MONTICIANO ☆☆ *Da Vestro*, Via Senese 4 (☎ 0577 756 618; ▤ 0577 756 466).
Near SAN LORENZO A MERSE ☆☆☆☆ *Locanda del Ponte*, at Ponte a Macereto (☎ 0577 757 108; ▤ 0577 757 110).

 Eating out
Restaurants

SCALVAIA € *Osteria-pizzeria La Capanna*, at the entrance to the village (☎ 0577 759 059). There is also a restaurant (€€) at **Frosini**.

San Galgano

The ruined **Abbey of San Galgano** (open daily 08.00–12.00, 14.00–sunset) is situated between Chiusdino and Monticiano, in beautiful farming country southwest of Siena.

History

The abbey was built by the Cistercians of Casamari between c 1224–88, in honour of St Galgano who was canonised in 1185. Galgano Guidotti (1148–81), born in Chiusdino of a noble family, decided to abandon a life of pleasure and become a Cistercian monk. He spent his last years living as a hermit on the hill of Monte Siepi where he built a little chapel.

The monastery became extremely powerful and the monks often ruled over disputes between cities such as Siena and Volterra; they also supervised the building of Siena cathedral. Subsequently there was a period of decline and corrupt administration. In the 16C the abbot sold the leading off the church roof which later collapsed. The buildings were subsequently abandoned and the church deconsecrated.

The **church** is a remarkable building modelled on the French Cistercian mother-house of Cîteaux. The façade, which remained unfinished, has three arched doorways separated by columns. The entrance to the church is on the right, past the chapter house and remains of the cloister. The roofless building, with a grass-grown nave, and a magnificent east end, is one of the most romantic sites in Tuscany. The majestic proportions of the structure and the effect of the windows framing the sky are particularly striking. There are remains of tracery in the smaller rose windows of the transept and in a few of the windows of the nave. The nave is divided by pillars with Gothic arches resting on finely carved capitals. The transept, forming a Latin-cross, is also divided by columns. The exterior of the apse and north flank of the church are built of beautifully cut regular stones, and one of the large gothic windows still preserves its carved mouldings. The little rectangular detached **cemetery chapel** also dates from the 13C.

The spacious **chapter house** is divided into two parts by low columns and has a fine vaulted ceiling and windows. On the upper floor are sixteen cells along the corridor and the monks' chapel.

On Monte Siepi (338m), the little adjacent hill, is the circular **Chapel of San Galgano** (open, as above). It was built in 1182 over the tomb of St Galgano and is unique of its kind. The exterior is built in stone to a height of 4m and then in alternate bands of stone and brick. The interior, one of the few centrally planned churches in Tuscany, has a conical-shaped cupola, built of concentric rings of red brick and white travertine. The sword in the stone at the centre commemorates St Galgano's renunciation of knightly pursuits in favour of a life of prayer before the Cross.

A doorway leads into another chapel, added in the 14C, which has frescoes and *sinopie* by Ambrogio Lorenzetti and his workshop (c 1344). In the central lunette is the *Virgin in Majesty adored by Saints and angels* holding baskets of flowers, with the figure of Eve reclining in the foreground. Below, divided by the window, are the *Virgin* and angel *Gabriel*; it is interesting to note the differences in composition between the frescoes and *sinopie*, which have been detached and hung on the adjacent wall. On the left wall are scenes from the *Life of St Galgano*: the saint conducted to Heaven and his vision of St Michael in Rome. In the vault are medallions with figures of prophets. There is a splendid view of the abbey from the hill.

Monticiano

To the southeast is the village of Monticiano, which came under Sienese dominion in the 13C. Although damaged in the Second World War, medieval houses survive above the former walls (there is a good view of them from the road leading south). In the piazza, above a flight of steps, is the Romanesque church of **Sant'Agostino**, with a travertine façade and a fine doorway and oculus. Here is preserved the funerary urn of Blessed Antonio Patrizi (d. c 1311), an important figure in the Augustinian monastic movement in medieval Tuscany. The single-naved interior, re-decorated in the Baroque period, has a 14C frescoed polyptych of the *Madonna and Child with Saints*, and a damaged *Crucifixion*. On the left side of the nave is a painting of the *Death of the Blessed Antonio Patrizi* by Rutilio Manetti (c 1629).

Off the cloister is the **chapter house** which houses a small **museum**. The collection includes an arched stained-glass window with *Christ on the cross between the Virgin and St John*, church silver, bells, vestments, reliquaries, illuminated choir-books and a few paintings. On the walls are interesting 15C frescoes by anonymous artists, including monochrome *Passion Scenes* silhouetted against a red ground, and a *Last Supper*. The *Madonna and Child enthroned between St Augustine and the Blessed Antonio Patrizi*, surmounted by the *Annunciation*, is attributed to a follower of Taddeo di Bartolo.

Farther uphill, in the older district, is the Romanesque church of **Santi Giusti e Clemente** dating from the 12C. The doorway is decorated with a motif of palmettes. Inside is a 14C Sienese *Crucifix*.

The Roccastrada road continues south past by-roads for **Luriano**, a group of farmhouses and villa, near which is a medieval mill, the **Molino della Pile**, and the village of **Scalvaia**. The area further south, in the province of Grosseto, is described on p 320.

A pretty road winds east from Monticiano to join the superstrada between Siena and Grosseto passing **San Lorenzo a Merse**, a small village above the river Merse (rice is cultivated in the valley). The main street leads up to the Romanesque church which has a stone façade decorated with green marble, in the Sienese style. It has a timber roof and an apse pierced by a single lancet window. To the left of the church is a chapel, and beyond is the old castle in a panoramic position.

North of San Galgano is **Frosini**, a medieval castle now a villa at the centre of a tiny village with a pretty Romanesque church. From the public garden situated on a slope facing south there is a fine view of the surrounding countryside.

Chiusdino

West of San Galgano, in beautiful countryside with interesting old farmhouses, is Chiusdino, St Galgano's birthplace. It is a typical hilltop village (564m), with a cluster of grey stone houses on narrow steep and winding streets, often with steps and archways. The simple Romanesque parish church has been extensively modernised. Nearby, in a picturesque little piazza, is the **Chapel of the Compagnia**, with a relief of *St Galgano* over the door by Urbano da Cortona dated 1466. Nearby is **St Galgano's house**, with horizontal bands of brick decorating the façade, and the copy of another relief showing the saint in a wood by Giovanni di Agostino. The original relief and a *Madonna and Child* by Niccolò di Segna of 1336, together with 12C–13C liturgical objects are kept in the nearby **Casa Parocchiale**. At 2 Via Mascagni is a small **museum** dedicated to the Cetine mines, with photographs, implements and objects relating to the mining industry in the metalliferous hills (☎ 0577 756 738; and see p 292).

Montalcino and Sant'Antimo

Montalcino (567m) is a charming little walled town, in a beautiful position above vines and olive groves, dominating the surrounding countryside. It is famed for its red wine; the remarkable *Brunello*, which keeps well and can be matured for many years, is one of the choicest Tuscan wines, and considered by some experts to be among Italy's finest. The abbey church of Sant'Antimo is one of the most beautiful churches in Tuscany in superb countryside.

Practical information

Getting there
By car

A by-road (14km) leads to Montalcino from Buonconvento 45km south of Siena on the Via Cassia, Sant'Antimo is on a lovely by-road, 10km further south. Car parks outside the fortress or outside the walls.

By bus

Buses (*TRA-IN*) from Siena (Piazza San Domenico) via Buonconvento for Montalcino and Sant'Antimo.

Information offices
Ufficio Turistico Comunale, Costa del Municipio 8 (☎/🖨 0577 849 331). *Pro-loco*, same address (☎ 0577 848 242).

Where to stay
Hotel

☆☆☆ *Il Giglio*, Via Soccorso Saloni 5, Montalcino (☎ 0577 848 167).

Eating out
Restaurants in Montalcino

€€ *Il Moro*, Via Mazzini.
€ *Trattoria Sciame*, Via Ricasoli and € *Osteria Porta al Cassero*, Via della Libertà 9.

Restaurants in the environs

€€ *La Taverna dei Barbi*, località I Barbi.
POGGIO ANTICO €€ *Poggio Antico*.
SANT'ANGELO IN COLLE € *Trattoria Il Pozzo*.

Festivals
A theatre festival is held in Montalcino in July. The *Sagra del Tordo*, on the last Sunday in October, features a bow and arrow competition, dancing and gastronomic regional specialities.

Montalcino

History

This area was already inhabited in the Palaeolithic era and later there were Etruscan and Roman settlements. In the Middle Ages, Montalcino became a flourishing and independent town, but was repeatedly attacked by Siena and defended by Florence, finally succumbing to Sienese rule after the Battle of Montaperti in 1260. There followed a period of peace and prosperity and in 1462 Montalcino received the title of city from Pius II. After successfully resisting two sieges in 1526 and 1553, the town was forced to capitulate to Florence, despite a heroic defence lasting four years. In 1559 it became part of the Grand Duchy of Tuscany.

Although particularly famous for its *Brunello*, other excellent wines produced locally include the *Rosso di Montalcino*, and *Moscadello*, a sweet fizzy wine. It is also known for its traditional white-and-turquoise coloured pottery, and for its honey.

Just outside Montalcino, on the approach from Buonconvento (see p 435), above a hill on the right, is the church of the **Osservanza**, founded in the 15C. The interior, which was rebuilt in the 18C, has an early 14C *Crucifix* and a *St Bernardine* by Sano di Pietro. The road climbs steeply, passing under the impressive ramparts dominated by the Medici arms.

The town has numerous medieval houses with gardens and orchards, and steep streets offering picturesque views. The 14C Sienese **fortress** (open daily, except Mon 09.00–13.00, 14.00–20.00; in winter 14.00–18.00) was provided with its notable ramparts by Cosimo I Medici in 1571. Inside the courtyard is the nave of a former church and, through an arch, a small garden with ilex trees. On the ground floor of the castle is an Enoteca, where it is possible to taste and buy the local wines. There are fine rooms on the upper floors and steps lead up to the towers and ramparts with a walkway from which there are magnificent views in all directions across the Orcia, Ombrone, and Asso valleys.

Via Ricasoli descends from the castle passing (left; no. 44) **Palazzo Pieri Nerli** which has a courtyard with a portico and wall. On the right is the monastery of **Sant'Agostino**. The 14C church has a fine marble doorway and rose-window. The interior preserves many of its original 14C frescoes (very worn); those in the choir of the *Life of St Augustine* are by Bartolo di Fredi. The stained-glass windows are modern.

The Museo Civico e Diocesano d'Arte Sacra

To the right, in the cloister, is the Museo Civico e Diocesano d'Arte Sacra which has been beautifully rearranged and all the works restored (open daily except Mon, Jan–Mar 10.00–13.00, 14.00–16.00; Apr–Dec 10.00–l8.00). It comprises a small archaeological section from local excavations, an important collection of 13C–16C Sienese painting and sculpture, and a unique group of polychrome, wooden life-size figures.

The first room has many important works, mostly from the town hall or churches in the town. A magnificent polyptych, signed and dated 1388, by Bartolo di Fredi has been restored and reassembled; the central panel of the *Coronation of the Virgin surrounded by angels* is considered to be the artist's masterpiece. There are several almost life-size figures in polychrome wood including the *Virgin and Angel Gabriel* (1370) by Maestro Angelo and two *Crucifixes* by Angelo di Nalduccio. Another important sculptor, Francesco di Valdambrino is represented by a seated figure of *St Peter* and a *Crucifix*. There is also an *Annunciation* group by Domenico di Niccolò dei Cori.

The collection of gold ground paintings includes a triptych by a close follower of Duccio, a charming *Madonna and Child* by Luca di Tommè, other works by Bartolo di Fredi, a *Madonna and Child* by a master close to Ambrogio Lorenzetti, a *Madonna* by the Maestro di Panzano and a *Madonna and Child* seated in a rose garden by Sano di Pietro.

Another section displays works from churches in the neighbourhood. These include two panels of *St Peter* and *St Paul* by Ambrogio Lorenzetti from Sant' Angelo in Colle, an extremely refined *Madonna and Child with two angels* by Giovanni di Paolo from Rocca d'Orcia, a *Madonna and Child crowned by angels* by Vecchietta from Castiglione d'Orcia, a *Madonna and Child* by Guidoccio Cozzarelli from San Giovanni d'Asso and another *Madonna* by Marco Pino from Argiano.

Two of the earliest works in the museum come from the Abbey of Sant'Antimo (see below): a late 12C *Crucifix*, painted in tempera on wood, showing Christ with open eyes, and two volumes of an illustrated Bible with exquisite miniatures, dating from the second half of the 12C.

The section of 15C–16C paintings includes works by Benvenuto di Giovanni, Girolamo di Benvenuto, Riccio, and Vincenzo Tamagni.

There is also a statue of *St Sebastian* by Andrea della Robbia and a group of della Robbian reliefs, other sculptures, miniatures, liturgical objects and vestments, and a rare collection of local pottery, mostly jugs, dating from the 13C.

A steep street leads down from Sant'Agostino to the triangular Piazza del Popolo above which looms the tall narrow tower of **Palazzo dei Priori** (1292). Numerous coats of arms decorate the front and side of the palace and beneath is a portico with a statue of *Cosimo I* by Giovanni Berti (1564). Inside the palace, which preserves some frescoed and sculpted coats of arms, is an office which provides information about the local wines (open daily except Mon 10.00–13.00, 15.30–18.30). Also facing the piazza is a grandiose **loggia**; the two first bays in stone date from the 14C, the four larger brick arches were built in the 15C. Opposite the loggia is an attractive, old-fashioned café.

To the right of Palazzo dei Priori, Via del Municipio leads into Piazza Garibaldi at the end of which is the church of **Sant'Egidio**. It contains a frescoed triptych by an artist close to Luca di Tommè, a *Madonna and Saints* by Francesco Cozza, and a painted *Crucifix* by Francesco di Valdambrino (c 1420).

Via Spagni leads uphill to the cathedral of **San Salvatore**, situated at the highest point of the town. It was built in 1818–32 by Agostino Fantastici to replace the Romanesque church. It has a grandiose brick portico and a spacious neo-Classical interior with Ionic columns. The two altarpieces of the *Immaculate Conception* and *St John the Baptist* in the nave are by Francesco Vanni (1588). In the baptistery chapel are interesting reliefs from the Romanesque church representing *Christ and the symbols of the Evangelists*. In front of the church is a small piazza with a view over the town. Via Spagni continues downhill to the **Madonna del Soccorso**, a sanctuary built in the 17C on the site of an ancient chapel. The elegant travertine façade is by Francesco Paccagnini (1829). The Baroque high altar encloses a venerated image of the *Madonna*, possibly 14C. To the right is an *Assumption of the Virgin* by Vincenzo Tamagni. From the terrace next to the sanctuary there is a splendid view towards Siena.

Viale Roma descends along the outside of the walls to Piazza Cavour where there is a little public garden. Here the former hospital of **Santa Maria della Croce** founded in the 13C (now the *Comune*) still preserves parts of its original structure. The old pharmacy, inside the main entrance, has frescoes of the *Madonna enthroned, Saints Jerome and Augustine*, figures in niches, and trompe-l'oeil cupboards by Vincenzo Tamagni (1510), visible through a window.

Downhill from Piazza Cavour are pretty streets leading to an old mill and public fountain and wash-house. Uphill again is the church of **San Francesco**, in front of which is a terrace with fine views of the town.

The church retains its 14C façade and tall square tower. It has been deconsecrated and is now incorporated into the local hospital, together with the 16C cloister and the remaining monastic buildings. There are two small chapels frescoed with scenes from the *Life of the Virgin* by Tamagni (key from the porter).

From Piazza Cavour the Corso leads back to Piazza del Popolo.

East of Montalcino, on the Cassia, is **Torrenieri**, a small industrial town important in the past for the production of bricks. The castle, remains of which still survive, was a stopping-point on the Via Francigena (see p 442) mentioned by Bishop Sigeric. The parish church has a small *Madonna and Child* by Domenico di Niccolò and a *Madonna and Child with Saints* by Francesco Bartalini.

Sant'Antimo

South of Montalcino is the picturesque village of **Castelnuovo dell'Abate**, overlooking the abbey church of Sant'Antimo. Open all day, but visitors are asked to come 10.30–12.30, 15.00–18.00; Sun 09.15–10.45, 15.00–18.00. The times of the offices with Gregorian chant are indicated in the church (☎ 0577 835 659). Organ concerts are held in the church in July and Aug.

One of the finest Romanesque religious buildings in Italy, it is in a beautiful setting in the Starcia valley, surrounded by olive groves and hills covered with ilex woods. The original abbey is said to have been founded by Charlemagne in 781, and as a Benedictine foundation it continued to enjoy the protection of the Holy Roman Emperor, besides receiving Papal privileges. A period of decline began in the 13C, and the abbey was suppressed by Pius II in 1462 and placed under the jurisdiction of the bishop of Montalcino. The present church probably dates from the early 12C (the date 1118 is inscribed on a column of the ambulatory). The style combines French and Lombard elements.

Abbey church of Sant'Antimo

The simple, lofty **façade** was never completed and was probably intended to have a double doorway. Originally, there was a portico supported on two columns resting on lions, which are now inside. The architrave over the doorway has stylised vine branches and other carved decoration. The exterior of the church is of monumental simplicity, its forms outlined by sequences of pilasters, corbels, and pierced openings. There are blind arches running along the nave under the roof. The prow-like choir gives an impression of compactness with its three eautiful apses. The decoration is subdued: two white columns with fine capitals linked by a row of carved corbels emphasise the curve of each apse. The bell-tower, which is divided into four storeys by a cornice and blind arches, is decorated with some stylised reliefs including a *Madonna and Child* on the east side. The stone varies in type and colour and the decorative effect is enhanced by some beautifully veined blocks. The older apse of the Carolingian chapel has an oculus at its base through which can be seen the 9C crypt, a small vaulted chamber with two apses facing each other and four columns, and a baptismal font let into the ground. There is a small finely carved doorway on the north side. The doorway on the south side is decorated with palmettes and interlaced bands beneath an architrave carved with eagles, gryphons, and monsters. Above, in the lunette, are the Sergardi arms and corbels with strange heads on either side.

The abbey has a basilican plan: the nave is supported on columns and four cruciform piers, with an upper gallery and a clerestory above. A timber roof covers the nave, whereas the side aisles are vaulted. The aisles become narrower towards the east end, leading into an ambulatory, with three radiating chapels, a feature which is rarely found in Italian architecture.

The interior is built of travertine of a particularly warm tonality, quarried locally. The luminous honey-coloured stone, and the numerous windows combine to create a wonderful, tranquil atmosphere. The light changes according to the season and the time of day, and the effect at sunset is particularly beautiful.

The sculptural decoration is of exceptionally high quality: the capitals of the nave present a variety of geometrical and leaf motifs. The finest is that of the second column on the right representing Daniel in the lions' den, which is now attributed to the Master of Cabestany, of French or Spanish origin. The sculptural decoration of the primitive church was subsequently adapted and re-used in some capitals of the ambulatory and gallery, or inserted into the outside walls.

The **gallery**, reached by a spiral staircase next to the sacristy, continues round the entire church. It was partially fitted up with rooms by the Bishop of Montalcino in the 15C one of which has a fireplace and wall paintings. Next to the entrance to the **sacristy** are carved pilasters from the Carolingian period and a stoup with two superimposed Romanesque capitals with the Piccolomini crescent in each corner. The sacristy occupies the primitive church or so-called **Carolingian chapel**, a small rectangular chapel with an apse (the vault was probably added later). It has a 15C cycle of grisaille frescoes of the *Life of St Benedict* by Giovanni di Asciano, and two anonymous 16C frescoes of *Christ on the Cross between Saints Anthony and Sebastian* and a *Pietà*.

The **ambulatory**, the design of which may have been borrowed from French prototypes, is supremely elegant and refined in every detail. There is great harmony in the play of light created by the columns, windows, vaults, and blind arches. Certain stones and the bases of some columns have been carved in onyx or alabaster instead of travertine and, when sunlight falls directly on them, they take on a translucent glow. Columns surround the high altar, on the steps of which is a long inscription referring to a benefactor, Count Bernardo, probably dating from the early 12C.

Over the altar is an impressive 13C painted *Crucifix*. The polychrome wood statue of the *Madonna del Carmine* in the nave is an Umbrian work (c 1260). To the right of the altar are steps leading down to a small rectangular crypt which has a barrel vault and a frescoed *Pietà*. At the foot of the bell-tower, at the north end of the ambulatory, is a small chapel with three niches, tall narrow pilasters in the corners, and three window openings. One of the bells is dated 1219.

Practically nothing remains of the monastic buildings or cloister, except for the well. The fine triple-arched window with cushion capitals, supposedly belonging to the chapter house, is pre-Romanesque.

A lovely road (partly unsurfaced) leads west from Sant'Antimo to **Sant'Angelo in Colle** (also reached by a direct road from Montalcino). This is an enchanting, well-preserved village on the top of a hill, still contained within its circle of walls. In the piazza at the centre is the Romanesque church of San Michele which has a *Madonna of the Rosary* by Francesco Rustici, dated 1625. There is a splendid view from the village across the Orcia valley towards Monte Amiata.

To the southwest is **Poggio alle Mura**, a former castle (now Villa Banfi) where a **Museo del Vetro** (open 11.00–13.00. 15.30–19.00) exhibits glass and a collection of farming implements. The surrounding vineyards produce the excellent Banfi red wine.

Asciano & Monte Oliveto Maggiore

Asciano is a delightful and interesting small town, with a good museum. Monte Oliveto Maggiore, one of the most important monasteries in Tuscany in a beautiful isolated position, is famous for its frescoes by Luca Signorelli and Sodoma. Both these places are approached from the Via Cassia, the old Roman road between Siena and Rome which runs through a remarkable landscape of bare clay hills known as *Le Crete*. **Beneath their deeply eroded slopes are clusters of trees. There are relatively few scattered farmhouses and the crests of the hills are often marked by pines and cypresses.**

This chapter also describes some lovely small villages including Buonconvento, whose museum has a fine collection of paintings, and Murlo, which has an interesting archeological collection.

Practical information

 ### Getting there
By car
Asciano can be reached direct from Siena on the N438; an alternative approach is by the Cassia (N2) as far as Monteroni d'Arbia where a particularly beautiful by-road diverges east for Asciano. Monte Oliveto Maggiore can either be reached from Asciano or by another by-road from Buonconvento.

By train
The branch railway line (some trains are substituted by buses) from Siena to Chiusi has stations at Asciano and Rapolano Terme. Another branch line from Siena to Grosseto has stations at Isola d'Arbia, Monteroni d'Arbia and Buonconvento.

By bus
Buses run by *TRA-IN* from Siena (Piazza San Domenico) to Asciano and Buonconvento (with a few services to Monte Oliveto Maggiore).

Information office
APT of **Siena** (☎ 0577 280 551).
Asciano information office, open in summer, Corso Matteotti 18 (☎ 0577 719 510). Comune, ☎ 0577 714 41.

 ### Where to stay
Hotels
ASCIANO ☆☆☆ *Il Bersagliere*, Via Roma 41 (☎/🖷 0577 718 629).
Accommodation is available at the abbey of **Monte Oliveto Maggiore** (☎ 0577 707 017).
BUONCONVENTO ☆☆ *Roma*, Via Soccini 14 (☎ 0577 806 021; 🖷 0577 807 284).

MURLO ☆☆☆ *L'Albergo di Murlo*,
Via Maritiri del Rigosecco, Vescovado
(☎ 0577 814 033; ✉ 0577 814 243).
RAPOLANO TERME has four
hotels.

Campsite

☆☆☆ *Le Soline* at Casciano di Murlo
(☎ 0577 817 410).

Eating out
Restaurants

ASCIANO €€ *Osteria della
Pievina*, 5km northwest on the SS438.
SANTE MARIE (7km north) €
Da Ottorino.
MURLO (8km south) at La Befa €
Osteria La Befa.

Asciano

Asciano is a little town in the *Crete* region southeast of Siena. The countryside here is particularly beautiful in spring, covered with yellow broom and red poppies. Access to the town is through the Porta dei Bianchi, but by car you should follow the road to the right, along the walls built by the Sienese in the 14C, to the gateway at the opposite end where there is a car park. There is a splendid view of the apse and tower of Sant'Agata from outside the walls.

An archway leads into the piazza which is dominated by the façade of the collegiate church of **Sant'Agata**, rising above a flight of steps. The original church dates from the 11C but it was rebuilt and enlarged in the following centuries. The geometrical simplicity of the exterior enhances the beauty of the travertine stone. The façade probably dates from the later 14C, at the time of the transition between the Romanesque and Gothic styles. It is composed of three slender blind arches, forming a triumphal arch, above which is a large oculus with blind arcading below the roof, separated by a string-course that creates the effect of a pediment. The decoration is confined to the inner arch surrounding the doorway and to the capitals of the pilasters.

The interior is unique to the district: a Latin cross plan with a single nave, with two side apses leading off the transept and a larger central apse. Above the crossing is a hemispherical dome resting on a drum, decorated with small columns and corbels, which is supported by four large arches springing from the piers. At the summit is an elegant lantern. On the right of the nave is a fresco of the *Madonna and Child with St Michael, Tobias, and the angel* by a follower of Sodoma, on the left is a *Pietà* by Riccio. A 15C *Crucifix* hangs over the altar.

To the left of the church is the **Oratorio di Santa Croce** which has some frescoes and an altarpiece by the Nasini.

About half-way down Corso Matteotti on the right is the little church of San Bernardino. Further down on the left is the municipal tower crowned with battlements, beneath which is a fountain. At the pharmacy opposite, which has elegant 19C cupboards displaying old jars, you can ask to see the large mosaic pavement belonging to a Roman villa.

Further down on the right is the church of **Sant'Agostino**, a Gothic church with a simple brick façade. The interior has transversal arches and altars of grey stone; the first two enclose damaged 16C frescoes. Behind the high altar (the *Madonna and Child* by Matteo di Giovanni is a reproduction) is the marble tombstone of Giacomo Scotti by Urbano da Cortona (1487).

Immediately beyond the church is **Palazzo Corboli**, which has been renovated to house the **Museo Civico, Archeologico e d'Arte Sacra** due to open in 2002. This is an interesting medieval building which still preserves some

14C frescoes.The collection of paintings comprises several masterpieces of Sienese art. There is a large altarpiece representing *St Michael slaying the dragon between two standing Saints*, with a *Madonna and Child* in the central pinnacle, by Ambrogio Lorenzetti, from the ruined abbey of Rofeno. One of the most fascinating works is the triptych representing the *Birth of the Virgin*, with the *Madonna of Humility* flanked by two smaller panels above, by the Master of the Osservanza, an artist close to Sassetta. The unusual *Nativity*, with *St Augustine* and *St Galgano* on either side, by Pietro di Giovanni d'Ambrogio is a somewhat naïf but charming rendition of the story, and the landscape in the background is clearly inspired by the *Crete* in this district. The polyptych with the *Madonna and Child enthroned*, surrounded by Saints James, Augustine, Bernardine and Margaret, with the *Annunciation and God the Father blessing* above, is by Matteo di Giovanni and comes from the church of Sant'Agostino. Other works include a *Madonna and Child* by Segna di Bonaventura, an *Annunciation* by Taddeo di Bartolo, an *Assumption of the Virgin* by Giovanni di Paolo and a charming *Madonna and Child* attributed to Lippo Memmi. Among the sculptural works are two polychrome wooden *Annunciation* figures of the *Virgin and Angel Gabriel* by Francesco di Valdambrino.

Also exhibited here is a small Etruscan collection with material dating from the 7C to 1C BC from Poggio Pinci (c 7km east of Asciano), Molinello, and other sites nearby, and includes ceramics, urns, and bronze objects.

A little street between Sant'Agostino and Palazzo Corboli leads to the walls which overlook the Bestima river. Further up is a view of the cascades, near which is a public park.

In Via Mameli nearby is the **Museo Cassioli** (open 10.00–12.30, 16.30–18.30 exc. Mon) which contains paintings, oil sketches and drawings by Amos Cassioli (1832–91), who was born in Asciano. A purist and romantic painter, he is best known for his frescoes representing scenes of the Risorgimento in Palazzo Pubblico in Siena. His son Giuseppe (1865–1942) was primarily a sculptor.

Off the far end of Corso Matteotti a pretty road (La Peschiera) runs left along the walls to Piazza del Grano. At the centre is a large marble fountain by Antonio Ghini (1450). The Palazzo del Podestà is studded with coats of arms. There are several charming medieval streets near the piazza.

From the piazza outside the walls, behind the Collegiata, a road leads uphill to **San Francesco**, in a panoramic position. The Gothic church was completely remodelled inside in the17C. Beneath the whitewash on the walls frescoes by Sienese artists of the 13C–15C are gradually coming to light. There is also a della Robbia relief of the *Madonna and Child with angels* and a marble holy-water stoup attributed to Antonio Ghini.

Northeast of Asciano is **Rapolano Terme**, a medieval town with spa waters and travertine quarries.

The Abbey of Monte Oliveto Maggiore

Eight kilometres south of Asciano is the Abbey of Monte Oliveto Maggiore, on a promontory in a dense cypress wood. It is one of the best known monasteries in Tuscany (open daily 09.15–12.00, 15.15–17.45). There is a car park outside the gate (and a bar and restaurant). Hospitality is available at the guest house.

History

The monastery was founded in 1313 by Giovanni Tolomei of Siena, a wealthy professor of law, who withdrew at the age of forty to this area on his family property called the Desert of Accona. Here he settled with his companions, founding the Olivetan order (a branch of the Benedictine order) which was approved by the bishop of Arezzo, Guido Tarlati, in 1319, and confirmed by Pope Clement VI in 1344. Giovanni Tolomei, who assumed the name of Bernardo, was later beatified. The order grew rapidly and by the early 15C there were already thirty houses in Tuscany and Umbria.

Pius II and Charles V sojourned here, the latter with 2000 followers. The monastery was suppressed by Napoleon in 1810. It was restored and made a National Monument in 1866. The Abbot General usually resides here and a number of monks work on the restoration of rare books.

The **entrance** is past a drawbridge and through a fortified building with an arched passage above which is a large niche with a glazed terracotta statue of the *Madonna and Child, crowned by two angels*, by Giovanni della Robbia. In a corresponding position on the other side is a seated figure of *St Benedict* also by Giovanni della Robbia. A path leads down to the **monastery** through an avenue of cypress trees. The huge monastic buildings extend beyond the church. In the surrounding cypress woods are small 18C chapels, dedicated to founder members of the Order and various saints. The large fish reservoir was built by the Sienese architect Giovanni Battista Pelori (1533).

The frescoes in the great cloister

The great cloister (1426–74), with two storeys of loggias, is famous for its frescoes illustrating the *Life of St Benedict*. The nine frescoes on the west wall are by Luca Signorelli (1497–98) and the others are by Sodoma (Giovanni Antonio Bazzi, 1505–08). The cycle is a masterpiece of fresco painting combining a picturesque and lively narrative style with charming naturalistic detail in a variety of landscape and architectural settings. In between the episodes are painted pilasters, several of which are decorated with grisailles and grotesques, also by Sodoma. The scenes follow the account of Benedict's life taken from the *Dialogues* of St Gregory the Great.

The cycle begins on the **east wall** with frescoes by Sodoma. 1. *Benedict departs from his home at Norcia to study in Rome*. 2. *Benedict leaves Rome*. 3. *Benedict miraculously mends a broken tray* (here Sodoma painted his own portrait in the richly clad young man with two tame badgers at his feet). 4. *The holy monk Romano gives Benedict a hermit's habit* (Subiaco is represented in the background). 5. *Benedict at prayer in front of his cave, with the devil about to break the bell of his bread basket*. 6. *A priest is inspired by Christ to take a meal to Benedict on Easter Day*. 7. *Benedict instructs a group of peasants*. 8. *Benedict overcomes temptation by throwing himself naked into brambles*. 9. *Benedict accepts the request of a group of monks to become their abbot*. 10. *Benedict, with the Sign of the Cross, shatters a glass of poisoned wine prepared by the monks who found his rule too strict*. 11. *Benedict founds the first twelve communities*. **South wall**: frescoes by Sodoma. 12. *Benedict welcomes Mauro and Placido into the Order*. 13. *Benedict chastises a monk tempted by the devil*. 14. *Benedict, in answer to the monks' prayers, makes water spring from Monte Oliveto*. 15. *Benedict retrieves a scythe which has fallen into a lake*. 16. *Mauro* *is sent to save Placido from drowning.* 17. *The miracle of the flask changed into a snake.* 18. *Fiorenzo attempts to poison Benedict.* 19. *To tempt the monks Fiorenzo sends a group of prostitutes to the monastery.*

West wall: 20. by Bartolomeo Neroni, called il Riccio. *Benedict sends Mauro to France and Placido to Sicily.* Nos. 21–29 are by Luca Signorelli: 21. *Fiorenzo's death.* 22. *Benedict converts the inhabitants of Monte Cassino.* 23. *Benedict defeats the devil.* 24. *Benedict rescues a young monk from beneath a collapsed wall.* 25. *Benedict tells two monks when and where they had dined outside the monastery.* 26. *Benedict reproaches Valeriano's brother for breaking the fast.* 27. *Benedict unmasks Riggo disguised as Totila, the Ostrogoth leader.* 28. *Benedict recognises and welcomes Totila.* The last fresco was destroyed when the door was enlarged. The following frescoes are by Sodoma: 30. *Benedict foretells the destruction of Monte Cassino* (by the Lombards in 581).

North wall: 31. *Benedict miraculously obtains flour for his monks.* 32. *Benedict appears to two monks in their sleep and instructs them on how to build a church.* 33. *Episode of two excommunicated nuns.* 34. *Miracle of the monk's burial.* 35. *Benedict forgives the monk who had escaped from the monastery.* 36. *Benedict releases a bound peasant by merely looking at him.*

In the passage leading to the church are two small frescoes of *Christ carrying the Cross* and *Christ at the column*, and *St Benedict giving the Rule to the founders of Monte Oliveto*, all by Sodoma. In the vestibule is a statue of the *Madonna and Child* by Fra Giovanni da Verona (1490) and a fresco of *Hermits in the desert* by an anonymous Sienese painter.

The **church**, which has a Latin-cross plan, was renovated by Giovanni Antinori in 1772. The magnificent choir-stalls of inlaid wood are by Fra Giovanni da Verona (1505) and the lectern by Raffaele da Brescia (1520). The *Assumption* in the cupola is by Jacopo Ligozzi, who also painted the *Nativity of the Virgin* behind the high altar. Off the north transept is the Chapel of the Holy Sacrament which has a large polychrome wooden *Crucifix* of the mid-13C. Opposite is the sacristy with cupboards dated 1417.

From the great cloister there is a passageway to the middle cloister, surrounded by a portico, with a *Madonna and Child and angels* over the entrance. A vestibule (with a 17C lavabo), surmounted by a fresco by Riccio gives access to the **refectory**, a large vaulted hall with frescoes by Paolo Novelli (1670). A staircase from the middle cloister leads up to the **library** which is preceded by a vestibule hung with portraits of Olivetan monks by Antonio Mueller. The library was built in 1518 to a basilican plan with Corinthian columns by Giovanni da Verona. He also executed the doorway and other carvings, as well as the Paschal candlestick. The library contains some forty thousand volumes, with important manuscripts, choirbooks and incunabula.

A double flight of steps leads to the **pharmacy** which has a fine collection of jars. The **chapter house** (called the Definitorio) dates from 1498. It has a chiaroscuro frieze and a fresco of the *Madonna and Child with Saints* attributed to Matteo Ripanda. In an adjacent room is a small collection of paintings: a *Maestà* by the Master of Monteoliveto, a follower of Duccio, a *Madonna and Child* by Segna di Bonaventura, *St Bernardine* by Neroccio di Bartolomeo, and a *Madonna and Child* by Vincenzo Tamagni. The **Hall of Justice** is also richly decorated and has a fresco of *Christ and the adulteress* by Riccio (1540).

From Monte Oliveto Maggiore a beautiful road leads south to **San Giovanni d'Asso**, on a hill (310m). An enormous **castle** towers over the village. The building is largely intact, with wooden doors, Gothic windows, and a large courtyard with a brick portico, added in the Renaissance period. The back entrance to the castle leads to a rectangular piazza from which there is a beautiful view. To the right, opposite an 18C chapel, is the church of **San Giovanni Battista**, which has a Romanesque brick façade decorated with blocks of travertine and a large oculus over the arched doorway. The interior has been restructured and the Sienese 14C triptych removed to Pienza for safe keeping.

At the far end of the piazza a path leads to the charming little church of **San Pietro in Villore**, surrounded by cypress trees. A very early church (11C–12C), it has an ancient, irregular façade decorated with blind arches and a doorway with carvings and strange anthropomorphic capitals. The structure, of sandstone and travertine, was restored in the upper part in brick at some later date. Beneath the church is a small crypt.

Montisi, nearby to the east, is described on p 457.

Buonconvento

Southwest of Monte Oliveto Maggiore, on the Via Cassia (see above), is Buonconvento, a picturesque fortified village at the confluence of the Arbia and Ombrone rivers. Emperor Henry VII, who was planning to lay siege to Siena, died of malaria here in 1313. Later, Buonconvento became one of the primary defences of Siena and its fine brick walls and gates are well preserved. On the charming main street, which crosses the town from north to south, are some medieval houses and Palazzo Pretorio, with a crenellated tower, all in brick. The parish church of Santi Pietro e Paolo dates from the 14C but was entirely rebuilt in the 18C. It preserves a *Madonna and Child* by Matteo di Giovanni and a *Madonna and Child with Saints* by Pietro di Francesco Orioli.

The **Museo d'Arte Sacra della Val d'Arbia** opposite Saint Pietro e Paolo is a museum of religious art from the Arbia Valley (open 10.00–12.00, 16.00–19.00 exc. Mon).

The collection includes several fine works from the parish church, the Compagnia del Corpus Domini, and other churches in the district. The most important include a charming *Madonna and Child* attributed to Duccio, a fine *Crucifix* by the so-called Master of the Buonconvento Cross, a *Madonna and Child with two angels* by Luca di Tommè, an *Annunciation* by Andrea di Bartolo, a large triptych with the *Madonna and Child enthroned and two Saints* by Sano di Pietro, a *Coronation of the Virgin* and other works by Matteo di Giovanni, and an *Annunciation*, by Benvenuto di Giovanni; a particularly luminous work with a charming landscape in the background. There are also some later paintings and liturgical objects including a fine early 14C incense-boat and a 15C copper gilt chalice.

The Val d'Arbia

Lucignano d'Arbia, a pretty village on a hill to the north off the Cassia, has two fortified gates, one at each end of the main street, which is lined with medieval and Renaissance houses built of brick. At the centre of the village, on a slight rise, is the Romanesque church of San Giovanni Battista beside which is a monumental bell-tower. Inside the church is a *Crucifixion* by Bartolomeo Neroni, called Il Riccio.

A by-road leads southwest to the village of **Vescovado**, which has some charming streets. The parish church is modern but contains a polyptych by Benvenuto di Giovanni of 1475, complete with its painted pinnacles, side-pilasters, and predella, and a small *Madonna and Child* by Andrea di Niccolò.

Murlo

Further south, on a hill, is the tiny village of Murlo (314m), dominating the surrounding countryside. The 12C walls form a complete circle and, although considerably restored, the village preserves its medieval character. The church of **San Fortunato**, medieval in origin and rebuilt in the 16C, has a *Madonna and Child with Saints* by Astolfo Petrazzi and an *Assumption* by Dionisio Montorselli.

In the same piazza is the former bishop's palace, called the Palazzone, which houses the **Museo Civico Archeologico** (open 09.30–12.30, 15.00–17.00 or 19.00, closed Mon).

The small but choice collection, beautifully displayed and well labelled, includes Etruscan objects excavated in recent years on the nearby hill of Poggio Civitate. A unique architectural complex with palatial villa has been discovered, dating from the 7C and 6C BC (see below). There are extensive remains of walls and roof tiles and terracotta decorations, including the bust of a bearded man wearing a broad brimmed hat, gorgons and other fantastic animals, besides panels with decoration in relief, some with horsemen. There are numerous refined objects in gold, silver, bronze, and ivory, some of them imported and therefore of interest in establishing the contacts that existed between Poggio Civitate, other districts on the peninsula and other countries. There is also an extensive collection of household objects for daily use, implements, earthenware, and personal ornaments.

A short distance southeast of Murlo are the excavations of the site of **Poggio Civitate**. These include a building dating from the last thirty years of the 7C BC and another archaic building dating from c 580 BC, which is one of the few known examples of domestic architecture of this period. The building was dismantled by the Etruscans at the end of the 6C BC, and walled in with stones and earth. The terracotta ornaments were buried in trenches and covered over. There is also an interesting large structure supported on three rows of piers which was used as a workshop by craftsmen producing objects in gold, ivory and bronze. All the material is now exhibited in the museum of Murlo (see above).

The area around Murlo is rich in castles, some of them romantic ruins in beautiful settings. A map of itineraries is available locally.

North of Lucignano, also on the Via Cassia, is **Monteroni d'Arbia**, the most developed industrial town in the district, specialising in the production of iron, glass and leather. The old borgo belonged to the hospital of Siena, Santa Maria della Scala, and preserves a large 14C fortified mill. This area is known for its excellent white wine.

A short distance north, in a conspicuous position above the Cassia, is **Cuna**, a rare example of a fortified medieval granary. Like Monteroni d'Arbia, it also belonged to Santa Maria della Scala, and is entirely built of brick with fortified walls, towers, and an arched gateway. Inside is a small chapel, with a 16C fresco of the *Madonna and Child with Saints*, various houses, beautifully preserved, and a central 13C fortress. An immense ramp leads up to the first floor where grain was stored. There is a fine view of Siena, about 12km north.

Pienza and the Val d'Orcia

Pienza is famous as an ideal Renaissance town built in the middle of the 15C in five years by Bernardo Rossellino. It is 12km west of Montepulciano and 50km south of Siena. San Quirico d'Orcia is a well kept interesting little medieval town. The landscape of the Val d'Orcia is perhaps one of the best preserved and one of the most beautiful in Tuscany. The river valley, with its characteristic eroded downs or clay hills, is in a majestic setting with the mountains of Cetona on one side, and Amiata on the other. In the wooded foothills are little towns and villages, often with their medieval castles towering above. There are also hot springs in the district known since Roman times.

Practical information

Getting there
By car

Pienza and the Val d'Orcia are close to the Via Cassia (N2) between Siena and Rome.

By bus

TRA-IN runs buses from Siena and Montepulciano to Pienza and San Quirico d'Orcia.

Information offices

For **Pienza**: *APT* Chianciano Terme Valdichiana, Chianciano Terme (☎ 0578 631 67), with offices in Pienza, Piazza Pio II (☎ 0578 749 071), and (*Pro-loco*) Via Case Nuove 22 (☎ 0578 748 072). For **San Quirico d'Orcia** and Bagno Vignoni, *APT* Siena (☎ 0577 422 09); information office in San Quirico, Via Dante Alighieri 33 (☎ 0577 897 211). For **Radicofani**, *APT* dell'Amiata, Abbadia San Salvatore (☎ 0577 778 608); information office in Radicofani, Via Renato Magi 31 (☎ 0578 556 84).

Where to stay

PIENZA ☆☆☆ *Corsignano*, Via della Madonnina 11 (☎ 0578 748 501; 📠 0578 748 166); *Il Chiostro di Pienza Relais*, Corso Rossellino 26 (☎ 0578 748 400; 📠 0578 748 440).

SAN QUIRICO D'ORCIA ☆☆☆ *Palazzuolo*, with restaurant, Via Santa Caterina 43 (☎ 0577 897 080; 📠 0577 898 264).

BAGNO VIGNONI ☆☆☆ *Posta Marcucci*, with hot thermal swimming pool (☎ 0577 887 112; 📠 0577 887 119), and *Le Terme* (☎ 0577 887 150; 📠 0577 887 497).

VIVO D'ORCIA ☆☆ *Amiata* (☎ 0577 873 790).

BAGNI SAN FILIPPO ☆☆☆ *Terme San Filippo* (☎ 0577 872 982).

RADICOFANI has ☆☆ hotels.

Eating out
Restaurants

PIENZA € *Latte di Luna*, Via San Carlo 2; *La Buca delle Fate*, Corso Rossellino 38.

SAN QUIRICO D'ORCIA €€ *Vecchio Forno*, Via della Piazzola.

Festivals

At **Monticchiello** a remarkable local **open-air theatre** season is held in July (information from the *Compagnia Popolare Teatro Povero*, ☎ 0578 755 118). On the estate of **La Foce** at the Castelluccio Bifolchi an **annual chamber music festival** is held in summer (*Incontri in Terra di Siena*), for information (☎ 0578 691 01).

Pienza

Pienza (491m) is a charming compact little Renaissance town (2400 inhab.) created by Aeneas Silvius Piccolomini, afterwards Pius II, on his election to the Papacy in 1458. He transformed the original fortified village of Corsignano, a Piccolomini feud and Aeneas's birthplace, and renamed it Pienza by papal bull in 1462. The architect Bernardo Rossellino was commissioned to design the monumental piazza with its splendid cathedral and palaces, all built between 1459–64. A particularly good sheep's cheese (*pecorino* or *cacio*) is made in the district.

Piazza Pio II, laid out by Bernardo Rossellino, is a remarkable example of Renaissance town planning. It shows the influence of Leon Battista Alberti, Rossellino's master. To one side of the beautifully paved piazza is an elegant well, also designed by Rossellino, flanked by two slender columns with finely carved capitals and an architrave.

The Duomo

The Duomo has a superb façade in Istrian stone. The motif of the triumphal arch and the choice of details are evidently inspired by classical Roman architecture. The proportions, the linear clarity and sober decoration conform to the aspirations of dignity, harmony and beauty of the Humanist architect. At the centre of the great pediment are the papal arms of Pius II, on an awe-inspiring scale.

The unusual lofty but compact interior has nave and aisles of equal height, divided by clustered columns with tall dosserets supporting the vault. Five large arched windows, decorated with tracery, one in each of the chapels encircling the east end, fill the church with light. The elegant architecture is clearly influenced by Northern European (French Gothic) models. The painted ribs of the vault, fanning out from the columns, add a beautiful touch of colour and enhance the etherial atmosphere of the church.

The five altarpieces were painted for the cathedral in 1461–63. In the south aisle, *Madonna and Child with Saints Bernardine, Anthony Abbot, Francis and Sabina*, and a *Pietà* in the lunette, by Giovanni di Paolo. First chapel: *Madonna and Child with Saints Catherine of Alexandria, Matthew, Bartholomew and Lucy*, and the *Flagellation* in the lunette, by Matteo di Giovanni. Second chapel: marble tabernacle attributed to Rossellino, which contains a relic of St Andrew. The central chapel has fine choir-stalls and a bishop's cathedra of 1462. Fourth chapel: triptych of the *Assumption with Saints Agatha, Callistus, Pius I and Catherine of Siena, Ecce Homo* in the predella, by Vecchietta. Fifth chapel: *Madonna and Child with Saints Mary Magdalen, Philip, James, and Anne, Ecce Homo* in the gable and *Annunciation* in the predella, by Sano di Pietro. In the north aisle, *Madonna and Child with Saints Jerome, Martin, Nicholas, and Augustine* by Matteo di Giovanni.

The north side of the church has had to be shored up in an attempt to stabilise the structure, and the crypt with a font in travertine by Rossellino is at present closed.

Palazzo Piccolomini

To the right of the Duomo is Palazzo Piccolomini, begun by Pius II and finished by Pius III, his nephew (the main rooms on the first floor are open to the public; guided tours 10.00–12.30, 15.00 or 16.00–18.00 or 19.00, except Mon). It is considered Rossellino's masterpiece, and shows the influence of Alberti's Palazzo Rucellai in Florence. The façade is built of sandstone with two elegant rows of

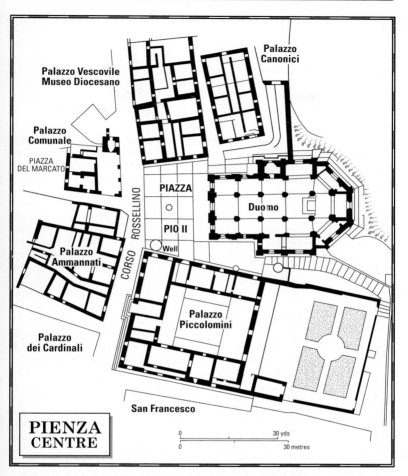

PIENZA CENTRE

Labels on map: Palazzo Canonici · Palazzo Vescovile Museo Diocesano · Palazzo Comunale · PIAZZA DEL MARCATO · CORSO ROSSELLINO · PIAZZA PIO II · Well · Duomo · Palazzo Ammannati · Palazzo dei Cardinali · Palazzo Piccolomini · San Francesco

0 — 30 yds
0 — 30 metres

arched mullioned windows alternating with pilasters, separated by horizontal cornices, and simple doorways. The base becomes a projecting bench on three sides of the palace. The elegant courtyard is surrounded by a portico supported on a splendid Corinthian order, above which are two storeys of square mullioned windows with a glazed loggia on two sides of the upper floor. On the right are stairs leading up to the first floor. Opposite, on the left, is the entrance to the hanging garden, onto which faces the magnificent garden front of the palace, composed of three superimposed open loggias. The Italian garden of evergreen box hedges and small trees, has remained unchanged (but is being restored). Seen against the backdrop of the Orcia valley, it is a supreme example of the Renaissance idea of the garden as the intermediary between architecture and nature.

The first floor was inhabited by the Piccolomini family until 1962. The Sala degli Antenati is hung with family portraits. The **dining room** has good furniture and tapestries. In the **music room** is a fine *scagliola* table representing a map of the Sienese State, and Cordova leather hangings. The large **Sala d'Armi** has a display of arms and battle paintings by Borgognone. From the Loggia is a view overlooking the garden and beyond, in the distance, Radicofani with Monte Cetona on the left and Monte Amiata on the right. The **bedroom** has a 17C bed and a fresco over the door with a portrait of *Pius II*. A passage leads to the **library**, interesting for its furniture, carpets, books and documents.

Museo Diocesano

Opposite Palazzo Piccolomini is **Palazzo Vescovile**, which was modified and enlarged by Roderigo Borgia, later Pope Alexander VI, whose arms it displays on the corner. This and the adjoining Palazzo Jouffroy di Arras, are now the seat of the Museo Diocesano, entered from the Corso (open 10.00–13.00, 15.00–18.30, exc. Tues; in winter only on weekends).

From the pretty courtyard with its well, stairs (or a lift) ascend to the second floor. The display is chronological and includes some very fine works of art from the cathedral and churches in the district. **Room I** displays a *Crucifix* of the late 12C, showing the influence of the Umbrian school, and another *Crucifix* by Segna di Bonaventura. The *Madonna and Child* by Pietro Lorenzetti from Montichiello is one of his masterpieces and a work of immense charm (1310–20). **Room 2** contains a charming little portable triptych by the Master of the Osservanza, and a rare portable altar with numerous scenes from the *Life of Christ* dating from the late 14C. The two polychrome wood statues are by Domenico di Niccolò dei Cori, and the *Madonna of the Misericordia* is by Bartolo di Fredi. **Room 3** displays three fine **Flemish tapestries** from Brussels and Arras, in particular a beautiful Crucifixion scene woven c 1460. **Room 4** contains a magnificent cope in *Opus Anglicanum* dating from the first half of the 14C, with scenes from the Life of the Virgin, saints and apostles embroidered in silk and silver gilt thread, one of the few surviving examples of English medieval ecclesiastical embroidery. **Room 5** contains the reliquary bust of St Andrew by Simone di Giovanni Ghini, and a precious Byzantine Cross in golden filigree and rock crystal. Pius II's superb **crozier** of gilded silver, inlaid with enamels, is a very fine example of Florentine goldsmiths' work (1460), with a charming *Annunciation* scene above a small temple containing six angels holding shields with the papal arms. Ten enamelled plaquettes from Pius's original mitre are now incorporated in a 19C mitre. The large **altarpiece** by Vecchietta has a charming predella and an *Annunciation* which demonstrates the artist's interest in perspective. Beyond a little room with a good view of the piazza, **room 6** has more 15C Sienese paintings. **Room 7** has scenes from the *Life of Christ* by Arcangelo Salimbeni and a Madonna by Il Riccio, as well as statuettes of *St Peter* and *St Paul* attributed to Giovanni Andrea Galletti. **Room 8** has a fine display of **choirbooks**, many of them illuminated by Sienese and Florentine artists of the mid-15C, and a showcase of 1901 containing the cathedral treasury including a little Cross in boxwood, and a 17C Florentine Crucifix. The last two rooms have late 16C and 17C works notably *St Bruno and the Madonna* by Francesco Trevisani.

Opposite the Duomo is **Palazzo Comunale**, with a fine portico supported on travertine columns with Ionic capitals and double windows on the upper floor, also designed by Rossellino. At the further end is a tall clock-tower.

Corso Rossellino leads out of the piazza along the north side of Palazzo Piccolomini, opposite which is **Palazzo Ammannati**, built by Cardinal Ammannati of Pavia, a close friend of Pius II. Its top floor loggia is now bricked in. Next to it is the smaller Palazzo dei Cardinali. A little further on, to the left, is **San Francesco**, an early Gothic church with some late 14C frescoes. The street ends at the 14C **Porta al Prato** (or Porta al Murello), beyond which is a public garden. From here there is a charming walk downhill, known as the Passeggiata di Santa Caterina, with a fine view.

Via delle Fonti leaves the piazza outside Porta al Prato and continues downhill (600m) to an old fountain. Nearby, beside some picturesque farm buildings, is the beautiful Romanesque **Pieve di Corsignano**, also known as Santi Vito e Modesto. The church is very ancient (10C–11C) and has an unusual circular tower with eight large arched windows. The doorway at the west end is decorated with reliefs of stylised flowers and palmettes and a strange double-tailed siren; the window has a female caryatid at the centre. On the architrave of the south doorway are carvings depicting the *Journey of the Magi* and the *Nativity*, with animals on the jambs. The lovely **interior** has a basilican plan and it still contains the simple baptismal font supported on a Romanesque capital in which Pius II was baptised.

Just inside Porta al Prato, Via Gozzante leads to a delightful raised walkway along the walls on the south side of the town which overlooks the valley. It passes beneath the garden of Palazzo Piccolomini and continues from the Canonica to the **Porta al Ciglio** at the far end of Corso Rossellino. Outside the gate is a fortified palace with two impressive round towers. The old medieval streets of Corsignano are extemely picturesque.

A road south from Pienza, providing the best view of the garden façade of Palazzo Piccolomini and the great apse of the Duomo, leads to **Monticchiello**, a lovely medieval village. Its 13C castle, walls and towers still exist in a relatively good state. The late 13C church of **Santi Leonardo e Cristoforo** has an elegant doorway and rose window. The interior, rebuilt in the 18C, has 14C and 15C frescoes of the Sienese school. The summer theatre festival is held in the adjacent Piazza San Martino (see above). A by-road leads southeast from Monticchiello to Montepulciano (see p 448).

San Quirico d'Orcia

San Quirico d'Orcia (409m). This little medieval town takes its name from the former church of San Quirico a Osenna, recorded as early as the 8C on the Via Francigena. Little is known of St Quirico (Cyricus) except that he was martyred, allegedly in the 4C. In the 13C the town walls were enlarged and several hospices and hospitals were built to accommodate pilgrims on their way to Rome. Stretches of the walls survive, as well as some of the former watch-towers, partly incorporated into other buildings.

From the medieval **Porta Cappuccini**, an unusual polygonal and well preserved gateway, Via Poliziano passes some interesting houses and ends at Piazza Chigi. The enormous **Palazzo Chigi** was built for Cardinal Flavio Chigi by Carlo Fontana in 1679. It was restored in 1999. The interior decorated with frescoes by Roman artists may be visited on request (☎ 0577 898 247).

The Via Francigena

The Via Francigena was the medieval pilgrims' way from France and Northern Europe to Rome, which was especially busy during Jubilee years. Sigeric (also called Siric) travelled along it on his way to Rome from Canterbury to receive the pallium (symbol of investiture) from the hands of the Pope as Archbishop of Canterbury. He described his return journey in 990, with its 80 stopping places, and the manuscript of his chronicle is still preserved in the British Museum in London. The archbishop studied to be a churchman at the Benedictine abbey at Glastonbury in England under St Dunstan.

In the 8C the road was used by the Lombards as a safe route from Pavia to the south, avoiding Byzantine territory, and in the following century it became known as the Francigena because it originated in Frankish territory (it is also sometimes called the Via Romea by medieval chroniclers). The route across France started at Calais and traversed Picardy, Champagne and the Ardennes, then from Switzerland, the Alps were crossed at the Great St Bernard Pass. From Aosta it passed through Northern Italy (Ivrea, Vercelli, Pavia, Piacenza, Fidenza and Parma) and from the Passo della Cisa on the Emilian border it entered Tuscany, where Pontremoli was the first centre of importance. It continued south to Lucca, crossed the Arno at Fucecchio, and then passed through the towns of San Gimignano, Siena, San Quirico d'Orcia, and left Tuscany at Radicofani to cross Lazio (Bolsena, Montefiascone, and Viterbo) before reaching Rome.

This route to Rome was one of three pilgrimage routes in medieval Europe; the other two led to Santiago de Compostela and Jerusalem. The journey from England to Rome took about two and a half months and ordinary pilgrims probably made the entire trip on foot (carrying a characteristic staff), although prelates such as Sigeric may have travelled on horseback. The road was rough and only paved in places, therefore unsuitable for wheeled vehicles. Numerous '*ospedali*' or stopping places grew up along the way which offered help and accommodation to travellers, some of them run by the church (such as the Ospedale di Santa Maria della Scala in Siena which ran many hospices south of the city). The hospice of La Magione (see p 421) is one of the best preserved to have survived. Castles and villages were also built near the route, and towns such as Lucca and Siena prospered as a result of their proximity to the Via Francigena. Apart from pilgrims, the road was used by merchants and traders and goods as well as works of art were transported along it. Some of the churches in Tuscany built close to the road show the influence of French Romanesque architecture, notably the abbey of Sant'Antimo.

The importance of the Via Francigena diminished after the 13C when other routes were opened over the Alps.

The collegiata

The Romanesque collegiata (open all day) was built in the 12C on the site of an earlier church. The exterior, built of travertine, has a simple structure, except for the three elaborately decorated **doorways**, parts of which are in contrasting sandstone. The main entrance, beneath a large rose window, dating from the late

12C, is the finest and most elaborate example of a Lombard portal in Sienese territory. It incorporates a frieze of strange animal heads and an arch above four slender clustered columns, tied together with a loop at their centre. These in turn have Lombard lions at their base. A sequence of inner arches, surrounding the lunette with a seated figure, said to be Pope St Damasus at the centre, are supported on five thin columns with unusual capitals. The sandstone architrave has two splendid dragons.

The doorway on the south side, with a porch supported on elegant telamons standing on lions, is slightly later in date and is attributed to the school of Giovanni Pisano. It has a fine architrave and is flanked by two elegant Gothic windows; the right window has a kneeling telamon and carved fantastic animals. The smaller doorway, at the end of the south transept, is dated 1298 (both were damaged by shell-fire). The remaining decoration is limited to small blind arches under the roofs. The bell-tower dates from the 18C.

The interior has a Latin-cross plan, with three arches supported on piers dividing the nave from the short north aisle. The timber ceiling, parts of which preserve the original paint, was discovered under the Baroque vault. The nave and transept chapels are divided from the crossing by arches. In the north transept is a fine polyptych by Sano di Pietro. The presence of St Quirico and the red-and-white arms of the town in the painting prove that it was painted for this church. The choir was enlarged in the mid-18C to house nine choir-stalls inlaid with trompe l'oeil scenes and half-length figures by Antonio di Neri Barili (possibly on designs by Signorelli) which originally formed a series of 19 in the Baptist's chapel in Siena cathedral. The 17C organ is attributed to Cesare Romani of Cortona; it is used for concerts. In the north aisle is a detached fresco of the **Madonna and Child**, by Girolamo di Benvenuto, known as the **Madonna delle Grazie** or **Madonna del Pomo**, a **Madonna of the Rosary** by Rutilio Manetti, and the marble pavement tombstone of Henry of Nassau by Urbano da Cortona, dated 1451.

To the left of the church is the **Oratory of the Misericordia** which has a **Madonna and Child with Saints** by Il Riccio.

The main street, Via Dante Alighieri, crosses the town past some well-preserved medieval houses and the Renaissance Palazzo Pretorio. In Piazza Libertà is the **Chiesa di Santa Maria di Vitaleta**, also known as San Francesco, which has a (restored) Gothic façade. The interior has a very beautiful white glazed enamel **Virgin Annunciate** by Andrea della Robbia of 1510 on the high altar and polychrome wood figures of the **Virgin** and **Angel Gabriel** by Francesco di Valdambrino. The **Preaching of the Baptist** is signed and dated 1597 by Empoli, who also painted the **Immaculate Conception** opposite. The **Miracle of the Loaves and Fishes** is by Vincenzo Rustici.

Across the piazza, next to the Porta Nuova, is the entrance to the **Horti Leonini** (open all day), a beautiful park with an Italian garden created by Diomede Leoni around 1580. At the centre is a marble statue of Cosimo III Medici by Giuseppe Mazzuoli (1688) which was removed from Palazzo Chigi. The garden, which follows the Renaissance pattern of box hedges in a geometrical design, leading to a *boschetto* or ilex wood on a slope, was intended as a resting place for pilgrims. It is surrounded by remains of the old ramparts, above which stood the tall castle tower.

Farther along Via Dante is a 14C house (no. 38) where St Catherine of Siena is supposed to have stayed. Towards the end of the street is the charming little church of **Santa Maria Assunta** (11C), built of beautiful stone blocks. It has a fine doorway with a porch (which may originally have been intended for Sant'Antimo). The simple interior is dimly lit by small lancet windows. The apse is decorated on the outside with blind arches and zoomorphic heads. The little walled **rose garden** opened here in 1993 has a gate leading into the Horti Leonini.

Opposite is the **Ospedale della Scala** (which belonged to the eponymous hospital of Siena) dating from the 13C. There are remains of a loggia giving on to the courtyard, which also preserves a 16C well.

The Val d'Orcia

South of San Quirico, approached from by-roads on either side of the Via Cassia, is the Val d'Orcia, the beautiful valley of the Orcia river. West of the Cassia are well-preserved villages, castles and thermal baths in the foothills of Monte Amiata, while to the east the valley widens out on either side of the river with a landscape of eroded clay slopes and small sharp ridges known as *calanchi*, much of it part of the huge estate of La Foce.

Just south of San Quirico, reached through beautiful countryside, is the tiny village of **Vignoni**, from which there is a fine view. It has a truncated medieval tower, and a 15C palace on the main street which leads to the Romanesque church on the edge of the hill.

The road continues to climb towards **Ripa d'Orcia**, a castle surrounded by ramparts in a spectacular, isolated position overlooking the Orcia Valley (it is now a hotel residence, ☎ 0577 530 23).

Bagno Vignoni is a tiny medieval spa on a small plateau. The hot water spring, known since Roman times, bubbles up into a large piscina, constructed by the Medici, in the charming and perfectly preserved piazza. It forms one of the most unusual and evocative sights in Tuscany, especially in winter when the condensation from the hot spring water creates a mist.

Castliglione d'Orcia (540m) is another picturesque little village, built round a ruined castle. The main **piazza**, named after the 15C artist Vecchietta, traditionally believed to have been born here, preserves its old paving of brick and pebbles and there is a well in the centre, dated 1618. The *pieve* of **Santi Stefano e Degna**, a Romanesque church with a Renaissance façade, has a *Madonna enthroned with four Saints* by Giovanni di Bartolomeo (1531), a large *Crucifixion* by Fabrizio Boschi and two early 16C frescoed lunettes. The pretty borgo has narrow streets with some medieval houses and a little Romanesque church, the Chiesa delle Sante Marie. There is a fine view over the Orcia valley.

Nearby is **Rocca d'Orcia** a particularly well-preserved medieval village on a slope, dominated by its spectacular castle, the **Rocca di Tentennano** where exhibitions are held (open in summer, 10.00–13.00, 15.30–19.30, in winter at weekends, reduced hours). The piazza has a large octagonal stone well in the centre. The parish church of **San Simeone** preserves a fresco of the *Madonna of Mercy* by a follower of Bartolo di Fredi and a *Madonna of the Rosary* by Francesco Rustici.

Farther south is **Campiglia d'Orcia** in an elevated position (811m) on the north slope of Monte Amiata, facing Radicofani. It has picturesque medieval streets and a tall bell-tower built on a rocky spur. In the church of San Biagio is a *Madonna and Child with Saints* attributed to Sebastiano Folli.

On the road to Monte Amiata is **Vivo d'Orcia** (870m), surrounded by woods, near the spring of the Vivo torrent. Near the bridge is the **Eremo del Vivo**, an impressive late Renaissance building overlooking the valley. A Camaldolese monastery in the early 12C, it became the property of the Cervini of Montepulciano who built a fortified palace here in 1536. The architect is said to have been Antonio da Sangallo the Younger. The church of San Pietro, opposite, has a Romanesque apse. Nearby are some interesting old farm buildings.

Close to the Cassia is **Bagni San Filippo**. Here the hot sulphurous springs, known since ancient times, are said to be named after St Filippo Benizzi (1238–85), of the Servite Order. There is a thermal station and beautiful cascades. In the village is the church of San Filippo which has an 18C stucco statue of *St Filippo* and busts of *St Filippo Benizzi* and *St Filippo Neri*.

La Foce

To the east of the Via Cassia (just south of San Quirico) a by-road leads past the fortified farm of **Spedaletto** which belonged to the hospital of Santa Maria della Scala in Siena, and was also used as a hospice for pilgrims on their way to Rome. A pretty lane diverges for Pienza (see above), while this road runs along the stony shallow river bed where there are gravel works. The interesting landscape has pasturelands and *calanchi* (see above). Its wild aspect was partly altered in the 1980s when certain areas were levelled to create arable land. At the end of the valley, where the road begins to climb up to the watershed between the Val d'Orcia and the Val di Chiana, the landscape is better preserved. This was part of the huge estate of **La Foce** (3000 acres) purchased by Iris and Antonio Origo in 1923 where they spent most of their lives reclaiming the land and cultivating it. They also started a school, nursery school and day clinic on the estate, and Antonio was the founder of the *Consorzio di bonifica* in the Val d'Orcia which ran other schools. During the war, children from Turin and Genoa were taken in by the Origos, and they ran an orphanage here. Iris Origo (1902–88), the historian and biographer, described her life here in her autobiography *Images and Shadows* and her war diary *War in Val d'Orcia*. Her book, *The Merchant of Prato*, about the life of Francesco di Marco Datini, provides a vivid description of life in medieval Italy.

On the skyline the **Castelluccio Bifolchi** can be seen, a small castle where a delightful annual chamber music festival (see p 437) is held in summer (in the courtyard and other localities nearby). From the main road, lined with cypresses and pines, there is also a view of the country road which zigzags up to a farmhouse on the estate, which was planted with widely spaced cypresses by the Origos to provide a picturesque view from the main villa.

At the top of the ridge is the main entrance to the **villa**, still owned by the Origo family and since 1998 the seat of a foundation for the study of the landscape and environment of the Val d'Orcia. The **gardens** may be visited on Wednesdays (15.00–dusk; entrance fee, which is donated to charity). Ask at the farm office in the courtyard to the left of the house. They are usually at their best in May, June and September.

The villa, built in 1498 as a hostel run by the Ospedale di Santa Maria della Scala of Siena, was restored for the Origos by the Englishman Cecil Pinsent, who designed a number of other gardens in Tuscany, most of them in the environs of Florence (see pp 109–110). Here he added the outside staircase and enlarged the house, as well as designing the lovely gardens and farm outbuildings (water was piped here from a spring seven kilometres away). The numerous cypresses he planted (which also served as wind-breaks) are now suffering from disease and some have had to be felled. Beside the house are two ilexes, one of which is very old, pruned to an unusual shape. The orangery is a handsome building by Pinsent (1924).

From the first garden close to the house (1924/5) which has a low hedge of dwarf pomegranates, a little stone ramp leads up to the gardens outside the larger house, partly built in the 19C (it was given its 16C appearance by Pinsent who added the two upper floors and courtyard), where bay and box hedges feature. The lemon garden, towards the Orcia valley, was designed in 1933. A splendid old wisteria flourishes here. The paths are paved in travertine from Rapolano. A terrace looks down onto a third garden, dating from just before the war. Here the box hedges are planted in an interesting design around four magnolias, and the hedge of cypresses is kept low for the view of the valley, which includes the cypress avenue mentioned above, which zigzags up the hill opposite. Above the second garden is the rose garden, with mixed flowerbeds bordered with lavender, and an herbaceous border. From here steps, lined with cypresses, lead up to the top of the hill. A paved pergola (of vines and wisteria) leads along the side of the hill from the rose garden, past grassy slopes planted with fruit trees and banksia roses. The pergola ends at a large wood crossed by paths, one of which leads to the little cemetery, also designed by Pinsent, where Iris and her husband are buried.

In the middle of the Orcia valley, on a hill is the little well-preserved village of **Contignano**, with a fine castle tower. The church, which was remodelled in the 17C, has a 14C altarpiece of the *Coronation of the Virgin*. There is a splendid panorama embracing Monte Amiata, Radicofani, Monte Cetona and Pienza across the Val d'Orcia.

Radicofani

Due south, in a spectacular position on a basaltic hill (783m) which divides the Orcia and the Paglia valleys, and close to the border with Lazio, is Radicofani. Its pretty medieval streets are mostly built of grey basaltic stone. The remains of the **Rocca** dominate the hill. It is associated with the legendary Ghino di Tacco who imprisoned the Abbot of Cluny here, as related by Boccaccio in the *Decameron*. The Rocca was taken in 1469 and rebuilt by the Sienese but was later forced to surrender, together with other Sienese strongholds, to Cosimo de' Medici in 1559. New fortifications of impressive proportions were constructed by the Medici. The castle was devastated by an explosion in the 18C and partly restored in the 1930s; further consolidation has been carried out in recent years. There are plans to create a local archaeological museum in part of the castle. The position offers a fine view over the Orcia valley to the north and of Monte Amiata to the west.

In the central piazza is the Romanesque church of **San Pietro** above a flight of steps, with a tall campanile rising from the façade. The fine interior has cross vaults over the transept and an apse supported on transversal arches. There are several good della Robbia statues and reliefs, a *Madonna and Child* in polychrome wood by Francesco di Valdambrino and over the high altar, a glazed terracotta *Crucifixion with the Magdalen*, by Benedetto and Santi Buglioni. Nearby, in Via Roma, is the Gothic church of **Sant'Agata**, the patron saint of Radicofani. The church was rebuilt in the 18C and has a terracotta altarpiece of the *Madonna and Child with Saints* by Andrea della Robbia.

On a road which descends towards the Via Cassia is a fountain erected by Ferdinando I dei Medici in 1603 with figures of Justice and Abundance flanking the Medici arms. Opposite is **Palazzo La Posta**, a hunting lodge with arched porticoes on two levels, which was built for grand-duke Ferdinando and is attributed to Simone Genga and Bernardo Buontalenti (1584). It later became an inn at which Montaigne, Chateaubriand, and Dickens all stayed. It is now in a sadly neglected state.

Montepulciano and environs

Montepulciano, in a lovely position, is one of the most interesting small towns in Tuscany and it has particularly attractive surroundings with well preserved little villages, well worth visiting.

Practical information

Getting there
By car

Montepulciano is just 12km east of Pienza (see p 438), reached by the Via Cassia south of Siena, but it can also be reached by the A1 motorway from Florence ('Val di Chiana' exit).

By train

There is a branch line between Siena and Chiusi with stations at Sinalunga, Torrita di Siena and Montepulciano Scalo, 11km north of Montepulciano, but the quickest approach from Florence or Rome is on the main line to Chiusi station where there is a bus service (*LFI*) c every hour for Montepulciano.

By bus

From Siena *TRA-IN* **bus service** (except on Sundays) to Montepulciano. *TRA-IN* buses also run between Montepulciano and Pienza.

Information office
APT Chianciano Terme e Valdichiana (☎ 0578 631 67). Information offices in

Montepulciano, Via di Gracciano nel Corso 59 (☎ 0578 757 341); Torrita di Siena, Biblioteca Comunale (☎ 0577 685 452); Sinalunga, Piazza Garibaldi 5 (☎ 0577 630 364); and Trequanda, Biblioteca Comunale (☎ 0577 685 452).

Where to stay
Hotels

MONTEPULCIANO ☆☆☆ *Il Marzocco*, Piazza Savonarola 18 (☎ 0578 757 262; ▯ 9578 757 530). In the environs, 3km southeast of Montepulciano on the road to Chianciano: ☆☆☆ *Panoramic*, Via di Villa Bianca 8 (☎ 0578 798 398; ▯ 0578 799 205).

TORRITA DI SIENA ☆☆☆ *La Stazione*, Via Mazzini 255 (☎/▯ 0577 685 158); ☆☆ *Belvedere*, Via Traversa Valdichiana Ovest 31 (☎ 0577 686 442).

SINALUNGA ☆☆☆☆ *Locanda dell'Amorosa*, with luxury (€€€) restaurant, Località Amorosa, 2km south of Sinalunga (☎ 0577 679 497;

0577 632 00).

TREQUANDA ☆☆ *Casal Mustia*, Piazza della Pieve 3, ☎ 0577 665 310.

Eating out
Restaurants

MONTEPULCIANO €€€
La Grotta, Viale della Rimembranza; **€€** *Il Cantuccio*, Via delle Cantine112; *Il Covo di Obelisk*, Strada per Chianciano (near San Biagio); **€** *Trattoria Diva e Maceo*, Via di Gracciano del Corso; *Il Cittino*, Via di Voltaia.
MONTEFOLLONICO €€€
La Chiusa, Via della Madonnina 88; **€€** *Conte Matto*.
PETROIO € *Madonnino dei Monti*.
MONTISI €€ *La Grancia*, Via Umberto I 3.
SINALUNGA €€€ *Locanda dell'Amorosa* (see above).
Café

Cafè in Montepulciano: *Antico Caffè Poliziano*, 27 Via di Voltaia nel Corso, founded in 1868 and retaining its charming old-fashioned furnishings.

Festivals

In Montepulciano the *Bravio delle Botti* is held on the last Sunday of **August**. Two men from each of the eight districts of the town compete in rolling a barrel (*botte*) weighing 80 kilos uphill, from Piazza Marzocco to Piazza Grande. The prize is a painted banner, the *Bravio*, and the privilege of offering the candle to the patron saint of Montepulciano, St Agnese, on her feast day on **1 May**, when an annual fair is held.

Since 1959 a *Convegno Internazionale di Studi Umanistici* has usually been held here, devoted to the study of Poliziano's work, which ends with a concert of Renaissance music in Palazzo Tarugi.

During the last week of July and the first week of **August**, the *Cantiere Internazionale d'Arte* has a programme of classical and modern music, with performances of plays and dance, and art exhibitions. Throughout August there is a *Mostra Interregionale dell'Artigianato*, an exhibition of local handicrafts.

At **Torrita di Siena** the *Palio dei Somari* is held on the Sunday following 19 March, with a mule race, flag throwing and various festivities.

Montepulciano

Montepulciano is a dignified and interesting hilltop town (14,300 inhab.) commanding the southeast part of Tuscany near the Umbrian border. It is particularly well preserved and has many handsome 16C palaces, including some by Antonio da Sangallo il Vecchio who also built the Tempio di San Biagio here. The area is noted for its red wines, the most famous being the *Vino Nobile di Montepulciano*.

History

After changing hands several times between Siena and Florence, Montepulciano came under permanent Florentine rule in 1511, and its fortifications, including the Porta di Gracciano, were rebuilt by Cosimo I. It was the birthplace of Angelo Ambrogini (1454–94), the great Classical scholar, who adopted the town's late Latin name **Poliziano**. Perhaps the most original genius among writers of his period, he was also famous for his eloquence. Although reputedly extremely ugly, with an enormous nose, Lorenzo il Magnifico employed him as tutor for his sons at Cafaggiolo in the Mugello, see p 129. He is famous for his poems in the vernacular including

Stanze per la giostra del magnifico Giuliano di Piero dei Medici (1475–78) and the *Fabula di Orfeo*. Another distinguished native was Cardinal Roberto Bellarmino (1542–1621), a Jesuit, author of the *Catechism of Christian Doctrine*, and hated by British Protestants in James I's days. Riccardo Cervini (1501–55), also from Montepulciano, later became Pope Marcellus II.

Outside Porta al Prato stands the 14C church of **Sant'Agnese**, on the site of the convent built by the Dominican abbess, Agnese Segni (1268–1317). She was canonised as St Agnese of Montepulciano in 1726. The modern **façade** incorporates a 14C doorway. The stained-glass rose window, representing St Agnese, is by Bano di Michelangelo da Cortona.

The interior has a single nave. In the first chapel to the right is a fresco of the *Madonna* attributed to Simone Martini. A door opens into the Camera di Sant' Agnese, where relics of the saint are preserved. Flanking the main altar on which is a marble urn containing the body of St Agnese, surmounted by a statue by Mazzuoli, are a *Birth of the Virgin* by Raffaello Vanni and the *Martyrdom of San Biagio* by Giovanni da San Giovanni. In the chapel on the left is a 13C *Crucifix*. The **cloister**, which was begun in the early 14C but only completed in the 17C, has frescoed lunettes with stories from the *Life of St Agnese*, by Salvi Castellucci (1652).

Opposite the church is the **Poggiofanti Garden**, dominated by the ramparts built by Antonio da Sangallo il Vecchio, with a fine view over the Val di Chiana.

From the fine **Porta al Prato**, Via di Gracciano del Corso winds up past several 16C palaces including **Palazzo Avignonesi** (no. 91; right), with a rusticated ground floor. Opposite is the Colonna del Marzocco, bearing a copy of the original lion (1511), now in the museum, made in 1856 by Antonio Sarrocchi. On the left is the church of **San Bernardo**, designed by the Baroque architect Padre Andrea Pozzo. The luminous oval interior has a *Madonna in Adoration* over the altar attributed to Andrea della Robbia.

The corso continues past Palazzo Batignani (no. 85; right), Palazzo Tarugi (no. 84; left), and **Palazzo Cocconi** (no. 70), attributed to Antonio da Sangallo il Vecchio (the top floor was added in the 19C). **Palazzo Bucelli** (no. 73) has Etruscan urns, reliefs, and inscriptions embedded in the lower part of its façade. It housed the Etruscan collection of finds from excavations in the region, created by the 18C scholar and antiquarian Pietro Bucelli, which was donated to Grand-duke Pietro Leopoldo I and is now in the Archaeological Museum in Florence.

Above a flight of steps on the right is the church of **Sant'Agostino**. The fine *façade in Istrian stone, and the doorway, with a terracotta high relief of the *Madonna and Child with Saints John the Baptist and Augustine*, are by Michelozzo. The interior was redesigned in 1784–91 when the apse and transepts were shortened. On the south side: *Raising of Lazarus* by Alessandro Allori; *St Bernardine* signed and dated 1456 by Giovanni di Paolo; and *Pietà* attributed to Cristoforo Roncalli. On the high altar, polychrome wooden *Crucifix* by Antonio da Sangallo il Vecchio (painted by Antonio di Bastiano). Behind the altar a door leads into the choir of the earlier church, with frescoes and paintings by Bartolomeo Barbiani of Montepulciano, and a *Crucifix* attributed to Pollaiolo. On the north side, the *Crucifixion* is by Lorenzo di Credi; the altarpiece of the *Madonna della Cintola* has been attributed to Federico Barocci and the altarpiece of the *Ascension* is by Cesare Nebbia (1585).

Facing the church, in Piazza Michelozzo, is an old tower house with a quaint

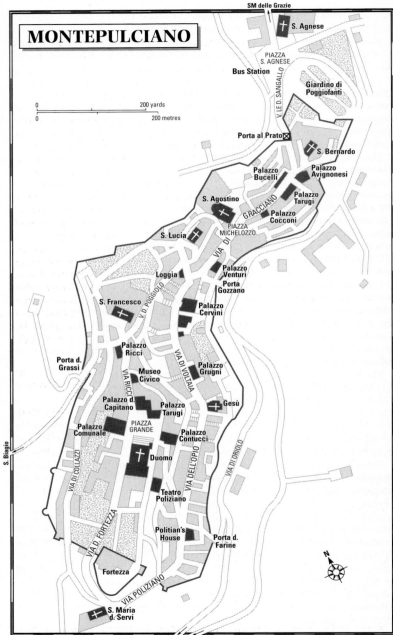

MONTEPULCIANO

SM delle Grazie

S. Agnese

PIAZZA
S. AGNESE

Bus Station

Giardino di
Poggiofanti

0 ___ 200 yards
0 ___ 200 metres

V. LE D. SANGALLO

Porta al Prato

S. Bernardo

Palazzo
Bucelli

Palazzo
Avignonesi

Palazzo
Tarugi

S. Agostino

GRACCIANO

Palazzo
Cocconi

PIAZZA
MICHELOZZO

S. Lucia

VIA DI

Palazzo
Venturi

Loggia

Porta
Gozzano

V. D. POGGIOLO

S. Francesco

Palazzo
Cervini

Palazzo
Ricci

Porta d.
Grassi

VIA DI VOLTAIA

Museo
Civico

Palazzo
Grugni

VIA RICCI

Palazzo d.
Capitano

Palazzo
Tarugi

Gesù

Palazzo
Comunale

PIAZZA
GRANDE

Palazzo
Contucci

VIA DELL'OPIO

VIA DI ORIOLO

Duomo

VIA DI COLLAZZI

Teatro
Poliziano

S. Biagio

Politian's
House

Porta d.
Farine

VIA D. FORTEZZA

Fortezza

VIA POLIZIANO

N

S. Maria
d. Servi

CHIANCIANO TERME (N146)

statue of Pulcinella on top which strikes the hours of the clock (the gift of a Neapolitan who settled in the city in the 17C).

The corso continues past **Palazzo Buratti-Bellarmino** (no. 28; left), with a 17C doorway and frescoes by Federico Zuccari in the vestibule. To the left, Borgo Buio leads to the Gothic **Porta di Gozzano**. Via di Gracciano begins to climb steeply uphill through the Arco della Cavina next to the former hospital of Santa Maria della Cavina, to reach Piazza delle Erbe, the market square. Here is the arched **Logge del Grano** (16C), with the Medici arms. Via di Voltaia continues left past the grandiose **Palazzo Cervini** (no. 21; left), begun for Marcellus II before his pontificate, perhaps by Antonio da Sangallo il Giovane, and **Palazzo Gagnoni-Grugni** (no. 55; left), with a balconied portal by Vignola. Farther on (left), next to the Jesuit College, is the church of the **Gesù**, with a Baroque interior by Andrea Pozzo and illusionistic paintings by his pupil Antonio Colli.

The corso now becomes Via dell'Opio, lined with more palaces, some of which still reveal their medieval origin. In Piazza dell'Opio, Via del Teatro leads right to Piazza Grande (see below) and Via della Farina leads left to **Porta delle Farine**, a typical example of a Sienese double gate. In Via Poliziano, the continuation of Via dell'Opio, is the 14C house (no. 5; plaque) where Poliziano was born.

Outside the town walls, at the end of Via Poliziano, is the church of **Santa Maria dei Servi**. The simple Gothic façade with an arched doorway and a rose window, dates from the 14C. The elegant Baroque interior is by Andrea Pozzo. On the north side (second altar) is a 15C fresco of the *Madonna della Santoreggia*, greatly venerated in the past, and (third altar) a *Madonna and Child* by the school of Duccio, inserted into a larger painting. The road, from which there is a beautiful view, then skirts the rebuilt **Fortezza** and re-enters the walls by Via della Fortezza to reach *Piazza Grande*, where there is a pretty well.

The Duomo

The Duomo in Piazza Grande was designed by Ippolito Scalza in 1592–1630. The façade, unlike the sides, is unfinished. The 14C campanile belonged to the earlier church of Santa Maria.

The interior has a Latin-cross plan with a nave and two aisles and a cupola over the crossing. Dismembered parts of the *tomb of Bartolomeo Aragazzi*, secretary to Pope Martin V, by Michelozzo (1427–36), are in various parts of the church. They include Aragazzi's effigy (right of the west door), two bas-reliefs on the first two nave pilasters, two statues, one on either side of the high altar, a statue in a niche of St Bartholomew on the right of the high altar, and the frieze of putti and festoons on the high altar (two kneeling angels from the same tomb are in the British Museum).

South aisle. First chapel, polychrome marble altar by Mazzuoli (1683); third chapel, two Sienese paintings with gold grounds of the *Redeemer* and the *Assumption*; fourth chapel, *Assumption* by Domenico Manetti and *St George* by Angelo Righi (1603). On the **high altar** is a *triptych by Taddeo di Bartolo of 1401, representing the *Assumption of the Virgin with Saints*, predella scenes and pinnacles. In the central nave, on the end piers, are two gilt-wood statues of the *Virgin Annunciate* and the angel *Gabriel* attributed to Francesco di Valdambrino. The marble tabernacle on the right pier of the choir is by Vecchietta.

North aisle. On the pilaster between the fifth and fourth chapels, modern copy of a *Madonna and Child* by Sano di Pietro (the original is in the museum);

in the **baptistery** there is a *font with six bas-reliefs on a base of three caryatid figures by Giovanni di Agostino, c 1340. On the wall, the so-called *Altare dei Gigli* (altar of the lilies), *with Saints Stephen, Bonaventura, Catherine, and Bernardine*, by Andrea della Robbia, enclose a bas-relief of the *Madonna and Child* attributed to Benedetto da Maiano. The statues of *Saints Peter and John the Baptist* in the side niches are attributed to Domenico di Agostino (c 1360).

The crenellated *Palazzo Comunale** is surmounted by an impressive clock tower. The building dates from the late 14C. The design of the façade, built in travertine with a rusticated ground floor, is now attributed to Michelozzo. There is a fine courtyard with a loggia on two sides and another on the upper floor. The **tower**, which recalls that of Palazzo Vecchio in Florence, is worth climbing to enjoy the view which stretches from Monte Amiata to Siena, and east to Lake Trasimene.

On the corner of Via Ricci is **Palazzo del Capitano del Popolo**, a Gothic palace considerably rebuilt (with fine Gothic arches on Via Ricci), and a bell-cote

Well in front of Palazzo del Capitano del Popolo, Montepulciano

on the roof. In front is the elegant ***Pozzo de' Griffi e de' Leoni** attributed to Antonio da Sangallo il Vecchio. The well is framed by an architrave resting on two columns, with the Medici arms, flanked by the lions of Florence and the griffins of Montepulciano. Next to it is the flank of ***Palazzo Tarugi**, with a triple arched arcade on the ground floor which continues round in the two left bays of the main front, facing the cathedral. The grandiose travertine façade, which is also attributed to Antonio da Sangallo il Vecchio, has Ionic half- columns on high pedestals supporting a balustrade above the pedimented windows of the main floor.

Opposite Palazzo Comunale is **Palazzo Contucci** which was begun for Cardinal Antonio Del Monte (his arms are on the corner) by Antonio da Sangallo il Vecchio. The fine stone façade has five windows on the piano nobile with pediments supported on Ionic columns; the top floor in brick was added later. Inside is an elegant courtyard, and the salone on the first floor is painted with trompe l'oeil frescoes by Andrea Pozzo (1705). The back of the palace rests on the old town walls: the gradient of the site on which the town is built can be appreciated here. The vast cellar extending beneath the piazza may be visited. To the right of Palazzo Contucci, Via del Teatro leads steeply down and then bends to the right past the **Teatro Poliziano**, built by Giacomo and Sebastiano Barchi and decorated by Giuseppe Castagnoli. It was inaugurated in 1796 by Ferdinando III. The interior is composed of four tiers of boxes.

Museo Civico and Pinacoteca

From Piazza Grande, opposite the Duomo, Via Ricci descends past the 12C–13C **Palazzo Sisti**. Opposite on the left is **Palazzo Ricci**, with a simple 16C façade; the back has a loggia and garden with a fine view overlooking San Biagio. On the right is **Palazzo Neri-Orselli** (no. 15), another Gothic palace, modified in later centuries, which houses the **Museo Civico e Pinacoteca Crociani** (reopened in 2000).

On the **ground floor (Room 1)** is the well displayed **archaeological section** with interesting Etruscan finds from the district, Bucchero ware of the 6C BC, black- and red-figure vases, bronzes, and the Bucelli collection of Etruscan urns. Stairs lead down to the **basement** past the Cocconi coat-of-arms and the original lion (1511) from the Colonna del Marzocco. In **room 2** a case displays the 14C–16C majolica found in the well here. The 16C bust in scagliola represents Marcellus II. **Room 3** has a display of epigraphs, including one dated 1277, and in **room 4** are architectural fragments, and a case of 17C silver, with the mask of St Agnese. On the stairs up to the **first floor** are displayed 19C works including a painting of the *Madonna* by Antonio Ciseri, a historical canvas by Tommaso Gazzarrini, and a portrait by Vincenzo Luchini of the tenor *Moriani* in *Lucia di Lammermoor*. **Room 5** (right) displays the earliest paintings: the 14C works include *St Francis* by Margaritone di Arezzo; *Madonna and Child with two angels* attributed to the Maestro di Badia a Isola; a charming little wood coffer; a *Coronation of the Virgin* by Jacopo di Mino del Pellicciaio; and a *Crucifixion* by Luca di Tommè. The little *Madonna and Child* by Sano di Pietro comes from the Duomo. The 15C and 16C works include a wood *Crucifix* from the church of Santa Chiara; *Nativity* attributed to Benvenuto di Giovanni, *Crucifixion* by the workshop of Filippino Lippi; tondo by the *bottega* of Raffaellino del Garbo; *Holy Family* by Sodoma; and an *Immaculate Conception* by Giovanni Antonio Lappoli (1545). Two 14C antiphonals are also displayed here. At the end, **Room 6** has a fine display of della Robbian works including two altarpieces by Andrea della Robbia: one with *God the Father and angels* surrounding a niche with a *Nativity and Adoration of the Magi* in the predella; and the other with the *Madonna and Child between Saints Bartholomew and Longinus and two angels holding a crown*. There are also figures of the *Virgin Annunciate* and angel *Gabriel*, and of *St John the Baptist*.

On the stairs is a painting of *Sant'Agnese* holding a model of Montepulciano. On the **second floor** one large hall with wood rafters displays a large collection of 16C–18C paintings, arranged by subject matter: **section 7** displays mythological and religious scenes including *Venus and Cupid* by Antonio Domenico Gabbiani, *Holy Family* by Rutilio Manetti, and works by lo Spadarino, Pier Dandini, Francesco Curradi, and Jacopo Vignali. The next section (**8**) has portraits including *Beata Caterina de' Ricci* by Giovanni Battista Naldini, a *Portrait of a lady* by Agostino Carracci, and works by Sustermans, François Xavier Fabre, and Santi di Tito. Dutch and Italian landscapes are displayed in **section 9**, including two 18C views of Arezzo Cathedral. The last section (**10**) exhibits still lifes and genre scenes mostly by painters from Naples and the Netherlands but also a beautiful *Still Life with musical instruments* by Cristoforo Munari (1712), an artist from Reggio Emilia.

We now return downstairs to the first floor where the last **room 11** has numerous small paintings, mostly 17C, from the Crociani collection, some by Flemish artists, and many in attractive frames.

Farther down Via Ricci, on the left, is the Baroque façade of the **Oratorio dei Cavalieri di Santo Stefano** and **Palazzo Benincasa**, with a bust of Gian Gastone de' Medici over the doorway. Beyond the Porta San Francesco (from which a street leads through the Porta dei Grassi down to San Biagio, see below) is a piazza with a fine view. Here, in the oldest part of the town, is the church of **San Francesco** which dates from the 13C. Next to the elegant Gothic doorway are the remains of a pulpit from which St Bernardine of Siena is reputed to have preached. The interior has been heavily restored. Via del Poggiolo passes the Piazzetta degli Archi and leads to the church of **Santa Lucia**, built in 1633, which has an elegant façade. On the high altar is a *Crucifix* by Giovanni Battista Alessi of Montepulciano. In the first chapel (right) is a fine, but damaged *Madonna* (c 1495) by Luca Signorelli (locked; light switch behind the grille, operated by a rod).

On the northern outskirts of the town, beyond Sant'Agnese (see above), Viale Calamandrei leads to the sanctuary of **Santa Maria delle Grazie**, designed by Ippolito Scalza, with a porticoed façade (1605). The interior was decorated with elegant stuccowork in the mid-18C by Andrea da Cremona. **South side**. *Madonna and Child with Saints* by Niccolò Betti, and (second altar) della Robbian *tabernacle, framing the *Madonna delle Grazie*, and two Annunciation figures attributed to Giovanni della Robbia. In the choir is a *Madonna and Child with St Simon Stock* by Giovan Battista Ferretti (1766). **North side**. *St Helen adoring the Cross* by Bartolomeo Barbiani of Montepulciano (1632), a German *Crucifix* (16C), with papier-mâché statues of the *Virgin* and *St John* (1740), and a *Madonna with Carmelite Saints* by Giuseppe Nicola Nasini. The late 16C organ is the only example of its kind in Italy (there is a comparable one at Innsbruck). Its pipes are of cypress wood and produce a particularly soft and gentle sound, which was recommended by Monteverdi for the accompaniment of his *Orfeo*. Since the organ's restoration in 1983, it has been played by organists from all over the world.

From Piazzale Sant'Agnese, Via Bernabei leads to Piazza del Mercato and the 16C Villa La Fantina (unfinished). About three kilometres from the centre of the town is the **Santuario della Madonna della Quercia**, built in the 18C round an earlier chapel. On the façade are two statuettes of the *Annunciation* by Giovanni della Robbia and, inside, an interesting collection of ex-votos.

Tempio di San Biagio

Just outside Montepulciano, off the road to Pienza, and approached by a beautiful cypress avenue, is the *Tempio di San Biagio (open 09.00–13.00, 15.00–19.00), one of the great church buildings of the High Renaissance. It was built by Antonio da Sangallo il Vecchio (1518–34) for the Ricci family on the site of an earlier church, also dedicated to St Biagio. It has a Greek-cross plan with a central dome. The exterior of travertine is of classical sobriety, and the beautifully proportioned design of the façade is repeated on the two sides. Only one of the towers was finished, and actually completed in 1545 by Baccio d'Agnolo, who also built the lantern of the dome.

The interior, which is also very beautiful, repeats and elaborates the classical features of the exterior, with sculptural decoration carved in high relief in the yellow sandstone. The marble high altar is by Giannozzo and Lisandro di Pietro Albertini (1584). The statues of *Saints John the Baptist, Agnes, Catherine of*

Tempio di San Biagio, Montepulciano

Siena, and *George*, are by Ottaviano Lazzari (1617). The venerated 14C fresco in the tabernacle represents the *Madonna and Child with St Francis*. The lunette fresco is by Antonio Righi (1648), and those in the vault are attributed to Bartolomeo Barbiani. The stained-glass window is by Bano di Michelangelo of Cortona (1568). Behind, in the area corresponding to the apse, is the sacristy, from which a staircase leads to the outside balcony. The canons' house, nearby, with open loggias on both floors, was built after Sangallo's death.

The environs of Montepulciano

Torrita di Siena

To the north of Montepulciano is the lovely little red-brick village of Torrita di Siena which was an important stronghold of the Sienese Republic until it became part of the Medici grand-duchy of Tuscany in 1554. It preserves parts of its walls and is a particularly well-kept village. It is thought to have been the birthplace of the 13C painter and mosaicist Fra Jacopo da Torrita (or Jacopo Torriti), and of Ghino di Tacco.

In the piazza, with a well, is **Palazzo Comunale** (13C; restored), with a bell-tower. Inside is the restored Teatro degli Oscuri (1824). Next to it is the Romanesque church of **Santa Flora e Lucilla**. In the pleasant brick interior, on the south side (light on the right) is an exquisite small *lunette of the *Blood of the Redeemer* carved **by Donatello** (owned by the Spedale Maestri outside Porta Nuova). Donatello's typical *schiacciato* technique is here used to portray the figure of Christ surrounded by eleven cherubim in the clouds and the busts of the two donors in a very small space. The church also has some fresco fragments and interesting paintings: on the south altar, triptych with the *Crucifixion and Saints* attributed to Michele di Matteo (1444). In the sanctuary, *Madonna in Glory with six Saints* by the school of Sodoma; north side, *Annunciation* (1592) by Francesco Vanni; (on the altar), triptych with the *Nativity and Saints Anthony Abbot and Augustine*, a charming work by Bartolo di Fredi; *Madonna and Saints, with the Trinity* in the lunette above by Benvenuto di Giovanni.

Just beyond the piazza is the church of **Santa Croce** (1642), with a Baroque interior and stucco statuary on the high altar. Outside Porta a Sole (reached along the side of Palazzo Comunale) is the **Madonna delle Nevi** (kept locked) a little brick chapel erected in 1525. It is preceded by a portico with two Ionic columns, and has a cast of Donatello's lunette depicting the *Blood of the Redeemer* (see above) over the portal. The altar wall has fine *frescoes attributed to Girolamo di Benvenuto. Outside Torrita, on the Sinalunga road (see below) is the 16C **Villa La Fratta**, attributed to Baldassarre Peruzzi, with a fine garden (admission sometimes on request).

Montefollonico

To the south of Torrita di Siena is Montefollonico, a quiet little fortified village with small houses, Sienese in atmosphere. It stands on a ridge (567m) between the Orcia and Chiana valleys. Probably of Roman origin, the village developed in the Middle Ages. Parts of its medieval walls with three gates remain, including the **Porta Nuova**, a 14C–15C double gate which provides the entrance to the delightful hamlet which has numerous doves and pigeons. The lovely old paving of the main street was destroyed in 1997.

The street leads left past the little 13C **Palazzo del Comune**, with a well-head next to it, to the 13C church of **San Leonardo** (if closed, ring at no. 38, by the east end). The pretty exterior is built of square blocks of local yellow-and-white stone, and is approached by steps on either side of outcrops of rock. The restored interior has a Baroque high altar. In a chapel to the left is a 13C wooden *Crucifix* between two paintings of the *Annunciation* in stone frames. In the nave are very worn frescoes and paintings of the *Birth of the Virgin* and a *Circumcision* (in a good frame). A *Madonna and two Saints* by Guidoccio Cozzarelli which belongs to the church and is now exhibited in the Museo Diocesano in Pienza, has been replaced by a copy.

In the other direction the street leads past the entrance to the little **Chiesa della Compagnia del Corpus Domini** (adm. as for San Leonardo), preceded by a tiny courtyard with the bell-tower at one corner. Inside is a *Deposition* by the school of Signorelli, and interesting 18C frescoed lunettes with amusing details.

The street leads on past (right) the church of **San Bartolomeo**, privately owned and recently restored (usually open in summer). High up on the façade there is a Romanesque sculpture of a mermaid. **Porta del Triano**, bearing the date 1278, frames a view of Montepulciano on the skyline. Outside the gate is a fine stretch of walls. A footpath continues down to the handsome **Chiesa del Triano** built on rocks in a group of horse-chestnut trees, with a lovely view of Monte Amiata. Its architectural features in brick and stone stand out against the white *intonaco*. It has a pretty domed bell-tower. The date 1609 is above the door. The interior has an attractive crossing with an unusual altar screen. The works of art which belong to the church are now exhibited in the Museo Diocesano in Pienza.

Sinalunga

Sinalunga is now a small industrial town. From the 12C up until 1864 it was known as *Asinalunga*. Here the Sienese defeated the English mercenaries of Niccolò da Montefeltro in 1363; here also Garibaldi was arrested in 1867 by Vittorio Emanuele II, to prevent an ill-timed descent on Rome.

In the ugly Piazza Garibaldi is the **collegiata** (San Martino). The interior has large white stucco statues of saints. On the south side, the third chapel contains a 16C *Crucifix*. In the south transept is a *Deposition* by Francesco Vanni (1563–1610), with a predella (in a good frame). On the south wall of the sanctuary, *Madonna and Saints* by Benvenuto di Giovanni (1509) with another good predella and frame. On the north wall of the sanctuary a tondo by Pseudo Pier Francesco Fiorentino has been removed. In the north transept, *Madonna and the standing Child* by Sodoma above *Christ supported by two angels flanked by Saints Bernardine and Catherine*.

To the right of the church is **Santa Croce** with an 18C façade. In the pretty interior is (right altar) a *Marriage of the Virgin* by the school of Luca Signorelli. Also in the piazza is the church of **Santa Maria delle Nevi** with a painting attributed to Benvenuto di Giovanni. On the right of the façade of the Collegiata Via Mazzini winds round to **Palazzo Pretorio**, in an unusual site, between two streets. It is built in brick, decorated with coats of arms and a tower. In front of the palace, a road continues down to **Santa Lucia** (deconsecrated; used by a musical society), which contains a fresco attributed to Benvenuto di Giovanni. Beyond is a view over the Valdichiana. Near Palazzo Pretorio is a **theatre** (1797–1807), with an inconspicuous exterior (no. 17). It is named after Ciro Pinsuti (1824–88), born in Sinalunga.

Outside the town is the Franciscan convent of **San Bernardino** (or the **Madonna del Riposo**; yellow signposts), approached by a short avenue. Off the 18C church (shown by a nun) is an octagonal chapel with some fine paintings: *Baptism of Christ* by Guidoccio Cozzarelli (1470); *Annunciation* by Benvenuto di Giovanni(1470); *Madonna and Child with Saints* by Guidoccio Cozzarelli (1486). A *Madonna and Child* by Sano di Pietro, stolen in 1971, is to be replaced by a copy. Over the high altar is a copy (the original has been removed for safe-keeping) of a *Madonna and Child* known as the *Madonna del Rifugio*, also attributed to Sano di Pietro.

Trequanda is a medieval village which was once under the dominion of Siena (car park below the fine round tower of the restored Castello dei Cacciaconti). The parish church of **Santi Pietro e Andrea** has a delightful façade chequered in brown-and-white stone. The interior contains frescoes by Sodoma and Bartolomeo Miranda and a triptych of the *Madonna and Saints* by Giovanni di Paolo over the high altar. Also here is the fine gilded wood sculptured coffer of Beata Bonizella (1235–1300). The seated wooden statue of the *Madonna and Child* is attributed to Jacopo Sansovino. The **Palazzo del Comune** has a tower reminiscent of a toy castle.

A lovely road leads south towards Pienza through the beautiful **Valdichiana Senese**, with wooded hills (ilexes and oaks) and cultivated fields past a number of interesting and well preserved small villages.

Montisi is a picturesque village south of Trequanda on a hill (413m). The **castle** preserves some Gothic windows. At the top of the hill, beside a clock tower, is the Romanesque church of the **Annunziata** (key with the caretaker at no. 11). The elegant interior has transversal arches supported on travertine columns. In the sanctuary is a large *polyptych of the Madonna and Child with Saints Peter, Louis, James and Paul*, signed and dated 1496 by Neroccio di Bartolomeo Landi in a fine frame. The predella is in the Museo Diocesano in Pienza. In the north transept chapel is a painted *Crucifix* attributed to Ugolino di Nerio. Among the numerous medieval buildings is a **granary** (at the entrance to the village) which belonged to the hospital of Santa Maria della Scala in Siena. San Giovanni d'Asso, a short way to the west, is described in p 435.

Further south, the village of **Castelmuzio** can be seen from the approach road. There are some lovely old olive trees in the vicinity. Of Etruscan and Roman foundations, and first mentioned in the 9C, it has simple brick and sandstone houses. It is built on a circular plan, so that all the streets are curving. In the piazza is a very unusual *casa-torre*, reconstructed in the 18C as **Palazzo Fratini**, restored. Also here is the **Museo della Confraternita della Santa Trinità e di San Bernardino** (opened on request locally). Next to a hostel for pilgrims on the Via Francigena, the Confraternity of Santa Trinità was founded in 1450. The collection contains a *Madonna and Child* by the school of Duccio; *St Bernardine*, by his friend Giovanni di Paolo; and a *Madonna and Saints*, attributed to Matteo di Giovanni or Pietro di Francesco Orioli. In the sacristy and a room on the upper floor is a charming little collection of Crosses, copes, chalices, musical instruments from the local band founded after the First World War (and disbanded in 1950), Etruscan urns and ceramics.

Outside the village (well signposted) is the **Pieve di Santo Stefano in Cennano**, founded in 1285 on the site of a Roman building. It stands in a group of olive trees beside a farmhouse, and the key is left in the side door. The impressive large church shows the influence of Lombard architecture, with a fine triple apse at the east end. The west door has an arch carved with animals and human heads. In the interior, which is awaiting restoration, the columns reach up to the roof. It was poorly restored in the 19C.

A beautiful road, with wide views of Radicofani, Montepulciano, Pienza, and Monte Amiata, leads east past fields and olive groves to **Petroio**. The medieval village is built on an interesting circular plan; a road forms a spiral, leading up to the tower of the impressive 13C brick castle, high above its clustered houses. The parish church of **San Pietro** has a large, but damaged, fresco of the *Crucifixion*, attributed to Andrea di Niccolò, in the choir. A beautiful fragment of a *Madonna and Child* by Taddeo di Bartolo also belongs to the church. **San Giorgio**, an older church, is in need of restoration. Petroio was the birthplace of a famous ascetic, Bartolomeo Carosi, known as Brandano (1483–1554), whose mottoes and prophesies have been handed down to this day.

The locality has been known since the 18C for its production of ceramic vases and pots, using the local ochre-coloured calcareous rock, and there is still a large terracotta works in the woods on the outskirts. To the north of Petroio (on the road to Sinalunga) is the **Abbadia a Sicille**, a 17C fortified farm on the site of a hospice for pilgrims, founded by the Knights Templar in the 11C. The church was built in 1263. The buildings were radically restored in the 19C.

Sant'Anna in Camprena

South of Castelmuzio is the large ex-Olivetan monastery of Sant'Anna in Camprena (accommodation available from Easter to September; information from the Curia at Montepulciano). Approached by a long cypress avenue, the monastery is beautifully situated on a peaceful hill which dominates the surrounding countryside (with views of picturesque farms and the little towns of Castelmuzio and Petroio). It was founded by Bernardo Tolomei in 1324, rebuilt in the 15C, and enlarged in the 17C. However, the monastery was abandoned at the end of the 18C. It is now being slowly restored, and can be visited (ring for the caretaker 09.00–12.00, 15.00–18.00).

The **refectory** has very well preserved *frescoes by Sodoma, his earliest works painted in 1503–05, at the age of 25. The splendid colours are extraordinarily vivid, and the landscapes and use of perspective, as well as the expressive figure studies, show remarkable ability. On the entrance wall: *Bishop Guido Tarlati approves the Rule of the Olivetan order*; the *Deposition* (a moving scene which includes the figures of St Anna and St Joachim); and *St Anna with the Virgin and Child and two Olivetan monks*. On the opposite wall: *Multiplication of the Loaves and Fishes*, divided into three scenes against a background in which the landscape incorporates the Colosseum and the arch of Constantine. The two long walls (the lower parts of which were formerly covered by the refectory benches), have two frescoed friezes (partially preserved) with roundels of *Saints Gregory, Catherine, and Bernardine*, alternating with monochrome scenes of the lives of St Anna and the Virgin, and grotesques.

Nearby is the splendid old **kitchen** and a charming **walled garden** with a pond. From the 16C **cloister** (which has been partially walled in) is an entrance to the **church** which was built in the 17C and provided with large paintings of the life of Bernardo Tolomei in the 18C.

Near the monastery, an unsurfaced road (signposted Siena) leads to the Cassia through superb countryside past little hamlets and *calanchi*, with exceptionally beautiful views.

Pienza, a few kilometres to the south, is described in p 438.

Chiusi and Chianciano Terme

Chiusi, on the south-eastern border of Tuscany close to Umbria, is well-known for its interesting Etruscan museum and painted Etruscan tombs. Nearby is the famous spa town of Chianciano Terme. Sarteano, with an archaeological museum, and Cetona, a picturesque place, are both villages worth a visit in the district to the south.

Practical information

Getting there
By car

Chiusi is very close to the A1 motorway from Florence and Rome, and Chianciano Terme is about 12km west of Chiusi. **Car parking** in Chiusi off Via Pietriccia and Via dei Longobardi.

By train

Railway station Chiusi-Chianciano Terme, 3km south of Chiusi on the main Florence–Rome line (mostly slow trains only, although a few of the faster trains also stop here).

By bus

Buses every half hour from Chiusi to the railway station. Bus services from Chiusi to Lago di Chiusi, and to Montepulciano via Chianciano Terme.

Information offices

APT Chianciano Terme-Valdichiana, Piazza Italia 67, Chianciano Terme (☎ 0578 631 67). The spa centre, Terme di Chianciano S.p.A., is at Via delle Rose 12 (☎ 0578 681 11). In Chiusi, **tourist office** in Piazza Duomo (☎ 0578 227 667). Sarteano: *Pro-Loco* information office, Corso Garibaldi 1 (☎ 0578 265 312). Cetona: *Pro-Loco* information office, Piazza Garibaldi (☎ 0578 239 143).

 Where to stay
Hotels

QUERCE AL PINO near Chiusi (4km west): ☆☆☆ *Il Patriarca* (☎ 0578 274 407; 📠 0578 274 594); *Ismaele* (☎ 0578 274 077; 📠 0578 274 069); *Rosati* (☎ 0578 274 408; 📠 0578 274 199).

CHIANCIANO TERME over 200 hotels of all categories.

SARTEANO ☆☆☆ *Residenza Santa Chiara*, with restaurant, Piazza Santa Chiara 30 (☎ 0578 265 412).

CETONA ☆☆☆ *Belverde*, just outside the town (☎ 0578 239 085; 📠 0578 239 084).

SAN CASCIANO BAGNI ☆☆☆ *Termina* (☎ 0578 581 35) and ☆☆ hotels.

Agriturist accommodation

Near SARTEANO *Montemelino*, Via di Chianciano 106 (☎ 0578 265 480). Near CETONA *Podere Verdino*, on the SS 321 Sud road (☎/📠 0578 238 777); *Caio Alto*, also on the SS 321 road (☎/📠 0578 226 666); *Fonterucola*, Via Fonterucola (☎ 0578 238 345).

Campsites

SARTEANO ☆☆☆☆ *Campeggio delle Piscine*, with hot sulphur swimming pool (☎ 0578 265 531; 📠 0578 265 889).

Two ☆ sites near **Lago di Chiusi**: *La Fattoria* (☎ 0578 214 07; 📠 0578 206 44) and *Pesce d'Oro* (☎ 0578 214 03).

 Eating out
Restaurants

CHIUSI € *La Solita Zuppa*, Via Porsenna 21.

SARTEANO €€€ *Santa Chiara* in the *Hotel Residenza Santa Chiara*; €€ *La Giara*, Viale Europa 2; € *Trattoria Tripolitania*, Via Garibaldi.

CETONA €€€ *La Frateria di Padre Eligio*, Via S.Francesco 2; €€ *Osteria Vecchia*, *Sobborgo*, Via Sobborgo 6/8 and *Osteria Vecchia*, Via Cherubini 11. € *Da Sacchetta*, Via del Polacco (pizzeria, just outside the centre). The *Podere Pornelleto*, Traversa Cassia Aurelia 8, an agriturist farm also has a restaurant.

Chiusi

Chiusi is a little hill-top town of 8700 inhabitants. It was an Etruscan town of great importance, as can be seen from the finds in its interesting museum, and the vast Etruscan necropolis which surrounds the town. Under the streets runs a labyrinth of Etruscan galleries.

History

Chiusi was the Etruscan Clevsins. One of the twelve cities of the Etruscan Confederation, it reached its greatest splendour around the 7C or 6C BC. The Latin authors often referred to the fertility of the surrounding countryside, which produced oil, wine, and wheat in abundance. Strabo described how the Lago di Chiusi could be reached by river from Rome up the Tiber and Chiana. Lars Porsena, the legendary Lucumo or king of Chiusi, attacked Rome in

507–06 BC, but after 296 BC the town became subject to Rome and took the Roman name of Clusium. It continued to flourish in the Augustan era, and was then occupied by the Goths from 540 probably up until the 10C, when it became part of the Lombard duchy. The unhealthy marshes of the Valdichiana caused malaria and brought about the decline of Chiusi, but the drainage works begun by Cosimo de' Medici restored some degree of prosperity.

The Duomo

The Duomo (San Secondiano) is in a pleasant little piazza with good paving and a loggia, beside a tall fortified tower (see below). It was founded in the 6C and the interior retains its basilican plan from that time. It was restored in 1887–94 when the porch was reconstructed and the nave and apses were carefully painted by Arturo Viligiardi in 1887 in imitation of antique mosaics. The splendid ★columns and capitals, including one in breccia marble at the west end, come from various local Roman edifices. Fragments of the old polychrome pavement dating from the 5C are preserved around the high altar. In the south aisle is an alabaster font, and in the north aisle an *Adoration of the Child* by Bernardino Fungai, and a monument to San Mustiola (1785).

Under the portico to the right of the façade is the **Museo della Cattedrale**, founded in 1932. It is well-arranged and labelled (open daily 1 June–15 Oct, 09.30–12.45, 16.30–19.30; winter 09.30–12.45).

Room I contains Roman finds from the Duomo including part of the mosaic floor, and a fragment of a huge sarcophagus with a high relief of a battle scene. The tombstones and inscriptions were found in the local catacombs of Santa Mustiola and Santa Caterina. At the top of the stairs there is a room with cases of church silver, vestments, and 15C ivories by the school of Baldassare degli Embriachi (based in Venice). Stairs continue up to a long passage above the portico with a fine display of **21 antiphonals** from the abbey of Monte Oliveto Maggiore dating from the second half of the 15C, illuminated by Liberale da Verona, Sano di Pietro, and others. The four rooms beyond display paintings and sculpture including: a remarkable late 14C polychrome wood figure of Christ (probably part of a Deposition group); a 14C Sienese Cross; a reliquary Cross dated 1436; and a tiny *Madonna and Child* by Sano di Pietro (in a silver frame dating from the 18C–19C). The *Madonna and Child with Saints* (very ruined) is by Girolamo di Benvenuto. The other rooms have 16C–18C works and an embroidered French cope (18C).

From the garden is the entrance to a remarkably long **Etruscan gallery**, known as the *Labirinto di Porsenna*, which may have served as a water channel, or as part of a defence system. Opened to the public in 1995 after 17 years of restoration work by local volunteers, it can be seen by appointment at the ticket office. The iron staircase in the garden provides a view of three lines of fortification, dating from the Etruscan (3C BC), Roman and medieval periods. The gallery is very narrow and low, and side galleries can also be seen, as it winds its way beneath the piazza and Duomo to emerge in a huge **cistern** with a remarkable double vault and central pilaster, dating from the end of the 2C BC or early 1C BC. Beside it is a tall fortified **tower** dating from the 12C, which was transformed into a campanile for the Duomo in 1585. It can be climbed up modern stairs and the view on a clear day takes in the rock of Orvieto, as well as the lakes of Trasimeno, Chiusi and Montepulciano, and Monte Amiata.

The **Catacombs of Santa Caterina**, near the station, can be seen on a guided tour, daily at 11.00, on request at the Museo della Cattedrale (a custodian accompanies visitors in their car). They date from the mid-3C AD and have been illuminated. The **Catacombs of Santa Mustiola**, dedicated to the Roman saint, beneath a farm house, and in use from the 3C to the 5C can also be visited (as for Santa Caterina).

The Etruscan Museum

The *Museo Nazionale Etrusco, opposite the side of the Duomo, was founded in 1871 and opened in this fitting neo-Classical building by Giuseppe Partini in 1901 (open daily 09.00–14.00; fest. 09.00–13.00; in summer usually 09.00–20.00 on weekdays, and fest. 09.00–13.00). It is one of the most important Etruscan museums in Italy, and there are plans to rearrange the ground floor. Chiusi was one of the first Etruscan cities to be explored, as early as the 15C, but unsystematic excavations, especially in the 19C, led to the dispersal of much of the material, and most of the objects in the museum are of unknown provenence; some have been poorly or incorrectly restored. A great number of inscriptions were found in and near Chiusi, but they are now in other museums.

In the **atrium** are six Roman statues from the funerary monument of the gens Allia. The **ground floor** illustrates the history of archaeological research in the area (right corridor), and (in the central hall) the chronological development of local products. The extremely fine prehistoric and Villanovian material includes finds dating from the 9C–8C BC, and canopic vases of the 7C–6C BC. In the central area are displayed beautiful Archaic reliefs (late 6C BC), showing Greek influence, and five sculptures of the 6C–5C BC. At the end of the hall are cases of Bucchero ware and 5C Attic black-figure and red-figure vases, terracotta architectural fragments, and 5C–4C bronzes. Another section has Etruscan vases and sarcophagi and cinerary urns (4C–2C BC) in alabaster and terracotta. The Roman material includes a head of Augustus, architectural and votive terracottas (3C–2C BC) and Hellenistic bronzes, ceramics and sarcophagi. In the **basement**, opened in 1992, the material is arranged topographically from excavations since 1930 in the centre of the city, in the necropoli on the outskirts, and in the sites discovered in the vicinity. The earliest finds date from the late Bronze Age. The remarkable alabaster tomb of Lars Sentinates is also displayed here.

The narrow Via della Misericordia leads past the 13C church of **Santa Maria della Morte**, with an unusually-shaped tower, to Piazza XX Settembre, with a clock tower and 14C loggia (altered), the town hall (enlarged in the 19C) and a 19C fountain. At the bottom of Via Lavinia, Porta Lavinia can be seen, with the countryside beyond. Near the clock tower is the church of **San Francesco**, founded in the 13C, with an ancient portal. The interior dates from the 18C; the stained glass windows at the east end were made in 1944 in Florence. Late 15C and early 16C frescoes were discovered and restored in 1998 on the north and south walls. On the left of the façade the attractively paved Via Paolozzi leads to Piazza Vittorio Veneto, with a view over unspoilt countryside. In the pretty little garden are Etruscan and Roman fragments. At the left end Via Arunte descends to a column of 1581 in Piazza Graziani, and then Via Porsenna continues up past several handsome 15C and 16C palaces back to Piazza Duomo.

On the outskirts of the town, in Via della Violella, off the Chianciano Terme road, part of the Etruscan walls of the city can be seen.

Etruscan tombs

At present just three of the many Etruscan tombs in the countryside around the town, a few kilometres outside the centre, can be visited. The Tomba della Pellegrina and Tomba del Leone can be visited during the opening hours of the Museo Nazionale Etrusco (and with the same ticket) by appointment (☎ 0578 201 77). The Tomba della Scimmia is only open on Tues, Thur, and Sat 11.00–12.00 and 16.00–17.00. The three tombs are close together approached along the same road, and a custodian accompanies you in your car (or you follow him in his car). The **Tomba della Pellegrina** dates from the early 3C BC and still contains a number of urns and sarcophagi. The **Tomba del Leone** first built in the early 5C BC was in use up until the 1C BC, the date in which the painted vaults were executed, in imitation of wood coffered ceilings. Between these two tombs is the **Tomba della Scimmia**, the most interesting tomb in Chiusi which preserves its wall-paintings. It was discovered in 1846 by Alessandro François and dates from 480–470 BC. It takes its name from an ape depicted on one of the walls.

All the other tombs in the neighbourhood have been closed indefinitely for conservation reasons.

To the north of Chiusi are two small picturesque lakes, with reedy shores, the **Lago di Chiusi** (387 hectares) and the **Lago di Montepulciano** (188 hectares), surrounded by cultivated fields and poplars. They are remnants of the huge marsh which once occupied this area. The interesting vegetation includes numerous varieties of aquatic plants, including water lilies. On the shores of Lago di Montepulciano is the Museo Naturalistico del Lago, a small museum illustrating the flora and fauna of the area (the lake can be visited by appointment, ☎ 0578 767 518). The lake is frequented by local fisherman.

Città della Pieve, south of Chiusi and Lago Trasimeno to the east of Chiusi, are described in *Blue Guide Umbria*.

Chianciano Terme

Chianciano Terme is one of the most important spa towns in Italy (6800 inhab.). It has warm saline and chalybeate waters. With over 200 hotels of all categories, it is well-equipped to receive its numerous visitors. The **Acqua Santa** (open all year round; high season June–Sept) waters are taken internally for liver complaints. The **Sillene** spring is used for baths.

The place was known to the Romans as *Fontes Clusinae*. In the Middle Ages it was contested between Siena and Orvieto. The spa developed in 1915–29, and most of the thermal buildings were rebuilt in the 1950s.

The pleasant old village of **Chianciano Vecchia** adjoins the spa. The town hall is in the first piazza. A street descends to a second little piazza with Palazzo del Podestà and Palazzo dell'Arcipretura, which contains the **Museo della Collegiata** (ring on the first floor: open 10.00–12.00, 16.00–19.00 except fest. & Mon; Nov–May only on request). The small collection is well labelled. The large *Crucifix* is attributed to the Maestro di San Polo in Rosso (school of Duccio), and the ancona (formerly on the high altar of the church) is attributed to the Maestro di Chianciano (early 14C). The Collegiata, beyond, has a detached fresco of the *Assunta*.

Outside the village, at the crossroads for Montepulciano, the **Museo Etrusco** (open 10.00–19.00 exc. Mon) was opened in the Granaio Simoneschi, an old granary, in 1997. It contains recent Etruscan and Roman finds from the area. Objects found in the tombs of the necropoli of La Pedata and Tolle include canopic vases, bronzes, and Bucchero ware. There are also finds from the baths at Mezzomiglio, and decorations from a temple pediment discovered at I Fucoli dating from the 2C BC, including a winged female deity.

Sarteano

Sarteano (573m) is a medieval village with its streets laid out in a semicircle at the foot of the castle hill. An Etruscan settlement, it was later contested between Perugia, Orvieto, and Siena, until it passed under the dominion of the latter in 1379. The locality has excellent olive oil. At the entrance to the village is the church of **San Francesco** with a fine Renaissance façade of 1480. In Piazza XXIV Giugno above is a war memorial by Arnaldo Zocchi (1923) and the 14C **Palazzo del Comune** (rebuilt in 1845) which contains the 18C **Teatro degli Arrischianti** (1740).

Via Roma leads up from the piazza past the fine Renaissance **Palazzo Piccolomini**. Opposite is the handsome Palazzo Gabrielli which houses the **Museo Civico Archeologico.** On the **ground floor** are displayed finds from the district made during excavations begun in the 19C and continued in the 20C. The material includes Bronze Age objects but is particularly important for Etruscan ware from 8C–2C BC necropoli (bronzes, vases, and canopic vases). Room 2 displays Bucchero ware with relief decoration (late 7C–early 6C BC). In Room 3 are red-figure vases, and a cippus found in the locality of Sant'Angelo with interesting reliefs (late 6C). Stairs lead down to the **basement** where the small private Bologni collection is displayed, as well as three unusual cinerary statuettes: the one on the left is a Hellenistic original, but the origins of the other two are uncertain. The bas-reliefs once decorated a building of the Augustan period, and two urns displayed here dating from the 1C BC are interesting because they bear the names of the dead in both Latin and Etruscan.

Via Roma continues downhill through an archway to the church of **San Martino**. In the interior, on the north side, is an **Annunciation* by Beccafumi, and a fine painting of the *Madonna with Saints Roch and Sebastian*, complete with its predella, by Andrea di Niccolò. On the south side are two works by Giacomo di Mino del Pellicciaio: *Madonna and Child*, and a triptych with the *Madonna and Saints John and Bartholomew*.

Corso Garibaldi leads from the other side of Piazza XXIV Giugno past several fine palaces including Palazzo Goti-Fanelli (1535), Palazzo Lichini (14C; enlarged in the 16C), and the 17C Palazzo Forneris, and the **Chiesa del Suffragio** with heavy yellow, black and white Baroque altars and some detached 15C frescoes.

The **Collegiata di San Lorenzo** lies beyond. Its foundations are 12C, its structure 16C. In the late 18C interior, on the left of the choir, is a chapel with two good paintings of the *Virgin Annunciate* and *Annunciatory angel* by Girolamo del Pacchia. In the chapel to the right of the choir is a marble ciborium by Marrina (1514). Opposite the Collegiata is the 15C Palazzo Cennini (rebuilt in the 18C). Just before Porta Monalda there is another fine palace (at no. 79) with an amusing mock Gothic pink-and-cream wing.

Outside the gate Via della Rocca (right) leads up to the imposing **castle**, first built in the 10C. The present building was fortified by the Sienese in

1467–74. Acquired by the Comune in 1997, there are plans to restore it.

Outside Sarteano, on the Cetona road, beside a tabernacle, a rough road leads to the **Tomba delle Pianacce**, an Etruscan tomb (5C BC) discovered in 1954, with a dromus some 30 metres long (some of the finds made here are in the Museo Civico Archeologico).

Cetona

Cetona is a beautifully preserved medieval village, which, in the last few decades has become a fashionable place to have a country house. It has fine views of Monte Cetona (see below), and is surrounded by pretty hills planted with cypresses and pine trees.

In the large pleasant **Piazza Garibaldi,** laid out in the 16C, at the bottom of the hill, is the church of **Sant'Angelo**. In the chapel to the right of the high altar (light by the side door) is a highly venerated seated wooden statue of the *Madonna and Child*, and on the second altar on the south side, a 16C painting of the *Madonna and Child with two Saints*.

At the other end of the piazza is a round tower, near which Via Roma goes up past the 16C ex-Palazzo Comunale with the **Museo Civico per la Preistoria del Monte Cetona** (open 09.30–12.30; Sat also 16.00–18.00; closed Mon. The same ticket allows admission to the archaeological park of Belverde; see below).

A delightful little museum, with children's corners and modern facilities, it documents the presence of Man on Monte Cetona from the Paleolithic era to the Bronze Age. Excavations were carried out in 1927–41 by Umberto Calzoni, and most of his finds are now exhibited in the Archaeological Museum of Perugia. Systematic excavations were resumed in 1984 and these finds are exhibited here. The most important material dates from the Bronze Age. The **first room** illustrates the geological formation of the mountain, which was an island in the Pliocene era. **Room 2** has remains of a huge bear found in a cave inhabited by Neanderthal man some 50,000 years ago. In **room 3** are Bronze Age finds made since 1984 on the Belverde site.

A street in Cetona

Via Roma continues uphill to the **collegiata** in a pretty little piazza with attractive paving. It contains a fresco of the *Assumption* attributed to Pinturicchio. From here there is a view of the Rocca above, surrounded by pine trees, and, in the other direction, of Monte Cetona. Farther on (keep left), Via della Fortezza leads up to the **Rocca** (privately owned), and there is a delightful walkway along the walls at the foot of the castle which leads past orchards and little terraces back towards Piazza Garibaldi.

Belverde archaeological park

Belverde (admission, see above; guided tours of c 30 minutes; open mid-Oct–end

June on request), 6km from Cetona, is the most important Bronze Age site in central Italy, where, for the first time, various phases of Bronze Age habitation were found in one place, untouched by later material. It is reached by taking the Sarteano road, and, just outside the village, Via di San Francesco. This leads up past the ex-**Convent of San Francesco**, founded in 1212. It has been restored by a Roman Catholic community called Mondo X which was founded by Padre Eligio to help young people in need. A member of the community will show visitors the convent including a 14C cloister. The well-known restaurant (*Convento di San Francesco*) is here (see above).

The road continues up to another road for Sarteano: the Monte Cetona road instead proceeds downhill to the left through spectacular countryside, with Monte Cetona conspicuous on the right. An unsurfaced road (yellow signpost) diverges from this road and continues left downhill to **Belverde** on the side of **Monte Cetona** (1148m), a beautiful wooded mountain (with its summit often hidden by clouds), visible, like Monte Amiata, for miles. A Cross was placed on the summit in 1968. Delightful walks may be taken on the mountain side. The road passes the **Parco Archeologico Naturalistico di Belverde**. If you decide on the tour, the guide will point out the interesting vegetation on the calcareous rock with marine deposits (sea-shells, etc). A cavern (lit by solar power), formed by the collapse of travertine outcrops, can be visited. Evidence of Neanderthal habitation was found here. The cave seems to have been used as a store in the Bronze Age. Below the road is an area (no admission) of excavations, begun in 1984, of a Bronze Age settlement.

Just beyond, the road pass the ex-**Convent of Santa Maria a Belverde**, surrounded by lovely old cypresses and ilex trees, with a fine view. A hermitage was founded here in 1367. This is now occupied by a Mondo X community (see above). Visitors are shown the **church**, preceded by a picturesque portico, divided into three oratories and frescoed in 1380–85. The lower church has a barrel vault and is covered with frescoes including a *Crucifixion* and *St Francis receiving the stigmata* attributed to Cola Petruccioli. Stairs lead up to the chapel of Santissimo Salvatore with more interesting frescoes of the *Life of Christ* (including the Resurrection) attributed to Petruccioli and Andrea di Giovanni. A few steps lead up to the adjoining chapel of Santa Maria Maddalena, with scenes from the *Life of Mary Magdalene*, also by Petruccioli.

San Casciano dei Bagni

South of Monte Cetona in lovely countryside with vineyards and wooded hills of oak, chestnut and pines is **San Casciano dei Bagni** (582m), a little spa town famous for its hot springs which have existed since Roman times. Mud baths are used here for alleviating rheumatism. The 13C–14C collegiata of **San Leonardo** has a high altarpiece of the *Coronation of the Virgin in a glory of angels, with Saints* (c 1490) by Pietro di Francesco Orioli. In the 16C **Oratorio della Santissima Concezione** is a fresco in a fine tabernacle attributed to Pomarancio. A neo-Gothic castle was built on the site of the Cassero. Just outside the town are the springs, where the Bagno del Portico was built by Ferdinando II. The Chiesa delle Terme is a primitive building founded in the 11C–12C. **Palazzone** to the east is known for its red wine.

Arezzo

Arezzo built on a low hillside (296m) about 5km south of the Arno, is now surrounded to the south by industrial suburbs. It is a lively agricultural provincial town (87,300 inhab.), with several notable churches and interesting museums. In the church of San Francesco is the famous fresco cycle of the *Legend of the True Cross* painted by Piero della Francesca. Its monthly antique market held in the streets of the old centre is one of the best known in Italy, and bargains can still sometimes be found here.

Practical information

Getting there
By car

Arezzo has an exit from the A1 motorway from Florence to Rome. A much longer, but prettier route from Florence is by the Casentino road (N70 and N71), see p 520. **Car parking** near the centre of the town (closed to traffic) is difficult, and most car parks (including those in Via Niccolò Aretino, Via Alberti, Via Pietro Aretino) charge an hourly tariff. Free parking in Viale Mecenate.

By train

Railway station, Piazza della Repubblica, about 500m southwest of San Francesco, on the main Florence–Rome line. Some fast Intercity trains stop here (from Florence in 45mins); otherwise slower trains (frequent service) in c 1hr. Local trains to Sinalunga via Monte San Savino, and (every hour) via Bibbiena and Poppi to Pratovecchio-Stia.

By bus

Country bus services run by *SITA* from Arezzo (Piazza Stazione) to Florence (in 1hr 20mins–2hrs); to Sansepolcro (via Anghiari) in c 1hr; to Città di Castello (in 1hr 30mins); to Caprese Michelangelo (in 1hr 30mins–2hrs). A few buses a day to Monterchi (in 45 min). Services run by *LFI* to Siena (in c 1hr 30mins); to Cortona (via Castiglion Fiorentino) in c 1hr; and to Urbino (in c 3hrs).

Information office

APT, Piazza della Repubblica 28, outside the railway station (☎ 0575 377 678).
✉: info@arezzo.turismo. toscana.it

Where to stay
Hotels

☆☆☆ *Continentale*, Piazza Guido Monaco 7 (Map 1; ☎ 0575 202 51, 🗐 0575 350 485); *Europa*, Via Spinello 43 (Map 2; ☎ 0575 357 701, 🗐 0575 357 703).

Hotels on the outskirts (towards the motorway)

☆☆☆☆ *Minerva*, Via Fiorentina 4 (☎ 0575 370 390, 🗐 0575 302 415). ☆☆☆☆ *Etrusco*, Via Fleming 39 (☎ 0575 984 066, 🗐 0575 382 131). ☆☆ *Astoria*, Via Guido Monaco 54 (Map 3; ☎ 0575 243 61, 🗐 0575 243 62); *Cecco*, Corso Italia 215 (Map 4; ☎ 0575 209 86, 🗐 0575 356 730).

Hotels in the environs

Montecchio Vesponi: ☆☆☆ *Villa Schiatti*, Via Montecchio 131 (☎ 0575 651 481, 🗐 0575 651 482).
Near Castiglion Fiorentino ☆☆☆ *Relais San Pietro*, with restaurant, at Polvano, 5km east (☎ 0575 650 100; 🗐 0575 650 255).

Youth hostel

Villa Severi, Via Redi 13 (beyond Borgo Santa Croce; bus no. 4 from Piazza Guido Monaco (☎/🗐 0575 299 047).

Eating out
Restaurants

€€€ *Le Tastevin*, Via dei Cenci 9 (off Corso Italia); *Lancia d'Oro*, Piazza Grande (with tables outside). €€ *La Torre di Gnicche*, Piaggia San Martino 8, with a good selection of wines; *Enoteca Vino di Vino*, Via Cesalpino. € *Trattoria Mazzoni*, Canto alla Croce 1; *L'Agania*, Via Mazzini 10; *Lucullo*, Borgo Santa Croce 10 (also excellent pizzeria); *La Vigna*, Via Spinello 27.

Picnics

Pleasant places to picnic include the Parco il Prato and Fortezza Medicea, and the Roman amphitheatre and adjoining public gardens (entrance on Via Francesco Crispi).

Pasticcerie

De' Redi—Dolcezze Savini, Piazza Sant'Agostino; *Carraturo*, Corso Italia; *Mignon*, Via Tolletta.

 Markets

A popular **antiques fair** is held in Piazza Grande and the surrounding streets on the first Sunday of every month (and the day before). A general market is held every Saturday.

 Festivals

An important international **choral festival** (*Concorso Polifonico Internazionale Guido d'Arezzo*) is held in the city in late August. The **Giostra del Saracino** is held twice a year: on the penultimate Sunday in June and the first Sunday in September. The contest starts in Piazza Grande at 17.00 and tickets are available in advance (information from the Tourist Office); standing room only on the day.

The Giostra del Saracino

The Giostra del Saracino goes back to the 13C and takes its name from the quintain which is in the form of a Saracen, which probably originated as a representation of the heathen enemy of the Crusader Knights. Two competitors from each of the four districts of the town, mounted and armed with lances, charge in turn across the piazza at a pivoting quintain called *Buratto Re delle Indie* (Puppet King of the Indies) which holds the target in its left hand and in its right a whip, ending in three wooden balls. Points are awarded (from 1–5) for aim, with bonus points for a broken lance, and penalties if the horseman is struck by the wooden balls as the figure turns on its pivot. Each of the four ancient districts of the town enters a team with a captain, standard-bearers, foot-soldiers, bowmen, and a band, which plays the Saracino hymn. The four districts have their own colours: Porta Sant'Andrea, white and green; Porta Crucifera, red and green; Porta del Foro, yellow and crimson; Porta Santo Spirito, yellow and blue. The team (not the individual) scoring the most marks is declared the winner.

History

Arretium was one of the more important of the twelve cities of the Etruscan Confederation. The bronze statues of *Minerva* and the famous *Chimera* (c 380 BC) found here in the 16C (now exhibited in the Archaeological Museum in Florence) testify to the quality of the work of local Etruscan artists. From the 3C BC the town became a faithful ally of Rome. It emerged as a free republic in the 10C. Generally supporting the Ghibelline party it was frequently at odds with Florence and was defeated by that city at Campaldino in the Casentino in 1289 when the Aretine leader, Bishop Guglielmino was killed. The town came under the control of Florence in 1384.

As a road junction, the town had tactical importance in the Second World War. Nearly every important building was damaged by bombing.

Ever since the Etruscan period Arezzo has produced notable artists and craftsmen. The famous Aretine pottery, with a bright red glossy finish, was first produced here c 50 BC, and was later mass produced and exported all over the world by some 90 firms working in Arezzo (up to the mid-1C AD).

Among the eminent citizens of Arezzo were C. Cilnius Maecenas (d. 8 BC), friend of Augustus and the patron of Virgil and Horace; Guido d'Arezzo (c 995–1050), the inventor of the musical scale; Margaritone, the painter (1216–93); Petrarch, the poet (1304–74); Spinello Aretino, the painter (c 1350–1410); Aretino (1492–1566), the most outspoken writer of the late Renaissance; and Giorgio Vasari (1512–74), the architect, painter, and art historian.

The most pleasant approach from the station is by **Corso Italia**, the main street of the medieval town, which leads gently uphill. Via Cavour branches left for **Piazza San Francesco**, a small square created in the 19C. The monument to Vittorio Fossombroni in front of San Francesco is by Pasquale Romanelli, 1863. Fossombroni was a mathematician and hydraulic engineer who drained the marshes of the Val di Chiana.

San Francesco

The church was built by Fra Giovanni da Pistoia in 1322. At the foot of the rough-hewn front is part of the facing which was never finished.

• **Open** 08.30–12.00, 14.00–18.30 or 19.00. For admission to the sanctuary to see the **frescoes** by Piero della Francesca close up, it is necessary to book in advance (☎ 0575 900 404 or 06 328 10). If tickets are available you can also book a visit on the same day at the office on the right of the church. For further information: ✉ www.pierodellafrancesca.it.

The bright Franciscan interior contains the world-famous frescoes by Piero della Francesca in the choir, but also numerous other frescoes (mostly fragments) in the nave, many of them showing his influence on the local school. West wall. The rose window has *stained glass showing *St Francis before Honorius III* by Guglielmo di Marcillat (William of Marseille, 1520), who also produced windows for the Duomo. The frescoes include: *Supper in the house of the Pharisee* by Giovanni di Balduccio, and the *Mystical Marriage of St Catherine of Alexandria*, an unusual scene with the figure of *St Christopher* attributed to Paolo Schiavo.

South wall. The first chapel has frescoes, dated 1463, showing *St Bernardine of Siena leading the Aretines from the church of San Francesco to destroy the Fons Tecta* (connected with a pagan cult), by Lorentino d'Andrea, an assistant of Piero della Francesca, and a painting of the *Sacred Conversation* by Niccolò Soggi. The frescoes in the second chapel include scenes from the *Life of St Bartholomew* by a follower of Piero della Francesca, a *Crucifixion*, and, above an unusual scene of two figures in monochrome guarding a door closed with chains (from the family name *Catenacci*). A 14C wooden *Crucifix*, and a fresco fragment by Antonio d'Anghiari, Piero della Francesca's master are surrounded by a tabernacle in *pietra serena*. Beyond the third chapel, with ruined frescoes attributed to Parri Spinelli, in a finely carved tabernacle, is a Roman sarcophagus, the tomb of Beato Benedetto Sinigardi (d. 1282), friend of St Francis. At the end of this wall, *Annunciation* by Spinello Aretino.

The chapel to the right of the sanctuary also has damaged frescoes (restored) by Spinello Aretino: right, *Deeds of St Michael*; left, *Legend of St Giles*. The triptych of the *Madonna of the Holy Girdle* is by Niccolò di Pietro Gerini.

In the **sanctuary** hangs a huge painted **Crucifix*, with St Francis at the foot of the Cross, attributed from this work to the Master of San Francesco (1250).

The ***Legend of the True Cross* by **Piero della Francesca**, on the walls of the choir, is his masterpiece, and one of the greatest fresco cycles ever produced in Italian painting. A general view of the restored frescoes can be had from the nave; but to enter the sanctuary you need to book in advance (see above).

In 1447 the Bacci, a rich Aretine family commissioned Bicci di Lorenzo to paint the sanctuary: he had only painted the *Four Evangelists* (with the help of assistants) on the vault and part of the *Last Judgement* on the triumphal arch before he left Arezzo in 1448 (he died in 1452). Piero della Francesca was called to complete the frescoes, possibly in 1448. He may have interrupted work on them during a stay in Rimini in 1451, and another in Rome in 1459, but the cycle was finished by 1466.

The frescoes underwent an extremely complicated restoration programme from 1985–2000. They had deteriorated alarmingly for a number of reasons: the wall is particularly thin, the circulation of air in the church had been altered when the roof was rebuilt and central heating was installed, and the delicate frescoes had been damaged by poor restorations in the past. During restoration work it was discovered that Piero, as well as using the technique of true fresco, had also painted parts of the scenes '*a secco*', using tempera on the dry (or slightly humid) *intonaco*, in order to provide even more colour, such as bright red and emerald green, to the scenes, a technique he apparantly learnt from Flemish painters. However these parts are those which have lost their colour over the centuries. All the preparatory drawings beneath the frescoes are by Piero's own hand (he made use of the '*spolvero*' technique by which the outlines were pricked with small holes over which a powder was dusted).

The frescoes illustrate the Legend of the True Cross, taken from the *Leggenda Aurea* by Fra Jacopo Varagine (13C), and the time span runs from the Death of Adam to the Battle of Chosroes in the 7C AD. The chronological order of the scenes is as follows: **right wall (lunette)**, *Death of Adam*. On the right, Adam seated on the ground, announces his imminent death from old age to his family; on the left is the dead figure of Adam, and Seth planting a fig tree on his grave (from which the Cross on which Christ is Crucified will be made; the leaves added in tempera have lost their colour). Many of the figures in this scene are derived from classical models. **Right wall (middle band)**, *the Queen of Sheba recognises the sacred wood* (used as a bridge over the Siloam river) and kneels in adoration before it, and (on the right) she is received by Solomon (thought to be a portrait of Cardinal Bessarion). **Right of the window** (middle panel), *the beam is buried deep in the ground by three men, by order of Solomon*. Right of the window (lower panel), *Constantine's Dream in 313 AD*. The Emperor, asleep in his tent at dawn before battle, dreams that an angel shows him the Cross and announces: 'By this sign, you shall conquer'. **Right wall (lower band)**, *Constantine's bloodless victory over Maxentius* early the next morning. Maxentius is portrayed as the Byzantine Emperor John Paleologus who had come to the Council of Florence in 1439 wearing this elaborate head-dress. **Left of the window** (middle panel), *Torture of a Jew named Judas*. He is kept in a dry well until he reveals the secret hiding place of the Cross, stolen after the Crucifixion. This scene, illuminated from the left, instead of from the east window (as in all the other scenes) was carried out by an assistant, probably Giovanni di Piamonte.

Left wall (middle band), *Finding of the True Cross*. Judas digs up the Cross before St Helena and her courtiers, and on the right, in a scene in front of a church, its authenticity is demonstrated by the raising of a young man from the dead, while Helena kneels in wonder. **Left wall (lower band)**, *Battle scene showing the victory of Heraclius over Chosroes in the 7C AD*, after Chosroes, king of the Persians, had seized the Cross and placed it near his throne (shown to the right). After his defeat he kneels awaiting execution. **Left wall (lunette)**, *Heraclius restores the Cross to Jerusalem*.

Also by Piero is the figure of a *Prophet* at the top of the **window wall** on the right (the *Prophet* on the left seems to be by the hand of an assistant) and the *Annunciation* (thought by some scholars to be St Helena receiving the news of her death and thus connected to the main cycle).

In the chapel to the left of the sanctuary is a fine painting of the *Annunciation* by Neri di Bicci, and a damaged fresco of the *Annunciation* attributed to Luca Signorelli or Bartolomeo della Gatta.

North wall. In the last chapel, terracotta funerary monument to Francesco Rosselli, attributed to Michele da Firenze (1439), and, in a 17C altar, *Ecstasy of St Francis* by Bernardino Santini. On a pilaster is a fine fresco of *St Elizabeth of Hungary*, by the school of Spinello Aretino. In the middle of this wall is a chapel with *frescoes of *St Anthony of Padua* and stories from his life, and a lunette of the *Visitation*, all by Lorentino d'Andrea, showing the influence of Piero della Francesca (and possibly on a cartoon by him). Beyond are remains of a fresco of *St Francis and Pope Honorius III* by Parri Spinello. The **lower church** (13C–14C) is open only for exhibitions.

The Pieve di Santa Maria

The *Pieve di Santa Maria, at the end of Corso Italia (see above; open 08.00–13.00, 15.00–18.30 or 19.00) is a 12C church replacing an earlier building, damaged in 1111. It is one of the most beautiful Romanesque churches in Tuscany. The superbly conceived *façade has a deep central portal flanked by blind arcades which support three tiers of colonnades, the intercolumnations of which diminish towards the top. The 68 diverse pillars include a human figure. The portal bears reliefs of the Madonna, angels and saints (1216) and the months are illustrated in the intrados.

The beautiful tall *interior has clustered pillars with good capitals and arches showing the transition to Gothic. The mullioned windows provide a diffused light on the mellow sandstone. The drum was to have supported a dome which was never built. In the raised presbytery is the *polyptych by Pietro Lorenzetti commissioned for the church by Bishop Guido Tarlati in 1320. The crypt below has good capitals, and a reliquary *bust of St Donato (1346) by a local goldsmith. In a chapel off the left side of the nave is a polychrome statue of the *Madonna and Child* by the 15C Florentine school.

Piazza Grande

The arcaded apse of the Pieve and its original **campanile** (1330) with its 40

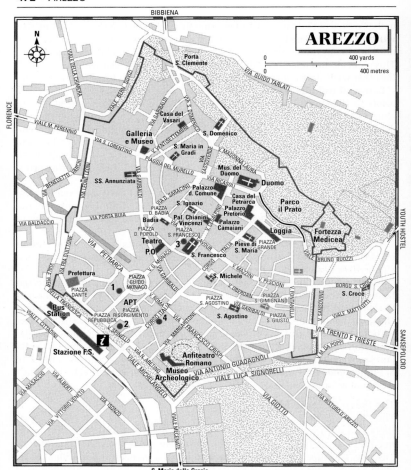

BIBBIENA

AREZZO

0   400 yards

0   400 metres

mullioned windows are best seen from the steeply-sloping ***Piazza Grande**, behind the church (reached by Via di Seteria which skirts the interesting flank of the church, opposite medieval shop-fronts). Piazza Grande was laid out c 1200 (some medieval houses and towers survive here; others were rebuilt in medieval style in the 19C). It is still the centre of city life, and the scene of the *Giostra del Saracino* in summer and of the monthly antiques fair.

Beside the apse of the *pieve* is the **Palazzo del Tribunale** (17C–18C) with pretty circular steps outside, and the elaborate little **Palazzo della Fraternità dei Laici** in a mixture of Gothic and Renaissance styles. The lower part dates from 1377 (with a detached fresco of *Christ in Pietà* by Spinello Aretino), and in 1434 Bernardo Rossellino added the relief of the *Madonna of the Misericordia* in the lunette above and two statues in niches on either side. The delicate cornice and loggia above were designed in 1460 by Giuliano da Settignano. The bell-cote and clock date from 1552.

One whole side of the square is occupied by Vasari's handsome ***Palazzo delle Logge** (1573). The long portico continues northwest back to Corso Italia in which is the 16C **Palazzo Camaiani**, now housing the State Archives. It was restored in 14C style at the beginning of the 20C and has painted decorations by Galileo Chini.

Via dei Pileati continues uphill past the 14C **Palazzo Pretorio**, its façade decorated with the armorial bearings of many podestà; it is occupied by the public library. The road curves uphill to the left, and at no. 28 Via dell'Orto is the **Casa Petrarca** (open on request here or at the Accademia Petrarca, Via degli Alberghetti, 10.00–12.00, 15.00–17.00; closed Sat afternoon and fest.), the supposed house of Petrarch reconstructed (after its destruction in the Second World War) as an academy and library for Petrarchian studies. Visitors are shown the library with MSS and an autograph letter of the poet (1370).

Petrarch

Petrarch (Francesco Petrarca), one of the most important Italian poets, was born in Arezzo in 1304. His father had been exiled here from Florence in 1302 because of his Guelf sympathies (Dante Alighieri, who was a friend, had been exiled the same year). The family apparantly soon moved to Ancisa in the Valdarno before following the Pope to Avignon in 1311. It was here in 1327 that Petrarch met a certain Laura and his unrequited love for her inspired some of his greatest sonnets. He travelled in Europe and studied at Bologna university and soon became famous for his learning and his writings in both prose and verse, mostly in Latin (although his masterpiece is considered the *Canzoniere*, a poem in Italian). He studied the writings of Cicero, Virgil, Livy and St Augustine and was particularly important because of the interest he revived in the classics and the culture of Greece and Rome. In many ways he anticipated the Humanist culture of the Renaissance. His beautiful poetry influenced generations of Italian writers and his verse was imitated for centuries, although by the 19C he was held in less esteem.

He became family chaplain and close friend of the Roman Cardinal Giovanni Colonna with whom he travelled widely, and in 1341 was crowned poet laureate on the Campidoglio. From 1353–61 he lived in Milan as a guest of the Visconti. He taught at the university of Padua but left the city in 1362 during an outbreak of the plague and went to Venice where he was offered a house on the Riva degli Schiavoni in return for his promise to leave his books to the city on his death (they formed the nucleus of the Biblioteca Marciana). He spent the last four years of his life in the quiet little village of Arquà in the Colli Euganei near Padua, where he is buried.

A huge monument to Petrarch (by Alessandro Lazzerini, 1928) stands in the **Parco il Prato**, an attractive large park with pine trees, lawns and pretty views of the Tuscan countryside. The 14C–16C **Fortezza** (open daily), also in a park, was rebuilt by Antonio da Sangallo the Younger (and partly dismantled in 1800).

The Duomo

The *Duomo (open 07.00–12.30, 15.00–18.30) was begun in 1278 and continued until 1510, with a campanile added at the east end in 1859 and a façade completed in 1914. Fine travertine steps (1525–29) surround the exterior. The handsome southern flank incorporates a good portal (1320–40), with worn reliefs, and terracotta statues of the *Madonna and*

Child between St Donato and Gregory X, attributed to Niccolò di Luca Spinelli.

The beautiful Gothic *interior has clustered columns and pointed arches. The splendid *stained glass windows** are by Guglielmo di Marcillat (1519–23), a French artist who lived in Arezzo. They are the most important example of stained glass of this date in Italy. He also painted the first three vaults of the nave and the first of the north aisle in 1521–27. The remaining vaults of the nave were painted in 1661 by Salvi Castellucci, a pupil of Pietro da Cortona.

South aisle. The funerary monument to Cardinal Stefano Bonucci (d. 1589) has a fine bust. The stained glass window by Marcillat illustrates the *Calling of St Matthew*. The sepulchral monument (1320–30) to Pope Gregory X who died at Arezzo in 1276 is a fine Gothic work. The second window by Marcillat shows the *Baptism of Christ*.

To the left of the altar there is a fragment of a 14C fresco of the *Madonna enthroned with Saints*, and a lunette of the *Risen Christ*, by Buffalmacco. The window by Marcillat shows the *Expulsion of the Merchants from the Temple*. On the third altar are 14C frescoes. The window of the *Woman taken in Adultery* is the last work in the church by Marcillat. The medieval **Tarlati Chapel** has a beautiful sculptured canopy by Giovanni di Agostino. The fresco of the *Crucifix and Saints* is attributed to a local painter known as the Maestro del Vescovado (mid-14C). The fine 4C early Christian sarcophagus rests on a marble tomb with a bas-relief of a bishop saint, and three inscriptions. The window by Marcillat shows the *Raising of Lazarus*. An 18C monument has two busts of members of the Maurizi family.

The chapel to the right of the apse has a marble ciborium of 1783 and a stained glass window of 1477. The Gothic sculptured *high altar**, by many 14C artists including Giovanni di Francesco and Betto di Giovanni, encloses the body of St Donato (martyred in 361), the patron saint of the city. The two lateral stained glass lancet windows in the tribune are by Domenico Pecori (16C); the central one dates from 1953.

North aisle. On the left of the sacristy door (and the entrance to the Museo del Duomo, see below) is a beautiful fresco of *St Mary Magdalene*, by Piero della Francesca (inconspicuous light on the nave pillar). Next to it is the unusual *tomb of Bishop Guido Tarlati, by Agostino di Giovanni and Agnolo di Ventura, with 16 panels representing the warlike life of this zealous Ghibelline (d. 1327). The small funerary monument to Girolamo Borro (d. 1592) bears his bust. The cantoria is Vasari's first architectural work (1535); the organ dates from 1534 (by Luca Boni da Cortona). Beneath it is a 13C wood statue of the *Madonna and Child* (thought to have been painted by Margaritone di Arezzo), and 14C fresco fragments. Beyond an altarpiece of the *Martyrdom of St Donato* by Pietro Benvenuti (1794) is a little fresco by Luigi Ademollo of the Aretines receiving the body of St Donato.

The large **Lady Chapel**, preceded by a pretty wrought-iron screen, was added in 1796. On the right, above a funerary monument to Bishop Albergotti (d. 1825), with reliefs by Odoardo Baratta, is an *Assumption* by Andrea della Robbia. On the right wall, large painting of *Judith* (1804) by Pietro Benvenuti, much admired by Canova. On the right wall of the chapel to the right of the main altar, *Trinity between Saints Donato and Bernard* by Andrea della Robbia (c 1485). The main altar was designed by Giuseppe Valadier (1823). The chapel to the left of the main altar has a statue of *Bishop Marcacci* by Stefano Ricci and, on the left wall, a polychrome terracotta attributed to Giovanni della Robbia. On the left wall, large painting of *David and Abigail* by Luigi Sabatelli. On the wall near the entrance to the chapel is a *Madonna and Child*, by Andrea della Robbia.

In the **north aisle**, funerary monument to Francesco Redi (d. 1697). The **baptistery** is at the west end of the aisle. The three beautiful *schiacciato* reliefs on the font are attributed to Donatello or his school.

The Museo Diocesano del Duomo

For admission to the museum (usually open Thur, Fri, and Sat 10.00–12.00) ask at the sacristy off the north aisle (from which the museum is usually entered).

Room 1 contains three wood *Crucifixes* from the 12C–13C: the oldest one is on the left of the entrance (it was painted in 1264 by Margaritone di Arezzo). The tabernacle with a terracotta bas-relief of the *Annunciation* is attributed to Bernardo Rossellino (1434). The frescoes include a fragment of an *Annunciation* and a *Madonna and Child with Saints James and Anthony Abbot*, both by Spinello Aretino. The tabernacle, also with an *Annunciation*, is by Parri di Spinello. The painting of the *Annunciation* is by Andrea di Nerio, master of Spinello. The Pax of Siena, in the base of a neo-Classical reliquary, is a 15C Flemish work in enamel surrounded by precious stones, depicting Christ supported by an angel, and the Madonna supported by an angel.

Room 2: a fresco and its sinopia of *St Jerome in the desert* by Bartolomeo della Gatta; detached fresco of the *Madonna and Child* by Lorentino d'Andrea; della Robbian polychrome bust of *St Donato*; *Madonna and Child with Saints Fabiano and Sebastian* by Bartolomeo della Gatta and Domenico Pecori; *Madonna in glory with Saints* by Domenico Pecori, *Founding of the Basilica Liberiana* by Niccolò Soggi; and panels from a predella by Luca Signorelli. Cases contain 14C–16C Crosses, reliquaries, and chalices.

Room 3: *Preaching of the Baptist, Baptism of Christ* and tondo of the *Madonna della Misericordia* (a processional standard) by Vasari; *Christ in the house of Martha* by Santi di Tito. The last room displays church vestments.

On the cathedral steps stands a statue of Ferdinando I, by Francavilla, after a design by Giambologna. It was erected by the Aretines in 1594 in gratitude for the Grand-duke's agricultural reforms and land reclamation in the Valdichiana. Across Piazza della Libertà is **Palazzo del Comune** of 1333. The tower, 41 metres high, can be climbed (10.00–16.00 or 18.00).

San Domenico

The old Via Sassoverde descends right from Via Ricasoli to San Domenico in a square of lime trees. The church, founded in 1275, has a Romanesque portal with a lunette frescoed by Angelo di Lorentino, and a Gothic campanile.

The bright interior has a miscellany of fresco fragments of particularly high quality. On the west wall, *Crucifixion and Saints* and (in the lunette) two scenes from the *Life of St Nicholas of Bari* by Parri di Spinello. On the south wall, in a Gothic canopied altar by Giovanni di Francesco, *Christ with the doctors in the temple* by Luca di Tommè. Above, between the windows, *Madonna and Child* by the school of Duccio. In a pretty carved polychrome niche, *St Peter Martyr* by the della Robbian school. The large detached fresco of a triptych with *St Catherine of Alexandria* is by the school of Spinello. Above an 18C wall monument there is a fragment of a fresco by Parri with angel musicians. Beside the steps, damaged fresco of *Christ blessing the faithful*.

East end. In the chapel to the right of the main altar has a fine stone 14C statue of the *Madonna and Child* and a fresco of the **Annunciation* by Spinello Aretino. The **Crucifix* in the main apse is by Cimabue, the only one to survive in tact by this great master (restored in 2001). It is an early work (1260–65) and was used as a model for his later famous Crucifix in Santa Croce in Florence, severely damaged in the Arno flood (see p 95). In the chapel to the left of the apse, triptych with *St Domenic, Archangel Michael, and St Paul* by Giovanni d'Agnolo.

On the north wall of the church are frescoes by Giovanni d'Agnolo, Parri di Spinello (*Marriage of St Catherine*), and Jacopo di Landino (stories of St Christopher). Vasari records that the last fresco on this wall of *St Vincent Ferrer* is the only known work by his great-grandfather Lazzaro Taldi Vasari. On the west wall is a large frescoed composition by Spinello Aretino.

Vasari's house

At no. 55 in Via XX Settembre is Vasari's house (open 08.30–19.30; fest. 08.30–12.30; ring). He finished building this house after he purchased it in 1540, and then carried out the painted decorations, with the help of assistants (restored in the 19C). It was acquired by the State in 1911 and contains a collection of 16C–17C paintings, many of them by artists in Vasari's circle.

Giorgio Vasari

Giorgio Vasari (1511–74) is well known as an art historian, painter and architect. His famous work *Le vite de' più eccellenti pittori, scultori e architettori,* which he first published in 1550, and later revised in 1568, has provided precious information about the lives of artists to generations of art historians and is still considered of fundamental importance to the study of the Renaissance and Mannerist periods. As a boy, Vasari worked in the studio of Giullaume de Marcillat in Arezzo but at 13 he was sent to Florence to study under Michelangelo, Andrea del Sarto and others. He then worked as a painter for the Medici, and in Rome received commissions from Cardinal Farnese and Pope Julius III. But it was under Cosimo I in Florence that he carried out his most important works, which include the Uffizi building and the corridor (known as the Corridoio Vasariano), which links Palazzo Vecchio with Palazzo Pitti across Ponte Vecchio. When Cosimo moved from his private Medici palace into Palazzo Vecchio Vasari was called in to redecorate the building, and he transformed the Salone dei Cinquecento in 1563–65 with frescoes celebrating the duke. He also designed the Studiolo for Francesco I in the same palace. In Florence he also founded the first art academy, the Accademia delle Arti del Disegno, and in 1572 he began the fresco of the *Last Judgement* in the dome of the cathedral. In Arezzo he designed the Palazzo delle Logge in Piazza Grande.

In the **hall** is a late 16C bust of *Vasari*. The **sala** has ceiling paintings by Vasari of *Virtue, Envy,* and *Fortune,* the *Four Seasons,* the *Four Ages of Man,* and allegorical figures and landscapes. The little **chapel**, with a worn majolica floor, has a *Madonna and Child* by Fra Paolino and small paintings by Michele di Ridolfo del Ghirlandaio, Bernardino Poccetti, and Leonardo Malatesta.

The **Camera d'Abramo**, with a ceiling painted by Vasari in 1548, contains paintings by Vasari (*Deposition*), Aurelio Lomi (*Ecce Homo*), Francesco Vanni (*Flagellation*), Perin del Vaga and Giovanni Stradano.

The **corridor** has a painting of *Ceres* in the vault, and small paintings by

Maso di San Friano and Lo Scarsellino. Beyond can be seen the little hanging **garden**. The room which was formerly the **kitchen** was frescoed in 1827 by Raimondo Zaballi. Here are hung portraits by Giovanni Maria Butteri and Scipione Pulzone, and two 16C marble bas-reliefs of *Aristotle* and *Plato*. The standard with the *Holy Trinity* is by Vasari.

The **Camera d'Apollo** has the best ceiling by Vasari. The paintings include works by Alessandro Allori, Jacopo Ligozzi, Maso di San Friano, Paolo Farinati and Il Poppi. The painting in a pretty frame of *Prudence* (which may have belonged to Vasari) is attributed to Il Doceno or Alessandro Allori.

The **Camera della Fama** has another good ceiling begun by Vasari and portraits in the lunettes of Lazzaro Vasari, Giorgio Vasari, Luca Signorelli, Spinello Aretino, Bartolomeo della Gatta, Michelangelo, and Andrea del Sarto. The paintings include works by Giovanni Stradano, Girolamo Macchietti, Carlo Portelli, and Giovanni Maria Butteri. The majolica relief of the head of *Galba* is attributed to Andrea Sansovino (purchased by Vasari). The last room has a wooden model by Vasari of the Logge in Piazza Grande, and works by Maso di San Friano. The precious family archives include letters to Vasari from Michelangelo.

The church of **Santa Maria in Gradi**, farther on (left), has a fine interior rebuilt in 1592 by Bartolomeo Ammannati. 17C frescoes of the Apostles on the pilasters have been uncovered and restored. On the first altar on the left, **Madonna del Soccorso* by the workshop of Andrea della Robbia. A staircase leads down to the remains of an earlier church or crypt (probably 10C) with a 13C wooden *Crucifix*. The two decorative cantorie (and chapels below) are by Salvi Castellucci (1633) and Bernardino Santini (1629).

The Museo Statale d'Arte Medioevale e Moderno

At the corner of Via Garibaldi this museum has a great variety of works of art from the medieval and later periods, first opened in the 1950s, and housed in the fine 15C **Palazzo Bruni** (open 08.30–19.30). It has one of the most important collections of majolica in Italy.

Off the 15C **courtyard**, which has fragments from the *pieve*, are two rooms with medieval sculptures and 14C *Madonnas* from gates in the walls, an early 14C statue of *St Michael Archangel*, a late 13C statue of a king (?) and a seated statue of *St Anthony Abbot* by Michele da Firenze.

First floor. **Room I** contains four colourful 13C works by Margaritone di Arezzo, including *St Francis* and a *Madonna*, both signed by him. **Room II** displays 15C frescoes by Giovanni d'Agnolo di Balduccio, a pupil of Spinello Aretino, one of the most famous painters of Arezzo but who carried out much of his work outside the city and returned to his native town only late in life. The processional Cross in majolica is by Piero di Martino Spigliati. In **room III** is a beautiful **Madonna of the Misericordia* by Parri di Spinello Aretino, Spinello's son, painted in a variety of red tones on a gold ground (1437), in the International Gothic style. The *Madonna of the Misericordia* was a favourite subject for painters in Arezzo since the Confraternita dei Laici, founded in 1262, has always been active in the city as a charitable brotherhood helping those in need (and it had its own museum of works of art). Also here are fragments of a fresco of the *Last Judgement* from a demolished church by Spinello Aretino. The early 14C painting of *St Michael Archangel* has recently been attributed to Buffalmacco.

Room IV has 15C ivories by the Embriachi workshop, a 14C rock crystal reliquary in the form of a Cross, and an ivory statuette of the Good Shephard thought to be an Indo-Portuguese work. **Room V** was designed in the 20C as a grand Renaissance hall, with a false ceiling and a 16C chimneypiece bought from another palace, one of Simone Mosca's most important works. The 15C works here include two votive paintings of *St Roch* (in 17C frames) by Bartolomeo della Gatta, painted at the time of the terrible plague in Arezzo in 1478. The smaller painting includes a view of medieval Arezzo, with the Piazza Grande and the seat of the Confraternita dei Laici. Bartolomeo was a Camaldolensian abbot, whose unusual style of painting shows Flemish influences. On the opposite wall, *Madonna and Saints* by Lorentino d'Arezzo. The gilded wood casket dates from 1490. **Room VI** has detached frescoes by Bartolomeo della Gatta, a *Madonna of the Misericordia* by Domenico Pecori, and a collection of small bronzes. **Room VII** contains della Robbian works including some by Andrea della Robbia. The other rooms on this floor contain a magnificent *collection of majolica* with examples from nearly all the most important Italian manufactories including Faenza, Gubbio, Deruta, Castel Durante, and Urbino (16C–18C), the oldest piece dated 1518 in lustre ware from Gubbio. There is also a 14C Chinese fiasca and Turkish Hispano-Moresque ware. Some 300 pieces are displayed (and another 300 are at present kept in the deposits).

The **Mario Salmi Bequest**, arranged in two rooms, includes small works by Il Poppi, Empoli, Agostino Ciampelli, Arcangelo Salimbeni, Franciabigio, Francesco Granacci, Alessandro Magnasco, Ludovico Carracci, and Adriano Cecioni. In the **gallery** is the *Banquet of Ester and Assuero*, Vasari's largest painting (1548).

Second floor. The **salone,** created in the 1950s (the freize was part of the room below) displays an altarpiece by Bernardino Poccetti, two late works by Luca Signorelli, and an *Allegory of the Immaculate Conception* by Giorgio Vasari (or Giovanni Balducci). **Room 2** has a display of 16C–19C glass, some of it from the Pharmacy of Camaldoli, and paintings by Vasari including *St Sebastian*, the *Standard of St Roch,* and the *Standard of Santissima Trinità with Abraham and the three angels,* his last known work (1570). **Room 3** has small paintings by Carlo Dolci and *Witches* (in its original frame) attributed to Angelo Caroseli. **Rooms 4** and **5** display 17C–19C works from the Fossombroni collection including paintings by Gaspare Dughet, Salvator Rosa, and the Macchiaioli school.

On the opposite side of Via Garibaldi is the Renaissance church of the **Santissima Annunziata**, with an *Annunciation* by Spinello Aretino on the outside. The beautiful Renaissance grey-and-white *interior is by Bartolomeo della Gatta (1491) and Giuliano and Antonio da Sangallo the Elder 1517). The interesting plan includes a columned atrium and a dome over the crossing; the capitals of the columns and pilasters are superbly carved. The stained glass tondo in the atrium is by Guglielmo di Marcillat.

In the chapel to the right of the high altar, *Madonna and St Francis* by Pietro da Cortona, and a 16C terracotta *Madonna and Child with Saints,* and a relief of *God the Father* above. The 17C high altar incorporates Renaissance statues in silver and a venerated statue of the *Madonna* attributed to Michele da Firenze. The chapel on the left of the high altar has an *Annunciation* by Matteo Rosselli and a *Nativity* by Niccolò Soggi (1522). On the third north altar is a 14C *Crucifix*, and on the first altar is a good painting of the *Deposition* painted by Vasari at the age of 18 on a cartoon by Rosso Fiorentino.

On the left, farther on, is the **Badia di Santi Fiora e Lucilla**, first built by the Benedictines in 1278 The octagonal campanile dates from 1650.

The interior is an interesting architectural work by Vasari (1565). On the west wall is a delightful *fresco of *St Lawrence,* by Bartolomeo della Gatta (1476). On the south side there is a wood *Crucifix* on the second altar by Baccio da Montelupo, and, beyond the third altar, a large painted *Crucifix* by Segna di Bonaventura (1320). In the **sacristy** is furniture decorated with intarsia attributed to Giuliano da Maiano.

The **high altar** has good paintings by Vasari, including the *Calling of the Apostles,* intended for his own tomb. On the right wall of the choir, the *Assumption* is also by Vasari. The cantoria of the fine organ dates from 1651 and bears two paintings by Raffaello Vanni. The cupola has a trompe l'oeil fresco by Andrea Pozzo (1702).

On the wall of the north side there is an exquisite marble tabernacle attributed to Benedetto da Maiano. The former monastery preserves a fine 15C cloister.

Via Cavour leads to Via Cesalpino where **Palazzo Chianini Vincenzi** has recently been restored as the seat of the **Galleria Comunale d'Arte Moderna** where exhibitions are held. The deconsecrated church of **Sant'Ignazio,** on the other side of Via Carducci, is also used for exhibitions.

Via Garibaldi continues southeast from the Badia, crossing the broad Via Guido Monaco to Piazza Sant'Agostino (where the daily market takes place). The church has a 13C campanile. On Corso Italia is a local Museum of Contemporary Art, containing works mostly dating from the 1960s.

From here Via Margaritone leads to the **Convento di San Bernardo** whose rebuilt double loggie follow the curve of the **Roman amphitheatre** (117–138 AD). The well-kept ruins, adjoining a public park entered from Via Crispi, are open at the same time as the archaeological museum.

The Archaeological Museum

The charming rooms of the convent, overlooking the amphitheatre, now house the Museo Archeologico Mecenate (open 08.30–19.30; ☎ 0575 20882). Other parts of the amphitheatre are visible in the museum rooms. The room numbering is erratic.

Ground floor. **Rooms 1** and **2** contain Archaic and Hellenistic finds from Arezzo (architectural fragments, small bronzes, and terracotta heads. **Room 3** (right) exhibits a krater by the potter and vase painter Euphronios (c 510–500 BC). **Rooms 4** and **5** contain material from the Valdichiana, including a fine red-figure amphora (420–410 BC) and kraters and stamnoi dating from the 5C BC.

Rooms 6 and **7** (right) have an excellent display of the famous Aretine vases which were mass-produced in Arezzo from 50 BC to 60 AD/70 AD, in a characteristic shiny red glaze, usually decorated with exquisite bas-reliefs. Moulds and instruments are displayed as well as the production of individual workshops. **Room 8** continues the display with superb early 1C AD works from the Ateius pottery (which had branch workshops in Pisa and Lyon).

Two small rooms contain a collection of grave-goods from the tomb of a young girl from Apulia (1C BC); a fragment of a circular monument dating from the Claudian era; a marble statue of a man in a toga (1C AD) found in Arezzo in 1994; and a head of Livia, wife of Augustus (35 BC), also found in Arezzo. The last rooms on the ground floor, overlooking the amphitheatre, display Roman mosaics, fragments of *opus sectile* marble pavement, and fragments of polychrome stucco wall decorations. There is also a marble head dating from the mid-1C AD, possibly a portrait of Agrippa, which was found in Arezzo, and bronzes, statues, sculpture and urns. A marble altar from the Augustan period is decorated with the legend of Romulus and Remus, and there is a wooden statuette of an Oriental divinity (1C–2C AD).

Upper floor. To the left are three rooms of vases: a curious urn with a human head and arms, from Chiusi (7C BC), a good red-figure Greek vases (5C BC) and bucchero ware. Two rooms to the left off a corridor display: Roman glass and a *portrait of a man moulded in gold (Aretine, 1C BC); small bronzes; and the Ceccatelli collection with finds from Vulci (7C–6C BC). Off the left side of the long corridor: the Gamurrini collection (small bronzes) and the Vincenzo Funghini (1828–96) collection (mostly 4C–3C BC). Off the opposite side of the corridor are the Palaeolithic and Neolithic collections from the territory of Arezzo. At the end of the long corridor is a display of casts illustrating the finds from the Tumolo del Sodo outside Cortona (see p 492).

Fifteen minutes' walk southeast of the station (reached through an ugly part of the town) is the church of **Santa Maria delle Grazie** in late Gothic style (1449), enclosed in a walled garden. The graceful early Renaissance *loggia is by Benedetto da Maiano. It contains a beautiful marble and terracotta *high altar by Andrea della Robbia and collaborators, which encloses a fresco of the *Madonna of the Misericordia* by Parri di Spinello. On the right wall is a very ruined fresco by Lorentino d'Arezzo. The adjacent oratory of St Bernardine (1450–56) has a pretty vault.

Environs of Arezzo ~ Castiglion Fiorentino

Between Arezzo and Cortona in the Valdichiana, its low hills planted with olives and vines, is Castiglion Fiorentino, a walled agricultural market town on a hill dominated by the oddly-shaped Torre del Cassero. From the Porta Fiorentina the Corso leads up past the church of **San Francesco**, in a piazza to the left, used for exhibitions. In **Piazza Municipio** there is a pretty 16C loggia with some arcades open to provide a view of the valley (the Collegiata is conspicuous on the side of the hill).

On the hillside above, built into the rock, is the ancient **Cassero** (castle), with the church of Sant'Angelo, founded in the 11C. It houses the delightful little **Pinacoteca Comunale** (open 10.00–12.30, 16.00–18.30 exc. Mon).

Visitors first enter the church of **Sant'Angelo**, with a high altar by Filippo Berrettini, and a painted *Cross* by the late 13C Umbrian school. On the left wall is a painting of the *Madonna and Child with Pope St Silvester and St Anthony*, by Vasari. In the **sacristy** are exhibited two *Crosses in gilded copper, one dating from the end of the 12C or beginning of the 13C showing northern European influence, and the other an exquisite work of 13C French manufacture. The silver gilt reliquary *bust of *Sant'Orsola* dates from the 14C and is attributed to a French master.

Stairs lead up to the **Pinacoteca** in the **Coro delle Monache**. In the first part of the room: painted *Cross by an Aretine master of the 13C; *St Francis* by the *bottega* of Margarito di Arezzo; fragment of the *Madonna and Child* by Taddeo Gaddi; *Adoration of the Child* by Pseudo Pier Francesco Fiorentino; *St Michael Archangel,* and *St Francis receiving the stigmata* both by Bartolomeo della Gatta; *St Catherine of Alexandria* by Giovanni di Paolo. Also here is a case of church silver. In the second part of the room: *Pool of Bethesda* by Jacopo del Sellaio; *St Teresa* (1723) by Gian Domenico Ferretti; *Adoration of the Shepherds*

PROVINCIA DI AREZZO

(1538) by Antonio di Donnino del Mazziere;*Madonna and Child with St Anne* by Papacello. Another flight of stairs leads up to the **Saletta della Torre**, decorated with 13C–16C coats of arms, with a fine view.

On the top of the hill is the **Torre del Cassero**. From Piazza Municipio, Via San Michele continues downhill to Piazza Verdi, and beside a pretty little Mannerist doorway, Vicolo dei Signori, with good views of the countryside leads steeply down to a piazza with three churches. The neo-classical **Collegiata** contains a della Robbian terracottas; a *Madonna enthroned with Saints* by Bartolomeo della Gatta (harshly restored; third south altar); and an *Adoration of the Child* by Lorenzo di Credi (chapel to the right of the main altar). In the north transept is a large *Maestà* signed by Segna di Bonaventura. The **pieve** (deconsecrated), next to the church (half of which was demolished) is entered from the right side of the Collegiata (unlocked on request). Near the 15C font is a *Deposition* by the school of Signorelli and a della Robbian *Baptism of Christ*. Behind the *pieve* is the church of the Gesù with a portico.

Via San Giuliano leads downhill to the Porta Romana, outside which is the octagonal **Madonna della Consolazione**. Nearby is the ex-church of **San Lazzaro**, now a small museum of frescoes (including a *Crucifixion* by the school of Giotto).

A short way south of Castiglion Fiorentino, off the road to Cortona, a narrow by-road (signposted) winds through charming countryside up a hill to the **castle of *Montecchio Vesponi**, acquired by Sir John Hawkwood in 1384. Born in England, he came to Italy as captain of a band of mercenaries in 1362, and from 1377 onwards, as captain of the Florentine army, he became one of the most famous *condottiere* in Italy. The splendid 13C walls (the crenellations were added in the 19C) enclosed a village up to the end of the 17C, but now only a tower and 16C house remain (usually shown 11.00–13.00 on Monday; or by appointment, ☎ 0575 651 272).

The main road continues south with a splendid view of Cortona and its monuments strung out along the skyline below Porta Colonia.

Northwest of Arezzo near Indicatore station is the **Arezzo British Military Cemetery**, with 1267 graves from the Second World War. Across the Arno at **Laterina** are long and almost intact stretches of the Roman road, Via Cassia Vetus, were unearthed in 1973.

Cortona

Cortona (22,600 inhab.) is a delightful, peaceful little town, particularly well preserved, with olive groves and vineyards reaching up to its walls. It is built on a long hillside with narrow, winding well-kept medieval streets covering the steep slopes. It has numerous interesting churches (including Santa Maria del Calcinaio, a famous Renaissance building), and two fine museums. Its works of art include paintings by Luca Signorelli who was born here. There are magnificent views over the wide agricultural plain which provides the main source of its economy.

Practical information

Getting there
By car

Cortona can be reached from Arezzo by N71, but from Florence the fastest approach is by the A1 motorway as far as the Val di Chiana exit and then the Perugia superstrada which has several exits for Cortona. **Car parking** (the centre is closed to traffic). Free car parks in Piazzale del Mercato, Porta Colonia, Porta Santa Maria, or Via Gino Severini.

By bus

Country buses (*LFI*) from Piazza Garibaldi to Camucia, Terontola, Castiglione Fiorentino, and Arezzo.

By train

There are bus connections from the two nearest stations. **Camucia**, 5km from Cortona, is the nearest station on the Florence–Rome secondary line (a few trains a day from Florence in 1hr 15mins). Bus from Camucia station c every 30mins in 10mins to Piazza Garibaldi. **Terontola**, 11km from Cortona, is on the main line between Florence and Rome, but only a few fast Intercity trains stop here; local trains in c 1hr 30mins from Florence. Bus from Terontola station c every hour in 25mins to Piazza Garibaldi.

Tourist information office
Via Nazionale 42 (☎ 0575 630 352).

Where to stay
Hotels
☆☆☆☆ *Il Falconiere Relais*, in the countryside at the bottom of the hill, off the road to Castiglion Fiorentino; località San Martino a Bocena (☎ 0575 612 679; 🖨 0575 612 927); *San Michele*, Via Guelfa 15 (Map 1; ☎ 0575 604 348, 🖨 0575 630 147).

☆☆☆ *Oasi*, località Le Contesse (just outside Cortona), with restaurant (☎ 0575 630 354, 🖨 0575 630 477); *San Luca*, Piazza Garibaldi 2 (Map 2; ☎ 0575 630 460, 🖨 0575 630 105); *Sabrina*, Via Roma 37 (Map 3; ☎ 0575 630 397, 🖨 0575 604 627); *Italia*, Via Ghibellina 5 (Map 4; ☎ 0575 630 254, 🖨 0575 630 564).

☆ *Athens*, Via Sant'Antonio 12 (Map 5), closed in winter (☎ 0575 630 508, 🖨 0575 604 457).

Youth hostel
Ostello per la Gioventù San Marco, Via Maffei 57 (closed in winter; ☎ 0575 601 392).

Agriturist accommodation

There are numerous agriturist hotels (information supplied by the **APT** office) including the following, both with swimming pools: località Landrucci, near Torontola, *Fattoria Landrucci* (☎ 0575 204 46); and località Burcinella, *Agrisalotto*, Santa Caterina di Cortona (☎ 0575 617 417).

Eating out
Restaurants
€€€ *Il Falconiere* (see above); *Il Cacciatore*, Via Roma 11; *Preludio*, Via Guelfa 11.
€€ *Osteria del Teatro*, Via Maffei 5.
€ *Dardano*, Via Dardano 19; *Taccone*, Via Dardano 46.

Restaurants in the environs

LOCALITÀ LE CONTESSE € *Oasi*.

OSSAIA € *La Tufa* (also pizzeria).
CASTEL GILARDI on the Città di Castello road, from Cortona (beyond the Porta Colonia), there is a trattoria (a cool place to eat in summer).

Café

Caffè degli Artisti, Via Nazionale. A snack bar, *La Casina dei Tigli*, in the public gardens near San Domenico is open in summer.

Picnic

Pleasant places to picnic include Piazza della Pescaia; near Porta Montanina; and in the little garden between San Benedetto and Sant'Agostino. Also on the hillside off Via Santa Margherita.

Festivals
An **antiques fair** is held in the town in September.

History

The hill on which Cortona stands was occupied by the Villanovan people in the 7C–6C BC. It was in an excellent strategic and commercial position dominating the Valdichiana, on the route between Rome and southern Etruria and northern Etruria and the Po valley, and mid-way between the Tyrrenian and Adriatic coasts. Little is known about the Etruscan town, which was one of the twelve cities of the Etruscan Confederation in the 4C BC. It is thought that the first walls (some 3km in circumference) were built as early as the 4C. By the end of the century the town had come under Roman influence, and large villas were built on the rich agricultural plain in the surrounding territory. However, this marshy area was abandoned in the Middle Ages because of malaria. In the 13C and 14C Cortona was a flourishing commune, ruled after 1325 by the Casali family. In the 15C and 16C it was a dominion of the Florentine Republic.

During the 14C and early 15C many Sienese artists were working in the town, including Sassetta. Fra Angelico painted two altarpieces in the 1430s for the church of San Domenico (now in the Museo Diocesano). The most famous painter born in Cortona was Luca Signorelli (1441–1523), the great precursor of Michelangelo, a number of whose paintings survive here. Another outstanding native painter (and architect) was Pietro Berrettini (1596–1669), called Pietro da Cortona. Gino Severini (1883–1966), the painter was also born here.

Santa Maria del Calcinaio

Half-way up to the town is the church of *Santa Maria del Calcinaio, a masterpiece of Renaissance architecture (open 15.00–17.00; summer 16.00–19.00; fest. 10.00–12.30). It is difficult to reach without a car; but there is a request stop outside the church served by buses to Camucia. Otherwise it is a walk of several kilometres (partly on the main road) from Porta Sant'Agostino. It is one of the few works to have survived certainly by Francesco di Giorgio Martini (1485). It is built on a Latin-cross plan with an octagonal cupola. It had been completed only as far

as the drum of the cupola at the death of Francesco di Giorgio in 1501. The building was finished under the direction of Pietro di Norbo in 1508–14, almost certainly following the design of Francesco di Giorgio.

Set into the hillside, its beautiful form can be fully appreciated as it is approached from above, along a short road with a

Santa Maria del Calcinaio, Cortona

few ancient cypresses. It was built on the site of a tannery (called a *calcinaio* from the use of lime), on the wall of which a miraculous image of the Madonna appeared. The Arte dei Calzolai (Guild of Shoe-makers) commissioned the church to house the venerated Madonna from Francesco di Giorgio, on the advice of Signorelli.

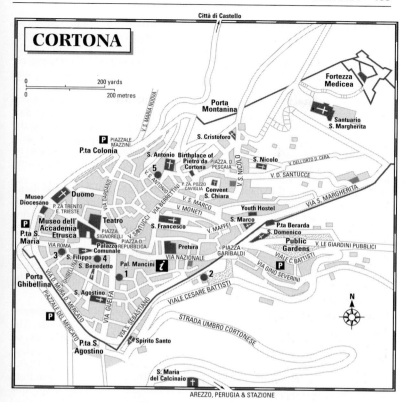

The beautiful light grey-and-white interior with clean architectural lines, has a handsome high altar of 1519 by Bernardino Covatti which encloses the devotional image of the *Madonna del Calcinaio* (14C or 15C). The stained glass in the rose window is by Guglielmo di Marcillat, and the two smaller windows are by his pupils.

On the right side, the first and third altars have an *Annunciation* and *Assumption* by the local painter, Tommaso Bernabei, called Papacello (1527 and 1526). The *Madonna and Child with Saints* by Alessandro Allori, in the right transept, has been removed for restoration for years. Left side: third altar, *Madonna and Saints* (including Thomas Becket), a good Florentine Mannerist painting by Jacopo di Giovanni di Sandro, called Jacone; second and first altars, *Immaculate Conception*, and *Epiphany*, both attributed to Papacello.

Town centre

The road continues up towards the centre (car parks signposted): to the right, near the main entrance to the town is the early 15C church of **San Domenico**. Over the portal is a worn fresco by Fra Angelico, who was a guest at the convent in 1438. The pleasant **interior** has 17C side altars designed by Ascanio Covatti. On the south side the detached fresco of *St Roch* is by Bartolomeo della Gatta, and on the first altar is a wood *Crucifix* of uncertain date. The bright *ancona on the high altar of the *Coronation of the Virgin* is a large, extremely well preserved work in its original elaborate frame, signed by Lorenzo di Nicolò Gerini (1402). In the chapel to the left of the high altar, **Madonna and Saints* by Luca Signorelli (1515). North side, third altar, *Assumption* signed by Palma Giovane; and second altar, *Circumcision* by Passignano.

The **Passeggiata** along the hillside behind the church through public gardens has fine views. In Via Santa Margherita is the façade of the lower church of **San Marco**, with a mosaic of St Mark by Gino Severini (1961). The frescoes on the vault of the oratory date from 1665. A staircase leads to the upper church with a 17C high altar sculpted by Andrea Sellari, and an altarpiece (on the right) by Andrea Commodi. Via Santa Margherita continues uphill, away from the centre, to the church of the same name (described below).

At the entrance to the town **Piazza Garibaldi** has a superb view of Santa Maria del Calcinaio and Lago Trasimeno. In **Via Nazionale**, popularly known as *Rugapiana*, because it is the main and only level street of the town, are several fine 16C palaces, and **Palazzo Ferretti** (no. 45; now the pretura) built in 1738 by Marco Tuscher.

Via Nazionale ends at **Piazza della Repubblica**, the centre of the town. The 13C **Palazzo Comunale** was enlarged in the 16C and extends to Piazza Signorelli, where the façade has a worn *Marzocco* (the Florentine lion) of 1508.

The Museo dell'Accademia Etrusca

Palazzo Casali (or Palazzo Pretorio), also in Piazza Signorelli, is a handsome 13C mansion of the Casali family who became governors of the city. The Renaissance façade was added by Filippo Berrettini in 1613. The 13C flank, on Via Casali, has numerous coats of arms of the governors of the city. The palace houses the *Museo dell'Accademia Etrusca (open 10.00–13.00, 16.00–19.00; winter 09.00–13.00, 15.00–17.00; closed Mon). The museum is entered from the outside staircase in the courtyard. This is also the seat of the Accademia Etrusca, a learned society founded in 1727 for historical and archaeological research. Famous throughout Europe in the 18C, Montesquieu and Voltaire were both early members. The important library has c 30,000 vols, and 620 codices.

On the **first floor** the splendid **main hall** (**2**) has a fine display of small bronzes. On the platform to the right is an Etruscan *chandelier, a very unusual work probably dating from the late 4C BC. It is decorated on the underside with intricate allegorical carved decorations between the 16 little oil lamps, surrounding a gorgon's head. Also displayed here is an inscription of 2C BC, formerly attached to the chandelier. On the platform to the left are eight fine wooden show-cases: in the first, Attic amphora of the mid-6C BC with *Hercules and the Nemean lion* and two lions in an heraldic pose, and an amphora in grey bucchero of the mid-6C BC.

In the first case on the right: statuette of *Zeus* (6C BC) and a bronze plaque with Etruscan letters, divinities, and figures of Hercules. 2nd case: statuettes of athletes, Kourai, votive figures, animals and warriors. 3rd case: 16C–17C bronzes including a statuette of *Marsyas* (perhaps derived from a work by Antonio Pollaiolo), and early 15C northern Italian ivories. In the double case at the end: *Christ crucified* (French or German, 12C–13C), Early Christian glass chalice and a globe of 1710 with the constellations.

In the cases on the left: 18C and 19C bronzes in imitation of Antique works, alabaster statuette of **Hecate** (with 3 bodies) of 1C AD; two votive statuettes (with inscriptions on their legs) of 3C–2C BC; and (last case) Italic and Etruscan votive statuettes.

In the small case opposite the entrance: the famous **Musa Polimnia**, an encaustic painting for long thought to be a Roman work of the 1C–2C AD, but now considered an excellent fake of c 1740. Other paintings displayed around the walls include: a tondo by Francesco Signorelli; **Adoration of the Shepherds** by Luca Signorelli; tondo of the **Madonna and Child** by Pinturicchio; works by Piazzetta, Pietro da Cortona (including an *Annunciation from San Francesco, his last work left unfinished, and **Madonna and Saints** from the church of Sant'Agostino), Ciro Ferri, Cristofano Allori (self-portrait with Ludovico Cigoli), Empoli, and Santi di Tito, as well as two 18C self-portraits by Zoffany and James Northcote.

In **room 3**, off the right end of the hall, is an interesting and representative Egyptian collection made by Monsignor Corbelli, Papal delegate in Egypt from 1891–96. It includes a rare wood model of a funerary boat (2060–1785 BC), statuettes, mummies, canopic vases, papyri, etc. In **Room 4**, off the hall, *Four Saints* by Niccolò Gerini; triptych by Bicci di Lorenzo; 12C–13C Tuscan mosaic of the **Madonna in prayer**. The architectural fragments from the *pieve* date from around 800. The small **rooms 5–7** to the right contain furniture, material relating to the military architect Francesco Laparelli (1521–70), born in Cortona, who designed La Valletta in Malta, fans, ivories, miniatures, swords, 18C–19C livery, and the portrait of an old lady by Bartolomeo Passarotti. The **hall (8)** has a good ceiling and two 18C globes, and a portrait by Zoffany. **Room 9** has a large remarkably elaborate porcelain *tempietto* presented by Carlo Ginori to the Accademia in 1756, which includes medallions of all the ruling members of the Medici family (copies of the medallions exhibited in the wall cases made in 1739 by Antonio Selvi), and allegorical figures. Also displayed here are seals including works by Pisanello and Matteo de' Pasti, and jewellery. **Room 10** (left) contains the numismatic collection, including rare Etruscan coins. The ceramics include Ginori, Delft, Deruta, and Gubbio ware. **Room 11** displays Roman and Etruscan bronzes and terracottas and votive statuettes. **Room 12** contains Etruscan cinerary urns, Bucchero ware, and Attic vases. A door leads out onto a walkway above the courtyard which leads back into the main hall. The last room, next to the ticket office, has a representative display of works by Gino Severini (1883–1966), born in Cortona.

At the top of the stairs on the **second floor** is a room (right) which displays portraits including marble busts of **Luca Signorelli** by Pietro Tenerani (1846) and of *Francesco Benedetti* by Lorenzo Bartolini. Beyond is the 18C **library**, a charming room with c 10,000 volumes in their original bookcases. To the left of the stairs are three rooms which display material from recent excavations in the Etruscan tumulus known as the Secondo Melone del Sodo on the plain below Cortona (described on p 492). These include fragments of Attic ceramics and a gold fibula dating from 480 BC found in the first tomb in 1990–91; jewellery found in 1991–92 in a second tomb in use from the 6C–2C BC; a cast of the stone griffin which decorates the right side of the altar platform; and models of the tumulus and the second tomb.

The Duomo

Via Casali descends to the Duomo on the site of an earlier church (open 08.00–12.30 or 13.00, and 15.00 or 15.30–18.30 or 19.00; you are not allowed in if wearing shorts or with bare shoulders).

It was rebuilt in the 16C probably by a local architect, a follower of Giuliano da Sangallo (but was later much modified). Remains of the Romanesque church can be seen in the façade (including a large capital with human heads). The campanile (1566) is by Francesco Laparelli. There is a fine view of the countryside from the terrace here. On the south side beneath a pretty 16C portico is a delightful *doorway by Cristofanello (1550).

The striking **interior**, with a barrel vault, has capitals similar to those in San Lorenzo in Florence. On the west wall is the impressive neo-Classical funerary monument to Giovanni Battista Tommasi, by Romualdo Galli (1806). South aisle. Second altar, *Transfiguration* by Raffaello Vanni; fourth altar, *St Joseph* by Lorenzo Berrettini. In the chapel to the right of the sanctuary, 13C terracotta *Pietà* (removed for restoration since 1977). The **high altar**, with four carved angels, is a fine work by the local sculptor Francesco Mazzuoli (1664). In the **choir** (light) are some good paintings (right to left): *Madonna of the Rosary* by Cigoli, *Consecration of the church of San Salvatore* by Andrea Commodi; *Descent of the Holy Spirit* by Pappacello; *Crucifixion* attributed to Luca Signorelli; *Incredulity of St Thomas* by Francesco Signorelli; *Madonna of the Holy Girdle* attributed to Cristofano Allori; *Madonna and Saints* by Giovanni Morandi, and *Assumption* by Andrea del Sarto (or his school). At the end of the north aisle, carved ciborium dated 1491 attributed to Cuccio di Nuccio or Urbano da Cortona, and two mosaics by Gino Severini. Fifth altar, *Madonna and Saints* by Lorenzo Berrettini; fourth altar, wood *Crucifix* by Andrea Sellari; third altar, *Adoration of the Shepherds* by Pietro da Cortona; second altar, *St Sebastian* by Lorenzo Baldi; first altar, 15C terracotta statue of the *Madonna and Child* (heavily decorated and repainted). On the west wall, fine funerary monument to Giovanni Alberti attributed to Santi di Tito.

A remarkable Byzantine ivory panel thought to date from the 9C preserved in a 17C reliquary which belongs to the church of San Francesco has been exhibited here while that church is closed.

The Museo Diocesano

Opposite the façade of the cathedral is the *Museo Diocesano which incorporates the former church of the Gesù, and is one of the most important diocescan museums in Tuscany with some beautiful paintings (open 09.30–13.00, 15.30–19.00; Oct–March: 10.00–13.00, 15.00–17.00; closed Mon).

Room 1, to the right of the entrance, has a Roman sarcophagus (end of the 2C) depicting the battle of the amazons and centaurs, known to have been admired by Donatello and Brunelleschi.

Beyond the stairs is the former **Church of the Gesù (3)** which has a fine wooden *ceiling by Michelangelo Leggi (1536), with symbols of the Passion and the Eucharist. Some beautiful paintings are displayed here: the *Madonna and Child with four Saints* by Sassetta was damaged when in storage during the last War, but the large painted *Crucifix* by Pietro Lorenzetti is, instead, very well preserved. The two works by Fra Angelico were painted for San Domenico: the *Madonna enthroned with Saints* has been recomposed: the central panel dates from 1433, while the side panels and exquisite predella were painted about five years later. The *Annunciation* (1428–30) is one of Angelico's most beautiful works, with a 'continuous' scene in the predella, which includes a view of a lake which may be Trasimeno. This was the last of three similar paintings to be painted by this master: the others are in the Prado in Madrid and San Giovanni Valdarno (see p 503). The *Assumption of the Virgin* is one of the best works of Bartolomeo della Gatta dating from the 1470s (the influence of Piero della Francesca as well as Van Eyck can be seen here). The church became the baptistery of the Duomo in the 18C and the font is by Cuccio di Nuccio.

In **room 2**, behind the font, *Madonna and Child* attributed to Niccolò di Segna; *Madonna enthroned with four angels*, signed and dated 1320 by Pietro Lorenzetti; and *St Margaret* and stories from her life (very damaged) by a 13C Aretine master. The Saint's unusual dress is particularly interesting, symbolising her poverty. The fresco fragments here include the *Way to Calvary* by Pietro Lorenzetti (from the old church of Santa Margherita). A long flight of stairs **(5)**, lined with cartoons (1944) by Gino Severini for his mosaics of the Via Crucis (see p 492), leads down past a painted *Crucifix* by Pietro Lorenzetti to the **lower church (6)**, the vault of which was painted by Giorgio Vasari in 1545, and the lunettes by Cristoforo Gherardi (Il Doceno). The plain stalls are by Vincenzo da Cortona (1517), and the terracotta *Deposition* group is a 15C Florentine work.

In **room 4** (at the end of room 1) is a *Deposition*, with a fine predella by Luca Signorelli; the *Communion of the Apostles* is attributed to him, and the other works are by his *bottega*. Off this room **room 9** has later works: *Ecstasy of St Margaret of Cortona* by Giuseppe Maria Crespi; *Assumption* by the 16C Roman school; and *Miracle of St Francesco da Paola* by Il Daggiù. Also here are displayed the symbolic bronzes made by Vincenzo Lapi in 1772 for the monument to St Margaret of Cortona in the piazza outside (replaced in situ by copies).

By the entrance another flight of stairs leads down to **room 8** with the Passerini church vestments of 1515, including a cope made for Leo X's visit to the town, embroidered on designs by Andrea del Sarto and Raffaellino del Garbo. Made of velvet with embroideries in gold thread these are the most important vestments made in Italy of their date. **Room 7** displays the Vagnucci reliquary signed and dated 1458 by Giusto da Firenze (the statuette of Christ is, instead, an early 15C French work), and church silver including a chalice by Michele di Tommaso da Siena (late 14C).

Lower town

From Piazza Signorelli, beyond the **Teatro Signorelli**, built in 1857 by Carlo Gatteschi, the pretty old Via Dardano leads uphill before descending to the simple **Porta Colonia** (which preserves its wooden doors). Here are the most considerable remains of the **Etruscan walls**, the huge blocks conspicuous below Roman and medieval masonry above. The walls stretch away up the hill towards the Fortezza Medicea, above the church of Santa Margherita, the top of which can just be seen in the woods (both described below). Outside the gate (reached by a pretty road), in beautiful countryside on the hillside below the town, the fine centrally-planned church of **Santa Maria Nuova** is well seen. It is known that both Cristofanello (in 1550–54) and Vasari were involved in the construction of the church, which was not finished until 1600 when the cupola was built. It is closed for restoration but contains altarpieces by Alessandro Allori and Empoli, and a 16C organ by Onofrio Zefferini. From the gate Via delle Mura del Duomo, a charming little lane with acacia trees, leads back along the top of the walls to the Duomo.

Via Janelli, Cortona

From **Piazza della Repubblica** three narrow old roads descend to gates in the walls. **Via Roma** passes beneath an archway of Palazzo Comunale and ends at the medieval Porta Santa Maria. On the left is the entrance to the church of **San Filippo** with a cupola, a fine work by Antonio Iannelli (1720). It contains altarpieces by Camillo Sagrestani (high altar) and Giovanni Battista Piazzetta (second altar on the left). Beside the church is the little Porta del Morto of **Palazzo Cinaglia** (no. 25), with a worn carved architrave. Many old houses in Cortona have a second small doorway usually raised above the level of the street (and now often used as a window). This was known as the Porta del Morto as it was popularly supposed that it was used only to carry out the coffin when an inhabitant of the house died. Instead it is now thought to have been used as the usual door of the house (which could easily be defended in times of trouble when the larger doorways were barred). On the right (no. 26) is the fine medieval **Palazzo Quintani**. Just before the gate is the pretty Via Jannelli (right) with medieval houses and wooden *sporti*.

Via Guelfa leads south from Piazza della Repubblica steeply down to Porta Sant'Agostino. At the beginning, on the right, is **Palazzo Mancini-Sernini** (no. 4) with an unusually tall *façade incorporating a loggia on the top storey. It was designed by Cristofanello for the Laparelli family in 1533. Lower down is the church and convent of **Sant'Agostino** with a Gothic exterior and a 17C interior (restored as a conference and exhibition centre). It contains side altars by Filippo Berrettini (1613) and an altarpiece by Empoli. Behind the church (reached by Via del Marzocco) is the unusual exterior of the church of **San Benedetto** (closed) built in 1722 on an elliptical plan. It contains an interesting wooden statue of *Christ at the Column*. Nearby is a medieval house with wooden *sporti* and a 13C public fountain. Outside Porta Sant'Agostino is the church of the **Spirito Santo** (closed) built in 1637 by Filippo Berrettini with a cupola of 1751. It contains an 18C *Madonna and Child with Saints* by Giuseppe Angeli, and a wood statue of the *Dead Christ* by Fabbrucci (1687–1767).

Via Ghibellina leads down from Piazza della Repubblica to the walls where the Etruscan **Porta Ghibellina** has been partially excavated. There is a pleasant walk from here back to Porta Sant'Agostino along the top of the walls.

Upper town

The stepped Via Santucci leads up beneath the **Palazzo del Popolo** in Piazza della Repubblica to the church of **San Francesco**, with a worn Gothic portal, the first church to be built outside of Assisi by the Franciscans after the death of St Francis. The architect was Brother Elias, friend and disciple of St Francis, who died in the convent of the church in 1253 and is buried behind the altar. It is thought that Luca Signorelli was buried in the crypt. The interesting interior, with many works of art, has been closed indefinitely for restoration.

Beneath the church steps is a 13C public fountain. Opposite the high wall of the church and convent in Via Maffei is the pretty Renaissance portico of the **Ospedale di Santa Maria della Misericordia**. Via Berrettini, a very steep road, leads up from San Francesco through a delightful, quiet residential part of the town, with colourful gardens and plants around the well-kept houses. Beyond a large circular water cistern is the **birthplace of Pietro da Cortona** (no. 33; plaque). The road follows the high convent wall of **Santa Chiara**. The convent and church were built in 1555 by Vasari. The church contains an *Immaculate Conception* by Andrea Commodi, and a *Deposition* attributed as an early work to Pietro da Cortona. In underground rooms are remains of a huge Roman cistern (the most important building of this date to survive in Cortona). The small triangular Piazza della Pescaia is beautifully planted with ilex trees.

Via Berrettini continues to ascend (keep left) towards the charming little Romanesque bellcote of **San Cristoforo** (entered to the left). It contains damaged detached frescoes by the 13C Umbrian school. Beside a large square water cistern a road, (right) descends shortly to the 15C church of **San Niccolò**, approached through a peaceful walled garden. The wooden porch, with Ionic capitals, was added in 1930 (opened by the custodian who lives here; ring at the door on the left, 09.00–12.00, 15.00–dusk). Over the altar is a standard painted on both sides by Luca Signorelli with a *Deposition (in excellent condition) and a *Madonna and Child* (shown by the custodian). On the north wall is a votive fresco of the *Madonna and Saints* by Signorelli or his school.

Via Santo Stefano continues uphill; on the left Via Porta Montanina leads to the edge of the hillside, planted with pine trees, beside the charming **Porta Montanina**, decorated with four arches, with its doors still intact. Remains of the Etruscan walls, and of a second fortified gate can be seen here. A fine stretch of walls leads steeply down the hillside beside orchards, and uphill to the Fortezza Medicea. Outside the gate there is a view of Santa Maria Nuova and the pretty countryside below the town.

Santa Margherita and the Fortezza Medicea

From Via Santo Stefano, Via Santa Croce (signposted for Santa Margherita), a stepped lane with gardens on either side continues uphill towards the sanctuary (which can also be reached by car off the Città di Castello road at Torreone). Via Santa Croce passes through cypress woods before reaching the sanctuary of **Santa Margherita**, dedicated to St Margaret of Cortona (1247–97).

Born at Laviano, in Umbria, she became a Franciscan tertiary, the third member of the Order after St Francis and St Clare. Her name was associated with numerous miracles after her death in a monastery here; a Gothic church, probably designed by Giovanni Pisano, was built on this site where she was buried. To celebrate her canonization in 1728, Ferdinando Ruggeri built a neo-Gothic cupola over her tomb five years later, but the whole church was rebuilt by Mariano Falcini in 1856–93 in Romanesque-Gothic style. A single rose window was retained from the original church. It contains her *sarcophagus, thought to have been designed by the native artists Angiolo and Francesco di Pietro (1362), but also attributed to Giovanni Pisano. The frescoes (1890–95) are by Giorgio Bandini.

Below the church, Via Santa Margherita descends to the public gardens (see above), past a Via Crucis in mosaic by Gino Severini, set up as a thanks-offering after Cortona was saved from severe war damage. A road continues up to the **Fortezza Medicea** or Girfalco, in a splendid position dominating the town (651m). There is a magnificent view of Lake Trasimene, and part of the outer circle of walls built by the Etruscans can be seen from here. The castle was built by order of Cosimo I in 1556, and was once thought to be the work of Francesco Laparelli, but is now considered to be by his friend Gabrio Serbelloni. At present the interior is open only for exhibitions in summer, 10.00–13.00, 15.00–19.00. Outside is a stone bench carved by Joe Tilson in 1990.

The environs of Cortona ~ Etruscan tombs

On the plain at the foot of the hill are a number of interesting Etruscan tombs. From the road junction, known as the Cinque Vie, near Santa Maria del Calcinaio (see above), a road (signposted for Sodo) leads to the **Tanella di Pitagora** (for adm. ☎ 0575 603 083), a vaulted circular Etruscan tomb, probably formerly covered by a tumulus. Restored in the 19C, it is now surrounded by cypresses. Despite its name (meaning 'cave-dwelling of Pythagoras'), it has nothing to do with Pythagoras (who lived at Crotone in Southern Italy). It had been discovered by the 16C when Vasari visited it, calling it the tomb of Archimedes. Formerly thought to date from the 4C BC, it may have been built in the 3C or even the 2C BC. Nearby, in Località Piaggette, is the **Tanella Angori**, similar in form, but less well preserved, discovered in 1949.

Near the railway station (entrance on Via Lauretana) is the **Melone di Camucia** ('Melone' or 'melon' refers to its shape), an Etruscan tumulus tomb excavated in 1842 by Alessandro François. It has a perimeter of 200 metres, and was in use from the 7C BC to the 4C BC. Finds from the two burial chambers (the second one discovered in 1964) are in the Archaeological Museum in Florence.

In the locality of Sodo, at the foot of the hill, off the road to Castiglion Fiorentino, are two more tumulus tombs. They are on either side of the road to Foiano. The **Primo Melone del Sodo** (for adm. ☎ 0575 612 778) was discovered in 1909 and is marked by a pine tree on top of the mound. It has a circumference of 185m, and was in use from the early 6C BC to the 3C BC. Inside is an inscription dating from the 4C BC. On the left of the Foiano road is the **Secondo Melone del Sodo** (usually open 08.00–14.00 exc. Mon; or ☎ 0575 612 565) excavated in 1927, and one of the largest tumuli so far found in Etruria. Excavations have been in progress here since 1990 when an altar was discovered on the exterior (east side) of the tumulus, approached by a monumental stairway either side of which are two large sphynxes with warriors carved in the early 6C (this is the only Eturscan tomb known which conserves sculptural elements in situ). Two tombs in use from the 6C–2C BC have been excavated in the tumulus, the finds from which are exhibited in the Museo dell'Accademia Etrusca in Cortona (see above).

Outside Porta Colonia (see above) on the Città di Castello road is the picturesque **Convento delle Celle**, in a beautiful position on the lower slopes of Monte Egidio. The pretty stone buildings, immaculately kept, are grouped beside a river torrent. A hermitage on this site was probably occupied by the Franciscans c 1214–17, who were visited by St Francis in 1226. The convent has been occupied by the Cappuccini since 1537. The hillside has had to be shored up above the convent to prevent landslides. Visitors can see various chapels including St Francis' cell.

Above the convent is **Torreone**, at the watershed between the Valdichiana and Val Tiberina, and **Castel Gilardi**. From here a rough road leads north along the wooded slopes of **Monte Egidio** (1056m) where Villa del Seminario is on the site of the Hermitage of St Egidio. There are particularly beautiful views from this road (of Cortona) and from the Città di Castello road (of Lake Trasimene). From Castel Gilardi a road leads over the Umbrian border to descend into the Tiber valley, joining the road from Umbertide to Città di Castello (see *Blue Guide Umbria*). Below the Public Gardens of Cortona (see above) Via delle Contesse and Via del Palazzone (left) lead to **Villa Passerini**, known as Il Palazzone. It was built for Cardinal Silvio Passerini by Giovanni Battista Caporali (1521), and is now used in the summer by the Scuola Normale di Pisa. The salone has frescoes by Papacello and the chapel is frescoed by Signorelli and his pupils. Nearby, at **Metelliano**, is the 11C church of Sant'Angelo.

A road leads southwest from Cortona towards Mercatale via the **Rocca di Pierle**, an impressive, large, square castle dating from before 1098, surrounded by a little hamlet. Mercatale is in Umbria (see *Blue Guide Umbria*).

A road leads across the plain from Camucia to the **Abbazia di Farneta**, probably founded in the 8C. The interesting Romanesque building has a beautiful 10C triple apse and *crypt, restored after 1940. In the priest's house (admission on request) is a local paleontological collection.

The Valdichiana

The Valdichiana is a plain southwest of Arezzo, named after the Chiana river which lies between the upper basins of the Arno and the Tiber. In prehistoric times this valley formed the bed of the Arno, which flowed not into the Tyrrhenian Sea but into the Tiber. The Chiana river was once an affluent of the Tiber but was deviated by the Romans into the Arno in an attempt to avoid flooding in Rome. By the late Roman period unhealthy marshes had formed on the plain. In 1388 the Florentines built a drainage ditch (called the Fosso Maestro) for the Chiana and in the 15C Leonardo da Vinci made studies of the area. However, the first serious attempt to drain the marshes was made by Cosimo I when he constructed the Canale Maestro della Chiana in 1551, and draining and irrigation operations continued until 1780 when the situation was more or less resolved by the construction of an artificial watershed between the Tiber and Arno rivers near Chiusi and the building of more canals. The most interesting little towns in this area are Monte San Savino and Lucignano. The southern part of the Valdichiana with Chiusi is described on p 460.

Practical information

Getting there
By car

The A1 motorway from Florence to Rome has exits at Monte San Savino (for Gargonza and Lucignano) and Valdichiana (for Foiano della Chiana).

By train

A secondary line from Arezzo has stations at Monte San Savino, Lucignano, and Foiano.

Information office

APT **Arezzo** (☎ 0575 377 678).

Where to stay
Hotels

MONTE SAN SAVINO
☆☆☆ *San Gallo*, Piazza Vittorio Veneto 16 (☎ 0575 810 049; ▯ 0575 810 220).

LUCIGNANO ☆☆☆ *Da Totò*, with restaurant, Piazza del Tribunale 6

(☎ 0575 836 763; ▯ 0575 836 988).

Agriturist accommodation

GARGONZA, near Monte San Savino: *Casa Contessa Francesca*, ☎ 0575 847 021; ▯ 0575 847 054 (with swimming pool and restaurant; houses or flats can be rented for short periods).

Eating out
Restaurant

LUCIGNANO € *La Rocca*, Via G. Matteotti 15.

Festivals

An annual **fair** (*Fiera di Santa Caterina*) is held on the last weekend in November in **Monte San Savino**, when locally-made ceramics are sold including decorative little hand-warmers with whistles on their handles which have been produced in the town for centuries. The carnival of **Foiano della Chiana** is a remarkable spectacle.

Above the northern part of the valley, in a beautiful position on a wooded ridge with fine views, is the delightful little hamlet of **Civitella in Val di Chiana**. Beside the Porta Senese is the **Cassero**, an impressive 13C castle with high ruined walls. It is now a public park. The delightful arcaded main street, with pretty brick paving (unfortunately unfeelingly renewed to a different design in 1995), continues past **Palazzo del Podestà** with coats of arms and a characteristic portico, the lines of which are repeated in the other buildings nearby. The rebuilt parish church in the piazza stands beside an inscription and bronze relief commemorating the inhabitants who lost their lives here in a brutal act of retaliation during the Second World War. An unsurfaced by-road leads downhill to the south through spectacular countryside, via Ciggiano to Gargonza (described below).

Monte San Savino

Monte San Savino, a pleasant little town (7300 inhab.), was the birthplace of the sculptor and architect Andrea Contucci, called Sansovino (1460–1529), and preserves a number of works by him.

History

Of Roman foundation, Monte San Savino is named after a church dedicated to the 5C bishop of Chiusi, San Savino. Long hostile to Arezzo, it was destroyed in 1325 by the Aretine bishop Guido Tarlati. Members of the local Di Monte family (who became Counts of the town in the 16C) included

Cardinal Antonio (friend and adviser of Julius II), and Pope Julius III.

The town has been known since ancient times for its production of ceramics and Andrea Sansovino began his artistic life here as a ceramist.

The town is entered by **Porta Fiorentina** built c 1550 by Nanni di Baccio Bigio (on a design by Giorgio Vasari). **Corso Sangallo** begins here and crosses the small town past several fine palaces. The street paving has been carefully restored. At the far end of Piazza Gamurrini an interesting palace has an unusual ground floor window with two carved herms. The obelisk was set up in honour of Mattias de' Medici who became ruler of the Principality in 1644. The **Cassero** (or castle) is attributed to the Sienese architect Bartolo di Bartolo (1383; restored). The exterior is now hidden by 17C houses. The castle was used as a Monte di Pietà (pawn shop) from 1595 until 1822 and then as a poorhouse (up until 1960). The **Museo del Cassero** (open 09.00–12.00, 16.00–19.00 exc. Mon) contains a collection of local ceramics from the Valdichiana (19C and early 20C), a statue of the *Madonna and Child* (16C–17C) and a wood 14C *Crucifix*. It is also used for exhibitions.

The church of **Santa Chiara**, built in 1652, now the property of the Comune is to be reopened. It contains a splendid *altarpiece of the *Madonna and Child with four Saints* by Andrea Sansovino (c 1490), glazed by Andrea or Giovanni della Robbia; an unglazed terracotta altarpiece of *St Lawrence between Saints Roch and Sebastian* (1486), also by Andrea Sansovino; a polychrome terracotta altarpiece of the *Nativity*, attributed to Giovanni della Robbia; and a statue of *St Anthony Abbot*, by Sansovino (with a glazed della Robbian frame).

Farther on in Corso Sangallo is the handsome ***Loggia dei Mercanti**, built in 1518–20 by Andrea Sansovino for Cardinal Antonio di Monte. The high arcade is borne on Corinthian columns and pilasters. Opposite it, in ***Palazzo Di Monte** is the town hall built in 1515 by Antonio da Sangallo the Elder, also for the Cardinal. It has a fine courtyard with two rectangular wells, beyond which is a charming hanging garden designed by Nanni di Baccio Bigio.

The **pieve** was built c 1100 and the interior remodelled in the mid-18C with stuccoes and marbling. On the left of the west door is the recomposed sarcophagus of Fabiano di Monte (father of Cardinal Antonio), an early work by Andrea Sansovino (1498). Above the benches towards the east end are two small square reliefs, possibly also early works by Sansovino. The organ dates from the 17C.

On the other side of the corso is the 14C tower of **Palazzo Pretorio** decorated with coats of arms: it can be climbed from May–Sept on fest. 09.30–12.30. Beyond is **Piazza Di Monte**, laid out by Andrea Sansovino in front of his house (plaque). Above the public fountain is a *Marzocco* lion.

The interior of the church of **Sant'Agostino** has a delightful double loggia with Ionic columns at the west end by Andrea Sansovino. The altars date from 1710, and the interesting terracotta pavement has numerous tomb slabs. On the west wall are good frescoes of the *Crucifixion*, *Adoration of the Magi*, and *Presentation in the Temple* by Giovanni d'Agnolo di Balduccio (1370–1452). Above is a rose window by Guglielmo di Marcillat. The high altarpiece of the *Assumption* is signed and dated 1539 by Vasari. It is flanked by a *Nativity and Adoration of the Magi* by Orazio Porta. On the left wall is a *Resurrection*, also by Porta.

Below the little pulpit is the worn tomb slab of Andrea Sansovino, found in 1969 beneath the pavement of the church. The damaged fresco of the *Pietà*, with five saints below, is by Paolo Schiavo. There is a fine cloister next to the church, probably designed by Sansovino (1528).

The church of **San Giovanni**, which has a door by Sansovino, is usually closed. In the northwestern district of the town (close to Porta Fiorentina) Via Salomone Fiorentino (named after a native Jewish poet, 1743–1815) recalls the **Ghetto** in this area inhabited from 1627–1799. The 17C synagogue is in a ruined state (there is also a Jewish cemetery outside the walls).

To the east of Monte San Savino (towards the motorway) is the sanctuary of **Santa Maria delle Vertighe** (open 07.00–12.00, 15.00–19.00), with a campanile attributed to Andrea Sansovino. In the primitive apse is an *altarpiece by Margaritone di Arezzo and Fra Ristoro (restored in 2000). The little museum (admission on request at the monastery) contains two saints by Ridolfo del Ghirlandaio, and a painted *Crucifix* by Lorenzo Monaco.

On the other side of the motorway is **Marciano della Chiana** which has remains of its walls and towers. A road leads south to **Pozzo**, beyond which, by the cemetery, is **Santa Vittoria**, an octagonal chapel with a cupola and lantern thought to have been designed by Ammannati or Vasari in 1572. It was commissioned by Cosimo I to commemorate the battle here of Scannagallo in 1554 in which the Florentines were victorious over the Sienese and French. It is an unusual, but well-proportioned building in brick and *pietra serena*.

Off the pretty Siena road (no. 73) which runs through woods west of Monte San Savino, is **Gargonza**, a charming little circular medieval hamlet in a peaceful position surrounded by wooded hills, and extremely well preserved. An Ubertini castle in the 13C, it was sold to Siena in 1381, but its possession was subsequently contested by Florence, who ordered the destruction of its walls in 1433. It has been carefully and unpretentiously restored by the Guicciardini family as a hotel-residence where houses or flats can be rented (see above).

Lucignano

Further south is Lucignano, a delightful, cheerful little medieval village laid out on an elliptical form, and well preserved. It has some interesting works of art, and fine views. Above the 14C **Cassero**, with a tall tower, is the large **Collegiata**, approached by a pretty flight of curving steps. The interior by Orazio Porta, dates from 1594. The gilded wooden angels were installed in 1706. In the south transept, *St Charles Borromeo* by Giacinto Gemignani. The high altar is by Andrea Pozzo (and the Crucifix dates from the 16C). In the north transept, *Visitation* by Matteo Rosselli. On the north side is a *Martyrdom of St Lucy* by Gemignani.

Beyond the Collegiata is the 14C **Palazzo Comunale** which houses the **Museo Comunale** (open 10.30–13.00, 15.30 or 16.00–17.30 or 19.00; closed Mon). In the entrance is a 16C fresco of the *Pietà*. In the entrance corridor is church silver of 1628, and a small painting of the *Madonna enthroned with Saints* attributed to Lippo Vanni. The vaulted **Sala del Tribunale** has delightful frescoes dating from 1438–65 of illustrious people from the Bible and Classical heroes, and a huge gold *reliquary* (over 2.5 metres high) known as the Tree of Lucignano, made in 1350–1471 and decorated with coral and exquisite miniatures. **Room 3**: lunette by Luca Signorelli of *St Francis receiving the stigmata* (with a lovely landscape), and a *Madonna and Child* attributed to him. **Room 4**:

Madonna and Child enthroned by the Sienese school (c 1320); triptych of the *Madonna with Saints John the Baptist and John the Evangelist* by Bartolo di Fredi; *St Bernardine* (1448) by Pietro di Giovanni Ambrogio; and a small *Crucifixion* by the 13C Sienese school.

Beside Palazzo Comunale is the church of **San Francesco** (1248), with a Romanesque façade. It has numerous interesting fresco fragments, some attributed to Bartolo di Fredi and Taddeo di Bartolo. On the last altar on the south side is a painted polychrome wood statue of the *Madonna and Child* by Mariano di Angelo Romanelli (1380–90). Behind the high altar, polyptych of the *Madonna with four Saints* by Luca di Tommè. The organ dates from the 16C.

The church of the **Madonna della Quercia** is outside the village (indicated by yellow signs). The road passes the ruins of the old Medici fortress on a hill, built by Cosimo I, and the cemetery. The church (in poor condition), next to a farm house, is only open for services at weekends. It was built in the late 16C perhaps on a design by Vasari. The fine interior is attributed to Giuliano da Sangallo.

On the other side of the motorway is **Foiano della Chiana**, a small agricultural town, with some light industries, near the Chiana plain. From the gate a road leads up to Piazza Cavour where Palazzo Comunale faces the well restored **Palazzo Monte Pio**. It was built by Ferdinando II de' Medici as a hunting lodge and used as such up to 1670 when it became the pawn shop. It now contains offices belonging to the Comune. A modern flight of steps leads down to the left and across Corso Vittorio Emanuele (which has an 18C loggia) to the church of **San Michele Arcangelo**, with a pretty exterior and campanile. It contains fine carved confessionals and benches dating from the 17C, and 15C choir stalls. On the second south altar is a *Madonna of the Rosary* by Lorenzo Lippi, and on the third north altar, an enamelled terracotta of the *Ascension* by Andrea della Robbia and his son Giovanni (1495–1500). Off the south side is an oratory with elaborate stuccoes in the vault and lunettes.

The corso continues to **Piazza della Collegiata** where there is a well, imposing brick fortifications (including a restored round tower) and a row of houses above brick bastions on either side of Porta Castello. The **Collegiata** has a Baroque façade. On the third south altar is a *Madonna della Cintola* (1502) by Andrea della Robbia, and on the second north altar, a *Coronation of the Virgin*, a late work by Luca Signorelli and his school. Steps lead up through Porta Castello, a double brick gate, to the church of **Santa Maria della Fraternità** (ask at the Comune for the key) which contains a 17C ceiling, cantoria, benches, organ, and gilded wood coffer. Four paintings are attributed to Giovanni Camillo Sagrestani, and the beautiful statue of the standing *Madonna and Child* is now thought to be by Andrea della Robbia (c 1460) probably on a model by his uncle, Luca.

On the outskirts of the town, by the hospital, is the church of **San Francesco** preceded by a portico (usually open in the afternoon). It contains 16C terracotta statuary, and a large della Robbian altarpiece of *Christ in Glory with Saints*.

From Foiano a road leads over the Chiana, via the Abbazia di Farneta (p 493), to Cortona, see p 482.

The Valdarno and Pratomagno

The Valdarno lies between Florence and Arezzo, overlooked by the Chianti hills and the western slopes of the Pratomagno. In the Pliocene era (about 3 million years ago) a huge lake occupied this area and on its shores were tropical forests inhabited by rhinoceros, hippopotamus, and elephants. It later became one of the most fertile areas of Italy, settled by the Etruscans and Romans.

The narrow Arno valley has always been important as the main route between Florence and the south. In the 14C the Florentine Republic founded *Terre nuove* here at San Giovanni Valdarno, Terranuova Bracciolini, and Castelfranco di Sopra. The Humanists Marsilio Ficino, Poggio Bracciolini, and Benedetto Varchi were all born in the Valdarno. The most interesting places to visit in the area include the small town of San Giovanni Valdarno, Montevarchi, and the monastery of Vallombrosa.

Many of the beautiful works of art in churches here by Florentine masters have been carefully restored in recent years: these include a triptych by Masaccio, born at San Giovanni Valdarno (now in the pieve at Cascia), an *Annunciation* by Fra Angelico (exhibited in the museum in San Giovanni Valdarno), and numerous della Robbian works. A fine red Chianti is produced on the *Colli Aretini*. The hills of the Pratomagno rise to nearly 1000 metres at **Vallombrosa**, famous for its monastery and forests.

Practical information

Getting there
By car
The A1 **motorway** from Florence to Arezzo follows the Valdarno with exits at Incisa (for Figline) and Valdarno (for San Giovanni Valdarno and Montevarchi).

By train
The main line from Florence–Rome via Pontassieve has stations at Incisa, Figline, San Giovanni, and Montevarchi (slow trains only).

By bus
Services run by *SITA* from Florence via San Donato in Collina to Incisa, Figline, San Giovanni, and Montevarchi. *CAT* services via Pontassieve to the above towns. *SITA* services via Pontassieve, Pelago and Tosi for Vallombrosa and Saltino.

Information offices
APT of **Florence** (☎ 055 290 832) for Incisa Valdarno, Figline Valdarno, Reggello, and Vallombrosa. *APT* of **Arezzo** (☎ 0575 377 678) for San Giovanni Valdarno and Montevarchi.

Where to stay
Hotels
FIGLINE ☆☆☆ *Antica Taverna Casa Grande* (with restaurant), Via Castelguinelli 84 (☎ 055 954 4851; 📠 055 954 4322) and *Torricelli*, Via San Biagio 2 (☎ 055 958 139; 📠 055 958 481).
SAN GIOVANNI VALDARNO ☆☆☆ *La Bianca*, Viale Don Minzoni 38 (☎ 055 912 3402; 📠 055 912 1423) and *River*, Via Fratelli Cervi 10 (☎ 055 912 2435; 📠 055 912 0219).

MONTEVARCHI ☆☆☆ *Delta*, Viale Diaz 137 (☎ 055 901 213; ▯ 055 901 727).

REGGELLO ☆☆☆☆ *Villa Rigacci* in the country at Vaggio (☎ 055 865 6718; ▯ 055 865 6537); ☆☆☆ *Fattoria degli Usignoli*, San Donato in Fronzano (☎ 055 865 2018; ▯ 055 865 2270).

PIETRAPIANA ☆☆☆ *Archimede*, with restaurant (☎ 055 869 055; ▯ 055 868 584).

SALTINO ☆☆☆ *Grand Hotel Vallombrosa*, Via Carducci 2 (☎ 055 862 012; ▯ 055 862 035) and ☆☆ *Villino Medici* (☎ 055 862 017).

Campsites

FIGLINE ☆☆☆☆ *Norcenni Girasole Club* (☎ 055 959 666).
CAVRIGLIA ☆☆ sites.

 **Eating out**
FIGLINE €€ *Papillon*, Piazza Ficino 83.
SAN GIOVANNI VALDARNO €€ *Adriano VII*, Piazza Masaccio 16, *Castellucci*, Corso Italia 44.
TERRANOVA BRACCIOLINI *Cooperativa Agricola Valdarnese*, open at weekends on a farm at Paterna (booking necessary, ☎ 055 977 052). At Penna Alta, €€ *Il canto di Maggio*.

The Valdarno

At the northern end of the Valdarno is **Incisa Valdarno**, so called from the deep chalky cutting made by the Arno, through which run the road, motorway, and railway. The conspicuous 14C Torre del Castellano was heavily restored in 1952. On the main road is the Municipio beside the church of **Sant'Alessandro** with three fragments of a polyptych by Andrea di Giusto. In the convent of **Santi Cosma e Damiano** (1538; reconstructed in the 17C), preceded by a portico of 1592, are 17C paintings and a polychrome terracotta bas-relief of the *Madonna and Child* attributed to Buggiano (on a design by Luca della Robbia.

A road beyond Sant'Alessandro climbs the hill to the locality known as Castello, where a few pine trees stand on the left of the road. This is the site of the old town of **Ancisa**, and the bellcote of the former church above the high pyramidal wall of the ruined castle provides an odd site. In the hamlet on the left is a house (plaques) where Petrarch spent the first seven years of his life. The road continues up to **Loppiano** in beautiful countryside, before which, on the left, is the **Pieve di Santi Vito e Modesto**. Of ancient foundation, it has a battlemented campanile, and owns a painting of the *Madonna of the Holy Girdle* by Francesco d'Antonio (1427).

To the south, in pretty countryside, near **Brollo**, is the tiny hamlet of **San Pietro al Terreno** (unsignposted), with farm buildings beside the church with a bellcote. In the fine 18C interior (if closed, ring on the right) are frescoes in grisaille, stuccoes, and marble confessionals. On the high altar, *Madonna and Child with four Saints* by an early 16C Florentine master. In the choir is a detached 14C fresco of the *Madonna and Saints*, and on the left altar, a 17C painting of the *Madonna of the Rosary*.

Figline Valdarno

Figline Valdarno has been an important market town (13,600 inhab.) since the 12C. The castle of Feghine was first mentioned in 1008, but the town on this site was laid out on a regular plan in 1259 by the Florentines, who also built its walls in 1356.

The lovely large **Piazza Ficino** (market on Tuesdays) is named after the great Humanist scholar Marsilio Ficino (1433–99) who was born here. A friend of Cosimo il Vecchio, he was a leading member of the Medici Platonic Academy in Florence. The square has porticoes and balconies, and a medley of houses. At one end is the 17C **Spedale Serristori** with a loggia. This was founded in 1399 by a certain Ser Ristoro, and the hospital was transferred to Villa di San Cerbone (see below) in 1890. Four very worn frescoes beneath the loggia are by Niccolò Lapi (late 17C).

At the other end of the piazza is the **Collegiata di Santa Maria**, founded in 1257, with a dark interior heavily restored in the 20C. **South wall**. *Madonna and Child with Saints* (including *St Romulus holding a model of Figline*), attributed to Giovanni Andrea de Magistris (1593). The pretty circular Chapel of the Holy Sacrament, with a colonnade of columns and a lantern above the cupola dates from the 19C. The seated statue of *St Joseph* in polychrome terracotta is attributed to Luca della Robbia 'il giovane' (great-nephew of Luca; c 1505–10. The **Maestà*, with remarkably subtle colouring, is ascribed to the Maestro di Figline, named from this work. On the **north wall** there is a 16C font and a painting of the *Transition of St Joseph* by the local painter Egisto Sarri (late 19C). A small **museum** (admission on request) has been arranged in two rooms beyond the sacristy. It contains a painting of the *Martyrdom of St Lawrence* by Lodovico Cigoli; two charming angels attributed to Bartolomeo di Giovanni (c 1480) which formerly surrounded the *Maestà* in the church; and church silver, chalices, vestments and illuminated choirbooks.

The narrow Vicolo Libri leads out of the square beside the Collegiata to the 14C **Palazzo Pretorio**, over-restored in 1931, next to a leaning bell tower, at the foot of which is a little open chapel which contains a *Madonna enthroned with Saints* in polychrome terracotta attributed to the workshop of Benedetto Buglioni (the garland, angels, and some details were added in 1930 by the Cantagalli workshop).

In the piazza is the church of **San Francesco**, founded in 1229 and preceded by an attractive portico beneath which, on the left, is a 14C statuette of the Madonna in a tabernacle. The interior was over restored at the beginning of the 20C. The **frescoes on the **west wall** are fine works by Francesco d'Antonio (*Crucifixion and Saints*, *Annunciation*, and *Coronation of the Virgin*, and *St Francis*). On the **south wall** is a frescoed lunette of the *Madonna and Child with two Saints* attributed to Pier Francesco Fiorentino (detached from the cloister). In the north transept are 14C frescoes of *Christ in Pietà between Saints* and a *Crucifixion* above. On the altar on the **north wall** is a late 15C fresco of the *Madonna of the Holy Girdle between Saints John the Baptist and Julian*, attributed to the school of Botticelli. A door leads into the **cloister** with very worn frescoes of the early 17C, off which is the **chapter house** (opened on request) which has a 14C fresco of the *Crucifixion* and a painting of the *Madonna and Child* signed and dated 1392 by Giovanni del Biondo.

On the opposite side of Piazza San Francesco is **Santa Croce** (entrance on Via Santa Croce), next to a convent (closed order). In the 18C interior is a 16C painting of the *Crucifixion* and a wooden *Crucifix* by a Tuscan sculptor of the late 15C or early 16C.

A road leads out of Piazza Ficino on the right of the Collegiata to Via Castelguinelli where at no. 86 (marked by two pine trees) is the **Casagrande dei**

Serristori, now a hotel and restaurant. The palace was built by the Serristori, the most important family of Figline, and has a Renaissance loggia and Italianate garden (incorporating part of the old walls) which can be seen on request at the restaurant.

Corso Matteotti leads out of the other end of Piazza Ficino beside the Spedale Serristori. It ends in Piazza Serristori with the **Teatro Garibaldi** built in 1868–70 by the local architect Andrea Pierallini and decorated by Egisto Sarri. A fine stretch of **town walls** (1356–75) and the Cassero can be seen here.

On the outskirts of the town (reached from Piazza Serristori by Via Vittorio Veneto), beyond the neo-Classical cemetery, and next to a palace of 1570, is the sanctuary of **Santa Maria al Ponterosso**, with a fine fresco of the *Madonna and Child* over the high altar by a follower of Perugino.

At the south end of the town (to the right off the main road) is the 17C **Villa di San Cerbone**, seat of the Ospedale Serristori since 1890 (admission on request at the convent). The chapel has an *Annunciation* by Lodovico Cigoli and paintings by Niccolò Lapi. Off the 15C courtyard is the refectory with a *Last Supper* attributed to Giorgio Vasari. The **pharmacy**, founded in 1399, has interesting 16C–19C majolica vases and glass, a painting of the *Madonna enthroned with angels* attributed to the Maestro del 1399, and the head of the *Redeemer* attributed to Matteo Rosselli.

This road (signposted Cesto and Gaville) continues past the inconspicuous church of **San Bartolomeo a Scampata**, re-founded in a farm building on the left of the road in 1970, when the old church on the hill above to the right was abandoned. It contains (right wall) a **Madonna and Child* attributed to Segna di Bonaventura or Ugolino di Nerio. The pretty road continues up to **Gaville** where the Ubertini castle was destroyed by the Florentines in 1252. A road (signposted for the Museo della Civiltà Contadina) continues up to the ancient **Pieve di San Romolo**, with a fine apse and campanile of 11C–12C, in a beautiful position. Inside is an *Annunciation* by the Florentine school (c 1500). Next door is a local **Ethnographical Museum** illustrating peasant life in the area (open Sat 16.00–18.00, Sun 15.00–19.00; or by appointment). The wide view takes in the lignite mines and blast furnaces on the plain (see below).

To the south off the main road for San Giovanni, near the locality of Restone is the church of **Sant'Andrea a Ripalta**, above the road on the right. It is usually locked but has an 18C stuccoed interior and a triptych with a fine predella dated 1436 by Andrea di Giusto.

San Giovanni Valdarno

San Giovanni Valdarno (19,000 inhab.) was founded in 1299 as one of the *Terre nuove* of the Florentine Republic. It is laid out with rectilinear streets, some with narrow porticoes, on either side of the two central piazze. San Giovanni was the birthplace of the painters Masaccio (Tommaso di Giovanni Cassai, 1401– c 1428), Mariotto di Cristofano, 1393–1457, and Giovanni da San Giovanni (Giovanni Mannozzi, 1592–1636).

*Palazzo Pretorio, with a tall central tower (restored in the 19C), stands in the centre of the two main squares, Piazza Cavour and Piazza Masaccio. It is surrounded on four sides by porticoes and covered with coats of arms dating from the 15C to the 18C, some in enamelled terracotta by the della Robbia work-

Coats of arms on
Palazzo Pretorio,
San Giovanni
Valdarno

shop. The palace was attributed by Vasari to Arnolfo di Cambio. Outside is a copy of the Florentine *Marzocco* (the original has been placed in the atrium).

In Piazza Cavour, with a monument to Garibaldi by Pietro Guerri (1902) is the 14C **Pieve di San Giovanni Battista** (restored in 1920; often closed), preceded by a portico. It contains a 17C terracotta *Pietà* and a 15C painting of the *Madonna and Child*. In the same square (at no. 12) is the convent of the **Augustinians** (now a school; adm. on request). In the oratory (**Santissima Annunziata**) are good works by Antonio Puglieschi (the ceiling fresco, side altarpiece, and high altarpiece of the *Annunciation*, c 1685). On the left altar is a tender **Madonna and Child* on a gold ground by the Maestro della Natività di Castello. In the corridor is a relief of the *Madonna and Child* derived from a prototype by Ghiberti.

The house at 83 Corso Italia is supposed to have belonged to Masaccio (there is a plaque); it is open for temporary exhibitions. In Piazza Masaccio, beyond the **Palazzaccio** (or Palazzetto Ricorboli) with three pretty loggias, is **San Lorenzo**, with a plain Gothic façade. The interior has been over restored. On the high altar, polyptych of the *Coronation of the Virgin* by Giovanni del Biondo. In the right aisle, remains of frescoes (very ruined) include a fragment of the *Martyrdom of St Sebastian*, the only known signed work by Scheggia (1457; Masaccio's brother, also known as Giovanni di ser Giovanni), and *St Anthony Abbot* with stories from his life (almost illegible) also sometimes attributed to him (or to Mariotto di Cristofano).

The Basilica of Santa Maria delle Grazie

In Piazza Masaccio is the basilica of Santa Maria delle Grazie, begun in 1484, with a façade of 1856–85, and an unusual portico and double staircase. The east end, with a dome, was rebuilt in the 1950s after severe war damage. At the foot of the staircase is a colourful lunette of the *Assumption of the Virgin with Saints* by Giovanni della Robbia (1515). The church is entered at the top of the right staircase. In the first part, dating from the 18C, with painted vaults, the elaborate high altar has 18C paintings of angels surrounding a venerated image of the *Madonna and Child*. On the altar wall, fresco of the plague which hit the town in 1479. Over a side altar, *Madonna enthroned with six Saints* by Domenico di Michelino. The unattractive **rotonda** (in very poor repair) dates from the 1950s. Here is a fresco of the *Marriage of the Virgin* by Giovanni da San Giovanni, detached from the exterior of the church.

The **Museo della Basilica** is entered from a door beside the high altar. (Open 11.00–13.00, 15.00–17.00; fest. 15.00–18.00; closed Mon). It is arranged in three rooms above the portico overlooking the piazza. In the **first room** Mariotto di Nardo, triptych with the *Trinity and four Saints*; Paolo Schiavo, *St Ansano, St Biagio, Chorus of angel musicians*; works by Lo Scheggia, including a *Chorus of angels*; Giovanni da Piamonte, *Tobias and the archangel Raphael* (also attributed to Bartolomeo della Gatta); Jacopo del Sellaio, *Annunciation*; and works by Mariotto di Cristofano, including *Christ in Pietà between the Virgin and St Lucy*. In the **room to the right** there is a beautiful painting of the *Annunciation*, from the convent of Montecarlo, almost certainly by Fra Angelico (c 1431). It is another version of the painting of the same subject by Angelico in the Museo Diocesano in Cortona. In the **room to the left**, *St John the Baptist, St Lawrence* by Gregorio Pagani, and *Beheading of St John the Baptist* by Giovanni da San Giovanni.

To the west of San Giovanni Valdarno is **Santa Barbara** laid out in the 1930s next to the open lignite mines and huge blast furnaces (visible from miles around) of an electrical plant. From **Castelnuovo dei Sabbioni** a road continues up through Massa Sabbioni to the **Parco Naturale di Cavriglia** (poorly signposted) on the wooded Chianti hills (800m) overlooking the Valdarno. This is a protected area created in 1978 with a well landscaped zoo (open daily 08.00–21.00) with bears, buffalo, wolves, llama, deer and wild fowl. There is a car park outside (if cars are driven into the zoo enclosure a fee is charged), and sports facilities, refreshments, and marked nature trails (wild deer can often be seen in the vicinity).

From Castelnuovo dei Sabbioni a road leads southeast to **Cavriglia**, where a lot of new building has taken place. Above the town is the church of San Giovanni Battista preceded by a garden of lime trees. Its square tower has unusual crenellations. The lunette over the church door of *St John the Baptist in the desert* is attributed to Benedetto Buglioni. The interior has fine Baroque side aisles. A small **Museo di Arte Sacra** has been opened here. It contains a 14C bronze *Crucifix*, and three white enamelled terracotta busts of angels attributed to Benedetto Buglioni. The Fondazione Carla Fineschi at Cavriglia is a remarkable rose garden open in May.

Southwest of San Giovanni is **Montecarlo**, a Franciscan convent founded in 1429, and now a religious community.

Montevarchi

Montevarchi was also laid out in the early 14C by the Florentine Republic. It has an interesting oval plan with two outer streets, slightly curved, parallel to the two main streets which pass through the central piazza. It is now an important market town (22,700 inhab.) with new suburbs. It is worth exploring for its Art Nouveau and Art Deco buildings.

The Collegiata di San Lorenzo

In the central **Piazza Varchi**, named after the Humanist Benedetto Varchi who was born here (1503–68), is the **Collegiata di San Lorenzo**, with an unusual façade dating partly from the 18C and partly from 1932 (when the bas-relief of the *Martyrdom of St Lawrence* was placed high up on the façade). The campanile (1440) was completed in 1560, and the statue of *St Lawrence* was added by Pietro Guerri in 1894.

The sober interior was redesigned in 1706–09 by the local architect and sculptor Massimiliano Soldani-Benzi. Pretty stucco frames surround paintings by Giovanni and Camillo Sagrestani and Matteo Bonechi. The two altarpieces on the right and left side of the *Madonna in glory with Saints* are by Giovanni Balducci (Il Cosci) and Carlo Maratta (1611). In the chapel on the right of the high altar, the dome paintings are attributed to the Sagrestani and Bonechi. At the east end, above the high altar, with the reliquary of the *Madonna del Latte*, by Gherardo Silvani are stuccoes of the *Madonna in Glory* by Giovanni Baratta. The terracotta bust of the *Madonna and Child* dates from the 15C and the bronze statue of the *Madonna* is by Soldani. In the left chapel, *Adoration of the Magi* by Matteo Rosselli.

The Museo della Collegiata

The Museo della Collegiata (open Tues, Thur, Sat 10.00–12.00; or enquire at the door on the right of the façade) is entered off the right side of the church. It is beautifully arranged in two rooms. In the **first room**: large wooden 17C *Crucifix*; three 14C illuminated manuscripts; 16C reliquary bust of one of the Virgins of St Orsola, by Simone di Antonio Pignoni; **Cross* with reliefs by Piero di Martino Spigliati, a pupil of Cellini; a reliquary in the form of a ciborium with 16C paintings by Giovanni del Brina; detached frescoes from the nearby convent of San Ludovico by Roberto (or Luberto) da Montevarchi (an assistant of Perugino).

In the **second room** is the beautiful **Tempietto Robbiano*. This was formerly the Cappella di Santa Maria del Latte, and it was partly destroyed when it was removed from the church in the 18C. It was reconstructed here in 1973. It was designed to contain a venerated reliquary given to the church in the 13C by Conte Guidoguerra dei Guidi (who had obtained it from Charles of Anjou in gratitude for his valour in a victorious battle in 1266). The enamelled terracottas are by Andrea della Robbia: above the altar are reliefs of *St John the Baptist* and *St Sebastian* in niches on either side of a copy of a terracotta *Madonna and Child*, now on the high altar of the church. Below are four angels protecting the reliquary and a beautiful *Pietà*. The chapel ceiling and friezes of cherubs are also by Andrea. On the wall (formerly on the façade of the church), is a fine della Robbian frieze, also attributed to Andrea, showing the reliquary being presented to the church. Also here are two della Robbian stemmae, fragments of ceramic oriental draperies, and a stone bas-relief dated 1283.

Via Bracciolini, in front of the church, leads left past **Palazzo del Podestà**, to a house with a portico, and **Palazzo Carapelli** with reliefs by Romano Romanelli (early 20C). The church of the **Gesù** has a 19C façade. It contains 18C wooden benches and a large wood statue of *Christ*. At no. 36 is the **Accademia Valdarnese del Poggio**, founded in 1804, in an old monastery with a fine courtyard. It has a library and an important **Paleontological Museum** (open Tues–Sat 09.00–12.30, 16.00–18.00; fest. 10.00–12.00; closed Mon). In the showcases (1870) are rock, vegetable and animal fossils found in the Valdarno, including the *Canis etruscus*, the fossilised head of a dog, studied by the paleontologist Professor F. Major of Glasgow who classified the collection in the 19C. Georges Cuvier, the great French naturalist came here in 1810 to study the fossils.

At the north end of the town, near the railway, is the church of the **Madonna del Giglio** with a handsome cupola attributed to Matteo Nigetti (1607–15), a portico, and an early 15C fresco fragment over the altar. In an unattractive part of town to the south (also near the railway), at La Ginestra is the church of **Santa Croce** on a little hill. Thought to have been founded in 614–20, the Benedictine monastery beside it was transformed into a spinning-mill in the 19C. Beyond a door on the right of the church a fresco of *St Benedict and St Scholastica* can be seen. A huge building, once a hat factory, below the hill, is being restored and beyond it can be seen the monumental **Palazzo Masini**, an extremely ornate Art Nouveau building with a tower (1924–27).

South of Montevarchi is **Galatrona** with a Romanesque church which contains important works by Giovanni della Robbia (1510–21; key at the priest's house in Mercatale), including a very fine font. Further south, in lovely countryside with farms and woods, is the peaceful little village of **Cennina**, with beautiful views, where a number of houses have been restored. The remains of its 12C–13C castle include an isolated gateway. In the attractive little piazza at the top of the hill with a well and houses covered with creepers, is the Sala d'Armi (enquire locally for the key) where concerts are held in August. Near the village is the castle of Lupinari, with a red tower.

Pratomagno

On the east side of the Arno and motorway, almost opposite Montevarchi, is **Terranuova Bracciolini**, now surrounded by ugly new buildings. This was another *Terra nuova* of the Florentine Republic, founded in 1337. The Humanist Poggio Bracciolini (1380–1459) was born here.

    Loro Ciuffena, to the east, is also now surrounded by new buildings. The old medieval village is in a fine position on rocks above the Ciuffena river. The church of Santa Maria Assunta has 16C paintings by Carlo Portelli who was born here. The town hall contains a museum (open 10.00–12.00; Sat & fest. 16.00–19.30) dedicated to the works of the local sculptor Venturino Venturi, born here in 1918.

    Gropina, in pine woods to the south, is a charming medieval hamlet built around a Romanesque *pieve (open 08.00–12.00, 15.00–17.00; or ring at the priest's house in front of the side door). The bare interior built in *pietra serena* has delightful carved capitals and a pulpit with interesting carvings. Beneath the right aisle, stairs lead down to remains of earlier buildings on this site (Roman and early Christian finds). On a secondary road to Arezzo is **San Giustino Valdarno**, with another Romanesque *pieve*.

    From Loro Ciuffena a beautiful road (the Strada dei Sette Ponti, or the road of the seven bridges), roughly on the line of the Roman *Cassia Vetus*, leads along the side of the **Pratomagno** hills back towards Florence. It passes the sanctuary of the **Madonna delle Grazie di Montemarciano**, built in 1532 and surrounded by a portico of the early 17C. It contains a fresco attributed to Francesco d'Antonio. The village of **Montemarciano** has remains of its castle destroyed by the Florentines in 1288.

    Castelfranco di Sopra was founded by the Florentines in 1299, and laid out on a circular plan perhaps to a design by Arnolfo di Cambio. Outside the village on the left is the Vallombrosan **Badia di San Salvatore a Soffena**, rebuilt in 1394. It contains interesting early 14C frescoes including works by Bicci di Lorenzo, Paolo Schiavo, Lo Scheggia, Mariotto di Cristofano, and Liberato da Rieti.

    At **Pian di Scò** the Romanesque pieve of Santa Maria (11C–12C) has interesting capitals, and a fresco attributed to Paolo Schiavo.

Outside **Reggello** (on the Figline Valdarno road) is **Cascia**, birthplace of the 14C musicians Giovanni and Donato da Cascia. Here is the Romanesque *pieve* of **San**

Pietro, marked by its tall bell-tower, and preceded by a 13C portico. It is traditionally thought to have been founded by Countess Matilda, but the present building dates from the late 12C or early 13C (open 07.30–12.00, 15.00–19.00; if closed ring at no. 1 in the piazza). At the end of the left aisle (light) is a beautiful small *triptych of the *Madonna and Child with Saints Bartolomeo, Biagio, Giovenale, and Antonio Abate*. Dated 1422, this is the first known work by Masaccio. It was rediscovered in 1961 in the nearby church of San Giovenale, restored in 1984, and installed here in 1988. The church also contains interesting capitals, an ancient *Crucifix* in the apse, an *Annunciation* on the left wall by Mariotto di Cristofano, brother-in-law of Masaccio, and a *Pietà* signed and dated 1601 by Santi di Tito.

Near Montanino, below Cascia, the yellow sandy hills (*calanchi*) have been eroded into strange forms.

Northwest of Reggello is the Romanesque church of **Sant'Agata in Arfoli** beside a Cedar of Lebanon. There is a splendid view of the Valdarno from the terrace. The porch was added in 1928, but the 13C cloister survives. In the interior (if closed ring at the house on the right) there is a medieval carved pluteus and a fresco of the *Madonna and Saints with the Pietà* surrounded by grotesques, attributed to Raffaellino del Garbo. The fine presbytery was designed in 1928 using old columns and pilasters.

A pretty road leads down between old walls and past vineyards to the hamlet of **Cancelli** and (right) the church of Santa Margherita. It contains a fresco of the *Crucifixion* and, on the left, a fragmentary fresco of good quality by the *bottega* of Paolo Schiavo. The road continues down past the entrance to the remarkable **Castello di Sammezzano** (a 4-star hotel which was closed in 2001). It is on the site of a castle which was visited by Charlemagne in 781 and was later owned by the Medici. In 1596 the Grand-duke Ferdinando I sold it to Sebastiano Ximenes of Aragon, a Spanish merchant who was trading in Tuscany. In the 19C it was transformed into a fantastic Oriental palace by a wealthy descendant, Ferdinando Panciatichi Ximenes d'Aragona (1813–97). A drive, 2km long, leads up through splendid woods, including numerous sequoia trees, to the huge 'castle', the exterior of which has elements which recall the Taj Mahal. The colourful interior has some splendidly decorated rooms on the piano nobile, some of them modelled on the Alhambra of Granada.

To the north on the main road along the Arno from Incisa (8km) to Pontassieve is the church of **San Clemente a Sociano** (on a curve of the road above to the right), with a portico. In the interior (if closed, ring at the house on the right) there are two lovely marble candle-bearing angels in the sanctuary attributed to Mino da Fiesole, and, in the left transept a marble *bas-relief of the *Madonna and Child* attributed to Antonio Rossellino. The two altarpieces are in poor condition: on the left, *St Michael and Saints* attributed to Giovanni Battista Naldini, and on the right, *Madonna and Saints* by the bottega of Santi di Tito.

Across the Arno is **Rignano**, on the railway on flat ground, surrounded by factories. The 20C church in the centre contains an *Assumption* by Matteo Confortini (1623), and (at the end of the left aisle) a hexagonal font in enamelled terracotta attributed to Benedetto and Santi Buglioni. In a chapel off the left side is a polychrome terracotta relief of the *Birth of the Virgin*, and a 16C *Crucifix* and painting of *St Roch*. At the west end is a fresco of a polyptych of the *Coronation of the Virgin* attributed to Cenni di Francesco di Ser Cenni (c 1370) detached from the Romanesque pieve of **San Leolino**, north of the town, which is in need of restoration.

North of Reggello, beyond Pietrapiana, another road (signposted Donnini) continues along the side of the hill with views of the valley to **San Donato in Fronzano** (if closed ring at the door on the right) with a 17C façade, and an interesting interior. Beyond is the **Pieve a Pitiana** with an 11C–12C campanile (if closed ring at the door on the left). Over the high altar is an *Annunciation* attributed to Ridolfo del Ghirlandaio. From Donnini another road, lined with cypresses and olives, leads up towards Tosi (see below) winding round the **Villa Pitiana** with a 19C yellow façade (and 14C and 16C elements).

Vallombrosa

From Pietrapiana the direct road for Vallombrosa winds up through **Saltino** (970m; good views), an old-fashioned resort with large hotels, some of them built at the end of the 19C or early 20C (open only in summer). A rack railway from Sant'Ellero on the Arno up to Saltino, in operation from 1892–1934, may be restored. **Vallombrosa** (997m) is surrounded by a thick forest of pines, firs and beeches, which has been owned by the State since 1867 when an important School of Forestry was established here. Cool in summer and conveniently close to Florence, it has a number of restaurants. It is famous for its monastery founded by St John Gualberto in 1040, and the first home of the Vallombrosan order. The monastery was suppressed in 1808, but the Order was reinstated in 1963 and some 20 monks now live here. An avenue leads to the **monastery** with a lawn and fish pond on the left. Beyond a walled garden is the splendid façade with numerous small windows by Gherardo Silvani (1610–40).

The **church** façade dates from 1644. Beneath the portico is a *Madonna and Child* by the *bottega* of Ghiberti and a statue of *St John Gualberto* by Giovanni Battista Caccini. The interior (open 09.00–12.00, 15.30–18.00) contains 18C frescoes and paintings. On the high altar, *Assumption* by Volterrano and 15C carved wooden choir stalls. In the south transept, *Martyrdom of St Sebastian* by Cesare Dandini, and in the north transept, *Trinity* by Lorenzo Lippi. The chapel in the north transept has a fine ceiling with frescoes and stuccoes by Alessandro Gherardini. In the **sacristy**, *Madonna and Saints with donors* by the *bottega* of Andrea della Robbia and paintings by Raffaellino del Garbo (*St John Gualberto and Saints*), and Luigi Sabatelli.

The **monastery** (for adm. ☎ 055 862 029; in summer usually open Tues & Fri 10.30–12.00) has an 18C refectory with paintings by Ignazio Hugford, an enamelled terracotta attributed to Santi Buglioni and a fine kitchen.

Milton was traditionally thought to have stayed in the guest house (known as the Paradisino) in 1638 (plaque set up in 1925). Although he mentions both the Valdarno and Vallombrosa in his *Paradise Lost* (Book I) he is not now thought to have come here on his visits to Tuscany in 1638 and 1639. However it became a famous place to visit for the English in the 18C and 19C, and when Wordsworth came here in 1837 he composed *At Vallombrosa*.

Fine walks can be taken in the forest, and a road leads up to **Monte Secchieta** (1450m), which has winter sports facilities. A road from Vallombrosa leads to the Passo della Consuma (see p 509), while the direct road to Florence descends steeply through woods past several streams to **Pian di Melosa**. The name of the main road here commemorates the art historian Bernard Berenson (see p 110) who often stayed nearby at San Miniato in Alpe. **Tosi** is known for its furniture makers. Beyond Pelago (p 119), a lovely hilly road continues down past open fields to Pontassieve and the main road for Florence.

The Casentino

The Casentino is the beautiful wooded upper valley of the Arno in the northeast corner of Tuscany. The scenery is superb and the area has prosperous and well-kept villages. One of the finest forests in Italy can be found at Camaldoli, on the border with Romagna.

The valley was dominated from the 10C until the middle of the 15C by the Guidi Counts, whose numerous castles are a feature of the region. Because of its position between Florence and Arezzo, it was long disputed between the two cities, but Florence remained the dominant force after its victory here on the plain of Campaldino in 1289. High up above the valley are the famous monasteries of La Verna and Camaldoli. Beautiful walks can be taken in the Casentino, and in particular in the Parco Nazionale delle Foreste Casentinesi, Monte Falterona e Campigna.

Practical information

Getting there
By car

From Florence, the Pontassieve road east of the city leads to the N70 which crosses the Passo della Consuma before descending into the valley of the Casentino.

By train

From Arezzo trains and buses run by *LFI* to Bibbiena, Poppi, and Stia.

By bus

SITA bus services (c 8 times daily) from **Florence** via the Consuma Pass to Poppi and Bibbiena (to Poppi in 2hrs; to Bibbiena in 2hrs 20mins). *SITA* buses daily also from Florence to Stia in 1hr 45mins. *SITA* buses from **Arezzo** to Caprese Michelangelo. From **Bibbiena** buses (*LFI*) to Camaldoli and La Verna.

Information offices

APT of **Arezzo** (☎ 0575 377 678). Information office at **Bibbiena**, Via Berni 25 (☎/🖷 0575 593 098). The administrative offices of the **Parco Nazionale delle Foreste Casentinesi, Monte Falterona e Campigna**, are at via G. Brocchi 7, Pratovecchio (☎ 0575 503 01).

Where to stay
Hotels

PASSO DELLA CONSUMA ☆☆ *Sbaragli*, Via Consuma, Montemignaio 3 (☎ 055 830 6651).
MONASTERY OF CAMALDOLI ☆☆☆ *Il Rustichello*, Via del Corniolo 14 (☎ 0575 556 020; 🖷 0575 556 046); ☆ *Camaldoli*, with restaurant, Via Camaldoli 13 (☎ 0575 556 019;

🗐 0575 556 073).
POPPI ☆☆ *Casentino*, Piazza
Repubblica 6, in front of the castle
(☎ 0575 529 090; 🗐 0575 529 067).
PONTE A POPPI ☆☆ *Campaldino*,
with restaurant (☎ 0575 529 008,
🗐 0575 529 032).
BIBBIENA ☆☆☆ *Brogi*, with restaurant (☎ 0575 536 222; 🗐 0575 536
223).
BADIA PRATAGLIA numerous
☆☆ hotels.
CHIUSI DELLA VERNA ☆☆ and
☆ hotels.
CAPRESE MICHELANGELO ☆☆
hotel, with restaurant, *Buca di
Michelangelo*, Via Roma 51 (☎ 0575
793 921; 🗐 0575 793 941).

Campsites

Campsites open in summer
MONASTERY OF CAMALDOLI
☆ *Camaldoli* (☎ 0575 556 157); ☆
Camaldoli Pucini (☎ 0575 556 006).
BADIA PRATAGLIA ☆ *Capanno*
(☎ 0575 518 015).
CHIUSI DELLA VERNA ☆
La Verna at Vezzano (☎ 0575 532
121).
CAPRESE MICHELANGELO ☆☆
Michelangelo at Zenzano (☎ 0575
793 886).

Eating out
Restaurants
PASSO DELLA

CONSUMA *Dal Consumi* has good
snacks.
STIA €€€ *Caranbar*, Via Adamo Ricci
19; €€ *Da Filetto*, Piazza Tanucci;
€ *La Rana (da Filetto)* in woods on the
Arno (by the sports stadium); *Fani
Sandro*, Piazza Tanucci (☎ 0575
58824; only by reservation for Sunday
lunch).
PRATOVECCHIO €€ *Gliaccaniti*,
Via Fiorentina 12; € *La Tana degli
Orsi*, Via Roma 1 (open in the
evening); *Toscana Twist*, 1 Via della
Libertà (good lunches with local
specialities).
MONASTERY OF CAMALDOLI
€€ *Pucini*, località Pucini.
POPPI €€ *Campaldino*, Via Roma 95,
Ponte a Poppi.
BIBBIENA €€ *Brogi (Da Marino)*,
Piazza Mazzoni 7; € *Mon Ami* (also
pizzeria). Outside Bibbiena: €€ *Il Bivio
di Querceto* at Querceto.
CHIUSI DELLA VERNA
€€ *La Beccia*, località la Beccia.
CAPRESE MICHELANGELO
€€ *La Faggeta*, *Il Cerro* and *La Buca
di San Francesco*.
TALLA € *L'Orcello*, Via Cesare Battisti
3.

Festival
BIBBIENA Traditional
Shrove Tuesday celebrations.

The approach to the Casentino from Florence is via the **Passo della Consuma**,
beyond which the road crosses bare hills where some replanting is taking place.
There is a fine distant view in the valley below of Poppi Castle with its tall tower.
To the north, a pretty by-road traverses woods and then winds downhill to end
just before the scanty ruins of **Castel Castagnaio**, an 11C castle.

Further on along the main road a road (well signposted) leads left to the
*Castello di Romena, built in the 11C and perhaps the most important castle in
the Casentino, belonged to the Guidi, the Ghibelline family who dominated the
area, with whom the exiled Dante sheltered after his expulsion from Florence.
Here in 1280 Maestro Adamo, recalled by Dante (*Divina Commedia, Inferno XXX*,
46–90), forged Florentine florins for the Guidi for which he was later burnt by
the Florentines. A short cypress avenue leads up to the impressive and well-kept
remains which include the three main towers and traces of three circles of walls

(open by appointment ☎ 0575 582 520). A room contains suits of armour, as well as a model of the castle, and there is a small archaeological collection. Stairs lead up to a loggia and walkway where the views are splendid.

A road (or path from the villa) descends past the **Fonte Branda** (plaque), an overgrown spring, mentioned by Dante (*Divina Commedia, Inferno*, XXX, 78), to the ***Pieve di Romena**, the most beautiful Romanesque church in the Casentino. It was built in 1152; remains of the 9C church can be seen beneath the building. It has a splendid east end with blind arcading. The lovely interior (only open by appointment, ☎ 0575 583 725) has a raised presbytery and fine capitals. All the paintings, which include works by Giovanni del Biondo and the Maestro di Varlungo, have been removed.

Stia

Stia is a pretty little town (3100 inhab.) where the Arno meets its first tributary, the Staggia. In the Middle Ages it was the residence of the Guidi family, and it is noted for its small woollen manufactories (some of the abandoned factories along the river are interesting for their architecture). Traditional, very fine hand-made textiles are still made here at 49 Via Sanarelli (the firm is called *T.A.C.S.*).

On the right bank of the river is the delightful, sloping **Piazza Tanucci** (with a local tourist office). The 18C public fountain is decorated with lions and snakes.

The Romanesque church of **Santa Maria Assunta** with a plain façade is in the piazza. The interior has fine capitals (illuminated by a light switch on the west wall). **South aisle**. First chapel, left wall, 16C *Nativity*, and, on the altar, triptych of the *Annunciation and Saints* with a good predella, by Bicci di Lorenzo. Beneath the altar is a della Robbian stemma. The marble font dates from 1526. On the right wall is another *Annunciation* by the Pistoian school. First altar, *Preaching of St John the Baptist* by Gian Domenico Ferretti. The quaint wooden pulpit dates from 1584.

In the chapel to the right of the high altar there is a good 16C Florentine painting of *Supper in the House of the Pharisee* (in very poor condition). On the left is an elaborate (damaged) della Robbian tabernacle. In the pretty **apse** with an ambulatory of four columns is a large 14C wooden *Crucifix*. In the chapel to the left of the high altar, **Madonna and Child* by the Maestro di Varlungo, and (on the right wall), *Madonna and Child* by Andrea della Robbia. **North aisle**. *Madonna enthroned with four Saints* by the Master of San Miniato; on the altar, an unusual painting of the *Assumption*, attributed to the Master of Borgo alla Collina. The 14C fresco of the *Madonna and Child* was detached from the Pieve of Stia.

To the right of the church is an archway with a fresco of *St Francis* by Pietro Annigoni (1985). The old streets off the piazza are well worth exploring.

On the other side of the river, an avenue ascends past (left) the church of the Madonna del Ponte with a della Robbian altarpiece. Opposite is a 16C painting of the *Holy Family*. The sanctuary is decorated with pretty angels. The avenue continues up to Piazza Mazzini with the modern town hall and a theatre. A road (signposted) leads left for the Castello di Palagio reconstructed in 1911 by Giuseppe Castellucci for Carlo Beni, historian of the Casentino. He left it to the Comune and it is open in summer for exhibitions and lectures; the garden, with some statuary, is open daily. A huge vault was built here a few years ago, over a spring.

Porciano

Just outside Stia is a by-road (signposted) right for Porciano, approached through pretty meadows. There is a car park below the castle and it is a short way on foot through the hamlet (reconstructed after an earthquake in 1919) to the massive tall square tower of the **castle**, privately owned. It was restored in 1963–75 (open from 15 May–15 Oct; on fest. 10.00–12.00, 16.00–19.00; or by previous appointment, ☎ 055 400 517). First mentioned in 1007, this may have been the first Guidi castle in the Casentino. It remained in their possession until the end of the 15C, and Dante Alighieri is known to have stayed here as their guest on a number of occasions when exiled from Florence. It was from here that he wrote to the Florentines and to Henry VII in 1311.

On the ground floor is a small display of agricultural implements and domestic tools, as well as a collection of native American material from North Dakota, made by the father of the present owner George A. Specht (1899–1973) when a child. The first floor has photographs of the castle before its restoration, and ceramics (including late 13C and early 14C ware) found during restoration work. On the second floor is a hall used for lectures. The views are splendid. The upper floors are private.

The church of **Santa Maria delle Grazie** is in an inconspicuous position above the Londa road, a few kilometres north-west of Stia. Beside the 15C church is the **Casa del Pellegrino**, built as a hospice for pilgrims with a lovely long loggia and stairs in the centre of the building. The **church** is only open for services at weekends. It con-

Castello di Porciano

tains a *Crucifix* attributed to Paolo Schiavo, a 15C *Madonna and Child*, a pulpit by Mino da Fiesole, and a fresco by Domenico Ghirlandaio (1485).

A fine walk of 4hrs leads north from Stia to the source of the Arno and from there to the summit of **Monte Falterona** (1654m), now part of a national park adjoining the Forest of Camaldoli (see p 512). The adjacent summit of **Monte Falco**, 4m higher, is more easily reached from the **Passo la Calla** (1296m), on the road from Stia into Emilia Romagna via the Bidente valley (see *Blue Guide Northern Italy*). On its slopes, visited by skiers, is a mountain refuge called the Rifugio La Burraia (1447m).

Pratovecchio

Adjoining Stia to the south is the large village of Pratovecchio surrounded by some small factories in the valley. From Piazza Paolo Uccello (named after the painter who was born here), Via Garibaldi with pretty porticoes leads (left) towards the attractive **Piazza Jacopo Landino** with a group of lime trees. Here is a fine palace (no. 18) with a coat of arms on the corner dated 1621. The parish **church** has a small della Robbian relief above the west door, and paintings by Jacopo Vignali and Francesco Botti inside. To the right of the church, at the end of the piazza, is the entrance (no. 20) to a courtyard in which is the church of **San Giovanni Evangelista** (if closed, ring at the Camaldolese convent). The unusual façade dates from 1909. Over the first left altar is a very well preserved painting of the *Assumption*, attributed to the Maestro di Pratovecchio, named from this work. It is very difficult to see as it is inserted behind a larger painting. The high altarpiece of the *Coronation of the Virgin* dates from the 16C. In Via XX Settembre, off the upper side of the piazza, is a large della Robbian tabernacle.

On the outskirts of Pratovecchio, just beyond a bridge beside several small factories on the main road to Bibbiena, is the inconspicuous church of **Santa Maria a Poppiena**, partly dating from the 12C, on the left of the road beside a few cypresses. It contains an *Annunciation* attributed to Giovanni dal Ponte. From Piazza Paolo Uccello a road leads down across the river with some interesting houses and from the bridge two roads are signposted for the Castello and Pieve di Romena (see p 509).

From Pratovecchio a beautiful road (signposted Santo Eremo), winds up a wooded valley with a view back of the castle of Romena. Before Lonnano it passes close to the little church of **Valiana** (San Romolo), on the right of the road (if closed, ring at no. 1). During restoration work by the local inhabitants in 1984 the original architrave of the door dated 1126 was found beneath the front steps (it is now displayed inside the church). The remarkable painting of **Christ in Pietà with symbols of the Passion* (late 14C or early 15C) is attributed to the Master of the Madonna Straus. From the church there is a delightful, distant view of the Castello di Romena and the wooded hills of the Casentino.

Camaldoli

The road continues up through Lonnano, entering the splendid **forest of Camaldoli** beyond Prato alle Cogne (1050m). Silver firs and beech trees predominate but other trees include sycamore, manna ash, laburnum, ilex, birch, willow, elm, yew, oak, chestnut, alder, poplar and lime. The forest is crossed by numerous streams and deer run wild here. In 1027 part of the forest was given to the Carthusian monks of Camaldoli, and in 1866 it became the property of the State. The road for the hermitage branches left from the road signposted for Camaldoli.

The forest is part of the **Parco Nazionale delle Foreste Castentinesi, Monte Falterona e Campigna**. The national park was instituted in 1991 to protect the forested area of the Casentino on the Apennine ridge which borders Tuscany and Romagna, and stretches from Monte Falterona (1654m; see above) to the Passo dei Mandrioli (1179m). It is one of the largest areas of forest left in Italy (36,000 hectares) and is administered by the *Ente Parco Nazionale Foreste Casentinesi* in Pratovecchio. Maps are available showing the lovely walks in the park.

The **Hermitage of Camaldoli** (1100m) was founded in 1012 by St Romuald in this *campo amabile*, or 'charming field'; its present name is a corruption of these two words. This is the most important of several hermitages and monasteries founded in Italy and the Pyrenees by this Benedictine saint. The hermits used to live in entire isolation: twelve monks now live here but they no longer choose to live a rigorous hermit's life, and meet for services, meals, and work. The church and cell of St Romuald are open 08.30–11.15, 15.00–18.00; fest. 08.30–10.45, 15.00–18.00. The **church** has a grey and white façade of 1713. In the vestibule is a bas-relief of the *Madonna and Child* attributed to Tommaso Fiamberti. The chapel of St Anthony Abbot, off the transept which precedes the nave has a tabernacle attributed to Andrea della Robbia and decorations by Adolfo Rollo (1930). The main church has elaborate gilded stucco decoration dating from 1669 and 17C frescoes. The choir stalls date from the 16C and the high altarpiece of the *Crucifixion and Four Saints* is attributed to Bronzino. On either side are large marble tabernacles by Gino da Settignano (1531) and in the apse a fresco of the *Transfiguration* by Ezio Giovannozzi (1937). In the **chapter house** is a painting of *St Romuald and his disciples in the forest* by Augusto Mussini (1915). The **refectory**, which dates from 1679, has a fine wood ceiling.

Outside the church is the gateway into the enclosure (no admission) with the 20 **hermits' cells**, really a little village of tiny self-contained houses. Opposite the church is the **cell of St Romuald**, which served as a model for the other cells. Above it the **library** was built in 1622.

A beautiful narrow road descends through the forest to the **Monastery of Camaldoli** (818m), founded in 1046, which now houses about 40 Carthusian monks (open daily 06.30–13.00, 15.00–20.00). The huge building on the road, called the *foresteria*, is used for visitors and meetings. Beyond is a piazza with the main entrance. Steps lead down to the **first cloister** (*di Maldolo*) dating from 1100 with primitive capitals, but restored. Off it is the ancient **chapel of Santo Spirito** with a barrel vault and a large column, asymmetrically placed. On the other side of the cloister is the former entrance to the monastery through a tunnel. The **second cloister** has a portico on three sides with pretty Ionic capitals. It was designed by Ambrogio Traversari (1386–1439), the friend and tutor of Cosimo il Vecchio, who was a monk here. From the piazza another door (no. 14) on the left leads into a small courtyard in which is the **church** with an 18C interior. It contains five fine paintings by Vasari, including a *Deposition*, and a *Nativity* and *Madonna with Saints John the Baptist and Jerome*. The **refectory** has a large painting by Pomarancio, a pulpit in *pietra serena*, and paintings attributed to Lorenzo Lippi.

At the other end of the *foresteria* is the entrance to the 16C **pharmacy** (open 09.00–12.30, 14.30–18.30; in winter closed on Wed), with lovely carved wood cupboards and panelling dating from 1543. Products made by the monks including honey, liquors and soap, are sold here. Another room is arranged as an apothecary's workshop.

In a separate building across the road is a private **Ornithological Museum**. At the bridge (by a lock) is a road for Bibbiena (another road for Poppi continues beyond the monastic buildings).

At a fork on the main road between Pratovecchio and Poppi a column marks the site of the battle of **Campaldino** on 11 June 1289. Here Dante fought as a young man in the Florentine Guelf army against the Ghibellines of Arezzo, who were defeated, and their leader Bishop Guglielmino Ubertino killed. It is estimated that some 2400 mounted knights and 18,000 foot soldiers took part in the battle which for centuries held almost mythical importance in the imagination of those who lived in the Casentino.

To the northwest is **Borgo alla Collina**, badly damaged in the Second World War. The road runs through a gate beside the tower of the castle. The church of **San Donato**, in a piazza with trees, contains a fine triptych and predella of the *Mystical Marriage of St Catherine*, now attributed to the Master of Borgo alla Collina (1408). The tomb of Cristofano Landini, the Dante scholar and tutor of Lorenzo il Magnifico, was erected in 1848 by Lorenzo Bartolini. Landini, as Secretary of the Florentine Republic, was given a palace here, where he died in 1504.

Nearby is **Castel San Niccolò** in a lovely position at the foot of the Pratomagno hills. Beyond Strada, on low ground to the left of the road by an avenue of lime trees, is the **Pieve di San Martino a Vado**. The simple interior, thought to date from the 11C, has charming historiated and foliated capitals. It contains an interesting font, and detached worn frescoes from the church of San Niccolò beside the castle, which is visible from outside the church. The road continues through two piazze and then narrows before reaching **Piazza Matteotti** (or Piazza della Fiera) with an attractive and unusual market building. A medieval paved bridge (reconstructed) leads across the stream and a narrow road (signposted) leads up to the **castle**. It is surrounded by a tiny hamlet and a Gothic postern gate beneath a tower with a huge clock survives on the side of the hill.

Beyond **Pagliericcio**, with a finely paved street, is **Cetica** in another pretty valley. Outside the village, near a modern school, is the 13C church of **Sant'Angiolo** with a low bell tower and steps at one corner of the building. In the wide interior, at the end of the right aisle, is a *Madonna and Child* by Francesco Pesellino in a beautiful tabernacle. The east end has lancet windows and a handsome altar table. The road ends at **Bagni di Cetica**, an ancient spa rediscovered in 1686, in a beautiful position.

Montemignaio is an attractive village which spreads out along the side of the valley, surrounded by numerous trees. As you approach the village across the valley, you see the very tall bell tower of its castle, and then the battlemented tower of the church. The road crosses the bridge: on the right is the **pieve**, probably dating from the 12C, with three rose windows above its three doors. The interior has a deep apse and massive capitals on the two shorter columns at the east end. The two hanging capitals on either side of the presbytery have interesting sculptures representing *Life and Death*. On the first north altar, *Madonna and Child* (a fragment of a polyptych) by Giovanni Toscani. The *Madonna enthroned with four doctors of the church* is by the school of Rodolfo del Ghirlandaio. In the south aisle is a della Robbian terracotta of the *Madonna and Child with two Saints*. On the pilasters are faded remains of frescoes.

A road leads along the side of the hill to another Guidi castle with an oddly-shaped tower. From here there is a distant view of the monastery of La Verna.

In the main valley, just outside Ponte a Poppi is the church of **Certomondo**, approached through an old gate and crumbling courtyard. A convent was founded here in 1262. The church was restored in 1987 when the rose window was exposed. On the right of the presbytery is a fine painting of the

Annunciation by Neri di Bicci. On pillars in the nave are fresco fragments of saints in very poor condition. On the right of the façade can be seen a few remains of the cloister.

Poppi

From Ponte a Poppi an avenue leads up past a war memorial to the delightful little town (6000 inhab.) of Poppi on a hill. Its splendid castle, which dominates the Casentino valley, can be seen from miles around. The hill is very well preserved, especially on its south side. Its streets have a medley of porticoes, some still built in wood. Poppi is famous as the residence of the Guidi counts who ruled the Casentino until it succumbed to the Florentine Republic in 1440. The sculptor Mino da Fiesole was born here in 1429.

The castle of the Guidi Counts

The approach road passes under a portico into Piazza Amerighi (described below). To the left, Via Conte Guidi continues up to the top of the hill where there is a car park in front of the *Castello (open daily 10.00–18.00; in Nov & Dec only on Sat & Sun) of the Guidi counts. It was begun in 1274 by Count Simone da Battifolle and is the best preserved castle in the Casentino. Built in two stages, the part on the right of the tower is attributed to Lapo, Arnolfo di Cambio's master, and the wing on the left was probably completed by Arnolfo di Cambio himself. Over the door is a relief of a disgruntled Florentine lion, set up by the local sculptor Jacopo di Baldassarre Torriani in 1477.

The *courtyard has a delightful staircase with old wooden balconies, and numerous coats of arms, and another Florentine *Marzocco*. On the left, a fine vaulted room with one huge column has a display of maps and diagrams illustrating the Battle of Campaldino (see p 513), and a room below has a delightful scale model of the battle.

First floor. The well-lit salone has a fine floor and painted walls. The *library (c 20,000 vols), in two rooms, has a remarkable collection of 519 medieval manuscripts and 780 incunabula (shown in exhibitions every year). Most of the material comes from the Fabrizio Rilli-Orsini collection (1825) and the convent of Camaldoli. At the top of the stairs is a fine stone caryatid representing Count Simone da Battifolle.

Top floor. The chapel has good frescoes by Taddeo Gaddi (1330–40). A room with a pretty little fireplace has a collection of 14C–17C documents from the archives, and the other rooms have painted walls and good views of the Campaldino plain and the castles of Romena and Porciano, and, in the distance, Monte Falterona. Also here is a detached fresco of the *Madonna and Saints*. Outside the castle is a huge underground cistern.

Behind the castle is the church of the **Agostiniani** which has a terracotta *Pietà* attributed to the *bottega* of Andrea della Robbia above the door. Inside (usually closed) is a *Nativity*, attributed to Benedetto Buglioni. Opposite Palazzo Pretorio is the ancient **Casa dei Guidi** (with a new outside stair) next to a gate into Villa Rita (ex-Giatteschi) in the garden of which can be seen a tower known as the Torre dei Diavoli or Devils' Tower.

Below the garden and piazza is Piazza Amerighi with the domed centrally-planned church of the **Madonna del Morbo** begun in 1657 and finished in 1705, dedicated to the Madonna in gratitude for deliverence from the plagues of

1530 and 1631. It is surrounded on three sides by porticoes. Over the high altar is a fine painting of the *Madonna and Child with the young St John* by Pier Francesco Fiorentino. Also in the piazza is the church of **San Marco** which contains a *Deposition* and a *Pentecost* by Francesco Morandini, named Il Poppi from his native town, and a *Raising of Lazarus* by Jacopo Ligozzi.

San Fedele

Via Cavour, the main street, entirely lined with picturesque porticoes, ends at the northern edge of the hill with the abbey church of San Fedele (open 09.00–18.30). Built in 1185–95, it is one of the most important churches in the Casentino.

On the south side, *Madonna and Child with Saints* by Ottavio Vannini; first altar, *Crucifixion with the Madonna* and *St John the Baptist and Mary Magdalen* (replica of a painting by Maso di San Friano). North side. First altar, 16C *Nativity*; *Martyrdom of St John* by Poppi; *Madonna and Child with angels*, a very unusual work by a Vallombrosan monk called Alessandro Davanzati (1506); *Martyrdom of St Laurence* by Pietro Sorri (1596); and *Three Saints* by Carlo Portelli. In the south transept is a **Madonna and Child* by the Maestro della Maddalena. On the high altar is a 14C painted Cross.

In the **apse**, *Madonna and Saints*, signed and dated 1527 by Antonio Solosmeo, the only known work by this artist; *Two Saints* by Passignano; *Assumption* and *St Benedict* by Jacopo Ligozzi. Beato Torello (1202–82) was born in Poppi and lived as a Vallombrosan recluse here, walled up in a cell for 60 years: he is buried in the **crypt**, which preserves his reliquary bust in gilded bronze (15C).

Below San Fedele is Porta a Porrena, still part of the walls which encircle the town, the other narrow streets of which are well worth exploring.

From Ponte a Poppi a road (signposted) leads beneath the railway up the hill-side to a **zoo** (open daily 08.00–dusk; picnic places are provided). Pleasantly laid out in 1972, it specialises in European fauna, and includes two bears, buffalo, deer, lynx, llamas, donkeys, and birds.

A by-road leads south from the foot of the hill of Poppi to the *pieve* of **Santa Maria a Buiano**, one of the oldest churches in the Casentino, built before 1000. It stands beside a farm with round silos (key at the house on the left). It has a charming deep brick apse and crypt. Excavations here in 1977 revealed remains of Roman baths and medieval tombs. This road continues to join another by-road in a pretty, unspoilt valley which passes fields and woods before reaching **Ortignano**. Outside the village, on a curve of the road, is the church of San Matteo. The road ends at the attractive village of **Raggiolo**, clearly visible on one side of the valley, in chestnut woods beneath its ruined castle. The view to the east, back down the valley takes in the headland of La Verna (see below).

Bibbiena

Bibbiena is one of the oldest towns in the Casentino: its name may be derived from *Vibia*, an Etruscan family. Built on a low hill, it is now the most important place in the valley (10,300 inhab.), surrounded by numerous small factories, especially on the plain to the south. It is documented from the 10C, but was destroyed by the Guelfs after their victory at Campaldino (see above). The castle was for centuries contested between Arezzo and Florence. Bernardo Dovizi, called Cardinal Bibbiena (1470–1520), famous statesman and man of letters, was born here. He was responsible for the election of Cardinal Giovanni de' Medici to the papal throne as Leo X, and was a friend and patron of Raphael, who painted his portrait (now in the Galleria Palatina in Palazzo Pitti in Florence). His best known work is his play *La Calandria*, written in Italian, which was first performed in 1513 with a prologue by Baldesar Castiglione.

The traditional Shrove Tuesday celebrations here date from the mid-14C. Called *Bello Ballo* the inhabitants dance and sing around a juniper bush set up in the piazza.

The approach road winds up to Via Dovizi, on the left of which is the early 16C **Palazzo Dovizi** (no. 26). Opposite is the 15C church of **San Lorenzo** (restored in 1917) with two fine enamelled terracotta altarpieces of the *Pietà* and *Nativity* (c 1513–20) attributed to Andrea and Girolamo della Robbia. From Piazza Roma, Via Giuseppe Borghi continues left to **Piazza Tarlati** (car parking). Here is a palace with a portico, a clock tower, and a terrace overlooking the valley.

Behind the clock tower is another tower, once part of the castle of the Tarlati family and on the right is the parish church of **Santi Ippolito e Donato**, usually called La Pieve. It was built at the beginning of the 12C as a chapel for the Tarlati castle. The wide interior has four large arches at the crossing. South side. 13C painted **Crucifix* by the Maestro di San Polo in Rosso; *Mystical Marriage of St Catherine* attributed to Jacopo Ligozzi; painted wooden statue of the seated *Madonna di Giona*, an unusual 12C Tuscan work. South transept. *Annunciation* by Il Poppi; **Madonna and Child enthroned with angels* by Arcangelo di Cola da Camerino. Over the high altar, a *Crucifix* replaces a triptych of the *Madonna and Child with Saints* by Bicci di Lorenzo. North transept. *Madonna and Child with Saints* signed and dated 1600 by Jacopo Ligozzi; organ of 1552 by Onofrio Zeffirini, brought here in 1700 from the abbey of Vallombrosa; 14C frescoed niche with the *Crucifixion*. North side. Good 14C frescoes by the Florentine school of the *Madonna and Child with Saints*, and, above, *Holy Trinity*.

Below the piazza is the neo-Classical façade of the **Teatro Dovizi**, a little theatre (200 seats; used for concerts) built in 1842 by Niccolò Matas. Nearby are the Biblioteca Comunale, the 16C Palazzo Comunale, and the restored 14C Palazzo della Pretura.

A short way northeast of Bibbiena is the 15C Dominican convent (closed order) and church of **Santa Maria del Sasso**. It has an attractive portico on the right of the façade with charming frescoed ex-votos in the lunettes (very worn).

In the domed interior is a Renaissance tabernacle by Bartolomeo Bozzolini (of Fiesole) with a della Robbian frieze. An elaborate silver frame encloses a fresco of the *Madonna and Child* by Bicci di Lorenzo, and on the back of the tabernacle is an *Annunciation* by Francesco Brina. On the south side there is an enamelled terracotta of *Christ and St John the Baptist* by Santi Buglioni, and in the south transept, *Birth of the Virgin with Saints*, signed and dated 1607 by Jacopo Ligozzi. North transept. *Madonna with St Giacinto* by Lodovico Buti. On the left wall of the church, *Madonna and Saints* (1525) by Paolino da Pistoia. Stairs lead down to the lower church and **crypt**, with a highly venerated polychrome wooden statue of the **Madonna del Buio*, attributed to Buggiano. The great rock (*sasso*), where legend relates that the Madonna appeared miraculously in 1347, and around which the sanctuary was built, can be seen here.

A road from Bibbiena leads northeast to the border with Romagna, passing the hamlet of **Serravalle** with views of Bibbiena and Poppi in the far distance. The impressive church was built in full Romanesque style in 1927. Beyond are remains of a castle around a tower (now privately owned).

The road continues up the deserted valley to **Badia Prataglia** (835m), the most important resort in the Casentino, surrounded by fine woods near the border with Romagna. The 11C **church** has a Romanesque crypt with interesting worn capitals and primitive reliefs, including one on the left of the altar of a figure in prayer. Fine **walks** may be taken in the wooded hills which surround the village. The main road continues over the Mandrioli Pass (1173m) and descends to Bagno di Romagna in Romagna (see *Blue Guide Northern Italy*).

La Verna

Another pretty road (for Pieve Santo Stefano) leads from Bibbiena up through woods. Ahead there is a view of the oddly shaped, wooded promontory on which the monastery of La Verna was built. Beyond the village of Dama there is another fine view of La Verna, and in the other direction the Pratomagno hills can be seen. From Case Nuove the panorama takes in the whole of the Casentino. The road continues across a plateau, with fewer trees, to the little resort of **Chiusi della Verna** (960m). Just outside (signposted Castello del Conti Orlando Cattani), on the right of the road, is a tiny group of houses with the house where the podestà resided and the church of **San Michele Arcangelo** (1338) below the ruins of a 10C castle, the highest in the Casentino, built on rocky outcrops.

A road diverges left from the Pieve Santo Stefano and Cesena road to climb up through plantations of fir trees to the famous **Monastery of La Verna**, in a remarkable position on a curiously shaped outcrop of rock (1129m) visible for many miles around. Count Orlando Cattani gave the site to St Francis in 1213, and here in 1224 the saint received the stigmata. It is still a Franciscan convent (with about 30 friars) and a retreat. The sanctuary was embellished in 1433 by order of Eugenius IV when a number of altars were commissioned from Andrea della Robbia, who here produced his masterpieces of enamelled terracotta sculpture.

The monastery is open 06.30–19.30 and there is a procession of the friars every day at 15.00 from the monastery to the Cappella delle Stimmate. A cobbled road leads through woods to the entrance arch, beyond which signs indicate the way (past the side of the Chiesa Maggiore) to the terrace from which there is a spectacular view of the Casentino, with Bibbiena in the distance.

The **Chiesa Maggiore** was begun in 1348, and continued in 1450–70. On the first south altar, *Madonna and Child enthroned between Saints*, attributed to Andrea della Robbia. The two *pietra serena* tabernacles on the right and left of the nave, one with the *Adoration of the Child* and the other with the **Annunciation*, are both also by him, as well as the **Ascension* surrounded by cherubs and fruit in the chapel on the left of the presbytery. At the entrance to the presbytery, the figures of *St Anthony Abbot* and *St Francis* are also by Andrea. The choir stalls date from 1495.

A covered **corridor** with frescoes of the *Life of St Francis* by the 20C Florentine painter Baccio Maria Bacci leads past several sites which recall the life of St Francis here. At the end steps descend to **St Francis' Cell**, with an 18C statue of the saint, beyond which is the tiny **Cappella delle Stimmate**. Above the door is a 13C bas-relief of the saint receiving the stigmata. This was built by order of Count Simone da Battifolle in 1263 on the spot where the Saint received the stigmata, marked by an inscription in the pavement. Over the door, on the inside wall, is a *tondo of the *Madonna and Child* by Luca della Robbia. The intarsia stalls date from 1531 (restored in 1906). The large enamelled terracotta *Crucifixion* (1480–81) by Andrea della Robbia (in a delightful frame), is one of the most monumental della Robbian works ever to have been made.

From the Chapel of San Bonaventura steps lead up and then down again to the Chapel of St Anthony of Padua. From here a door admits to a walkway which leads to the Precipizio (where there is a remarkable view of the sheer rock face), and a cave where St Francis used to pray. Other holy spots are pointed out by the friars.

A ramp leads down from the terrace to the small church of **Santa Maria degli Angeli** (or the Chiesina, begun in 1216–18) which contains an altarscreen with two polychrome terracotta altars attributed to Andrea or Giovanni della Robbia, and, beyond, in the earliest church, a blue-and-white altarpiece of the *Assumption of the Virgin*, another fine work by Andrea, and Renaissance stalls. Count Orlando Cattani is buried here. A path leads up to the summit of the rock (La Penna, 1283m).

Caprese Michelangelo

From Chiusi della Verna (see above) a narrow road winds down through lovely scenery to Caprese Michelangelo, a tiny isolated hamlet (200 inhabitants), with fine views. It is famous because this is where Michelangelo was born in 1475. His father, Leonardo Buonarroti, was appointed *podestà* here the same year, but a short time after Michelangelo's birth the family moved back to Florence.

Cars must be left below the little hill. Beyond the gate is the restored **castle** with the ticket office (open daily 09.30–18.30; Nov–mid-June 10.00–17.00 exc. Mon) in the ground-floor hall. Opposite the **Palazzo Pretorio**, with the room where Michelangelo may have been born, is now a (disappointing) museum with some of Michelangelo's works reproduced in photographs. A garden enclosed by the castle walls has been decorated with sculptures (including works by Emilio Greco and Antonio Berti). A modern building has casts of Michelangelo's most famous works. The great artist was christened in the 13C chapel of San Giovanni Battista below the hill. The district is known for its delicious wild mushrooms (*porcini*).

From Chiusi della Verna the main road continues east to Pieve Santo Stefano (see p 528). A lovely by-road leads southwest from Chiusi della Verna through beautiful countryside to Chitignano and Rassina (see below).

To the south of Bibbiena, the Arezzo road follows the Arno, but soon leaves the Casentino valley. At **Rassina**, a busy place with a large gravel works, is **Pieve Socana**. The 11C church has a fine campanile, round below and hexagonal above, beside its lovely apse. The interior (if closed ring at the priest's house on the right) has been heavily restored. A gate on the right of the façade leads to a path which runs beneath a vine trellis and through an orchard to the east end of the church. A large rectangular Etruscan altar (5C BC) and remains of steps which led up to a temple can be seen here.

A by-road leads from Pieve Socana through a pretty valley up to **Castel Focognano**, a compact little village. Beyond the Torre Grande the road leads up to the church beside the Podesteria (early 15C), decorated with coats of arms. Beyond a narrow archway on the left, beneath the campanile, its old loggia with a wooden roof and more coats of arms can be seen, beneath which is an old bread oven. On the right is a palace with two lions. The road continues up through woods with views ahead of the wooded slopes of the Pratomagno. It then descends into a valley with a stream in which is **Carda** a quiet, well-kept little village. In the old district on a hill (keep left) is the church (ring for the key at the priest's house) which contains a precious triptych attributed to Mariotto di Cristofano.

Another road from Rassina leads southwest to **Talla**, birthplace of Guido Monaco (990–c 1050). There is a beautiful carved 16C organ case in San Niccolò.

Another by-road leads east from Rassina to **Chitignano**, just before which a signpost (right) indicates the castle of the counts (now privately owned) above the road on a little hill surrounded by cypresses, with statues high up on its wall. It was from here that Bishop Guglielmino Ubertini, the famous condottiere, set out on 11 June 1289, at the head of the Ghibelline army of Arezzo for the Battle of Campaldino, where he lost his life. The scattered village has mineral water springs.

The main road leads south from Rassina through Giovi, near **Pieve a Sietina**, a lovely little church (adm. only by appointment, ☎ 0575 451 207), to Arezzo (see p 467).

Sansepolcro, Anghiari and Monterchi

Sansepolcro is in the north-east corner Tuscany on the Umbrian border. It can be reached most easily from Arezzo. It is famous as the birthplace of Piero della Francesca and preserves some beautiful works by him. Nearby at Monterchi there is another famous fresco by Piero. The little, well preserved medieval town of Anghiari is of interest for its churches and delightful museum.

Practical information

Getting there
By car

Sansepolcro is reached from Arezzo by N73 which passes close to Monterchi. Another road from Arezzo via the pretty Scheggia Pass skirts Anghiari before reaching Sansepolcro. **Car parking**. In **Sansepolcro** there is free parking in Via dei Molini, outside Porta del Castello, and Via Alessandro Volta. Car park with an hourly tariff outside Porta Fiorentina. In **Anghiari** there is a car park off Via Matteotti below Piazza Baldaccio.

By train

The *Ferrovia Centrale Umbra* links

Perugia (see *Blue Guide Umbria*) via Città di Castello with Sansepolcro.

By bus

Buses run by *SITA* (☎ 0575 742 999) from Arezzo and Florence to Anghiari, Monterchi, and Sansepolcro.

Information offices

APT Arezzo, Piazza della Repubblica 22 (☎ 0575 377 678). In **Sansepolcro**, Piazza Garibaldi 2 (☎ 0575 740 536). *Comunità Montana Valtiberina Toscana*, Via San Giuseppe 32. **Anghiari**: *Pro Loco*, Corso Matteotti 103 (next to the post office; ☎ 0575 749 279).

Where to stay
Hotels in Sansepolcro

☆☆☆ *Fiorentino*, Via Luca Pacioli 60 (☎ 0575 740 350; 📠 0575 740 370).

☆☆ *Da Ventura*, Via Niccolò Agguinti 30 (☎/📠 0575 742 560).

Hotels on the outskirts of Sansepolcro

☆☆☆ *Oroscopo*, Piazza Togliatti 66, località Pieve Vecchia (☎ 0575 734 875, 📠 0575 735 051).

ANGHIARI ☆☆☆ *Oliver*, Via della Battaglia 16 (☎ 0575 789 933; 📠 0575 789 944); *La Meridiana*, Piazza IV Novembre 8 (☎/📠 0575 788 102).
BADIA TEDALDA has a ☆☆ hotel.

Eating out
Restaurants

SANSEPOLCRO

€€€ *Oroscopo*, Via Togliatti 78.

€€€ *Da Ventura*, Via Niccolò Agguinti 30 (excellent white truffles).

€€ *Fiorentino*, Via Luca Pacioli 60; *Enoteca Tirartardi*.

€ *Da Totò*, Via XX Settembre 140; *Calisti*, Via Pacioli 50.

There is a student canteen (*mensa*; anyone welcome) open at lunchtime in the convent next to the church of the Cappuccini (outside Porta Fiorentina).

ANGHIARI €€ *La Nena*, Via Gramsci 12; € *Da Alighiero*, Via Garibaldi 8.

SORCI €€ *Castello di Sorci*

SCHEGGIA 10km west € *Antico Posto di Ristoro* (a cool place in summer).

TAVERNELLE € *Vecchia Osteria La Pergola* with a couple of rooms to let.

MONTERCHI € *La Vecchia Osteria*, Via dell'Ospedale 19.

Festivals

At **Sansepolcro**, the *Palio della Balestra* is held on the second Sunday in September, with a crossbow contest in medieval costume against Gubbio. The town is famous for the skill of its flag-throwers, the *Sbandieratori*. A large fair, the *Mezza Quaresima* is held after the fourth Sunday in Lent, and on 16 August, the *Festa Popolare di San Rocco*, there are various festivities.

At **Anghiari** there is a fair of artisans' work in late April and early May in the streets of the old town.

Sansepolcro

Sansepolcro (properly Borgo San Sepolcro) is an attractive little town (15,500 inhab.) in a plain in the upper Tiber valley, where tobacco is grown. Most of its buildings date from the 15C. It is famous as the birthplace of Piero della Francesca (1416–92). The Buitoni family began their pasta business here in 1827.

History

According to an ancient tradition Sansepolcro is named in honour of relics brought back from the Holy Sepulchre in Jerusalem by two pilgrims named

Arcano and Egidio who settled here on their return. An abbey built in the town in 1012 soon became very powerful after it was granted privileges by popes and emperors, and Sansepolcro became seat of a bishopric in 1520. The town was contested between its powerful neighbours Perugia, Città di Castello, Rimini and the Pontifical States, as well as Milan, until it came under Florentine dominion in 1441. It was severely shaken by earthquake in 1351–52, and was again damaged in the Second World War.

Other painters born here besides Piero, were Matteo di Giovanni (c 1430–95), Raffaellino del Colle (1490–1566) and Santi di Tito (1538–1603).

At the centre of the city is **Piazza Torre di Berta**, named after a tower (destroyed in 1944) through which runs the main street of the town, **Via XX Settembre** (usually called the Corso). **Palazzo Pichi-Sermolli** has a fine 16C façade with handsome windows and a central balcony. On the corner of the corso is another palace with two balconies.

The Duomo

The wide Via Matteotti leads out of Piazza Torre di Berta past the **Duomo** which has an imposing Romanesque interior (13C–14C) with Gothic elements. On the west wall are two high reliefs of *St Benedict* and *St Augustine* by Andrea della Robbia and a collaborator. South wall. Fine fresco of the *Madonna with Saints Catherine of Alexandria and Thomas Becket* by the Riminese school (1383); first altar: *Incredulity of St Thomas* (1575) by Santi di Tito; fresco of the *Crucifixion* by Bartolomeo della Gatta; second altar: *Nativity* by Durante Alberti. At the end of the aisle is a delightful Baroque altar, lit from above by a little oval dome decorated with cherubs. In the **sanctuary**, the polyptych with the *Resurrection of Christ* attributed to Niccolò di Segna, later influenced Piero della Francesca (see below). The organ was built by Tamburini.

In the chapel to the left of the high altar the ***Volto Santo** is a huge wood Crucifix, probably dating from the 10C or earlier. North side. On the right of the sacristy door, polychrome statue of the *Madonna and Child* (14C or 15C), and on the left of the door a della Robbian tabernacle. Second altar, *Assumption* signed and dated 1602 by Palma Giovane; *Ascension* attributed to Perugino (or Gerino da Pistoia on a cartoon by Perugino). Beyond the wall monument to Simone Graziani (1509) is a *Resurrection* by Raffaellino del Colle,and a 16C *Crucifixion* by Romano Alberti on the first altar.

On the right of the façade, at no.3, is a covered way which leads past part of the cloister with fine capitals towards Via Piero della Francesca. On the wall is a Roman cippus. On the right is the **Cappella del Monacato** or di San Leonardo. It contains a 17C altar and a fresco attributed to Cherubino Alberti around a 15C sculpted *Crucifix*. It is thought that Piero della Francesca is buried here. Opposite the Duomo is Palazzo Gherardi with two 12C towers. Next to the Duomo is **Palazzo delle Laudi** (1592–1609) by Alberto Alberti and Antonio Cantagallina, with a monumental portico. It is now the town hall. Opposite is the 16C Palazzo Aggiunti. In Piazza Garibaldi is **Palazzo Pretorio**, decorated with della Robbian coats of arms. First built in the 14C it was restored in 1843. The Gothic hall on the ground floor with a 16C fresco is used for exhibitions. The fine Gothic windows at the west end are best seen from the museum (see below).

Museo Civico

The Arco della Pesa connects Palazzo Pretorio with the ex-Palazzo Comunale, which has an outside stair. It is now the seat of the Museo Civico (entered around the corner at no. 65 Via Aggiunti), famous for its masterpieces by Piero della Francesca (open every day 09.30–13.00, 14.30–18.00; summer 09.00–13.30, 14.30–19.30). In 1998, the garden courtyard was enclosed for use as a ticket office and bookshop.

Beyond the **Sala del Camino**, the room on the right displays the *polyptych of the *Madonna of the Misericordia,* commissioned from Piero della Francesca by the local confraternity of the Misericordia (1445–62). The **Sala della Resurrezione** contains masterpieces by Piero della Francesca. The *Resurrection* was brought to the attention of a new generation of art historians after it had been described by Aldous Huxley in 1925 as the best picture in the world in his *Notes and Essays of a Tourist* (*Along the Road*). Justly one of Piero's most famous works, the remarkable figure of Christ is one of the most haunting images ever produced in Christian art. His head shows the influence of Masaccio, but the expression has a new spiritual intensity. The soldiers asleep in the peaceful scene below offers a striking contrast. Christ's foot is shown in perfect perspective. Some scholars once believed that it was frescoed in another room of the palace in 1463, and moved here in 1480, but it is now usually agreed that it must have been originally painted for its present position.

Also here are two frescoes by Piero: fragment of the bust of a *Saint (St Julian?)*, found in the former church of Santa Chiara, and *St Louis of Toulouse*. The stalls with 15C intarsia come from the church of San Francesco.

The **Sala di Matteo di Giovanni** contains a triptych by Matteo di Giovanni (removed from the Duomo). The central panel, with the *Baptism of Christ*, by Piero della Francesca, is now in the National Gallery, London. Also here are a *standard painted on both sides (*Crucifixion and Saints*) by Luca Signorelli; *Saints Peter and Paul* and *Assumption* by Gerino da Pistoia; a tabernacle in glazed terracotta of the *Nativity*, recently attributed to Andrea della Robbia (c 1485) and a tondo of the *Madonna and Child* also thought to be by him. From here there is access to a series of small rooms with engravings.

The **Sala di Raffaellino del Colle** contains a fresco and a painting by Raffaellino del Colle and the *Martyrdom of St Quinten* by Pontormo. The **Sala di Giovanni de' Vecchi** has works by the local artist Giovanni de' Vecchi (1537–1615). In the large **Sala di Santi di Tito** are four works by Santi di Tito (*Annunciation, St Nicholas of Tolentino, Pope St Clement among the faithful,* and *Pietà*), and paintings by Agostino Ciampelli (*Destruction of the idols*); and Leandro Bassano (*Adoration of the Magi*).

On the other side of the Sala del Camino (see above), beyond a room with an *Immaculate Conception* by Giovanni Battista Mercati, and an *Adoration of the Magi* by Leandro Bassano, stairs mount to two rooms with 14C (detached) frescoes, and a view of the two Gothic windows of Palazzo Pretorio (see above). From the courtyard a new flight of stairs leads down to vaulted rooms in the **basement** which display an archaeological collection of finds from the area, including Roman material. In another room the **Cathedral treasury** is displayed including church vestments and ecclesiastical objects belonging to Bishop Costaguti (18C), and the crown and vestments (mid-14C) used to adorn the Volto Santo in the cathedral, as well as 13C sculpture.

Piazza San Francesco

In Piazza San Francesco, planted with trees, are two churches. **San Francesco** was founded in 1285, but transformed in 1752. Interior. South side, second altar, *St Francis receiving the stigmata* (1614) by Giovanni de' Vecchi, and, to the right, a profile in marble of the native painter Cristoforo Gherardi (c 1556). The altar table (1304) in sandstone has reliefs and is surrounded by little Gothic arches. *North side*. Second altar, *Eternal Father and Saints* attributed to Francesco Curradi; first altar, *Christ among the Doctors in the Temple* by Passignano (in very poor condition). In the adjoining cloister are lunette frescoes (1681–83) of the *Life of St Anthony* (also in very poor condition).

On the other side of the piazza is the church of **Santa Maria delle Grazie**, with a pretty double loggia (1518). The interior has fine carved altars. The high altar has a delightful decorated niche around the *Madonna in Prayer* by Raffaellino del Colle, flanked by two marble angels. The carved wood ceiling is by Alberto Alberti. On the south altar is a wooden *Crucifix* and on the north altar a painting of *Saints* by Francesco Gambacciani. The organ dates from the 17C. An interesting (but damaged) detached fresco of *St Lucy with two Saints* also belongs to the church. Beneath the loggia beside the church is a pretty **oratory** (now used for exhibitions) with a vault and 15 frescoed lunettes attributed to Giovanni Alberti and Raffaello Schiaminossi. The *Assumption* in the centre of the ceiling is by Federico Zoi.

In Via Niccolò Aggiunti are a number of interesting palaces: at no.47 is a very unusual brick building (17C), and at no. 57 a 16C palace with graffiti decoration. On the opposite side is a 15C palace (no. 84). At no.71 is the **Casa di Piero della Francesca**, a large palace which was probably designed by the famous artist (restored in the mid-16C), and where he may have lived for a time. It has a fine row of windows high up on the façade and has been restored as a study centre. In the garden opposite is a monument to the painter by Arnaldo Zocchi (1892). Just beyond, next to the headquarters of the Misericordia is the church of **San Rocco** (ring for admission). It contains two angels attributed to Alessandro and Giovanni Alberti, and *St Sebastian* attributed to Leonardo Cungi (d. 1569). On the left side is an 18C painting of three saints. Behind the carved and gilded altar is a statue of the *Dead Christ*. The **oratory** beneath the church (also shown on request; ring in Via della Fonte), has frescoed lunettes by the Alberti and a replica of the *Resurrection of Christ* by Raffaellino del Colle in the Duomo. Behind is a copy of the *Holy Sepulchre in Jerusalem*, an imitation of the work by Leon Battista Alberti in the Cappella di San Sepolcro in Florence.

Via XX Settembre (the Corso), which runs across the town from the 16C Porta Fiorentina, beside a fine stretch of walls, to the site of Porta Romana, is well worth exploring, especially at the east end. Outside the gate, a road leads up to the church of the **Cappuccini** (San Michele Arcangelo) which has an interesting high altarpiece of *Paradise* by Paolo Piazza dated 1608. At the west end of the Corso is the church of **Sant'Agostino**, rebuilt in 1771 by Vincenzo Righi with a bright interior decorated with white stuccoes. South side, second altar, *Annunciation* (1762) by Annibale Lancisi; third altar, 14C *Crucifix*. In front of the high altar, painted wood sarcophagus of 1230, and in the apse, *Madonna della Cintola* by Giovanni Cimica. North side, third altar, *Birth of the Virgin* by the 17C Florentine school, first altar, *Madonna in glory with St Nicholas of Tolentino* by Giovanni Cimica.

At no.46 Via XX Settembre is the 18C Palazzo Alberti with a bust of Cosimo II. Beyond Piazza Torre di Berta, Via XX Settembre passes (right) **Palazzo Graziani**, a handsome early 17C palace. Across Via del Buon Umore, with four flying arches, is the 16C **Palazzo Ducci Del Rossi** (no. 131), seat of the town library. On the left is **Teatro Dante** (now a cinema) built in 1835, and (no. 139) Palazzo Turini with an old tower. The last part of the Corso, with numerous shops, has small side streets, many with arches.

In the southern part of the town (reached from Piazza Torre di Berta by the pretty Via della Fraternità) is the church of **Santa Maria dei Servi**. On the right of the high altar, *Madonna in Glory*, a fine but damaged painting attributed to Matteo di Giovanni. On either side are two paintings of four *Saints* (with the *Annunciation* in tondoes above), all once part of one work by Matteo di Giovanni. In Via Santa Croce is the deconsecrated church of **San Lorenzo** (open 09.00–13.00, 15.00–19.00), with a Renaissance loggia on one corner. It contains a *Deposition* by Rosso Fiorentino (1528), a dark and crowded composition. Above is a lunette with *God the Father* by Raffaellino del Colle.

The **Fortezza Medicea** (no admission; in urgent need of restoration), at the north-east corner of the old town, was built for Cosimo I in 1561–63 by Alberto Alberti on a design by Giuliano da Sangallo; at the northwest corner is the Cannoniere del Buontalenti, a bastion erected in the 16C in the walls by Bernardo Buontalenti. Other pretty steets in the town include Via San Giuseppe, Via Sant'Antonio, Via Piero della Francesca, and Via Luca Pacioli. To the north of Piazza San Francesco is the old Buitoni factory; a new factory has been erected on the southern outskirts of the town.

Anghiari

From Sansepolcro, beyond the *superstrada* a remarkably long and straight road crosses the plain on the site of the famous battle of Anghiari (see below) and then climbs to Anghiari (6000 inhab.), once called *Castrum Angulare*, in a spectacular position (430m) above the plain. It has a well-preserved old centre, typical of a medieval walled town. In 1440 it was the scene of a Florentine victory, under Francesco Sforza, over the Visconti of Milan (the subject of a fresco commissioned from Leonardo da Vinci for Palazzo Vecchio in Florence, the completed fragment of which is lost). Later, in 1796, the French defeated the Austrians here.

The local artisans are particularly skilled cabinet makers, and there is an institute for the restoration of antique furniture. On weekends, various artisans' workshops in the old town can be visited.

There is a car park off Via Matteotti below Piazza Baldaccio, with a pretty walk (signposted; keep left) up to an old gate in the walls, which provides an entrance to the medieval town, near Palazzo Pubblico. In **Piazza Baldaccio**, the old market-place, with a statue of Garibaldi, is a monumental arcade, the **Galleria Magi** (1889), an unexpected sight. Beyond it, in Piazza IV Novembre, is the neo-Classical **Teatro dei Ricomposti**, with a façade crowned by statues.

On the other side of Piazza Baldaccio is the unspoilt, walled medieval town. From the piazza, the higher road (right) leads to the scenographic Via Trieste, which ascends steeply to **Santa Maria delle Grazie** (the Propositura) at the top.

It has an 18C neo-Classical interior with a barrel vault. In the north transept are two charming paintings in their original frames by Sogliani: *Last Supper* and *Christ washing the disciples' feet*. The high altar and tabernacle were made in the della Robbian workshop. On the right of the high altar is a *Madonna and Child with four Saints and two angels* by Matteo di Giovanni (from the church of Sant'Agostino, see below). In the right transept is a *Deposition* by Domenico Puligo. Beside the church the town walls and a clock tower can be seen.

The lower road out of Piazza Baldaccio leads shortly to Piazza Mameli which has a number of old houses including the fine Renaissance Palazzo Taglieschi, probably built in 1437 by Matteo Cane (Taglieschi). It now contains the **Museo Statale di Palazzo Taglieschi**, a good local museum, well maintained and carefully labelled (open 09.00–18.30; fest. 09.00–12.30; closed Mon).

In the **basement** are architectural fragments, and at the foot of the stairs an enamelled terracotta lunette by Benedetto and Santi Buglioni. **Upper floor**. The first room contains a precious 16C organ (still in working order) from Santo Stefano and wooden sculptures including 13C and 14C *Madonnas*, and a seated statue of *St Anthony Abbot* by Giovanni di Turino. In a separate room a *Madonna* in polychrome wood is displayed; very well preserved, it is one of the best works of Jacopo della Quercia (c 1420). It was made for a church in Anghiari and purchased by the State in 1977. The *Child*, formerly on the Madonna's knee, has been exhibited separately since its restoration. It is not known if it was sculpted at the same time, nor whether it was intended as part of this group. Another room displays an enamelled terracotta *Nativity and Saints* by Andrea della Robbia (from the church of the Badia).

On the **second floor** the 17C paintings include works by Matteo Rosselli, and Giovanni Battista Ghidoni. The collection also includes dolls, terracotta statuettes by Francesco Maria Angiolini, ecclesiastical objects, copes and furniture.

The church of **Sant'Agostino**, also in the piazza, has been closed for many years during excavation work on an earlier church below the foundations. The 12C building was enlarged in 1464. St Thomas Becket is supposed to have stayed here. Beside it a tunnel (signposted) leads down to Porta Sant'Angelo and the walls.

A road continues up left from the piazza to the inconspicuous church of the **Badia**, reconstructed in the 14C, with an unusual asymmetrical interior. A carved dossal attributed to Desiderio da Settignano surrounds a painted, wooden high relief of the seated *Madonna, with the standing Child* by Tino da Camaino. Dating from c 1316 this is the only wooden sculpture known by Tino di Camaino. Around the high altar are four 18C statues.

Opposite the church is the former headquarters (with an interesting old window) of the **Misericordia**, now a delightful little museum (for adm. ring at no. 13 Via Nenci, or ☎ 0575 789 577) illustrating the history of this charitable institution, still very active all over Tuscany. In the hall, dating from the early 16C, are displayed a carriage (1861) and a litter (1909), surgical instruments, and costumes worn by members of the brotherhood. The archives are kept in a room with traces of 15C frescoes. Uphill to the right (beneath an archway) is **Palazzo Pubblico**, with coats of arms on its façade.

In the other part of the town (see above) Via Matteotti leads straight downhill from the 16C porticoed church of **Santa Croce**, through Piazza Baldaccio, and, near the bottom, past the church of **Santo Stefano** (ring at no. 13), with its little bellcote. This is a remarkable church on a Byzantine Greek-cross plan, thought to date from the 7C–8C, partly enclosed in a later building. It is one of the earliest buildings to have survived in the upper Tiber valley.

Environs of Anghiari

To the east of Anghiari is **San Leo**, near which can be seen **Santa Maria a Corsano**, dating from around 1000, next to an abandoned farm house. It has an unusual campanile attached to the façade, beneath which is the west door of the church.

From Anghiari, a pretty secondary road for Arezzo winds around the hill with wonderful views of the town to the left. It follows an undulating ridge of hills planted with trees and passes a turn left (yellow signpost) for **Pieve a Sovara**, reached in less than 1km along an unsurfaced road. The pieve stands beside a group of farm buildings. The church, has a prominent campanile and was founded in the 9C but mostly rebuilt in 1480. It contains a 15C font.

The Arezzo road continues to **Tavernelle** where a castellated villa, with a tall central tower, called La Barbolana is conspicuous on a hill to the right. The valley now narrows and the road climbs gently uphill past thick woods (and few houses) to a summit level of 575m at **Scheggia**. It then descends past cypresses, pines, and chestnuts to Arezzo.

A short way north of Anghiari is the church of **Santa Maria a Micciano**, of ancient foundation. It contains a 15C altarpiece of the *Madonna and two Saints*.

Monterchi

Monterchi, south of Anghiari and Sansepolcro, is a quiet little fortified village, damaged by earthquakes in the past, the birthplace of the mother of Piero della Francesca. The famous *Madonna del Parto* by Piero has been kept here, since its restoration in 1993. It is displayed in an old school building in Via della Reglia (open 09.00–13.00, 14.00–18.00 or 19.00 exc. Mon; in July and Aug it is also open 21.00–24.00). The fresco was formerly in the church of Momentana, partially demolished in 1785, and was then included in a chapel in the cemetery at the foot of the hill, just outside the village. It was detached in 1910, and in 1956–69 the chapel was transformed to isolate it from the cemetery. It now seems unlikely that the fresco will be returned to the little chapel: its present display in a stark black glass case with harsh lighting has been justly criticised.

The fresco was painted c 1460 and shows the pregnant Madonna revealed by two angels pulling back the curtains of a tent. It is thought that Piero's mother was buried in the cemetery and this work was intended as a memorial to her. A 14C fresco fragment of the *Madonna and Child*, found beneath the *Madonna del Parto* is displayed in the same room. In other rooms there are instructive displays relating to Piero's fresco technique and recent restorations. There is a fine view from the little garden, where concerts are sometimes held.

At the top of the hill, near a piazza with lime trees, is the **Pieve di San Simeone**, rebuilt in 1966. Its works of art are in poor condition. In the interior (only open for services), the first chapel on the south side has a 16C detached fresco of the *Madonna of the Misericordia*. The second south chapel contains a little polychrome terracotta ciborium (its original painted wooden door has recently been stolen). Between the second and third chapels are three interesting

15C bas-reliefs of the *Pietà*. On the third north altar is a 15C wooden *Crucifix*. Behind the church is a lovely old medieval passageway. Palazzo Massi-Alberti in Via XX Settembre is used for exhibitions.

At the foot of the hill, the main road to Città di Castello passes the cemetery and the avenue which leads (left) to the chapel which formerly contained the *Madonna del Parto*. A by-road continues from the chapel over the hill to the lovely little village of Citerna in Umbria, described in *Blue Guide Umbria*. The interesting town of Città di Castello, to the east, is also described in *Blue Guide Umbria*.

West of Monterchi, on the main road to Arezzo in the Cerfone valley is **Pieve a Ranco** (blue signpost). Approached over a very narrow bridge, the church of **Santi Lorentino e Pergentino** (if closed, ring at the priest's house beside the east end of the church) was damaged by an earthquake in 1916. It contains a beautiful 14C polychrome wooden seated statue of the *Madonna and Child* at the east end.

North of Sansepolcro is **Pieve Santo Stefano** (433m), which was systematically mined in the Second World War. The collegiata was left standing almost alone, amid ruins. The **church**, rebuilt in 1844–81 in neo-Classical style, contains a *Martyrdom of St Stephen*, attributed to Spagnoletto, a dossal in enamelled terracotta of the *Assumption* (1514; by Andrea della Robbia), and a 16C polychrome *Madonna*. The church of the **Madonna dei Lumi**, on a domed Greek-cross plan, dates from 1590–1625. In **Palazzo Comunale** is a fine terracotta of the *Good Samaritan* (1511). The Loggia del Grano is an old covered marketplace. The main road continues north to cross the border into Emilia Romagna (see *Blue Guide Northern Italy*).

Another road leads north from Sansepolcro across the Passo di Viamaggio (983m). Here a rough road leads west to the hermitage of **Cerbaiolo**, founded in 722 by the Benedictines and owned by the Franciscans since 1216. The 13C church and cloister survive, in beautiful countryside.

The main road continues to **Badia Tedalda**, a little hill resort (756m). The parish **church** contains enamelled terracotta altarpieces by the Buglioni, including the high altarpiece of the *Madonna and four Saints* commissioned in 1516 from Benedetto Buglioni, a *Madonna of the holy Girdle* (1521), and *Saints Julian, Sebastian, and Anthony* (1522), by Santi Buglioni.

The road continues to **Sestino** an ancient Roman municipium, in the eastern corner of Tuscany, on the border with the Marche. An **antiquarium** (open weekdays 10.00–12.00, 16.00–18.00) founded here in 1930–36 displays local Roman finds including statues of the Imperial era. The ancient **Pieve of San Pancrazio** contains a huge painted Cross by the 14C Riminese school. The primitive crypt is also interesting.

To the northeast of Sansepolcro, a by-road leads past the 14C church of Santa Maria near **Montagna**, with 14C frescoes. The rough road continues up to the convent of **Montecasale**, surrounded by fine woods and cypresses. A hermitage was built here by St Francis (now occupied by Cappuchin fathers). The church contains a 12C wood statue of the *Madonna and Child*.

West of Sansepolcro, on the left bank of the Tiber, is the church of **San Martino di Montedoglio**, probably founded before 1000. It contains a fresco of *St Martin* attributed to the school of Piero della Francesca or to Gerino da Pistoia, and a 15C terracotta statue of *St Sebastian*.

The Islands of Elba and Capraia

The Parco Nazionale dell'Arcipelago Toscano which includes the small islands of Gorgona, Pianosa, Montecristo and Giannutri, half of Elba and Giglio, and most of Capraia, was instituted in 1996, a victory for the conservationists after years of debate and considerable local opposition. The Reserve will protect the beautiful landscape of the islands which are covered with low vegetation known as the *macchia mediterranea*, or Mediterranean scrub, which usually includes ilex, broom, strawberry tree, myrtle, cistus rockrose, rosemary, juniper and mastic. Migratory birds visit the islands, and many nest here (shearwaters, shags, Adouin's gulls and herring gulls).

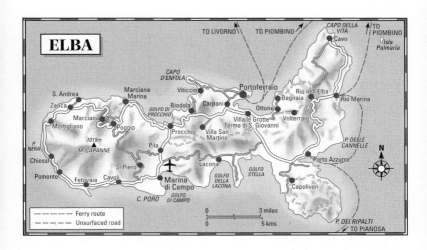

Practical information

Getting there and getting around
By sea

The mainland port for Elba is Piombino (see p 309). **Maritime services** are run by *Toremar* and *Mobylines*. It is always advisable to book the outward and return trip for cars in advance, especially on holidays and in summer.
Toremar: Piombino office, Piazzale Premuda 13 (☎ 0565 311 00);

Portoferraio office, Calata Italia 22 (☎ 0565 918 080).
Mobylines: Piombino office, Piazzale Premuda 13 (☎ 0565 221 212); Portoferraio office, Viale Elba 4 (☎ 0565 914 133). Frequent car ferries and hydrofoils (much more expensive) run to Portoferraio on the north coast in c 1hr (hydrofoils in 30mins). Another boat serves Porto Azzurro and Rio Marina on the east coast. Hydrofoil to Cavo.

By air

Airport at Marina di Campo (☎ 0565 976 011) with flights from Milan and Rome, as well as Zurich, Munich, Vienna.

By train

The slower trains on the main line from Pisa and Livorno to Rome stop at Campiglia Marittima, where there are frequent services to Piombino Marittima for the ferry. There is one return train a day from Florence direct to Piombino Marittima (the *Freccia dell'Elba*) in c 2hrs 15mins connecting with the ferry.

Transport on the island

Bus services run by *ATL* (information ☎ 0565 914 392) from near the ferry quay at Portoferraio to numerous localities on the island.

Car and bicycle hire available at Portoferraio.

 ### Information offices
Agenzia per il Turismo dell'Arcipelago Toscano, Calata Italia 26, Portoferraio, Elba (☎ 0565 914 671; ▤ 0565 916 350; ✉: info@aptelba.it). *Comunità Montana dell'Elba e Capraia*, Viale Manzoni, Portoferraio (who publish a map of the numerous footpaths on the island).

 ### Where to stay
Hotels
There are some 200 hotels and residences of all categories on the island, and only a very small selection is given below.

Near **PORTOFERRAIO** ☆☆☆☆ *Villa Ottone*, località Ottone (☎ 0565 933 042; ▤ 0565 933 257), and

Le Picchiaie, località Picchiaie (☎ 0565 933 110; ▤ 0565 933 186). **BIODOLA** ☆☆☆☆ *Hermitage* (☎ 0565 936 911; ▤ 0565 969 984) and *Biodola* (☎ 0565 936 811; ▤ 0565 969 852).

Near **CAPOLIVERI** ☆☆☆ *Capo Sud*, località Lacona (☎ 0565 964 021; ▤ 0565 964 263) and Residence *Costa dei Gabbiani*, località Ripalte (☎ 0565 935 122; ▤ 0565 935 233).

RIO MARINA ☆☆☆ *Rio*, Via Palestro 31 (☎ 0565 924 225; ▤ 0565 924 162).

There is also some **agriturist accommodation** on the island: a list is supplied by the *APT* and information from Terranostra Isola d'Elba, ☎ 0565 914 220 and *Turismo Verde Toscana* in Portoferraio, ☎ 0565 915 111.

Campsites

There are numerous campsites all over the island. These include the ☆☆☆ *Rosselba Le Palme* at località Ottone, east of Portoferraio (☎ 0565 933 101; ▤ 0565 933 041). Others on the south coast, particularly near Lacona.

 ### Eating out
Restaurants
PORTOFERRAIO
€€ *Da Vittorio*, Via dell'Amore 54 (near the old port); *La Ferrigna*, Piazza della Repubblica; € *Da Elbano Benassi*, località Casaccia.

CAPOLIVERI €€ *Il Chiasso*, Via N. Sauro.

RIO MARINA € *La Canocchia*, Via Palestro.

POGGIO €€ *Publius*.

Elba

Elba (29,000 inhab.), is the largest island in the Tuscan archipelago, and is only 10km from Piombino on the mainland. It has an area of 223 sq km, and is 27km long and 18km across at its broadest. The climate is mild and sunny and the sea bathing good, although it is crowded with visitors in August. It is especially popular as a holiday place with German visitors, many of whom come here in September. It has a particularly interesting geological formation, with numerous varieties of different minerals. The inhabited part of the island has pretty hills covered with the *macchia mediterranea*, while other parts are barren and deserted. The beauty of the island has been threatened in recent years by forest fires, but about half of the island has been protected since 1996 as part of the **Parco Nazionale dell'Arcipelago Toscano**. The excellent red and white wines once produced here are now difficult to find, although the sweet desert wines Aleatico and Moscato are still sold on the island.

The island became famous in 1814–15 as Napoleon's place of exile, and the two villas where he passed his time can be visited: one is in Portoferraio, but Villa San Martino nearby is more interesting.

Although Portoferraio is the main port, perhaps the most attractive place on the island is Marciana Marina near the scenic Monte Capanne (1019m), covered with chestnut, oak and ilex woods. The resort of Porto Azzurro is in the eastern part of the island.

History

The Greek *Aethalia* and the Roman *Ilva*, Elba has been known since ancient times for its iron ore, which was mined here up until the last century. In the 11C the island was in the possession of Pisa and in 1399 it came under the control of Piombino. In 1548 Cosimo I built Portoferraio, and the south-eastern part of the island was taken over by the Spaniards in the 17C as part of the Stato dei Presidi (see p 332). It officially became part of Tuscany in 1809. The English have been coming here since the end of the 18C, and Joseph Conrad based his last unfinished novel, *Suspense* (begun in 1905), on Elba, although he never visited the island. Aldous Huxley probably came here in 1924, and Dylan Thomas in 1947.

Portoferraio

The chief town and port is Portoferraio (11,500 inhab.), where once huge blast furnaces smelted iron ore. It was founded in 1548 by the Medici grand-duke Cosimo I when the remarkable fortifications were begun by Giovanni Battista Bellucci and Giovanni Camerini. The modern seafront, where the ferries dock, is unattractive; the old port, now used by private boats, is at the end of the promontory. It was occupied by the British fleet in 1795–97 under Nelson (the Mediterranean fell under British control the following year).

The fortified **Porta a Mare** (1637) leads into the old district, still the centre of the town, with a covered market. The **Museo Archeologico della Linguella,** housed in the old salt warehouses, is at present closed. It contains late Bronze Age finds, as well as Etruscan and Roman material. In the Caserma de Laugier is the **Pinacoteca Foresiana** (open summer 09.00–19.00, winter 09.30–12.30 exc. fest., with 16C–19C Tuscan paintings.

A road (or steps) lead up from the main Piazza della Repubblica to the Medici **Forte Stella** which dominates the port and from which there is a good view. Napoleon's principal residence was the **Villa dei Mulini**, nearby, overlooking the sea. The modest house (usually open 09.00–19.00; fest. 09.00–13.00) contains Napoleonic souvenirs.

The main defensive system is to the west around **Forte Falcone**; this can be visited on the descent from the fort to the **Porta a Terra** on the sea front.

Along the coast west of Portoferraio is **Capo d'Enfola** on a rocky promontory with beaches and a camp site.

On the Marciana road southwest of Portoferraio, beyond the junction with the road for Porto Azzurro (see below) is the by-road left for the **Villa San Martino** (adm. as for the Villa dei Mulini), in a fertile valley, Napoleon's summer residence. The large one-storey neo-Classical edifice was built in front of Napoleon's house by Prince Anatolio Demidoff in 1851 as a memorial to him. The Galleria Demidoff, with a collection of engravings was opened here in 1987. Napoleon's simple house above is reached by a path on the left. It is charmingly decorated in the style known as *retour d'Egypte* with frescoes commemorating Napoleon's Egyptian campaign in 1798–1800. They were painted by his official court painter, Vincenzo Antonio Revelli in 1814.

Napoleon Bonaparte

The name of Napoleon Bonaparte is indelibly associated with the island since his enforced residence here. He was born in Corsica in 1769 which up until the year before had belonged to Genoa, and his parents' families were from mainland Italy. He became a general at the age of 26 and his first Italian campaign was an immediate success. He established the Cisalpine and Cispadane republics in Northern Italy and by the Treaty of Campoformio handed over Venice to Austria. He returned to Italy in 1800 after his Egyptian expedition. The year after he became Emperor (in 1804) he was appointed king of the new 'Kingdom of Italy'. His rule lasted until 1813 when he was defeated at Leipzig. Deposed by the Tallyrand government in Paris in 1814, he was forced to abdicate, but managed to obtain Elba as a principality. He arrived on the island with a guard of honour of some 800 men. In March 1815 he set sail from here for Cannes and re-entered Paris for the 'One Hundred Days' before his final defeat at Waterloo.

Biodola, a holiday village on a pretty little bay with a sandy beach, has bungalows and hotels. **Procchio** is a busy resort, with a good beach. Nearby, beyond the small airport, is **Marina di Campo**, an attractive bathing resort on the coast, with perhaps the best beach on the island, and numerous hotels.

Access to the sea is limited between Procchio and Marciana Marina along the north coast. **Marciana Marina** is a pretty little fishing port with sardine fisheries. The cylindrical tower on the waterfront was built by the Pisans in the 12C. There are long-term plans to expand the harbour. From here the road runs uphill through chestnut woods to the most beautiful part of the island around **Poggio** (330m) and **Marciana Alta**, both delightful little villages. A cable-car (open Apr–Sept 10.00–12.00, 14.30–18.00) ascends to the summit of **Monte Capanne** (1019m), which can also be climbed by marked paths in c 2hrs.

The western shore of the island has splendid views and wild scenery. **Sant'Andrea** is an elegant resort, and **Chiessi** is a pretty village amidst vineyards.

The main town in the eastern part of the island is **Porto Azzurro**, a fashionable resort overlooking a beautiful bay. With its great Spanish fort of 1602 (now a prison), it was formerly called Porto Longone.

On the road from Portoferraio to Porto Azzurro are the **Terme di San Giovanni**, a small spa, with mud baths rich in sulphur (used to help alleviate rheumatism). Nearby, on the shore, are the remains of **Villa Le Grotte** (open summer daily, 09.00–dusk), a Roman villa of the Imperial era, excavated in 1960. Its swimming pool is one of the largest ever discovered.

In the southern part of the island is **Capoliveri**, a delightful little old miners' town in a charming position. North of Porto Azzurro, reached by an inland road, is **Rio Marina**, of interest as it was once the chief ore-port and centre of the mining area, with tall, grim houses. The local Mineral Museum is no longer open regularly. **Cavo**, reached by a coast road from Rio Marina, is at the northernmost point of the island.

Some of the most beautiful scenery on the island can be seen on the unsurfaced road from Bagnaia (east of Portoferraio) to **Rio nell'Elba**, where there is another mineral museum. Another scenic road, the *Volterraio*, leads from Ottone to Rio nell'Elba.

The Tuscan archipelago

Capraia

To the north of Elba, 55km from the mainland at Piombino, is the mountainous volcanic islet of Capraia (20 sq km). The prison here was closed in 1986, and most of the island was protected in 1996, together with the rest of the archipelago, as part of a national park.

Practical information

Getting there
By sea

Ferry (*Toremar*) in 2hr 30mins from Livorno once a day (via Gorgona on Tuesdays). At some periods of the year there is also a service once a week from Portoferraio (in 2hrs). *Toremar* office in Livorno, Porto Mediceo (☎ 0586 896 113); in Capraia, Via Assunzione (☎ 9586 905 069); in Portoferraio, Calata Italia 22 (☎ 0565 918 080).

Information offices
APT dell'Arcipelago Toscano (☎ 0565 914 671).
Cooperativa Parco Naturale Isola di Capraia (☎ 0586 905 071), and *Pro-Loco* (☎ 0586 905 138).

Where to stay
Hotels

☆☆☆☆ *Il Saracino* (☎ 0586 905 018; ▤ 0586 905 062); ☆☆☆ *Da Beppone* (☎/▤ 0586 905 001). There are also a number of residences and rooms to let.
Campsite

☆☆☆ *Le Sughere* (☎ 0586 905 066).

The only settlement is **Capraia** (300 inhab.), beneath Forte San Giorgio, reached from the port by the only road on the island. From here paths lead over the wild volcanic countryside, with beautiful vegetation, where cormorants nest. The highest hills reach a level of 400 metres above sea level, and there is a little inland lake. The island was named by navigators from ancient Greece who found numerous goats (*capre*) here. There is good skin diving along the rocky shore, with numerous caves.

Gorgona

The tiny island of Gorgona (2.2 sq km), is the northernmost island in the archipelago, 44km north of Capraia, and 37km off the mainland at Livorno. It is still used as a prison. It is also a beautiful wild place, with numerous pine trees and interesting bird life (the island became part of the **Parco Nazionale dell'Arcipelago Toscano** in 1996). To visit the island it is necessary to book at least one month in advance at the Comune of Livorno (☎ 0586 884 522; ▤ 0586 895 237): a maximum of 40 people are allowed to visit the island on Tuesdays (by the *Toremar* boat from Livorno to Capraia).

Pianosa

14km south of Elba is the low-lying islet of Pianosa, also used as a prison for a hundred years until it was closed down in 1998. There are plans to introduce boat services to the island and open it up to visitors. With an area of 10 sq km, it rises to a maximum of 29 metres above sea level, and has a particularly mild climate which accounts for its interesting flora and fauna. Some 90 amphorae were discovered in 1991 offshore: they have probably remained here exactly as they fell from a Roman shipwreck. The island has been part of the **Parco Nazionale dell'Arcipelago Toscano** since 1996.

Montecristo

Montecristo, the most isolated of the islands in the Tuscan archipelago is 40km south of Elba, and 63km west of the Argentario. It has an area of 10 sq km. This romantic island, now deserted (except for some goats) and declared a European nature reserve in 1988, and part of the **Parco Nazionale dell'Arcipelago Toscano** in 1996, cannot normally be visited. It is formed of a granite mass covered with woods, rising in the centre to Monte Fortezza (645m). Here are the ruins of the Benedictine monastery of San Salvatore and San Mamiliano, devastated by the pirate Dragut in 1553. A legend that the monks had buried their treasure here before abandoning the island inspired Alexandre Dumas (Dumas père) to write his historical novel, *Le Comte de Monte-Cristo* (1844). From the 15C to the 18C expeditions were made from Piombino to search for the treasure.

The island was acquired in 1852 by a wealthy Englishman, George Watson Taylor, who built a villa at Cala Maestra (the only port of the island), later used as a hunting lodge by Vittorio Emanuele III, and surrounded by a luxuriant garden. While in residence here (1853–60) Taylor, who liked to call himself the 'Count of Montecristo', produced an herbarium of the 335 species of flora to be found on the island.

The islands of Giglio and Giannutri, reached by boat from Monte Argentario, are both described in pp 335–336.

Glossary

Aedicule, small opening framed by two columns and a pediment, originally used in classical architecture

Albarello (pl. *albarelli*), cylindrical shaped pharmacy jars, usually slightly waisted and produced by numerous potteries in Italy from the 15C to 18C

Alberese, white building stone used in Tuscany (especially in the Garfagnana)

Amphora, antique vase, usually of large dimensions, for oil and other liquids

Ancona, retable or large altarpiece (painted or sculpted) in an architectural frame

Antefix, ornament placed at the lower corners of the tiled roof of a temple to conceal the space between the tiles and the cornice

Antiphonal, choir-book containing a collection of antiphonae—verses sung in response by two choirs

Apse, vaulted semicircular end wall of the chancel of a church or of a chapel

Arca, wooden chest with a lid, for sacred or secular use. Also, monumental sarcophagus in stone, used by Christians and pagans

Archaic, period in Greek civilisation preceding the classical era: from about 750 BC–480 BC

Architrave, lowest part of an entablature, horizontal frame above a door

Archivolt, moulded architrave carried round an arch

Atlantes (or Telamones), male figures used as supporting columns

Atrium, forecourt, usually of a Byzantine church or a classical Roman house

Attic, topmost storey of a classical building, hiding the spring of the roof

Badia, Abbazia, abbey.

Baldacchino, canopy supported by columns, usually over an altar

Basilica, originally a Roman building used for public administration; in Christian architecture, an aisled church with a clerestory and apse, and no transepts

Bas-relief, sculpture in low relief

Borgo, a suburb; street leading away from the centre of a town

Bottega, the studio of an artist: the pupils who worked under his direction

Bozzetto, sketch for a painting or a small model for a piece of sculpture

Broccatello, a clouded veined marble from Siena

Bucchero, Etruscan black terracotta ware

Bucrania, a form of classical decoration—skulls of oxen garlanded with flowers

Campanile, bell-tower, often detached from the building to which it belongs

Camposanto, cemetery

Canephora, figure bearing a basket, often used as a caryatid

Canopic vase, Egyptian or Etruscan vase enclosing the entrails of the dead

Cantoria, singing-gallery in a church

Cappella, chapel

Capomaestro, Director of Works or masterbuilder

Cartoon, from cartone, meaning large sheet of paper. A full-size preparatory drawing for a painting or fresco

Caryatid, female figure used as a supporting column

Cassone, a decorated chest, usually a dower chest

Cavea, the part of a theatre or amphitheatre occupied by the rows of seats

Cella, sanctuary of a temple, usually in the centre of the building

Cenacolo, scene of the Last Supper (often in the refectory of a convent)

Chalice, wine cup used in the celebration of Mass

Chasuble long, sleeveless outer garment worn by a priest when celebrating Mass

Chiaroscuro, distribution of light and shade, apart from colour in a painting

Ciborium, casket or tabernacle containing the Host

Cinquecento, Italian term for the 'fifteen-hundreds' i.e. the 16C

Cipollino, onion-marble; a greyish marble with streaks of white or green

Cippus, sepulchral monument in the form of an altar

Cista, casket, usually of bronze and cylindrical in shape, to hold jewels, toilet articles, etc., and decorated with mythological subjects

Cloisonné, type of enamel decoration

Columbarium, a building (usually subterranean) with niches to hold urns containing the ashes of the dead

Commune, a town or city which adopted a form of independent self-government in the Middle Ages

Comune, municipal government (Palazzo del Comune, town hall)

Condottiere, professional military commander

Confessio, crypt beneath the high altar and raised choir of a church, usually containing the relics of a saint

Corbel, a projecting block, usually of stone

Corso, main street of a town

Crater, *see* krater

Crenellations, battlements

Cupola, dome

Cyclopean, the term applied to walls of unmortared masonry, older than the Etruscan civilisation, and attributed by the ancients to the giant Cyclopes

Diptych, painting or ivory panel in two sections

Dossal, altarpiece

Dosseret, a second block above the capital of a column

Duomo, cathedral

Edicola, *see* aedicule

Exedra, semicircular recess

Ex-voto, tablet or small painting expressing gratitude to a saint

Fresco (in Italian, *affresco*), painting executed on wet plaster (*intonaco*). On the rough plaster (*arriccio*) beneath, the artist made a sketch (or *sinopia*) which was covered little by little as work on the fresco proceeded. Since the *intonaco* had to be wet during this work, it was applied each day only to that part of the wall on which the artist was sure that he could complete the fresco (these areas, which can now often be detected by restorers, are known as *giornate*). From the 16C onwards cartoons (*cartoni*) were used to help the artist with the over-all design: the *cartone* was transferred on to the *intonaco* either by pricking the outline with small holes over which a powder was dusted, or by means of a stylus which left an incised line on the wet plaster. In the 1960s and 1970s, many frescoes were detached from the walls on which they were executed and so the *sinopie* beneath were discovered (and sometimes also detached)

Giallo Antico, red-veined yellow marble from Numidia

Gonfalon, banner of a medieval guild or commune

Gonfaloniere, chief magistrate or official of a medieval Italian Republic, the bearer of the Republic's *gonfalone*

Graffiti, design on a wall made with an iron tool on a prepared surface, the design showing in white. Also used loosely to describe scratched designs or words on walls

Greek-cross, cross with the arms of equal length

Grisaille, painting in various tones of grey

Grotteschi (or grotesques), a style of painting or stucco decoration used by the ancient Romans and discovered in the 1490s in the Domus Aurea in Rome (then underground, hence its name, from 'grotto'). The delicate ornamental decoration, normally on a light background, is characterised by fantastical motifs with intricate patterns of volutes, festoons, garlands, and borders of twisted vegetation and flowers interspersed with small winged human or animal figures, birds, masques, griffins, and sphynxes. This type of decoration became very fashionable and was widely copied by late Renaissance artists

Herm (pl. *hermae*), quadrangular pillar decreasing in girth towards the ground surmounted by a bust

Hypogeum, subterranean excavation for the burial of the dead (usually Etruscan)

Iconostasis, high balustrade with figures of saints, guarding the sanctuary of a Byzantine church

Impasto, early Etruscan ware made of inferior clay

Intarsia (or *tarsia*), inlay of wood, marble, ivory, or metal

Intonaco, plaster

Intrados, underside or soffit of an arch

Krater, Antique mixing-bowl, conical in shape with rounded base

Kylix, wide shallow vase with two handles and short stem

Latin-cross, cross with a long vertical arm

Lavabo, hand-basin usually outside a refectory or sacristy

Loggia, covered gallery or balcony, usually preceding a larger building

Lunette, semicircular space in a vault or ceiling, or above a door or window, often decorated with a painting or relief

Macchia mediterranea, see p 303

Maestà, representation of the Madonna and Child enthroned in majesty

Majolica (or *maiolica*), a type of earthernware glazed with bright metallic oxides that was originally imported to Italy from Majorca and was extensively made in Italy during the Renaissance

Matroneum, gallery reserved for women in early Christian churches

Medallion, large medal; loosely, a circular ornament

Menhir, a long megalithic stone planted vertically in the ground

Meta, turning-post at either end of a Roman circus

Monochrome, painting or drawing in one colour only

Monolith, single stone (usually a column)

Narthex, vestibule of a Christian basilica

Niello, black substance (usually a compound of sulphur and silver) used in an engraved design, or an object so decorated

Nimbus, luminous ring surrounding the heads of saints in paintings; a square nimbus denoted that the person was living at that time

Oculus, round window

Opera (Del Duomo), the office in charge of the fabric of a building (i.e. the Cathedral)

Opus Reticulatum, masonry arranged in squares or diamonds so that the mortar joints make a network pattern

Opus Tessellatum, mosaic formed entirely of square tesserae

Pala, large altarpiece

Palazzo, any dignified and important building

Palombino, fine-grained white marble

Pavonazzetto, yellow marble blotched with blue

Pax, sacred object used by a priest for the blessing of peace, and offered for the kiss of the faithful. It can be circular or rectangular, and engraved enamelled or painted, usually in a gold or silver frame

Pendentive, concave spandrel beneath a dome

Peristyle, court or garden surrounded by a columned portico

Pietà, representation of the Virgin mourning the dead Christ

Pietre dure, hard or semi-precious stones, often used in the form of mosaics to decorate cabinets, table-tops, etc., known as *commesso* work in Italian

Pietra forte, fine-grained limey sandstone used as a building material in Florence, and often for the rustication of palace façades

Pietra serena, fine-grained dark grey sandstone, easy to carve. Although generally not sufficiently resistant for the exterior of buildings, it was used to decorate many Renaissance interiors in Florence

Pieve, parish church, often isolated in the countryside (rather than in a town), and the most important in the district

Piscina, Roman tank; a basin for an officiating priest to wash his hands before Mass

Plaquette, small metal tablet with relief decoration

Pluteus (pl. *plutei*), marble panel, usually decorated; a series of them used to form a parapet to precede the altar of a church

Podestà, chief magistrate who ruled a medieval city with the help of a council and representatives from the corporations. Also a military leader

Polyptych, painting or panel in more than three sections

Porta, gate (or door)

Porta del Morto, in certain old mansions of Umbria and Tuscany, a narrow raised doorway, said to be for the passage of biers of the dead, but more probably for use in troubled times when the main gate would be barred

Predella, small painting or panel, usually in sections, attached below a large altarpiece, illustrating the story of a saint, the life of the Virgin, etc.

Presepio, literally, crib or manger. A group of statuary of which the central subject is the Infant Jesus in the manger

Pronaos, porch in front of the cella of a temple

Putto (pl. *putti*), figure of a small child sculpted or painted, usually nude

Quadratura, painted architectural perspectives

Quatrefoil, four-lobed design

Quattrocento, Italian term for the 'fourteen hundreds' i.e. the 15C

Reredos, decorated screen rising behind an altar

Rhyton, drinking-horn usually ending in an animal's head

Rood-screen, a screen below the Rood or Crucifix dividing the nave from the chancel of a church

Scagliola, a material made from selenite and used to imitate marble or pietre dure, often used for altar frontals and columns

Scena, the stage of a Roman theatre

Schiacciato, term used to describe very low relief in sculpture, where there is an emphasis on the delicate line rather than the depth of the panel

Schola cantorum, enclosure for the choristers in the nave of an early Christian church, adjoining the sanctuary

Sinopia, large sketch for a fresco made on the rough wall in a red earth pigment called sinopia (because it originally came from Sinope on the Black Sea). When a fresco is detached for restoration, it is possible to see the sinpoia beneath, which can also be separated from the wall

Soffit, underside or intrados of an arch

Spandrel, surface between two arches in an arcade or the triangular space on either side of an arch

Stamnos, big-bellied vase with two small handles at the sides, closed by a lid

Stele, upright stone bearing a monumental inscription

Stemma, coat of arms or heraldic device

Stereobate, basement of a temple or other building

Stoup, vessel for Holy Water, usually near the west door of a church

Stucco (pl. *stucchi*), plaster-work

Stylobate, basement of a columned temple or other building

Tablinum, room in a Roman house with one side opening onto the central courtyard

Telamones, *see* Atlantes

Tempera, a painting medium of powdered pigment bound together, in its simplest form, by a mixture of egg yolk and water

Tessera, a small cube of marble, glass, etc., used in mosaic work

Thermae, Roman baths

Tholos, a circular building

Tondo, round painting or bas-relief

Transenna, open grille or screen, usually of marble, in an early Christian church

Travertine, tufa quarried near Tivoli

Trecento, Italian term for the 'thirteen hundreds', i.e. the 14C

Triclinium, dining room and reception room of a Roman house

Triptych, painting or panel in three sections

Trompe-l'oeil, literally, a deception of the eye. Used to describe illusionist decoration, painted architectural perspectives, etc.

Tufa, porous volcanic rock used as a building stone

Tympanum, the area between the top of a doorway and the arch above it; also the triangular space enclosed by the mouldings of a pediment

Viale (pl. *viali*), wide avenue

Villa, country house with its garden

Westwork, west end of a Carolingian or Romanesque church with a massive central tower and, inside, a double story, with the upper room open to the nave

Index of artists

This index lists painters, sculptors and architects mentioned in the Guide, with their dates. Only a few foreign artists who worked in the region are included.

General index